Reading Across the Disciplines

College Reading and Beyond

SIXTH EDITION

Kathleen T. McWhorter
Niagara County Community College

Boston Columbus Indianapolis New York San Francisco Upper Saddle River
Amsterdam Cape Town Dubai London Madrid Milan Munich Paris Montreal Toronto
Delhi Mexico City São Paulo Sydney Hong Kong Seoul Singapore Taipei Tokyo

Editor in Chief: Eric Stano
Senior Development Editor: Gill Cook
Assistant Development Editor: Phoebe Mathews
Executive Marketing Manager: Roxanne McCarley
Senior Supplements Editor: Donna Campion
Executive Digital Producer: Stefanie Snajder
Content Specialist: Erin Jenkins
Digital Editor: Sara Gordus
Production Manager: Denise Phillip Grant

Project Coordination, Text Design, and Electronic Page Makeup: PreMediaGlobal
Cover Designer: John Callahan
Cover: Images (clockwise from top): © Steve Apps/Alamy, © Masterpics/Alamy, © inga spence/Alamy, © SPL/Science Source
Senior Manufacturing Buyer: Dennis J. Para
Printer/Binder: R. R. Donnelley/Crawfordsville
Cover Printer: Lehigh-Phoenix Color Corp.

Credits and acknowledgments borrowed from other sources and reproduced, with permission, in this textbook appear on the appropriate page within text [or on pages 643–648].

Library of Congress Cataloging-in-Publication Data

McWhorter, Kathleen T.
Reading across the disciplines : college reading and beyond / Kathleen T. McWhorter, Niagara County Community College.—Sixth edition.
    pages cm
Includes index.
ISBN-13: 978-0-321-92148-2
ISBN-10: 0-321-92148-8
1. College readers.   2. Reading (Higher education)   3. Interdisciplinary approach in education.   I. Title.
PE1122.M37 2015
428.6—dc23

2013038590

10 9 8 7 6 5 4 3 2 1—DOC—17 16 15 14

Student ISBN 10: 0-321-92148-8
Student ISBN 13: 978-0-321-92148-2
A la Carte Edition ISBN-10: 0-321-96520-5
A la Carte Edition ISBN-13: 978-0-321-96520-2

Brief Contents

Detailed Contents

PART TWO   **Readings for Academic Disciplines 241**

Preface

Reading Across the Disciplines, Sixth Edition, is designed to improve college students' reading and thinking skills through brief skill instruction and extensive guided practice with academic discipline-based readings. The text is structured around ten academic disciplines. The 30 readings—all of which aim to motivate students—are selected from college textbooks as well as from books, periodicals and popular magazines, newspapers, and Internet sources. The objective is to show the relevance of college studies to events and issues in everyday life through the use of engaging readings.

PURPOSE

The primary purposes of the text are to teach essential college reading skills and to guide their application in each of ten academic disciplines and career fields. The text develops basic vocabulary and comprehension skills, as well as inferential and critical-reading and -thinking skills. In addition to developing overall reading skills, the text also introduces students to discipline-specific reading skills. Each chapter in Part Two, "Readings for Academic Disciplines," begins with a tip list for applying reading and thinking skills to texts with the unique characteristics of academic and career fields. Questions and activities that precede and follow each reading demonstrate the application of vocabulary, comprehension, and critical-reading and -thinking skills to the particular discipline. Part Three, "Classroom Simulation: Textbook Reading and Writing" provides a realistic model for reading and learning from textbooks within a classroom setting.

Another important goal of the text is to demonstrate to students the relevance and utility of college courses to their daily lives. The book attempts to answer the long-standing question frequently asked by students, "Why do I have to take a course in history, biology, etc.?" The book presents readings that show students how academic disciplines embrace and investigate topics of interest and concern to everyday human experience.

NEW TO THE SIXTH EDITION

This revision focused on strengthening the book's focus on textbook reading skills within the academic disciplines. Specific goals of this revision were to create a new handbook chapter that focuses on textbook reading, provide a classroom simulation model for reading and writing using textbooks, provide a new chapter that explores the use of technology across academic disciplines, and to merge and consolidate skill coverage in the handbook.

NEW Handbook Chapter on Textbook Learning Strategies. To further the new emphasis on textbook reading skills, a new chapter, "Textbook Learning Strategies," has been added to Part One. This chapter offers strategies for reading textbooks, presents the SQ3R system, teaches learning and recall strategies, and covers numerous methods of organizing information: highlighting, annotating, paraphrasing, outlining, mapping, and summarizing.

NEW Classroom Simulation of Textbook Reading and Writing Skills. Part Three contains a unique classroom simulation built around a textbook chapter excerpt. The excerpt from an interpersonal communication textbook is treated as a classroom reading assignment. Students prepare for a class lecture on the assignment, read the assignment, review the assignment, attend the lecture and participate in simulated class activities, write about the assignment, take quizzes based on the assignment, and take an exam based on the assignment.

NEW Chapter on Technology in Academic Disciplines. Because technology is pervasive in many academic disciplines, Chapter 14 has been added to examine the expanding role of technology in a variety of academic disciplines. The topics include DNA fingerprinting, which represents use of technology in career fields; robotics, which examines advances in robotic technology that influence the way companies do business; and citizen science, which reports on the contributions to scientific research by everyday citizens.

NEW Reading Selections. Fourteen new readings have been added to this edition of the text. An effort was made to choose readings from textbooks within the discipline as well as other sources students may have contact with as they study within the discipline. New topics include sports fans, movie and television genres, censorship of art, media news reporting, robotics, the importance of darkness, and eco-tourism.

NEW Success Strategies. Three new or revised strategies have been added to the Ten Success Strategies for Learning and Studying Academic Disciplines. The new strategies focus on understanding the importance of reading in academic disciplines, developing time management skills, and using electronic study and information resources.

NEW Handbook Reorganization. The handbook has been reorganized to make it more compact and to integrate related skills. Content from former Chapter 8, "Organizing Ideas," has been integrated into the new Chapter 5. Former Chapter 10, "Reading and Evaluating Electronic Sources," has been condensed and merged into Chapter 7, "Critical Reading." Former Chapter 9, "Improving and Adjusting Your Reading Rate," has been dropped.

NEW Lexile Measures. A Lexile® measure—the most widely used reading metric in U.S. schools—provides valuable information about a student's reading ability and the complexity of text. It helps match students with reading resources and activities that are targeted to their ability level.

Lexile measures indicate the reading levels of content in MyReadingLab and the longer selections in the Annotated Instructor's Editions of all Pearson's reading books. See the Annotated Instructor's Edition of *Reading Across the Disciplines* and the Instructor's Manual for more details.

NEW Modules Available as Ancillaries. Instructors may supplement or vary their instruction by using the additional McWhorter modules available through the Pearson Custom Library. See page xiv, "A Modularized Approach and Customization," for more details.

MyReadingLab   **NEW Part Two Reading Selections and Exercises Now Available Online.** All of the readings and related exercises in Part Two can be accessed online and the objective exercises can be computer-scored with grades feeding into a gradebook.

CONTENT OVERVIEW

The book is organized into three parts:

- **Part One, "A Handbook for Reading and Thinking in College,"** presents a brief skill introduction. Written in handbook format (1a, 1b, etc.), this part introduces students to essential vocabulary, comprehension, and critical-reading skills.
- **Part Two, "Readings for Academic Disciplines,"** has ten chapters, each containing readings representative of a different academic or career field. Each chapter has three reading selections. The readings in each chapter are chosen from textbooks, books, periodicals, newspapers, and Internet sources that contain material relevant to the discipline. The readings in each chapter vary in length as well as difficulty, providing students with the opportunity to strengthen their skills, experience success, and build positive attitudes toward reading. Each reading is accompanied by an extensive apparatus that guides student learning.
- **Part Three, "Classroom Simulation: Textbook Reading and Writing,"** models a classroom reading assignment and corresponding classroom activities. The section contains an excerpt from an interpersonal communication textbook chapter, which is treated as an assignment. Students perform typical classroom activities related to the assignment including preparing for a lecture on the assignment, reading and reviewing the assignment, attending a lecture and participating in class, writing about the assignment, and taking quizzes and exams.

FEATURES

Reading Across the Disciplines guides students in learning reading and thinking skills essential for college success.

Students Approach Reading as Thinking

Reading is approached as a thinking process—a process of interacting with textual material and sorting, evaluating, and reacting to its organization and content.

The apparatus preceding and following each reading focuses, guides, and shapes students' thought processes.

Students Develop Active Reading Skills

Students learn to approach reading as a process that requires involvement and response. In doing so, they are able to master the skills that are essential to college reading. The reading apparatus provides a model for active reading.

Students Learn Essential Reading Skills

Vocabulary, comprehension, and critical-reading skills are presented concisely in Part One, "A Handbook for Reading and Thinking in College," and are accompanied by several exercises.

Students Learn Discipline-Specific Reading Skills

The high-interest readings in Part Two are grouped according to academic discipline and career fields. Each chapter begins with a brief list of tips for reading and learning within the particular discipline. Students are encouraged to apply these techniques as they read the selections within the chapter.

Students Learn as They Work

Unlike many books, which simply test students after they have read a selection, this text teaches students as they work. Some of the apparatus provides new material on vocabulary, methods of organizing information, transitions, and reading/study strategies.

Students Understand the Importance of Academic Disciplines to Their Daily Lives

Through the high-interest topics selected, students will come to understand the relevance of various academic disciplines to their daily lives, careers, and workplace.

Students Learn Visually

Increasingly, college students are becoming visual learners, and visual literacy is critical to success in today's world, so this text includes an entire chapter on how to read and interpret photographs, graphics, graphic organizers (maps), charts, and diagrams.

Students Appreciate Consistent Format

Because students often need structure and organization, this text uses a consistent format for each reading selection. Students always know what to expect and what is expected of them.

Students Refer to Part One, "A Handbook for Reading and Thinking in College," to Get Help Answering Questions

The activities following each reading parallel the topics in Part One of the book, which presents a brief skill overview in a handbook format. For example, if students have difficulty answering inferential questions, they may refer to the section in Part One that explains how to make inferences. The handbook also includes a section on reading and evaluating electronic sources.

Format of the Exercises

The exercises for each reading selection follow a consistent format. The sections vary in the number of questions and the specific skills reviewed. Exercises that can be scored objectively are available online. Each reading selection has the following parts:

- **Headnote.** A headnote introduces the reading, identifies its source, provokes the students' interest, and most important, establishes a framework or purpose for reading.
- **Previewing the Reading.** Students are directed to preview the reading using the guidelines provided in Part One and to answer several questions based on their preview.
- **Making Connections.** This brief section encourages students to draw connections between the topic of the reading and their own knowledge and experience.
- **Reading Tip.** The reading tip is intended to help students approach and work through the reading. A different reading tip is offered for each reading. For example, a reading tip might suggest how to highlight to strengthen comprehension or how to write annotations to enhance critical thinking.
- **Reading Selection/Vocabulary Annotation.** Most reading selections contain difficult vocabulary words that are essential to the meaning of the selection. Often these are words that students are unlikely to know and cannot figure out from context. These words are highlighted, and their meanings are given as marginal annotations. Preferable to a list of words preceding the reading, this format allows students to check meanings on an as-needed basis, within the context of the selection. Annotations are also used occasionally to provide necessary background information that students may need to grasp concepts in a reading.
- **Understanding the Thesis and Other Main Ideas.** This section helps students figure out the thesis of the reading and identify the main idea of selected paragraphs.
- **Identifying Details.** This section focuses on recognizing the relationship between main ideas and details, as well as distinguishing primary from secondary details. The format of questions within this section varies to expose students to a variety of thinking strategies.
- **Recognizing Methods of Organization and Transitions.** This part of the apparatus guides students in identifying the overall organizational pattern of the selection and in identifying transitional words and phrases within the reading. Prompts are provided that serve as teaching tips or review strategies.
- **Reviewing and Organizing Ideas.** Since many students are proficient at literal recall of information but have difficulty seeing relationships and

organizing information into usable formats for study and review, this section emphasizes important review and organizational skills such as paraphrasing, mapping, outlining, and summarizing.

- **Reading and Thinking Visually.** Since textbooks and electronic media are becoming increasingly visual, students need to be able to interpret and analyze visuals. This section guides students in responding to any visuals that accompany the reading.

- **Figuring Out Implied Meanings.** The ability to think inferentially is expected of college students. This section guides students in making inferences based on information presented in the reading selection.

- **Thinking Critically.** This section covers essential critical-thinking skills, including distinguishing fact from opinion, identifying the author's purpose, recognizing bias, evaluating the source, identifying tone, making judgments, and evaluating supporting evidence.

- **Building Vocabulary.** The first part of this section focuses on vocabulary in context, while the second is concerned with word parts. Using words from the reading selection, exercises are structured to encourage students to expand their vocabulary and strengthen their word-analysis skills. A brief review of the meanings of prefixes, roots, and suffixes used in the exercise is provided for ease of reference and to create a meaningful learning situation. The third vocabulary section focuses on a wide range of interesting features of language, drawing upon unusual or striking usage within the reading. Topics such as figurative language, idioms, and connotative meanings are included.

- **Selecting a Learning/Study Strategy.** College students are responsible for studying and learning what they read; many use the same study method for all disciplines and all types of material. This section helps students to choose appropriate study methods and to adapt their study methods to suit particular academic disciplines.

- **Exploring Ideas Through Discussion and Writing.** Questions provided in this section are intended to stimulate thought, provoke discussion, and serve as a springboard to writing about the reading.

- **Beyond the Classroom to the Web.** These activities draw on the skills students have learned by directing them to the Internet, where they search for information on topics related to the chapter readings. These activities also demonstrate the relevance of the academic discipline beyond the classroom and provide guidance in using Web sources.

A MODULARIZED APPROACH AND CUSTOMIZATION

Reading and Writing About Contemporary Issues (ISBN: 0-321-84442-4), also by Kathleen McWhorter, emphasizes an integrated approach to teaching reading and writing. It has a similar structure to *Reading Across the Disciplines*, including a handbook, but Part Two chapters are organized by contemporary themes, and Part Three consists of a Casebook of eight readings from a variety of sources that offer a focused, in-depth examination of a single contemporary issue—global warming and climate change. The introduction to the Casebook provides tips for reading about the issue, synthesizing sources, and previewing. Each selection is followed by critical thinking questions and a collaborative exercise. A section titled "Synthesis and Integration Questions and Activities" at the end of the Casebook contains questions, activities, and writing prompts that encourage students to synthesize the information in the sources.

Both books are modular in structure and can be customized to meet instructor's needs. However, instructor's may also draw chapters from both books to create a custom text with a mix of instructional topics and academic and contemporarily themed readings to accommodate student needs and interests. Additional modules written by Kathleen McWhorter (including a chapter on academic reading and writing, a casebook on the digital revolution, a biology based classroom simulation, and discipline and issue themed chapters) are also available through the Pearson Custom Library.

BOOK-SPECIFIC ANCILLARIES

- **Annotated Instructor's Edition (ISBN 0-321-96532-9).** The Annotated Instructor's Edition is identical to the student text, but it includes answers printed directly on the pages where questions and exercises appear. Lexile levels and word counts are included for all readings in Part Two.
- **Online Instructor's Manual/Test Bank (ISBN 0-321-96540-X).** The manual includes teaching suggestions for each section of Part One. For each reading in Part Two, the manual provides numerous suggestions for introducing the reading and offers a variety of follow-up activities designed to review and reinforce skills. The Test Bank contains numerous tests for each chapter, formatted for easy distribution and scoring. It includes content review quizzes and skill-based mastery tests for Part One and a discipline-based test and two discipline-based mastery tests for Part Two.

ACKNOWLEDGMENTS

I wish to express my gratitude to my reviewers for their excellent ideas, suggestions, and advice on the preparation and revision of this text:

Bonnie Arnett, Washtenaw Community College; Susan Banach, South Suburban College; Kathleen S. Britton, Florence-Darlington Technical College; Laraine Croall, South Louisiana Community College; Suzanne R. Franklin, Johnson County Community College; Richard A. Gair, Valencia College; Kimberly S. Hall, Harrisburg Area Community College; Tracy Harrison, Valencia Community College; Anne Hepfer, Seattle University; Debra Herrera,

Cisco Junior College; Valerie Hicks, Community College Beaver County; Janice Johnson, Missouri State University–West Plains; Kelly Johnson, Front Range Community College; Kimberly Jones, College of Southern Idaho; Lisa Jones, Pasco Hernando Community College; Diane Lerma, Palo Alto College; Linda Maitland, Lone Star; Dianne Miller, Phoenix College; Julie Monroe, Madison College; Lance Morita, Leeward Community College; Cindy Ortega, Phoenix College; Lynette D. Shaw-Smith, Springfield College Illinois/Benedictine University; Jeffrey Siddall, College of DuPage; Ursula Sohns, LSC North Harris; Maria Spelleri, State College of Florida, Manatee-Sarasota; Kitty Spires, Midlands Technical College; Rakesh Swamy, Ohlone College; Michelle Van de Sande, Arapahoe Community College; Michael Vensel, Miami Dade College; Carl Vinas, Nassau Community College; and Sylvia D. Ybarra, San Antonio College.

I also wish to thank Gillian Cook, my development editor, for her creative vision of the project, her helpful suggestions, guidance, and creative energy. I would like to acknowledge Eric Stano, Editor-in-Chief of Developmental Reading and Writing, for his enthusiastic support and valuable advice. I want to thank Phoebe Mathews for her valuable assistance in the development and preparation of the manuscript.

Kathleen T. McWhorter

Success Strategies for Learning and Studying Academic Disciplines

STRATEGIES

TEN

Success Strategies for Learning and Studying Academic Disciplines

Each academic discipline has a specialized approach for studying the world. To illustrate, let's consider how various disciplines might approach the study of human beings.

- A **PSYCHOLOGIST** might study how people attempt to meet basic human needs (love, safety, friendship, community).

- An **ARTIST** might consider a human being as an object of beauty and record a person's fluid, flexible muscular structure and subtle facial expressions on canvas.

- A **HISTORIAN** might research the historical importance of human actions and decisions—for example, the decisions to enter wars or form alliances with other countries.

- An **ECONOMIST** might focus on the supply of and demand for the goods and services that human beings want (food, clothing, shelter, transportation) and the amount of business these goods and services generate.

- A **BIOLOGIST** would categorize a human being as a member of *Homo sapiens.*

- A **MATHEMATICIAN** might calculate human life expectancies based on lifestyle, sex, race, and other categories.

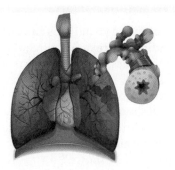

- An **ANATOMIST** would study the parts of the human body (lungs, heart, stomach) and a **PHYSIOLOGIST** would study those parts' functions (breathing, blood circulation, digestion).

Each academic discipline, then, approaches a given object or event with a different focus or perspective. Each discipline has its own special purposes and interests that help it. You will also find that each discipline has its own methodology for studying the topics with which it is concerned. Because each discipline is unique, each requires somewhat different study and learning strategies. The purpose of this introduction is to show you how to modify and adapt your learning, thinking, and study strategies to a variety of specific academic areas.

3

STRATEGY 1

Understand the Importance of Reading in Each Academic Discipline

There is no getting around it: reading will be required in every college course you take. For thousands of years, reading has been one of the primary ways in which knowledge and learning are conveyed. (The other methods include training, experience, and demonstrations.) As you begin your college studies, keep the following reading pointers in mind:

1. **Attending lectures is not a substitute for doing the required reading.** Most college instructors assign readings so that students will come to class prepared to discuss the reading materials. They make the assumption that students have read and understood the reading assignment, and their lectures expand on the reading. If you skip the reading assignment, you enter the class at a disadvantage.

2. **Examining the visual aids in your reading materials is not a substitute for reading the text.** Although the world has become extremely visual—videos, graphics, diagrams, charts, and photographs are everywhere—these visual aids are not a substitute for reading. Most often, visual aids are a supplement to the text, not a replacement for it. For maximum comprehension, you should read text and visual aids together, going back and forth between the text and the visual aid. Textbook authors tell you when to look at the visual aid. They might say, for example, "See Figure 1" or "As the photo to the left shows."

3. **Reading textbooks helps you develop the logical thinking that is required for college success.** When you are surfing the Internet, it is easy to become distracted. Links on a Web site make it easy to jump around from topic to topic. So, for example, you may start reading a Web site about a major American poet, and before you know it you may end up on a completely unrelated Web site, reading about a musician or a Hollywood celebrity. In a textbook, these distractions are not present, which allows you to follow the topic carefully and closely. By reading your textbook, you learn how to think about the topic and how to make logical connections.

4. **The more you read, the better your grade.** Many students are concerned with grades because they believe (correctly) that employers look at grade

point averages when they make hiring decisions. Because quizzes and exams are usually based on a combination of the reading assignments and the lectures, students who read their assignments (and review them as they prepare for exams) get better grades. You can think about success in college this way:

D and F students	Skip classes, don't read their assignments, and don't make their college studies a priority in their lives
C students	Do just enough to get by, skim their assignments instead of reading them, pay too much attention to visuals and not enough attention to the text, and are satisfied with just getting by
B students	Read all their assignments, show up prepared for class, hand in all their assignments on time, and use the proven study techniques in this introduction to maximize their comprehension and recall
A students	Do everything B students do, but also go the extra mile, demonstrating their ability to think critically, demanding excellence of themselves, and asking for help when they need it

Resisting Shortcuts

Textbooks provide many features to help students learn and review material. Keep in mind, though, that most of these features are intended to summarize material, not serve as a replacement for reading the text.

Consider the following example from a nutrition textbook. Like many other textbooks, this nutrition textbook begins each chapter with a list of learning objectives (that is, what students should be able to do after they have read the chapter). The chapter includes this learning objective:

- List at least one good food source for each of vitamins A, D, E, and K.

At the end of the chapter, the textbook provides a summary of the "Top Ten Points to Remember" in the chapter, including the following points:

- Vitamins are essential nutrients needed by your body to grow, reproduce, and maintain good health.
- Antioxidants, such as vitamins E and C, suppress harmful oxygen-containing molecules called free radicals that can damage cells.
- Vitamin A is needed for strong vision, reproduction, and healthy fetal development.
- Vitamin D is necessary for absorption of calcium and phosphorous.
- Vitamin E is an antioxidant that protects your cells' membranes.

—adapted from Blake, *Nutrition and You*, pp. 226, 273

Did you notice that you cannot fulfill the learning objective simply by reading this summary, which does not mention vitamin K and does not list good food sources for each of the vitamins listed? To discover these food sources, you must read the text. There you will discover that you will find vitamin A in milk, eggs, carrots, and spinach; vitamin D in milk and fortified yogurts; vitamin E vegetable oils and avocados; and vitamin K in broccoli, spinach, and Brussels sprouts.

Now consider the following visual aid, which appears in a psychology textbook.

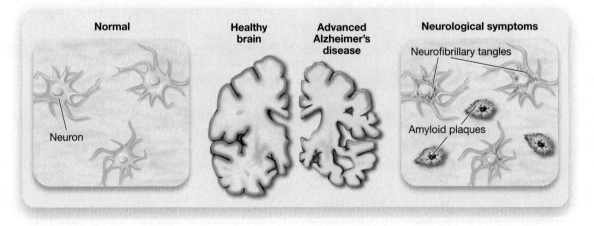

How Alzheimer's Disease Affects the Brain Advanced Alzheimer's disease is marked by significant loss of both gray and white matter throughout the brain. The brain of a person with Alzheimer's disease typically has a large buildup of plaques of a protein called beta-amyloid, which kills nerve cells. Also, tau proteins maintain the structure of nerve cells in the normal brain; these proteins are often found to be defective in the Alzheimer's brain, resulting in neurofibrillary tangles.

—Krause and Corts, Psychological Science, p. 385

Suppose you skip your reading assignment and choose to skim this visual aid instead. How well will you be prepared for the following exam question?

Define Alzheimer's disease, explaining its symptoms and the age at which it usually occurs.

While the visual aid helps explain Alzheimer's disease, it focuses on what happens in the brain of a person who has Alzheimer's. It does not define the disease, explain its symptoms, or identify the age at which it typically occurs. For this information, you have to read the text that accompanies the diagram:

Approximately 14% of people older than 71 years of age have dementia. Nearly 10% of these cases involve a type of dementia called **Alzheimer's disease**—a degenerative and terminal condition resulting in severe damage of the entire brain. Alzheimer's disease rarely appears before age 60, and it usually lasts 7 to 10 years from onset to death (although some individuals may live for 20 years with it). Early symptoms include forgetfulness for recent events, poor judgment, and some mood and personality changes. As the disease progresses, people struggle to recognize family members, have frequent memory loss, and experience confusion. In the most advanced stages of Alzheimer's disease, affected individuals may fail to recognize themselves and develop difficulty with basic bodily processes such as swallowing and bowel and bladder control.

—Krause and Corts, *Psychological Science*, p. 384

EXERCISE 1 THINKING ABOUT THE CONNECTION BETWEEN READING AND VISUAL AIDS

Directions: *Examine the following visual aid, which appears in a business textbook.*

—Bovee and Thill, *Business in Action*, p. 222

Which of the following exam questions could you answer by reading the visual aid only? Which would you not be able to answer as a result of reading the visual aid?

1. Provide an example of each of the five levels of Maslow's hierarchy of needs.

2. Define the term *self-actualization.*

3. Discuss the work of the psychologists and researchers who have criticized Maslow's needs hierarchy.

4. Summarize Abraham Maslow's hierarchy of needs. Which of these needs is at the lowest level? The highest level?

Students would be able to answer questions 1 and 4 based on reading the figure only.

FOR FURTHER INFORMATION AND STUDY

Part One of this book, "A Handbook for Reading and Thinking in College," provides an overview of the reading skills you will need to maximize your comprehension and recall.

STRATEGY 2
Manage Your Time and Balance Your Life

Think about a typical day in your life. Assuming you spend eight hours sleeping, that leaves 16 hours for school, work, family responsibilities, errands, and a social life. Now consider that you should plan to spend two hours studying outside of class for every one hour you spend in class. Let's say you are taking 12 credits this term. That means you spend 12 hours in class per week. To do well in these courses, you should plan to spend $12 \times 2 = 24$ hours per week reading and studying.

Now divide the 24 hours of study time by seven days per week ($24 \div 7$), and you can see that you will need to spend on average almost 3½ hours per day studying!

What does this mean? *You must carve out time for reading and studying every day.* Only you can determine how best to schedule your time, but here are some tips:

- **Consider waking up early.** An extra hour of quiet time in the morning can be very effective. Do not deprive yourself of the sleep you need, however.
- **Take study breaks during the day.** If you have a job, you can use part of your lunch hour to read or study.
- **Schedule your classes so that you have a break between classes.** During the break, go to the library, find a quiet place, and read.
- **Set your priorities.** You might need to skip a night out with friends so that you can study for an exam.
- **Monitor your feelings.** Your college reading and writing assignments take time. When feeling overwhelmed, you may be tempted to skip materials or simply not do an assignment. Such feelings are normal. Try breaking material up into chunks. Instead of reading an entire chapter all at once, try reading five pages per day over the course of a week.

Focusing Your Attention and Avoiding Distractions

We are a society bombarded by information—millions of Web sites, hundreds of cable TV channels, the constant ringing of the cell phone or beeping of incoming text messages.

As a result of all the interruptions we face, our attention spans have decreased significantly. Some experts now estimate that the average attention span is just seven minutes. How much do you think you can read, write, or research in just seven minutes? The answer is probably "Not much." If you are constantly interrupted, the chances of accomplishing your tasks and meeting your goals are quite slim.

Thus it is essential that you find ways to focus your attention and eliminate distractions. Here are some specific tips for achieving these goals:

- **Set up a study space.** If possible, always use the same area of your home to study. Make it conducive to study by keeping it clutter-free.
- **Turn off the TV, the iPod, the computer, the iPad.** It is difficult to understand complicated materials when electronic gadgets are competing for your attention.
- **Turn off the smartphone.** Don't turn it on again until you have completed your assignment.
- **Monitor your attention span.** It is normal to lose focus occasionally, to feel tired or hungry. It is perfectly fine to take study breaks. But a break should be just a brief "time out," not an extended vacation from study.
- **Work in places conducive to study.** A quiet library is usually a much better place to read than a busy student center or a bustling cafeteria.
- **Avoid social networking sites during study time.** Facebook, Twitter, and other social media sites are massive time wasters. Students report losing hours a day simply checking text messages and Facebook.

Balancing School, Family, and Work

Juggling your schoolwork with family, parenting, and/or work responsibilities can be challenging. Here are some suggestions for finding a healthy balance among the various components of your life:

- **Understand how much you can handle.** It is good to be ambitious, but don't take on too much. For example, you may feel much less stress if you think about taking an extra year to complete your degree. You will have more time for work and family.
- **Have a family conversation.** Your family benefits from your college degree. Discuss all family members' responsibilities and the roles they play in your college success. It is important for everyone to understand that some sacrifices must be made for the family's benefit.
- **If you have children, get help with childcare.** Arrange to have a friend or relative look after your children for specific hours each night or during the weekend. You can return the favor when school is not in session.
- **Schedule your classes on selected days.** This will minimize the time you spend traveling to and from campus.
- **Increase your efficiency by running errands at off-peak times.** Don't go to the grocery store on a busy Saturday morning. Instead, go late at night when the store is empty and you won't have to wait in long lines.
- **Use weekends wisely.** Some students think of weekdays as the time to concentrate on school and work, and weekends as the time to have fun.

This approach can lead to very stressful weeks. Make your weekdays less stressful by scheduling study or reading time each weekend.

- **Take advantage of campus services.** Many campuses now offer free or inexpensive childcare for parents, as well as evening, weekend, and Internet classes.
- **Most important, take care of yourself.** Eat a healthy diet, get some exercise, and take some time for yourself occasionally. "Reward" yourself with small things when you accomplish important tasks—for example, a new song for your iPod when you have finished writing your paper, or a cup of coffee at the local coffeehouse after you have taken your exam.

EXERCISE 2 CREATING A WEEKLY SCHEDULE

Directions: *The best way to manage your time is to make a weekly schedule and stick to it. Do this at the start of every week, filling in your obligations (classes, job hours, meals, travel time, appointments), as well as the hours you plan to study. A blank weekly plan is provided on the next page. Plan your upcoming week in detail, being sure to schedule the required number of hours for study.*

EXERCISE 3 EXAMINING YOUR DISTRACTIONS

Directions: *Many electronic advances—such as e-mail and the Internet—have become primarily forms of entertainment. Answer the following questions to get a sense of the type and number of distractions in your life and how they affect your ability to read, focus, and study.*

1. How many text messages do you send and receive per day? _____ How many of these are "important"? _____ Do you stop what you are doing to check your phone the second a text message arrives? _____ Have you ever texted while driving? _____
2. How many calls do you receive on your cell phone each day? _____ Do you leave your cell phone on all the time? _____ Do you answer it every time it rings, even when you're in class or studying? _____ Do you ever use your cell phone as a way to procrastinate? _____
3. How many hours a day do you spend surfing the Internet or posting on social networking sites like Facebook? _____ How often do you check your Facebook page or Twitter account? _____ Does this socializing affect your studying, concentration, and grades? _____

	Monday	Tuesday	Wednesday	Thursday	Friday	Saturday	Sunday
7:00							
8:00							
9:00							
10:00							
11:00							
12:00							
1:00							
2:00							
3:00							
4:00							
5:00							
6:00							
7:00							
8:00							
9:00							
10:00							
11:00							

FOR FURTHER INFORMATION AND STUDY

When you feel overwhelmed, reread this introductory section. Talk with friends or classmates about techniques they have developed for managing their time and their lives. Think positively and focus on achieving your goals.

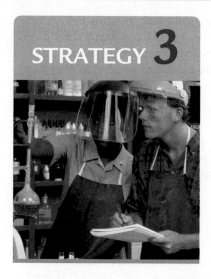

STRATEGY **3**

Develop New Skills for Each Academic Discipline

In college, you are likely to encounter disciplines with which you have little or no prior experience. For example, sociology, political science, and chemistry may be new to you. At first, you may feel lost, confused, or frustrated in such courses. These feelings may result from unfamiliarity with the specialized language of the discipline; with the types of learning and thinking that are expected of you; or with the conventions, approaches, and methodology of the discipline. One student described this feeling as "being on the outside looking in," watching other students participate in the class but being unable to do so himself.

Strategies for Reading in New Disciplines

When approaching a new field of study, try the following:

1. **Understand the baseline for success in the course.** Each discipline uses a specific set of tools. Identifying and understanding these tools is essential. If you do not use them, you will not learn the material properly. For example, case studies are common in business courses, so business majors need to develop a system for identifying and summarizing their key points. In economics, you cannot get a good grade without understanding how to create and analyze graphs.

2. **Establish an overview of the field.** Study your textbook's table of contents; it provides an outline of the course. Look for patterns, progression of ideas, and recurring themes, approaches, or problems. Before you read each chapter, preview the material at the beginning of the chapter (which often includes learning goals) as well as the material at the end of the chapter (which often includes study questions). Then use these goals and questions to guide your reading.

3. **Overlearn until you discover what is expected.** Until you discover what is important in the course and figure out the best way to learn it, learn more information than you may need. That is, err on the side of learning too much rather than too little. As an example, consider a criminal justice class. Until you know whether the instructor's focus is on trends, patterns, and theories—or on facts, research findings, and specific laws—it is safer to learn both.

4. **Use several different methods to learn the same information.** For example, in an anthropology course, you might learn events and discoveries chronologically (according to occurrence in time) as well as comparatively (according to similarities and differences among them). In a sociology course you might highlight textbook information (to promote factual recall) as well as write outlines and summaries (to interpret and consolidate ideas). You might also draw diagrams to map the relationships between concepts and ideas.

5. **Look for similarities between the new subject matter and other academic fields that are more familiar to you.** If similarities exist, you may be able to modify or adapt learning approaches and strategies with which you are already familiar. For instance, if you are familiar with mathematics, some of the learning strategies you use in math courses may help you in physics and chemistry courses.

6. **Develop a support network.** Ask students who've taken the class about their experiences. Which Web sites and other resources are helpful as study tools? What kinds of questions does the instructor tend to ask on exams? Which chapters in the textbook are the most important?

7. **Think in new ways.** Many college courses ask you to change your way of thinking. For example, many economics instructors say they want their students to "think like an economist," which means understanding the trade-offs involved whenever you make a choice. Geography instructors ask students to "think geographically," which means looking at how human beings interact with their locations.

EXERCISE 4 THINKING IN NEW WAYS

Directions: *Sociologists often discuss two different perspectives on society. The* functionalist perspective *maintains that social institutions (such as the education system and the family) work in society's best interests. The* conflict perspective *maintains that these same institutions set up systems in which certain people benefit at the expense of others.*

Think about the idea of arranged marriages, in which parents arrange for their children to marry suitable partners. What would sociologists with a functionalist perspective think about these marriages? What would sociologists with a conflict perspective think about the same topic?

FOR FURTHER INFORMATION AND STUDY

Part Two of this book, "Readings for Academic Disciplines," provides readings from a wide variety of subject areas. Use the suggestions outlined above, as well as the tips at the start of each chapter, as you begin reading in each new discipline.

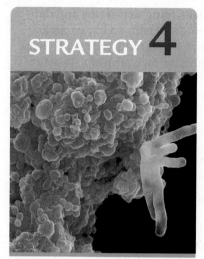

A white blood cell ingests bacteria using phagocytosis.

Learn the Language of the Discipline

Each academic discipline has a set of specialized words that allow precise communication through accurate and concise descriptions of events, principles, concepts, problems, and occurrences. One of the first tasks you face in a new course, then, is learning that course's specialized language. You cannot learn a new discipline without being able to use its terminology!

This task is especially important in introductory courses in which the subject is new and unfamiliar. In an introductory psychology course, for example, you must learn many new terms—*assimilation, autonomic nervous system, conditioning, reinforcement, defense mechanism,* and *phobia* are a few examples. You will encounter this specialized vocabulary in class lectures and in textbooks and will be expected to use it in assignments and on exams.

Class Lectures

Often, the first few lectures in a course are devoted to acquainting you with the nature and scope of the field and introducing you to its vocabulary. Use the following tips to keep track of and learn new words during lectures:

- **Read Chapter 1 of your textbook before the first lecture.** The textbook's first chapter usually introduces key terminology that will be used throughout the course. For example, in a widely used psychology textbook, 34 new terms are introduced in the first two chapters (40 pages). In a popular chemistry textbook, 56 vocabulary words are introduced in the first two chapters (28 pages). Understanding some of the key terms before you go to class will make that first class much easier.
- **Record each new term for later review and study.** If you don't fully understand a word during the lecture, look up its meaning in the textbook or ask your instructor for clarification.
- **Pay attention to your instructor's clues about what terms are important.** Some instructors make a habit of writing key vocabulary on the board. Others emphasize new terms and definitions by slowing down, almost dictating, so that you can record definitions in your notebook. Still other instructors may repeat a word and its definition several times. After each class session, compare notes with a classmate to ensure that you haven't missed any key terms.

- **Develop a consistent way of easily identifying new terms and definitions recorded in your notes.** You might (1) draw a box or circle around each new term, (2) underline each new term in red as you review your notes, (3) write "def." in the margin near each term and its definition, or (4) use a special mark or symbol to indicate an important term. The particular mark or symbol you use is your choice; the important thing is to find some way to mark definitions for further study.

> ### Sample Lecture Notes
>
> A. Types of Aging
> 1. Primary—normal progressive aging
> 2. Secondary—aging due to extrinsic factors
>   - ex. disease, smoking, environmental pollution

- **Never stop learning.** In some courses, key vocabulary can be learned in just the first few weeks of class. But in most courses—especially those in the sciences—you will be learning new vocabulary in just about every class, from the first week of the term until the last. Adjust your expectations accordingly!

Textbook Assignments

Some of the terms you'll encounter in your textbooks are words common in everyday usage that have specialized meanings when used in a specific discipline. For example, the word *drive* is commonly used to mean "to control a vehicle," but in psychology it means a biologically based motivation. *Ground*, commonly used to refer to the solid surface on which we stand, means *background*—the area around and between figures—in the field of visual arts. Other technical terms are used only in a specific subject area. For example, the terms *distal tubing*, *endodermis*, and *photosynthesis* are unique to biology-related fields.

Most textbooks use various methods to emphasize and explain new terminology. These include:

- **Typeface variations.** *Italic* type, **boldface** type, or colored print often identify important terms and/or definitions.
- **Marginal definitions.** New terms are sometimes defined in the margin of a page next to where they appear in the text.
- **Key terms lists.** These appear at the beginning or end of each chapter, often with a page number to indicate the page on which the term is introduced and defined.
- **Glossaries.** These comprehensive lists of the terms in the textbook are usually found at the end of the book. They list all the key terms alphabetically, along with their definitions and sometimes the page number on which the term is introduced.

An excellent way to test your vocabulary is to make and use flash cards. Write the word on one side of an index card and the definition on the other side. (Just writing the word and its definition will help you learn them.) Test yourself or a classmate. Many textbook Web sites include electronic flash cards to help you study.

EXERCISE 5 LEARNING ACADEMIC VOCABULARY

Directions: *In the following chart are five terms used often in sociology courses. Using an online sociology dictionary (or any other dictionary of sociology), match each term with its correct definition.*

_____	1. altruistic love	a.	the role we perform in relation to a particular audience
_____	2. social script	b.	nonconformity to social norms
_____	3. lifeboat ethics	c.	placing another's happiness before one's own
_____	4. deviance	d.	marriage between a man and more than one woman
_____	5. polygyny	e.	a model of resource distribution that presents rich nations as lifeboats and poor nations as swimmers

FOR FURTHER INFORMATION AND STUDY

Chapter 2, "Vocabulary Building," offers additional tips for building your vocabulary. In addition, each reading in this book includes vocabulary exercises to help you master academic vocabulary.

STRATEGY 5

Communicate, Network, and Collaborate

In college as in life, success is often determined by your ability to build a support network and to work with others. Developing strong networks can help you in even the most challenging courses.

In most courses, your classmates and instructors are your most valuable and important resources. Talking with classmates in person or by phone was once the primary form of communication. Now computers, the Internet, social media, and smart phones offer convenient ways of communicating, sharing information, and studying.

Tips for Communicating with Classmates

Here are some tips for communicating electronically with classmates:

- **E-mail.** Try to get the e-mail addresses of some classmates the first week of class. If you miss a class or are confused by an assignment, you can contact a classmate for help. If you are taking an online class, you may be able to communicate directly with your classmates through the course Web site. To make e-mail communication easy, keep your e-mail address simple. For example, FirstName.LastName@gmail.com is much better than Rv3rGur1@hotmail.com.
- **Text messages.** Text messages (brief messages usually sent from one cell phone to another, or from a computer to a cell phone) can be effective in sharing quick bits of information, but they are usually ineffective for substantive communication. Typing on a cell phone can be very time-consuming—which can make it difficult to convey information efficiently. If you need to take part in an online conversation, it can be more efficient to use an IM (instant message) service that allows real-time conversation online, with fewer limits on the number of characters in a particular message.
- **Online study groups.** If you take notes on a computer, sharing them is easy. E-mail, social media, and applications like Skype make it easy to share notes and ideas. Group chat rooms that offer text and audio are often preferable to walking a mile in the rain to participate in a study group. Many of the course management systems now used on college campuses have built-in chat rooms.

- **Professor-operated message boards.** In some courses, your professor may create a message board where class members can post and share information. Remember that anything you post here is public and available for anyone to read. Avoid posting complaints about assignments or the workload. Instead, use the message board positively: get other students' points of view on topics and issues, or share study tips and information sources.

- **Social networks.** Many students communicate through social networks such as Facebook, posting photographs, status updates, or personal opinions. Use these networks with caution, and be sure not to provide information that may jeopardize your safety or security. If you are using a public network, remember that what you post now may hurt you later. Many employers check these networks to learn about potential employees' backgrounds. You would not want a potential employer to see a photo of you in embarrassing or inappropriate poses, for example.

  While social networks are often used for nonacademic purposes, they can be quite useful in building an academic network. At some schools, students list all their current and past classes on Facebook; this allows them to create a support community. A freshman can ask a junior for tips on how to succeed in the course, and friendships developed through Facebook in this way have led to many job offers.

Tips for Communicating with Instructors

The best way to communicate with instructors is in person, before or after class or during their office hours. But many instructors now make themselves available through e-mail and other electronic means, including:

- **E-mail.** Most instructors give students an e-mail address at which to contact them. You can generally find the instructor's e-mail on the course syllabus. Some professors check their e-mail several times a day; others may check it as little as once a week. Until you are certain an instructor checks e-mail frequently, do not e-mail time-sensitive questions or information.

  Although e-mail is more informal than other types of writing, use a more formal level of communication with professors than you would with friends. Use correct grammar, spelling, and punctuation; avoid slang. Try to keep your e-mails short and focused. Do not be overly familiar, and don't send attachments or pictures unless requested. Some professors won't discuss grades or other personal information over e-mail.

- **Phone and text messages.** Be cautious with professors' phone numbers, and call only at appropriate or approved times. If an instructor has provided a cell phone number, do not text him or her without permission and do not post it in any public forum.

The culture of the Internet has made many people expect immediate responses to their e-mails or text messages. Be aware that most instructors are not "on call" 24 hours a day, so your messages may go unanswered longer than you would like. Plan accordingly; don't wait until the last minute to ask important questions or get essential information.

Tips for Collaborating on Group Projects

Many college assignments involve working with a partner or small group of classmates. For example, a sociology professor might divide the class into groups and ask each group to brainstorm solutions to the economic or social problems of recent immigrants. Group presentations may be required in a business course, or groups in your American history class might be asked to research and present a topic.

Group, or *collaborative*, projects are designed to help students learn from one another. They are excellent learning opportunities and good preparation for the workplace. Use the following suggestions to work effectively in a group setting:

- **Think of group work as training for your career.** Almost every job requires you to work with others as part of a team. It is valuable to learn about the ins and outs of collaboration early in your college career.
- **Select alert, energetic classmates if you are permitted to choose group members.**
- **Create a roster of group members with all contact information (cell phone, e-mail, and so forth).** Get to know your group members. It is always easier to work together when you know something about your collaborators.
- **Approach each activity seriously.** Save joking and socializing until the group work has been completed.
- **Be an active, responsible participant.** Accept your share of the work and ask others to do the same.
- **Choose a leader who will keep the group focused.** The leader should direct the group in analyzing the assignment, organizing a plan of action, distributing the assignments, establishing deadlines, and keeping the group on track.
- **Take advantage of individual strengths.** Members bring different strengths and experiences to the group. For instance, a person who has strong organizational skills might be assigned the task of recording the group's findings. A person with strong communication skills might be chosen to present group results to the class.
- **Treat others as you would like to be treated.** Offer praise when it is deserved. Listen to others, but be willing to disagree with them if doing so is in the group's best interests.
- **Hold group members accountable.** Establish ground rules. Everyone must come prepared, and everyone must do his or her share of the work.

If someone is not pulling his or her share of the weight, the other members should mention this politely.

EXERCISE 6 COMMUNICATION SKILLS

Directions: *Suppose you are preparing for an exam that will take place next week. You have decided to assemble a study group of five students. You have identified five possible ways of getting together to study:*

- Meeting at the library for a two-hour study session
- Sitting in front of your computers with Skype
- Texting each other
- Setting up a chat room that you all join
- Starting an e-mail chain in which one person asks a question and everyone else answers

What are the pros and cons of each method?

FOR FURTHER INFORMATION AND STUDY

Chapter 10 of this text provides additional tips for effective communication via readings from the Communication and Speech disciplines.

STRATEGY 6

Demonstrate Academic Integrity

Academic integrity is a code of honest and ethical academic conduct. It applies to both students and instructors, and it means:

- Doing your own work
- Not representing the work of others as your own
- Conducting yourself in class in a serious, respectful manner

Cheating

There are many forms of cheating—some obvious, some subtle. Obvious forms of cheating include sharing homework assignments, buying term papers online, exchanging information with other students during exams, or getting answers from students who've taken the class before you. Less obvious, but still very serious, forms of cheating include (but are not limited to):

- Using unauthorized notes during an exam
- Changing exam answers after grading and requesting a new grade
- Falsifying or making up results for a lab report
- Submitting the same essay or paper for more than one course without instructor authorization
- Not following rules on take-home exams
- Using someone else's work or ideas as if they are your own (plagiarism)

Most colleges have very strict anti-cheating policies. Getting caught cheating just once can cause you to fail a course. In some cases, college officials may ask cheaters to leave the school entirely.

Plagiarism

Plagiarism means borrowing someone else's ideas or exact words without giving that person credit. If you take information about Frank Lloyd Wright's architecture from a reference source (such as an encyclopedia, scholarly journal, or Web site) but do not specifically indicate where you found it, you have plagiarized. If you take the six-word phrase "Peterson, the vengeful, despicable drug czar" from an online news article, you have plagiarized.

Plagiarism can be intentional (planned) or unintentional (done by accident or oversight). Either way, it carries the same academic penalty—failing the course or dismissal from the college. Here are some guidelines to help you understand exactly what constitutes plagiarism.

WHAT IS PLAGIARISM?

- **Plagiarism** is the use of another person's words without crediting that person.
- **Plagiarism** is the use of another person's theory, opinion, or idea without listing the source of that information.
- **Plagiarism** results when another person's exact words are not placed inside quotation marks. Both the quotation marks and a citation (reference) to the original source are required.
- Paraphrasing (rewording) another person's ideas or words without credit is **plagiarism**.
- Using facts, data, graphs, and charts without stating their source(s) is **plagiarism**.
- Using commonly known facts or information is **not plagiarism**, and you need not provide a source for such information. For example, the fact that Neil Armstrong set foot on the moon in 1969 is widely known and does not require documentation.

To avoid plagiarism, do the following:

- **Use quotation marks.** When you take notes from any published or Internet source, place anything you copy directly in quotation marks.
- **Separate your ideas from those of the sources you use.** As you read and take notes, separate your ideas from ideas you have taken from the sources you are consulting. You might use different colors of ink or different sections of a notebook page for each. Separating ideas this way will prevent you from mistakenly presenting other people's ideas as your own.
- **Keep track of all the sources you use,** clearly identifying where each idea comes from.
- **When paraphrasing someone else's words, change as many words as possible and try to organize them differently.** Be sure to credit the original source of the information. For more information about writing a paraphrase, see Chapter 5.
- **Write paraphrases without looking at the original text** so that you rephrase information using your own words.
- **Use citations to indicate the source of quotations and all information and ideas that are not your own.** A citation is a parenthetical

notation referring to a complete list of sources provided at the end of the paper. The most common documentation styles are:

MLA (Modern Language Association). Used in English, some humanities, and foreign language studies. (www.mla.org/style)

APA (American Psychological Association). Widely used in the social sciences. (www.apastyle.org)

CSE (Council of Science Editors). Used in the life sciences, physical sciences, and mathematics. (www.councilscienceeditors.org)

Chicago Style. Commonly used in history, art history, philosophy, and some humanities. (www.chicagomanualofstyle.org)

Avoiding Cyberplagiarism

Cyberplagiarism is a specific type of plagiarism. It involves using information from the Internet without giving credit to the Web site that posted the information. It is also called *cut-and-paste plagiarism*, due to the ease of copying something from the Internet and pasting it into an essay or paper. Cyberplagiarism can also refer to buying prewritten papers from the Internet and submitting them as your own work. Because many instructors have access to programs that identify shared or purchased papers, they can easily identify plagiarism.

Use the following suggestions to avoid unintentional cyberplagiarism:

- **If you cut and paste information from an Internet source into your notes, add quotation marks at the beginning and end of the excerpt.** Also record the author's name, the name of the Web site or page, the date you accessed the material, and the exact URL (no matter how long it is). Consult a documentation manual for details on how to format your sources and citations.
- **Keep source information for *all* the information you have taken from the Internet** regardless of whether it takes the form of direct quotes, paraphrases, facts, opinions, ideas, theory, data, or summaries of someone else's ideas.
- **Never copy and paste directly from a Web site into your essay or paper** without enclosing the words in quotation marks and listing the source.

As you encounter new disciplines, you may ask yourself, "How can I possibly write a paper without using someone else's ideas? I don't know enough about the subject!" The good news is that it is perfectly acceptable to use other people's ideas in your research and writing. The key things to remember are that (1) you must *credit* all information taken from any published or Internet source, and (2) you must provide a *specific citation* for the publication from which you took your information. Identifying your sources serves two important purposes. First, it credits the person who originally wrote the material or thought of the idea. Second, it helps those who want to explore the subject in more detail locate the sources you've used.

EXERCISE 7 AVOIDING PLAGIARISM

Directions: *Read the following passage from the sociology textbook* Sociology for the Twenty-First Century *by Tim Curry, Robert Jiobu, and Kent Schwirian. Then read the statements that follow and use a check mark to indicate the correct use of credit and citation.*

> **Mexican Americans.** Currently, Mexican Americans are the second-largest racial or ethnic minority group in the United States, but within two decades they will be the largest group. Their numbers will swell as a result of continual immigration from Mexico and the relatively high Mexican birth rate. Mexican Americans are one of the oldest racial-ethnic groups in the United States. Under the terms of the treaty ending the Mexican-American War in 1848, Mexicans living in territories acquired by the United States could remain there and be treated as American citizens. Those who did stay became known as "Californios," "Tejanos," or "Hispanos."
>
> —Curry, Jiobu, and Schwirian,
> *Sociology for the Twenty-First Century,* p. 207

_____ a. Mexican Americans are the second-largest minority in the United States. Their numbers grow as more people immigrate from Mexico.

_____ b. After the Mexican-American War, those Mexicans living in territories owned by the United States became American citizens and were known as Hispanos, Californios, or Tejanos (Curry, Jiobu, and Schwirian, 207).

_____ c. "Mexican Americans are one of the oldest racial-ethnic groups in the United States."

FOR FURTHER INFORMATION AND STUDY

As you work through this textbook, note how each reading selection provides specific information regarding the author and the publication from which it was taken. The "Credits" at the end of the book (pages 643–648) are the equivalent of the "Works Cited" page in an academic essay or paper.

Make the Most of Online Courses and Assignments

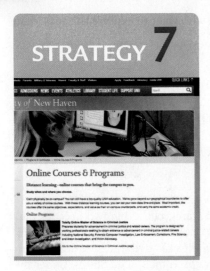

Many colleges now offer online courses. Rather than attending class in person, students complete all or most of the course requirements electronically. Some of these courses are *hybrid courses*, a mixture of occasional trips to campus with a strong online component.

In online courses, instructors post reading assignments, sponsor and monitor discussions, and interact with individual students by e-mail, instant messages, or chat rooms. Some online classes are conducted in **real time**, meaning that the instructor and students are online together at given times. Other classes permit students to work independently, choosing the times they want to participate, work, and study.

Many online courses make use of sophisticated electronic systems, such as BlackBoard, WebCT, or Moodle. These **course management systems** allow the instructor to control the course, set deadlines, post announcements, provide specific resources and assignments, and give exams. They also allow students to submit assignments, organize discussion groups, send e-mail, and post announcements. Many of these systems also provide additional resources for student learning, such as test-yourself quizzes, electronic tutorials, and electronic flash cards.

While online courses may seem easy, they require a great deal of self-discipline and the ability to work alone. Use the following tips to maximize your success in online courses.

1. **Avoid taking online courses your first year of college.** Your first year of college is likely to be transitional. You'll go from a world in which you're very comfortable (especially if you go to college right after high school) to one in which you are expected to manage your own education. Attending traditional on-campus classes makes it easier to learn what is expected in college. Once you have learned how to manage your time and workload, you will be better prepared to take online courses.

2. **Take online courses for distribution requirements or other courses not required for your major.** While scheduling difficulties may require you

to take online courses for your major, it is better to attend majors courses in person. Your major is your area of specialty, and the benefits of being on campus for these courses are strong. You'll forge a stronger relationship with your instructors and network live with other students, which can help you when you begin looking for a job in your field.

3. **Read, read, read.** Whether you attend a class on campus or take an online course, reading is your primary source of information. In fact, the reading requirements for online courses may be heavier than they are for lecture courses, simply because your professor isn't physically present to reinforce textbook concepts. If you aren't a strong reader or need personal contact with instructors and other students, online courses may not be appropriate for you.

4. **Keep up with the work and meet all due dates.** Most students who fail online courses do so because they fall hopelessly behind with the required reading assignments and cannot catch up. The course's home page usually provides a list of what is due and when. Due dates for papers and other assignments are not flexible just because the course is online. For example, if the course's home page indicates that a paper is due on March 15th, be sure to submit that paper no later than March 15th.

5. **Treat your online course exactly as you would treat other courses.** Prepare a work/study schedule and follow it for your online course, just as you would for any other class.

6. **Focus.** Turn off music, TV, your cell phone, text messaging, and e-mail.

7. **Make use of optional resources.** With online courses, consider the computer your study partner. Use the resources provided by the textbook's Web site or the course's home page to help you learn and quiz yourself. Take advantage of the textbook's built-in learning aids, such as chapter quizzes and test reviews, even if your instructor does not officially assign them.

8. **Take screen breaks.** Your eyes can become tired and dry if you spend hours staring at a computer screen. To keep yourself alert, take occasional breaks from the screen. Use this time to have a healthy snack or to work with the printed textbook. If you are using an e-book, you may find it helpful to print out important pages and work with those instead.

Using Course Management Web Sites

Here are some tips for using course management Web sites:

- **Be sure you do not submit materials until you have finalized them.** Take the time to ensure your work is top quality and does not need further revision. Once you click "send," your work is submitted and you may not be given the chance to resubmit.

- **Be sure you use the recommended Web browser.** While most course management Web sites work with Firefox, Safari, and Chrome, some are still Internet Explorer–only. Make sure you are using the latest version of the browser.
- **Install the most recent plug-ins for QuickTime, Flash, Adobe Reader, and anything else the site requires.** Course Web sites usually provide links to safe, reliable sites that allow you to download and install these plug-ins.
- **Be cautious about using real-time instant messages or other chat features.** It is easy to get distracted from course materials if you are chatting or socializing with friends.
- **Keep backups of all your work.** Most course management systems are reliable, but some can be prone to technological glitches. Save a copy of your work on your own computer or on a flash/thumb drive.
- **Write down the system's technical support phone number and e-mail in a safe place, or store this information in your smartphone.** Don't hesitate to contact tech support if you need it. Most calls to tech support involve lost usernames and passwords, so be sure to keep track of that information.

EXDRCISE 8 WORKING WITH ONLINE COURSES

Directions: *The best way to understand the demands of an online course is to talk to other students who've taken them. At the student center or some other location, try to find students who've taken an online class and ask them about their experiences. What do they see as the pros and cons of online courses? Report your findings to a small group or to the class.*

FOR FURTHER INFORMATION AND STUDY

A relevant Web site or Web search for each reading in Part Two of this book is included as part "K" following the reading. Be sure to check out the additional resources offered by these sites.

STRATEGY 8

Develop and Use Electronic Study and Information Resources

While print textbooks, instructor handouts, and print library sources are still important primary sources of information, you also need to be familiar with newer electronic information delivery systems, including e-books, online class notes, and on-line information sources.

Reading E-books

E-books are textbooks that you can purchase in electronic form. E-books have one major advantage—they are usually cheaper than print textbooks. They are also convenient and portable via computer (and therefore much lighter than traditional textbooks). However, they do have their draw-backs. Some can be difficult to read outdoors on a sunny day, and most are sold through a subscription model. This means that you have access to the content for a limited period of time (usually one semester), after which the content disappears. If you need the textbook to serve as a reference in later courses or your career, it may be better to purchase the printed textbook. Finally, reading e-books can be tough on the eyes, though most e-book readers allow you to increase the size of the type and adjust the screen contrast.

Here are some suggestions for reading and using e-books:

- **Use the search function.** In most e-books, you can use the search function to find useful information (such as key terms) not only in the chapter you're currently studying, but also elsewhere in the text.
- **Experiment with the toolbar.** Many e-books have premium features that may come in handy, such as the ability to highlight, type notes in the margin, and click on key terms for their definitions. Use whichever tools work with your personal learning goals and styles.
- **Sometimes paper is better for the task at hand.** Feel free to print out what you need. And if you prefer traditional printed textbooks to e-books, you are not alone. Many studies show that most students still prefer printed textbooks over e-books.

Reading and Using Online Notes

Some instructors post notes on their personal Web sites or on the department's Web site. These notes may be guides to upcoming lectures, summaries of previous lectures, or Microsoft PowerPoint presentations they used in their lectures. All of these resources are useful because they identify what the instructor feels is important and necessary to learn. Here are a few tips for reading and using online notes.

1. **Do not skip the lecture and rely on online notes.** Online notes are intended as an outline or summary of a particular lecture. They are a tool for review, not a substitute for the lecture. Missing a lecture also means missing the class discussion, one of the best ways to learn new concepts.

2. **Do not use online notes as a substitute for taking your own notes in class.** Lectures often cover different aspects of the material and go into greater detail than the notes do. In addition, because notes are often prepared *prior* to class, they usually will not include the answers to questions that come up in class.

3. **Devise a system for placing your own notes with the online notes.** Use a split screen or a different color to add your notes to the online notes. If you are annotating a PowerPoint presentation, print the slides and write in the white spaces, or type your notes into the "Notes" section at the bottom of each slide.

4. **Test yourself on the content of online notes.** Reading online notes is not enough to ensure that you have learned the material. Unlike notes that you have taken yourself, you have little ownership of online notes. Reading only the online notes (and not the textbook assignment) means you have not thought about the material, condensed it, and expressed it in your own words. To maximize your learning, read the assignment, attend the lecture, and then interact with the online notes by summarizing, rewriting, reorganizing, or testing yourself on the contents.

Lecture Capture

Lecture capture software allows instructors to record their lectures and place them online afterward. While watching recorded lectures, not only will you see and hear your instructor, but you will also be able to see what has been written on the "whiteboard." Watching captured lectures can be extremely helpful in subject areas that require a lot of board work, such as mathematics, statistics, and the sciences. Because the lectures are captured in real time, you're able to hear all the questions asked by the class, as well as the instructor's answers.

Lecture captures are very useful for review sessions. You can "rewind" the video as many times as you like or watch the same mathematical problem get solved until you understand the solution. Remember, though, that watching a lecture video is mostly a passive process. To get a good grade in the course, you must still do all the reading, complete all the assignments, and participate in class. Like online notes, lecture captures are a helpful review but not a substitute for attending class.

EXERCISE 9 WORKING WITH NEW TECHNOLOGIES

Directions: *If you haven't seen an e-book, visit the campus library and ask the librarian to demonstrate one for you. What do you see as the benefits of e-books? The drawbacks?*

FOR FURTHER INFORMATION AND STUDY

Chapter 14 of this book, "Technology in Academic Disciplines," offers a series of readings on new and developing technologies, exploring their use in a variety of disciplines.

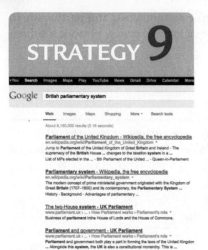

STRATEGY 9

Google and the Google logo are registered trademarks of Google Inc., used with permission.

Focus Your Research

Twenty years ago, anyone who conducted research had to sit in a library, sort through a card catalog, and wander the stacks looking for the books and journals they needed. The Internet has changed all that. Today's students can conduct research and work on assignments anywhere they have a computer and an Internet connection.

Although convenient, the Internet contains a vast amount of information that is not organized in any particular way. It becomes important, then, to limit or qualify your information search to yield the best results.

Starting with Google and Wikipedia

While many Internet search engines are available, most information searches today start with Google (www.google.com). No matter what your topic, Google is likely to return highly relevant results on the first try, which is what has made this search engine so popular.

It often helps to use Google's "Advanced Search" feature, which is located at the bottom of the first page of results. After clicking on "Advanced Search," type your search term in the box labeled "this exact word or phrase," then click the "Advanced Search" button. This type of search allows you to find the phrase that corresponds *exactly* to your search term.

Wikipedia (www.wikipedia.org) is an online encyclopedia that has no specific author. Rather, anyone is permitted to adjust, change, or add to any entry. For this reason, Wikipedia is almost never acceptable as a source in a term paper or project. However, many of the discussions in Wikipedia come with footnotes that cite credible sources. Clicking on the relevant citations can take you to credible Web sites with good information. The best overall guideline for using Wikipedia is this: Use it as a place to start or to develop a general understanding, but be cautious anytime you see a statement labeled "Citation needed." This means that the statement has not been verified by an expert. In general, remember that you need at least two credible sources to confirm any piece of information.

Remember to keep track of every URL you have visited so that you do not engage in unintentional plagiarism. Also remember that it is difficult to get full books online, unless you purchase them. Because many instructors require a combination of sources in term papers—including published books, articles, and Web sites—you will likely end up taking a trip to the library at some point.

Focus

In a world of information overload, it's easy to get distracted by all the materials coming at you on the Web. In general, you can often ignore the results that appear in a tinted box at the top of the first Google results page and the right-hand column of the results page. These are paid ads, usually from businesses that are trying to sell a product or service. In other search engines, you will see a list of "sponsored results" at the top or bottom of the results page. *Sponsored results* is another term for *advertisements*, so you can ignore these results, too. In some cases, however, Google uses the right-hand column to offer a snapshot of key information about the search term. For instance, if you conduct a Google search for the novelist Stephen King, the right-hand column of the first results page will provide photos of the author, a brief biography, and related searches.

Recent studies have shown that many students assume that the first page of Google results are the best results for the search. But the first results are not necessarily the best. You may sometimes have to dig deeper into the results to find the best sources of information.

Many Web sites, even those managed by credible information sources, have begun to accept advertisements. Often these advertisements are placed at the top, bottom, left, or right of the screen. Ignore the advertisements and focus on the center of the screen, where you're likely to find the best information.

Finally, remember that, in general, you are likely to get the best information from Web sites that end in *.edu* (indicating a college or university domain), *.org* (indicating a nonprofit organization), or *.gov* (indicating a government Web site that is home to reliable information and data). However, these Web sites may not be completely free of bias. For more information about bias, see Chapter 7.

EXERCISE 10 CONDUCTING AN ONLINE SEARCH

Directions: *List the courses you are taking this term. Conduct a Google search to identify at least three helpful Web sites for each course. How did you find these Web sites? Were they included on the first page of your Google results page, or did you have to dig deeper to find them?*

FOR FURTHER INFORMATION AND STUDY

Once you find information on a Web site, be sure to evaluate its purpose, content, and accuracy using the suggestions provided in Chapter 7, "Critical Reading," in the section titled "How Reliable Are Printed and Electronic Source Materials?"

STRATEGY **10**

Learn to Take Tests

Quizzes, midterms, and final exams are often the basis on which grades are awarded. But they are also valuable thinking and learning experiences. Quizzes force you to keep up with reading assignments, while longer exams require you to consolidate and integrate concepts and information. Exam questions fall into two general categories: objective (multiple-choice, true/false, matching) and essay exams.

Multiple-Choice and True/False Questions

Here are some tips for answering multiple-choice and true/false questions on exams:

- **Read the directions thoroughly.** The directions may contain crucial information you need to answer the questions correctly.
- **Answer every question.** Even if you guess at the answer, you have nothing to lose.
- **Watch for absolute words such as *all, none, always,* and *never.*** Absolute statements tend to be false or incorrect.
- **Read two-part statements carefully in true/false questions.** If both parts are not correct, then the answer must be "false."
- **Read all choices before choosing your answer,** even if you think you have found the correct one. In multiple-choice tests, remember that your job is to choose the best answer.
- **Avoid selecting answers that are unfamiliar or that you do not understand.**
- **When you have to guess at an answer, pick the one that seems complete and contains the most information.** Instructors are usually careful to make the best answer completely correct and recognizable. Such a choice often becomes long or detailed.
- **Play the odds.** In a multiple-choice test, if you can eliminate a couple of choices that are absolutely incorrect, you greatly increase your chances of getting the answer right.
- **If two of the answer choices are opposites, it is likely that one of them is the correct answer.**
- **If two similar answer choices are presented, one is likely to be correct.**
- **Don't change answers without a good reason.** When reviewing your answers before you turn in your exam, don't make a change unless you have a good reason for doing so. Very often your first impressions are correct.

- **Mark any item that contains unfamiliar terminology as false.** If you have studied the material thoroughly, trust that you would recognize as true anything that was part of the course content.
- **When all else fails, it is usually better to guess true rather than false.** It is more difficult for instructors to write plausible false statements than true statements. As a result, many exams have more true items than false items.
- **Choose a midrange number.** When a question asks you to select a number (such as a percentage or other statistic) and you don't know the correct answer, choose a midrange number. Test writers often include choices that are both higher and lower than the correct answer.

Essay Exams

Here are some tips for preparing for and taking essay exams:

- **Determine the likely questions on the exam.** You can do this by reviewing your lecture notes, thinking about the topics your instructor emphasized in class, rereading parts of your textbook, or talking with your classmates about possible questions. Write up the possible questions and practice answering them.
- **Remember that an essay exam requires an essay with a good topic sentence and adequate support.** Before you start writing, quickly outline your answer so that your essay has form and structure.
- **Keep your eye on the time.** Bring a watch to class and plan how much time you will spend on each question. You must answer each question to get a good grade.
- **Read the directions carefully before you start the exam,** looking for clues that will tell you what the instructor is looking for.
- **If you have a choice of questions, select carefully.** Read all the questions first, and then choose the questions on which you will be able to score the most points.
- **If you don't know the answer, do not leave the page blank; write something.** In attempting to answer the question, you may hit upon some partially correct information. However, the main reason for writing something is to give the instructor an opportunity to give you at least a few points for trying. If you leave a blank page, your instructor has no choice but to give you zero points.

Be sure to begin studying for each major exam at least a week before the test. Research has shown that early preparation leads to higher grades than an all-night cram session the day before the test. Show up for the exam a few minutes early, sit at the front of the room (to minimize distractions and be one of the first to get the exam), and bring the necessary materials (including pens, pencils, and erasers).

EXERCISE 11 ANALYZING TEST QUESTIONS

Directions: *The following multiple-choice items appeared on a psychology exam. Study each item and use your reasoning skills to eliminate items that seem incorrect. Then, making an educated guess, select the best answer.*

_____ 1. If a psychologist were personally to witness the effects of a tornado on the residents of a small town, what technique would she be using?

    a. experimentation
    b. correlational research
    c. observation
    d. none of the above

_____ 2. A case study is a(n)

    a. synonym for a longitudinal study.
    b. comparison of similar events.
    c. study of changes and their effects.
    d. intense investigation of a particular occurrence.

_____ 3. Approximately what percentage of men are color blind?

    a. 1 percent
    b. 10 percent
    c. 99 percent
    d. 100 percent

_____ 4. Jane Goodall has studied the behavior of chimpanzees in their own habitat. She exemplifies a school of psychology that is concerned with

    a. theories.
    b. mental processes.
    c. human behavior.
    d. naturalistic behavior.

FOR FURTHER INFORMATION AND STUDY

Many of the questions in this book are multiple-choice or true/false. Use the techniques you learned here to help you determine the correct answers.

A Handbook for Reading and Thinking in College

PART ONE

1 Active Reading and Thinking Strategies

LEARNING OBJECTIVES

In this chapter, you will learn how to . . .

1 Read actively
2 Preview before reading
3 Activate your background knowledge
4 Write as you read
5 Check your comprehension
6 Strengthen your comprehension

What does it take to do well in biology? In psychology? In history? In business? In answer to these questions, college students are likely to say:

- "Knowing how to study."
- "You have to like the course."
- "Hard work!"
- "Background in the subject area."
- "A good teacher!"

Students seldom mention reading as an essential skill. In a sense, reading is a hidden factor in college success. When you think of college, you think of attending classes and labs, completing assignments, studying for and taking exams, and writing papers. A closer look at these activities, however, reveals that reading is an important part of each.

Reading stays "behind the scenes" because instructors rarely evaluate it directly. Grades are based on production: how well you express your ideas in papers or how well you do on exams. Yet reading is the primary means by which you acquire your ideas and gather information.

Throughout this handbook you will learn numerous ways to use reading as a tool for college success.

1a   ACTIVE READING: THE KEY TO ACADEMIC SUCCESS

LEARNING OBJECTIVE 1
Read actively

Reading involves much more than moving your eyes across lines of print, more than recognizing words, and more than reading sentences. Reading is thinking. It is an active process of identifying important ideas and comparing, evaluating, and applying them.

Have you ever gone to a ball game and watched the fans? Most do not sit and watch passively. Instead, they direct the plays, criticize the calls, encourage the players, and reprimand the coach. They care enough to get actively involved in the game. Just like interested fans, active readers get involved. They question, challenge, and criticize, as well as understand. Table 1-1 below contrasts the active strategies of successful readers with the passive ones of less successful readers. Not all strategies will work for everyone. Experiment to discover those that work particularly well for you.

TABLE 1-1 ACTIVE VERSUS PASSIVE READING

ACTIVE READERS ...	PASSIVE READERS ...
Tailor their reading to suit each assignment.	Read all assignments the same way.
Analyze the purpose of an assignment.	Read an assignment because it was assigned.
Adjust their speed to suit their purpose.	Read everything at the same speed.
Question ideas in the assignment.	Accept whatever is in print as true.
Compare and connect textbook material with lecture content.	Study lecture notes and the textbook separately.
Skim headings to find out what an assignment is about before beginning to read.	Check the length of an assignment and then begin reading.
Make sure they understand what they are reading as they go along.	Read until the assignment is completed.
Read with pencil in hand, highlighting, jotting notes, and marking key vocabulary.	Read.
Develop personalized strategies that are particularly effective.	Follow routine, standard methods. Read all assignments the same way.
Look for the relevance of the assignment to their own lives.	Fixate on memorizing terms and definitions solely to pass the exam or get a good grade.
Engage with the contemporary issues under discussion with an open mind.	React emotionally to reading assignments without taking the time to carefully consider the author's key points.

EXERCISE 1-1 ACTIVE READING

Directions: *Consider each of the following reading assignments. List ways to get actively involved in each assignment.*

1. Reading two poems by Maya Angelou for an American literature class.

   _____

   _____

2. Reading the procedures for your next biology lab.

   _____

   _____

3. Reading an article in *Time* magazine assigned by your political science instructor in preparation for a class discussion.

   _____

   _____

1b   PREVIEWING

LEARNING OBJECTIVE 2
Preview before
reading

Previewing is a means of familiarizing yourself with the content and organization of an assignment *before* you read it. Think of previewing as getting a "sneak preview" of what a chapter or reading will be about. You can then read the material more easily and more rapidly.

How to Preview Reading Assignments

Use the following steps to become familiar with the content and organization of a chapter, essay, or article.

1. **Read the title.** The title indicates the topic of the article or chapter; the subtitle suggests the specific focus of, or approach to, the topic.
2. **Check the author and the source of an article and essay.** This information may provide clues about the article's content or focus.
3. **Read the introduction or the first paragraph.** The introduction or first paragraph serves as a lead-in, establishing the overall subject and suggesting how it will be developed.
4. **Read each boldfaced (dark print) heading.** Headings label the contents of each section and announce the major topic covered.
5. **Read the first sentence under each major heading.** This sentence often states the main point of the section. By reading first sentences, you will encounter most of the key ideas in the article. If there are no headings, read the first sentence of several paragraphs per page. If the first sentence seems introductory, read the last sentence; often this sentence states or restates the central thought.

6. **Note any typographical aids.** Colored print, **boldfaced** font, and *italics* are used to emphasize important terminology and definitions, distinguishing them from the rest of a passage. Material that is numbered 1, 2, 3; lettered a, b, c; or presented in list form is also of special importance.

7. **Note any graphic aids.** Graphs, charts, photographs, and tables often suggest what is important. Be sure to read the captions of photographs and the legends on graphs, charts, or tables.

8. **Read the last paragraph or summary.** This provides a condensed view of the article or chapter, often outlining the key points.

9. **Read quickly any end-of-article or end-of-chapter material.** This might include references, study questions, discussion questions, chapter outlines, or vocabulary lists. If there are study questions, read them through quickly because they tell you what is important to remember in the chapter. If a vocabulary list is included, rapidly skim through it to identify the terms you will be learning as you read.

A section of an interpersonal communication textbook chapter discussing types of body gestures is reprinted here to illustrate how previewing is done. The portions to focus on when previewing are shaded. Read only those portions. After you have finished, test how well your previewing worked by completing Exercise 1-2, "What Did You Learn from Previewing?"

Body Gestures

1   Nonverbal communication involves a variety of channels, including body gestures. An especially useful classification in **kinesics**—or the study of communication through body movement—identifies five types: emblems, illustrators, affect displays, regulators, and adaptors. The table on page 42 summarizes and provides examples of these five types of movements.

Emblems

2   **Emblems** are substitutes for words; they're body movements that have rather specific verbal translations, such as the nonverbal signs for "OK," "Peace," "Come here," "Go away," "Who, me?" "Be quiet," "I'm warning you," "I'm tired," and "It's cold." Emblems are as arbitrary as any words in any language. Consequently, your present culture's emblems are not necessarily the same as your culture's emblems of 300 years ago or the same as the emblems of other cultures. For example, the sign made by forming a circle with the thumb and index finger may mean "nothing" or "zero" in France, "money" in Japan, and something sexual in certain southern European cultures.

Illustrators

3   **Illustrators** accompany and literally illustrate verbal messages. Illustrators make your communications more vivid and help to maintain your listener's attention. They also help to clarify and intensify your verbal messages. In saying, "Let's go up," for example, you probably move your head and perhaps your finger in an upward direction.

In describing a circle or a square, you more than likely make circular or square movements with your hands. Research points to another advantage of illustrators: that they increase your ability to remember. People who illustrated their verbal messages with gestures remembered some 20 percent more than those who didn't gesture.

4 We are aware of illustrators only part of the time; at times, they may have to be brought to our attention. Illustrators are more universal than emblems; illustrators will be recognized and understood by members of more different cultures than will emblems.

Affect Displays

5 **Affect displays** are the movements of the face that convey emotional meaning—the expressions that show anger and fear, happiness and surprise, eagerness and fatigue. They're the facial expressions that give you away when you try to present a false image and that lead people to say, "You look angry. What's wrong?" We can, however, consciously control affect displays, as actors do when they play a role. Affect displays may be unintentional (as when they give you away) or intentional (as when you want to show anger, love, or surprise). A particular kind of affect display is the poker player's "tell," a bit of nonverbal behavior that communicates bluffing; it's a nonverbal cue that tells others that a player is lying. In much the same way that you may want to conceal certain feelings from friends or relatives, the poker player tries to conceal any such tells.

Regulators

6 **Regulators** monitor, maintain, or control the speaking of another individual. When you listen to another, you're not passive; you nod your head, purse your lips, adjust your eye focus, and make various paralinguistic sounds such as "mm-mm" or "tsk." Regulators are culture-bound: Each culture develops its own rules for the regulation of conversation. Regulators also include such broad movements as shaking your head to show disbelief or leaning forward in your chair to show that you want to hear more.

TABLE 6.2	Five Types of Body Movements

Can you identify similar gestures that mean different things in different cultures and that might create interpersonal misunderstandings?

Movement and Function	Examples
Emblems directly translate words or phrases.	"OK" sign, "Come here" wave, hitchhiker's sign
Illustrators accompany and literally "illustrate" verbal messages.	Circular hand movements when talking of a circle, hands far apart when talking of something large
Affect displays communicate emotional meaning.	Expressions of happiness, surprise, fear, anger, sadness, disgust
Regulators monitor, maintain, or control the speaking of another.	Facial expressions and hand gestures indicating "Keep going," "Slow down," or "What else happened?"
Adaptors satisfy some need.	Scratching head, chewing on pencil, adjusting glasses

7   Regulators communicate what you expect or want speakers to do as they're talking; for example, "Keep going," "Tell me what else happened," "I don't believe that. Are you sure?" "Speed up," and "Slow down." Speakers often receive these nonverbal signals without being consciously aware of them. Depending on their degree of sensitivity, speakers modify their speaking behavior in accordance with these regulators.

Adaptors

8   Adaptors satisfy some need and usually occur without conscious awareness; they're unintentional movements that usually go unnoticed. Nonverbal researchers identify three types of adaptors based on their focus, direction, or target: self-adaptors, alter-adaptors, and object-adaptors.

- *Self-adaptors* usually satisfy a physical need, generally serving to make you more comfortable. Examples include scratching your head to relieve an itch, moistening your lips because they feel dry, or pushing your hair out of your eyes. When these adaptors occur in private, they occur in their entirety: You scratch until the itch is gone. But in public these adaptors usually occur in abbreviated form. When people are watching you, for example, you might put your fingers to your head and move them around a bit but probably not scratch with the same vigor as when in private.
- *Alter-adaptors* are the body movements you make in response to your current interactions. Examples include crossing your arms over your chest when someone unpleasant approaches or moving closer to someone you like.
- *Object-adaptors* are movements that involve your manipulation of some object. Frequently observed examples include punching holes in or drawing on a styrofoam coffee cup, clicking a ballpoint pen, or chewing on a pencil. Object-adaptors are usually signs of negative feelings; for example, you emit more adaptors when feeling hostile than when feeling friendly. Further, as anxiety and uneasiness increase, so does the frequency of object-adaptors.

—adapted from DeVito, *The Interpersonal Communication Book*, pp. 143–144

EXERCISE 1-2 WHAT DID YOU LEARN FROM PREVIEWING?

Directions: *Without referr ing to the passage, answer each of the following true/false questions.*

_____ 1. Kinesics is the study of communication through body movement.

_____ 2. The nonverbal signs for "OK" and "I'm cold" are examples of emblems.

_____ 3. Facial expressions that convey emotional meaning are called illustrators.

_____ 4. Regulators communicate what you want speakers to do as they are talking, such as speed up or slow down.

_____ 5. Nonverbal researchers have identified five types of adaptors.

You probably were able to answer all (or most) of the questions in Exercise 1-2 correctly. Previewing, then, does provide you with a great deal of information. If you were to return to the passage from the textbook and read the entire section, you would find it easier to do than if you hadn't previewed it.

Why Previewing Is Effective

Previewing is effective for several reasons:

- **Previewing helps you to make decisions about how you will approach the material.** On the basis of what you discover about the assignment's organization and content, you can select the reading and study strategies that will be most effective.
- **Previewing puts your mind in gear and helps you start thinking about the subject.**
- **Previewing also gives you a mental outline of the chapter's content.** It enables you to see how ideas are connected, and since you know where the author is headed, reading will be easier than if you had not previewed. Previewing, however, is never a substitute for careful, thorough reading.

EXERCISE 1-3 PREVIEWING

Directions: *Assume you are taking a sociology course. Your instructor has assigned the following article from the* Utne Reader, *a periodical that focuses on current issues reported in a variety of alternative and independent presses. Preview, but do not read, the article using the procedure described on pages 40–41. When you have finished, answer the questions that follow.*

Treating Wounded Soldiers: Polytrauma

Joan O'C. Hamilton

1   Corporal Jason Poole was 17 when he joined the U.S. Marine Corps in 2000. On his third tour of duty in Iraq in 2004, Poole was in a group patrolling near the Syrian border when an improvised explosive device detonated, killing two Marines and an interpreter, and ripping off the top left part of Poole's head. He had surgery to repair and seal his skull and remained in a coma for almost two months. When he finally awoke to see the excited face of his twin sister, he was frightened and disoriented—although he laughs at the memory of reaching immediately for his head. "I thought I'd have some big Afro after two months," Poole says, "but my head was shaved."

2   Five years after that horrific blast, he sits in a visitors' lounge at the Veterans Affairs Palo Alto Health Care System. He is blind in his left eye, deaf in his left ear. His right

side is weak and his right arm heavily scarred. His hands and arms still contain scores of faint, freckle-sized black specks of shrapnel. But many subsequent surgeries have given Poole back a friendly and good-looking face whose scars do not overshadow his easy, bright smile. That in itself is something of a miracle. Not to mention the fact that he has relearned how to speak, how to eat, how to read, how to walk.

Jason Poole, at left.

What Is Polytrauma?

3   There is no official definition for polytrauma in most dictionaries, although it's easy enough to figure out: *Trauma* is bodily shock or emotional injury; *Poly* is from the ancient Greek for *many*. But at the VA Palo Alto's Ward 7D, the Polytrauma Rehabilitation Center (PRC), the idea of "many" shocks and injuries barely does justice to reality. Palo Alto is one of four PRCs—along with those in Minneapolis, in Tampa, Florida, and in Richmond, Virginia—chartered in 2005 to address what the U.S. military acknowledges is a signature injury of its operations in Afghanistan and Iraq: traumatic brain injury (TBI) in combination with other combat wounds. Service members patrolling debris-strewn streets and crowded areas are vulnerable to booby-trapped roadside bombs that not only hurl shrapnel into and through body tissue at tremendous force and create burns, but also produce a shock wave that can severely damage the brain without any visible sign of injury.

4   Veterans with polytrauma often return with profound physical disfigurements, missing limbs, and serious organ damage. But their TBIs also produce myriad neurological symptoms, which can include amnesia, headaches, dizziness, vision problems, and the inability to concentrate, swallow, speak, or read. They also suffer from insomnia and nightmares. And they battle other common symptoms of posttraumatic stress disorder, such as a lack of impulse control, flashbacks, and irritability. Together, these issues affect their ability to think, to sleep, to see, to interact normally with others—even to recognize their spouses and children.

5   In March 2009 Pentagon officials reported that more than 350,000 service members that returned from deployment in Iraq and Afghanistan might have suffered some form of brain injury. (This includes mild TBI, or concussion.) The Department of Veterans Affairs estimates that it has treated 8,000 brain injuries in this group. So far about 700 of the most gravely injured have been treated in the four PRCs, almost 200 of them in Palo Alto.

Treatment at the Polytrauma Research Center

6   Patients spend an average of 42 days in Ward 7D. Those who are in a coma spend at least 90 days, most at least six months. During that time, an extraordinary number of specialists work with them. When program director Sandy Lai settles into a chair at her team's biweekly meeting to discuss cases, she joins about 20 team members from physiatry, rehabilitation nursing, blind rehabilitation, neuropsychology, psychology, speech-language pathology, occupational therapy, physical therapy, social work, chaplaincy, nutrition, therapeutic recreation, and prosthetics. Virtually everyone has an opinion and a therapeutic or diagnostic angle on the patients under discussion; they comment on everything from the growing strength in one person's injured leg to how to convince another person to take his medications. All are encouraged to contribute any insight or observation that may help. A speech pathology aide, for example, shares her discovery that one of the patients is particularly interested in basketball. These are the seemingly small but significant insights that can provide a window on motivating someone in a new way.

7   One aspect of these patients' lives that demands a new approach is their youth. Before the wars in Afghanistan and Iraq, the VA facilities mostly were dealing with Vietnam veterans, who are much older, Lai explains. The Afghanistan and Iraq service members "do not want to play bingo as rehabilitation," Lai says. "They have more energy, they are more technology oriented. They even have bigger appetites. We have redesigned the kitchens so they and their families can access food more easily; we have brought in Wii systems and personal computers for their recreational therapy."

Family-Centered Care

8   Because of their youth, these veterans also have families who are far more involved in their care than many older veterans' families, and those families have expectations for recovery that the staff have to both support and manage. Lai, whose background is in family medicine, was instrumental in developing the four PRCs' "family-centered care" philosophy, which from day one strikes a partnership with the injured service members' families, including parents and, often, very young spouses who are overwhelmed by the tragedy. "We always try to focus on the possibilities," Lai says. "When we admit the patient, he or she may have a serious disfigurement. We try to focus on what we know is possible, that a prosthetic, for example, will eventually restore a normal-looking head to the patient, and that young people's ability to heal is quite amazing."

9   Jason Poole's sunny demeanor masks the lingering consequences of his brain injury. He has no memory of the explosion that changed his life. He sometimes has trouble finding the right words, and it's hard to concentrate when he reads. As we talk, a slight, pale young man who has been standing a bit uncomfortably near us suddenly pulls up a chair and announces, "I find when I join a group, the group stops functioning as it has been."

10   Such jarring comments are not uncommon here. TBI robs many patients of the ability to empathize, read social situations, or interact as expected. Poole's compassion and social skills are intact. He leans toward the anxious young man with genuine concern and reassures him that we're simply in the middle of a conversation we

need to finish. No hard feelings, nothing to worry about. In fact, he says, "I'll catch up with you later, man."

—Hamilton, *Stanford* magazine, November/December 2009

1. What is the overall subject of this article?

_____

2. What caused Jason Poole's injuries?

_____

3. What is polytrauma?

_____

4. Why do recovery expectations differ for these veterans?

_____

5. On a scale of 1 to 5 (1 = easy, 5 = very difficult), how difficult do you expect the article to be?

_____

1c   ACTIVATING BACKGROUND KNOWLEDGE

LEARNING OBJECTIVE 3
Activate your background knowledge

After previewing your assignment, you should take a moment to think about what you already know about the topic. Whatever the topic, you probably know *something* about it: This is your background knowledge. For example, a student was about to read an article titled "Growing Urban Problems" for a sociology class. His first thought was that he knew very little about urban problems because he lived in a rural area. But when he thought of a recent trip to a nearby city, he remembered seeing the homeless people and crowded conditions. This recollection helped him remember reading about drug problems, drive-by shootings, and muggings.

Activating your background knowledge aids your reading in three ways. First, it makes reading easier because you have already thought about the topic. Second, the material is easier to remember because you can connect the new information with what you already know. Third, topics become more interesting if you can link them to your own experiences. Here are some techniques to help you activate your background knowledge:

- **Ask questions, and try to answer them.** If a chapter in your biology textbook titled "Human Diseases" contains headings such as "Infectious diseases," "Sexually transmitted diseases," "Cancer," and "Vascular diseases," you might ask and try to answer such questions as the following: What kinds of infectious diseases have I seen? What caused them? What do I know about preventing cancer and other diseases?

- **Draw on your own experience.** If a chapter in your business textbook is titled "Advertising: Its Purpose and Design," you might think of several ads you have seen and then analyze the purpose of each and how it was constructed.
- **Brainstorm.** Write down everything that comes to mind about the topic. Suppose you're about to read a chapter in your sociology textbook on domestic violence. You might list types of violence—child abuse, rape, and so on. You might write questions such as "What causes child abuse?" and "How can it be prevented?" Alternatively, you might list incidents of domestic violence you have heard or read about. Any of these approaches will help to make the topic interesting.

EXERCISE 1–4 ACTIVATING BACKGROUND KNOWLEDGE

Directions: Use one of the three strategies listed above to discover what you already know about injuries veterans have sustained in the wars in Iraq and Afghanistan.

1d WRITING TO STRENGTHEN YOUR READING AND RECALL

LEARNING OBJECTIVE 4
Write as you read

Many students find that reading with a pen or a highlighter in their hand is an excellent way to continue their active-reading mind-set. Highlighting key information in a reading helps you focus your attention, sort ideas, and create a document that helps you review the material at a later date. Consider the following passages. One is highlighted; the other is not.

The major challenge facing single people through the ages has been building a satisfying life in a society highly geared toward marriage. Until recently, the general tendency in U.S. popular culture has been to portray singles as belonging in one of two stereotypical groups. On the one side is the "swinging single"—the partygoer who is carefree, uncommitted, sexually adventuresome, and the subject of envy by married friends. Poles apart from this image is the "lonely loser"—the unhappy, frustrated, depressed single who lives alone and survives on TV dinners, a fate few people would envy.

The major challenge facing single people through the ages has been building a satisfying life in a society highly geared toward marriage. Until recently, the general tendency in U.S. popular culture has been to portray singles as belonging in one of two stereotypical groups. On the one side is the "swinging single"—the partygoer who is carefree, uncommitted, sexually adventuresome, and the subject of envy by married friends. Poles apart from this image is the "lonely loser"—the unhappy, frustrated, depressed single who lives alone and survives on TV dinners, a fate few people would envy.

—Schwartz and Scott, *Marriages and Families*, p. 212

Which version would you prefer to study and why? You likely prefer the highlighted version, because it identifies the selection's key points and makes review easier and faster.

To highlight effectively, read the selection completely through first, then go back and highlight during your second reading. Do not highlight too much or too little. If you highlight too much, you have not selected the reading's main points. If you highlight too little, you will miss key points during your review. Avoid highlighting complete sentences. Highlight only enough so that your highlighting makes sense when you read it. (For more information on highlighting, see section 5d.)

Highlighting is beneficial for several reasons:

- Highlighting forces you to sift through what you have read to identify important information. This sifting or sorting helps you weigh and evaluate what you read.
- Highlighting keeps you physically active while you read and improves concentration.
- Highlighting can help you discover the organization of facts and ideas as well as their connections and relationships.
- Highlighting helps you determine whether you have understood a passage you just read. If you don't know what to highlight, you don't understand it.

A word of caution: Do not assume that what is highlighted is learned. You must process the information by organizing it, expressing it in your own words, and testing yourself periodically.

Two additional active reading strategies are *annotating* (using a pen to underline key phrases, make notes in the margin, and so on) and *summarizing* (writing a brief summary of the reading's key points). Both of these strategies use writing to increase recall and engagement with the material. We discuss annotation in detail in section 5e and summarizing in section 5i.

1e   CHECKING YOUR COMPREHENSION

LEARNING OBJECTIVE 5
Check your comprehension

What happens when you read material you can understand easily? Does it seem that everything "clicks"? Do ideas seem to fit together and make sense? Is that "click" noticeably absent at other times?

Table 1-2 on page 50 lists and compares common signals to assist you in checking your comprehension. Not all the signals appear at the same time, and not all the signals work for everyone. But becoming aware of these positive and negative signals will help you gain more control over your reading.

TABLE 1-2 COMPREHENSION SIGNALS

POSITIVE SIGNALS	NEGATIVE SIGNALS
You feel comfortable and have some knowledge about the topic.	The topic is unfamiliar, yet the author assumes you understand it.
You recognize most words or can figure them out from context.	Many words are unfamiliar.
You can express the main ideas in your own words.	You must reread the main ideas and use the author's language to explain them.
You understand why the material was assigned.	You do not know why the material was assigned and cannot explain why it is important.
You read at a regular, comfortable pace.	You often slow down or reread.
You are able to make connections among ideas.	You are unable to detect relationships; the organization is not apparent.
You are able to see where the author is heading.	You feel as if you are struggling to stay with the author and are unable to predict what will follow.
You understand what is important.	Nothing (or everything) seems important.
You read calmly and try to assess the author's points without becoming too emotionally involved.	When you encounter a controversial topic, you close your mind to alternative viewpoints or opinions.

EXERCISE 1-5 CHECKING YOUR COMPREHENSION

Directions: *Read the article titled "Treating Wounded Soldiers: Polytrauma" that appears on pages 44–47. Be alert for positive and negative comprehension signals as you read. After reading the article, answer the following questions.*

1. On a scale of 1 to 5 (1 = very poor, 5 = excellent), how would you rate your overall comprehension? _____

2. What positive signals did you sense? List them below.

   _____

   _____

   _____

3. What negative signals did you experience, if any? List them below.

   _____

   _____

   _____

4. In which sections was your comprehension strongest? List the paragraph numbers. _____

5. Did you feel at any time that you had lost, or were about to lose, comprehension? If so, go back to that part now. What made it difficult to read?

_____

_____

1f   STRENGTHENING YOUR COMPREHENSION

LEARNING OBJECTIVE 6
Strengthen your comprehension

Here are some suggestions to follow when you realize you need to strengthen your comprehension.

1. **Analyze the time and place in which you are reading.** If you've been reading or studying for several hours, mental fatigue may be the source of the problem. If you are reading in a place with distractions or interruptions, you might not be able to understand what you're reading.
2. **Rephrase each paragraph in your own words.** You might need to approach complicated material sentence by sentence, expressing each in your own words.
3. **Read aloud sentences or sections that are particularly difficult.** Reading out loud sometimes makes complicated material easier to understand.
4. **Reread difficult or complicated sections.** In fact, at times several readings are appropriate and necessary.
5. **Slow down your reading rate.** On occasion, simply reading more slowly and carefully will provide you with the needed boost in comprehension.
6. **Write questions next to headings.** Refer to your questions frequently and jot down or underline answers.
7. **Write a brief outline of major points.** This will help you see the overall organization and progression of ideas.
8. **Highlight key ideas.** After you've read a section, go back and think about and underline what is important. Underlining forces you to sort out what is important, and this sorting process builds comprehension and recall. (Refer to section 5d for suggestions on how to highlight effectively.)
9. **Write notes in the margins.** Explain or rephrase difficult or complicated ideas or sections.
10. **Determine whether you lack background knowledge.** Comprehension is difficult, or at times impossible, if you lack essential information that the writer assumes you have. Suppose you are reading a section of a political science text in which the author describes implications of the balance of power in the Third World. If you do not understand the concept of balance of power, your comprehension will break down. When

you lack background information, take immediate steps to correct the problem:

- Consult other sections of your text, using the glossary and index.
- Obtain a more basic text that reviews fundamental principles and concepts.
- Consult reference materials (encyclopedias, subject or biographical dictionaries).
- Ask your instructor to recommend additional sources, guidebooks, or review texts.

SUMMARY OF LEARNING OBJECTIVES

1	**Read actively** **What is active reading?**	Reading is thinking. **Active reading** is the process of identifying important ideas in a reading selection and comparing, evaluating, and applying them. To read actively, determine the purpose of a reading assignment and then adjust your speed to suit your purpose.
2	**Preview before reading** **Why is it important to preview before you read, and what does it entail?**	**Previewing** is a means of familiarizing yourself with the content and organization of an assignment **before** you read it. Previewing entails using the title and subtitle, headings, the introductory and concluding paragraphs, key sentences, and typographical aids to get a "sneak preview" of what a reading selection will be about.
3	**Activate your background knowledge** **Why is it important to activate background knowledge?**	Effective readers connect their **background knowledge**—what they already know about a topic—to what they are reading. Activating your background knowledge makes reading easier because you have already thought about the topic; the material easier to remember because you can connect the new information with what you already know; and the topics become more interesting because you connect them to your own experiences.
4	**Write as you read** **What does it mean to "write as you read"?**	One way to write as you read is by **highlighting key information,** which helps you focus your attention, sort ideas, and review easier and faster. To highlight effectively, read the selection first, then go back and highlight key points. Two additional active reading strategies are **annotating** (using a pen to underline key phrases, make notes in the margin, and so on) and **summarizing** (writing a brief summary of the reading's key points), both of which increase recall and engagement with the material.

5	Check your comprehension **How do you check your comprehension?**	**Use comprehension signals** (such as the level of the vocabulary and your ability to make connections among ideas) while you read to determine how well you understand the material. If you experience a low level of comprehension, adjust your reading strategy.
6	Strengthen your comprehension **How do you strengthen your reading comprehension?**	To **strengthen comprehension,** ensure your reading area is free of distractions. Rephrase paragraphs and ideas in your own words, and reread complicated sections. Decrease your reading rate or read sentences aloud. Use questions, outlines, highlighting, and margin notes to engage with the reading. Assess your background knowledge and consult other sources if necessary.

2 Vocabulary Building

LEARNING OBJECTIVES

In this chapter, you will learn how to . . .

1 Use context clues

2 Use prefixes, roots, and suffixes

3 Use unusual words and idioms

Your vocabulary can be one of your strongest assets or one of your greatest liabilities. It defines and describes you by revealing a great deal about your level of education and your experience. Your vocabulary contributes to that all-important first impression people form when they meet you. A strong vocabulary provides both immediate academic benefits and long-term career effects. This chapter describes two methods of strengthening your vocabulary: using context clues and word parts. It also introduces *idioms*, which are phrases with a meaning different from their individual words.

2a USING CONTEXT CLUES

LEARNING OBJECTIVE 1
Use context clues

Read the following brief paragraph in which several words are missing. Try to figure out the missing words and write them in the blanks.

> Rate refers to the _____ at which you speak. If you speak too _____, your listeners will not have time to understand your message. If you speak too _____, your listeners' minds will wander.

Did you insert the word *speed* in the first blank, *fast* in the second blank, and *slowly* in the third blank? Most likely you correctly identified all three missing words. You could tell from the sentence which word to put in. The words around the missing words—the sentence **context**—provided clues as to which word would fit and make sense. Such clues are called **context clues**.

While you probably won't find missing words on a printed page, you will often find words whose meaning you do not know. Context clues can help you figure out the meanings of unfamiliar words.

Example

> **Phobias**, such as fear of heights, water, snakes, or confined spaces, can make it difficult for people to function.

From the sentence, you can tell that *phobia* means "fear of specific objects or situations."

Here's another example:

> The couple finally **secured** a table at the crowded restaurant.

You can figure out that *secured* means "got" or "succeeded in getting" the table.

There are four types of context clues to look for: (1) definition, (2) example, (3) contrast, and (4) logic of the passage.

Definition Clues

Many times a writer defines a word immediately following its use. The writer may directly define the word by giving a brief definition or a *synonym* (a word that has the same meaning). To signal a definition, the writer will often use such words and phrases as *means, is, refers to,* and *can be defined as*. Here are some examples:

> **Corona** refers to *the outermost part of the sun's atmosphere.*
>
> A **soliloquy** is *a speech made by a character in a play that reveals his or her thoughts to the audience.*

At other times, a writer may provide you with clues rather than formally define the word. Punctuation is often used to signal that a definition clue will follow. Punctuation separates the meaning clue from the rest of the sentence. Three types of punctuation—commas, parentheses, and dashes—are used in this way. In the examples below, notice that punctuation separates the meaning clue from the rest of the sentence.

1. **Commas**

> *Five-line rhyming poems,* or **limericks**, are among the simplest forms of poetry.
>
> **Equity**, *a catch-all term for the general principles of fairness and justice*, is used in law when existing laws do not apply or are inadequate.

2. **Parentheses**

> **Lithium** (*an alkali metal*) is so soft it can be cut with a knife.
>
> A leading cause of heart disease is a diet with too much **cholesterol** (*a fatty substance made of carbon, hydrogen, and oxygen*).

3. **Dashes**

> We would like our country's **gross national product**—*the total market value of its national output of goods and services*—to increase steadily.
>
> Ancient Egyptians wrote in **hieroglyphics**—*pictures used to represent words.*
>
> **Facets**—*small flat surfaces at different angles*—bring out the beauty of a diamond.

EXERCISE 2-1 USING DEFINITION CLUES 1

Directions: *Read each sentence and write a definition or synonym for each bold-faced word or phrase. Use the definition context clue to help you determine word meaning.*

1. The judge's **candor**—his sharp, open frankness—shocked the jury.

   _____

2. A **chemical bond** is a strong attractive force that holds two or more atoms together.

   _____

3. Hearing, technically known as **audition**, begins when a sound wave reaches the outer ear.

   _____

4. A **species** is a group of animals or plants that share similar characteristics and are able to interbreed.

   _____

   _____

5. Many diseases have **latent periods**, periods of time between the infection and the first appearance of a symptom.

   _____

EXERCISE 2-2 USING DEFINITION CLUES 2

Directions: *Read the following paragraphs and use definition clues to help you de-termine the meaning of each boldfaced word or phrase.*

During **adolescence** (the period of growth from childhood to maturity), friendship choices are directed overwhelmingly to other students in the same school. Adolescent students may be involved in an informal network of friendship subsystems that operate primarily within the boundaries of the school world.

Cliques are relatively small, tightly knit groups of friends who spend considerable and often exclusive time with each other. Although cliques are the most common and important friendship structure for adolescents, not everyone belongs to one; in fact, fewer than half of adolescents do. About 30 percent of students are **liaisons**—individuals who have friends from several different cliques but belong to none. The remaining students are **social isolates**—individuals with few friends. Schools also contain **crowds**, which are loose associations of cliques that usually get together on weekends.

—adapted from Rice and Dolgin, *The Adolescent*, pp. 250–251

1. adolescence _____

2. cliques _____

   _____

3. liaisons _____

4. social isolates _____

5. crowds _____

Example Clues

Writers often include examples that help to explain or clarify a word. Suppose you do not know the meaning of the word *toxic*, and you find it used in the following sentence:

> **Toxic** materials, such as arsenic, asbestos, pesticides, and lead, can cause bodily damage.

This sentence gives four examples of toxic materials. From the examples given, which are all poisonous substances, you could conclude that *toxic* means "poisonous."

> Perceiving, learning, and thinking are examples of **cognitive** processes.

Cognitive processes, then, are mental processes.

> **Legumes**, such as peas and beans, produce pods.

Legumes, then, are vegetable plants that produce pods.

> Many **pharmaceuticals**, including morphine and other sedatives, are not readily available in some countries.

From the examples of morphine and sedatives, you know that pharmaceuticals are drugs.

EXERCISE 2-3 USING EXAMPLE CLUES 1

Directions: *Read each sentence and write a definition or synonym for each boldfaced word or phrase. Use the example context clues to help you determine word meaning.*

1. The child was **reticent** in every respect; she would not speak, refused to answer questions, and avoided looking at anyone.

   _____

2. Instructors provide their students with **feedback** through test grades and comments on papers.

   _____

3. Clothing is available in a variety of **fabrics**, including cotton, wool, polyester, and linen.

   _____

4. **Involuntary reflexes**, like breathing and beating of the heart, are easily measured.

   _____

5. The student had a difficult time distinguishing between **homonyms**—words such as *see* and *sea*, *wore* and *war*, and *deer* and *dear*.

   _____

EXERCISE 2-4 USING EXAMPLE CLUES 2

Directions: *Read the following paragraphs and use definition and example clues to help you determine the meaning of each boldfaced word or phrase.*

Freshwater lakes have three life zones. The **littoral zone**, nearest to shore, is rich in light and nutrients and supports the most diverse community—from cattails and bulrushes close to shore, to water lilies and algae at the deepest reaches of the zone. Inhabitants include snails, frogs, minnows, snakes, and turtles, as well as two categories of the microscopic organisms called plankton: photosynthetic **phytoplankton**, including bacteria and algae, and non-photosynthetic **zooplankton**, such as protists and tiny crustaceans.

The **limnetic zone** is the open-water region of a lake where enough light penetrates to support photosynthesis. Inhabitants of the limnetic zone include cyanobacteria, zooplankton, small crustaceans, and fish. Below the limnetic zone lies the **profundal zone**, which is too dark for photosynthesis. This zone is inhabited primarily by decomposers and detritus feeders, such as bacteria, snails, and insect larvae, and by fish that swim freely among the different zones.

—adapted from Audesirk et al., *Life on Earth*, pp. 622–624, 632

1. littoral zone _____

   _____

2. phytoplankton _____

_____

3. zooplankton _____

_____

4. limnetic zone _____

_____

5. profundal zone _____

_____

6. The selection may contain words whose meanings you cannot guess from context. List at least three of them here. Where might you find definitions of these words? _____

_____

_____

Contrast Clues

It is sometimes possible to determine the meaning of an unknown word from another word or phrase in the context with an opposite meaning (or *antonym*). In the following sentence, notice how a word opposite in meaning from the boldfaced word provides a clue to its meaning:

> One of the dinner guests **succumbed** to the temptation to have a second slice of pie, but the others resisted.

Although you may not know the meaning of *succumbed*, you know that the one guest who succumbed was different from the others who resisted. The word *but* suggests this. Because the others resisted a second dessert, you can tell that one guest gave in and had a second slice. Thus, *succumbed* means the opposite of *resist*; that is, *succumb* means "to give in to."

Examples

> Most of the graduates were **elated**, though a few felt sad and depressed.
> (The opposite of *sad and depressed* is joyful.)

> The old man seemed **morose**, but his grandson was very lively.
> (The opposite of *lively* is quiet and sullen.)

> The gentleman was quite **portly**, but his wife was thin.
> (The opposite of *thin* is heavy or fat.)

EXERCISE 2-5 USING CONTRAST CLUES 1

Directions: *Read each sentence and write a definition or synonym for each bold-faced word. Use the contrast context clue to help you determine word meaning.*

1. Some city dwellers are **affluent**; others live in or near poverty.

   _____

2. I am certain that the hotel will hold our reservation; however, if you are **dubious**, call to make sure.

   _____

3. Although most experts **concurred** with the research findings, several strongly disagreed.

   _____

4. The speaker **denounced** certain legal changes while praising other reforms.

   _____

5. When the couple moved into their new home, they **revamped** the kitchen and bathroom but did not change the rest of the rooms.

   _____

EXERCISE 2-6 USING CONTRAST CLUES 2

Directions: *Read the following paragraph and use contrast clues to help you determine the meaning of each boldfaced word. Consult a dictionary, if necessary.*

The Whigs chose General William Henry Harrison to run against President Martin Van Buren in 1840, using a **specious** but effective argument: General Harrison is a plain man of the people who lives in a log cabin. Contrast him with the suave Van Buren, **luxuriating** amid "the Regal Splendor of the President's Palace." Harrison drinks ordinary hard cider with his hog meat and grits, while Van Buren **eschews** plain food in favor of expensive foreign wines and fancy French cuisine. The general's furniture is **unpretentious** and sturdy; the president dines off gold plates and treads on carpets that cost the people $5 a yard. In a country where all are equal, the people will reject an **aristocrat** like Van Buren and put their trust in General Harrison, a simple, brave, honest, public-spirited common man. (In fact, Harrison came from a distinguished family, was well educated and financially comfortable, and certainly did not live in a log cabin.)

—adapted from Carnes and Garraty, *The American Nation*, p. 267

1. specious _____

2. luxuriating _____

3. eschews _____

4. unpretentious _____

5. aristocrat _____

Logic of the Passage Clues

Many times you can figure out the meaning of an unknown word by using logic and reasoning skills. For instance, look at the following sentence:

> Bob is quite **versatile**; he is a good student, a top athlete, an excellent car mechanic, and a gourmet cook.

You can see that Bob is successful at many different types of activities, and you could reason that *versatile* means "capable of doing many things competently."

> When the customer tried to pay with British **pounds**, the clerk explained that the store accepted only U.S. dollars.

Logic tells you that customers pay with money; *pounds*, then, are a type of British currency.

> We had to leave the car and walk up because the **incline** was too steep to drive.

Something that is too steep must be slanted or have a slope; *incline* means a slope.

> Because Reginald was nervous, he brought his rabbit's foot **talisman** with him to the exam.

A rabbit's foot is often thought to be a good luck charm; *talisman* means good luck charm.

EXERCISE 2-7 USING LOGIC OF THE PASSAGE CLUES 1

Directions: *Read each sentence and write a definition or synonym for each bold-faced word. Use information provided in the context to help you determine the word's meaning.*

1. The foreign students quickly **assimilated** many aspects of American culture.

_____

2. The legal aid clinic was **subsidized** by city and county funds.

_____

3. When the bank robber reached his **haven**, he breathed a sigh of relief and began to count his money.

_____

4. The teenager was **intimidated** by the presence of a police officer walking the beat and decided not to spray-paint the school wall.

_____

5. If the plan did not work, the colonel had a **contingency** plan ready.

_____

EXERCISE 2-8 USING LOGIC OF THE PASSAGE CLUES 2

Directions: _Read the following paragraph and use the logic of the passage clues to help you select the correct meaning of each boldfaced word or phrase._

Fashion is regarded as a national industry in France, and as such it is **fostered**, protected, and financed by its government. The French fashion industry is supported by devoted and skilled dressmakers. Dressmaking is a most honorable profession in France; **legions** of well-trained seamstresses are available to **execute** a designer's work. A great spirit of cooperation exists among the **allied** trades; for example, buttonmakers will provide the exact fastener that the designer requests or needs. Entire cities such as Alencon, Chantilly, Valenciennes, and Calais exist to support the fashion industry with their **exquisite** laces and trims.

—adapted from Marshall et al., _Individuality in Clothing Selection and Personal Appearance_, p. 111

_____ 1. fostered
   a. prevented
   b. promoted
   c. controlled
   d. allowed

_____ 2. legions
   a. groups
   b. businesses
   c. programs
   d. marketers

_____ 3. execute
   a. destroy
   b. combine
   c. produce
   d. criticize

_____ 4. allied
   a. related
   b. competitive
   c. separated
   d. selected

_____ 5. exquisite
   a. complicated
   b. expensive
   c. basic
   d. beautiful

SUMMING IT UP

CONTEXT CLUES

CONTEXT CLUE	HOW TO FIND MEANING	EXAMPLE
Definition	1. Look for words that announce that a meaning will follow (*is, are, refers to, are called, means*).	Broad, flat noodles that are served with sauce or butter are called **fettucine.**
	2. Look for parentheses, dashes, or commas that set apart synonyms or brief definitions.	Psychologists often wonder whether **stereotypes**—the assumptions we make about what people are like—might be self-fulfilling.
Example	Figure out what the examples have in common. (For example, both peas and beans are vegetables and grow in pods, so are in the *legume* family; plants whose seeds are set in pods.)	Most **condiments,** such as pepper, mustard, and ketchup, are used to improve the flavor of foods.
Contrast	Look for a word or phrase that is the opposite of a word whose meaning you don't know.	Before their classes in manners, the children were disorderly; after graduation, they acted with more **decorum.**
Logic of the Passage	Use the rest of the sentence to help you. Pretend the word is a blank line and fill in the blank with a word that makes sense.	On hot, humid afternoons, I often feel **languid.**

2b LEARNING PREFIXES, ROOTS, AND SUFFIXES

LEARNING OBJECTIVE 2
Use prefixes, roots, and suffixes

Suppose you come across the following sentence in a human anatomy textbook:

> Trichromatic plates are used frequently in the text to illustrate the position of body organs.

If you did not know the meaning of *trichromatic*, how could you determine it? There are no context clues in the sentence. One solution is to look up the word in a dictionary. An easier and faster way is to break the word into parts and analyze the meaning of each part. Many words in the English language are made up of word parts called **prefixes**, **roots**, and **suffixes**. These word parts have specific meanings that, when added together, can help you determine the meaning of the word as a whole.

The word *trichromatic* can be divided into three parts: its prefix, root, and suffix.

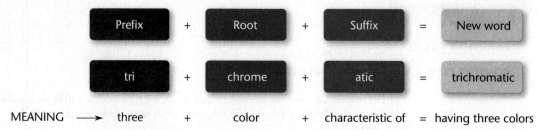

| Prefix | + | Root | + | Suffix | = | New word |
| tri | + | chrome | + | atic | = | trichromatic |

MEANING → three + color + characteristic of = having three colors

You can see from this analysis that *trichromatic* means "having three colors."

Here are two other examples of words that you can figure out by using prefixes, roots, and suffixes:

> The parents thought the child was **unteachable**.
> **un-** = not
> **teach** = help someone learn
> **-able** = able to do something
> **unteachable** = not able to be taught

> The student was a **nonconformist**.
> **non-** = not
> **conform** = go along with others
> **-ist** = one who does something
> **nonconformist** = someone who does not go along with others

The first step in using the prefix–root–suffix method is to become familiar with the most commonly used word parts. The prefixes and roots listed in Tables 2-1 and 2-2 (pp. 66 and 69) will give you a good start in determining the meanings of thousands of words without having to look them up in the dictionary. Before you begin to use word parts to figure out new words, there are a few things you need to know:

1. **In most cases, a word is built upon at least one root.**
2. **Words can have more than one prefix, root, or suffix.**
   a. Words can be made up of two or more roots (*geo/logy*).
   b. Some words have two prefixes (*in/sub/ordination*).
   c. Some words have two suffixes (*beauti/ful/ly*).
3. **Words do not always have a prefix and a suffix.**
   a. Some words have neither a prefix nor a suffix (*heat*).
   b. Others have a suffix but no prefix (*heat/ing*).
   c. Others have a prefix but no suffix (*pre/heat*).
4. **The spelling of roots may change as they are combined with suffixes.** Some common variations are included in Table 2-2 (p. 69).

5. **Different prefixes, roots, or suffixes may have the same meaning.** For example, the prefixes *bi-*, *di-*, and *duo-* all mean "two." The prefixes *un-*, *in-*, and *non-* all mean "not."

6. **Some roots, prefixes, and suffixes have different meanings in different words.** The meaning is based on whether the word part comes from Latin or Greek. For example, the biological term for mankind is *homo sapiens.* Here, *homo* means "man." In the word *homogenous*, which means "all of the same kind," *homo* means "same." Other words that use the Greek meaning of *homo* are *homogenize* (to make uniform or similar) and *homonym* (two words that sound the same).

7. **Sometimes you may identify a group of letters as a prefix or root but find that it does not carry the meaning of that prefix or root.** For example, the letters *mis* in the word *missile* are part of the root and are not the prefix *mis-*, which means "wrong; bad."

Prefixes

Prefixes appear at the beginning of many English words. They alter the meaning of the root to which they are connected. For example, if you add the prefix *re-* to the word *read*, the word *reread* is formed, meaning "to read again." If *pre-* is added to the word *reading*, the word *pre-reading* is formed, meaning "before reading." If the prefix *post-* is added, the word *post-reading* is formed, meaning "after reading." Table 2-1 (p. 66) lists common prefixes grouped according to meaning.

EXERCISE 2-9 USING PREFIXES 1

Directions: *Read the following paragraph and choose the correct prefix from the box below to fill in the blank next to each boldfaced word part. One prefix will not be used.*

multi	uni	pseudo
tri	bi	sub

   Neurons, or nerve cells, can be classified structurally according to the number of axons and dendrites that project from the cell body. (1) _____ **po-lar** neurons have a single projection from the cell body and are rare in humans. (2) _____ **polar** neurons have two projections, an axon and a dendrite, extending from the cell body. Other sensory neurons are (3) _____ **unipolar** neurons, a (4) _____ **class** of bipolar neurons. Although only one projection seems to extend from the cell body of this type of neuron, there are actually two projections that extend in opposite directions. (5) _____ **polar** neurons, the most common neurons, have multiple projections from the cell body; one projection is an axon, all the others are dendrites.

—adapted from Germann and Stanfield, *Principles of Human Physiology*, p. 174

TABLE 2-1 COMMON PREFIXES

PREFIX	MEANING	SAMPLE WORD
Prefixes referring to amount or number		
mono-/uni-	one	monocle/unicycle
bi-/di-/duo-	two	bimonthly/divorce/duet
tri-	three	triangle
quad-	four	quadrant
quint-/pent-	five	quintet/pentagon
dec-/deci-	ten	decimal
centi-	hundred	centigrade
homo-	same	homogenized
mega-	large	megaphone
milli-	thousand	milligram
micro-	small	microscope
multi-/poly-	many	multipurpose/polygon
nano-	extremely small	nanoplankton
semi-	half	semicircle
equi-	equal	equidistant
ultra-	beyond, extreme	ultrasweet
Prefixes meaning "not" (negative)		
a-	not	asymmetrical
anti-	against	antiwar
contra-/counter-	against, opposite	contradict
dis-	apart, away, not	disagree
in-/il-/ir-/im-	not	incorrect/illogical/irreducible/ impossible
mal-	poorly, wrongly	malnourished
mis-	wrongly	misunderstand
non-	not	nonfiction
un-	not	unpopular
pseudo-	false	pseudoscientific
Prefix meaning "good" or "well"		
eu-	good, well	eustress (a good type of stress)

(*continued on next page*)

(continued from preceding page)

PREFIX	MEANING	SAMPLE WORD
Prefixes giving direction, location, or placement		
ab-	away	absent
ad-	toward	adhesive
ante-/pre-	before	antecedent/premarital
circum-/peri-	around	circumference/perimeter
com-/col-/con-	with, together	compile/collide/convene
de-	away, from	depart
dia-	through	diameter
ex-/extra-	from, out of, former	ex-wife/extramarital
hyper-	over, excessive	hyperactive
hypo-	below, beneath	hypodermic
inter-	between	interpersonal
intro-/intra-/in-	within, into, in	introduction
post-	after	posttest
pre-	before	preview
re-	back, again	review
retro-	backward	retrospect
sub-	under, below	submarine
super-	above, extra	supercharge
tele-	far	telescope
trans-	cross, over	transcontinental
Prefix meaning "together"		
co-	joint, mutual, common	cooperate

EXERCISE 2–10 USING PREFIXES 2

Directions: *Read each of the following sentences. Use your knowledge of prefixes to fill in the blank and complete the word.*

1. A person who speaks two languages is _____ lingual.

2. A letter or number written beneath a line of print is called a _____ script.

3. The new sweater had a snag, and I returned it to the store because it was _____ perfect.

4. The flood damage was permanent and _____ reversible.

5. I was not given the correct date and time; I was _____ informed.

6. People who speak several different languages are _____ lingual.

7. A musical _____ lude was played between the events in the ceremony.

8. I decided the magazine was uninteresting, so I _____ continued my subscription.

9. Merchandise that does not pass factory inspection is considered _____ standard and is sold at a discount in outlet stores.

10. The tuition refund policy approved this week will apply to last year's tuition as well; the policy will be _____ active to January 1 of last year.

Roots

Roots carry the basic or core meaning of a word. Hundreds of root words are used to build words in the English language. Some of the most common and most useful are listed in Table 2-2. Knowing the meanings of these roots will help you unlock the meanings of many words. For example, if you know that the root *dic/dict* means "tell or say," then you have a clue to the meanings of such words as *dictate* (to speak for someone to write down), *diction* (wording or manner of speaking), and *dictionary* (book that lists what words say).

TABLE 2-2 COMMON ROOTS

COMMON ROOT	MEANING	SAMPLE WORD
aero	air	aeronautics
agr, agro	agriculture	agrobusiness
anthro/anthropo	human being	anthropology
archaeo	ancient or past	archeology
aster/astro	star	astronaut
aud/audit	hear	audible
bene	good, well	benefit
bio	life	biology
cap	take, seize	captive
cardi	heart	cardiology
chron(o)	time	chronology

COMMON ROOT	MEANING	SAMPLE WORD
corp	body	corpse
cred	believe	incredible
dict/dic	tell, say	predict
duc/duct	lead	introduce
eco	earth	ecological
fact/fac	make, do	factory
fem	female	feminine
gen	create	generate
geo	earth	geophysics
graph	write	telegraph
gyn, gyneco	woman	gynecology
hetero	different, other	heterosexual
log/logo/logy	study, thought	psychology
mit/miss	send	permit/dismiss
mort/mor	die, death	immortal
neuro	nerve	neurology
nom	name	nomenclature
osteo	bone	osteopath
path, patho	feeling	sympathy
	suffering/disease	pathology
phono	sound, voice	telephone
photo	light	photosensitive
phys	body	physiology
port	carry	transport
pulmo	lungs	pulmonary
psych	mind	psychology
scop	see	microscope
scrib/script	write	inscription
sen/sent	feel	insensitive
spec/spic/spect	look, see	retrospect
tend/tent/tens	stretch or strain	tension
terr/terre	land, earth	territory
theo	god	theology

(*continued on next page*)

(continued from preceding page)

COMMON ROOT	MEANING	SAMPLE WORD
vasc	blood vessels	vascular
ven/vent	come	convention
vert/vers	turn	invert
vis/vid	see	invisible/video
voc	call	vocation
xeno	foreign	xenophobia

EXERCISE 2-11 USING ROOTS 1

Directions: *Use the list of common roots in Table 2-2 to determine the meanings of the following words. Write a brief definition or synonym for each, checking a dictionary if necessary.*

1. photocopy

   _____

2. visibility

   _____

3. credentials

   _____

4. speculate

   _____

5. terrain

   _____

6. audition

   _____

7. astrophysics

   _____

8. chronicle

   _____

9. autograph

   _____

10. geology

    _____

EXERCISE 2-12 USING ROOTS 2

Directions: *Read the following paragraph and choose the correct root from the box below to fill in the blank next to each boldfaced word part. One root will not be used.*

bene	gyneco	voc
mit	bio	logy

People take different paths to their chosen profession. For example, Erin was only 11 when she decided on medicine as her (1) _____ **ation** after her grandfather had a stroke. Although she knew she wanted to be in the medical profession, she had a variety of options to consider. In college, Erin's advisor suggested that she major in (2) _____ **logy**, the study of life, because the coursework would be (3) _____ **ficial** to someone planning a career in medicine. Erin was also intrigued by the study of human behavior, so she minored in (4) **socio** _____. During her senior year, Erin travelled to Haiti as part of a health-care team. Through that experience, Erin realized that she was most interested in medical issues facing women; she is now in medical school on her way to becoming a (5) _____ **logist**.

Suffixes

Suffixes are word endings that often change the word's tense and/or part of speech. For example, adding the suffix *-y* to the noun *cloud* forms the adjective *cloudy*. Accompanying the change in part of speech is a shift in meaning (*cloudy* means "resembling clouds; overcast with clouds; dimmed or dulled as if by clouds").

Often, several different words can be formed from a single root word with different suffixes. If you know the meaning of the root word and the ways in which different suffixes affect the meaning of the root word, you will be able to figure out a word's meaning when a suffix is added. A list of common suffixes and their meanings appears in Table 2-3.

TABLE 2-3 COMMON SUFFIXES

SUFFIX	SAMPLE WORD
Suffixes that refer to a state, condition, or quality	
-able	touchable
-ance	assistance
-ation	confrontation
-ence	reference

(continued on next page)

(continued from preceding page)

SUFFIX	SAMPLE WORD
-ful	joyful
-ible	tangible
-ic	chronic
-ion	discussion
-ish	girlish
-ity	superiority
-ive	permissive
-less	hopeless
-ment	amazement
-ness	kindness
-ous	jealous
-tion	action
-ty	loyalty
-y	creamy

Suffixes that mean "one who"

SUFFIX	SAMPLE WORD
-an/-ian	Italian
-ant	participant
-ee	referee
-eer	engineer
-ent	resident
-er	teacher
-ist	activist
-or	advisor

Suffixes that mean "pertaining to or referring to"

SUFFIX	SAMPLE WORD
-ac	cardiac
-al	autumnal
-ary	secondary
-hood	brotherhood
-ship	friendship
-ward	homeward

Suffix that means "to make or become"

SUFFIX	SAMPLE WORD
-ize	mechanize

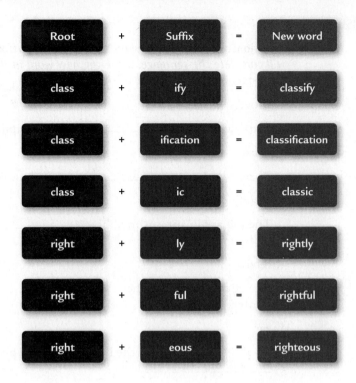

You can expand your vocabulary by learning the variations in meaning that occur when suffixes are added to words you already know. When you find a word whose meaning you do not know, look for the root. Then, using context, figure out what the word means with the suffix added. Occasionally you may find that the spelling of the root word has changed. For instance, a final *e* may be dropped, a final consonant may be doubled, or a final *y* may be changed to *i*. Consider the possibility of such changes when trying to identify the root word.

Examples

The article was a **compilation** of facts.
   root + suffix
compil(e) + -ation = something that has been compiled, or put together into an orderly form
I was concerned with the **legality** of my decision to change my name.
   root + suffix
legal + -ity = pertaining to legal matters
Our college is one of the most **prestigious** in the state.
   root + suffix
prestig(e) + -ous = having prestige or distinction

EXERCISE 2-13 USING SUFFIXES 1

Directions: *For each of the words listed, add a suffix so that the new word will complete the sentence. Write the new word in the space provided. Check a dictionary if you are unsure of the spelling.*

1. converse

   Our phone _____ lasted ten minutes.

2. assist

   The medical _____ labeled the patient's blood samples.

3. qualify

   The job applicant outlined his _____ to the interviewer.

4. intern

   The doctor completed her _____ at Memorial Medical Center.

5. eat

   We did not realize that the blossoms of the plant could be

   _____.

6. audio

   She spoke so softly that her voice was not _____.

7. season

   It is usually very dry in July, but this year it has rained constantly. The weather isn't very _____.

8. permit

   The professor granted me _____ to miss her class.

9. instruct

   The lecture on Freud was very _____.

10. remember

    The wealthy businessman donated the building in _____ of his deceased father.

EXERCISE 2-14 USING SUFFIXES 2

Directions: *Read the following paragraph. For each pair of words in parentheses, underline the word that correctly completes the sentence.*

How do new species form? Most evolutionary (1) (biologists / biological) believe that the most common source of new species, especially among animals, has been geographic isolation. When an (2) (impassable / impassor) barrier physically separates different parts of a population, a new species may result. Such physical separation could occur if, for example, some members of a population of land-dwelling organisms drifted, swam, or flew to a remote (3) (oceany / oceanic) island. Populations of water-dwelling organisms might be split when (4) (geological / geologist) processes such as volcanism or continental drift create new land barriers that divide previously (5) (continuous / continuation) seas or lakes. You can probably imagine many other scenarios that could lead to the geographic subdivision of a population.

—adapted from Audesirk et al., *Life on Earth*, p. 237

SUMMING IT UP

WORD PARTS

WORD PARTS	LOCATION	HOW TO USE THEM
Prefixes	Beginnings of words	Notice how the prefix changes the meaning of the root or base word. (How does meaning change when *un-* is added to the word *reliable?*)
Roots	Beginning or middle of words	Use roots to figure out the basic meaning of the word.
Suffixes	Endings of words	Notice how the suffix changes the meaning of the root or base word. (How does meaning change when *-ship* is added to the word *friend?*)

2c LEARNING UNUSUAL WORDS AND IDIOMS

LEARNING OBJECTIVE 3
Understand idioms

English is a rich language filled with unusual words and phrases, many of them borrowed from other languages or shaped into meaning over time. An **idiom** is a phrase with a meaning different from the phrase's individual words. Sometimes you can figure out an idiom's meaning from context within the sentence or paragraph, but more commonly you must simply know the idiom to understand it.

Examples

> The $10,000 he embezzled was just the **tip of the iceberg** (a small, observable part of something much larger).
>
> While the company's sales are excellent, its **bottom line** (total profit) is awful. ("Bottom line" refers to the last line of a financial statement, showing the company's overall profit or loss.)
>
> The only **sure-fire** (guaranteed to work) method of losing weight is diet and exercise.
>
> We have **buried our head in the sand** (denied reality) about our nation's deficit for far too long.

As you read, be on the lookout for phrases that use common words but do not make sense no matter how many times you reread them. When you find such a phrase, you have likely encountered an idiom. (It is estimated that English has almost 25,000 idiomatic expressions.)

EXERCISE 2-15 UNDERSTANDING IDIOMS

Directions: *For each sentence, write the meaning of the idiomatic expression in boldface.*

1. The kidnapping of the twins from Utah in 1985 has turned into a **cold case**.

   _____

2. Jake decided to **zero in on** his goal of becoming a firefighter.

   _____

3. I am trying to make an appointment with my academic advisor, but she's been hard to **pin down**.

   _____

4. The mystery novels of P. D. James **blur the line** between popular fiction and literature.

   _____

5. Milton **saw red** when someone rear-ended his car.

   _____

SUMMARY OF LEARNING OBJECTIVES

1	**Use context clues** **What are the four types of context clues?**	Context clues help readers figure out the meaning of unfamiliar words. Context clues fall into four categories: (1) definition clues, (2) example clues, (3) contrast clues, and (4) logic of the passage clues.
2	**Use prefixes, roots, and suffixes** **What are prefixes, roots, and suffixes?**	Many words are composed of some combination of prefix, root, and suffix. The prefix precedes the main part of the word; the root is the key part of the word that carries its core meaning; and the suffix appears at the end of the word. In the word *unteachable*, *un-* is the prefix, *teach* is the root, and *-able* is the suffix. Knowing the meanings of key prefixes, roots, and suffixes will help you unlock the meaning of many unfamiliar words.
3	**Understand idioms** **What are idioms?**	An idiom is a phrase with a meaning different from the phrase's individual words (such as "it's raining cats and dogs").

3 Thesis, Main Ideas, Supporting Details, and Transitions

LEARNING OBJECTIVES

In this chapter you will learn how to

1 Identify the thesis
2 Find stated main ideas
3 Recognize supporting details
4 Find implied main ideas
5 Recognize transitions

Most articles, essays, and textbook chapters contain numerous ideas. Some are more important than others. As you read, your job is to sort out the important ideas from those that are less important. For exams, your instructors expect that you have discovered and learned what is important in the assigned reading materials. In class, your instructors expect you to be able to discuss the important ideas from an assignment. In this chapter, you will learn to identify the thesis of a reading assignment and to distinguish main ideas and supporting details. You will also learn about transitions that writers use to link ideas together.

3a IDENTIFYING THE THESIS

LEARNING OBJECTIVE 1
Identify the thesis

The **thesis** is what the entire reading selection is about. Think of it as the one most important, general idea that the entire article or assignment explains. In articles and essays the thesis is quite specific and is often stated in one sentence, usually near the beginning of the article. In textbook chapters the thesis of the entire chapter is much more general. Individual sections of the chapter may have more specific theses. A psychology textbook chapter on stress, for example, may have as its thesis that stress can negatively affect us but there are ways to control it. A section within the chapter may discuss the thesis that there are five main sources of stress. A magazine article on stress in the workplace, because it is much shorter, would have an even more specific thesis. It might, for instance, express the thesis that building strong relationships with co-workers can help to alleviate stress.

Now look again at the article from *Stanford* magazine on the topic of polytrauma that appears on page 8.

The thesis of this reading is that polytrauma involves numerous physical and emotional injuries. The remainder of the article presents details that explain this thesis.

EXERCISE 3-1 IDENTIFYING THESIS STATEMENTS 1

Directions: *Underline the thesis statement in each group of sentences. Remember that thesis statements tend to be general.*

1. a. Monotheism is a belief in one supreme being.

   b. Polytheism is a belief in more than one supreme being.

   c. Theism is a belief in the existence of a god or gods.

   d. Monotheistic religions include Christianity, Judaism, and Islam.

2. a. Vincent Van Gogh is an internationally known and respected artist.

   b. Vincent Van Gogh's art displays a revolutionary approach to color.

   c. Vincent Van Gogh created seventy paintings in the last two months of his life.

   d. Vincent Van Gogh's art is respected for its attention to detail.

3. a. The Individuals with Disability Education Act offers guidelines for inclusive education.

   b. The inclusive theory of education says that children with special needs should be placed in regular classrooms and have services brought to them.

   c. The first movement toward inclusion was mainstreaming—a plan in which children with special needs were placed in regular classrooms for a portion of the day and sent to other classrooms for special services.

   d. Families play an important role in making inclusive education policies work.

4. a. Stress can have a negative effect on friendships and marital relationships.

   b. Stress can affect job performance.

   c. Stress is a pervasive problem in our culture.

   d. Some health problems appear to be stress related.

3b   FINDING STATED MAIN IDEAS

LEARNING OBJECTIVE 2
Find stated main ideas

A **paragraph** is a group of related sentences. The sentences are all about one thing, called the **topic.** A paragraph expresses a single idea about that topic. This idea is called the **main idea.** All the other sentences in the paragraph support this main idea. These sentences are called **supporting details.** Not all details in a paragraph are equally important.

In most paragraphs the main idea is expressed in a single sentence called the **topic sentence.** Occasionally, you will find a paragraph in which the main idea is not expressed in any single sentence. The main idea is **implied;** that is, it is suggested but not directly stated in the paragraph.

You can visualize a paragraph as shown in the accompanying diagram.*

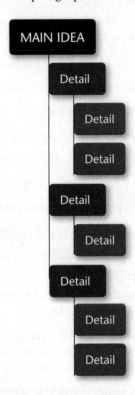

Distinguishing Between General and Specific Ideas

A *general* idea applies to a large number of individual items. The term *television programs* is general because it refers to a large collection of shows—soap operas, sports specials, sitcoms, and so on. A *specific* idea or term is more detailed or particular. It refers to an individual item. The term *reality TV*, for example, is more specific than the word *program*. The title *The Real Housewives of Atlanta* is even more specific.

Examples

General:	Continents	General:	Parts of Speech
Specific:	Asia	Specific:	noun
	Africa		verb
	Australia		adjective

*The number of details will vary.

EXERCISE 3-2 IDENTIFYING GENERAL IDEAS

Directions: *For each list of items, select the choice that best describes that grouping.*

_____ 1. dodo bird, tyrannosaurus rex, wooly mammoth, stegosaurus
    a. extinct animals
    b. animals
    c. endangered animals
    d. zoo animals

_____ 2. single-parent, divorced, two-career, married
    a. children
    b. incomes
    c. families
    d. societies

_____ 3. for money, for experience, to meet people
    a. reasons to attend a party
    b. reasons to get a part-time job
    c. reasons to apply for loans
    d. reasons to attend a basketball game

_____ 4. U.S. Constitution, Bill of Rights, Federalist Papers, First Amendment
    a. policies
    b. historical events
    c. historical documents
    d. party politics

_____ 5. Mars, Saturn, Jupiter, Mercury
    a. asteroids
    b. solar systems
    c. galaxies
    d. planets

Now that you are familiar with the difference between general and specific, you will be able to use these concepts in the rest of the chapter.

Finding the Topic

We have defined a paragraph as a group of related ideas. The sentences are related to one another, and all are about the same person, place, thing, or idea.

The common subject or idea is called the **topic**—what the entire paragraph is about. As you read the following paragraph, you will see that its topic is the functions of political parties.

> Political parties perform a variety of functions. Along with interest groups and the mass media, parties play a role in keeping the public informed about current political issues and helping people form opinions on those issues. The minority political party—the one that does not control Congress or the presidency—serves as a check on the majority party. It examines and criticizes the proposals of the majority party and often suggests alternatives. The functions of political parties also include the recruitment and selection of leaders, the representation and integration of group interests, and the control and direction of government. Party activities center on recruiting, electing, and appointing legislative, executive, and judicial leaders to office. They provide the conditions under which many thousands of elective offices can be filled in an organized manner. By proposing and campaigning for specific lists of candidates, the parties bring a degree of order and predictability to the political process.
>
> —Volkomer, *American Government*, p. 114

Each sentence of this paragraph discusses or describes the functions of political parties. To identify the topic of a paragraph, then, ask yourself: *"What or whom is the paragraph about?"*

EXERCISE 3-3 IDENTIFYING THE TOPIC

Directions: *After reading each of the following paragraphs, select the choice that best represents the topic of the paragraph.*

_____ 1.   Mars is a world of wonders, with ancient volcanoes that dwarf the largest mountains on Earth, a great canyon that runs nearly one-fifth of the way around the planet, and polar caps made of frozen carbon dioxide ("dry ice") and water. Although Mars is frozen today, the presence of dried-up riverbeds, rock-strewn floodplains, and minerals that form in water offers clear evidence that Mars had at least some warm and wet periods in the past. Major flows of liquid water probably ceased at least 3 billion years ago, but some liquid water could persist underground, perhaps flowing to the surface on occasion.

—Bennett et al., *The Essential Cosmic Perspective*, p. 150

    a. planets

    b. Earth

    c. Mars

    d. astronomy

_____ 2.   The importance of status varies between cultures. The French, for example, are extremely status conscious. Also, countries differ on the criteria that confer status. For instance, in Latin America and Asia, status tends to come from family position and formal roles held in organizations. In contrast, while status is important in countries like the United States and Australia, it tends to be less "in your face." And it tends to be given based on accomplishments rather than on titles and family history.

—Robbins and Coulter, *Management*, p. 362

a. status

b. culture

c. organizations

d. the French

_____ 3.   Baseball's first professional team, the Cincinnati Red Stockings, appeared in 1869, and baseball soon became the preeminent national sport. Fans sang songs about it ("Take Me Out to the Ballgame"), wrote poems about it ("Casey at the Bat"), and made up riddles about it ("What has 18 feet and catches flies?"). Modern rules were adopted. Umpires were designated to call balls and strikes; catchers wore masks and chest protectors and moved closer to the plate instead of staying back to catch the ball on the bounce. Fielders had to catch the ball on the fly rather than on one bounce in their caps. By 1890, professional baseball games were drawing crowds of 60,000. In 1901, the American League was organized. Two years later the Boston Red Sox beat the Pittsburgh Pirates in the first modern World Series.

—Brands et al., *American Stories*, p. 481

a. professional sports

b. baseball

c. modern sports rules

d. the World Series

_____ 4.   Snakebites require special care but are usually not life threatening. Nearly 50,000 people in the United States are bitten by snakes each year. Although over 8,000 of these cases involve poisonous snakes, on the average fewer than 10 deaths each year are reported from snakebites. (In the United States, more people die each year from bee and wasp stings than from snakebites.) The signs and symptoms of snakebite poisoning may take several hours to appear. If death does result, it is usually not a rapidly occurring event unless anaphylactic shock develops.

—Limmer and O'Keefe, *Emergency Care*, p. 828

a. poisonous snakes

b. bee and wasp stings

c. anaphylactic shock

d. snakebites

_____ 5.   There is no reference to the First Lady in the U.S. Constitution, nor is there any other official recognition of the role of the president's wife in the federal government. Yet throughout American history, First Ladies have often participated in their husbands' administrations. Their activities have varied greatly over the years, depending on their personalities and interests as well as on the customs of the time. During the War of 1812, Dolley Madison remained in the White House as long as possible, finally packing the original drafts of the Constitution and the Declaration of Independence and departing as the British drew near. Sarah Polk served as her husband's personal secretary, and Helen Taft attended cabinet meetings. Edith Wilson could be said to have served as acting president after Woodrow Wilson suffered a stroke in 1919. She handled all correspondence addressed to the president from the Senate, the cabinet, and the public.

—Volkomer, *American Government*, p. 242

    a. the U.S. Constitution

    b. the presidency

    c. First Ladies

    d. the War of 1812

Stated Main Ideas

The **main idea** of a paragraph is what the author wants you to know about the topic. It is the broadest, most important idea that the writer develops throughout the paragraph. The entire paragraph explains, develops, and supports this main idea. A question that will guide you in finding the main idea is *"What key point is the author making about the topic?"* In the paragraph about political parties on page 82, the writer's main idea is that political parties perform a variety of functions.

Often, but not always, one sentence expresses the main idea. This sentence is called the **topic sentence.**

Finding the Topic Sentence

To find the topic sentence, search for the one general sentence that explains what the writer wants you to know about the topic. A topic sentence is a broad, general statement; the remaining sentences of the paragraph provide details about or explain the topic sentence.

In the following paragraph, the topic is generational values. Read the paragraph to find out what the writer wants you to know about this topic. Look for the one sentence that states this.

> Each generation brings with it a set of values that tend to characterize the group. **Generation Y**, the **Millennials**, born from 1982 to 2000, are optimistic and tolerant; they value diversity, challenge, and creativity. They are self-confident, technological wizards and multitaskers who value a fun, team-oriented work environment. **Gen Xers**, born from 1961 to 1982, want to know "What's in it for me?" They are independent, self-reliant, flexible, technologically confident, informal, quick paced, and often irreverent. Although they have high performance expectations and want to be rewarded for merit alone, they are unwilling to sacrifice life balance for work. **Baby Boomers**, born from 1943 to 1960, value achievement, accomplishment, hard work, the traditional work ethic, and a democratic work environment where anything is possible given enough effort expended. **The Matures**, born from 1925 to 1942, are disciplined, responsible, conservative and loyal, and willing to sacrifice. They value security, history, tradition, and a clearly defined set of rules and hierarchy.
>
> —Sukiennik et al., *The Career Fitness Program*, pp. 50–51

The paragraph opens with a statement and then proceeds to explain it by providing examples. This first sentence is the topic sentence, and it states the paragraph's main point: Each generation is characterized by a set of values.

Tips for Locating the Topic Sentence.   Here are some tips that will help you find the topic sentence.

1. **Identify the topic.** Figure out the general subject of the entire paragraph. In the preceding sample paragraph, "each generation's values" is the topic.
2. **Locate the most general sentence (the topic sentence).** This sentence must be broad enough to include all of the other ideas in the paragraph. The topic sentence in the sample paragraph ("Each generation brings with it a set of values that tend to characterize the group") covers all of the other details in the paragraph.

The topic sentence can be located anywhere in the paragraph. However, there are several positions where it is most likely to be found.

Common Positions for the Topic Sentence

General

Specific

Topic Sentence
Detail
Detail
Detail

Topic Sentence First.   Most often the topic sentence is placed first in the paragraph. In this type of paragraph, the writer first states his or her main point and then explains it.

> Several planets are easy to find with the naked eye. Mercury is visible infrequently, and only just after sunset or just before sunrise because it is so close to the Sun. Venus often shines brightly in the early evening in the west or before dawn in the east. If you see a very bright "star" in the early evening or early morning, it is probably Venus. Jupiter, when it is visible at night, is the brightest object in the sky besides the Moon and Venus. Mars is often recognizable by its reddish color, though you should check a star chart to make sure you aren't looking at a bright red star. Saturn is also easy to see with the naked eye, but because many

> stars are just as bright as Saturn, it helps to know where to look. (It also helps to know that planets tend not to twinkle as much as stars.)
>
> —adapted from Bennett et al., *The Essential Cosmic Perspective*, p. 48

Here the writer first states that there are several planets that are easily seen with the naked eye. The rest of the paragraph describes those planets.

Topic Sentence Last.   The second most likely place for a topic sentence to appear is last in the paragraph. When using this arrangement, a writer leads up to the main point and then directly states it at the end.

> Most people are familiar with the common uses of many basic metals, including aluminum in beverage cans, copper in electrical wiring, and gold and silver in jewelry. But some people are not aware that pencil lead contains the greasy-feeling mineral graphite and that bath powders and many cosmetics contain the mineral talc. Moreover, many do not know that drill bits impregnated with diamonds are employed by dentists to drill through tooth enamel, or that the common mineral quartz is the source of silicon for computer chips. In fact, practically every manufactured product contains materials obtained from minerals.
>
> —Tarbuck and Lutgens, *Earth*, p. 74

In this paragraph, the authors describe a variety of uses for minerals and conclude with the paragraph's main point: most manufactured products contain materials obtained from minerals.

Topic Sentence in the Middle.   If it is placed neither first nor last, then the topic sentence appears somewhere in the middle of the paragraph. In this arrangement, the sentences before the topic sentence lead up to or introduce the main idea. Those that follow the main idea explain or describe it.

> How many types of living things are there on Earth? How many varieties of life-forms are there that we can recognize as being fundamentally different from one another? It may surprise you to learn that we haven't the foggiest idea. The lowest estimate is about 3 million species, but higher-end estimates often come in at 10 to 15 million, and the highest of them all is 100 million. Scientists simply have been unable to catalogue the vast diversity that exists on our planet. In 250 years of watching, digging, netting, and bagging, they have identified about 1.8 million species—a large number, to be sure, but only a fraction of the species that actually exist, even if our lowest estimates are correct.
>
> —Krogh, *Biology*, p. 319

In this paragraph, the author first explores the question of how many species exist on Earth and offers several estimates. Then he states his main point: Scientists have not been able to determine how many species there are on Earth. The remainder of the paragraph describes attempts to identify Earth's species.

Topic Sentence First and Last.   Occasionally the main idea is stated at the beginning of a paragraph and again at the end, or elsewhere in the paragraph.

Writers may use this organization to emphasize an important idea or to explain an idea that needs clarification. At other times, the first and last sentences together express the paragraph's main idea.

> The way you decorate your private spaces communicates something about who you are. The office with a mahogany desk, bookcases, and oriental rugs communicates importance and status within the organization, just as a metal desk and bare floor communicate a status much farther down in the hierarchy. At home, the cost of your furnishings may communicate your status and wealth, and their coordination may communicate your sense of style. The magazines may communicate your interests. The arrangement of chairs around a television set may reveal how important watching television is. Bookcases lining the walls reveal the importance of reading. In fact, there is probably little in your home that does not send messages to others and that others do not use for making inferences about you.
>
> —DeVito, *The Interpersonal Communication Book*, p. 161

The first and last sentences together explain that how you decorate your private spaces communicates information about you.

EXERCISE 3-4 FINDING TOPIC SENTENCES 1

Directions: *Underline the topic sentence of each of the following paragraphs.*

Paragraph 1

Sociologists have several different ways of defining poverty. *Transitional poverty* is a temporary state that occurs when someone loses a job for a short time. *Marginal poverty* occurs when a person lacks stable employment (for example, if your job is lifeguarding at a pool during the summer season, you might experience marginal poverty when the season ends). The next, more serious level, *residual poverty*, is chronic and multigenerational. A person who experiences *absolute poverty* is so poor that he or she doesn't have resources to survive. *Relative poverty* is a state that occurs when we compare ourselves with those around us.

—adapted from Carl, *Think Sociology*, p. 122

Paragraph 2

State and local governments, or subnational governments, touch our lives every day. They pick up our garbage, educate us, keep us safe from criminals, protect our water supply, and perform a myriad of other vital services. Odds are that you are attending a state or city university right now. You will drive home on locally maintained streets. Subnational governments regulate a wide range of business activities, from generating electric power to cutting hair. The state government is also the single largest employer in every state; moreover, local governments, taken together, employ even more people than do the states. So, as a consumer of government services, as a regulated businessperson, and/or as an employee, we live lives that are intimately touched by subnational governments.

—Edwards et al., *Government in America*, p. 608

Paragraph 3

Gross anatomy, or macroscopic anatomy, considers features visible with the unaided eye. There are many ways to approach gross anatomy. **Surface anatomy** refers to the study of general form and superficial markings. **Regional anatomy** considers all the superficial and internal features in a specific region of the body such as the head, neck, or trunk. **Systemic** anatomy considers the structure of major organ systems, which are groups of organs that function together in a coordinated manner. For example, the heart, blood, and blood vessels form the cardiovascular system, which circulates oxygen and nutrients throughout the body.

—Martini and Bartholomew, *Essentials of Anatomy and Physiology*, p. 3

Paragraph 4

Some artists, such as Picasso, demonstrated exceptional drawing ability as young children. Others, such as Paul Cezanne and Vincent van Gogh, did not show obvious drawing ability when they committed themselves to art. Their skills developed through diligent effort. In spite of early difficulties, they succeeded in teaching themselves to draw. Seeing and drawing are learned processes, not just inborn gifts.

—Frank, *Prebles' Artforms*, p. 104

Paragraph 5

With so many people participating in social networking sites and keeping personal blogs, it's increasingly common for a single disgruntled customer to wage war online against a company for poor service or faulty products. Unhappy customers have taken to the Web to complain about broken computers or poor customer service. Individuals may post negative reviews of products on blogs, upload angry videos outlining complaints on YouTube, or join public discussion forums where they can voice their opinion about the good and the bad. In the same way that companies celebrate the viral spread of good news, they must also be on guard for online backlash that can damage a reputation.

—adapted from Ebert and Griffin, *Business Essentials*, p. 161

Paragraph 6

Elections serve a critical function in American society. They make it possible for most political participation to be channeled through the electoral process rather than bubbling up through demonstrations, riots, or revolutions. Elections provide regular access to political power, so that leaders can be replaced without being overthrown. This is possible because elections are almost universally accepted as a fair and free method of selecting political leaders. Furthermore, by choosing who is to lead the country, the people—if they make their choices carefully—can also guide the policy direction of the government.

—adapted from Edwards et al., *Government in America*, p. 306

Paragraph 7

A gunnysack is a large bag, usually made of burlap. As a conflict strategy, gunny sacking refers to the practice of storing up grievances so we may unload them at another time. The immediate occasion for unloading may be relatively simple (or so it might seem at first), such as someone's coming home late without calling. Instead of arguing about this, the gunnysacker unloads all past grievances. As you probably know from experience, gunnysacking begets gunnysacking. When one person gunnysacks, the other person often reciprocates. Frequently the original problem never gets addressed. Instead, resentment and hostility escalate.

—DeVito, *Human Communication*, p. 217

Paragraph 8

As just about everyone today knows, e-mail has virtually become the standard method of communication in the business world. Most people enjoy its speed, ease and casual nature. But e-mail also has its share of problems and pitfalls, including privacy. Many people assume the contents of their e-mail are private, but there may in fact be any number of people authorized to see it. Some experts have even likened e-mail to postcards sent through U.S. mail: They pass through a lot of hands and before a lot of eyes, and, theoretically, many different people can read them.

—adapted from Ebert and Griffin, *Business Essentials*, p. 64

Paragraph 9

Patrescence, or becoming a father, usually is less socially noted than matrescence. The practice of **couvade** is an interesting exception to this generalization. Couvade refers to "a variety of customs applying to the behavior of fathers during the pregnancies of their wives and during and shortly after the births of their children." The father may take to his bed before, during, or after the delivery. He may also experience pain and exhaustion during and after the delivery. More common is a pattern of couvade that involves a set of prohibitions and prescriptions for male behavior. Couvade occurs in societies where paternal roles in child care are prominent. One interpretation views couvade as one phase of men's participation in parenting: Their good behavior as expectant fathers helps ensure a good delivery for the baby. Another interpretation of couvade is that it offers support for the mother. In Estonia, a folk belief is that a woman's birth pains will be less if her husband helps by taking some of them on himself.

—adapted from Miller, *Cultural Anthropology*, pp. 144–145

Paragraph 10

Everything moves. Even things that appear at rest move. They move relative to the sun and stars. As you're reading this you're moving at about 107,000 kilometers per hour relative to the sun. And you're moving even faster relative to the center of our galaxy. When we discuss the motion of something, we describe motion relative to something else. If you walk down the aisle of a moving bus, your speed relative to the floor of the bus is likely quite different from your speed relative to the road. When we say a racing car reaches a speed of 300 kilometers per hour, we mean relative to the track. Unless stated otherwise, when we discuss the speeds of things in our environment we mean relative to the surface of the earth; motion is relative.

—adapted from Hewitt, *Conceptual Physics*, p. 39

EXERCISE 3-5 FINDING TOPIC SENTENCES 2

Directions: *Underline the topic sentence of each of the following paragraphs.*

Semiotics: The Symbols Around Us

What does a cowboy have to do with a bit of tobacco rolled into a paper tube? How can a celebrity such as the basketball player LeBron James or the singer Rihanna enhance the image of a soft drink or a fast-food restaurant? To help them understand how consumers interpret the meanings of symbols, some marketers turn to **semiotics,** a field that studies the correspondence between signs and symbols and their roles in how we assign meanings. Semiotics is a key link to consumer behavior because consumers use products to express their social identities. Products carry learned meanings, and we rely on marketers to help us figure out what those meanings are.

From a semiotic perspective, every marketing message has three basic components: an *object*, a *sign*, and an *interpretant*. The **object** is the product that is the focus of the message (e.g., Marlboro cigarettes). The **sign** is the sensory image that represents the intended meanings of the object (e.g., the Marlboro cowboy). The **interpretant** is the meaning we derive from the sign (e.g., rugged, individualistic, American).

According to semiotician Charles Sanders Peirce, signs relate to objects in one of three ways: They can resemble objects, connect to them, or tie to them conventionally. An **icon** is a sign that resembles the product in some way (e.g., the Ford Mustang has a galloping horse on the hood). An **index** is a sign that connects to a product because they share some property (e.g., the pine tree on some of Procter and Gamble's cleanser products conveys the shared property of fresh scent). A **symbol** is a sign that relates to a product by either conventional or agreed-on associations (e.g., the lion in Dreyfus Fund ads provides the conventional association with fearlessness and strength that it carries [or hopes to carry] over to the company's approach to investments).

—adapted from Solomon, *Consumer Behavior*, p. 73

EXERCISE 3-6 FINDING MAIN IDEAS

Directions: *After reading the following passage, select the choice that best completes each of the statements that follow.*

Picking Partners

Just as males and females may find different ways to express emotions themselves, the process of partner selection also shows distinctly different patterns. For both males and females, more than just chemical and psychological processes influence the choice of partners. One of these factors is *proximity*, or being in the same place at the same time. The more you see a person in your hometown, at social gatherings, or at work, the more likely that an interaction will occur. Thus, if you live in New York, you'll probably end up with another New Yorker. If you live in northern Wisconsin, you'll probably end up with another Wisconsinite.

The old adage that "opposites attract" usually isn't true. You also pick a partner based on *similarities* (attitudes, values, intellect, interests). If your potential partner expresses interest or liking, you may react with mutual regard known as *reciprocity*. The more you express interest, the safer it is for someone else to return the regard, and the cycle spirals onward.

Another factor that apparently plays a significant role in selecting a partner is *physical attraction*. Whether such attraction is caused by a chemical reaction or a socially learned behavior, males and females appear to have different attraction criteria. Men tend to select their mates primarily on the basis of youth and physical attractiveness. Although physical attractiveness is an important criterion for women in mate selection, they tend to place higher emphasis on partners who are somewhat older, have good financial prospects, and are dependable and industrious.

—Donatelle, *Health*, p. 105

_____ 1. The thesis of the entire selection is
   a. several factors influence choice of partners.
   b. physical attraction is more important to men than for women.
   c. proximity is the key to mate selection.
   d. opposites attract.

_____ 2. The topic sentence of the first paragraph begins with the words
   a. "For both."
   b. "One of these."
   c. "The more."
   d. "Just as."

_____ 3. The topic of the second paragraph is
   a. physical attraction.
   b. similarities.
   c. the old adage.
   d. interaction.

_____ 4. In the second paragraph, the topic sentence begins with the words
   a. "You also pick."
   b. "The more you express."
   c. "If your potential."
   d. "The old adage."

_____ 5. The topic sentence of the third paragraph is the
   a. first sentence.
   b. second sentence.
   c. third sentence.
   d. fourth sentence.

3c   RECOGNIZING SUPPORTING DETAILS

Supporting details are those facts and ideas that prove or explain the main idea of a paragraph. While all the details in a paragraph support the main idea, not all details are equally important. As you read, try to identify and pay attention to the most important details. Pay less attention to details of lesser importance. The key details directly explain the main idea. Other details may provide additional information, offer an example, or further explain one of the key details.

Figure A shows how details relate to the main idea and how details range in degree of importance. In the diagram, more important details are placed toward the left; less important details are closer to the right.

Figure A   **Figure B**

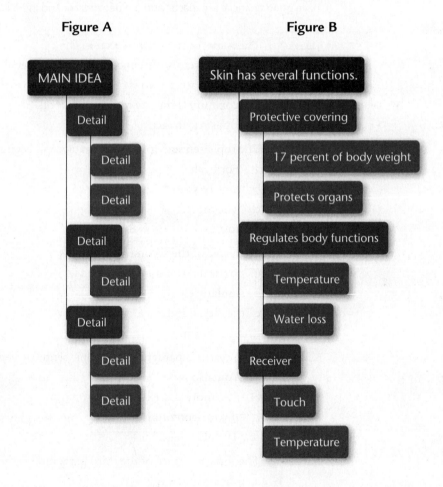

Read the following paragraph and study Figure B.

> The skin of the human body has several functions. First, it serves as a protective covering. In doing so, it accounts for 17 percent of the body weight. Skin also protects the organs within the body from damage or harm. The skin serves as a regulator of body functions. It controls body temperature and water loss. Finally, the skin serves as a receiver. It is sensitive to touch and temperature.

From this diagram you can see that the details stating the three functions of skin are the key details. Other details, such as "protects the organs," provide further information and are less important.

Read the following paragraph and try to pick out the more important details.

> Many cultures have different rules for men and women engaging in conflict. Asian cultures are more strongly prohibitive of women's conflict strategies. Asian women are expected to be exceptionally polite; this is even more important when women are in conflict with men and when the conflict is public. In the United States, there is a verbalized equality; men and women have equal rights when it comes to permissible conflict strategies. In reality, there are many who expect women to be more polite, to pursue conflict in a nonargumentative way, while men are expected to argue forcefully and logically.

This paragraph could be diagrammed as follows (key details only):

Many cultures have different rules for men and women engaging in conflict.

Rules in Asian cultures

Rules in the United States

EXERCISE 3-7 RECOGNIZING SUPPORTING DETAILS 1

Directions: *Each of the following topic sentences states the main idea of a paragraph. After each topic sentence are five sentences containing details that may or may not support the topic sentence. Read each sentence and put an "S" beside those that contain details that support the topic sentence.*

1. **Topic Sentence:** An oligopoly is a market structure in which only a few companies sell a certain product.

   _S_ a. The automobile industry is a good example of an oligopoly, even though it gives the appearance of being highly competitive.

   _S_ b. The breakfast cereal, soap, and cigarette industries, although basic to our economy, operate as oligopolies.

_____ c. Monopolies refer to market structures in which only one industry produces a particular product.

_____ d. Monopolies exert significant control over prices.

_____ e. The market for many agricultural products, such as wheat and sugar, is quite competitive because there is little or no difference among the products.

2. **Topic Sentence:** *Mens rea,* a term that refers to a person's criminal intent when committing a crime, or his or her state of mind, can be evaluated in several ways.

_____ a. Confessions by criminals are direct evidence of their criminal intent.

_____ b. Circumstantial evidence can be used to suggest mental intent.

_____ c. *Actus rea* is a person's actions that make up a crime.

_____ d. A person may unknowingly commit a crime.

_____ e. Expert witnesses may offer an opinion about a person's criminal intent.

3. **Topic Sentence:** Food irradiation is a process in which food is treated with radiation to kill bacteria.

_____ a. Gamma radiation is made up of radioactive cobalt, cesium, and X-rays.

_____ b. The radioactive rays pass through the food without damaging it or changing it.

_____ c. The newest form of irradiation uses electricity as the energy source for irradiation.

_____ d. Irradiation increases the shelf life of food because it kills all bacteria present in the food.

_____ e. *E. coli*, salmonella, and listeria cause many illnesses each year.

4. **Topic Sentence:** Overtraining is the most common type of fitness-related injury, and it can be easily avoided.

_____ a. A physical fitness program will improve your health and well-being.

_____ b. Our bodies usually provide warning signs of potential overtraining and muscle damage.

_____ c. People often injure themselves by doing too much too soon when they exercise.

_____ d. To avoid injury, do not engage in repetitive motion activities like running or step aerobics for long periods of time.

_____ e. Varying an exercise program can allow muscles time to rest and recover from strain.

5. **Topic Sentence:** Frank Lloyd Wright was a radically innovative architect.

_____ a. Wright was born in Richland Center, Wisconsin.

__S__ b. He popularized the use of steel cantilevers in homes at a time when they were only used commercially.

__S__ c. He built the Kaufmann Residence over a waterfall without disturbing the waterfall at all.

__S__ d. Wright had plans to build a mile-high skyscraper but died before he could achieve his goal.

_____ e. Wright designed the Guggenheim Museum.

EXERCISE 3-8 RECOGNIZING SUPPORTING DETAILS 2

Directions: *Underline only the most important details in each of the following paragraphs.*

Paragraph 1

States earn money from gambling in three main ways. First, states may run a gambling operation outright. State lotteries are the best example. State skim off as much as 50 percent of the receipts from lottery tickets, offering most of the rest as prize money. Second, states may earn money from gambling by taxing bets and winnings heavily, as is commonly done with casino and racetrack gambling. Third, states can levy a variety of fees, including licensing fees.

—Edwards et al., *Government in America*, p. 639

Paragraph 2

Withdrawal reflexes move stimulated parts of the body away from a source of stimulation. The strongest withdrawal reflexes are triggered by painful stimuli, but these reflexes are also initiated by the stimulation of touch or pressure receptors. A **flexor reflex** is a withdrawal reflex affecting the muscles of a limb. If you grab an unexpectedly hot pan on the stove, a dramatic flexor reflex will occur. When the pain receptors in your hand are stimulated, the sensory neurons activate interneurons in the spinal cord that stimulate motor neurons in the anterior gray horns. The result is a contraction of flexor muscles that yanks your forearm and hand away from the stove.

—Martini and Bartholomew, *Essentials of Anatomy and Physiology*, p. 283

Paragraph 3

A theme park in Japan offers "amusement baths" to visitors, including a wine bath, a green-tea bath, a coffee bath, a sake bath, and even a ramen-noodle bath. When they don their bathing suits and jump into the ramen bath (which looks like a soup bowl), they frolic in pepper-flavored water that contains collagen and garlic extracts the Japanese believe will improve the skin. A man dressed as a chef dispenses noodle-shaped bath additives and soy sauce to everyone in the tub. A **fad** is a very short-lived fashion. Relatively few people adopt a fad product, but it can spread very quickly. Adopters may all belong to a common subculture, and the fad "trickles across" members but rarely breaks out of that specific group.

—Solomon, *Consumer Behavior,* p. 565

Paragraph 4

There are three familiar states of matter: solid, liquid, and gas. A **solid** object maintains its shape and volume regardless of its location. A **liquid** occupies a definite volume but assumes the shape of the portion of a container that it occupies. If you have 355 milliliters (mL) of a soft drink, you have 355 mL whether the soft drink is in a can, in a bottle, or, through a mishap, on the floor—which demonstrates another property of liquids. Unlike solids, liquids flow readily. A **gas** maintains neither shape nor volume. It expands to fill completely whatever container it occupies. Gases flow and are easily compressed. For example, enough air for many minutes of breathing can be compressed into a steel tank for SCUBA diving.

—adapted from Hill et al., *Chemistry for Changing Times,* p. 16

Paragraph 5

Observational research involves gathering primary data by observing relevant people, actions, and situations. For example, Trader Joe's might evaluate possible new store locations by checking traffic patterns, neighborhood conditions, and the locations of competing Whole Foods, Fresh Market, and other retail chains. Researchers often observe consumer behavior to glean customer insights they can't obtain by simply asking customers questions. For instance, Fisher-Price has established an observation lab in which it can observe the reactions little tots have to new toys. The Fisher-Price Play Lab is a sunny, toy-strewn space where lucky kids get to test Fisher-Price prototypes, under the watchful eyes of designers who hope to learn what will get them worked up into a new-toy frenzy.

—Armstrong and Kotler, *Marketing,* p. 103

EXERCISE 3-9 RECOGNIZING SUPPORTING DETAILS 3

Directions: *Reread the article "Treating Wounded Soldiers: Polytrauma" on pp. 8–11 and underline the most important supporting details in each paragraph.*

3d UNDERSTANDING IMPLIED MAIN IDEAS

LEARNING OBJECTIVE 4
Find implied main ideas

Study the cartoon at right. What main point is it making? Although the cartoonist's message is not directly stated, you were able to figure it out by looking at the details in the cartoon. Just as you figured out the cartoonist's main point, you often have to figure out the implied main ideas of speakers and writers. When an idea is **implied**, it is suggested but not stated outright. Suppose your favorite shirt is missing from your closet and you know that your roommate often borrows your clothes. You might say to your roommate, "If my blue plaid shirt is back in my closet by noon, I'll forget it was missing." This state-

Roadkill

ment does not directly accuse your roommate of borrowing the shirt, but your message is clear—Return my shirt! Your statement implies or suggests to your roommate that he has borrowed the shirt and should return it.

EXERCISE 3-10 UNDERSTANDING IMPLIED MAIN IDEAS

Directions: *For each of the following statements, select the choice that best explains what the writer is implying or suggesting.*

_____ 1. Allie's hair looked as if she had been on a roller coaster ride.

    a. Allie needs a haircut.

    b. Allie's hair is messed up.

    c. Allie needs a hat.

    d. Allie's hair needs coloring.

_____ 2. Dino would not recommend Professor Wright's class to his worst enemy.

    a. Dino likes Professor Wright's class.

    b. Dino dislikes Professor Wright's class.

    c. Professor Wright's class is popular.

    d. Professor Wright's class is unpopular.

_____ 3. The steak was overcooked and tough, the mashed potatoes were cold, the green beans were withered, and the chocolate pie was mushy.

    a. The dinner was tasty.

    b. The dinner was nutritious.

    c. The dinner was prepared poorly.

    d. The dinner was served carelessly.

When trying to figure out the implied main idea in a paragraph, it is important to remember the distinction between general and specific ideas (see p. 80). You know that a *general* idea applies to many items or ideas, while a *specific* idea refers to a particular item. The word *color,* for instance, is general because it refers to many other specific colors—purple, yellow, red, and so forth. The word *shoe* is general because it can apply to many types, such as running shoes, high heels, loafers, and slippers.

You also know that the main idea of a paragraph is not only its most important point but also its most *general* idea. *Specific* details back up or support the main idea. Although most paragraphs have a topic sentence, some do not. Instead, they contain only details or specifics that, taken together, point to the main idea. The main idea, then, is implied but not directly stated. In such paragraphs you must **infer**, or reason out, the main idea. **Inference** is a process of adding up the details and deciding what they mean together or what main idea they all support or explain.

What general idea do the following specific sentences suggest?

> The doctor kept patients waiting hours for an appointment.
> The doctor was hasty and abrupt when talking with patients.
> The doctor took days to return phone calls from patients.

You probably determined that the doctor is inconsiderate and manages her practice poorly.

What larger, more general idea do the following specific details and the accompanying photograph point to?

> The wind began to howl at over 90 mph.
> A dark gray funnel cloud was visible in the sky.
> Severe storms had been predicted by the weather service.

Together these three details and the photograph suggest that a tornado has devastated the area.

EXERCISE 3-11 WRITING GENERAL IDEAS

Directions: *For each item, read the specific details. Then select the word or phrase from the box below that best completes the general idea in the sentence that follows. Make sure that each general idea fits all of its specific details. Not all words or phrases in the box will be used.*

different factors	genetic	contributes	nonverbal messages
store's image	advertisers	characteristics	
process	problems	dangerous effects	

1. a. Major life catastrophes, such as natural disasters, can cause stress.

   b. Significant life changes, such as the death of a loved one, elevate one's level of stress.

   c. Daily hassles, such as long lines at the drugstore, take their toll on a person's well-being.

   General idea: A number of _____ contribute to stress.

2. a. Humorous commercials catch consumers' attention.

   b. Fear emphasizes negative consequences unless a particular product or service is purchased.

   c. "Sex sells" is a common motto among those who write commercials.

   General idea: _____ use a variety of appeals to sell products.

3. a. Acid rain may aggravate respiratory problems.

   b. Each year millions of trees are destroyed by acid rain.

   c. Acid rain may be hazardous to a pregnant woman's unborn child.

   General idea: Acid rain has _____.

4. a. Facial expressions reveal emotions.

   b. Hand gestures have meanings.

   c. Posture can reveal how a person feels.

   General idea: The body communicates _____.

5. a. The smell of a store can be appealing to shoppers.

   b. Colors can create tension or help shoppers relax.

   c. The type of background music playing in a store creates a distinct impression.

   General idea: Retailers create a _____ to appeal to consumers.

6. a. Creative people are risk takers.

   b. Creative people recognize patterns and make connections easily.

   c. Creative people are self-motivated.

   General idea: A number of different _____ contribute to creativity.

How to Find Implied Main Ideas in Paragraphs

When a writer leaves his or her main idea unstated, it is up to you to look at the details in the paragraph and figure out the writer's main point. The details, when taken together, will all point to a general and more important idea. Use the following steps as a guide to find implied main ideas:

1. **Find the topic.** As you know from earlier sections in this chapter, the *topic* is the general subject of the entire paragraph. Ask yourself: "What *one thing* is the author discussing throughout the paragraph?"

2. **Figure out the most important idea the writer wants you to know about that topic.** Look at each detail and decide what larger idea is being explained.

3. **Express the main idea in your own words.** Make sure that the main idea is a reasonable one. Ask yourself: "Does it apply to all of the details in the paragraph?"

Here is a sample paragraph; identify the main idea.

> What marks the beginning of adulthood? Young Israelis view completing military service as important for becoming an adult, reflecting Israel's requirement of mandatory military service. Young Argentines especially value being able to support a family financially, perhaps reflecting the economic upheavals Argentina has experienced for many years. Emerging adults in Korea and China view being able to support their parents financially as necessary for adulthood, reflecting the value of obligation to parents found in Asian societies. In India, emotional self-control is one of the top criteria for adulthood. This is consistent with the emphasis in Indian culture on consideration of the well-being of others.
>
> —adapted from Arnett, *Human Development*, p. 459

The topic of this paragraph is adulthood. The author's main point is that young people in various cultures have different criteria for adulthood. You can figure out this writer's main idea even though no single sentence states this directly. You can visualize this paragraph as follows:

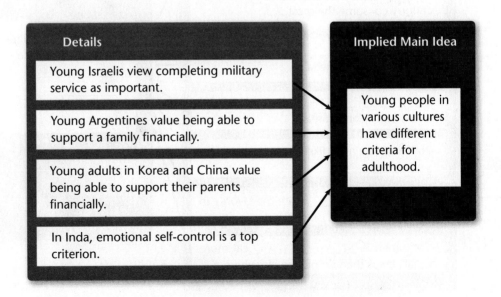

EXERCISE 3-12 FINDING IMPLIED MAIN IDEAS 1

Directions: *After reading each of the paragraphs, complete the diagram that follows by filling in the missing information.*

Paragraph 1

The average American consumer eats 21 pounds of snack foods in a year, but people in the West Central part of the country consume the most (24 pounds per person) whereas those in the Pacific and Southeast regions eat "only" 19 pounds per person. Pretzels are the most popular snack in the mid-Atlantic area, pork rinds are most likely to be eaten in the South, and multigrain chips turn up as a favorite in the West. Not surprisingly, the Hispanic influence in the Southwest has influenced snacking preferences—consumers in that part of the United States eat about 50 percent more tortilla chips than do people elsewhere.

—adapted from Solomon, *Consumer Behavior*, p. 184

Topic: _____

Details

The average consumer eats _____ of snack food in a year.

People in _____ part of the country consume the most.

People in _____ regions consume the least.

_____ are the most popular snack in the mid-Atlantic area.

Pork rinds are most likely to be eaten in _____.

_____ are the favorite in the West.

Consumers in _____ eat more tortilla chips than do people elsewhere.

Implied Main Idea

_____ differ in their preferences for _____ _____ according to where they live.

Paragraph 2

The constellation [group of stars] that the Greeks named Orion, the hunter, was seen by the ancient Chinese as a supreme warrior called *Shen*. Hindus in ancient India also saw a warrior, called *Skanda*, who rode a peacock. The three stars of Orion's belt were seen as three fishermen in a canoe by Aborigines of northern Australia. As seen from southern California, these three stars climb almost straight up into the sky as they rise in the east, which may explain why the Chemehuevi Indians of the California desert saw them as a line of three sure-footed mountain sheep.

—adapted from Bennett et al., *The Cosmic Perspective*, p. 28

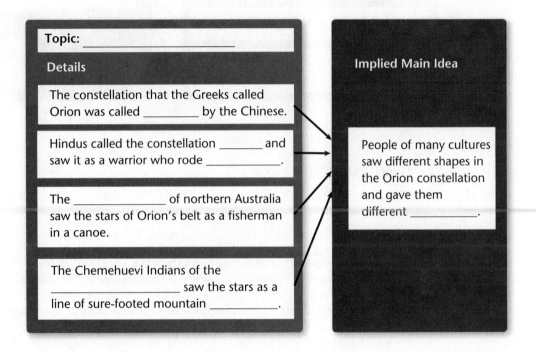

Topic: _____

Details

The constellation that the Greeks called Orion was called _____ by the Chinese.

Hindus called the constellation _____ and saw it as a warrior who rode _____.

The _____ of northern Australia saw the stars of Orion's belt as a fisherman in a canoe.

The Chemehuevi Indians of the _____ saw the stars as a line of sure-footed mountain _____.

Implied Main Idea

People of many cultures saw different shapes in the Orion constellation and gave them different _____.

Paragraph 3

More than 30 percent of all food borne illnesses result from unsafe handling of food at home. Among the most basic of precautions are to wash your hands and to wash all produce before eating it. Avoid cross-contamination in the kitchen by using separate cutting boards and utensils for meats and produce. Temperature control is also important; hot foods must be kept hot and cold foods kept cold in order to avoid unchecked bacterial growth. Leftovers need to be eaten within 3 days, and if you're unsure how long something has been sitting in the fridge, don't take chances. When in doubt, throw it out.

—adapted from Donatelle, *Health*, p. 280

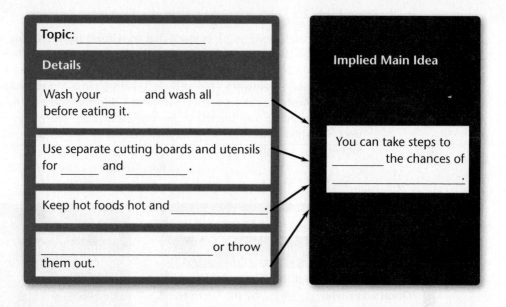

EXERCISE 3-13 FINDING IMPLIED MAIN IDEAS 2

Directions: *Write a sentence that states the main idea for each of the following paragraphs.*

Paragraph 1

A vital element of professionalism is **etiquette**, the expected norms of behaviour in any particular situation. The way you conduct yourself, interact with others, and handle conflict can have a profound influence on your company's success and on your career. Etiquette blunders can have serious financial costs through lower productivity and lost business opportunities. When executives hire and promote you, they expect your behaviour to protect the company's reputation. The more you understand such expectations, the better chance you have of avoiding career-damaging mistakes. Moreover, etiquette is an important way to show respect for others and contribute to a smooth-running workplace.

—Bovée and Thill, *Business in Action*, p. 20

Main idea: _____

_____

Paragraph 2

Many farmers and artisans in developing countries are unable to borrow from banks the money they need to invest in their businesses. By banding together in fair trade cooperatives, they can get credit, reduce their raw material costs, and maintain higher and fairer prices for their products. Cooperatives are managed democratically, so farmers and artisans learn leadership and organizational skills. The people who grow or make the products have a say in how local resources are utilized and sold. Safe and healthy working conditions can be protected. Cooperatives thus benefit the local farmers and artisans who are members, rather than absentee corporate owners interested only in maximizing profits.

—Rubenstein, *Contemporary Human Geography*, p. 214

Main idea: _____

_____

Paragraph 3

When Richard Nixon was under fire for ordering a cover-up of the Watergate break-in, he went months without a news conference. His aides plotted his movements to avoid even informal, shouted questions from reporters. He hunkered down in the White House in a classic example of **stonewalling**. Experts in the branch of public relations called political communications generally advise against stonewalling because people infer guilt or something to hide. Nonetheless, it is one way to deal with difficult media questions.

—Vivian, *The Media of Mass Communication*, p. 378

Main idea: _____

_____

Paragraph 4

If your peers listen to rap, Nortec, death metal, rock and roll, country, or gospel, it is almost inevitable that you also prefer that kind of music. In high school, if your friends take math courses, you probably do, too. It is the same for clothing styles and dating standards. Peer influences also extend to behaviors that violate social norms. If your peers are college-bound and upwardly striving, this is most likely what you will be; but if they use drugs, cheat, and steal, you are likely to do so, too.

—adapted from Henslin, *Sociology*, p. 81

Main idea: _____

_____

EXERCISE 3-14 FINDING IMPLIED MAIN IDEAS 3

Directions: *After reading each of the following paragraphs, select the choice that best answers each of the questions that follow.*

Paragraph A

John Kennedy, the first "television president," held considerably more public appearances than did his predecessors. Kennedy's successors, with the notable exception of Richard Nixon, have been even more active in making public appearances. Indeed, they have averaged more than one appearance every weekday of the year. Bill Clinton invested enormous time and energy in attempting to sell his programs to the public. George W. Bush followed the same pattern.

—adapted from Edwards et al., *Government in America*, p. 422

_____ 1. What is the topic?

    a. the presidency

    b. the effects of television

    c. President Kennedy

    d. public appearances of the president

_____ 2. What main idea is the writer implying?

    a. U.S. presidents all enjoy being in the public eye.

    b. The successors of President Kennedy have tried to imitate him.

    c. Presidents have placed increasing importance on making public appearances.

    d. Presidents spend too much time making public appearances.

Paragraph B

When registering for online services under a screen name, it can be tempting to think your identity is a secret to other users. Many people will say or do things on the Internet that they would never do in real life because they believe that they are acting anonymously. However, most blogs, e-mail and instant messenger services, and social networking sites are tied to your real identity in some way. While your identity may be superficially concealed by a screen name, it often takes little more than a quick Google search to uncover your name, address, and other personal and possibly sensitive information.

—Ebert and Griffin, *Business Essentials*, p. 188

_____ 3. What is the topic?

    a. online identity

    b. screen names

    c. online services

    d. Google searches

_____ 4. What is the writer saying about the topic?

    a. Google searches offer clues to your identity.

    b. People write things on the Internet they would never say face-to-face.

    c. Your identity is not secret on the Internet.

    d. Screen names help conceal your identity.

Paragraph C

All the nutrients in the world are useless to humans unless oxygen is also available. Because the chemical reactions that release energy from foods require oxygen, human cells can survive for only a few minutes without oxygen. Approximately 20% of the air we breathe is oxygen. It is made available to the blood and body cells by the cooperative efforts of the respiratory and cardiovascular systems.

—adapted from Marieb, *Human Anatomy and Physiology,* p. 9

_____ 5. What is the topic?

    a. humans

    b. nutrients

    c. oxygen

    d. the respiratory system

_____ 6. What main idea is the writer implying?

    a. All chemical reactions require oxygen.

    b. Oxygen is vital to human life.

    c. Less than a fourth of the air we breathe is oxygen.

    d. The respiratory system and the cardiovascular system work together.

_____ 7. Which one of the following details does *not* support the paragraph's implied main idea?

    a. All the nutrients in the world are useless to humans.

    b. The chemical reactions that release energy from foods use oxygen.

    c. Oxygen is an important component of the air we breathe.

    d. The respiratory and cardiovascular systems supply oxygen to the blood and body cells.

Paragraph D

People's acceptance of a product may be largely determined by its packaging. In one study the very same coffee taken from a yellow can was described as weak, from a dark brown can as too strong, from a red can as rich, and from a blue can as mild. Even your acceptance of a person may depend on the colors worn. Consider, for example, the comments of one color expert: "If you have to pick the wardrobe for your defense lawyer heading into court and choose anything but blue, you deserve to lose the case. . . ." Black is so powerful it could work against the lawyer with the jury. Brown lacks sufficient authority. Green would probably elicit a negative response.

—adapted from DeVito, *Messages,* p. 161

_____ 8. What is the topic?

    a. packaging

    b. marketing

    c. colors

    d. dressing for success

_____ 9. What is the writer saying about the topic?

    a. Colors influence how we think and act.

    b. A product's packaging determines whether or not we accept it.

    c. A lawyer's success depends on the color of his or her wardrobe.

    d. Color experts consider blue to be the most influential color.

_____ 10. Which one of the following details does *not* support the paragraph's implied main idea?

    a. The same coffee is judged differently depending on the color of the coffee can.

    b. The colors a person is wearing may influence your opinion of that person.

    c. Defense lawyers who do not wear blue in court deserve to be defeated.

    d. Green is an appropriate color for almost all occasions.

EXERCISE 3-15 FINDING STATED AND IMPLIED MAIN IDEAS

Directions: *Turn to the article titled "Treating Wounded Soldiers: Polytrauma" on pages 8–11. Using your own paper, number the lines from 1 to 10, to correspond to the ten paragraphs in the article. For each paragraph number, if the main idea is stated, record the sentence number in which it appears (first, second, etc.). If the main idea is unstated and implied, write a sentence that expresses the main idea.*

3e   RECOGNIZING TRANSITIONS

LEARNING OBJECTIVE 5
Recognize transitions

Transitions are linking words or phrases used to lead the reader from one idea to another. If you get in the habit of recognizing transitions, you will see that they often guide you through a paragraph, helping you to read it more easily.

    In the following paragraph, notice how the underlined transitions lead you from one important detail to the next.

Example

> Assuming you have adequate skills and background and that you have identified a job for which you are 100 percent enthusiastic, the following approach will work for you. First, you must make a contract with yourself to complete all the tasks necessary to get the job. Next, you must become totally informed about the tasks and responsibilities of the job you are seeking. Additionally, you will need to augment any researched information by making personal contacts with insiders. Furthermore, once you have identified your ideal job situation, investigate activities that may be indispensable first steps toward your goal. Such activities may be temporary, volunteer, or entry-level jobs in your chosen field. They can be critical in adding to your experience and connecting you with the right people to make you a better candidate for your preferred job.
>
> —adapted from Sukiennik et al., *The Career Fitness Program*, p. 185

Not all paragraphs contain such obvious transitions, and not all transitions serve as such clear markers of major details. Often, however, transitions are used to alert you to what will come next in the paragraph. If you see the phrase *for instance* at the beginning of a sentence, then you know that an example will follow. When you see the phrase *on the other hand*, you can predict that a different, opposing idea will follow. Table 3-1 lists some of the most common transitions used within a paragraph and indicates what they tell you.

TABLE 3-1 COMMON TRANSITIONS

TYPES OF TRANSITIONS	EXAMPLES	WHAT THEY TELL THE READER
Time or Sequence	first, later, next, finally	The author is arranging ideas in the order in which they happened.
Example	for example, for instance, to illustrate, such as	An example will follow.
Enumeration	first, second, third, last, another, next	The author is marking or identifying each major point (sometimes these may be used to suggest order of importance).
Continuation	also, in addition, and, further, another	The author is continuing with the same idea and is going to provide additional information.
Contrast	on the other hand, in contrast, however	The author is switching to a different, opposite, or contrasting idea than previously discussed.
Comparison	like, likewise, similarly	The writer will show how the previous idea is similar to what follows.
Cause and Effect	because, thus, therefore, since, consequently	The writer will show a connection between two or more things, how one thing caused another, or how something happened as a result of something else.

EXERCISE 3-16 RECOGNIZING TRANSITIONS 1

Directions: *Select the transitional word or phrase from the box below that best completes each of the following sentences.*

another	however	more important
for example	because	

1. The function of taste buds is to enable us to select healthy foods. _____ function is to warn us away from foods that are potentially dangerous, by detecting a sour, bitter, or rancid taste.

2. Michelangelo considered himself to be primarily a sculptor; _____, the painting on the ceiling of the Sistine Chapel is one of his best known works of art.

3. Failure to floss and brush teeth and gums can cause bad breath. _____, this failure can also lead to periodontal disease.

4. Businesses use symbols to represent their products; _____, the golden arches have come to represent the McDonald's chain.

5. In the 1800s, the "Wild West" was made up of territories that did not belong to states. _____ there was no local government, vigilantes and outlaws ruled the land, answering only to U.S. marshals.

EXERCISE 3-17 RECOGNIZING TRANSITIONS 2

Directions: *Select the transitional word or phrase from the box below that best completes each of the following sentences. Two of the transitions in the box may be used more than once.*

on the other hand	for example	because	in addition
similarly	after	next	however
also			

1. Typically, those suffering from post-traumatic stress disorder (PTSD) are soldiers after combat. Civilians who witnessed or lived through events such as the World Trade Center destruction can _____ experience PTSD.

2. Columbus was determined to find an oceanic passage to China _____ finding a direct route would mean increased trading and huge profits.

3. In the event of a heart attack, it is first important to identify the symptoms. _____, call 911 or drive the victim to the nearest hospital.

4. In the 1920s, courtship between men and women changed dramatically. _____, instead of visiting the woman's home with her parents present, men began to invite women out on dates.

5. Direct exposure to sunlight is dangerous because the sun's ultraviolet rays can lead to skin cancer. _____, tanning booths emit ultra-violet rays and are as dangerous as, if not more dangerous than, exposure to sunlight.

6. Lie detector tests are often used by law enforcement to help determine guilt or innocence. _____, because these tests often have an accuracy rate of only 60 to 80 percent, the results are not admissible in court.

7. The temporal lobes of the brain process sound and comprehend language. _____, the temporal lobes are responsible for storing visual memories.

8. The theory of multiple intelligences holds that there are many differ-ent kinds of intelligence, or abilities. _____, musical ability, control of bodily movements (athletics), spatial understand-ing, and observational abilities are all classified as different types of intelligence.

9. During World War II, Japanese Americans were held in relocation camps. _____ the war was over, the United States paid reparations and issued an apology to those who were wrongfully detained.

10. Many believe that the United States should adopt a flat tax in which every person pays the same tax rate. _____, it is unlikely that the tax code will be overhauled any time soon.

EXERCISE 3-18 RECOGNIZING TRANSITIONS 3

Directions: *Many transitions have similar meanings and can sometimes be used interchangeably. Match each transition in column A with a similar transition in column B. Write the letter of your choice in the space provided.*

Column A	Column B
_____ 1. because	a. therefore
_____ 2. in contrast	b. also
_____ 3. for instance	c. likewise
_____ 4. thus	d. after that
_____ 5. first	e. since
_____ 6. one way	f. in conclusion
_____ 7. similarly	g. on the other hand
_____ 8. next	h. one approach
_____ 9. in addition	i. in the beginning
_____ 10. to sum up	j. for example

EXERCISE 3-19 RECOGNIZING TRANSITIONS 4

Directions: *Each of the following beginnings of paragraphs uses a transitional word or phrase to tell the reader what will follow. Read each, paying particular attention to the underlined word or phrase. Then, in the space provided, specifically describe what you would expect to find immediately after the transitional word or phrase.*

1. Price is not the only factor to consider in choosing a pharmacy. Many provide valuable services that should be considered. <u>For instance</u> . . .

   _____

2. There are a number of things you can do to prevent a home burglary. <u>First,</u> . . .

   _____

3. Most mail order businesses are reliable and honest. <u>However,</u> . . .

   _____

   _____

4. One advantage of a laptop computer is that all the components are built into the unit. <u>Another</u> . . .

   _____

5. To select the presidential candidate you will vote for, you should examine his or her philosophy of government. Next . . .

SUMMARY OF LEARNING OBJECTIVES

1	Identify the thesis What is a thesis?	The thesis is what the entire reading is about. It is the one most important, general idea (or central thought) that the entire reading selection explains. It is sometimes expressed in a thesis sentence or thesis statement.
2	Find stated main ideas What are stated main ideas and where are they located?	A main idea expresses a single idea about the topic of a paragraph. Main ideas are often expressed directly in a topic sentence. The topic sentence is the most general sentence in the paragraph. The topic sentence often appears first in a paragraph, but it may also appear in the middle or at the end of the paragraph. Sometimes it appears both at the beginning and at the end of the paragraph.
3	Recognize supporting details What are supporting details?	Supporting details are facts and ideas that prove or explain a paragraph's main idea. Not all details are equally important.
4	Find implied main ideas How can you find implied main ideas?	When a main idea is implied, it is not stated outright. To state an implied main idea, look at the details in the paragraph and figure out the writer's main point. The details, when taken together, will point to a general and more important idea. This is the implied main idea.
5	Recognize transitions What is the function of transitions?	Transitions are linking words or phrases that lead the reader from one idea to another. They are often used to alert the reader to what is coming next.

4 Organizational Patterns

LEARNING OBJECTIVES

In this chapter, you will learn how to

1 Recognize definition

2 Recognize classification

3 Recognize order or sequence

4 Recognize cause and effect

5 Recognize comparison and contrast

6 Recognize listing/enumeration

7 Recognize mixed patterns

8 Recognize other patterns of organization

Most college students take courses in several different disciplines each semester. They may study psychology, anatomy and physiology, mathematics, and English composition all in one semester. During one day they may read a poem, solve math problems, and study early developments in psychology.

What few students realize is that biologists and psychologists, for example, think about and approach their subject matter in similar ways. Both carefully define terms, examine causes and effects, study similarities and differences, describe sequences of events, classify information, solve problems, and enumerate characteristics. They may study different subject matter and use different language, but their approaches to their studies are basically the same. Researchers, textbook authors, your professors, and professional writers use standard approaches, or **organizational patterns**, to express their ideas.

In academic writing, commonly used organizational patterns include definition, classification, order or sequence, cause and effect, comparison and contrast, and listing/enumeration. Other important patterns include statement and clarification, summary, generalization and example, and addition. Each of these patterns can work alone or with other patterns.

These patterns can work for you in several ways:

- Patterns help you anticipate the author's thought development and thus focus your reading.
- Patterns help you remember and recall what you read.

- Patterns are useful in your own writing; they help you organize and express your ideas in a coherent, comprehensible form.

The following sections describe each pattern listed on the preceding page. In subsequent chapters, you will see how these patterns are used in specific academic disciplines.

4a DEFINITION

LEARNING OBJECTIVE 1
Recognize definition

Each academic discipline has its own specialized vocabulary. One of the primary purposes of introductory textbooks is to introduce students to this new language. Consequently, **definition** is a commonly used pattern throughout most introductory-level texts.

Suppose you were asked to define the word *comedian* for someone unfamiliar with the term. First, you would probably say that a comedian is a person who entertains. Then you might distinguish a comedian from other types of entertainers by saying that a comedian is an entertainer who tells jokes and makes others laugh. Finally, you might mention, by way of example, the names of several well-known comedians who have appeared on television. Although you may have presented it informally, your definition would have followed the standard, classic pattern. The first part of your definition tells what general class or group the term belongs to (entertainers). The second part tells what distinguishes the term from other items in the same class or category. The third part includes further explanation, characteristics, examples, or applications.

See how the term *rap* is defined in the following paragraph, and notice how the term and the general class are presented in the first sentence. The remainder of the paragraph presents the distinguishing characteristics. Sometimes writers use typographical aids, such as *italics*, **boldface**, or **color** to emphasize the term being defined.

Example

> One of the most interesting musical and literary developments of the 1980s was the emergence of **rap**, a form of popular music in which words are recited to a driving rhythmic beat. It differs from mainstream popular music in several ways, but, most interesting in literary terms, rap lyrics are spoken rather than sung. In that sense, rap is a form of popular poetry as well as popular music. In most rap songs, the lead performer or "M.C." talks or recites, usually at top speed, long, rhythmic, four-stress lines that end in rimes.

—Kennedy and Gioia, *Literature*, p. 762

You can visualize the definition pattern as follows:

TERM		RAP	
General group		Popular music	
	Distinguishing feature		Words are recited to a beat
	Distinguishing feature		Lyrics are spoken, not sung
	Distinguishing feature		Is a form of popular poetry
	Distinguishing feature		Lines usually end in rimes (rhymes)

Writers often provide clues called **transitions** that signal the organizational pattern being used. These signals may occur within single sentences or as connections between sentences. (Transitional words that occur in phrases are italicized in the box below to help you spot them.)

TRANSITIONS FOR THE DEFINITION PATTERN

Genetics *is* . . .
Bureaucracy *means* . . .
Patronage *refers to* . . .
Aggression *can be defined* as . . .
Deficit is *another term* that . . .
Balance of power *also means* . . .

EXERCISE 4–1 USING DEFINITION

Directions: *Read each of the following paragraphs and answer the questions that follow.*

A.   A *pidgin* is a contact language that emerges when different cultures with different languages come to live in close proximity and therefore need to communicate. Pidgins are generally limited to highly functional domains, such as trade, since that is what they were developed for. A pidgin therefore is no one's first language. Many pidgins of the Western hemisphere developed out of slavery, where owners needed to communicate with their slaves. A pidgin is always learned as a second language. Tok Pisin, the pidgin language of Papua New Guinea, consists of a mixture of many languages, some English, Samoan, Chinese, and Malayan. Tok Pisin has been declared one of the national languages of Papua New Guinea, where it is transforming into a *creole*, or a language descended from pidgin with its own native speakers and involving linguistic expansion and elaboration. About two hundred pidgin and creole languages exist today, mainly in West Africa, the Caribbean, and the South Pacific.

—Miller, *Cultural Anthropology*, pp. 308–309

1. What terms are being defined?

   _____

2. Explain the meaning of the terms in your own words.

   _____

   _____

   _____

3. Give an example of the first term that is defined.

   _____

B.   A **tariff** is a tax that is imposed on a good when it is imported. For example, the government of India imposes a 100 percent tariff on wine imported from California. When an Indian firm imports a $10 bottle of Californian wine, it pays the Indian government a $10 import duty. The incentive for governments to impose tariffs is strong. First, they provide revenue to the government. Second, they enable the government to satisfy the self-interest of people who earn their incomes in import-competing industries.

—Bade and Parkin, *Essential Foundations of Economics*, p. 205

4. What term is being defined, and what is the definition?

   _____

5. What are two reasons that governments impose tariffs?

   _____

   _____

4b   CLASSIFICATION

LEARNING OBJECTIVE 2
Recognize classification

If you were asked to describe types of computers, you might mention desktops, laptops, and handhelds. By dividing a broad topic into its major categories, you are using the **classification** pattern.

This pattern is widely used in many academic subjects. For example, a psychology text might explain human needs by classifying them into two categories: primary and secondary. In a chemistry textbook, various compounds may be grouped and discussed according to common characteristics, such as the presence of hydrogen or oxygen. The classification pattern divides a topic into parts, on the basis of common or shared characteristics.

Here are a few examples of topics and the classifications or categories into which each might be divided:

- **movies:** comedy, horror, mystery, drama
- **motives:** achievement, power, affiliation, money
- **plants:** leaves, stem, roots, flower

Note how the following paragraph classifies the various types of clouds.

> In 1803, Luke Howard, an English naturalist, published a cloud classification that serves as the basis of our present-day system. According to Howard's system, three basic cloud forms or shapes are recognized. **Cirrus** clouds are high, white, and thin. They form delicate veil-like patches or wisplike strands and often have a feathery appearance. **Cumulus** clouds consist of globular cloud masses that are often described as cottonlike in appearance. Normally cumulus clouds exhibit a flat base and appear as rising domes or towers. **Stratus** clouds are best described as sheets or layers that cover much or all of the sky. Although there may be minor breaks, there are no distinct individual cloud units. All clouds have at least one of these three basic forms, and some are a combination of two of them (for example, cirro-cumulus clouds).
>
> —adapted from Lutgens and Tarbuck, *The Atmosphere*, pp. 131–132

You can visualize the classification pattern as follows:

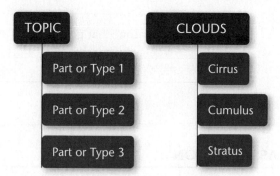

> ## TRANSITIONS FOR THE CLASSIFICATION PATTERN
> There are *several kinds* of chemical bonding . . .
> There are *numerous types of* . . .
> Reproduction can be *classified as* . . .
> The human skeleton is *composed of* . . .
> Muscles *comprise* . . .
> *One type of* communication . . .
> *Another type of* communication . . .
> *Finally*, there is . . .

EXERCISE 4-2 USING CLASSIFICATION

Directions: *Read each of the following selections and answer the questions that follow.*

A. Communication between two entities, whether they are people or computers, can be separated into two broad classes: synchronous and asynchronous. **Synchronous communication** requires that both the sender and the receiver are active at the same time. A telephone conversation is an example of synchronous communication because both people in the conversation must perform one of the two parts of the communication—sending (talking) or receiving (listening)—simultaneously. In **asynchronous communication**, the sending and receiving occur at different times. Postcards and text messages are examples of asynchronous communication because they are written at one time and read at another. Answering machines and voice mail make synchronous telephones asynchronous because the caller leaves a message and the receiver listens to it later. Email is asynchronous; applications like Skype and iChat are synchronous computer communication.

—Snyder, *Fluency with Information Technology*, p. 51

1. List the classification of communication included in this paragraph.

   _____

2. Underline the transitional phrase used in the paragraph to indicate the classification pattern.

B. Astronomers classify galaxies into three major categories. **Spiral galaxies**, such as our own Milky Way, look like flat white disks with yellowish bulges at their centers. The disks are filled with cool gas and dust, interspersed with hotter ionized gas, and usually display beautiful spiral arms. **Elliptical galaxies** are redder, rounder, and often longer in one direction than in the other, like a football. Compared with spiral galaxies, elliptical galaxies contain very little cool gas and dust, though they often contain very hot ionized gas. **Irregular galaxies** appear neither disklike nor rounded. The differing colors of galaxies arise from the different kinds of stars that populate them: Spiral and irregular galaxies look white because they contain stars of all different colors and ages, while elliptical galaxies look redder because old, reddish stars produce most of their light.

—Bennett et al., *The Essential Cosmic Perspective*, pp. 412–413

3. What are the three classifications of galaxies?

_____

4. Underline the transitional words used in the paragraph to indicate the classification pattern.

4c   ORDER OR SEQUENCE

LEARNING OBJECTIVE 3
Recognize order or sequence

If you were asked to summarize what you did today, you probably would mention key events in the order in which they occurred. In describing how to write a particular computer program, you would detail the process step-by-step. In each case, you are presenting information in a particular sequence or order. Each of these examples illustrates a form of the organizational pattern known as *order* or *sequence*. Let's look at several types of order.

Chronology

Chronological order refers to the sequence in which events occur in time. This pattern is essential in the academic disciplines concerned with the interpretation of events in the past. History, government, and anthropology are prime examples. In various forms of literature, chronological order is evident; the narrative form (used in novels, short stories, and narrative essays) relies on chronological order.

The following paragraph uses chronology to describe the sinking of the *Lusitania*.

> At 12:30 on the afternoon of May 1, 1915, the British steamship *Lusitania* set sail from New York to Liverpool. The passenger list of 1,257 was the largest since the outbreak of war in Europe in 1914. Six days later, the *Lusitania* reached the coast of Ireland. The passengers lounged on the deck. As if it were peacetime, the ship sailed straight ahead, with no zigzag maneuvers to throw off pursuit. But the submarine U-20 was there, and its commander, seeing a large ship, fired a single torpedo. Seconds after it hit, a boiler exploded and blew a hole in the *Lusitania's* side. The ship listed immediately, hindering the launching of lifeboats, and in eighteen minutes it sank. Nearly 1,200 people died, including 128 Americans. As the ship's bow lifted and went under, the U-20 commander for the first time read the name: *Lusitania*.
>
> —adapted from Divine et al., *America Past and Present*, p. 596

You can visualize the chronological order pattern as follows:

EVENT

1. Action

2. Action

3. Action

4. Action

5. Action

6. Action

> **TRANSITIONS FOR THE CHRONOLOGICAL ORDER PATTERN**
>
> *In* ancient times . . .
> *At* the start of the battle . . .
> *On* September 12 . . .
> The *first* primate species . . .
> *Later* efforts . . .
> Other chronological transitions are *then, before, during, by the time, while, afterward, as, after, thereafter, meanwhile,* and *at that point.*

EXERCISE 4–3 USING ORDER OR SEQUENCE

Directions: *Read each of the following selections and answer the questions that follow.*

A. Railroads: Pioneers of Big Business

Completion of efficient and speedy national transportation and communications networks encouraged mass production and mass marketing. Beginning in 1862, federal and state governments vigorously promoted railroad construction with land grants from the public domain. Eventually, railroads received lands one and a half times the size of Texas. Local governments gave everything from land for stations to tax breaks.

With such incentives, the first transcontinental railroad was finished in 1869. Four additional transcontinental lines and miles of feeder and branch roads were laid down in the 1870s and 1880s. By 1890, trains rumbled across 165,000 miles of tracks. Telegraph lines arose alongside them.

—Nash et al., *The American People*, pp. 611–613

1. What events does the excerpt detail?

_____

2. What is the importance of these events?

_____

3. Underline the transitional words used in the excerpt.

B. Ending the Cold War

A far more promising trend toward freedom began in Europe in mid-1989. In June, Lech Walesa and his Solidarity movement won free elections in Poland. Soon the winds of change were sweeping over the former Iron Curtain countries. Hungary opened its borders to the West in September, allowing thousands of East Germans to flee to freedom. One by one, the repressive governments of East Germany, Czechoslovakia, Bulgaria, and Romania fell. The most heartening scene took place in East Germany in early November when new communist leaders suddenly announced the opening of the Berlin Wall. Workers quickly demolished a 12-foot-high section of this despised symbol of the Cold War, joyously singing a German version of "For He's a Jolly Good Fellow."

—Brands et al., *American Stories*, p. 807

4. What events in history does this paragraph describe?

_____

_____

5. Underline the transitional words used in the excerpt.

Process

In disciplines that focus on the procedures, steps, or stages by which actions are accomplished, the **process** pattern is often employed. These subjects include mathematics, natural and life sciences, engineering, and many career fields. The process pattern is similar to chronological order in that the steps or stages follow each other in time. Transitional words and phrases used with the process pattern are similar to those used for chronological order.

Note how the process pattern is used in a paragraph explaining how memory works.

Memory is a process of acquiring information and storing it over time so that it will be available when we need it. Contemporary approaches to the study of memory employ an information-processing approach. They assume that the mind is in some ways like a computer: Data are input, processed, and output for later use in revised form. In the **encoding** stage, information enters in a way the system will recognize. In the **storage** stage, we integrate this knowledge with what is already in memory and "warehouse" it until it is needed. During **retrieval**, we access the desired information.

—Solomon, *Consumer Behavior*, p. 95

You can visualize the process pattern as follows:

PROCESS

1. Step

2. Step

3. Step

4. Step

EXERCISE 4-4 USING PROCESS

Directions: *Read each of the following selections and answer the questions that follow.*

A.   The **initiative** is the purest form of direct democracy. Although its details vary from state to state, the basic procedure is as follows. First, a citizen decides that he or she wants to see a law passed. The specific language of that proposal is then registered with a state official (typically the secretary of state), and permission to circulate a petition is given. The advocates of the proposal then try to get a specified number of eligible voters (typically 5 to 10 percent of those voting in the previous election) to sign a petition saying they would like to see the proposal on the ballot. When the appropriate number of signatures has been verified, the proposal is placed on the next general election ballot for an approve/disapprove vote. If a majority of voters approve it, the proposal becomes law.

—Edwards et al., *Government in America*, p. 627

1. What process does this passage explain?

_____

2. Underline the transitional words used in the paragraph.

B.   BMI [body mass index] is an index of the relationship of height and weight. It is one of the most accurate indicators of a person's health risk due to excessive weight, rather than "fatness" per se. Although many people recoil in fright when they see they have to convert pounds to kilograms and inches to meters to calculate BMI, it really is not as difficult as it may seem. To get your kilogram weight, just divide your weight in pounds (without shoes or clothing) by 2.2. To convert your height to meters squared, divide your height in inches (without shoes) by 39.4, then square this result. Sounds pretty easy and it actually is. Once you have these basic values, calculating your BMI involves dividing your weight in kilograms by your height in meters squared.

$$\text{BMI} = \frac{\text{Weight (in lbs)} \times 2.2 \text{ (to determine weight in kg)}}{(\text{Height [in inches]} \div 39.4)^2 \text{ (to determine height in meters squared)}}$$

Healthy weights have been defined as those associated with BMIs of 19 to 25, the range of the lowest statistical health risk. A BMI greater than 25 indicates overweight and potentially significant health risks. The desirable range for females is between 21 and 23; for males, it is between 22 and 24. A body mass index of over 30 is considered obese. Many experts believe this number is too high, particularly for younger adults.

—Donatelle, *Access to Health*, p. 264

3. What process is being described in this paragraph?

_____

4. How do you convert height in inches to meters squared?

_____

5. What does BMI measure and why is it useful?

_____

_____

Order of Importance

Almost all fields of study use a pattern that expresses ideas in order of priority or preference. In this pattern, ideas can be arranged in one of two ways: from most to least important, or from least to most important. In the following paragraph, cities are placed in **order of importance** based on the business services they provide.

Geographers distinguish settlements according to their importance in the provision of business services. At the top of the hierarchy are settlements known as **world cities** that play an especially important role in global business services. World cities are most closely integrated into the global economic system because they are at the center of the flow of information and capital. Below the first tier of world cities are three other tiers of settlements according to type and extent of business services. In the second tier are **command and control centers**. These contain the headquarters of many large corporations, well-developed banking facilities, and concentrations of other business services, including insurance, accounting, advertising, law, and public relations. In the third tier are **specialized producer-service centers**. These offer narrower and more highly specialized services. In the fourth tier are **dependent centers**, which provide relatively unskilled jobs.

—adapted from Rubenstein, *Contemporary Human Geography*, pp. 278–279

TRANSITIONS FOR ORDER OF IMPORTANCE

is *less* essential than . . .
More revealing is . . .
Of *primary* interest is . . .
Other transitions that show the order of importance are *first, next, last, most important, primarily,* and *secondarily*.

EXERCISE 4–5 USING ORDER OF IMPORTANCE

Directions: *Read the following paragraph and answer the questions that follow.*

A health claim on a food product label must contain two important components: a food or a dietary compound, such as fiber, and a corresponding disease or health-related condition that is associated with the claim. There are three types of health claims: (1) authorized health claims, (2) health claims based on authoritative statements, and (3) qualified health claims. The differences between them lie in the amount of supporting research and agreement among scientists about the strength of the relationship between the food or dietary ingredient and the disease or condition. Authorized health claims and health claims based on authoritative statements are the strongest, as they are based on years of accumulated research or an authoritative statement. Qualified health claims are less convincing. They are made on potentially healthful foods or dietary ingredients, but, because the evidence is still emerging, the claim has to be "qualified" as such.

—adapted from Blake, *Nutrition and You*, pp. 52–56

1. What is the topic of this paragraph?

_____

2. Which types of health claims are the strongest and why?

_____

_____

3. What makes qualified health claims less convincing?

_____

4. Underline transition words that indicate order of importance.

Spatial Order

Information organized according to its physical location, or position or order in space, exhibits the **spatial order** pattern. Spatial order is used in academic disciplines and careers in which physical descriptions are important. These include numerous technical fields, engineering, and the biological sciences.

You can see how the following description of the human eye relies on spatial relationships.

> Light comes into our eyes through the transparent cornea and passes through the opening known as the pupil. Surrounding the pupil is the iris, which is composed partly of smooth muscle and thus is capable of contracting or dilating, meaning it can let in less light in a bright environment or more light in a darkened one. The incoming light is bound for the layer of cells at the back of the eye called the retina: an inner layer of tissue in the eye containing cells that transform light into nervous system signals.
>
> —Krogh, *Biology*, p. 526

Diagramming is of the utmost importance in working with this pattern; often, a diagram accompanies text material that uses spatial order. For example, a diagram makes the functions of the various parts of the human brain easier to understand. Instructors often refer to a visual aid or drawing when providing spatial descriptions.

TRANSITIONS FOR SPATIAL ORDER

The *left side* of the brain . . .
The *lower* portion . . .
The *outer* covering . . .
Beneath the surface . . .
Other spatial transitions are *next to, beside, above, to the left, to the right, in the center, internally*, and *externally*.

EXERCISE 4-6 USING SPATIAL ORDER

Directions: *Read the following selection and answer the questions that follow.*

Taste receptors, or *gustatory receptors*, are distributed over the surface of the tongue and adjacent portions of the pharynx and larynx. The most important taste receptors are on the tongue; by the time we reach adulthood, those on the pharynx and larynx have decreased in importance and abundance. Taste receptors and specialized epithelial cells form sensory structures called **taste buds**. The taste buds are well protected from the mechanical stress due to chewing, for they lie along the sides of epithelial projections called **papillae**. The greatest numbers of taste buds are associated with the large *circumvallate papillae*, which form a V that points toward the base of the tongue. Each taste bud contains slender sensory receptors known as **gustatory cells** and supporting cells. Each gustatory cell extends slender microvilli, sometimes called *taste hairs*, into the surrounding fluids through a narrow opening, the **taste pore**. The mechanism behind gustatory reception seems to parallel that of olfaction (the sense of smell).

—adapted from Martini and Bartholomew, *Essentials of Anatomy and Physiology*, p. 312

1. Where are taste receptors located?

   _____

2. Underline the transitional words in the passage.

3. Why are taste buds protected from the stress of chewing?

   _____

4. What is the other sense that seems to have a parallel mechanism to gustatory reception?

   _____

   _____

4d   CAUSE AND EFFECT

LEARNING OBJECTIVE 4
Recognize cause and effect

The **cause-and-effect** pattern expresses a relationship between two or more actions, events, or occurrences that are connected in time. The relationship differs, however, from chronological order. In the cause-and-effect pattern, one event leads to another by *causing* it. Information organized with the cause-and-effect pattern may:

- explain causes, sources, reasons, motives, and actions
- explain the effect, result, or consequence of a particular action
- explain both causes and effects

You can visualize the cause-and-effect pattern as follows:

Cause and effect is clearly illustrated by the paragraph on the following page, which explains the phenomenon known as a mirage.

You have undoubtedly seen a mirage while traveling along a highway on a hot summer afternoon. The most common highway mirages are in the form of "wet areas" that appear on the pavement ahead, only to disappear as you approach. Because these "wet areas" always disappear as a person gets closer, many people believe they are optical illusions. This is not the case. Highway mirages, as well as all other types of mirages, are as real as the images observed in a mirror. What causes the "wet areas" that appear on dry pavement? On hot summer days, the layer of air near Earth's surface is much warmer than the air aloft. Sunlight traveling from a region of colder (more dense) air into the warmer (less dense) air near the surface bends in a direction opposite to Earth's curvature. As a consequence, light rays that began traveling downward from the sky are refracted upward and appear to the observer to have originated on the pavement ahead. What appears to the traveler as water is really just an inverted image of the sky.

—adapted from Lutgens and Tarbuck, *The Atmosphere*, p. 454

The cause-and-effect pattern is used extensively in many academic fields. All disciplines that ask the question "Why?" employ the cause-and-effect thought pattern. It is widely used in careers in the sciences, technologies, and social sciences.

Many statements expressing cause-and-effect relationships appear in direct order, with the cause stated first and the effect stated second: "When demand for a product increases, prices rise." However, reverse order is sometimes used, as in the following statement: "Prices rise when a product's demand increases."

The cause-and-effect pattern is not limited to an expression of a simple one-cause, one-effect relationship. There may be multiple causes, or multiple effects, or both multiple causes and multiple effects. For example, both slippery road conditions and your failure to buy snow tires (causes) may contribute to your car sliding into the ditch or into another car (effects).

In other instances, a chain of causes or effects may occur. For instance, failing to set your alarm clock may force you to miss your 8:00 A.M. class, which in turn may cause you not to submit your term paper on time, which may result in a penalty grade.

TRANSITIONS FOR THE CAUSE-AND-EFFECT PATTERN

Stress *causes* . . .
Aggression *creates* . . .
Depression *leads to* . . .
Forethought *yields* . . .
Mental retardation *stems from* . . .
Good hygiene *helps to* . . .
Life changes *produce* . . .
Hostility *breeds* . . .
Avoidance *results in* . . .
Other cause-and-effect transitions are *therefore, consequently, hence, thus, for this reason,* and *since.*

EXERCISE 4-7 USING CAUSE AND EFFECT

Directions: *Read each of the following selections and answer the questions that follow.*

A.   Something that all allergic reactions share is that people do not have them the first time they are exposed to an allergen. This is because the body's immune system has not "learned" to recognize the allergen yet. The first time someone is exposed to an allergen, the immune system forms antibodies in response. These antibodies are the body's attempt to attack the foreign substances. A particular antibody will combine with only the allergen it was formed in response to (or another allergen very similar to the original one).

The second time the person is exposed to the allergen, the antibodies already exist in the person's body. This time, the antibody combines with the allergen, leading to the release of histamine and other chemicals into the bloodstream. Together, these substances have several effects that may lead to a spectrum of allergic reactions including, at times, the life-threatening condition known as anaphylaxis: They dilate blood vessels, decrease the ability of capillaries to contain fluid, cause bronchoconstriction, and promote the production of thick mucus in the lungs.

—Limmer and O'Keefe, *Emergency Care*, p. 533

1. What happens the first time someone is exposed to an allergen?

_____

2. What effects result from a second exposure to an allergen?

_____

_____

_____

_____

3. Underline the transitional words used in the selection.

B.   It's the end of the term and you have dutifully completed the last of several papers. After hours of nonstop typing, you find that your hands are numb, and you feel an intense, burning pain that makes the thought of typing one more word almost unbearable. If you are like one of the thousands of students and workers who every year must quit a particular task due to pain, you may be suffering from a repetitive stress injury (RSI). These are injuries to nerves, soft tissue or joints that result from the physical stress of repeated motions. One of the most common RSIs is carpal tunnel syndrome, a product of both the information age and the age of technology in general. Hours spent typing at the computer, flipping groceries through computerized scanners, or other jobs "made simpler" by technology can result in irritation to the median nerve in the wrist, causing numbness, tingling, and pain in the fingers and hands.

—adapted from Donatelle, *Access to Health*, p. 516

4. What is the cause of RSIs?

_____

5. What kind of damage causes carpal tunnel syndrome?

_____

6. What do students often do that can cause RSIs?

_____

7. What kinds of symptoms can result from RSI?

_____

8. Underline the transitional words used in the passage.

4e   COMPARISON AND CONTRAST

LEARNING OBJECTIVE 5
Recognize comparison and contrast

The **comparison** organizational pattern emphasizes or discusses similarities between or among ideas, theories, concepts, or events. The **contrast** pattern emphasizes differences. When a speaker or writer is concerned with both similarities and differences, a combination pattern called **comparison–contrast** is used. You can visualize these three variations of the pattern as follows:

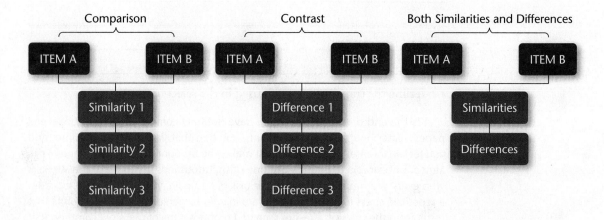

The comparison-and-contrast pattern is widely used in the social sciences, which study different groups, societies, cultures, and behaviors. Literature courses may require comparisons among poets, among several literary works, or among stylistic features. A business course may examine various management styles, compare organizational structures, or contrast retailing plans.

A contrast is shown in the following paragraph, which describes differences in parenting according to social class.

> Working-class and middle-class parents have different ideas of how children develop, ideas that have fascinating consequences for children's play. For working-class parents, children are like wild flowers—they develop naturally. Since the child's development will take care of itself, good parenting primarily means to provide food, shelter, and comfort. These parents set limits on their children's play ("Don't go near the railroad tracks") and let them play as they wish. To middle-class parents, in contrast, children are like tender house plants—they need a lot of guidance to develop correctly. These parents want their children's play to accomplish something. They may want them to play baseball, for example, not for the enjoyment of the sport, but to help them learn how to be team players.
>
> —adapted from Henslin, *Sociology*, p. 78

Depending on whether the speaker or writer is concerned with similarities, differences, or both similarities and differences, the pattern might be organized in different ways. Suppose a professor of American literature asks you to compare the work of two American poets, Walt Whitman and Robert Frost. Each of the following assignments is possible:

1. **Compare and then contrast the two.** That is, first discuss how Frost's poetry and Whitman's poetry are similar, and then discuss how they are different.
2. **Discuss by author.** Discuss the characteristics of Whitman's poetry, then discuss the characteristics of Frost's poetry, and then summarize their similarities and differences.
3. **Discuss by characteristic.** First discuss the two poets' use of metaphor, next discuss their use of rhyme, and then discuss their common themes.

TRANSITIONS THAT SHOW CONTRAST

Unlike Whitman, Frost . . .
Less wordy *than* Whitman . . .
Contrasted with Whitman, Frost . . .
Frost *differs from* . . .
Other transitions of contrast are *in contrast, however, on the other hand, as opposed to,* and *whereas.*

TRANSITIONS THAT SHOW COMPARISON

Similarities between Frost and Whitman . . .
Frost is *as* powerful *as* . . .
Like Frost, Whitman . . .
Both Frost and Whitman . . .
Frost *resembles* Whitman in that . . .
Other transitions of comparison are *in a like manner, similarly, similar to, likewise, correspondingly,* and *in the same way.*

EXERCISE 4-8 USING COMPARISON AND CONTRAST

Directions: *Read each of the following paragraphs and answer the questions that follow.*

A.   In the national election in Vietnam in 2011, it was reported that 99.5 percent of the adults voted, whereas in the United States, 41.6 percent of the citizens voted in the 2010 national election. What best accounts for this difference? In Vietnam, voting is an obligatory act, a required gesture of support for the current political leadership, rather than a genuine selection among candidates—indeed, there is no choice. Most Vietnamese vote because someone who does not vote risks unwanted scrutiny by Communist Party authorities. In the United States, voting has always been a voluntary act, and there are no sanctions for not voting. Thus, the citizen decides whether her sense of civic responsibility or her desire to affect the outcome on ballot choices merits the effort of going to vote.

—Danziger, *Understanding the Political World*, p. 87

1. What two countries are discussed?

   _____

2. Does this paragraph mainly use comparison, contrast, or both?

   _____

3. According to the author, what accounts for the difference in voting in each country?

   _____

4. Underline the transitional words in the paragraph.

B.   Star clusters come in two basic types: modest-size **open clusters** and densely packed **globular clusters**. The two types differ not only how densely they are packed with stars, but also in their locations and ages. Recall that most of the stars, gas, and dust in the Milky Way Galaxy, including our Sun, lie in the relatively flat *galactic disk*; the region above and below the disk is called the *halo* of the galaxy. Open clusters are always found in the disk of the galaxy, and their stars tend to be quite young. They can contain up to several thousand stars and typically are about 30 light-years across. In contrast, most globular clusters are found in the halo, and their stars are among the oldest in the universe. A globular cluster can contain more than a million stars concentrated in a ball typically 60 to 150 light-years across. Its central region can have 10,000 stars packed into a space just a few light-years across. The view from a planet in a globular cluster would be marvelous, with thousands of stars lying closer to that planet than Alpha Centauri is to the Sun.

—adapted from Bennett et al., *The Essential Cosmic Perspective*, pp. 325–326

5. What two things are being compared or contrasted?

   _____

6. What three characteristics are used to differentiate the star clusters?

   _____

7. Which type of cluster has younger stars?

   _____

8. Underline the transitional words used in the paragraph.

4f   LISTING/ENUMERATION

LEARNING OBJECTIVE 6
Recognize listing/
enumeration

If someone asks you to evaluate a film you saw, you might describe the characters, plot, and technical effects. These details about the film could be arranged in any order; each detail provides information about the film, but they need not be discussed in any particular order. This arrangement of ideas is known as **listing** or **enumeration**—giving information on a topic by stating details one after the other, often with no specific method of organizing those details.

You can visualize the listing/enumeration patterns as follows:

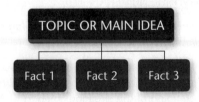

The following list of advertising objectives could have been presented in any order without altering the meaning of the paragraph.

> Advertising has three primary objectives—to inform, to persuade, and to remind. **Informative advertising** is used to provide consumers with information on the product or service, as well as to build awareness and initial demand of a new product. It can also be used to explain the features and functions of a product or to correct false impressions. **Persuasive advertising** is used to develop brand preferences and is also effective at increasing customer loyalty. Marketers often use comparative advertising to persuade consumers to switch brands. **Reminder advertising** is used by well-established brands to maintain brand awareness and remind customers to buy.
>
> —Levens, *Marketing: Defined, Explained, Applied*, p. 228

This pattern is widely used in college textbooks in most academic disciplines. In its loosest form, the pattern may be simply a list of items: factors that influence light emission, characteristics of a particular poet, the reasons for supporting a particular social program, a description of an atom, a list of characteristics that define poverty.

Somewhat tighter is the use of listing to explain, support, or provide evidence. Support may take the form of facts, statistics, or examples. For instance, the statement, "The incidence of white collar crime has dramatically increased over the past ten years" would be followed by facts and statistics documenting the increase.

TRANSITIONS FOR LISTING

One aspect of relativity . . .
A second feature of relativity . . .
Also, relativity . . .
There are *several characteristics of* . . .
(1) . . . , *(2)* . . . , *and (3)* . . . ,
(a) . . . , *(b)* . . . , *and (c)* . . . ,
Other transitional words and phrases are *in addition, first, second, third, finally,* and *another.*

EXERCISE 4-9 USING LISTING/ENUMERATION

Directions: *Read each of the following paragraphs and answer the questions that follow.*

A.   In the past few decades, few issues in the public dialog have become as politicized and polarized as pollution and resource depletion. To reach a clearer understanding of this situation, keep three important points in mind. First, the creation, delivery, use, and disposal of products that society values virtually always generate pollution and consume natural resources. For example, it's tempting to assume that web-based businesses are "clean" because there is no visible pollution. However, the Internet and all the computers attached to it have a voracious appetite for electricity; Google is one of the largest users of electricity in the world, for example. Moreover, generation of electricity seriously affects the environment, as over 70 percent of the electricity used in the United States is generated by burning coal, oil, or natural gas. Second, "environmental" causes are often as much about human health and safety as they are about forests, rivers, and wildlife. The availability of clean air, water, and soil affects everyone, not just people concerned with wild spaces. Third, many of these issues are neither easy nor simple. They often require tough trade-offs, occasional sacrifice, disruptive change, and decision making in the face of uncertainty.

—adapted from Bovée and Thill, *Business in Action,* p. 80

1. What does this paragraph list?

_____

_____

2. Underline the transitional words used in the paragraph.

B.   During toddlerhood, emotional self-regulation advances in four ways. First, toddlers develop *behaviors* that can help them regulate their emotions. For example, toddlers who are frightened may run to a trusted adult or older sibling, or cling to a comforting blanket or stuffed animal. Second, toddlers use *language* to promotion emotional self-regulation. Throughout toddlerhood and beyond, talking about feelings with others enhances children's understanding of their own and others' emotions, which in turn promotes their emotional self-regulation. Third, *external requirements* by others extend toddlers' capacities for emotional self-regulation. In toddlerhood, parents begin to convey and enforce rules that require emotional self-regulation: no hitting others no matter how angry you are, no jumping on the table no matter how happy you are, and so on. Fourth and finally, emotional self-regulation in toddlerhood is promoted by the development of the *sociomoral emotions*. Becoming capable of guilt, shame, and embarrassment motivates toddlers to avoid these unpleasant emotional states. Because they may be admonished by others for expressing primary emotions too strongly or in the wrong context, they learn emotional self-regulation as part of an effort to win approval from others and avoid their disapproval.

—adapted from Arnett, *Human Development*, pp. 200–201

3. What does this paragraph list?

_____

4. Underline the transitional words used in the paragraph.

5. How does the development of sociomoral emotions promote self-regulation?

_____

_____

4g   MIXED PATTERNS

LEARNING OBJECTIVE 7
Recognize mixed patterns

Organizational patterns are often combined. In describing a process, a writer may also give reasons why each step must be followed in the prescribed order. An instructor may define a concept by comparing it with something similar or familiar. Suppose a chapter in your political science textbook opens by stating, "The distinction between 'power' and 'power potential' is an important one in considering the balance of power." You might expect a definition pattern (where the two terms are defined), but you also might anticipate that the chapter would discuss the difference between the two terms (contrast pattern). The longer the reading selection, the more likely it combines multiple patterns of organization.

In the following paragraph, notice how the author combines three patterns: definition, contrast, and listing/enumeration.

Definition #1 →	A city's central business district, or CBD, grows around the city's most accessible point, and it typically contains a dense concentration of offices and stores. CBDs grow with the needs of the community; they expand and contract organi-
Contrast →	cally as the city grows and changes. In contrast, a master-
Definition #2 →	planned community is a residential suburban development. In master-planned developments, houses are designed to look alike and "match," and the community also offers private recreational facilities (such as tennis courts and swimming pools) for its residents. Often, the community is gated
Listing →	to prevent non-residents from entering. Weston is a master-planned community that covers 10,000 acres in Florida. In Weston, almost all aspects of the community are controlled and regulated. Shrubs are planted to shield residents from having to look at the interstate highway. Road signs have a uniform style, each in a stylish frame. Weston offers different areas to cater to different incomes and lifestyles. The houses in the Tequesta Point section come with Roman bathtubs, while an even wealthier section provides larger plots of land for people who own horses.

EXERCISE 4-10 USING ORGANIZATIONAL PATTERNS 1

Directions: *For each of the following topic sentences, anticipate what organizational pattern(s) the paragraph is likely to exhibit. Record your prediction in the space provided.*

1. The Enlightenment celebrated the power of reason; however, an opposite reaction, Romanticism, soon followed.

   Pattern: _____

2. Psychogenic amnesia—a severe and often permanent memory loss—results in disorientation and the inability to draw on past experiences.

   Pattern: _____

3. Several statistical procedures are used to track the changes in the divorce rate.

   Pattern: _____

4. The GNP (gross national product) is an economic measure that considers the total value of goods and services that a country produces during a given year.

   Pattern: _____

5. Large numbers of European immigrants first began to arrive in the United States in the 1920s.

   Pattern: _____

6. There are sources of information about corporations that might help an investor evaluate them. One of the most useful is the Value Line Investment Survey.

   Pattern: _____

7. Diseases of the heart and blood vessels—cardiovascular diseases—are the leading cause of death in the United States today.

   Pattern: _____

8. The spinal cord is located within the spinal column; it looks like a section of rope or twine.

   Pattern: _____

9. Think of the hardware in a computer system as the kitchen in a short-order restaurant: It's equipped to produce whatever output a customer (user) requests, but sits idle until an order (command) is placed.

   Pattern: _____

10. The purpose of a résumé is to sell the qualities of the person writing it; it should include several important kinds of information.

    Pattern: _____

EXERCISE 4–11 USING ORGANIZATIONAL PATTERNS 2

Directions: Read each of the following paragraphs and identify the primary organizational pattern used in each.

Paragraph 1

The founder of Buddhism, Siddharta Gautama, was born about 563 B.C. in Lumbini, in present-day Nepal. The son of a lord, Gautama led a privileged life, with a beautiful wife, palaces, and servants. According to Buddhist legend, Gautama's life changed after a series of four trips. He encountered a decrepit old man on the first trip, a disease-ridden man on the second trip, and a corpse on the third trip. After witnessing these scenes of pain and suffering, Gautama began to feel he could no longer enjoy his life of comfort and security. On a fourth trip, Gautama saw a monk, who taught him about withdrawal from the world. Gautama lived under a Bodhi (or bo) tree in a forest for seven weeks, thinking and experimenting with forms of meditation. He emerged as the Buddha, the "awakened or enlightened one."

— Rubenstein, *Contemporary Human Geography*, p. 131

Pattern: _____

Paragraph 2

Dyslexia is a disorder affecting the comprehension and use of words. Developmental dyslexia affects children; estimates indicate that up to 15 percent of children in the United States suffer from some degree of dyslexia. These children have difficulty reading and writing, although their other intellectual functions may be normal or above normal. Their writing looks uneven and unorganized; letters are typically written in the wrong order (*dig* becomes *gid*) or reversed (*E* becomes Ǝ). Recent evidence suggests that at least some forms of dyslexia result from problems in processing and sorting visual information.

—Martini and Bartholomew, *Essentials of Anatomy and Physiology*, p. 271

Pattern: _____

Paragraph 3

The process of digestion begins at the upper end of the gastrointestinal tract. The *mouth* is where food enters and where the processes of mechanical breakdown and digestion begin. In the mouth, food is chewed (a process called mastication) and mechanically broken down into smaller particles by the cutting and grinding actions of the teeth. The food is also mixed with saliva, which lubricates it and contains an enzyme which begins the digestion of carbohydrates by breaking down starch and glycogen.

From the mouth, the food-saliva mixture is propelled by the tongue into the pharynx (commonly known as the *throat*), a common passageway for food and air. From the pharynx, the passageways for food and air diverge. Whereas air enters the larynx and trachea and proceeds toward the lungs, food enters the esophagus, which runs parallel to the trachea.

The esophagus is a muscular tube whose primary function is to conduct food from the pharynx to the stomach. It can easily stretch to accommodate food as it is swallowed; when food is not present, however, it is normally collapsed.

—adapted from German and Stanfield, *Principles of Human Physiology*, pp. 606–607

Pattern: _____

Paragraph 4

Organized crime falls into three basic categories: provision of illicit services, provision of illicit goods, and infiltration of legitimate businesses. Provision of illicit services involves attempts to satisfy the public's demand for certain services that may not be offered by legitimate society. Specific crimes in this category include loan-sharking, prostitution, and certain forms of gambling. Provision of illicit goods involves offering particular products that a segment of the public desires but cannot obtain through legitimate channels. The sale and distribution of drugs and the fencing and distribution of stolen property are examples of crimes in this category. The third category of organized crime is infiltration of legitimate business. This is often characterized by racketeering, which involves an ongoing criminal enterprise that is maintained through a pattern of criminal activity. Labor racketeering and the takeover of waste disposal companies are examples of this type of crime.

—adapted from Albanese, *Criminal Justice*, p. 421

Pattern: _____

Paragraph 5

Not all tumors are malignant (cancerous); in fact, most are benign (noncancerous). Benign and malignant tumors differ in several key ways. Benign tumors are generally composed of ordinary-looking cells enclosed in a fibrous shell or capsule that prevents their spreading to other body areas. Malignant tumors, in contrast, are usually not enclosed in a protective capsule and can therefore spread to other organs. Unlike benign tumors, which merely expand to take over a given space, malignant cells invade surrounding tissue, emitting clawlike protrusions that disrupt chemical processes within healthy cells.

—adapted from Donatelle, *Health*, p. 324

Pattern: _____

4h   OTHER PATTERNS OF ORGANIZATION

LEARNING OBJECTIVE 8 Recognize other patterns of organization

Although the patterns presented in the previous sections of this chapter are the most common, writers do not limit themselves to these six patterns. Especially in academic writing, you may also find statement and clarification, summary, generalization and example, and addition. Transitions associated with these different patterns are listed in the "Summing It Up" table on pages 144–145.

Statement and Clarification

Many writers make a statement of fact and then proceed to clarify or explain that statement. For instance, a writer may open a paragraph by stating "The best education for you may not be the best education for someone else." The remainder of the paragraph would then discuss and clarify that statement by explaining how educational needs are based on an individual's talents, skills, and goals. Here is a sample **statement-and-clarification** paragraph about sex ratios.

> Sex ratios in the poor countries do not show a consistent pattern. In some poor countries men outnumber women, but in others (in tropical Africa, for example) women outnumber men. In fact, variations in sex ratios can be explained only by a combination of national economic and cultural factors. In the countries of North America and Europe and in Japan, women may suffer many kinds of discrimination, but they are not generally discriminated against when it comes to access to medical care.
>
> —Bergman and Renwick, *Introduction to Geography*, p. 185

Notice that the writer begins with a statement about sex ratios in poor countries and then goes on to clarify this fact. The author uses the transitional phrase *in fact*.

Summary

A **summary** is a condensed statement that provides the key points of a larger idea or piece of writing. Often writers summarize what they have already said or what someone else has said. For example, in a psychology textbook you will find many summaries of research. Instead of asking you to read an entire research study, the textbook author will summarize the study's findings. Other times a writer may repeat in condensed form what he or she has already said in order to emphasize or clarify a main point. Frequently, summaries at the end of a textbook chapter, or the closing paragraphs of an article or essay, provide a quick review of the contents.

In the following paragraph about public policy, the author uses the summary method of organization.

> In summary, public policy is purposeful, goal-oriented action that is taken by government to deal with problems, real or perceived, that arise in a society. Public policy generally does one or more of the following: reconcile conflicting claims made on scarce resources, create incentives for collective action, prohibit morally unacceptable behavior, protect the rights and activities of individuals and groups, and provide direct benefits to individuals.
>
> —Volkomer, *American Government*, p. 344

Notice that the author summarizes what public policy does and that the transitional phrase *in summary* is used.

Generalization and Example

Examples are one of the best ways to explain something that is unfamiliar or unknown. **Examples** are specific instances or situations that illustrate a concept or idea. Often writers make a general statement, or **generalization**, and then explain it by giving examples to make its meaning clear. In a business magazine, for instance, you may find the following generalization: "Employee theft is increasing." The section may then go on to offer examples from specific companies in which employees insert fictitious information into the company's computer program and steal company funds.

In the following paragraph about dreams, the writer uses **generalization and example**:

> Different cultures place varying emphases on dreams and support different beliefs concerning dreams. For example, many people in the United States view dreams as irrelevant fantasy with no connection to everyday life. By contrast, people in other cultures view dreams as key sources of information about the future, the spiritual world, and the dreamer. Such cultural views can influence the probability of dream recall. In many modern Western cultures, people rarely remember their dreams upon awakening. The Parintintin of South America, however, typically remember several dreams every night and the Senoi of Malaysia discuss their dreams with family members in the morning.
>
> —Davis and Palladino, *Psychology*, p. 210

Notice that the authors begin with the generalization that different cultures place different emphases on dreams. They then go on to give examples of the way specific cultures treat dreams. Note the use of the transitional phrase *for example*.

Addition

Writers often introduce an idea or make a statement and then supply additional information about that idea or statement. For instance, a parenting magazine may introduce the concept of homeschooling and then provide in-depth information about its benefits. This pattern is often used to expand, elaborate, or discuss an idea in greater detail.

In the following paragraph about pathogens, the writers use the **addition** pattern.

> Some pathogens [disease-causing organisms] evolve and mutate naturally. Also, patients who fail to complete the full portion of their antibiotic prescriptions allow drug-resistant pathogens to multiply. The use of antibiotics in animal feed and to spray on fruits and vegetables during food processing increases opportunities for resistant organisms to evolve and thrive. Furthermore, there is evidence that the disruption of Earth's natural habitats can trigger the evolution of new pathogens.
>
> —Bergman and Renwick, *Introduction to Geography*, p. 182

Notice that the writers state that some pathogens mutate naturally. They then go on to add that they also mutate as a result of human activities. Note the use of the transitional words *also* and *furthermore*.

EXERCISE 4-12 USING ORGANIZATIONAL PATTERNS 3

Directions: *For each of the following statements, identify the organizational pattern. Choose from the following patterns: process, statement and clarification, summary, generalization and example, addition, and spatial order.*

1. If our criminal justice system works, the recidivism rate—the percentage of people released from prison who later return to prison—should decrease. In other words, in a successful criminal justice system, there should be a decrease in the number of criminals who are released from prison and become repeat offenders.

   Pattern: _____

2. Students who are informed about drugs tend to use them in moderation. Furthermore, they tend to help educate others.

   Pattern: _____

3. A kernel of grain consists of a coarse outer layer called the bran which is high in fiber and mineral ash. Underneath the bran layer is the aleurone layer which contains protein and other important minerals. The central portion of the grain is called the endosperm and makes up roughly 80 percent of the kernel.

   Pattern: _____

4. In conclusion, it is safe to say that crime by women is likely to increase as greater numbers of women assume roles traditionally held by men.

   Pattern: _____

5. The digestive system breaks down food into smaller and smaller units as it passes through the alimentary canal. Food breakdown begins with chewing and continues with chemical digestion.

   Pattern: _____

6. Sociologists study how we are socialized into sex roles, the attitudes expected of males and females. Sex roles, in fact, identify some activities and behaviors as clearly male and others as clearly female.

   Pattern: _____

7. Patients often consult a lay referral network to discuss their medical problems. Cancer patients, for instance, can access Internet discussion groups that provide both information and support.

   Pattern: _____

EXERCISE 4–13 USING ORGANIZATIONAL PATTERNS 4

Directions: *Read each of the following paragraphs and identify the predominant organizational pattern used. Write the name of the pattern in the space provided. Choose from among the following patterns: statement and clarification, summary, generalization and example, and addition.*

1. Environmental features influence food preferences as well as avoidances. In Asia, for example, soybeans are widely grown, but raw they are toxic and indigestible. Lengthy cooking renders them edible, but in Asia fuel is scarce. Asians have adapted to this environmental dilemma by deriving foods from soybeans that do not require extensive cooking. These include bean sprouts, soy sauce, and bean curd. In Europe, traditional preferences for quick-frying foods resulted in part from fuel shortages in Italy. In northern Europe, an abundant wood supply may have encouraged the slow stewing and roasting of foods over fires, which also provided home heat in the colder climate.

   —adapted from Rubenstein, *Contemporary Human Geography*, p. 89

   Pattern: _____

2. A serious problem with some drugs is addiction, or drug dependence. That is, people come to depend on the regular consumption of a drug in order to make it through the day. When people think of drug addiction, they are likely to think of addicts huddled in slum doorways, the dregs of society who seldom venture into daylight—unless it is to rob someone. They don't associate addiction with "good," middle-class neighborhoods and "solid citizens." But let's look at drug addiction a little more closely. Although most people may think of heroin as the prime example of an addictive drug, I suggest that nicotine is the better case to consider. I remember a next-door neighbor who stood in his backyard, a lit cigarette in his hand, and told me about the operation in which one of his lungs was removed. I say "I remember," because soon after our conversation he died from his addiction.

   —Henslin, *Social Problems*, p. 93

   Pattern: _____

3. Human migration has by no means come to an end. Large-scale migrations still make daily news. The United Nations' Universal Declaration of Human Rights affirms anyone's right to leave his or her homeland to seek a better life elsewhere, but it cannot guarantee that there will be any place willing to take anyone. As in the past, the major push and pull factors behind contemporary migration are economic and political. Also, people are trying to move from the poor countries to the rich countries and from the politically repressed countries to more democratic countries. In addition, millions of people are fleeing civil and international warfare. Pressures for migration are growing, and in coming years they may constitute the world's greatest political and economic problem.

   —Bergman and Renwick, *Introduction to Geography*, p. 197

   Pattern: _____

4.   "Sentencing by public humiliation" has taken many different forms over its long history. In ancient Greece, deserters from the army were displayed in public wearing women's clothes. In England, public drunkards were walked through the streets wearing only a barrel. Bridles were used on certain offenders in England and colonial America. These devices looked like cages that fit over the head with a metal place that fit into the mouth. Any movement of the tongue was painful. Bridles were used primarily on "scolds," women who habitually lied or found fault with others. Use of stocks, pillories, and the ducking stool continued in England, France, and America until the early 1800s. These devices held the offender in public view in extremely uncomfortable positions for the purpose of ridicule and punishment.

—Albanese, *Criminal Justice*, p. 370

Pattern: _____

5.   In sum, psychologically healthy people are emotionally, mentally, socially, and spiritually resilient. They most often respond to challenges and frustrations in appropriate ways, despite occasional slips. When they do slip, they recognize that fact and take action to rectify the situation.

—Donatelle, *My Health*, p. 23

Pattern: _____

SUMMING IT UP

PATTERNS AND TRANSITIONS

PATTERN	CHARACTERISTICS	TRANSITIONS
Definition	Explains the meaning of a word or phrase	is, refers to, can be defined as, means, consists of, involves, is a term that, is called, is characterized by, occurs when, are those that, entails, corresponds to, is literally
Classification	Divides a topic into parts based on shared characteristics	classified as, comprises, is composed of, several varieties of, different stages of, different groups that, includes, one, first, second, another, finally, last
Chronological Order	Describes events, processes, procedures	first, second, later, before, next, as soon as, after, then, finally, meanwhile, following, last, during, in, on, when, until

(continued on next page)

(continued from preceding page)

PATTERN	CHARACTERISTICS	TRANSITIONS
Process	Describes the order in which things are done or how things work	first, second, next, then, following, after that, last, finally
Order of Importance	Describes ideas in order of priority or preference	less, more, primary, first, next, last, most important, primarily, secondarily
Spatial Order	Describes physical location or position in space	above, below, beside, next to, in front of, behind, inside, outside, opposite, within, nearby
Cause and Effect	Describes how one or more things cause or are related to another	*Causes:* because, because of, for, since, stems from, one cause is, one reason is, leads to, causes, creates, yields, due to, breeds, for this reason *Effects:* consequently, results in, one result is, therefore, thus, as a result, hence, produces
Comparison and Contrast	Discusses similarities and/or differences among ideas, theories, concepts, objects, or persons	*Similarities:* both, also, similarly, like, likewise, too, as well as, resembles, correspondingly, in the same way, to compare, in comparison, share *Differences:* unlike, differs from, in contrast, on the other hand, instead, despite, nevertheless, however, in spite of, whereas, as opposed to
Listing/Enumeration	Organizes lists of information: characteristics, features, parts, or categories	the following, several, for example, for instance, one, another, also, too, in other words, first, second, numerals (1, 2, 3), letters (a, b, c), most important, the largest, the least, finally
Statement and Clarification	Indicates that information explaining an idea or concept will follow	in fact, in other words, clearly, evidently, obviously
Summary	Indicates that a condensed review of an idea or piece of writing is to follow	in summary, in conclusion, in brief, to summarize, to sum up, in short, on the whole
Generalization and Example	Provides examples that clarify a broad, general statement	for example, for instance, that is, to illustrate, thus
Addition	Indicates that additional information will follow	furthermore, additionally, also, besides, further, in addition, moreover, again

SUMMARY OF LEARNING OBJECTIVES

1	**Recognize definition** **What is the definition pattern?**	In the definition pattern, a key word, phrase, or concept is defined and explained.
2	**Recognize classification** **What is the classification pattern?**	In the classification pattern, a broad topic is divided into its major categories.
3	**Recognize order or sequence** **What is the order or sequence pattern?**	Several organizational patterns make use of order or sequence. Chronological order refers to the sequence in which events occur in time. Process focuses on the procedures, steps, or stages by which actions are accomplished. In order of importance, details are expressed in order from most to least important, or least to most important. Spatial order organizes information based on its physical location, position, or order in space.
4	**Recognize cause and effect** **What is the cause and effect pattern?**	The cause-and-effect pattern expresses a relationship between two or more actions, events, or occurrences that are connected in time. One event leads to another by causing it. There may be multiple causes and/or effects.
5	**Recognize comparison and contrast** **What is the comparison and contrast pattern**	The comparison pattern emphasizes or discusses similarities among ideas, theories, concepts, or events. The contrast pattern emphasizes differences. Both patterns can be used together, creating the comparison–contrast pattern.
6	**Recognize listing/enumeration** **What is the listing/enumeration pattern?**	The listing/enumeration pattern gives information on a topic by stating details one after the other, in no particular order.
7	**Recognize mixed patterns** **What are mixed patterns?**	Organizational patterns are often combined in paragraphs, essays, and longer readings. The longer the reading selection, the more likely it combines multiple patterns of organization.
8	**Recognize other patterns of organization** **What other patterns of organization do writers use?**	In the statement-and-clarification pattern, the writer makes a statement of fact and then clarifies or explains that statement. A summary is a condensed statement that provides the key points of a larger idea or piece of writing. In the generalization-and-example pattern, the writer makes a general statement and then explains it by way of examples. In the addition pattern, a writer introduces an idea and then supplies additional information about it.

5 Textbook Learning Strategies

LEARNING OBJECTIVES

In this chapter, you will learn how to

1 Use strategies for reading textbooks
2 Use the SQ3R system
3 Use learning and recall strategies
4 Highlight effectively
5 Use annotation to record your thinking
6 Paraphrase ideas
7 Outline text
8 Draw maps to show relationships
9 Summarize text

Have you ever wondered how you will learn all the facts and ideas from your textbooks and instructors? The key to handling the volume of information presented in each course is to use your textbooks effectively. This involves using textbook learning aids the author provides and reading textbooks in a way to help you learn and remember what you read. It is also helpful to use strategies to organize the information to make it more meaningful and easier to learn. These include highlighting and annotating textbooks, mapping and outlining to organize ideas, and writing paraphrases and summaries of what you read.

5a STRATEGIES FOR READING TEXTBOOKS

LEARNING OBJECTIVE 1
Use strategies for reading textbooks

While textbooks may seem to be long and impersonal, they are actually carefully crafted teaching and learning systems. They are designed to work with your instructor's lecture to provide you with reliable and accurate information and to help you practice your skills.

Why Buy and Study Textbooks?

Did you know the following facts about textbooks?

- Nearly all textbook authors are college teachers. They work with students daily and understand students' needs.
- Along with your instructor, your textbook is the single best source of information for the subject you are studying.
- The average textbook costs only about $7 a week. For the price of a movie ticket, you are getting a complete learning system that includes not only a textbook but also a companion Web site and other study materials.
- Your textbook can be a valuable reference tool in your profession. For example, many nursing majors keep their textbooks and refer to them often when they begin their career.

Textbooks are an investment in your education and in your future. A textbook is your ally—your partner in learning.

Textbook Learning Aids and How to Use Them

Because most textbooks are written by professors, the authors know their subject matter and they also know their students. They know what topics you may have difficulty with and know the best way to explain them. Because textbooks are written by teachers, they contain numerous features to help you learn. Table 5-1 summarizes these features and explains how to use each.

TABLE 5-1 TEXTBOOK AIDS TO LEARNING

FEATURE	HOW TO USE IT
Preface or "To the Student"	• Read it to find out how the book is organized, what topics it covers, and what learning features it contains.
Chapter Opener (may include chapter objectives, photographs, and chapter outlines)	• Read it to find out what the chapter is about. • Use it to test yourself later to see if you can recall the main points.
Marginal Vocabulary Definitions	• Learn the definition of each term. • Create a vocabulary log (in a notebook or computer file) and enter words you need to learn.
Photographs and Graphics	• Determine their purpose: what important information do they illustrate? • For diagrams, charts, and tables, note the process or trend they illustrate. Make marginal notes. • Practice redrawing diagrams without referring to the originals.

(*continued on next page*)

(continued from preceding page)

FEATURE	HOW TO USE IT
Test Yourself Questions (after sections within the chapter)	• Always check to see if you can answer them before going on to the next section. • Use them to check your recall of chapter content when studying for an exam.
Special Interest Inserts (can coverage of related issues, critical thinking topics, etc.)	• Discover how the inserts are related to the chapter content: include profiles of people, what key concepts do they illustrate?
Review Questions/Problems/Discussion Questions	• Read them once *before* you read the chapter to discover what you are expected to learn. • Use them after you have read the chapter to test your recall.
Chapter Summary	• Test yourself by converting summary statements into questions using the words *Who? Why? When? How?* and *So what?*
Chapter Review Quiz	• Use this to prepare for an exam. Pay extra attention to items you get wrong.

EXERCISE 5-1 EVALUATING TEXTBOOK LEARNING AIDS

Directions: *Using this textbook or a textbook from one of your other courses, use Table 5-1 to analyze the features the author includes to guide your learning. Identify particularly useful features and decide how you will use each when you study.*

5b   USE THE SQ3R SYSTEM FOR LEARNING FROM TEXTBOOKS

LEARNING OBJECTIVE 2
Use the SQ3R
system

SQ3R is an established method of actively learning while you read. Instead of reading now and studying later when an exam is scheduled, the SQ3R method enables you to integrate reading and learning by using the five steps listed on page 150. By using SQ3R, you will strengthen your comprehension, remember more of what you read, and need less time to prepare for an exam. Don't get discouraged if you don't see dramatic results the first time you use it. It may take a few practice sessions to get used to the system.

Feel free to adapt the SQ3R method to suit how you learn and the type of material you are studying. For example, if writing helps you recall information, you might add an *Outline* step and make the *Review* step a *Review of Outline* step. Or, if you are studying a course in which terminology is especially important, such as biology, then add a *Vocabulary Check* step.

STEPS IN THE SQ3R SYSTEM

Survey Become familiar with the overall content and organization of the material using the steps for previewing from Chapter 1 on page 40.

Question Ask questions about the material that you expect to be able to answer as you read. As you read each successive heading, turn it into a question.

Read As you read each section, actively search for the answers to your guide questions. When you find the answers, underline or mark the portions of the text that concisely state the information.

Recite Probably the most important part of the system, "recite" means that after each section or after each major heading, you should stop, look away from the page, and try to remember the answer to your question. If you are unable to remember, look back at the page and reread the material. Then test yourself again by looking away from the page and "reciting" the answer to your question.

Review Immediately after you have finished reading, go back through the material again, reading headings and summaries. As you read each heading, recall your question and test yourself to see whether you can still remember the answer. If you cannot, reread that section. Once you are satisfied that you have understood and recalled key information, move toward the higher-level thinking skills. Ask application, analysis, evaluation, and creation questions. Some students like to add a fourth "R" step—for "React."

EXERCISE 5-2 USING SQ3R

Directions: *Apply the SQ3R system to a section of a chapter in one of your textbooks. List your questions in the margin or on a separate sheet of paper, and highlight the answers in your textbook. After you have finished the section, evaluate how well SQ3R worked for you, and note how you might adapt it.*

5c　USE LEARNING AND RECALL STRATEGIES

LEARNING OBJECTIVE 3
Use learning and recall strategies

Some students think that as long as they spend time studying they will get good grades. However, spending time is not enough. You have to plan when to study and use the right techniques to get the most out of the time you spend. Use the following strategies.

Immediate Review

Forgetting occurs most rapidly right after learning. **Immediate review** means reviewing new information as soon as possible after you hear or read it. Think of immediate review as a way of fixing in your mind what you have just learned. Here are some ways to use immediate review:

- **Review your lecture notes as soon as possible after taking them.** This review will help the ideas stick in your mind.
- **Review a textbook chapter as soon as you finish reading it.** Do this by rereading each chapter heading and then rereading the summary.
- **Review all new course materials again at the end of each day of classes.** This review will help you pull together information and make it more meaningful.

Periodic Review

To keep from forgetting material you have learned, you will need to review it several times throughout the semester. Periodic review, then, means returning to and quickly reviewing previously learned material on a regular basis. Suppose you learned the material in the first three chapters of your criminology text during the first two weeks of the course. Unless you review that material regularly, you are likely to forget it and have to relearn it by the time your final exam is given. Therefore, you should establish a periodic review schedule in which you quickly review these chapters every three weeks or so.

Final Review

Final review means making a last check of material before a test or exam. This should not be a lengthy session; instead, it should be a quick once-over of everything you have learned. A final review is helpful because it fixes in your mind what you have learned. Be sure to schedule your final review as close as possible to the exam in which you will need to recall the material.

Building an Intent to Remember

Very few people remember things that they do not intend to remember. Before you begin to read an assignment, define as clearly as possible what you need to remember. Your decision will depend on the type of material, why you are reading it, and how familiar you are with the topic. For instance, if you are reading an essay assigned in preparation for a class discussion, plan to remember not only key ideas but also points of controversy, applications, and opinions with which you disagree. Your intent might be quite different in reviewing a chapter for an essay exam. Here you would be looking for important ideas, trends, and significance of events.

As you read a text assignment, sort important information from that which is less important. Continually ask and answer questions such as:

1. How important is this information?
2. Will I need to know this for the exam?
3. Is this a key idea or is it an explanation of a key idea?
4. Why did the writer include this?

Organizing and Categorizing

Information that is organized, or that has a pattern or structure, is easier to remember than material that is randomly arranged. One effective way to organize information is to *categorize* it, to arrange it in groups according to similar characteristics. Suppose, for example, that you had to remember the following list of items to buy for a picnic: *cooler, candy, 7-Up, Pepsi, napkins, potato chips, lemonade, peanuts, paper plates.* The easiest way to remember this list would be to divide it into groups. You might arrange it as follows:

DRINKS	SNACKS	PICNIC SUPPLIES
7-Up	peanuts	cooler
Pepsi	candy	paper plates
lemonade	potato chips	napkins

By grouping the items into categories, you are putting similar items together. Then, rather than learning one long list of unorganized items, you are learning three shorter, organized lists.

Now imagine you are reading an essay on discipline in public high schools. Instead of learning one long list of reasons for disruptive student behavior, you might divide the reasons into groups such as peer conflicts, teacher–student conflicts, and so forth.

Associating Ideas

Association involves connecting new information with previously acquired knowledge. For instance, if you are reading about divorce in a sociology class and are trying to remember a list of common causes, you might try to associate each cause with a person you know who exhibits that problem. Suppose one cause of divorce is lack of communication between the partners. You might remember this by thinking of a couple you know whose lack of communication has caused relationship difficulties.

Using a Variety of Sensory Modes

Your senses of sight, hearing, and touch can all help you remember what you read. Most of the time, most of us use just one sense—sight—as we read. However, if you are able to use more than one sense, you will find that recall is easier.

Activities such as highlighting, note taking, and outlining involve your sense of touch and reinforce your learning. Or, if you are having particular difficulty remembering something, try to use your auditory sense as well. You might try repeating the information out loud or listening to someone else repeat it.

Visualizing

Visualizing, or creating a mental picture of what you have read, often aids recall. In reading about events, people, processes, or procedures, visualization is relatively simple. However, visualization of abstract ideas, theories, philosophies, and concepts may not be possible. Instead, you may be able to create a visual picture of the relationship of ideas in your mind or on paper. For example, suppose you are reading about invasion of privacy and learn that there are arguments for and against the storage of personal data about each citizen by online companies like Google. You might create a visual image of two lists of information—advantages and disadvantages.

Using Mnemonic Devices

Memory tricks and devices, often called **mnemonics**, are useful in helping you recall lists of factual information. You might use a rhyme, such as the one used for remembering the number of days in each month: "Thirty days hath September, April, June, and November. . . ." Another device involves making up a word or phrase in which each letter represents an item you are trying to remember. If you remember the name *Roy G. Biv*, for example, you will be able to recall the colors in the light spectrum: **r**ed, **o**range, **y**ellow, **g**reen, **b**lue, **i**ndigo, **v**iolet.

EXERCISE 5-3 USING RECALL STRATEGIES

Directions: *Read each of the following study situations. Choose one of the strategies suggested for each situation, then briefly explain how you would apply that strategy.*

1. For an exam in economics, you must be able to define each of the four market types and provide key features and examples of each type. You have read each of the assigned chapters once and now you are ready to study. Describe how *organization/categorization* or *using a variety of sensory modes* could help you learn these details.

   _____

   _____

   _____

2. In an environmental science course, you are reading an essay about deforestation to prepare for a class discussion. You have also witnessed the loss of forests due to fire and urban development on family trips to Colorado.

Describe how you would use *building an intent to remember* or *association* to prepare to discuss the different causes of deforestation.

_____

_____

_____

_____

3. For an anatomy and physiology exam, you must be able to identify the bones of wrist and hand. Describe how you would use *mnemonic devices* or *visualization* to learn the names and locations of the wrist and hand bones.

_____

_____

_____

5d HIGHLIGHTING

LEARNING OBJECTIVE 4
Highlight effectively

Highlighting is an excellent way to improve your comprehension and recall of textbook assignments. Highlighting forces you to decide what is important and sort the key information from less important material. Sorting ideas this way improves both comprehension and recall. To decide what to highlight, you must think about and evaluate the relative importance of each idea. To highlight most effectively, use these guidelines.

1. **Analyze the assignment.** Preview the assignment and define what type of learning is required. This will help you determine how much and what type of information you need to highlight.
2. **Assess your familiarity with the subject.** Depending on your background knowledge, you may need to highlight only a little or a great deal. Do not waste time highlighting what you already know.
3. **Read first, then highlight.** Finish a paragraph or self-contained section before you highlight. As you read, look for signals to organizational patterns (see Chapter 4). Each idea may seem important as you first encounter it, but you must see how it fits in with the others before you can judge its relative importance.
4. **Use the boldfaced headings.** Headings are labels that indicate the overall topic of a section. These headings serve as indicators of what is important to highlight.
5. **Highlight main ideas and only key supporting details.** Avoid highlighting examples and secondary details.
6. **Avoid highlighting complete sentences.** Highlight only enough so that your highlighting makes sense when you reread it. In the following selection, note that only key words and phrases are highlighted. Now read only the highlighted words. Can you grasp the key idea of the passage?

> Rocks can be grouped into three basic categories that reflect how they form. **Igneous rocks** are formed when molten crustal material cools and solidifies. The name derives from the Greek word for *fire*, which is the same root as for the English word *ignite*. Examples of igneous rocks are basalt, which is common in volcanic areas, including much of the ocean floor, and granite, which is common in continental areas. **Sedimentary rocks** result when rocks eroded from higher elevations (mountains, hills, plains) accumulate at lower elevations (like swamps and ocean bottoms). When subjected to high pressure and the presence of cementing materials to bind their grains together, rocks like sandstone, shale, conglomerate, and limestone are formed. **Metamorphic rocks** are created when rocks are exposed to great pressure and heat, altering them into more compact, crystalline rocks. In Greek, the name means "to change form." Examples include marble (which metamorphosed from limestone) and slate (which metamorphosed from shale).
>
> —Dahlman et al., *Introduction to Geography*, p. 95

7. **Move quickly through the document as you highlight.** If you have understood a paragraph or section, then your highlighting should be fast and efficient.
8. **Develop a consistent system of highlighting.** Decide, for example, how you will mark main ideas, how you will distinguish main ideas from details, and how you will highlight new terminology. Some students use a system of single and double highlighting, brackets, asterisks, and circles to distinguish various types of information; others use different colors of ink or combinations of pens and pencils.
9. **Use the 15–25 percent rule of thumb.** Although the amount you will highlight will vary from course to course, try to highlight no more than 15 to 25 percent of any given page. If you exceed this figure, it often means that you are not sorting ideas as efficiently as possible. Other times, it may mean that you should choose a different strategy for reviewing the material. Remember, the more you highlight, the smaller your time-saving dividends will be as you review. The following excerpt provides an example of effective highlighting.

> When organizations decide to go international, they might use licensing or franchising, which are similar approaches involving one organization giving another organization the right to use its brand name, technology, or product specifications in return for a lump sum payment or a fee usually based on sales. The only difference is that licensing is primarily used by manufacturing organizations that make or sell another company's products and franchising is primarily used by service organizations that want to use another company's name and operating methods. For example, Chicago consumers can enjoy Guatemalan Pollo Campero fried chicken, South Koreans can indulge in Dunkin' Brands' coffee, Hong Kong residents can dine on Shakey's Pizza, and Malaysians can consume Schlotsky's deli sandwiches—all because of *franchises* in these countries. On the other hand,

Anheuser-Busch InBev has *licensed* the right to brew and market its Budweiser beer to brewers such as Kirin in Japan and Crown Beers in India.

—adapted from Robbins and Coulter, *Management*, p. 79

EXERCISE 5-4 HIGHLIGHTING 1

Directions: *Read the following pairs of paragraphs, which have been highlighted in two different ways. Look at each highlighted version, and then write your answers to the questions that follow in the spaces provided.*

Example A

Murders, especially mass murders and serial murders, fascinate the public and criminologists. Murder is the least committed crime but receives the most attention. Murder trials often capture the attention of the entire nation. The O. J. Simpson murder trial was one of the most watched television programs in the history of network Nielson ratings.

—Fagin, *Criminal Justice*, p. 78

Example B

Murders, especially mass murders and serial murders, fascinate the public and criminologists. Murder is the least committed crime but receives the most attention. Murder trials often capture the attention of the entire nation. The O. J. Simpson murder trial was one of the most watched television programs in the history of network Nielson ratings.

1. Is Example A or Example B the better example of effective highlighting?

_____

2. Why isn't the highlighting in the other example effective?

_____

_____

Example C

Air pollution results when several factors combine to lower air quality. Carbon monoxide emitted by automobiles contributes to air pollution, as do smoke and other chemicals from manufacturing plants. Air quality is usually worst in certain geographic locations, such as the Denver area and the Los Angeles basin, where pollutants tend to get trapped in the atmosphere. For this very reason, the air around Mexico City is generally considered to be the most polluted in the entire world.

—Ebert and Griffin, *Business Essentials*, p. 71

Example D

Air pollution results when several factors combine to lower air quality. Carbon monoxide emitted by automobiles contributes to air pollution, as do smoke and other chemicals from manufacturing plants. Air quality is usually worst in certain geographic locations, such as the Denver area and the Los Angeles basin, where pollutants tend to get trapped in the atmosphere. For this very reason, the air around Mexico City is generally considered to be the most polluted in the entire world.

3. Is Example C or Example D the better example of effective highlighting?

___

4. Why isn't the highlighting in the other example effective?

___

EXERCISE 5-5 HIGHLIGHTING 2

Directions: *Highlight the following article, "What Is Crime?"*

TEXTBOOK
EXCERPT

What Is Crime?

Deviance vs. Crime

1   Most prisoners are incarcerated because they've broken a law. But how do we determine which behaviors are criminal? **Deviance** is the violation of norms that a society agrees upon. For example, teens who dye their hair in neon colors would be considered deviant in most parts of society. However, some acts that may be considered socially deviant, like refusing to bathe, for instance, aren't necessarily illegal, no matter how much you might wish they were. For something to be considered a **crime**, it has to be a violation of norms that have been written into law. Going above the speed limit is an example of a crime. Sociologists who specialize in **criminology** scientifically study crime, deviance, and social policies that the criminal justice system applies.

What Is Deviance?

2   If deviance refers to violating socially agreed upon norms, then how do we determine what is and what isn't considered deviant? There are four specific characteristics that sociologists use to define deviance:

1. **Deviance is linked to time.** History changes the definition of deviance, so what is considered deviant today may not be deviant tomorrow. One hundred years ago, it was considered deviant for women to wear trousers. Today, it's normal for women to dress in trousers.

2. **Deviance is linked to cultural values.** How we label an issue determines our moral point of view. Cultural values come from religious, political, economic, or philosophical principles. For example, in Holland, active euthanasia for the terminally ill, or "mercy killing," is legal within some circumstances. In the United States, euthanasia is considered murder and is punished accordingly. Each culture defines euthanasia differently.

3. **Deviance is a cultural universal.** You can find deviants in every culture on the planet. Regardless of what norms a society establishes, you can always find a small number of nonconformists who will break those rules.

4. **Deviance is a social construct.** Each society views actions differently. If society tolerates a behavior, it is no longer deviant. For example, Prohibition in the 1920s and early 30s made drinking alcohol illegal in the United States, but today it's normal.

Street Crime

3   Although there are many different types of crime, when most people talk about "crime," they're likely talking about **street crime**, which refers to many different types of criminal acts, such as burglary, rape, and assault. Street crime has been the focus of most criminological research, but you may wonder how much street crime actually exists. The next section will discuss street crime and how it is measured.

Crime Statistics

4   After spending an hour watching a show like *CSI*, you'd think the police are able to solve crimes like they do on TV. Unfortunately, real life isn't as convenient as

television. For example, when someone stole the tires off my car, I asked the police officer when I might get my wheels back. He said, "Probably never. These kinds of crimes are difficult to solve."

Uniform Crime Reports and the National Crime Victimization Survey

5   Another aspect of detective work often omitted from television is the paperwork that officers must file. The information in those files is vital to understand crime statistics. Criminologists use two primary sources of data to measure the amount of street crime: the UCRs and the NCVS. The Federal Bureau of Investigation (FBI) collects **Uniform Crime Reports (UCRs),** the official police statistics of reported crimes. The **National Crime Victimization Survey (NCVS)** measures crime victimization by contacting a representative sample of over 70,000 households in the United States.

6   UCRs only contain data on reported crimes, so when a car is reported as stolen, it becomes a UCR statistic. This report also lists the **crime index,** which consists of eight offenses used to measure crime. These include four violent offenses: homicide, rape, robbery, and aggravated assault, as well as four property crimes: burglary, larceny-theft, motor vehicle theft, and arson.

7   Criminologists understand that many crimes go unreported, so they also refer to the NCVS statistics. NCVS data always account for more crime than UCR data. For example, in 2002 UCR reported fewer than 12 million offenses, whereas NCVS showed approximately 23 million crimes. This supports the criminologist's rule of thumb—about half the crimes committed go unreported.

Crime Trends

8   UCR and NCVS data are also used to determine crime trends, and the trend that seems most constant is that the crime rates change over time. The vast majority of crime in the United States is property crime. In 2006, property crimes made up 88 percent of all reported crimes, whereas violent crimes constituted less than 12 percent. These trends are in stark contrast to the media's portrayal of crime.

Gender and Crime

9   Throughout history, men have traditionally committed more crime than women. The demographic characteristics of street criminals in the United States have not changed much over time. In fact, 77 percent of people arrested are men. This is a significant statistic because men make up less than 50 percent of the population. However, several other factors also figure in crime trends.

Race and Crime

10   Although the gender differences in crime statistics are fairly easy to distinguish, discussing a link between race and crime is controversial. The major problem is the long history of racism in the United States. African Americans make up about 12 percent of the population, but they represent 27 percent of those arrested in the United States. Does this disproportionate representation suggest African Americans commit more crimes, or does the criminal justice system unfairly pursue them?

11   Some argue that the police's different enforcement practices are responsible for these data. Racial profiling is a controversial police practice of targeting criminals based on their race. Cole shows that traffic police disproportionately stop people of color. Jeffrey Reiman suggests that the police seek out the poor for arrest because the poor are easier to catch and easier to convict of crimes. Wealthy people can hire expensive lawyers; poor people must use the public defender system. This increases the odds that official statistics have an inherent racial bias because racial minorities disproportionately represent the poor in the United States.

Social Class and Crime

12   Although crime rates are higher in poorer neighborhoods, that doesn't necessarily mean people in lower classes actually commit more crime. This makes data on the link between social class and crime difficult to interpret. A number of studies have shown that poorer people are arrested at higher rates, but that doesn't mean everyone who lives in poor neighborhoods breaks the law or is more likely to break the law.

13   On the other side of the spectrum, Reiman shows that the upper classes' crimes are not prosecuted at the same rates. For example, in all 50 states, getting caught with five grams of crack cocaine can earn you up to five years in prison. However, a person would have to possess 500 grams of cocaine powder to receive the same sentence. So what's the difference? People convicted of crack possession tend to be poor, while people caught with cocaine powder are usually wealthy.

14   Reiman believes that social class makes a huge difference in who gets caught and who goes to prison. He argues that laws are applied differently and that dangerous activities performed by the "elite" are not even considered crimes.

15   For example, doctors who accidentally kill a patient during an unnecessary surgery are not accused of manslaughter. Similarly, Reiman suggests that white-collar crimes are not reported because people want to avoid a scandal. Furthermore, we do not keep official records of white-collar crimes, so there is no way of knowing exactly how much of this occurs.

Age and Crime

16   Essentially, crime is a young person's game. This idea is supported by the relationship between age and crime. It indicates that the majority of arrests peak between the ages of 15 to 25. After that point, they follow a slow but steady decrease throughout life. Arrest data from other cultures and times in history also support this claim.

17   The link between age and crime is very clear in criminology. According to Steffensmeier and Harer, a 60 percent decrease in crime rates in the 1980s is attributable to a decrease in the total number of 15- to 24-year-olds. Clearly, age matters when discussing crime.

International Comparisons of Street Crime

18   In order to gain a better perspective on crime in the United States, sociologists often make international comparisons. However, making international comparisons of crime data creates certain problems for the researcher. Therefore, for this text I selected countries that are similar to the United States in a number of ways: they are all generally wealthy, and all keep good crime data. Here is a list of potentially complicating factors:
1. Crime numbers may or may not be accurate. Some countries deliberately skew their data to show lower crime rates in order to keep tourism high.
2. Legal definitions of crimes differ among nations. Some nations do not recognize marital rape as a crime; others have legalized drugs that are illegal in the United States.
3. Different methods of collecting data can result in differences in reported crimes. Some nations have extraordinarily reliable data collection systems, while others do not.
4. Cultures vary, as do programs to prevent, punish, and curb crime.

United States: Number One with a Bullet

19   Why does the United States have the highest murder rate in the industrialized world? Some blame easy access to guns, and others claim it's our violent history as a nation. Still others argue that it is the level of inequality in our country. Whatever the reasons, one thing is clear: U.S. citizens are three times more likely to be murdered compared to people in other developed nations.

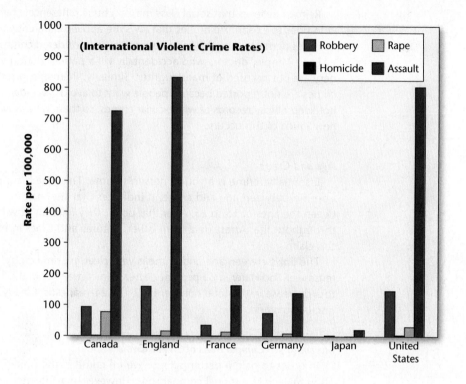

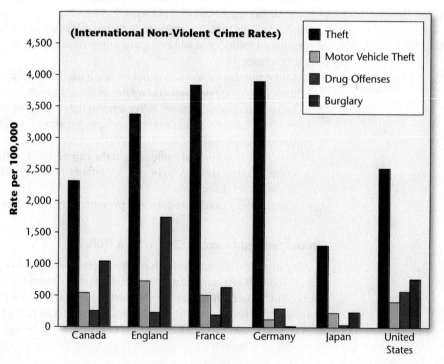

20   However, the graphs on page 162 present a somewhat different picture of violence with regard to international rates of rape and robbery. The countries selected are similar to the United States and give you a quick way to compare crime in the United States to that of other countries. As you can see from these data, England leads these nations in robbery, and Canada has the highest rate of rape. The United States has high rates of both crimes, but clearly is not the worst.

21   Property crimes present a different picture. The second graph provides data on four nonviolent crimes: theft, motor vehicle theft, drug offenses, and burglary. Generally speaking, occurrences of property crime are higher in other industrialized nations than in the United States.

22   These data leave a mixed picture for the international comparison of crime. Living in the United States increases the odds that one might be murdered, but it also decreases the chance of being a victim of most property crimes.

23   Comparing international crime rates shows that crime is common to all industrial societies. Some suggest this occurs because industrial societies have more high-value, lightweight items—such as iPods or laptops—that are easily stolen and sold.

—Carl, *Think Sociology*, pp. 228–231

5e   ANNOTATING

LEARNING OBJECTIVE 5
Use annotation to record your thinking

In many situations, highlighting alone is not a sufficient means of identifying what to learn. It does not give you any opportunity to comment on or react to the material. For this, you might want to use annotation. Annotating is an active reading process. It forces you to keep track of your comprehension as well as react to ideas. The chart on page 164 suggests various types of annotation used in marking a political science textbook chapter.

EXERCISE 5-6 ANNOTATING 1

Directions: *Review the chart on page 164 and then add annotations to the reading "What Is Crime?" on pages 157–163.*

EXERCISE 5-7 ANNOTATING 2

Directions: *Add annotations to the reading "Human Population Growth—What's the Problem?" on page 192.*

MARGINAL ANNOTATION	TYPES OF ANNOTATION	EXAMPLE
	Circling unknown words	. . . redressing the apparent asymmetry of their relationship
	Marking definitions	To say that the balance of power favors one party over another is to introduce a disequilibrium.
	Marking examples	. . . concessions may include negative sanctions, trade agreements . . .
	Numbering lists of ideas, causes, reasons, or events	components of power include

self-image, population, natural resources, and geography |
	Placing asterisks next to important passages	Power comes from three primary sources . . .
	Putting question marks next to confusing passages	war prevention occurs through institutionalization of mediation . . .
	Making notes to yourself	power is the ability of an actor on the international stage to . . .
	Marking possible test items	There are several key features in the relationship . . .
	Drawing arrows to show relationships	. . . natural resources . . . , . . . control of industrial manufacture capacity
	Writing comments, noting disagreements and similarities	war prevention through balance of power is . . .
	Marking summary statements	the greater the degree of conflict, the more intricate will be . . .

5f   PARAPHRASING

LEARNING OBJECTIVE 6
Paraphrase ideas

A **paraphrase** is a restatement of a passage's ideas in your own words. The author's meaning is retained, but your wording, *not* the author's, is used. We use paraphrasing frequently in everyday speech. For example, when you relay a message from one person to another you convey the meaning but do not use the person's exact wording. A paraphrase can be used to make a passage's meaning clearer and often more concise. Paraphrasing is also an effective learning and review strategy in several situations.

First, paraphrasing is useful for portions of a text for which exact, detailed comprehension is required. For example, you might paraphrase the steps in solving a math problem, the process by which a blood transfusion is administered, or the levels of jurisdiction of the Supreme Court.

Paraphrasing is also a useful way to be certain you understand difficult or complicated material. If you can express the author's ideas in your own words, you can be certain you understand it, and if you find yourself at a loss for words—except for those of the author—you will know your understanding is incomplete.

Paraphrasing is also a useful strategy when working with material that is stylistically complex, poorly written, or overly formal, awkward, or biased. Below is a paraphrase of a paragraph from "What Is Crime?"

A SAMPLE PARAPHRASE

PARAGRAPH	PARAPHRASE
Essentially, crime is a young person's game. This idea is supported by the relationship between age and crime. It indicates that the majority of arrests peak between the ages of 15 and 25. After that point, they follow a slow but steady decrease throughout life. Arrest data from other cultures and times in history also support this claim.	Age and likelihood to commit a crime are related. Crime is mostly committed by young people. Most arrests are made for people between 15 and 25 years old. After that, as age increases, there is a steady decrease in arrests. This pattern is consistent with data from other cultures and other historical periods.

Use the following suggestions to paraphrase effectively.

1. **Read slowly and carefully.**
2. **Read the material through entirely before writing anything.**
3. **As you read, pay attention to exact meanings and relationships among ideas.**
4. **Paraphrase sentence by sentence.**
5. **Read each sentence and express the key idea in your own words.** Reread the original sentence; then look away and write your own sentence. Then reread the original and add anything you missed.
6. **Don't try to paraphrase word by word. Instead, work with ideas.**
7. **For words or phrases you are unsure of** or that are not words you feel comfortable using, check a dictionary to locate a more familiar meaning.
8. **You may combine several original sentences into a more concise paraphrase.**

EXERCISE 5-8 PARAPHRASING 1

Directions: *Read each paragraph and the paraphrases following them. Answer the questions about the paraphrases.*

Paragraph A

The use of silence can be an effective form of communication, but its messages and implications differ cross culturally. In Siberian households, the lowest status person is the in-marrying daughter, and she tends to speak very little. However, silence does not always indicate powerlessness. In American courts, comparison of speaking frequency between the judge, jury, and lawyers shows that lawyers, who have the least power, speak most, while the silent jury holds the most power.

—Miller, *Cultural Anthropology*, p. 302

Paraphrase 1

Silence carries a message as well as serves as a form of communication. Young married Siberian women speak very little, lawyers (who are powerless) speak a great deal, and the jury (which is most powerful) is silent.

Paraphrase 2

Silence is a way to communicate, but its meaning varies from culture to culture. In Siberia, women have low status in their husband's family and speak very little. In American courts, however, the most powerful group, the jury, is silent, while the least powerful—attorneys—speak the most.

Paraphrase 3

Silence has many meanings. Siberian women speak very little, indicating their low status. Lawyers speak a great deal, while a jury is silent.

1. Which is the best paraphrase of the paragraph? _____

2. Why are the other paraphrases less good?

   _____

   _____

   _____

   _____

   _____

Paragraph B

Today, the dominant family form in the United States is the child-free family, where a couple resides together and there are no children present in the household. With the aging of the baby boomer cohort, this family type is expected to increase steadily over time. If current trends continue, nearly three out of four U.S. households will be childless in another decade or so.

—Thompson and Hickey, *Society in Focus*, p. 355

Paraphrase 1

A child-free family is one where two adults live together and have no children. It is the dominant family form.

Paraphrase 2

The child-free family is dominant in the United States. Baby boomers are having fewer children. Three out of four homes do not have children in them.

Paraphrase 3

The child-free family is dominant in the United States. As baby boomers get older, there will be even more of these families. Three-quarters of all U.S. homes will be childless ten years from now.

3. Which is the best paraphrase of the paragraph? _____

4. Why are the other paraphrases less good?

_____

_____

_____

EXERCISE 5-9 PARAPHRASING 2

Directions: *Write a paraphrase of paragraph 11 in the reading "What Is Crime?" on page 160.*

5g   OUTLINING TO ORGANIZE IDEAS

LEARNING OBJECTIVE 7
Outline text

Outlining is a writing strategy that can assist you in organizing information and pulling ideas together. It is also an effective way to pull together information from two or more sources—your textbook and class lectures, for example. Finally, outlining is a way to assess your comprehension and strengthen your recall. Use the following tips to write an effective outline.

1. **Read an entire section and then jot down notes.** Do not try to outline while you are reading the material for the first time.
2. **As you read, be alert for organizational patterns (see Chapter 4).** These patterns will help you organize your notes.
3. **Record all the most important ideas in the briefest possible form.**
4. **Think of your outline as a list of the main ideas and supporting details of a selection.** Organize it to show how the ideas are related or to reflect the organization of the material.

5. **Write in your own words; do not copy sentences or parts of sentences from the selection.** Use words and short phrases to summarize ideas. Do not write in complete sentences.

6. **Use a system of indentation to separate main ideas and details.** As a general rule, the greater the importance of an idea, the closer it is placed to the left margin. Ideas of lesser importance are indented and appear closer to the center of the page. Your notes might follow a format like that shown below:

OUTLINE FORMAT

> TOPIC
> Main Idea
> > Supporting detail
> > > fact
> > > fact
> > Supporting detail
> Main Idea
> > Supporting detail
> > Supporting detail
> > > fact
> > > fact

To further illustrate the techniques of outlining, study the notes shown in the sample outline below. They are based on paragraphs 1 and 2 of the textbook excerpt "Body Gestures" on page 41.

A SAMPLE OUTLINE

I. Body Gestures

   A. Kinesics—the study of communication through body movement

   B. Five types of movements

      1. Emblems

         a. substitutes for words

         b. specific verbal translations

         c. not the same across time or cultures

EXERCISE 5-10 OUTLINING 1

Directions: Read the following passage and complete the outline.

Gender Characteristics

Masculinity refers to attributes considered appropriate for males. In American society, these traditionally include being aggressive, athletic, physically active, logical, and dominant in social relationships with females. Conversely, femininity refers to attributes associated with appropriate behavior for females, which in America include passivity, docility, fragility, emotionality, and subordination to males. Research conducted by Carol Gilligan and her students at Harvard's Gender Studies Department indicate that children are acutely aware of and feel pressure to conform to these powerful gender traits by the age of 4. Some people insist that gender traits such as male aggressiveness are innate characteristics linked to sex and do not depend on cultural definitions. However, the preponderance of research indicates that females and males can be equally aggressive under different social and cultural conditions and that levels of aggression vary as widely within the sexes as between them.

—adapted from Thompson and Hickey, *Society in Focus*, p. 285

Gender Characteristics

A. Masculinity

    1. attributes society believes appropriate for males

    2. include _____

    _____

B. Femininity

    1. _____

    2. include _____
    and subordination to males

C. _____ are aware of and feel pressure to conform to gender expectations by _____

D. Link to Sex

    1. some people believe linked to sex

    2. research shows both sexes can be equally aggressive and levels of

    _____

EXERCISE 5-11 OUTLINING 2

Directions: *Finish outlining the textbook excerpt "Body Gestures" on pages 41–43.*

5h   MAPPING TO SHOW RELATIONSHIPS

LEARNING OBJECTIVE 8
Draw maps to show relationships

Mapping is a way of drawing a diagram to describe how a topic and its related ideas are connected. Mapping is a visual means of learning by writing; it organizes and consolidates information.

This section discusses four types of maps: conceptual maps, process diagrams, time lines, and part and function diagrams.

Conceptual Maps

A conceptual map is a diagram that presents ideas spatially rather than in list form. It is a "picture" of how ideas are related. Use the following steps in constructing a conceptual map.

1. **Identify the topic and write it in the center of the page.**
2. **Identify ideas, aspects, parts, and definitions that are related to the topic.** Draw each one on a line radiating from the topic.
3. **As you discover details that further explain an idea already recorded, draw new lines branching from the idea that the details explain.**

A conceptual map of Part One of this book is shown below. This map shows only the major topics included in Part One. Maps can be much more detailed and include more information than the one shown, depending on the purpose for drawing it.

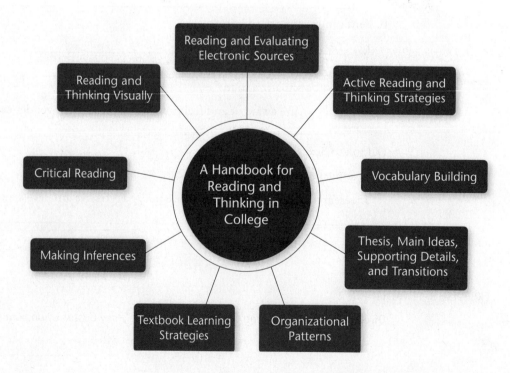

EXERCISE 5-12 DRAWING A CONCEPTUAL MAP 1

Directions: *Read the following paragraph about social institutions. Complete the conceptual map that presents the ideas contained in this paragraph.*

Society cannot survive without social institutions. A social institution is a set of widely shared beliefs, norms and procedures necessary for meeting the basic needs of society. The most important institutions are family, education, religion, economy, and politics. They have stood the test of time, serving society well. The family institution leads countless people to produce and raise children to ensure that they can eventually take over from the older generation the task of keeping society going. The educational institution teaches the young to become effective contributors to the welfare—such as the order, stability, or prosperity—of society. The religious institution fulfills spiritual needs, making earthly lives seem more meaningful and therefore more bearable or satisfying. The economic institution provides food, clothing, shelter, employment, banking, and other goods and services that we need to live. The political institution makes and enforces laws to prevent criminals and other similar forces from destabilizing society.

—Thio, *Sociology*, pp. 35–36

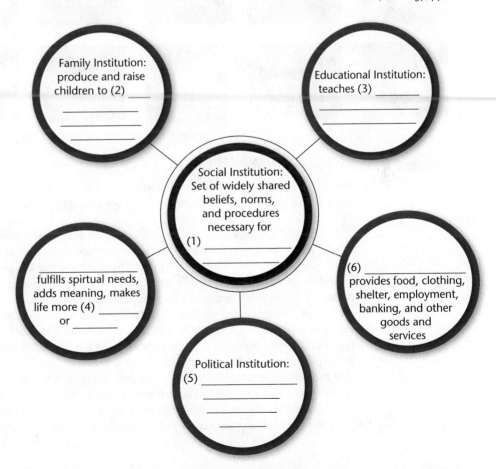

Directions: *Draw a conceptual map for the textbook excerpt "Body Gestures" on pages 41–43.*

Process Diagrams

In the technologies and the natural sciences, as well as in many other courses, *processes* are an important part of the course content. A diagram that visually describes the steps, variables, or parts of a process will make learning easier. For example, the diagram below visually describes the steps in the process of conducting research.

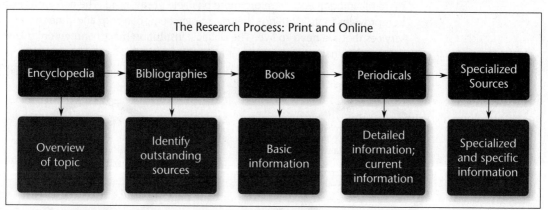

The Research Process: Print and Online

Encyclopedia →	Bibliographies →	Books →	Periodicals →	Specialized Sources
Overview of topic	Identify outstanding sources	Basic information	Detailed information; current information	Specialized and specific information

Directions: *The following paragraph describes how a bill becomes a law. Read the paragraph and then complete the process diagram that illustrates this procedure.*

Federal criminal laws must originate in the House of Representatives or the U.S. Senate. A senator or representative introduces a proposal (known as a bill) to create a new law or modify an existing law. The merits of the bill are debated in the House or Senate and a vote is taken. If the bill receives a majority vote, it is passed on to the other house of Congress where it is again debated and put to a vote. If any changes are made, the amended bill must be returned to the house of Congress where it originated and voted on again. This process continues until the House and Senate agree on a single version of the bill. The bill is then forwarded to the president, who can sign the bill into law, veto it or take no action, in which case the bill dies automatically when Congress adjourns. If the president vetoes a bill, Congress can pass the law over the president's veto by a two-thirds vote of both houses. Whether approved by the president and the Congress or by the Congress alone, a bill becomes a law when it is published in the *U.S. Criminal Codes*.

—Fagin, *Criminal Justice*, p. 152

Drawing a Process Diagram

The Making of Federal Criminal Laws

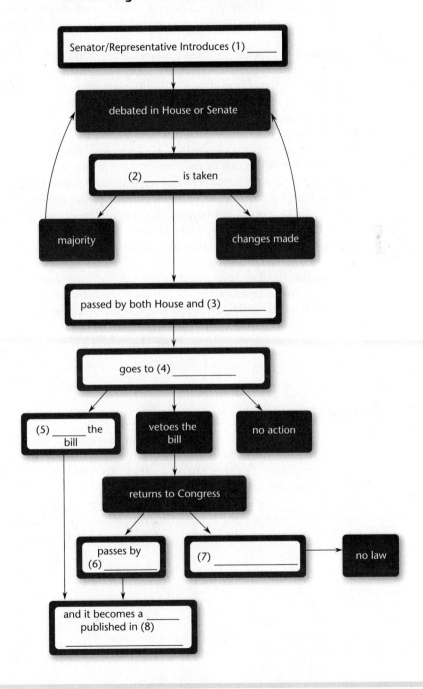

EXERCISE 5–15 DRAWING A PROCESS DIAGRAM 2

Directions: *The following paragraphs describe the body's response to stress. Read the paragraphs and then draw a process diagram that describes this response sequence. Compare your diagram with those of several other students.*

The body's response to stress (*general adaptation syndrome*) has three stages. During the first stage (*alarm reaction*), your sympathetic nervous system increases its activity in what is known as the "fight-or-flight" syndrome. Your pupils dilate, your heart rate increases, and your bronchial passages dilate. In addition, your blood sugar increases, your digestive system slows, your blood pressure rises, and blood flow to your skeletal muscles increases. At the same time, the endocrine system produces more cortisol, a hormone that influences your metabolism and your immune response. Cortisol is critical to your body's ability to adapt to and cope with stress.

In the second stage (*stage of resistance*), your body systems return to normal functioning. The physiologic effects of sympathetic nervous system stimulation and the excess cortisol are gone. You have adapted to the stimulus and it no longer produces stress for you. You are coping. Many factors contribute to your ability to cope; these include your physical and mental health, education, experiences, and support systems, such as family, friends, and coworkers.

Exhaustion, the third stage of the general adaptation syndrome, occurs when exposure to a stressor is prolonged or the stressor is particularly severe. At this point the individual has lost the ability to resist or adapt to the stressor and may become seriously ill as a consequence. Fortunately, most individuals do not reach this stage.

—adapted from Limmer and O'Keefe, *Emergency Care*, p. 36

Time Lines

When you are studying a topic in which the sequence or order of events is a central focus, a time line is a helpful way to organize the information. Time lines are especially useful in history courses. To map a sequence of events, draw a single line and mark it off in year intervals, just as a ruler is marked off in inches. Then write events next to the correct year. For example, the following time line displays major events during the presidency of Franklin D. Roosevelt. The time line shows the sequence of events and helps you to visualize them clearly.

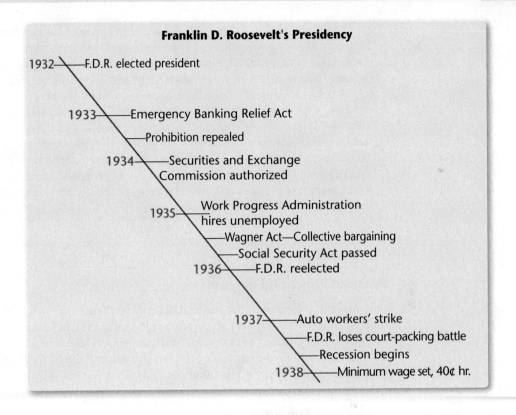

Franklin D. Roosevelt's Presidency

1932 —— F.D.R. elected president

1933 —— Emergency Banking Relief Act
—— Prohibition repealed

1934 —— Securities and Exchange
Commission authorized

1935 —— Work Progress Administration
hires unemployed
—— Wagner Act—Collective bargaining
—— Social Security Act passed

1936 —— F.D.R. reelected

1937 —— Auto workers' strike
—— F.D.R. loses court-packing battle
—— Recession begins

1938 —— Minimum wage set, 40¢ hr.

EXERCISE 5-16 DRAWING A TIME LINE

Directions: The following passage reviews the chronology of events in public school desegregation. Read the selection and then draw a time line that will help you to visualize these historical events.

Desegregating the Schools

Schools soon became the primary target of civil rights advocates. The NAACP concentrated first on universities, winning admission for qualified African Americans to state graduate and professional schools. Led by Thurgood Marshall, NAACP lawyers then attacked segregation in the public schools. Challenging *Plessy v. Ferguson*, the 1896 Supreme Court decision that upheld the constitutionality of separate but equal public facilities, Marshall argued that even substantially equal but separate schools did profound psychological damage to African American children and thus violated the Fourteenth Amendment.

In 1954, in the case of *Brown v. Board of Education of Topeka*, the Supreme Court unanimously agreed. Chief Justice Earl Warren, recently appointed by President Eisenhower, flatly declared that "separate educational facilities are inherently unequal." To divide grade-school children "solely because of their race," he argued, "generates a feeling of inferiority as to their status in the community that may affect their hearts and minds in a way unlikely ever to be undone." Despite this sweeping language, Warren realized that changing historic patterns of segregation would be difficult. Accordingly, in 1955 the Court ruled that school desegregation should proceed "with all deliberate speed" and left the details to the lower federal courts.

"All deliberate speed" proved to be agonizingly slow. The border states quickly complied with the Court's ruling, but the Deep South responded with massive resistance. White citizens' councils organized to retain racial separation; 101 representatives and senators signed a Southern Manifesto in 1956 denouncing the *Brown* decision as "a clear abuse of judicial power." School boards found ways to evade the Court's ruling. These tactics led to long disputes in the federal courts; by 1960, less than 1 percent of the black children in the Deep South attended school with whites.

—adapted from Brands et al., *American Stories*, pp. 735–736

Part and Function Diagrams

In courses that deal with the use and description or classification of physical objects, labeled drawings are an important learning tool. In a human anatomy and physiology course, for example, the easiest way to learn the parts and functions of the brain is to draw it. To study it, you would sketch the brain and test your recall of each part and its function.

EXERCISE 5–17 DRAWING A PART AND FUNCTION DIAGRAM

Directions: *The following paragraph describes a model showing where different types of people tend to live in an urban area. Read the paragraph and then draw a diagram that will help you to visualize this model of urban structure.*

In 1923, sociologist E. W. Burgess created the concentric zone model to describe the internal structure of cities. According to this model, a city grows outward from a central area in a series of five concentric rings, like the growth rings of a tree. The innermost zone is the central business district (CBD), where nonresidential activities are concentrated. A second ring, the zone in transition, contains industry and poorer-quality housing. Immigrants to the city first live in this zone in high-rise apartment buildings. The third ring, the zone of working-class homes, contains modest older houses occupied by stable, working-class families. The fourth zone has newer and more spacious houses for middle-class families. A commuters' zone beyond the continuous built-up area of the city is inhabited by people who work in the center but choose to live in "bedroom communities" for commuters.

—adapted from Rubenstein, *Contemporary Human Geography*, p. 296

5i   SUMMARIZING TO CONDENSE IDEAS

LEARNING OBJECTIVE 9
Summarize text

Like outlining, summarizing is an excellent way to learn from your reading and to increase recall. A **summary** is a brief statement that reviews the key points of what you have read. It condenses an author's ideas or arguments into sentences written in your own words. A summary contains only the gist of the text, with limited explanation, background information, or supporting detail. Writing a summary is a step beyond recording the author's ideas; a summary must pull together the writer's ideas by condensing and grouping them. Before writing a summary, be sure you understand the material and have identified the writer's major points. Then use the following suggestions:

1. **As a first step, highlight or write brief notes on the material.**
2. **Write one sentence that states the writer's overall concern or most important idea.** To do this, ask yourself what one topic the material is about. Then ask what point the writer is trying to make about that topic. This sentence will be the topic sentence of your summary.
3. **Be sure to paraphrase, using your own words rather than those of the author.**
4. **Review the major supporting information that the author gives to explain the major idea.**
5. **The amount of detail you include, if any, depends on your purpose for writing the summary.** For example, if you are writing a summary of a television documentary for a research paper, it might be more detailed than if you were writing it to jog your memory for a class discussion.
6. **Normally, present ideas in the summary in the same order in which they appeared in the original material.**
7. **If the writer presents a clear opinion or expresses an attitude toward the subject matter, include it in your summary.**
8. **If the summary is for your own use only and is not to be submitted as an assignment, do not worry about sentence structure.** Some students prefer to write summaries using words and phrases rather than complete sentences.

A sample summary of the textbook excerpt "Body Gestures," which appears on page 41, is shown below.

A SAMPLE SUMMARY

> Nonverbal messages can be communicated through body gestures. Kinesics (the study of communication through body movement) classifies movements as emblems, illustrators, affect displays, regulators, and adaptors. Emblems take the place of words. Illustrators complement and enhance verbal messages and they also improve recall. Affect displays are facial expressions that communicate emotions either intentionally or unintentionally. Regulators are

body gestures that help control conversation and send signals about what you want a speaker to do. Adaptors are unintentional movements that satisfy a need. They include self-adaptors, which usually involve physical comfort; alter-adaptors, which are responses to an interaction; and object-adaptors, which involve manipulating an object, usually in a negative way.

EXERCISE 5-18 SUMMARIZING 1

Directions: *Complete this summary of the passage about stress on page 174.*

There are three stages in the general adaptation syndrome, which is the body's response to _____. In the first stage, called _____, the _____ increases activity as part of the "fight-or-flight" syndrome. This response includes dilated _____ and _____, a slowed _____, and increases in heart rate, blood sugar, blood pressure, and blood flow to _____. The endocrine system also produces more cortisol, which is a critical hormone in the body's response to _____. Body systems return to normal in the second stage, called _____. In this stage, _____ has ceased to produce stress because the person is able to _____. Factors that contribute to this coping ability include _____, education, experiences, and support networks. The third stage is _____, which results from _____ or _____. In this stage, a person is unable to _____ to the stressor, which may result in _____; however, most people do not get to this stage.

EXERCISE 5-19 SUMMARIZING 2

Directions: *Write a summary of the section titled "Social Class and Crime" (paragraphs 12–15) of the article "What Is Crime?" on pages 160–161.*

SUMMARY OF LEARNING OBJECTIVES

1	**Use strategies for reading textbooks** **What textbook features help you read and learn from textbooks?**	Textbooks are designed to work with your instructor's lecture to provide you with reliable and accurate information and to help you practice your skills. Refer to Table 5-1 on pages 148–149 for a list of textbook features and how to use them.
2	**Use the SQ3R system** **What are the steps in the SQ3R system?**	The SQ3R method enables you to integrate reading and learning by using the following steps: Survey, Question, Read, Recite, and Review. You may also adapt the SQ3R method to suit how you learn and the type of material you are studying.
3	**Use learning and recall strategies** **What learning and recall strategies are useful for textbook reading?**	Learning and recall strategies include immediate review, periodic review, final review, building an intent to remember, organizing and categorizing, association, using a variety of sensory modes, visualization, and mnemonic devices.
4	**Highlight effectively** **What does effective highlighting involve?**	To highlight most effectively, you should analyze the assignment; assess your familiarity with the subject; read first, then highlight; use the boldfaced headings; highlight main ideas and only key supporting details; and avoid highlighting complete sentences.
5	**Use annotation to record your thinking** **Why is annotation useful?**	Annotating forces you to keep track of your comprehension as well as react to ideas. Refer to the chart on page 164 for examples of different types of annotation.
6	**Paraphrase ideas** **What is a paraphrase and why is paraphrasing useful?**	A paraphrase is a restatement of a passage's ideas in your own words. Paraphrasing is useful for portions of a text for which exact, detailed comprehension is required. It is also helpful for understanding complicated material or material that is stylistically complex, poorly written, overly formal, or biased.
7	**Outline text** **Why is outlining useful?**	Outlining can help you organize information and ideas, pull together information from two or more sources, assess your comprehension, and strengthen your recall.
8	**Draw maps to show relationships** **What is mapping and what are the types of maps?**	Mapping is a way of drawing a diagram to describe how a topic and its related ideas are connected. Types of maps include conceptual maps, process diagrams, part and function diagrams, and time lines.
9	**Summarize text** **What is the purpose of a summary?**	A summary is a brief statement that reviews the key points of what you have read. It condenses an author's ideas or arguments into sentences written in your own words.

6 Making Inferences

LEARNING OBJECTIVES

In this chapter, you will learn how to

1 Make inferences from facts
2 Make inferences from written material
3 Make accurate inferences

Look at the photograph below, which appeared in a psychology textbook. What do you think is happening here? What is the man's occupation? What are the feelings of the subjects in the photograph?

In order to answer these questions, you had to use any information you could get from the photo and make guesses based on it. The facial expressions, body language, clothing, and other objects present in this photo provided clues. This reasoning process is called "making an inference."

6a MAKING INFERENCES FROM THE GIVEN FACTS

LEARNING OBJECTIVE 1
Make inferences from facts

An **inference** is a reasoned guess about what you don't know made on the basis of what you do know. Inferences are common in our everyday lives. When you get on an expressway and see a long, slow-moving line of traffic, you might predict that there is an accident or roadwork ahead. When you see a puddle of water under the kitchen sink, you can infer that you have a plumbing problem. The inferences you make may not always be correct, even though you based them on the available information. The water under the sink might have been the result of a spill. The traffic you encountered on the expressway might be normal for that time of day, but you didn't know it because you aren't normally on the road then. An inference is only the best guess you can make in a situation, given the information you have.

EXERCISE 6-1 MAKING INFERENCES 1

Directions: *Study the photograph below. Use your skills in making inferences to write a statement explaining what is happening in this photograph.*

_____

_____

_____

_____

_____

EXERCISE 6-2 MAKING INFERENCES 2

Directions: *Read each of the following statements. Place a check mark in front of each sentence that follows that is a reasonable inference that can be made from the statement.*

1. Twice as many couples seek marriage counseling as did 20 years ago.
   - _____ a. There are more married people now than 20 years ago.
   - _____ b. There has been an increased demand for licensed marriage counselors.
   - _____ c. Marriage is more legalistic than it used to be.
   - _____ d. Couples are more willing to discuss their differences than they were 20 years ago.

2. More than half of all Americans are overweight.
   - _____ a. Many Americans are at high risk for heart disease.
   - _____ b. Teaching children about nutrition and exercise should be a high priority in public schools.
   - _____ c. Americans place great emphasis on appearance.
   - _____ d. The weight-loss industry is an important sector of business.

3. Many courts now permit lawyers to file papers and handle some court work over the Internet.
   - _____ a. Courtrooms will no longer be needed.
   - _____ b. Attorneys will be able to check the status of their cases from their home computers.
   - _____ c. Some cases may proceed more quickly now.
   - _____ d. More lawyers will carry laptops.

6b   MAKING INFERENCES FROM WRITTEN MATERIAL

LEARNING OBJECTIVE 2
Make inferences from written material

When you read the material associated with your college courses, you need to make inferences frequently. Writers do not always present their ideas directly. Instead, they often leave it to you to add up and think beyond the facts they present. You are expected to reason out or infer the meaning an author intended (but did not say) on the basis of what he or she did say. In a sense, the inferences you make act as bridges between what is said and what is not said, but is meant.

6c HOW TO MAKE ACCURATE INFERENCES

LEARNING OBJECTIVE 3
Make accurate
inferences
Each inference you make depends on the situation, the facts provided, and your own knowledge and experience. Here are a few guidelines to help you see beyond the factual level and make solid inferences.

Understand the Literal Meaning

Be sure you have a firm grasp of the literal meaning. You must understand the stated ideas and facts before you can move to higher levels of thinking, which include inference making. You should recognize the topic, main idea, key details, and organizational pattern of each paragraph you have read.

Notice Details

As you are reading, pay particular attention to details that are unusual or stand out. Often such details will offer you clues to help you make inferences. Ask yourself:

- **What is unusual or striking about this piece of information?**
- **Why is it included here?**

Read the following excerpt, which is taken from an essay about a young Polish immigrant to the U.K., and mark any details that seem unusual or striking.

An Immigration Plan Gone Awry

Due to her own hardship, Katja was not thrilled when her younger brother called her from Warsaw and said that he was going to join her in the U.K. Katja warned him that opportunities were scarce in London for a Polish immigrant. "Don't worry," he said in an effort to soothe her anxiety. "I already have a job in a factory." An advertisement in a Warsaw paper had promised good pay for Polish workers in Birmingham. A broker's fee of $500 and airfare were required, so her brother borrowed the money from their mother. He made the trip with a dozen other young Polish men.

The "broker" picked the young men up at Heathrow and piled them in a van. They drove directly to Birmingham, and at nightfall the broker dropped the whole crew off at a ramshackle house inside the city. He ordered them to be ready to be picked up in the morning for their first day of work. A bit dazed by the pace, they stretched out on the floor to sleep.

Their rest was brief. In the wee hours of the night, the broker returned with a gang of 10 or so thugs armed with cricket bats. They beat the young Polish boys to a pulp and robbed them of all their valuables. Katja's brother took some heavy kicks to the ribs and head, then stumbled out of the house. Once outside, he saw two police cars parked across the street. The officers in the cars obviously chose to

> ignore the mayhem playing out in front of their eyes. Katja's brother knew better than try to convince them otherwise; the police in Poland would act no differently. Who knows, maybe they were part of the broker's scam. Or maybe they just didn't care about a bunch of poor Polish immigrants "invading" their town.
>
> —Batstone, "Katja's Story"

Did you mark details such as the $500 broker's fee, the promise of a well-paying job despite scarce job opportunities for Polish immigrants, and the beating and robbery of the boys?

Add Up the Facts

Consider all of the facts taken together. To help you do this, ask yourself such questions as the following:

- **What is the writer trying to suggest with this set of facts?**
- **What do all these facts and ideas seem to point toward or add up to?**
- **Why did the author include these facts and details?**

Making an inference is somewhat like assembling a complicated jigsaw puzzle; you try to make all the pieces fit together to form a recognizable picture. Answering these questions requires you to add together all the individual pieces of information, which will enable you to arrive at an inference.

When you add up the facts in the article "An Immigration Plan Gone Awry" you realize that Katja's brother is the victim of a scam.

Be Alert to Clues

Writers often provide you with numerous hints that can point you toward accurate inferences. An awareness of word choices, details included (and omitted), ideas emphasized, and direct commentary can help you determine a textbook author's attitude toward the topic at hand. In "An Immigration Plan Gone Awry," the "ramshackle" house, the men "piled" into a van, and sleeping on the floor are all clues that something is amiss.

Consider the Author's Purpose

Also study the author's purpose for writing. What does he or she hope to accomplish? In "An Immigration Plan Gone Awry" the writer seems critical of immigrant brokers and of the police.

Verify Your Inference

Once you have made an inference, check that it is accurate. Look back at the stated facts to be sure that you have sufficient evidence to support the inference. Also, be certain that you have not overlooked other equally plausible or more plausible inferences that could be drawn from the same set of facts.

EXERCISE 6-3 MAKING INFERENCES 3

Directions: *Study the cartoon below and place a check mark in front of each statement that is a reasonable inference that can be made from the cartoon.*

_____ 1. The cartoonist thinks workers are physically abused.

_____ 2. The cartoonist is critical of those in management.

_____ 3. Many conflicts exist between workers and supervisors.

_____ 4. The cartoonist believes that people change when they become managers.

_____ 5. The cartoonist is a labor relations specialist.

"We get it, Tom—you're management now."

EXERCISE 6-4 MAKING INFERENCES 4

Directions: *Read each of the following statements. Place a check mark in front of each sentence that follows that is a reasonable inference that can be made from the statement.*

1. Political candidates must now include the Internet in their campaign plans.

_____ a. Political candidates may host online chats to assess voter opinion.

_____ b. Informal debates between candidates may be conducted online.

_____ c. Internet campaigning will drastically increase overall campaign expenditures.

_____ d. Television campaigning is likely to remain the same.

2. Half of the public education classrooms in the United States are now hooked up to the Internet.

_____ a. Children are more computer literate than their parents were when they were in school.

_____ b. Students now have access to current world news and happenings.

_____ c. Books are no longer considered the sole source of information on a subject.

_____ d. Teachers have become better teachers now that they have Internet access.

3. The Internet can make doctors more efficient through the use of new software and databases that make patient diagnosis more accurate.

_____ a. The cost of in-person medical care is likely to decrease.

_____ b. Doctors may be able to identify patients with serious illnesses sooner.

_____ c. Doctors are likely to pay less attention to their patients' descriptions of symptoms.

_____ d. Information on the symptoms and treatment of rare illnesses is more readily available.

EXERCISE 6-5 MAKING INFERENCES 5

Directions: *Read each of the following passages. Using inference, determine whether the statements following each passage are true or not. Place an X next to each untrue statement.*

A. Each year, the government's Department of Housing and Urban Development conducts a national survey of cities and towns to find out how many people in the United States are homeless. The 2010 survey found about 649,917 people living in shelters, in transitional housing, and on the street on a single night in January. But, the government estimates, a much larger number—approximately 1.6 million people—are homeless for at least some time during the course of the year. As with earlier estimates of the homeless population, critics claimed that the HUD estimate undercounted the homeless, who may well have numbered several million people. Some estimates suggest that as many as 3 million people are homeless for at least one night in a given year. In addition, they add, evidence suggests that the number of homeless people in the United States is increasing.

—adapted from Macionis, *Society*, p. 216

_____ 1. The Department of Housing and Urban Development does not consider homelessness to be a problem.

_____ 2. Gaining an accurate count of the homeless population is difficult.

_____ 3. The number of homeless people remains the same at different times throughout the year.

_____ 4. People who are homeless for short periods may not be counted in estimates of the homeless population.

_____ 5. The number of homeless people in the United States will probably decrease.

B.   Blowfish is one of the most prized delicacies in the restaurants of Japan. This fish is prized not only for its taste, but for the tingling sensation one gets around the lips when eating it. In blowfish TTX (a neurotoxin) is concentrated in certain organs, including the liver and gonads. Its preparation takes great skill and can only be done by licensed chefs who are skilled at removing the poison-containing organs without crushing them, which can lead to contamination of normally edible parts. The toxin cannot be destroyed by cooking. Lore has it that the most skilled chefs intentionally leave a bit of the poison in, so that diners can enjoy the tingling sensation caused by blockage of nerve signals from the sense receptors on the lips.

—adapted from Germann and Stanfield, _Principles of Human Physiology_, p. 185

_____ 6. Consuming TTX has potentially dangerous consequences.

_____ 7. The United States has strict rules about the preparation of blowfish.

_____ 8. Japanese diners enjoy blowfish partly because of the sense of danger involved.

_____ 9. TTX causes blockage of signals from nerves.

_____ 10. Blowfish is always unsafe to eat.

C.   Your culture instills in you a variety of beliefs, values, and attitudes about such things as success (how you define it and how you should achieve it); the relevance of religion, race, or nationality; and the ethical principles you should follow in business and in your personal life. These teachings provide benchmarks against which you can measure yourself. Your ability to achieve what your culture defines as success, for example, contributes to a positive self-concept; in the same way, your failure to achieve what your culture encourages will contribute to a negative self-concept.

—DeVito, _Human Communication_, p. 52

_____ 11. People with positive self-concepts often have achieved their culture's notion of success.

_____ 12. Most cultures do not believe that race or religion are relevant.

_____ 13. People often ignore their culture's beliefs about ethical principles.

_____ 14. Self-concept is affected by both success and failure.

_____ 15. Your self-concept can never change.

EXERCISE 6-6 MAKING INFERENCES 6

Directions: *Read each of the following paragraphs. A number of statements follow them; each statement is an inference. Label each inference as either:*

PA—Probably accurate—there is substantial evidence in the paragraph to support the statement.

IE—Insufficient evidence—there is little or no evidence in the paragraph to support the statement.

A.   We could use more wind power. The kinetic energy of moving air is readily converted to mechanical energy to pump water, grind grain, or turn turbines and generate electricity. Wind power currently supplies only about 2% of U.S. energy production, but it is the fastest-growing energy source, increasing at an annual rate of 20–30%. Wind is clean, free, and abundant. However, it does not blow constantly, and some means of energy storage or an alternative source of energy is needed. Not all regions have enough wind to make wind power feasible. Some environmentalists oppose wind power because the rotating blades kill thousands of birds each year, but so do domestic cats and collisions with television and microwave towers. The amount of land required for windmills might become a problem if wind power were used widely, but the land under windmills could be used for farming or grazing.

—Hill et al., *Chemistry for Changing Times*, p. 446

_____ 1. The United States will continue developing wind power as a source of energy.

_____ 2. Some parts of the country may always have to rely on other forms of energy.

_____ 3. Environmentalists prefer solar power to wind power.

_____ 4. Farmers oppose the use of land for wind turbines.

_____ 5. Every renewable energy source has advantages and disadvantages that must be considered.

B.   Artist Georgia O'Keeffe was born in Sun Prairie, Wisconsin, and spent her childhood on her family's farm. While in high school, she had a memorable experience that gave her a new perspective on the art-making process. As she passed the door to the art room, O'Keeffe stopped to watch as a teacher held up a jack-in-the-pulpit plant so that the students could appreciate its unusual shapes and subtle colors. Although O'Keeffe had enjoyed flowers in the marshes and meadows of Wisconsin, she had done all of her drawing and painting from plaster casts or had copied them from photographs or reproductions. This was the first time she realized that one could draw and paint from real life. Twenty-five years later she produced a powerful series of paintings based on flowers.

—adapted from Frank, *Prebles' Artforms*, p. 37

_____ 6. O'Keeffe's artistic style was influenced by her high-school art teacher.

_____ 7. O'Keeffe's paintings from plaster casts were unsuccessful.

_____ 8. O'Keeffe was deeply influenced by nature.

_____ 9. O'Keeffe was not influenced by modern art.

_____ 10. O'Keeffe never copied flowers from other paintings.

EXERCISE 6–7 MAKING INFERENCES 7

Directions: *Read the following paragraphs and the statements that follow. Place a check mark next to the statements that are reasonable inferences.*

August Vollmer was the chief of police of Berkeley, California, from 1905 to 1932. Vollmer's vision of policing was quite different from most of his contemporaries. He believed the police should be a "dedicated body of educated persons comprising a distinctive corporate entity with a prescribed code of behavior." He was critical of his contemporaries and they of him. San Francisco police administrator Charley Dullea, who later became president of the International Association of Chiefs of Police, refused to drive through Berkeley in protest against Vollmer. Fellow California police chiefs may have felt their opposition to Vollmer was justified, given his vocal and strong criticism of other California police departments. For example, Vollmer publicly referred to San Francisco cops as "morons," and in an interview with a newspaper reporter, he called Los Angeles cops "low grade mental defectives."

Because of his emphasis on education, professionalism, and administrative reform, Vollmer often is seen as the counterpart of London's Sir Robert Peel and is sometimes called the "father of modern American policing." Vollmer was decades ahead of his contemporaries, but he was not able to implement significant change in policing during his lifetime. It remained for Vollmer's students to implement change. For example, O.W. Wilson, who became chief of police of Chicago, promoted college education for police officers and wrote a book on police administration that reflected many of Vollmer's philosophies. It was adopted widely by police executives and used as a college textbook well into the 1960s.

Vollmer is credited with a number of innovations. He was an early adopter of the automobile for patrol and the use of radios in police cars. He recruited college-educated police officers. He developed and implemented a 3-year training curriculum for police officers, including classes in physics, chemistry, biology, physiology, anatomy, psychology, psychiatry, anthropology, and criminology. He developed a system of signal boxes for hailing police officers. He adopted the use of typewriters to fill out police reports and records, and officers received training in typing. He surveyed other police departments to gather information about their practices. Many of his initiatives have become common practice within contemporary police departments.

—Fagin, *Criminal Justice*, pp. 245–246

_____ 1. Vollmer did not have a college degree.

_____ 2. Most police officers of Vollmer's time had limited educations.

_____ 3. Vollmer believed police should be held accountable for their actions.

_____ 4. Sir Robert Peel dramatically changed policing procedures in England.

_____ 5. Vollmer received support from most police officers on the street.

_____ 6. Vollmer would support technological advances in policing.

_____ 7. Police departments of Vollmer's time were run with a careful eye toward accuracy.

_____ 8. Vollmer outlawed billy clubs.

SUMMARY OF LEARNING OBJECTIVES

1	**Make inferences from facts** **What is an inference?**	An inference is a reasoned guess about what you don't know based on what you do know. It is the best guess you can make in a situation, given the facts you have.
2	**Make inferences from written material** **Why do authors leave ideas unstated?**	Writers do not always present their ideas directly. Instead, they often leave it to you to think beyond the facts presented and infer the meaning they intended (but did not say).
3	**Make accurate inferences** **How do you make accurate inferences?**	To make accurate inferences, first understand the literal meaning of the reading selection. Pay attention to details, asking what is unusual or striking about them and why they have been included. Add up the facts, asking what they point to. Be alert to clues and consider the writer's purpose. Once you have made an inference, verify that it is accurate.

7 Critical Reading

LEARNING OBJECTIVES

In this chapter, you will learn how to

1 Distinguish fact from opinion
2 Identify the author's purpose
3 Evaluate tone
4 Identify bias
5 Evaluate data and evidence
6 Understand connotative language
7 Interpret figurative language
8 Think critically about source materials

In college you will be reading many new kinds of material: research articles, essays, critiques, reports, and analyses. Your instructors expect you to be able to do much more than understand and remember the basic content. They often demand that you read critically, interpreting, evaluating, and reacting to readings. To meet these expectations, you'll need to distinguish facts from opinions, identify the author's purpose, recognize the author's tone, detect bias, evaluate data and evidence, understand connotative language, interpret figurative language, and evaluate electronic resources.

7a IS THE MATERIAL FACT OR OPINION?

LEARNING OBJECTIVE 1
Distinguish fact from opinion

When working with any source, try to determine whether the material is factual or an expression of opinion. **Facts** are statements that can be verified—that is, proven true or false. **Opinions** are statements that express feelings, attitudes, or beliefs, and they are neither true nor false. Following are examples of each:

Facts

1. More than one million teenagers become pregnant every year.
2. The costs of medical care increase every year.

Opinions

> 1. Government regulation of our private lives should be halted immediately.
> 2. By the year 2025, most Americans will not be able to afford routine health care.

Verified facts from a reputable source can be accepted and regarded as reliable information. Opinions, on the other hand, are not reliable sources of information and should be carefully evaluated. Look for evidence that supports the opinion and indicates that it is reasonable. For example, opinion 2 is written to sound like a fact, but read closely. What basis or agenda does the author reveal?

Some writers are careful to signal the reader when they are presenting an opinion. Watch for words and phrases such as:

According to	It is believed that	Presumably
Apparently	It is likely that	Seemingly
In my opinion	One explanation is	This suggests
In my view	Possibly	

In the following excerpt from an environmental science textbook, notice how the author carefully distinguishes factual statements from opinion using qualifying words and phrases (underlined).

Human Population Growth—What's the Problem?

At some point during the autumn of 2011, the global human population passed the 7 billion mark. We don't know the exact day, much less the hour or minute; United Nations census data and estimates of world population growth are just not that precise. Nevertheless, many noted this milestone in human history. Some people feel that the rapid growth in our numbers is the "mother of all environmental problems." And they have a point. Our numbers have doubled twice over the past century. If you are 20 years old, Earth's population has grown by nearly 30% (1.6 billion) since your birth. Many argue that the growing number of humans is the primary factor driving our increasing impact on our planet and its life-support systems. From other commentators you will hear, "It's not that simple." Yes, the growth in our numbers is a concern, but the growth in our consumption is even more troubling. As a measure of the change in our consumption, they point to a milestone related to energy use. Sometime between 2007 and 2009 the amount of energy that the average person uses per year rose above 80 billion joules, which is equivalent to the energy in about 615 gallons of gasoline. This milestone represents an increase in personal energy use of more than 40% over the past century.

—Christensen, *The Environment and You*, p. 118

Other authors do just the opposite; they try to make opinions sound like facts (as in opinion 2), or they mix fact and opinion without making clear distinctions. This is particularly true in the case of *expert opinion*, which is the opinion of an authority. For example, those who write for *Car and Driver* magazine are often considered experts on cars. Textbook authors, too, often offer expert opinion, as in the following statement from an American government text.

> Ours is a complex system of justice. Sitting at the pinnacle of the judicial system is the Supreme Court, but its importance is often exaggerated.
> —Lineberry, *Government in America*, p. 540

The author of this statement has reviewed the available evidence and provides his expert opinion as to what the evidence indicates about the Supreme Court. The reader is free to disagree and to offer evidence to support an opposing view.

The article "Treating Wounded Soldiers: Polytrauma," reprinted in Chapter 1, uses expert opinion, as well. The opinions of Sandy Lai, program director of the Palo Alto Polytrauma Rehabilitation Center, are given as evidence.

EXERCISE 7-1 DISTINGUISHING FACT AND OPINION 1

Directions: *Read each of the following statements and identify whether it is fact (F), opinion (O), or expert opinion (EO).*

_____ 1. United Parcel Service (UPS) is the nation's largest delivery service.

_____ 2. United Parcel Service will become even more successful because it uses sophisticated management techniques.

_____ 3. Americans spend $13.7 billion per year on alternative medicine.

_____ 4. The best way to keep up with world news is to read the newspaper.

_____ 5. A community, as defined by sociologists, is a collection of people who share some purpose, activity, or characteristic.

_____ 6. The Bill of Rights comprises the first ten amendments to the Constitution.

_____ 7. Archaeologists believe that the stone monument known as Stonehenge was built to serve a religious purpose.

_____ 8. According to Dr. Richard Sobol, a communication specialist, conflict in interpersonal relationships is not only inevitable, it can also be beneficial.

_____ 9. The finest examples of landscape photography can be found in the work of Ansel Adams.

_____ 10. The symbol of Islam—a crescent and star—appears on the flags of nations that have a Muslim majority, such as Turkey and Pakistan.

EXERCISE 7-2 DISTINGUISHING FACT AND OPINION 2

Directions: *Each of the following paragraphs contains both facts and opinions. Read each paragraph and label each sentence as fact (F), opinion (O), or expert opinion (EO).*

A.   [1]Almost half of all Americans drink coffee every day, and many others consume caffeine in some other form, mainly for its well-known "wake-up" effect. [2]That jolt of caffeine has seemingly become an essential element of many people's morning ritual. [3]Caffeine is derived from the chemical family called *xanthines*, which are found in plant products from which coffee, tea, and chocolate are made. [4]In addition to enhancing mental alertness and reducing fatigue, the xanthines can produce side effects including insomnia, irregular heartbeat, dizziness, nausea, indigestion, and heartburn. [5]Apparently, these rather unpleasant side effects are not enough to deter millions of Americans from their daily caffeine "fix."

—adapted from Donatelle, *My Health*, p. 131

Sentences: 1. _____ 2. _____ 3. _____ 4. _____ 5. _____

B.   [1]Harriet Tubman was born a slave in Maryland in 1820 and escaped to Philadelphia in 1849. [2]We can guess that her own escape from slavery required tremendous courage, but that was only the beginning. [3]Through her work on the Underground Railroad, Harriet Tubman led hundreds of slaves to freedom. [4]During the Civil War, she continued her efforts toward the abolition of slavery by working as a nurse and a spy for the Union forces. [5]Today, Americans of all races consider Harriet Tubman one of the most heroic figures in our country's history.

Sentences: 1. _____ 2. _____ 3. _____ 4. _____ 5. _____

C.   [1]Smokeless tobacco products include chewing tobacco (tobacco leaves treated with molasses and other flavorings) and snuff (a finely ground form of tobacco that can be inhaled, chewed, or placed against the gums). [2]One possible explanation for the popularity of smokeless tobacco among young men is that they are emulating professional athletes who chew tobacco during games. [3]It is time to banish the notion that smokeless tobacco is safe. [4]Chewing tobacco and snuff contain *more* nicotine than cigarettes, and just as many toxic and carcinogenic chemicals. [5]Smokeless tobacco is prohibited in minor league baseball, a move that should be extended to all professional sports to help discourage the use of smokeless tobacco products.

—adapted from Donatelle, *My Health*, p. 161

Sentences: 1. _____ 2. _____ 3. _____ 4. _____ 5. _____

D.   [1]Some sociologists believe that if any nation deserves the "pro-family" label, it is Sweden. [2]The typical Swedish family today consists of two working parents, with the majority of women working part time and more than 90 percent of men working full time. [3]To support women's and men's dual roles in the family and work, the state has devised a benefit package that *all* families receive, regardless of class or income. [4]Benefits include public-supported child care, parental leave insurance for both men and women, a basic child allowance per year of around $900, and a housing allowance based on income and number of children in the family. [5]Despite deficiencies (for example, women occupy only 5 percent of upper management positions), the way Sweden combines family and employment appears to be far superior to the situations in most other countries.

—adapted from Thompson and Hickey, *Society in Focus*, p. 383

Sentences: 1. _____ 2. _____ 3. _____ 4. _____ 5. _____

E.   [1]In 2006, Congress passed a ban on Internet gambling, making it illegal for banks and credit card companies to process online gaming payments from the United States. [2]Some are concerned that Internet gambling lures minors and compulsive gamblers playing online games at home in their pajamas, resulting in huge debts. [3]On the other side, it is claimed that even an outright ban does not stop people from online gambling. [4]It is possible that this effort to ban Internet gambling might move the Internet gambling market underground, resulting in more unscrupulous operators and organized crime. [5]However, some states are considering legalization of instate Internet gambling, which has not yet been legally tested.

—adapted from Albanese, *Criminal Justice*, pp. 435–436

Sentences: 1. _____ 2. _____ 3. _____ 4. _____ 5. _____

7b   WHAT IS THE AUTHOR'S PURPOSE?

LEARNING OBJECTIVE 2
Identify the author's purpose

Writers have many different reasons or purposes for writing. Read the following statements and try to decide why each was written:

1. About 14,000 ocean-going ships pass through the Panama Canal each year. This averages to about three ships per day.
2. *New Unsalted Dry Roasted Almonds.* Finally, a natural snack without added salt. We simply shell the nuts and dry-roast them until they're crispy and crunchy. Try a jar this week.
3. Man is the only animal that blushes. Or needs to. (Mark Twain)
4. If a choking person has fallen down, first turn him or her faceup. Then knit together the fingers of both your hands and apply pressure with the heel of your bottom hand to the victim's abdomen.
5. If your boat capsizes, it is usually safer to cling to the boat than to try to swim ashore.

Statement 1 was written to give information, 2 to persuade you to buy almonds, 3 to amuse you and make a comment on human behavior, 4 to explain, and 5 to give advice.

In each of the examples, the writer's purpose is fairly clear, as it is in most textbooks (to present information), newspaper articles (to communicate daily events), and reference books (to compile facts, figures, and basic knowledge about a topic). However, in many other types of writing, authors have varied, sometimes less obvious, purposes. In these cases, the author's purpose must be inferred. (For more on inference, see Chapter 6.)

Often a writer's purpose is to express an opinion indirectly. The writer may also want to encourage the reader to think about a particular issue or problem. Writers achieve their purposes by manipulating and controlling what they say and how they say it.

Writers may vary their styles to suit their intended audiences. A writer may write for a general-interest audience (anyone who is interested in the subject but is not considered an expert). Most newspapers and periodicals, such as *Time* and *The Week*, appeal to a general-interest audience. The article "Treating Wounded Soldiers: Polytrauma," seems to be written for the general public. It does not assume that readers have a special knowledge of polytrauma or its treatment.

On the other hand, a writer may have a particular interest group in mind. A writer may write for medical doctors in *The New England Journal of Medicine*, for skiing enthusiasts in *Skiing Today*, or for antique collectors in *The World of Antiques*. A writer may also target his or her writing to an audience with particular political, moral, or religious attitudes. Articles in *The New Republic* often appeal to those interested in a particular political viewpoint, whereas articles in the *Catholic Digest* appeal to a specific religious group.

Depending on the group of people for whom the author is writing, he or she will change the level of language, choice of words, and method of presentation. One step toward identifying an author's purpose, then, is to ask yourself the question: Who is the intended audience? Your response will be your first clue to determining why the author wrote the article.

EXERCISE 7-3 IDENTIFYING THE AUTHOR'S PURPOSE 1

Directions: *Read each of the following statements. Then find the author's purpose for each statement in the box below and write it in the space provided.*

to persuade	to entertain	to inform
to advise	to criticize	

1. _____ If you are looking for specialized information on the Internet, the best approach is to use a metasearch engine such as ProFusion.

2. _____ Good judgment comes from experience, and a lot of that comes from bad judgment. (Will Rogers)

3. _____ The Constitution of the United States prescribes a separation of powers among the executive, legislative, and judicial branches of government.

4. _____ Members of the art gallery enjoy benefits such as free admission and discounts on special gallery exhibits.

5. _____ The governor's ill-advised plan to attach a "sin tax" to sales of tobacco and alcohol can only have a negative effect on tourism in our state.

EXERCISE 7-4 IDENTIFYING THE AUTHOR'S PURPOSE 2

Directions: *Read each of the following statements and identify the author's purpose. Write a sentence that describes the intended audience.*

1. Chances are you're going to be putting money away over the next five years or so. You are hoping for the right things in life. Right now, a smart place to put your money is in mutual funds or bonds.

   _____

   _____

2. Think about all the places your drinking water has been before you drink another drop. Most likely it has been chemically treated to remove bacteria and chemical pollutants. Soon you may begin to feel the side effects of these treatments. Consider switching to filtered, distilled water today.

   _____

   _____

3. Introducing the new, high-powered Supertuner III, a sound system guaranteed to keep your mother out of your car.

   _____

   _____

4. Bright and White laundry detergent removes dirt and stains faster than any other brand.

   _____

   _____

5. As a driver, you're ahead if you can learn to spot car trouble before it's too late. If you can learn the difference between drips and squeaks that occur under normal conditions and those that mean that big trouble is just down the road, then you'll be ahead of expensive repair bills and won't find yourself stranded on a lonely road.

   _____

   _____

7c   WHAT IS THE TONE?

LEARNING OBJECTIVE 3
Evaluate tone

The tone of a speaker's voice helps you interpret what he or she is saying. If the following sentence were read aloud, the speaker's voice would tell you how to interpret it: "Would you mind closing the door?" In print you cannot tell whether the speaker is polite, insistent, or angry. In speech you could tell by whether the speaker emphasized the word *would*, *mind*, or *door*.

Just as a speaker's tone of voice tells how the speaker feels, a writer conveys a tone, or feeling, through his or her writing. **Tone** refers to the attitude or feeling a writer expresses about his or her subject. The tone of the article "Treating Wounded Soldiers: Polytrauma" is informative. The author presents facts, statistics, and other evidence to support the thesis.

A writer's tone may be sentimental, angry, humorous, sympathetic, instructive, persuasive, and so forth. Here are a few examples of different tones. How does each make you feel?

- **Instructive**

  When purchasing a piece of clothing, one must be concerned with quality as well as with price. Be certain to check for the following: double-stitched seams, matched patterns, and ample linings.

- **Sympathetic**

  The forlorn, frightened-looking child wandered through the streets alone, searching for someone who would help her find her parents.

- **Persuasive**

  Child abuse is all too common in our society. Strong legislation is needed to control the abuse of innocent victims and to punish those who trample the rights and feelings of others.

- **Humorous**

  ACQUAINTANCE, n. A person whom we know well enough to borrow from, but not well enough to lend to.

  CABBAGE, n. A familiar kitchen-garden vegetable about as large and wise as a man's head.

  CIRCUS, n. A place where horses, ponies and elephants are permitted to see men, women and children acting the fool.

  LOVE, n. A temporary insanity curable by marriage or by removal of the patient from the influences under which he incurred the disorder.

  —Ambrose Bierce

- **Nostalgic**

> Things change, times change, but when school starts, my little grand-
> daughter will run up the same wooden stairs that creaked for all of the
> previous generations and I will still hate it when the summer ends.
>
> —Hastreiter, "Not Every Mother Is Glad Kids Are Back in School." *Buffalo Evening News*

In the first example, the writer offers advice in a straightforward, informative style. In the second, the writer wants you to feel sorry for the child and accomplishes that goal through description. In the third example, the writer tries to convince the reader that action must be taken to prevent child abuse. The use of such words as *innocent* and *trample* establish this tone. In the fourth example, the writer tries to amuse the reader with mocking definitions, and in the fifth example, the writer fondly reminisces about the start of school in the fall.

To identify an author's tone, pay particular attention to descriptive language and shades of meaning. Ask yourself: "How does the author feel about his or her subject and how are these feelings revealed?" It is sometimes difficult to find the right word to describe the author's tone. Table 7-1 lists words that are often used to describe the tone of a piece of writing. Use this list to provoke your thinking when identifying tone. If any of these words are unfamiliar, check their meanings in a dictionary.

TABLE 7.1 WORDS FREQUENTLY USED TO DESCRIBE TONE

abstract	condemning	formal	joyful	reverent
absurd	condescending	frustrated	loving	righteous
amused	cynical	gentle	malicious	sarcastic
angry	depressing	grim	melancholic	satiric
apathetic	detached	hateful	mocking	sensational
arrogant	disapproving	humorous	nostalgic	serious
assertive	distressed	impassioned	objective	solemn
awestruck	docile	incredulous	obsequious	sympathetic
bitter	earnest	indignant	optimistic	tragic
caustic	excited	indirect	outraged	uncomfortable
celebratory	fanciful	informative	pathetic	vindictive
cheerful	farcical	intimate	persuasive	worried
comic	flippant	ironic	pessimistic	
compassionate	forgiving	irreverent	playful	

EXERCISE 7–5 RECOGNIZING TONE 1

Directions: *Read each of the following statements. Then choose a word from the box that describes the tone it illustrates, and write it in the space provided.*

optimistic	angry	admiring	cynical/bitter
excited	humorous	nostalgic	disapproving
formal	informative	sarcastic	

1. _____ Taking a young child to a PG-13 movie is inappropriate and shows poor judgment on the part of the parents.

2. _____ The brown recluse spider has a dark, violin-shaped marking on the upper section of its body.

3. _____ The dedication and determination of the young men and women participating in the Special Olympics were an inspiration to everyone there.

4. _____ The first tomato of the summer always makes me think fondly of my grandfather's garden.

5. _____ Nobody is ever a complete failure; he or she can always serve as a bad example.

6. _____ The councilman once again demonstrated his sensitivity toward the environment when he voted to allow commercial development in an area set aside as a nature preserve.

7. _____ The success of the company's youth mentoring program will inspire other business groups to establish similar programs.

8. _____ Professional athletes have no loyalty toward their teams or their fans anymore, just their own wallets.

9. _____ We were thrilled to learn that next year's convention will be held in San Antonio—we've always wanted to see the Alamo!

10. _____ To be considered for the president's student-of-the-year award, an individual must demonstrate academic excellence as well as outstanding community service, and the individual must furnish no fewer than four letters of reference from faculty members.

EXERCISE 7-6 RECOGNIZING TONE 2

Directions: *Read each of the following statements, paying particular attention to the tone. Then write a sentence that describes the tone. Prove your point by listing some of the words that reveal the author's feelings.*

1. No one says that nuclear power is risk-free. There are risks involved in all methods of producing energy. However, the scientific evidence is clear and obvious. Nuclear power is at least as safe as any other means used to generate electricity.

   _____

   _____

   _____

2. The condition of our city streets is outrageous. The sidewalks are littered with paper and other garbage—you could trip while walking to the store. The streets themselves are in even worse condition. Deep potholes and crumbling curbs make it unsafe to drive. Where are our city tax dollars going if not to correct these problems?

   _____

   _____

   _____

3. I am a tired American. I am tired of watching criminals walk free while they wait for their day in court. I'm tired of hearing about victims getting hassled as much or more than criminals. I'm tired of reading about courts of law that accept lawsuits in which criminals sue their intended victims.

   _____

   _____

   _____

4. Cross-country skis have heel plates of different shapes and materials. They may be made of metal, plastic, or rubber. Be sure that they are tacked on the ski right where the heel of your boot will fall. They will keep snow from collecting under your foot and offer some stability.

   _____

   _____

   _____

5. My daughter, Lucy, was born with an underdeveloped brain. She was a beautiful little girl—at least to me and my husband—but her disabilities were severe. By the time she was two weeks old we knew that she would never walk, talk, feed herself, or even understand the concept of mother and father. It's impossible to describe the effect that her five-and-a-half-month life had on us; suffice it to say that she was the purest experience of love and pain that we will ever have, that she changed us forever, and that we will never cease to mourn her death, even though we know that for her it was a triumphant passing.

—Armstrong, in *The Choices We Made*, p. 165

_____

_____

_____

| 7d | **IS THE AUTHOR BIASED?** |

LEARNING OBJECTIVE 4
Identify bias

Bias refers to an author's partiality, prejudice, or inclination toward a particular viewpoint. A writer is biased if he or she takes one side of a controversial issue and does not recognize opposing viewpoints. Perhaps the best example of bias is in advertising. A magazine advertisement for a new car model, for instance, describes only positive, marketable features—the ad does not recognize the car's limitations or faults. In some materials the writer might be direct and forthright in expressing his or her bias; other times a writer's bias might be hidden and discovered only through careful analysis.

Read the following selection entitled "Ethanol Madness." As the title suggests, the authors have a negative attitude toward federal law requiring the use of ethanol in gasoline. Notice, in particular, the underlined words and phrases.

Henry Ford built his first automobile in 1896 to run on pure ethanol. If Congress has its way, the cars of the future will be built the same way. But what made good economic sense in the late nineteenth century doesn't necessarily make economic sense today—although it does make for good politics. Indeed, the ethanol story is a classic illustration of how good politics routinely trumps good economics to yield bad policies.

Federal law requires that ethanol be added to gasoline in increasing amounts through 2022. This requirement is supposed to conserve resources and improve the environment. It does neither. Instead, it lines the pockets of American corn farmers and ethanol makers and incidentally enriches some Brazilian sugarcane farmers along the way.

—adapted from Miller, Benjamin, and North, *The Economics of Public Issues*, p. 10

To identify bias, use the following suggestions:

1. **Analyze connotative meanings.** Does the author use a large number of positive or negative terms to describe the subject?
2. **Notice descriptive language.** What impression is created?
3. **Analyze the tone.** The author's tone often provides important clues.
4. **Look for opposing viewpoints.**

EXERCISE 7-7 DETECTING BIAS 1

Directions: *Read each of the following statements and place a check mark in front of each one that reveals bias.*

_____ 1. Testing the harmful effects of cosmetics on innocent animals is an outrage.

_____ 2. Judaism, Christianity, and Islam share a common belief in an all-powerful creator.

_____ 3. One of Shakespeare's wittiest and most delightful romantic comedies is *The Taming of the Shrew*.

_____ 4. Each fall, thousands of greater sandhill cranes leave their nesting grounds in Idaho and fly south to the Rio Grande.

_____ 5. A laissez-faire policy asserts that businesses should be able to charge whatever they want for their goods and services without interference from the government.

_____ 6. Campaign finance reform is essential to restoring both the integrity of the election process and the faith of Americans in our political system.

_____ 7. The longest siege of the Civil War took place in Petersburg, Virginia, when Union troops blocked Confederate supply lines from June 1864 to April 1865.

_____ 8. Students should not waste their time joining fraternities and sororities; they should concentrate on their academic coursework.

_____ 9. Bicycling is the only way to fully experience the beautiful scenery of southern France.

_____ 10. The hardware in a computer system includes the physical system itself, which may consist of a keyboard, a monitor, a central processing unit (CPU), and a printer.

EXERCISE 7-8 DETECTING BIAS 2

Directions: *Read the following passage and underline words and phrases that reveal the author's bias*

The Beatles caught on as no group ever did—before or since. Young women proved to be their most enthusiastic fans, some even fainting from sheer ecstasy. They were mobbed wherever they went. Sales of their records hit the stratosphere. Older audiences, as with Elvis, shook their heads in despair over the decline of not only music but of an entire generation. The Beatles knew perfectly well they were performing for a young audience who wanted the *new*. The well-groomed foursome—John, Paul, George, and Ringo—with the unfamiliar new style, not to mention a repertoire destined to take its place among the all-time classics, appealed almost uncontrollably to a rising subculture of "hippies," young people who championed freedom from all social and moral restraints. In all of its phases since the 1950s, rock has retained its revolutionary social battle cry.

—Janaro and Altshuler, *The Art of Being Human*, p. 183

7e　HOW STRONG ARE THE DATA AND EVIDENCE?

LEARNING OBJECTIVE 5
Evaluate data and evidence

Many writers who express their opinions or state viewpoints provide the reader with data or evidence to support their ideas. Your task as a critical reader is to weigh and evaluate the quality of this evidence. You must examine the evidence and assess its adequacy. You should be concerned with two factors: the type of evidence being presented, and the relevance of that evidence. Types of evidence include:

- personal experience or observation
- expert opinion
- research citation
- statistical data
- examples, descriptions of particular events, or illustrative situations
- analogies (comparisons with similar situations)
- historical documentation
- quotations
- description

Each type of evidence must be weighed in relation to the statement it supports. Acceptable evidence should directly, clearly, and indisputably support the case or issue in question.

EXERCISE 7-9 EVALUATING DATA AND EVIDENCE

Directions: *Refer to the article "Treating Wounded Soldiers: Polytrauma," on page 44. For each of the following paragraphs, identify the type(s) of evidence the author provides.*

1. Paragraph 1 _____

2. Paragraph 4 _____

3. Paragraph 5 _____

4. Paragraph 7 _____

7f   HOW IS CONNOTATIVE LANGUAGE USED?

LEARNING OBJECTIVE 6
Understand connotative language

Which of the following would you like to be a part of: a crowd, mob, gang, audience, congregation, gathering, or class? Each of these words has the same basic meaning: "an assembled group of people." But each has a different *shade* of meaning. *Crowd* suggests a large, disorganized group. *Audience*, on the other hand, suggests a quiet, controlled group. Try to decide what meaning each of the other words in the list suggests.

This example shows that words have two levels of meanings—a literal meaning and an additional shade of meaning. A word's **denotation** is the meaning stated in the dictionary—its literal meaning. A word's **connotations** are the additional implied meanings, or nuances, that the word takes on. Often a connotation carries either a positive or negative, favorable or unfavorable impression. The words *mob* and *gang* have negative connotations because they imply disorderly, disorganized groups. *Congregation, gathering, audience,* and *class* have positive connotations because they suggest orderly, organized groups.

Here are a few more examples. Would you prefer to be described as "slim" or "skinny"? As "intelligent" or "brainy"? As "heavy" or "fat"? As "particular" or "picky"? Notice that each pair of words has a similar literal meaning, but that each word within the pair has a different connotation.

Depending on the words they choose, writers can suggest favorable or unfavorable impressions of the person, object, or event they are describing. For example, through the writer's choice of words, the two sentences below create two entirely different impressions. As you read them, notice the underlined words. Does each have a positive connotation or a negative connotation?

> The unruly crowd forced its way through the restraint barriers and ruthlessly attacked the rock star.
> The enthusiastic group of fans burst through the fence and rushed toward the rock star.

When reading any type of informative or persuasive material, pay attention to the writer's choice of words. Often a writer may communicate subtle or hidden messages, or he or she may encourage the reader to have positive or negative feelings toward the subject.

EXERCISE 7-10 USING CONNOTATIVE LANGUAGE 1

Directions: *For each of the following pairs of words, underline the word with the more positive connotation.*

1. request   demand
2. overlook   neglect
3. ridicule   tease
4. display   expose
5. garment   gown
6. gaudy   showy
7. artificial   fake
8. costly   extravagant
9. choosy   picky
10. seize   take

EXERCISE 7-11 USING CONNOTATIVE LANGUAGE 2

Directions: *For each of the following sentences, underline the word in parentheses that has the more appropriate connotative meaning. Consult a dictionary, if necessary.*

1. The new superintendent spoke (extensively / enormously) about the issues facing the school system.

2. The day after we hiked ten miles, my legs felt extremely (rigid /stiff).

3. Carlos thought that he could be more (productive / fruitful) if he had a home office.

4. The (stubborn /persistent) ringing of the telephone finally woke me up.

5. The investment seemed too (perilous /risky) so we decided against it.

7g   HOW IS FIGURATIVE LANGUAGE USED?

LEARNING OBJECTIVE 7
Interpret figurative language

Figurative language is a way of describing something that makes sense on an imaginative level but not on a literal or factual level. Many common expressions are figurative:

> The exam was a piece of cake.
>
> Sam eats like a horse.
>
> He walks like a gazelle.

In each of these expressions, two unlike objects are compared on the basis of some quality they have in common. Take, for example, Hamlet's statement "I will speak daggers to her, but use none." Here Shakespeare is comparing the features of daggers (sharp, pointed, dangerous, harmful) with something that can be used like daggers—words.

Figurative language is striking, often surprising, even shocking. This reaction is created by the unlikeness of the two objects being compared. To find the similarity and understand the figurative expression, focus on connotative meanings rather than literal meanings. For example, in reading the lines

> In every cry of every man . . .
>
> The mind-forg'd manacles* I hear.

from a William Blake poem, you must think not only of handcuffs but also of their characteristics: restraint, limitation, loss of freedom. Then you can see that the lines mean that people's cries reveal the restraints created by the mind. Figurative words and phrases, which are also called **figures of speech**, are used to communicate and emphasize relationships that cannot be communicated through literal meaning. For example, the statement by Jonathan Swift, "She wears her clothes as if they were thrown on by a pitchfork," creates a stronger image and conveys a more meaningful description than saying "She dressed sloppily."

The two most common types of figurative expressions are similes and metaphors. Similes make the comparison explicit by using the word *like* or *as*. Metaphors, on the other hand, directly equate the two objects. Here are several examples of each.

- **Similes**

> We lie back to back. Curtains
>
> lift and fall,
>
> like the chest of someone sleeping.
>
> —Kenyon

*****manacles** handcuffs, shackles

> Life, like a dome of many-colored glass,
> stains the white radiance of Eternity.
>
> —Shelley

● **Metaphors**

> All the world's a stage,
> And all the men and women merely players.
> They have their exits and their entrances,
> And one man in his time plays many parts,
> His acts being seven ages.
>
> —William Shakespeare
>
> . . . his hair lengthened into sunbeams . . .
>
> —Gustave Flaubert

EXERCISE 7-12 USING FIGURATIVE LANGUAGE 1

Directions: *Each of the following sentences uses figurative language. For each figurative expression, write the letter of the choice that best explains its meaning.*

_____ 1. Craig looked like a deer caught by headlights when I found him eating the last piece of pie.

    a. startled into immobility

    b. worried he would be injured

    c. comfortable in the spotlight

    d. ready to be admired

_____ 2. Rosa was walking on air after she learned that she had made the dean's list.

    a. hurrying

    b. happy and lighthearted

    c. unable to get her footing

    d. numb

_____ 3. Throughout my grandmother's life, her church has been her rock.

    a. hard

    b. unfeeling

    c. source of strength

    d. heavy weight

_____ 4. Our computer is a dinosaur.

    a. very large

    b. frightening

    c. unique

    d. outdated

_____ 5. The food at the sales meeting tasted like cardboard.

    a. artificial

    b. tasteless

    c. stiff

    d. sturdy

EXERCISE 7-13 USING FIGURATIVE LANGUAGE 2

Directions: *Study the figurative expression in each of the following statements. Then, in the space provided, explain the meaning of each.*

1. Hope is like a feather, ready to blow away.

    _____

    _____

    _____

2. Once Alma realized she had made an embarrassing error, the blush spread across her face like spilled paint.

    _____

    _____

    _____

3. A powerboat, or any other sports vehicle, is a hungry animal that devours money.

    _____

    _____

    _____

4. Sally's skin was like a smooth, highly polished apple.

_____

_____

_____

5. Upon hearing the news, I took shears and shredded my dreams.

_____

_____

_____

7h HOW RELIABLE ARE PRINTED AND ELECTRONIC SOURCE MATERIALS?

LEARNING OBJECTIVE 8
Think critically about source materials

Throughout your college career, you will be consulting a wide variety of resources, both printed and electronic. These include, but are not limited to, books, magazines, newspapers, journals, dictionaries, monographs (academic papers on a single, focused topic), encyclopedias, online databases, and Web sites. Before the rise of the Internet, most printed materials were professionally written and edited. Now, desktop publishing and other technologies permit writers to publish their own work, whether it is accurate or not. Anyone can start and maintain a Web site, and anyone can adjust a Wikipedia entry.

All of this means that you must carefully determine the reliability of the sources you consult. You can do so by evaluating the source's content, accuracy, authority, timeliness, and objectivity.

Evaluating Content

When evaluating the content of a source, carefully assess its appropriateness, its level of technical detail, its completeness, and its own sources and citations.

Appropriateness	To be worthwhile, a source should contain the information you need. It should answer one or more of your questions. If it does not answer your questions, search for a more useful source. Do not be shy about asking your instructor or a librarian for recommendations.

Level of technical detail	A useful source should contain a level of technical detail that is suited to your purpose. Some sites may provide only limited or basic information; others assume a level of background knowledge or technical sophistication that you lack. In many courses, your textbook will be your single best source of introductory information. It will provide the basic understanding you need. You can then use other sources to build on the foundation of knowledge provided by your textbook.
Completeness	Determine whether the source provides complete information on its topic. Does it address all aspects of the topic that you feel it should? For example, if a book about important American poets does not mention Walt Whitman, Robert Frost, or Emily Dickinson, then it is incomplete. In this case, you would be right to wonder about the qualifications of an author who leaves such important literary figures out of his discussion. Note, however, that no source can contain *everything*. Be sure to limit your topic accordingly so that your search for information does not become overwhelming.
Sources and Citations	Most reliable sources provide a list of their own sources. For example, many books provide a lengthy list of the books that the author consulted when writing the book. Credible research papers refer to the work of other researchers and their results in a Works Cited section at the end of the paper. Some Web sites (such as Wikipedia) provide links to sources. In general, the presence of a source list indicates a serious scholarly work. Works without citations or sources may be reliable, but they are just as likely to be opinion-based or biased.

Evaluating Accuracy

When writing an academic paper or preparing an academic presentation, it is important to find and use accurate information. Sources provide clues about the accuracy of the information they contains, so ask the following questions about each source you consult.

Can the information in the source be verified?	Compare the information you find with information from other sources on the same topic, either in print or online. If you find discrepancies, further research is called for.

Could the source be a parody?	Some sources that appear serious are actually spoofs, hoaxes, or satires designed to poke fun at topics and issues. An example is **www.theonion.com**. This Web site appears to offer legitimate information but actually provides political and social commentary through made-up (and often funny) stories, such as "Bo Obama Receives Visiting Dognitaries from Furuguay." There is no such thing as a dognitary, and there is no such place as Furuguay.
Is the information provided by an organization that is widely respected?	For instance, information provided by the United Nations, the U.S. Geological Survey, and the World Bank is widely considered accurate and reliable. The information provided in sources that are published by advocacy groups (that is, groups with a specific agenda, such as political parties or environmental-awareness organizations) may be (but is not necessarily) biased.
Is the information complete, condensed, or summarized?	If you find a summary of information, attempt to locate the original source. Original information is less likely to contain errors, and most instructors prefer students to use original sources in academic papers.

Evaluating Authority

Before quoting a source, use the following questions to evaluate the authority of the person or group presenting the information.

Who is the author?	Does the author have academic credentials from a reputable university? Does he or she work for an organization devoted to unbiased scholarship and research? If so, the source provides credible authority. In the case of a Web site or blog, is the author's name provided, or only the Webmaster's? (The Webmaster handles the technical details of a Web site but is not responsible for, and does not create, content.) If the author's name is not given, the site lacks authority. If the author's name is given, is the author an expert in his or her field? Is he or she professionally trained, unbiased, credible, and respected? If not, the information may not be trustworthy.
Does the author provide contact information?	Often, serious scholars and researchers provide an e-mail address or other contact information. As professional researchers, they wish to engage in a dialogue with readers and other interested parties. If a source does not provide contact information for the author, the source may not be reliable.

Who is the publisher or sponsor?	Is the publisher (of a printed work) or the sponsor (of a Web site) a private individual, an institution, a corporation, a government agency, or a nonprofit organization? A source's publisher or sponsor often suggests its purpose. For example, books published by a university press (such as Oxford University Press or Princeton University Press) have the approval of prestigious, highly respected universities behind them. A Web site sponsored by a local library may be designed by its librarians to help patrons learn to use the library's resources more effectively, while a Web site sponsored by Nike is designed to promote its products. Often, a Web site's URL (address) can help you identify the sponsor. For example, suppose you find a paper about Berlin during World War II on the Internet and you want to track its source. Its URL is **hti.math.uh.edu/curriculum/units/2004/01/04.01.09.php**. If you shorten this URL to **hti.math.uh.edu/**, you are taken to the University of Houston Teachers Institute, where this paper was submitted as a curriculum unit. In general, if a Web site's sponsor is not identified, the site lacks authority.

Evaluating Timeliness

In some disciplines, the foundations of knowledge never change. The human body is very much the same as it was hundreds of years ago; the principles of physics and the basic rules of mathematics have not changed much, either. In these disciplines, a book published in 1900 may be just as informative as a book published in 2014.

However, many books that represented the most current thinking or research when they were first published can become dated or even obsolete as new information comes to light. Such books may be useful for historical information, but in most academic areas—whether the business disciplines, the life sciences, or literary criticism—you will generally want to consult recently published materials.

The same holds true for Web sites. Although the Web often provides up-to-the-minute information, not all Web sites are current. Evaluate a Web site's timeliness by checking

- the date on which the materials were posted to the Web site
- the date when the site was last revised or updated
- the date when the links were last checked

Evaluating Objectivity

When consulting sources, be sure that they are objective—that is, that they treat the topic in a fair, unbiased manner. (See Section 7d, p. 202 for more about bias.) On the following page are a few questions to ask about each source.

What is the goal of the source?	Is it to present information or the results of research? Or is it to persuade you to accept a particular point of view or to take a specific action? If the source's goal is not to present information, you should question its objectivity.
Are opinions clearly identified?	An author is free to express opinions, but these opinions should be clearly identified as such. Look for words and phrases that identify ideas as opinions. (See Section 7a, p. 192 for a list of these words and phrases.) If a source presents opinions as facts or does not distinguish between facts and opinions, the source may be biased or unreliable.
Is the source actually advertising in disguise?	Be cautious of sources that present information to persuade you to purchase a product or service. If a selection in a newspaper looks like an article but has the word "advertisement" above it in small print, the information is likely biased. If a Web site resembles an infomercial you might see on television, be just as suspicious of it as you would be of an infomercial.

EXERCISE 7-14 EVALUATING WEB SITES

Directions: Conduct a Google search on a topic related to one of the courses you are taking this term. For instance, for a psychology course you might choose to search on the topic of "mental illness." Choose two Web sites to examine. Evaluate the content, accuracy, authority, timeliness, and objectivity of each.

SUMMARY OF LEARNING OBJECTIVES

| 1 | **Distinguish fact from opinion** **What are facts and opinions?** | Facts are verifiable statements; you can determine whether they are true or false. Opinions express attitudes, feelings, or personal beliefs. By distinguishing statements of fact from opinions you will know what ideas to accept or verify and which to question. |
| 2 | **Identify the author's purpose** **How can you identify the author's purpose?** | Authors usually address specific audiences. Depending on their purpose, authors adjust content, language, and method of presentation to suit their audience. Recognizing the author's purpose will help you to grasp meaning more quickly and evaluate the author's work. |

3	Evaluate tone What is tone and why is it useful to recognize it?	Tone refers to the attitude or feeling an author expresses about his or her subject. Recognizing tone will help you evaluate what the writer is attempting to accomplish through his or her writing.
4	Identify bias What is bias and why is it helpful to identify it?	Bias refers to an author's partiality toward a particular viewpoint. Recognizing bias will help you evaluate whether the author is providing objective, complete information or selectively presenting information that furthers his or her purpose.
5	Evaluate data and evidence What are data and evidence and why should you evaluate them?	Data and evidence are used to support statements, opinions, and viewpoints. By evaluating the data and evidence, you will be able to decide whether to accept a writer's position.
6	Understand connotative language What is connotative language and why should you analyze it?	Connotative language refers to a word's implied meanings or nuances. By analyzing connotative language you will uncover writers' efforts to create favorable or unfavorable impressions of their subjects.
7	Interpret figurative language What is figurative language an why should you analyze it?	Figurative language is a way of describing something that makes sense on an imaginative level but not on a literal level. It compares two unlike things that have some quality in common. By understanding figurative language you will more fully appreciate the writer's use of language and gain a fuller understanding of how the writer views his or her subject.
8	Think critically about source materials What factors should you consider in evaluating source materials?	To determine the reliability of the sources you consult, you must evaluate each source's content, accuracy, authority, timeliness, and objectivity.

8 Reading and Thinking Visually

If you preview this (or any other) textbook, you will probably notice many photos, figures, tables, and other learning aids. **Visual aids**, such as photographs, graphs, and illustrations, are common not only in college textbooks, but also in other reading materials, from magazines to Web sites to newspapers.

All visual aids share one goal: to illustrate concepts and help you understand them better. As a reader, your key goal is to extract important information from them. Visual aids work best when you read them *in addition to* the text, not *instead of* the text.

8a READING AND ANALYZING PHOTOGRAPHS

LEARNING OBJECTIVE 1
Read and analyze photographs

An old saying goes, "A picture is worth a thousand words." Photographs can help writers achieve many different goals. For example, photos can be used to

- **spark interest**
- **provide perspective**
- **elicit an emotional response**
- **introduce new ideas**
- **offer examples**

Just as you can learn specific techniques to improve your reading comprehension, you can use a process for reading and analyzing photos.

1. **First read the text that refers to the photo.** Photos are not a substitute for the text. They are meant to be examined *along with* the text. In fact, most textbooks will include specific references to each photo, usually directly after a key point. For example:

> A common term for a shantytown, especially in Latin American countries, is *favela* (Figure 8-1).

Examine the photo as soon as you see the reference. The photo will help you visualize the concept, making it easier to remember.

2. **Read the photo's title and/or caption.** The **caption** is the text that accompanies the photo. It is usually placed above, below, or to the side of the photo. The caption generally explains how the photo fits into the discussion.

3. **Ask: What is my first overall impression?** Because photos can be powerful, they are often chosen to elicit a strong reaction. Analyze your response to the photo. Ask yourself: Why has the author included this photo?

4. **Examine the details.** Look closely at the picture, examining both the foreground and the background. Details can provide clues regarding the date the photograph was taken and its location. For example, people's hairstyles and clothing often give hints as to the year or decade. Landmarks help point to location. If you saw a photo of a smiling couple with the Eiffel Tower in the background, you would know that the photo was taken in Paris, France.

5. **Look for connections to the textbook, society, or your life.** Ask yourself how the photo relates to what you are reading or to your own experiences. Putting the image in context will help you learn the concepts *and* help you prepare for exams.

Now apply this method to Figure 8-1 on page 218.

1. **Read the text that refers to the photo.** Note that this photo is from a geography textbook. The text it illustrates might read as follows:

> On the outskirts of many cities in developing countries are large shantytowns with no access to utilities or running water (see photo).

Note that the reference comes directly after a key point.

2. **Read the caption.** In reading the caption, you learn where the photo was taken (Rio de Janeiro, Brazil). You also learn key vocabulary terms: *favelas, barrios, colonias,* and *barriadas.*

3. **Examine your first impression.** This is clearly a settlement of some sort. The homes are built on a hill, and the surrounding area looks quite pleasant, with trees. But would you want to live here? Why or why not? (Most people probably would not want to live in a shantytown.)

4. **Examine the details.** In examining the details, you may notice the absence of power lines. What does this suggest about the income level of the people who live in a favela? Notice too the crowded conditions and the size of the houses. What do these details suggest about the people who live there? (All these details suggest the people are probably poor.)

FIGURE 8-1 PHOTOGRAPH FROM A GEOGRAPHY TEXTBOOK

A favela in Rio de Janeiro. Shantytowns are common in South American countries, where they often develop close to wealthy neighborhoods in big cities with large populations. These shantytowns are called *favelas, barrios, colonias, or barriadas.*

5. **Look for connections.** Thinking about connections to American society or your life, you might contrast the way poor people live in a favela to the way poor people live in the United States. How is this favela similar to low-income neighborhoods in U.S. cities? How is it different? It is similar in that many people live in a small area. It is different in that the setting is natural rather than urban.

EXERCISE 8-1 ANALYZING A PHOTOGRAPH

Directions: *Analyze the photo and answer the accompanying questions.*

1. What does the term "culturally diverse society" mean?

_____

_____

In a society as culturally diverse as the United States, companies try to ensure that their advertising is appealing to as many people as possible.

2. Which culturally diverse groups are represented in this photo?

   _____

   _____

3. What do the hairstyles and clothing of the people in the photo tell you about their income level? (Also notice the type of car being driven.)

   _____

   _____

4. What audience do you think the advertiser is trying to reach with this photo? For example, is this ad trying to appeal to senior citizens? To recent college graduates?

   _____

   _____

5. Can you think of any groups *not* represented in this photo?

   _____

   _____

8b   A GENERAL APPROACH TO READING GRAPHICS

LEARNING OBJECTIVE 2
Approach graphics

In addition to photographs, you will encounter many other types of graphics in your reading materials. These include

- tables
- graphs
- charts
- diagrams

- maps
- time lines
- infographics
- cartoons

Here is a step-by-step approach to reading graphics. As you read, apply each step to the graph shown in Figure 8-2.

FIGURE 8-2 A SAMPLE GRAPH

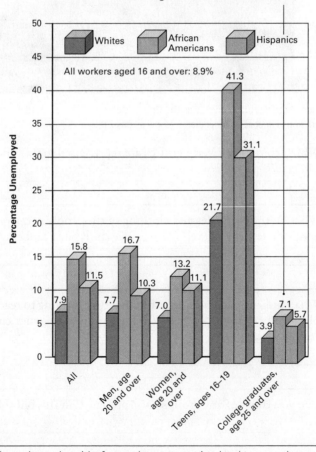

- The best strategy to reduce your risk of being without a job is to complete a college education.

All workers aged 16 and over: 8.9%

Although college graduates have a low risk of unemployment, race is related to unemployment for all categories of people.

Source: Macionis, *Society,* p. 313

1. **Look for the reference in the text.** The textbook author will refer you to each specific graphic. When you see the reference in the text, finish reading the sentence, and then look at the graphic. In some cases, you will need to go back and forth between the text and the graphic, especially if the graphic has multiple parts.

2. **Read the title and caption.** The title will identify the subject, and the caption will provide important information. In some cases, the caption will specify the key take-away point for the graphic.

3. **Examine how the graphic is organized.** Read all headings and labels. Sometimes a label is turned sideways, like the words "Percentage Unemployed" in Figure 8-2. Labels tell you what topics or categories are being discussed, and they are important. For example, if Figure 8-2 did not specify "Percentage," you might incorrectly think that the numbers along the left side are *numbers* of people instead of *percentages* of people.

4. **Look at the legend.** The **legend** is the guide to the colors, terms, and other important information in the graphic. In Figure 8-2, the legend appears at the top and shows blue for Whites, orange for African Americans, and green for Hispanics.

5. **Analyze the graphic.** Based on what you see, determine the graphic's key purpose. For example, is its purpose to show change over time, describe a process, present statistics? The purpose of Figure 8-2 is clear: it compares unemployment rates by age and race.

6. **Study the data to identify trends or patterns.** If the graphic includes numbers, look for unusual statistics or unexplained variations. For instance, note that the unemployment rate is highest for black teenagers, similar for men and women over age 20, and less than the national average for all college graduates. What conclusions can you draw from these observations?

7. **Make a brief summary note.** In the margin, jot a brief note summarizing the graphic's trend, pattern, or key point. Writing will help cement the idea in your mind. A summary note of Figure 8-2 might read, "Race and education are key factors in unemployment rates."

EXERCISE 8–2 READING GRAPHICS

Directions: Choose any graphic or visual aid from this chapter and go through it step-by-step, following the seven-step process outlined above.

8c   TABLES

LEARNING OBJECTIVE 3
Analyze tables

A **table** lists factual information in an organized manner, usually in rows or columns. Tables are often composed of numbers (Figure 8-3, page 222), but they can also contain words (Figure 8-4, page 223). Tables condense or summarize large amounts of data into an easily readable format, but they can sometimes seem over-whelming because they include so much information. To understand tables, follow a step-by-step process:

1. **Look for the reference in the text.**
2. **Determine how the information is divided and arranged.**
3. **Look for key data points, make comparisons, and determine trends.**
4. **Draw conclusions.**

FIGURE 8-3 A SAMPLE TABLE: NUMBERS

ESTIMATED DAILY CALORIE NEEDS

Calorie Range			
	Sedentary	→	Active
Children			
2–3 years old	1,000	→	1,400
Females			
4–8 years old	1,200	→	1,800
9–13	1,600	→	2,200
14–18	1,800	→	2,400
19–30	2,000	→	2,400
31–50	1,800	→	2,200
51+	1,600	→	2,200
Males			
4–8 years old	1,400	→	2,000
9–13	1,800	→	2,600
14–18	2,200	→	3,200
19–30	2,400	→	3,000
31–50	2,200	→	3,000
51+	2,000	→	2,800

Source: Donatelle, *Health,* p. 257

EXERCISE 8-3 READING TABLES

Directions: *Use Figures 8-3 and 8-4 to answer the following questions.*

FIGURE 8-3

Indicate whether each statement is true (T) or false (F).

_____ 1. Starting at age 4, males require more calories than females.

_____ 2. In general, those who lead more active lifestyles tend to need fewer calories.

_____ 3. The highest calorie requirements are needed by active females in the 14–30 age range.

FIGURE 8-4 A SAMPLE TABLE: WORDS

MAJOR STORE RETAILER TYPES

TYPE	DESCRIPTION	EXAMPLES
Specialty stores	Carry a narrow product line with a deep assortment, such as apparel stores, sporting-good stores, furniture stores, and florists.	Tiffany, Radio Shack, Williams-Sonoma
Department stores	Carry several product lines—typically clothing, home furnishings, and household goods—with each line operated as a separate department managed by specialist buyers.	Macy's, Sears, Neiman Marcus
Supermarkets	Relatively large, low-cost, low-margin, high-volume, self-service operations designed to serve the consumer's total needs for grocery and household products.	Kroger, Safeway, A&P, Stop & Shop, Hannaford
Convenience stores	Relatively small stores located near residential areas, open long hours seven days a week, and carrying a limited line of high-turnover convenience products at slightly higher prices.	7-Eleven, Wawa, Circle K, Sheetz
Discount stores	Carry standard merchandise sold at lower prices with lower margins and higher volumes.	Walmart, Target, Kohl's, Kmart
Off-price retailers	Sell merchandise bought at less-than-regular wholesale prices and sold at less than retail, often leftover goods, over-runs, and irregulars obtained at lower prices from manufacturers and other retailers. This category also includes retailers that sell items in bulk.	Home Goods, T.J. Maxx, Marshall's, Sam's Club, BJ's Wholesale Club
Superstores	Very large stores aimed at meeting consumers' total needs for routinely purchased food and nonfood items.	Walmart Supercenter, BestBuy, PetSmart

Source: Armstrong and Kotler, *Marketing,* p. 326

FIGURE 8-4

1. What type of store is a bookstore? _____

2. Into what category of store would factory outlets fall? _____

3. Provide an additional example of each of the seven types of stores in the table.

_____

_____

_____

4. At which type of store are you likely to pay a higher price for a gallon of milk: a supermarket or a convenience store? _____

8d   GRAPHS

LEARNING OBJECTIVE 4
Analyze graphs

A **graph** shows the relationship between two ideas, sometimes called *variables* because they can change depending on the circumstances. Graphs are extremely common in business and science textbooks and fall into two general categories:

- bar graphs
- line graphs

To understand a graph, do the following:

- **Read all the labels, which identify the variables.**
- **Read the legend, which explains how the information is presented.**
- **Summarize the graph's key points in a few sentences.**

Bar Graphs

Bar graphs illustrate relationships with thick bars. They are often used to make comparisons between amounts, and they are particularly useful for showing changes over time. In a well-constructed bar graph, it is easy to see key differences.

The bars shown on a bar graph can be either horizontal or vertical. Figure 8-5 is a simple vertical bar graph showing the importance of small business in the United States. Part (a) of the graph shows that almost 86 percent of all U.S. companies have fewer than 20 employees. Part (b) shows that 25.6 percent of U.S. workers work at a company with fewer than 20 employees. Note a special feature of this graph: the author has included a built-in note summarizing the key point.

FIGURE 8-5 A SAMPLE BAR GRAPH

THE IMPORTANCE OF SMALL BUSINESS IN THE UNITED STATES

*Almost 86 percent of all U.S. businesses have **no more than 20 employees.** The total number of people employed by these businesses is approximately one-fourth of the entire U.S. workforce. Another 29 percent work for companies with **fewer than 100 employees.***

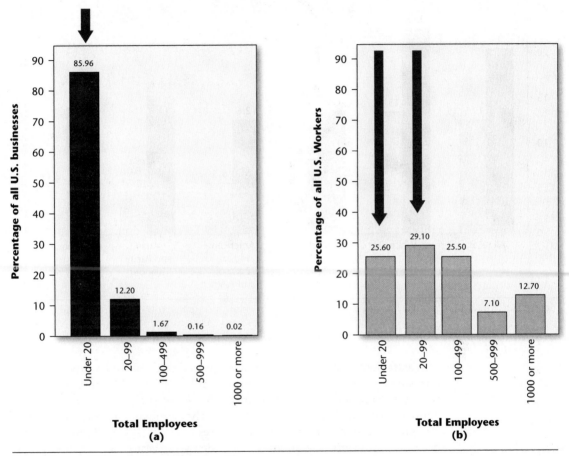

Source: Ebert and Griffin, *Business Essentials*, p. 38.

In a **multiple bar graph,** two or three comparisons are made simultaneously, which makes reading the labels and the legend particularly important. Figure 8-6 (p. 226) shows the breakdown of the elderly population in the United States by race and ethnicity. Note that two bars are included for each racial and ethnic group: the actual percentages for 1990, and the estimated percentages for 2050.

FIGURE 8-6 A SAMPLE MULTIPLE BAR GRAPH

PERCENTAGE OF ELDERLY, BY RACE AND ETHNICITY, 1990 AND 2050

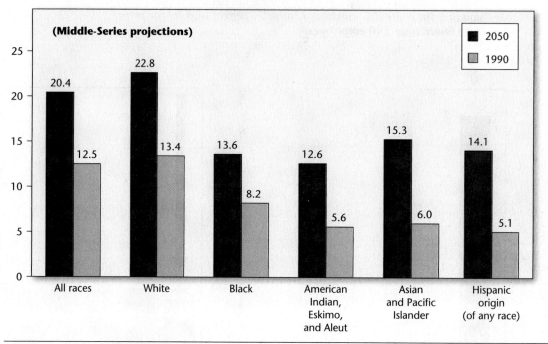

Source: Kunz, *THINK Marriages and Families*, p. 173

In a **stacked bar graph**, the bars are placed one on top of another rather than side by side. The goal is often to emphasize whole/part relationships (that is, the relationship of one part of the bar to the entire group or class). Figure 8-7 is a stacked bar graph showing the home regions and numbers of immigrants who moved to the United States from 1971 to 2008. By looking at the colors of the graph, you can see that the two largest groups of immigrants over this time period have come from Latin America and Asia.

Line Graphs

Line graphs connect data points along a line. Connecting points in this manner often gives a sense of trends or changes over time. Sometimes only one variable is shown in a line graph, but it is common to see line graphs with multiple variables, as in Figure 8-8, which shows how Americans' answer to the question "How much of the time do you think you can trust the government?" changed over the period 1958–2006.

FIGURE 8-7 A SAMPLE STACKED BAR GRAPH

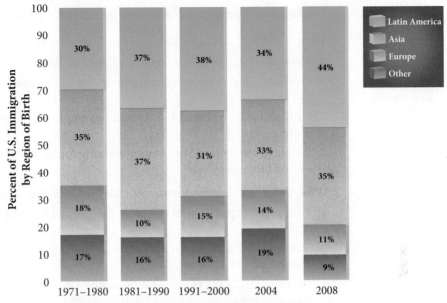

Because of rounding, percentages may not add up to 100.

Source: Thompson and Hickey, *Society in Focus,* p. 282

FIGURE 8-8 A SAMPLE LINE GRAPH

THE DECLINE OF TRUST IN GOVERNMENT, 1958–2006

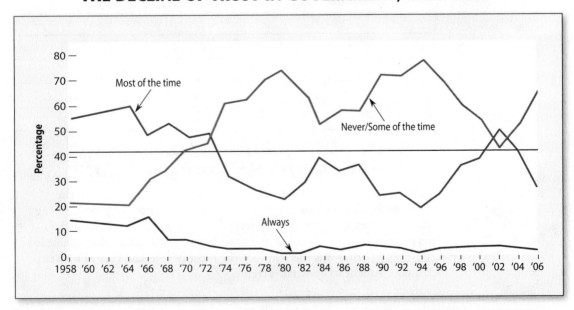

The graph shows how people have responded to the following question: How much of the time do you think can trust the government in Washington to do what is right—just about always, most of the time, or only some of the time?

Source: Edwards, Wattenberg, and Lineberry, *Government in America,* p. 201

EXERCISE 8-4 READING GRAPHS

Directions: *Use Figures 8-5 through 8-8 to answer the following questions.*

_____ 1. What is the best summary statement for **Figure 8-5** (p. 225)?

    a. Most U.S. businesses employ a minimum of 500 workers.

    b. Small businesses are more common in the United States than in Europe.

    c. Only about 2 percent of U.S. companies employ 100 workers or more.

    d. People in the United States enjoy working for small, family-owned businesses.

_____ 2. What is the best summary statement for **Figure 8-6** (p. 226)?

    a. The Hispanic population is growing significantly in the United States.

    b. The Hispanic population in the United States is expected to decrease between 1990 and 2050.

    c. There were roughly the same numbers of American Indians and Hispanic people in the United States in 1990.

    d. Regardless of race or ethnicity, the U.S. population is getting older, and elderly people will make up much larger chunks of the population in 2050 than in 1990.

3. Using **Figure 8-7** (p. 227), write a brief summary of the immigration patterns of Latin Americans, Asians, and Europeans from 1971 to 2008.

_____

_____

_____

_____

_____

_____

4. Use **Figure 8-8** (p. 227) to complete this statement:

The number of people saying they trust the government most of the time reached its peak in _____, while the number of people saying that they trust the government never or only some of the time reached its peak in _____. Absolute trust in government was the highest in _____; that was the year that the most people said they always trust the government to do what is right.

8e   CHARTS

LEARNING OBJECTIVE 5
Analyze charts

Unlike graphs, which illustrate two or more variables, a **chart** often focuses on illustrating just one variable or concept.

Pie Charts

Pie charts, also called *circle graphs*, show whole/part relationships. The pie or circle represents the whole (or 100 percent), and each "slice" of the pie represents a smaller part. Figure 8-9, a pie chart illustrating world religious affiliations, indicates that Christianity has more adherents than any other world religion.

FIGURE 8-9 A SAMPLE PIE CHART

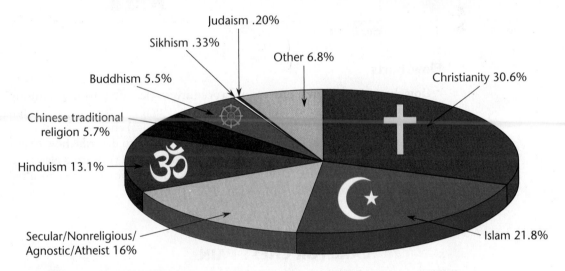

WORLD RELIGIOUS AFFILIATIONS

Judaism .20%
Sikhism .33%
Other 6.8%
Buddhism 5.5%
Chinese traditional religion 5.7%
Christianity 30.6%
Hinduism 13.1%
Secular/Nonreligious/ Agnostic/Atheist 16%
Islam 21.8%

Note: Total equals more than 100% due to rounding.

Source: Carl, *Think Sociology,* p. 271

Organizational Charts

Organizational charts divide an organization (such as a corporation, university, or hospital) into its administrative departments, staff positions, or lines of authority. Figure 8-10 (p. 230) shows an organization chart for a typical U.S. corporation. In general, bosses and other higher-ups appear higher in the chart, while lower-level workers appear lower on the chart.

FIGURE 8-10 A SAMPLE ORGANIZATIONAL CHART

ORGANIZATIONAL CHART OF A TYPICAL U.S. CORPORATION

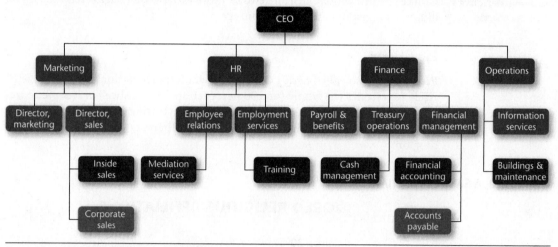

Source: Solomon, Poatsy, and Martin, *Better Business,* p. 205

Flowcharts

A **flowchart** shows how a process or procedure works, often from beginning to end. Lines or arrows indicate the direction in which to follow steps through the procedure. Various shapes (boxes, circles, rectangles) enclose what is done at each step. You could, for example, draw a flowchart to describe how to apply for a student loan or how to locate a malfunction in your car's electrical system. Figure 8-11 shows a flowchart for emergency medical technicians illustrating how to care for patients who have chest pain.

FIGURE 8-11 A SAMPLE FLOWCHART

CARE FOR CHEST PAIN

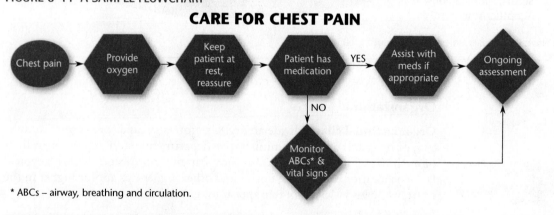

* ABCs – airway, breathing and circulation.

Source: Bergeron and Le Baudour, *First Responder,* p. 257

Many flowcharts flow from left to right, and some (such as Figure 8-11) have junction points at which you choose which path to follow based on your answer to a specific question. To check that you fully understand the process outlined in a flowchart, summarize it in your own words.

EXERCISE 8-5 READING CHARTS

Directions: *Use Figure 8-9 through Figure 8-11 to answer the following questions.*

_____ 1. According to **Figure 8-9** (p. 229), which of the following is not one of the world's top three religions in terms of the number of people practicing that religion?

    a. Judaism

    b. Islam

    c. Christianity

    d. Hinduism

_____ 2. According to **Figure 8-10** (p. 230), which of the following departments has the lowest rank in the company?

    a. payroll and benefits

    b. information services

    c. accounts payable

    d. employee relations

_____ 3. Which of the following is not part of caring for someone who has chest pain, according to **Figure 8-11** (p. 230)?

    a. keeping the patient at rest

    b. providing oxygen

    c. assessing whether the patient has medication or not

    d. applying pressure to the area of pain

8f DIAGRAMS

LEARNING OBJECTIVE 6
Analyze diagrams

A **diagram** is a simplified drawing showing the appearance, structure, or workings of something. Diagrams can have many purposes, including

- **to introduce key vocabulary**
- **to show the parts of a system**
- **to illustrate relationships**

Diagrams are common in technical and scientific books. They often correspond to fairly large segments of text, requiring you to switch back and forth frequently between the text and the diagram. Consider the following excerpt from a human anatomy textbook and the diagram that illustrates it:

> A **nail** is a scalelike modification of the epidermis that corresponds to the hoof or claw of other animals. Each nail has a *free edge*, a *body* (visible attached portion), and a *root* (embedded in the skin). The borders of the nail are overlapped by skin folds, called *nail folds*. The thick proximal nail is commonly called the *cuticle* (Figure 8-12). The *stratum basale* of the epidermis extends beneath the nail as the *nail bed*. Its thickened proximal area, called the *nail matrix*, is responsible for nail growth. The region over the thickened nail matrix that appears as a white crescent is called the *lunula*.
>
> —Marieb, *Essentials of Human Anatomy and Physiology*, p. 106

FIGURE 8-12 A SAMPLE DIAGRAM

THE STRUCTURE OF A NAIL

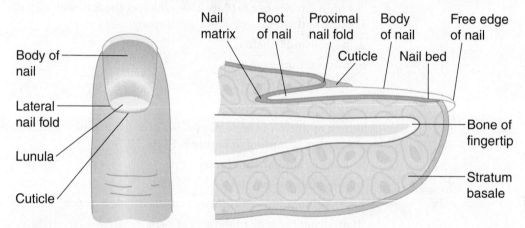

Structure of a nail. Surface view (left) and longitudinal section of the distal part of a finger (right), showing nail parts and the nail matrix that forms the nail.

Source: Mareib, *Essentials of Human Anatomy and Physiology,* p. 106

Because diagrams and their explanations are often complicated, plan on reading these sections more than once. Read first to grasp the overall process or structure. In subsequent readings, focus on the details or progression.

One of the best ways to study a diagram is to redraw it in as much detail as possible without referring to the original. Or, test your understanding and recall of the process outlined in a diagram by explaining it, step-by-step, in your own words.

Directions: *Use Figure 8-12 (p. 232) and the accompanying text discussion to answer the following questions.*

Indicate whether the following statement is true (T) or false (F).

_____ 1. The human fingernail is similar to a horse's hoof.

Select the best answer.

_____ 2. Most men cut their fingernails when the _____ extends beyond the finger.
   a. lunula
   b. cuticle
   c. free edge
   d. nail matrix

_____ 3. Which of the following is not a part of the human fingernail?
   a. stratum basale
   b. free edge
   c. root
   d. body

8g   MAPS AND TIME LINES

LEARNING OBJECTIVE 7
Analyze maps and time lines

Maps and time lines are used to show how information is related in terms of place and time.

Maps

Maps describe relationships and provide information about location and direction. They are commonly found in geography, history, and economics texts. They can cover a very small area (for example, just one block in a city) or an area as large as the entire world.

While we often think of maps as showing distances and place names, they are also used to show the distribution of all kinds of data—public opinion, population concentration, area in which a particular language is spoken, and so on. When reading maps, use the following steps:

1. **Read the title and caption,** which will identify the subject of the map.
2. **Use the legend or key to identify the symbols or codes used.**
3. **Note the *scale*, which explains how distances on the map correspond to distances in the real world.** For example, a map may be scaled so that one inch on the map represents one mile.

4. **Study the map, looking for trends.** Often the text accompanying the map states the key points.

5. **Write, in your own words, a statement of what the map shows.**

Figure 8-13 is a map showing the U.S. states with the highest numbers of millionaires. Note that the person who created the map has built in study questions to help you read and analyze it.

FIGURE 8-13 A SAMPLE MAP

MILLIONAIRES IN THE UNITED STATES

More wealth is located on the coasts – Washington, California, New York, Pennsylvania, Florida, and New Jersey have the highest number of millionaires.

Texas
• One of the richest states with the 9th highest poverty rate. Why might this be?

New York
• 368,388 millionaires live in New York
• Has the 15th highest poverty rate in the United States, which could be related to Wilson's claim that urban areas are prone to higher poverty.

Number of millionaires in the United States, by State

0-49,999   50,000-99,999   100,000-199,999   200,000-700,000

Source: Carl, *Think Sociology*, p. 122

Time Lines

A **time line** is a graphic representation of the passage of time as a line. Very common in history textbooks, time lines can help you keep track of key dates, social movements, and trends. Time lines usually focus on major events and are extremely useful for learning the "big picture," but they generally do not provide a lot of detail. To fully understand what is happening in a time line, you must read the accompanying text. Figure 8-14 is a time line showing the birth and development of feminism (women's rights) in the United States.

FIGURE 8-14 A SAMPLE TIME LINE

The History of Feminism

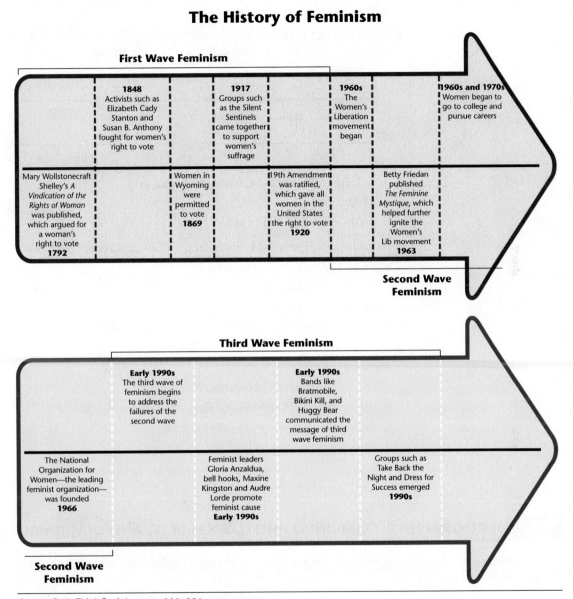

Source: Carl, *Think Sociology*, pp. 200–201

Directions: *Use Figures 8-13 (p. 234) and 8-14 above to answer the following questions.*

_____ 1. According to **Figure 8-13**, which of the following states has the smallest number of millionaires?

a. New Jersey   c. Florida

b. Montana   d. Texas

2. According to **Figure 8-13**, Texas is one of the richest states in the United States, but it also has the ninth highest poverty rate.

a. What might explain the wealth?

_____

b. What might explain the poverty?

_____

_____

_____ 3. According to **Figure 8-14**, feminism began in

a. 1792.   c. 1920.

b. 1860.   d. 1966.

_____ 4. According to **Figure 8-14**, the earliest feminism was concerned with

a. equal pay for men and women.

b. women's right to vote.

c. women's right to attend college.

d. women's right to inherit wealth from their parents.

_____ 5. Which was not a key event in the history of feminism, according to **Figure 8-14**?

a. the publication of *The Feminine Mystique*

b. the founding of the National Organization for Women

c. the ratification of the 1st Amendment

d. women's attending college and pursuing careers

8h   INFOGRAPHICS: COMBINED PHOTOS, CHARTS, AND DIAGRAMS

LEARNING OBJECTIVE 8
Analyze infographics

Graphic designers are always looking for new, visually interesting ways to present information. In recent years, a new type of visual aid called an *infographic* has become popular. While the definition is not precise, **infographics** usually combine several types of visual aids into one, often merging photos with text, diagrams, or tables.

Unlike other graphics, infographics are sometimes designed to stand on their own; they do not necessarily repeat what is in the text. Consider the following excerpt from a health textbook:

> Within our society, some gender-specific communication patterns are obvious to the casual observer. Recognizing these differences and how they make us unique is a good step in avoiding unnecessary frustrations and irritations.
>
> —Donatelle, *My Health*, p. 73

Figure 8-15 lists many differences in male and female communication styles, which are *not* listed in the text. To understand this material, you must carefully read and learn the infographic, because the information cannot be found in the text.

FIGURE 8-15 A SAMPLE INFOGRAPHIC

HE SAYS/SHE SAYS

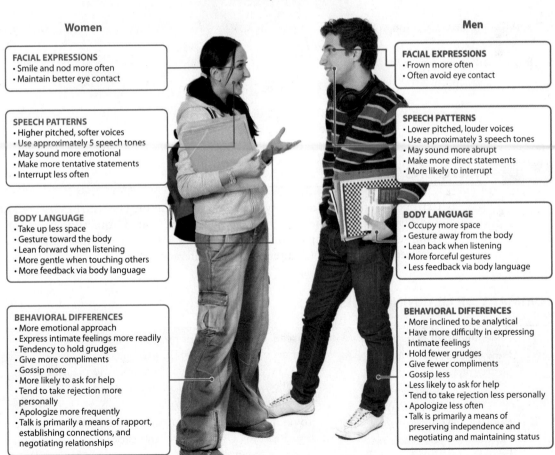

Women

FACIAL EXPRESSIONS
- Smile and nod more often
- Maintain better eye contact

SPEECH PATTERNS
- Higher pitched, softer voices
- Use approximately 5 speech tones
- May sound more emotional
- Make more tentative statements
- Interrupt less often

BODY LANGUAGE
- Take up less space
- Gesture toward the body
- Lean forward when listening
- More gentle when touching others
- More feedback via body language

BEHAVIORAL DIFFERENCES
- More emotional approach
- Express intimate feelings more readily
- Tendency to hold grudges
- Give more compliments
- Gossip more
- More likely to ask for help
- Tend to take rejection more personally
- Apologize more frequently
- Talk is primarily a means of rapport, establishing connections, and negotiating relationships

Men

FACIAL EXPRESSIONS
- Frown more often
- Often avoid eye contact

SPEECH PATTERNS
- Lower pitched, louder voices
- Use approximately 3 speech tones
- May sound more abrupt
- Make more direct statements
- More likely to interrupt

BODY LANGUAGE
- Occupy more space
- Gesture away from the body
- Lean back when listening
- More forceful gestures
- Less feedback via body language

BEHAVIORAL DIFFERENCES
- More inclined to be analytical
- Have more difficulty in expressing intimate feelings
- Hold fewer grudges
- Give fewer compliments
- Gossip less
- Less likely to ask for help
- Tend to take rejection less personally
- Apologize less often
- Talk is primarily a means of preserving independence and negotiating and maintaining status

Source: Donatelle, *My Health*, p. 73

EXERCISE 8-8 READING INFOGRAPHICS

Directions: *Use Figure 8-15 (p. 237) to complete the following table. Check off which characteristics are more common in men and which are more common in women. The first answer has been provided for you.*

CHARACTERISTIC	MORE COMMON IN MEN	MORE COMMON IN WOMEN
1. Apologizing		√
2. Leaning forward while listening		
3. Using approximately 3 speech tones		
4. Asking for help		
5. Interrupting		
6. Frowning		
7. Providing feedback through body language		
8. Taking rejection personally		

8i   CARTOONS

Cartoons express an idea and make a point with humor. They can be very broad and easy to understand, or very subtle and complicated. Analyzing cartoons requires you to pick up on unstated messages. For more information about unstated messages, see Chapter 6, Making Inferences.

SUMMARY OF LEARNING OBJECTIVES

1	Read and analyze photographs How do you read and interepret photographs?	To read and analyze a photograph, first read the text that accompanies the photo and the photo caption. Examine your first overall impression and the details of the photo. Then look for connections to the reading selection, to society, or to your life.
2	Approach graphics How should you read and interpret graphics?	To understand a graphic, first look for a reference in the text. Read the graphic's title and caption, and examine how it is organized. Look at the legend and analyze the graphic, studying the data to indentify trends or patterns. Then make brief summary notes.

3	Analyze tables What is a table and how do you analyze it?	A table lists facts in an organized manner, usually in rows or columns. To understand tables, first look for the reference in the text, then determine how the information in the table is divided and arranged. Look for key data points, make comparisons, determine trends, and draw conclusions.
4	Analyze graphs What is a graph and how do you analyze them?	A graph shows the relationship between two ideas or variables. To analyze a graph, first read the labels and identify the variables. Then read the legend, which explains how the information is presented. Finally, summarize the graph's key points in a few sentences.
5	Analyze charts What is a chart and how do you analyze them?	A chart usually illustrates just one variable or concept. Use the overall approach to graphics to analyze pie charts, organizational charts, and flowcharts, ensuring that you read the chart in the correct order (if a specific order is specified).
6	Analyze diagrams What is a diagram and how do you analyze them?	A diagram is a simplified drawing showing the appearance, structure, or workings of something. Diagrams introduce key vocabulary, show parts of a system, and/or illustrate relationships. When reading a diagram, go back and forth between the diagram and the text that accompanies it. Plan to read the diagram more than once, and test your understanding by explaining the diagram, step-by-step, in your own words.
7	Analyze maps and time lines What are maps and timelines and how do you analyze them?	A map describes relationships and provides information about direction and location. To analyze a map, read the title, caption, and legend. Note the map's scale, look for trends, and write a summary statement. A time line is a graphic representation of the passage of time as a line, which helps organize key dates, social movements, and trends. To fully understand what is happening in a time line, be sure to read the accompanying text closely.
8	Analyze infographics What are infographics and how do you analyze them?	Infographics combine several types of visual aids into one. Unlike other graphics, they sometimes stand on their own. In these cases, you must carefully read and analyze them as if they were included within the reading selection, because they provide information not found in the text.

Readings for Academic Disciplines

PART

TWO

Introduction: Reading Across the Disciplines

Brian was a first-year student taking a full-time course load: Introductory Psychology, College Writing, Biology, and World History. He had received good grades in high school and was confident he would do well at a community college where he was majoring in pre-elementary education. After about the fourth week of the term, Brian realized he was not doing as well as he expected to do in his courses. He spent approximately 30 hours per week studying but was not earning top grades. He got C's on three biology labs, a B minus on a response essay for his writing class, a 70 on his first history exam, and 65, 75, and 70 on the first three psychology quizzes. Brian knew he would probably pass all of his courses, but his goal was to earn grades that would ensure his transfer to a four-year college of his choice.

Brian visited the campus Academic Skills Center and requested tutors for three of his courses. After the first few tutoring sessions he realized that his tutors used a unique approach to each of the disciplines. Specifically, they seemed to read, study, and think differently in each. Brian learned to vary his approach to the material he was studying in different courses. Before, he had studied each course the same way; now he has realized that different disciplines require specialized thinking skills.

Brian's realization is confirmed by a national research study titled "Understanding University Success"; it identified the critical thinking skills essential to success in various disciplines. The table on the facing page demonstrates that different disciplines require different types of thinking and includes many of the skills identified in the research study. Read the table to get an idea of the types of thinking skills involved in each disciplinary grouping.

READINGS FOR ACADEMIC DISCIPLINES

Each college course you take will be different; in each you will be asked to master a unique set of information, learn new terminology, and demonstrate what you have learned. This section of the text provides you with opportunities to practice reading material from a wide range of disciplines, learn new terminology, and demonstrate your mastery of content through a variety of test-taking methods.

ADAPTING YOUR THINKING TO ACADEMIC DISCIPLINES

DISCIPLINE	SPECIALIZED TYPES OF THINKING REQUIRED	EXAMPLES
Social Sciences (sociology, psychology, anthropology, economics)	Evaluate ideas, make generalizations, be aware of bias, follow and evaluate arguments	Studying patterns of child development, examining causes of age discrimination, comparing cultures
Mathematics	Think sequentially, reason logically, evaluate solutions	Solving word problems, understanding theorems
Natural and Life Sciences (biology, chemistry, physiology, physics, astronomy, earth science)	Grasp relationships, ask questions, understand processes, evaluate evidence	Studying the theory of evolution, examining the question of life in outer space
Arts (literature, music, painting, sculpture)	Evaluate the work of others, express your own ideas, critique your own work	Evaluating a sculpture, revising a musical score
Applied Fields (career fields, technology, business)	Follow processes and procedures, make applications, make and evaluate decisions	Evaluating a patient (nursing), finding a bug in a computer program (computer technology)

Part Two contains 30 readings, three readings for each of the following disciplines: social sciences, communication/speech, arts/humanities/literature, political science/government/history, business/advertising/economics, technology/computers, health-related fields, life sciences, physical sciences/mathematics, and career fields.

When taking courses in these fields, you will read textbooks, but you will also read a variety of print and online sources, as well. To give you practice reading a wide range of sources, most chapters in Part Two contain one textbook reading and two non-textbook readings. The readings are preceded by information, tips, and questions intended to guide your reading. They are followed by questions that will help you evaluate your reading and practice with different test-taking formats. The types of questions and activities are intended to prepare you for future work in the different disciplines. They are in different formats so as to familiarize you with the variety of testing and evaluation methods used in these disciplines. Included are multiple-choice, fill-in-the-blank, true/false, and matching tests, as well as open-ended questions and brief writing assignments. Here is a review of the types of questions and activities you will work with.

- **Understanding the Thesis and Other Main Ideas.** These questions help you identify the most important information in each reading.
- **Identifying Details.** These questions help you discover the relationship between main ideas and details and distinguish between more and less important details.

- **Recognizing Methods of Organization and Transitions.** This activity guides you in discovering organizational patterns and using transitions.
- **Reviewing and Organizing Ideas.** This activity shows you how to learn the material in a reading. You will learn and practice a number of different review and study strategies, including mapping, summarizing, outlining, and paraphrasing.
- **Reading and Thinking Visually.** These questions help you examine graphic elements and integrate them with the rest of your reading.
- **Figuring Out Implied Meanings and Thinking Critically.** These two sections demonstrate the types of thinking and reasoning that are expected in college courses. The questions take you beyond the literal (factual) content of the selection and guide you in applying many of the critical thinking skills you learned in Part One.
- **Building Vocabulary.** This section gives you practice in learning the terminology that is an essential part of each new academic discipline. You will learn how to use both context and word parts to master new terminology.
- **Selecting a Learning/Study Strategy.** Choosing appropriate learning and study methods is important in every discipline. This activity guides you in identifying appropriate ways to learn and study the material in a selection.
- **Exploring Ideas Through Discussion and Writing.** Because class participation is an important part of many college courses, this activity provides topics that can be used for class discussion. As many college courses involve writing papers and research reports and taking written exams, this activity also provides an opportunity for you to begin to apply your writing skills to various disciplines.
- **Beyond the Classroom to the Web.** Many instructors expect their students to extend and apply their learning to situations outside the classroom. This activity extends your learning beyond the reading selection and provides ways you can use or apply new information.

9 Social Sciences

The **social sciences** are concerned with the study of people, their history and development, and how they interact and function together. These disciplines deal with the political, economic, social, cultural, and behavioral aspects of people. Social scientists study how we live, how we act, how we dress, how we get along with others, and how our culture is similar to and different from other cultures. By reading in the social sciences, you will learn a great deal about yourself and those around you. In "A Surveillance Society" you will read about how surveillance cameras make our daily activities more public. In "Child-free by Choice" you will read about the current trend for couples to choose not to have children. "Are Sports Fans Happier?" examines a major social institution—sports—and discusses the social benefits of following sports (athletes and teams). Use the following tips when reading in the social sciences.

TIPS FOR READING IN THE SOCIAL SCIENCES

- **Pay attention to terminology.** The social sciences use precise terminology to describe their subject matter. Learn terms that describe behavior, name stages and processes, and label principles, theories, and models. Also learn the names of important researchers and theorists. As you read, highlight new terms. You can transfer them later to index cards or a vocabulary log for that course.
- **Understand explanations and theories.** The social sciences are devoted, in part, to explaining how and why people behave as they do. In this chapter you will read an explanation of the reasons people decide not to have children, for example. As you read theories and explanations, ask these questions: What behavior is being explained? What evidence is offered that it is correct? Of what use is the explanation?
- **Look for supporting evidence.** As you read, look for details, examples, anecdotes, or research evidence that demonstrates that the writer's explanations are reasonable or correct. For example, when reading "Are Sports Fans Happier?" look for the scientific evidence the author provides to support his main ideas. Often, too, in the social sciences, the examples and applications are highly interesting and will help you remember the theories they illustrate.
- **Make comparisons and connections.** Try to see relationships and make comparisons. Draw connections between topics. Sketch charts or maps that compare different explanations, and closely examine the visual aids that accompany the reading.
- **Make practical applications.** As you read, consider how the information is useful to you in real-life situations. Make marginal notes of situations that illustrate what you are reading about. Write comments, for example, about what you have observed about surveillance in our society, adults without children, and sports fans.

245

SELECTION 1

A Surveillance Society

William E. Thompson and Joseph V. Hickey

TEXTBOOK EXCERPT
Contemporary Issues Reading

This reading selection from a textbook titled *Society in Focus* describes the increasing use of surveillance systems in public places. Read the selection to discover the benefits and risks of high-tech surveillance.

PREVIEWING THE READING

Using the steps listed on pages 40–41, preview the reading selection. When you have finished, complete the following items.

1. What is the subject of this selection? _____

2. List four questions you expect to be able to answer after reading this selection.

    a. _____

    b. _____

    c. _____

    d. _____

 MAKING CONNECTIONS

Think about public places in which you have noticed security cameras. Do these cameras make you feel safer? Why or why not?

READING TIP

As you read, look for and highlight the risks and benefits of surveillance systems.

A Surveillance Society

1   The cameras are familiar to most people, perhaps even comforting to some. They are perched high atop almost every lamppost, rooftop, and streetlight. Elsewhere, they are undetectable, except to the authorities. Video cameras are never turned off. They pan up and down, left and right, surveying traffic, pedestrians, and everything else in public view, day and night.

Here, a surveillance camera is disguised as a light.

Growing Trends

2   You might be thinking that this scene offers a glimpse of the future. Perhaps it is a dark, futuristic vision, much like George Orwell's nightmare of **Big Brother** monitoring and controlling people's lives down to the smallest details. But by now you are aware that *things are not necessarily what they seem.*

Big Brother
a fictional character from George Orwell's futuristic novel *Nineteen Eighty-Four*

3   This is not some grim, dystopian vision of the future, but a growing trend almost everywhere in the world—including most shopping malls and stores, almost all government and corporate offices, and many other social arenas. In the name of public security, the British have been most active of all nations in installing surveillance monitoring systems. In the beginning, they were tried in a handful of "trouble spots." Now more than 4.2 million cameras have been installed throughout Britain, and the average Londoner can expect his or her picture to be taken hundreds of times each day. Alarmed at the amount of surveillance and the astonishing amount of personal data that is hoarded by the state and by commercial organizations, Ross Clark asks whom should we fear most: the government agencies that are spying on us or the criminals who seem to prosper in the swirling fog of excessive data collection?

4   Since the 9/11 terrorist attacks, the United States has been trying to catch up. Times Square in New York and the nation's capital have seen a proliferation of surveillance cameras installed in public places. Experiments in face-recognition technology have been expanded, and "photo radar" that uses cameras and computers to photograph license plates, identify traffic violators, and issue citations is catching on as well. And in all cases, the technology has also grown more sophisticated. The USA PATRIOT Act, passed after 9/11 and renewed in 2006, expanded the government's authority to "spy" on private citizens.

5   In the private sector, cameras and computers are abundant and socially accepted. Today, there are millions of tiny private security cameras at hotels, malls, parking lots—everywhere businesses and shoppers can be found. The new digital surveillance systems are more sophisticated than those from just a few years ago. Today's technology not only can scan businesses and malls, but also analyze what it is watching and recording and, if something is unusual, alert security. Likewise, digital security systems can now record, store, and index images, making it possible for security personnel to "instantly retrieve images of every person who passed through a door on any given day."

Surveillance Technologies

6   High-tech surveillance devices are becoming more common across the urban landscape. Although many people may be wary of these devices, few are aware that they are but a small part of surveillance technologies that now routinely monitor all of our personal histories, daily routines, and tastes. And 9/11 and global terrorist threats have increased public willingness for added security and new surveillance technologies.

7   Police and military surveillance is impressive—with video scanners, electronic ankle monitors, night-vision goggles, and pilotless airborne spy vehicles, to name just a few. But high-tech surveillance has expanded well beyond the police and military to thousands of corporations, government agencies, and even individuals who routinely monitor the workplace, marketplace, and almost all other social arenas. As one sociologist noted, "Being able to hide and remain anonymous has become more difficult . . . we are moving toward a glass village in which everyone is available for view online."

Information Sharing

8   Today, corporations and government agencies routinely share databases. In "computer matching," organizations swap back and forth personal information on different kinds of populations and combine them to suit their own needs. The Pentagon's "Total Information Awareness Program" is one of the most ambitious plans to combine computer databases. The Pentagon maintains that it relies mainly on information from government, law enforcement, and intelligence databases to "forestall terrorism," but its use of other kinds of data—like personal financial and health records—remains unresolved. Critics argue that because such a system could (and some say already has) tap into e-mail, culling records, and credit card and banking transactions as well as travel documents, it poses a direct threat to civil liberties.

9   Similar arguments were made after the passage of the USA PATRIOT Act in 2001, which gave the government the right to "search suspected terrorists' library records—and add them to government databases—without the patron ever knowing." By early 2002, one study found that over 85 libraries had already been asked for information on patrons in connection with the 9/11 investigation.

10   Post-9/11 surveillance surfaced as a controversial political issue in 2006 when it was discovered that after the 9/11 attacks the government gave approval to the highly secretive National Security Agency (NSA) to solicit phone records of private citizens from the nation's largest phone companies. Only weeks later it was revealed that the government also had begun monitoring the banking habits of private citizens in an effort to thwart terrorist activities. Open debates developed over how much personal privacy Americans were willing to relinquish for the promise of safety from terrorism. Nevertheless, the act was renewed in 2006.

11   The government is not the only one in the spying business. Some of the most sophisticated surveillance devices are available to the public and can be ordered from retail catalogues. For example, night-vision goggles can be had for the price of a good video camera. High-tech scanners are available that can trace ink patterns and read the content of letters "without ever breaking the seal." There is a good possibility that as cameras get smaller and more mobile we should expect "mosquito-scale drones" that fly in and out of office and home windows, making privacy difficult or impossible. Of course, cell phones and other mobile devices with digital cameras have proliferated, as have pinhole cameras, microvideo systems, and wireless video that potentially could make everyone part of the security **apparatus**.

apparatus
structure or system

The Impact of Surveillance

12   Journalists have largely focused their attention on how surveillance relates to political citizenship and "privacy" issues, but much more is involved. According to sociologist David Lyon, new surveillance systems have expanded to the point at which they have become a major social institution that affects all social relationships, as well as people's very identities, personal space, freedom, and dignity. Increasingly, data images—computer-integrated profiles of each individual's finances, health, consumer preferences, ethnicity, neighborhood, education, criminal record, and other "significant" characteristics—are the "looking-glass" that provides social judgments about "who we are" and our life changes. Using the old South Africa as his guide, Lyon asks, will the new "non-persons," segregated by surveillance systems, be bankrupt individuals or perhaps non consumers?

13   Many people see the benefits of new surveillance as far outweighing the risks and argue that only criminals and terrorists should be concerned about the intensification of surveillance. They assert, "Why should I worry about privacy? I have nothing to hide." Lyon himself makes the point that dark visions about corporate and government Big Brothers may be counterproductive in that they may produce nothing more than paranoia, **fatalism**, and inaction. New surveillance, in fact, both constrains and enables. Although it is unequally distributed, with large organizations controlling most information technologies, these same technologies have given ordinary people access to many new channels of participation and protest, not only nationally but globally. However, today's increases in identity theft, spying, selling of personal information, and other technological invasions of privacy prompted one sociologist to conclude that "public access to private information has taken on even more ominous tones."

fatalism
the belief that
events are determined
by fate and cannot
be changed by
human actions

A. UNDERSTANDING THE THESIS AND OTHER MAIN IDEAS

Select the best answer.

_____ 1. The authors' primary purpose in this selection is to

    a. promote the use of high-tech surveillance systems for public security.

    b. criticize the government's widespread use of surveillance technologies.

    c. describe the growing use of surveillance systems in public places.

    d. compare and contrast surveillance techniques in other countries.

_____ 2. The main focus of paragraph 4 is on

    a. where surveillance cameras have been installed.

    b. how face-recognition technology is expanding.

    c. when photo radar is used most effectively.

    d. how the United States has increased surveillance since 9/11.

_____ 3. The statement that best expresses the main idea of paragraph 7 is

    a. "Police and military surveillance is impressive."

    b. "High-tech surveillance has expanded beyond the police and military to corporations, government agencies, and individuals."

    c. "Individuals routinely monitor the workplace, marketplace, and almost all other social arenas."

    d. "Police and the military use video scanners, electronic ankle monitors, night-vision goggles, and airborne spy vehicles."

_____ 4. According to the selection, data images are computer-integrated profiles that include information about an individual's

    a. health and finances.

    b. consumer preferences.

    c. criminal record.

    d. all of the above.

_____ 5. The topic of paragraph 11 is

    a. the government.

    b. spies.

    c. surveillance devices.

    d. privacy.

B. IDENTIFYING DETAILS

Complete each of the following statements by underlining the word in parentheses that makes the statement true.

1. The USA PATRIOT Act was originally passed (before/after) the terrorist attacks of 9/11.

2. The USA PATRIOT Act (was/was not) renewed in 2006.

3. The USA PATRIOT Act authorized the government to search suspected terrorists' library records (with/without) their knowledge.

4. After 9/11, the NSA solicited the phone records of private citizens (with/without) government approval.

5. The government's post-9/11 antiterrorism efforts (did/did not) include monitoring the banking habits of private citizens.

C. RECOGNIZING METHODS OF ORGANIZATION AND TRANSITIONS

Complete the sentences by filling in the blanks.

1. In paragraph 5, the transition word that points out a similarity between digital surveillance and security systems is _____.

2. In paragraph 10, two transitions that indicate the chronological order of events are _____ and _____. A contrasting idea is also indicated in this paragraph by the transition _____.

3. In paragraph 11, the authors use the generalization-and-example organizational pattern to explain that the government is not alone in the spying business. A transitional phrase that indicates this pattern is

_____.

D. REVIEWING AND ORGANIZING IDEAS: MAPPING

Complete the following map of paragraphs 3–5 by filling in the blanks.

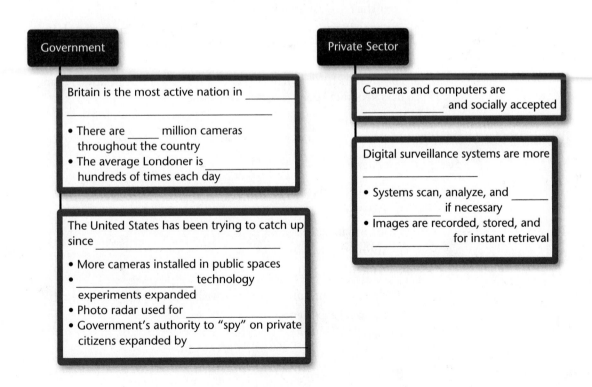

Government

Britain is the most active nation in _____

- There are _____ million cameras throughout the country
- The average Londoner is _____ hundreds of times each day

The United States has been trying to catch up since _____

- More cameras installed in public spaces
- _____ technology experiments expanded
- Photo radar used for _____
- Government's authority to "spy" on private citizens expanded by _____

Private Sector

Cameras and computers are _____ and socially accepted

Digital surveillance systems are more _____

- Systems scan, analyze, and _____ _____ if necessary
- Images are recorded, stored, and _____ for instant retrieval

E. READING AND THINKING VISUALLY

Answer each of the following questions.

1. What concepts in the selection are illustrated by the photograph?

   _____

2. What can you tell about the people shown in the photograph?

   _____

F. FIGURING OUT IMPLIED MEANINGS

Indicate whether each statement is true (T) or false (F).

_____ 1. In the opening paragraphs, the authors acknowledge that people respond differently to surveillance cameras in public places.

_____ 2. Ross Clark's question in paragraph 3 indicates that he supports increased surveillance and the collection of personal data.

_____ 3. The public became more willing to tolerate increased surveillance after the terrorist attacks of 9/11.

_____ 4. The sociologist's comment about a "glass village" in paragraph 7 refers to the increased transparency of government actions and policies.

_____ 5. The authors believe that the Pentagon's "Total Information Awareness Program" poses a direct threat to civil liberties.

G. THINKING CRITICALLY

Select the best answer.

_____ 1. The tone of this selection can best be described as
   a. apathetic.
   b. informative.
   c. angry.
   d. amused.

_____ 2. The authors support their thesis with all of the following *except*
   a. personal experience.
   b. facts.
   c. descriptions.
   d. examples.

_____ 3. Of the following words in paragraphs 3, the only one with a positive connotation is
   a. grim.
   b. hoarded.
   c. prosper.
   d. excessive.

_____ 4. The most important point the authors make at the end of this selection is that new surveillance technologies
   a. should concern only those who are breaking the law.
   b. produce dark visions about corporations and government.
   c. have had outcomes that are negative as well as beneficial.
   d. increase identity theft and other invasions of privacy.

_____ 5. The intended audience for this selection is most likely to be
   a. government officials.
   b. surveillance professionals.
   c. security consultants.
   d. sociology students.

H. BUILDING VOCABULARY

Context

Using context and a dictionary, if necessary, determine the meaning of each word as it is used in the selection.

_____ 1. pan (paragraph 1)
   a. move
   b. criticize
   c. contain
   d. separate

_____ 2. proliferation (paragraph 4)
   a. clear decline
   b. major alteration
   c. excessive increase
   d. preservation

_____ 3. abundant (paragraph 5)
   a. unusual
   b. plentiful
   c. expensive
   d. simple

———— 4. wary (paragraph 6)

    a. upset

    b. indifferent

    c. comfortable

    d. cautious

———— 5. ominous (paragraph 13)

    a. risky

    b. threatening

    c. illegal

    d. weak

Word Parts

A REVIEW OF PREFIXES

UN- means *not*
DYS- means *bad or difficult*
COUNTER- means *against or opposite*
IN- means *not*

Use your knowledge of word parts and the review above to fill in the blanks in the following sentences.

1. Something that is **undetectable** (paragraph 1) is ———————————— visible.

2. If the term *utopia* refers to a perfect or ideal state, then a **dystopian** (paragraph 3) vision of the future is one that is ———————————— .

3. When a problem or issue is **unresolved** (paragraph 8), it has ———————————— been settled or decided.

4. Ideas that are **counterproductive** (paragraph 13) tend to produce the ———————————— of the desired effect.

5. A belief that leads to **inaction** (paragraph 13) results in ———————————— action.

I. SELECTING A LEARNING/STUDY STRATEGY

Assume you will be tested on this selection on an upcoming exam. Evaluate the usefulness of the map you completed on page 251 as a study tool. Which other paragraphs would be useful to map?

J. EXPLORING IDEAS THROUGH DISCUSSION AND WRITING

1. Evaluate this selection's introduction. How effective was it in capturing your attention?

2. Over the course of a week, keep a list of the public places you go, and observe which places have installed security cameras. At the end of the week, write a paragraph describing the different types of public places you visited that are under surveillance.

3. Do you agree with those who say that only criminals and terrorists should be concerned about the intensification of surveillance? Why or why not?

K. BEYOND THE CLASSROOM TO THE WEB

Paragraph 11 refers to a controversial technology: "mosquito-scale drones." What exactly is a drone, and for what purposes are drones used? Conduct a Web search to find information about government and business uses of drones, and prepare a list of these uses. What arguments are made in favor of using drones? What arguments are made against the use of drones?

TRACKING YOUR PROGRESS

Selection 1

Section	Number Correct		Score
A. Thesis and Main Ideas (5 items)	_____	× 4	_____
B. Details (5 items)	_____	× 2	_____
C. Organization and Transitions (5 items)	_____	× 2	_____
F. Implied Meanings (5 items)	_____	× 4	_____
G. Thinking Critically (5 items)	_____	× 4	_____
H. Vocabulary			
Context (5 items)	_____	× 2	_____
Word Parts (5 items)	_____	× 2	_____
		Total Score	_____%

SELECTION 2

Childfree by Choice

Kelly J. Welch

TEXTBOOK
EXCERPT

This reading originally appeared in a family studies textbook, *Family Life Now*. The author, Kelly J. Welch, teaches sociology at Kansas State University.

PREVIEWING THE READING

Using the steps listed on page 40–41, preview the reading selection. When you have finished, complete the following items.

1. Indicate whether each statement is true (T) or false (F).

      _____ a. Dr. Seuss, the children's book author, had only one child.

      _____ b. In 2006, the level of childlessness in the United States was about twice what it was in 1976.

      _____ c. The trend toward childlessness is limited mostly to the United States.

2. According to Baum's 1999 research, childless women fall into four categories: _____, _____, _____, and _____.

MAKING
CONNECTIONS

Do you know any single people or any married couples who have made the decision not to have children? Have you identified how you feel about having children of your own? If you are a parent, do you have any opinions regarding people who have decided not to have children?

READING TIP

Like many readings in the social sciences, this selection focuses on presenting research. Look for research citations in parentheses—for example, (Cartwright, 1999) in paragraph 2. As you read, make a brief note in the margin summarizing the results of each research study.

Childfree by Choice

1 The **childfree-by-choice** trend is certainly nothing new as a quick glance at A-list celebrities shows: Kim Cattrall, Stockard Channing, Jay Leno, Steve Martin, George Clooney, and Oprah Winfrey all have opted to remain childfree. Even Dr. Seuss, the infamous children's book author, was childfree by choice. But the "no kids, no thanks" trend is moving beyond the borders of Hollywood and extending to mainstream USA. In 2006, U.S. Census Bureau data showed that the level of childlessness was 18.8 percent—twice the level as 1976 (Current Population Reports, 2008). In the last 30 years, the number of women ages 40 to 44 with no children has almost doubled to 18.8 percent (U.S. Census Bureau, Current Population Survey, 2010). This no-kids trend is not isolated to the United States. One body of research from Australia estimated that one in five women in the child-bearing years opted to not have children (Merlo & Rowland, 2000).

2 To date, there has been little empirical research in family studies, sociology, or psychology that examines the motives of women and men who are voluntarily childless; however, there are a few studies that help us understand why people opt to remain childfree. For example, one body of research found that there are certain categories or groups among those who elect not to become parents. These groups include those who are certain they do not want children, those who are certain they do not want children at this point in their lives, those who are ambivalent to having children, and those who feel the decision was made for them due to health reasons or lack of a partner (Cartwright, 1999).

COUPLES may adopt the no-kids/no-thanks track so they can pursue other endeavors, such as volunteering for Habitat for Humanity.

3 The reasons people remain childfree are as many and varying as those reasons people opt to become parents. Rathus and Nevid (1992) found in their study of hundreds of couples that there are various reasons why individuals and couples opt for the no-kids track: more time with one another, freedom from the responsibility of raising children, financial freedom, able to devote more time to careers, and concerns about worldwide overpopulation.

4   Other research found that beyond individual factors ("micro" factors), social factors ("macro" factors"), such as the increase in women's education levels and their participation in the job market, "compete with raising children" (Weston & Qu, 2001). Changing social values, decreasing importance of religion, access to legal abortion, and effective **contraceptives** also alter childbearing. These research findings indicated that those who choose to be childless do so because of their dislike of children, choice of lifestyle, lack of interest in children and parenting, or a belief that the world is too dangerous for children.

contraceptive
birth control

5   Similar to Rathus and Nevid, other studies similarly found that financial security and job security are also factors closely linked to an individual's decision to become a parent (MacKay, 1994; McDonald, 2000, Wooden, 1999). An additional study appears to confirm the findings from prior research. Sociologist Kristin Park (2005) analyzed the motives of 23 childless men and women. Through in-depth interviews, she found that women believed parenting would conflict with their careers and/or leisure activities. The women also indicated that they lacked a "maternal instinct," or they were generally uninterested in children. Men, more than women, believed that parenting required too many sacrifices, including great financial expense. Both men and women indicated that they felt their personalities were not suited to parenting.

6   Other research into childlessness categorizes childless women in the following groups (Baum, 1999):

- *Hedonists.* These women are not willing to, nor do they have a desire to, sacrifice money, energy, time, or themselves in rearing children.
- *Emotional.* Some women who choose not to become mothers have no "maternal instincts"; these women report that they have no emotional connection or feelings toward babies or children.
- *Idealistic.* These women indicate that they feel the world is not a safe place to bring a child into. They also feel that the world's resources are limited and they raise environmental concerns in their decision not to have children.
- *Practical.* Women in this category desire to remain childfree for practical reasons, such as educational or career goals.

7   Although to some it may appear that women remain childfree for selfish reasons, this is not necessarily the case. Couples must be honest when assessing whether or not to become parents. Some people feel their lives are complete and full without children. Others choose to be childfree because of unfortunate circumstances, and in these instances, the decision can be a painful one. For instance, a close friend of mine desperately desired to be a mother but because she is a genetic carrier of an always-fatal type of muscular dystrophy, she opted to remain childless. Other couples may not consciously decide not to have children—they simply fall into childlessness.

Are Childfree-by-Choice Couples Selfish?

8   Recently in Britain, senior Anglican Bishop of Rochester, Rev. Michael Nazir-Ali, condemned couples that chose to not have children as "self-indulgent." The bishop asserted that the basic good of marriage is having children, and that not to have children would doom a marriage to failure. He further asserted that couples who opt out of having children have abandoned the societal and cultural duty of all married people—to ensure that the society continues by reproducing. Finally, the reverend stated that those who do not have children are "following the religion of the new 'me,'" are selfish, and have excessive self-regard.

9   Our study in this chapter has shown us that childfree-by-choice couples are an emerging demographic in our society.

1. Have you decided that children won't fit into your married life? If so, why? if not, why not?
2. Do you believe that children are part and parcel of the whole concept of "marriage"?
3. Why do you think that the decision to remain childfree is met with such criticism?

A. UNDERSTANDING THE THESIS AND OTHER MAIN IDEAS

Select the best answer.

_____ 1. Which of the following best states the thesis or central thought of "Childfree by Choice"?

a. Many men and women throughout the world are choosing not to have children, but the trend is particularly visible in the United States and Australia.

b. In general, research has shown that men are more likely to live a childfree life than women are.

c. According to Rev. Michael Nazir-Ali, those who choose not to have children are selfish and have abandoned their primary cultural duty, but it is not too late for these people to change their minds.

d. The rate of childlessness has grown significantly in the last three decades, and several research studies have suggested some of the reasons for this trend, which some have criticized as self-indulgent.

_____ 2. Which of the following best states the implied main idea of paragraph 5?

  a. Rathus and Nevid conducted the original research into the question of why people choose to remain childless.

  b. Men are more likely than women to believe that parenting requires too many personal sacrifices, and women are more likely
than men to believe that parenting will be too expensive.

  c. Several studies have been undertaken to understand why people
choose not to have children; these studies identified a number of
factors that contribute to the decision.

  d. In general, studies that have studied childless couples have been
unable to come to any conclusions regarding the most important factor in that decision.

_____ 3. The topic of paragraph 6 is

  a. the categories identified in Baum's research.

  b. the maternal instinct and the paternal instinct.

  c. the differences between idealism and pragmatism.

  d. the role of education in the decision to remain childfree.

_____ 4. Which of the following best states the implied main idea of paragraph 8?

  a. Childbearing should be the primary reason that people get married, not only in the United States but also across the world.

  b. Those who choose not to have children are self-indulgent.

  c. Attitudes toward being childfree in Great Britain differ from
attitudes in the United States.

  d. The Rev. Michael Nazir-Ali has pointed out several reasons why
those who choose to remain childfree are selfish.

B. IDENTIFYING DETAILS

Select the best answer.

_____ 1. Which of the following people mentioned in the selection is likely a
parent?

  a. Oprah Winfrey

  b. George Clooney

  c. Michael Nazir-Ali

  d. Kim Cattrall

_____ 2. Which of the following was not one of the reasons for remaining childfree identified in the Rathus and Nevid study?

   a. financial freedom

   b. concerns about global population

   c. freedom from the responsibility of raising children

   d. inability to conceive due to medical problems

_____ 3. Over the last three decades, the number of women in the United States between the ages of 40 and 44 who've never had children has

   a. remained constant.

   b. doubled.

   c. tripled.

   d. decreased by about half.

_____ 4. The author tells the story of a friend who chose not to have children because she (the friend) carries the gene for _____.

   a. cancer

   b. diabetes

   c. sickle cell anemia

   d. muscular dystrophy

C. RECOGNIZING METHODS OF ORGANIZATION AND TRANSITIONS

Select the best answer.

_____ 1. The overall pattern of organization used in the selection is

   a. chronological order.

   b. listing.

   c. process.

   d. spatial order.

_____ 2. The main pattern of organization used in paragraph 6 is

   a. cause and effect.

   b. process.

   c. chronological order.

   d. classification.

_____ 3. The transitional word or phrase that signals the generalization-and-example pattern in paragraph 7 is

   a. although.   c. because of.

   b. others.   d. for instance.

D. REVIEWING AND ORGANIZING IDEAS: WRITING A SUMMARY

Write a summary of the reading. The first few sentences have been provided for you.

In "Childfree by Choice," Kelly J. Welch begins by listing top Hollywood celebrities who have chosen not to have children. This trend is not limited to Hollywood, however. In fact, recent data have shown that the overall level of childlessness in the United States doubled between 1976 and 2006.

_____

_____

_____

_____

_____

_____

_____

E. READING AND THINKING VISUALLY

Select the best answer.

_____ 1. The author likely included the photo and caption shown on page 257 in order to

    a. provide an example of one reason that people may choose not to have children.

    b. encourage students to volunteer for Habitat for Humanity.

    c. imply that men are more likely to choose a childfree life than women are.

    d. show why the decision not to have children is as selfish as the decision not to volunteer.

F. FIGURING OUT IMPLIED MEANINGS

Indicate whether each statement is true (T) or false (F).

_____ 1. A hedonist pursues pleasure.

_____ 2. Some research has shown that 20% of Australian women in their childbearing years have chosen not to have children.

_____ 3. In general, it seems that childfree men often think they are too old to be a good father to their children.

_____ 4. Women who do not want to have children because they prefer to further their educational or career goals would fall into Baum's "idealistic" category.

_____ 5. Some people fall into childlessness rather than making a conscious choice not to have children.

_____ 6. Overall, the decision to remain childfree is exceedingly well researched, and a large body of knowledge has been developed on the subject.

_____ 7. Weston & Qu believe that women's increasing levels of education and career advancement sometimes compete with the idea of raising children.

G. THINKING CRITICALLY

Select the best answer.

_____ 1. The tone of the reading selection is best described as
   a. hostile.   c. puzzled.
   b. informative.   d. skeptical.

_____ 2. The author's main purpose in "Childfree by Choice" is to
   a. discuss the trend toward childlessness and the results of some of the research that has studied the trend.
   b. persuade young people to think very seriously about having children before they make up their minds.
   c. help readers understand why childfree people tend to be selfish or too focused on money or their career.
   d. offer an overview of the many activities in which childfree couples can take part after they've made the decision not to have children.

_____ 3. The author uses all of the following types of evidence to support her thesis *except*
   a. personal anecdotes from her own life.
   b. U.S. government data.
   c. sociological research studies.
   d. statistics from the American Sociological Association.

_____ 4. Which of the following is an opinion, not a fact?
   a. "Even Dr. Seuss was childfree by choice." (paragraph 1)
   b. "To date, there has been little empirical research that examines the motives or women and men who are voluntarily childless." (paragraph 2)
   c. "These research findings indicated that those who choose to be childless do so because of their dislike of children." (paragraph 4)
   d. "Couples who opt out of having children have abandoned the societal and cultural duty of all married people—to ensure that society keeps reproducing." (paragraph 8)

_____ 5. The most recent study cited in the article is

    a. Current Population Reports.

    b. U.S. Census Bureau, Current Population Survey.

    c. Weston & Qu.

    d. Cartwright.

_____ 6. Which statement best characterizes the research of Kristin Park?

    a. It was conducted in 1999.

    b. It focused exclusively on women's choice not to have children.

    c. It included in-depth interviews with a relatively small number of people.

    d. It identified the maternal instinct as the single most important factor in the decision to have children.

_____ 7. Which of the following best states the author's approach to having children?

    a. She agrees with Bishop Michael Nazir-Ali.

    b. She believes that people over the age of 40 should not have children.

    c. She thinks young women should postpone the decision to have children as long as possible.

    d. She believes the choice is a very personal one and she does not express any opinion beyond that.

_____ 8. The fact that Dr. Seuss, a well-known children's book author, chose not to have children might be considered

    a. symbolic.

    b. ironic.

    c. metaphorical.

    d. literary.

_____ 9. In paragraph 4, the author refers to the "micro" factors and "macro" factors. Which of the following would be a "macro" factor?

    a. a woman's relationship with her mother

    b. a man's salary and the company for which he works

    c. a couple's city of residence

    d. an overall increase in women's education levels

H. BUILDING VOCABULARY

Context

Using context and a dictionary if necessary, determine the meaning of each word as it is used in the selection.

_____ 1. opted (paragraph 1)

    a. learned

    b. chosen

    c. angered

    d. departed

_____ 2. empirical (paragraph 2)

    a. based on observation

    b. out of date

    c. psychological

    d. serious

_____ 3. ambivalent (paragraph 2)

    a. determined

    b. unsure

    c. incapable

    d. young

_____ 4. assess (paragraph 7)

    a. measure

    b. teach

    c. evaluate

    d. tax

Word Parts

> **A REVIEW OF PREFIXES AND SUFFIXES**
>
> **-FREE** means without.
> **UN-** means nost.

Use your knowledge of word parts and the review above to fill in the blanks in the following sentences.

1. A person who is *childfree* (paragraph 1) is _____ children.

2. Those who are *uninterested* (paragraph 5) in a topic are _____ interested in that topic.

I. SELECTING A LEARNING/STUDY STRATEGY

This textbook excerpt uses the cause-and-effect organizational pattern. Create a map or chart that summarizes the reasons for childlessness.

J. EXPLORING IDEAS THROUGH DISCUSSION AND WRITING

Write a paragraph or essay in response to the following writing prompts.

1. In general, women in developed countries (such as those in North America and Europe) tend to have fewer children than women in developing countries (such as those in Asia and Africa). Write a paragraph offering some insights into the factors that might be at work in this situation.

2. Write a paragraph in which you answer this question: How is the decision to put off having children similar to a decision not to have children? How is it different?

3. This reading lists numerous reasons why people decide to be childfree. Write a paragraph in which you list and discuss three additional possible reasons.

4. Write an essay in which you explore the idea of having children of your own. Do you know whether you want children or not? If you are already a parent, would you have more children? Why or why not?

5. Write an essay in which you respond to Rev. Michael Nazir-Ali, whose opinions of the childfree lifestyle are found in paragraph 8.

6. Write an essay in which you answer one of the questions found in paragraph 9 of the reading.

K. BEYOND THE CLASSROOM TO THE WEB

Conduct a Web search to locate current statistics about the level of childlessness in the U.S. Compare those statistics with those cited in the article. Write a paragraph summary of your findings and offer possible explanations for whatever change is noted.

TRACKING YOUR PROGRESS

Selection 2

Section	Number Correct	Score
A. Understanding the Thesis and Other Main Ideas (4 items)	_____ × 3	_____
B. Identifying Details (4 items)	_____ × 3	_____
C. Recognizing Methods of Organization and Transitions (3 items)	_____ × 2	_____
E. Reading and Thinking Visually (1 item)	_____ × 4	_____
F. Figuring Out Implied Meanings (7 items)	_____ × 3	_____
G. Thinking Critically: Analyzing the Author's Technique (9 items)	_____ × 3	_____
H. Building Vocabulary (6 items)	_____ × 3	_____
	Total Score	_____ %

SELECTION 3

Are Sports Fans Happier?

Sid Kirchheimer

This selection originally appeared in *The Saturday Evening Post*, a popular American magazine. The author, Sid Kirchheimer, is a former newspaper reporter and the author of *The Doctors Book of Home Remedies II*. He writes mostly about health-related matters.

PREVIEWING THE READING

Using the steps listed on pages 40–41, preview the reading selection. When you have finished, complete the following items.

1. Recent studies suggest that _____ are happier and healthier in mind, body, and spirit.

2. Indicate whether each statement is true (T) or false (F).

   _____ a. Sports fans tend to have lower self-esteem than people who are not sports fans.

   _____ b. Many experts believe that "March Madness" benefits the workplace in the long run.

 MAKING CONNECTIONS

The selection discusses the benefits of being a sports fan. Do you follow any team or individual sports? If so, which ones? Why are you drawn to those specific sports? Which teams or athletes do you root for? Why?

READING TIP

As you read, connect the examples to your own experiences. What benefits has sports fandom brought to your life? Have you experienced any drawbacks or negative effects?

Are Sports Fans Happier?

New studies reveal that rooting passionately is good for your mind, body, and spirit.

vasectomy
a voluntary surgical procedure that results in male sterility

1   LET THE MADNESS BEGIN! March is the time when **vasectomies** increase by 50 percent thanks to the much-anticipated opportunity for patients to "recover" in front of their TVs.

2   March is also the time when workplaces do some real number-crunching; on the expected loss in employee productivity (estimated at 8.4 million hours and $192 million last year); on money bet on office pools (a hefty chunk of the $2.5 billion in total sports wagering each year); and even on the number of times workers hit the so-called "Boss Button" (computer software that instantly hides live video of games with a phony business spreadsheet), which was activated more than 3.3 million times during the first four days of last year's tournament.

3   But mostly, the NCAA Basketball Championship—better known as "March Madness" or "The Big Dance"—is a time that gives us something to cheer about beyond the same itself. If history and science hold true, no matter the outcome of the three-week tournament that begins in March, most of the millions who will follow its hard-court action will emerge as winners, "That's because in the long run it's really not the games that matter," says Daniel Wann, Ph.D., a professor of psychology at Murray State University in Kentucky and author of *Sports Fans: The Psychology and Social Impact of Spectators*. "Being a fan gives us something to talk about, to share and bond with others. And for the vast majority of people, it's psychologically healthier when you can increase social connections with others."

4   After conducting some 200 studies over the past two decades, Wann, a leading researcher on "sports fandom," finds consistent results; people who identify

primal
essential,
fundamental

themselves as sports fans tend to have lower rates of depression and higher self-esteem than those who don't. Blame it on our **primal** nature. "Sports fandom is really a tribal thing," says Wann, a phenomenon that can help fulfill our psychological need to belong—providing similar benefits to the social support achieved through religious, professional, or other affiliations, "We've known for decades that social support—our tribal network—is largely responsible for keeping people mentally sound. We really do have a need to connect with others in some way."

5   But when it comes to opportunities to connect, the Big Dance may have a foot-hold over other sporting events. "The beauty of March Madness is that it attracts people of all levels of sports fandom—and for different reasons," says Edward Hirt, PhD., a professor of psychology at Indiana University who researches how fanship affects social identity.

6   Some watch, whether or not they usually follow sports, because they are alumni or have another previous affiliation to these "tribal networks"—the 60-plus participating college teams. Others connect on the spot, perhaps because it's easier to form emotional allegiances with gutsy amateur athletes who compete with heart and soul (and while juggling midterm exams) rather than for the paychecks collected by millionaire pros.

7   Also consider the unique nature of the tournament itself—a series of back-to-back games over the course of several weeks with little to no idle time in between during which a casual fan might lose interest. "I have not seen any **empirical** evidence to support that March Madness is necessarily better than other sports events" for promoting mood and mindset enhancements. "But theoretically I expect it could be," says Wann. "There are only a couple of events—the Super Bowl also comes to mind—that seem to transcend typical fandom into being akin to a national holiday . . . a reason for people to get together. But with the Super Bowl, everything leads to one game—and most of the time it's an **anticlimactic** one that's over by half-time."

empirical
based on data

anticlimactic
disappointing in the
end after
excitement

8   With March Madness, however, Wann notes, "there's a longer, more drawn out event that provides more opportunities to engage in social opportunities and connections. And bonds tend to be stronger with a longer passage of time."

9   Do the math: More games + more time = more opportunities to share for better bonding. "Because upsets are a normal occurrence, and you get runs by Cinderella teams knocking off the perennial favorites, there's enough uncertainty and unpredictability in this tournament to get people excited—and keep them exalted," adds Hirt. "Early games affect later decisions; there's a cascading effect, as opposed to a one-time pick . . . and that allows for the pride that comes with someone with no sports expertise being able to win the office pool."

10   Maybe that's why despite a short-term productivity loss many experts believe that March Madness actually benefits the workplace in the long term. Bonds formed in office pools and post-game water-cooler chatter build morale and inspire teamwork. At afterwork get-togethers in front of the tube, buddies can share chicken wings—and their emotions. "You have guys hugging each other, cursing at the ref, and bonding by sharing a sense of commonality," says Hirt. "Where else can guys express their emotions like that?"

11   And those other relationships? Although studies show that two to four percent of marriages are negatively affected when one spouse is an ardent fan (think of the so-called "football widow"), sports fandom has a positive or neutral effect on nearly half of relationships, says Wann. "It gives many couples something to do together or allows one to have time to go off and do their own thing."

12   Even if you watch in solitude, March Madness and other sporting events provide a diversion from the woes of everyday life—if only for a few hours. "Older people, especially when widowed or physically incapacitated, are more likely than others to relate to televised events," says Stuart Fischoff, Ph.D., senior editor of the *Journal of Media Psychology* and a California State University, Los Angeles, professor **emeritus** of psychology. "Watching sports helps us get outside ourselves."

emeritus
retired

bona fide
real

13   With the thrill of victory, many fans experience **bona fide** joy—complete with hormonal and other physiological changes such as increased pulse and feelings of elation. And with defeat, the overwhelming majority may initially feel sadness and disappointment, but usually rebound within a day or two, studies show.

14   However, lest we present too rosy a picture, it must be said that sports fandom can also be a health hazard. In a 2008 study published in the *New England Journal of Medicine*, researchers found that on days when Germany's soccer team played in the World Cup, cardiac emergencies more than tripled for German men and nearly doubled for women. Of course, European soccer fans are an extreme bunch; but even in the U.S., although visits to hospital emergency rooms tend to decrease during a much-anticipated sports game, there's a higher-than-usual surge immediately after the game ends. The explanation: To see a game's final outcome, some die-hard fans delay making that trip to the ER.

15   And, of course, no story about March Madness would be complete without mention of gambling. The odds of predicting all game winners are about 9.2 quintillion to one. Yet when it comes to sports betting, nothing turns John Q. Fan into Jimmy the Greek more than the NCAA tournament. Workplace camaraderie is one reason. But there's another important factor.

16   Bragging rights.

17   With Super Bowl pools there's just a series of boxes with different scores. If you're lucky enough to pick the right one, you win. "But it's a more complex task in filling out all the March Madness brackets, and a seductive pleasure in trying to predict the upsets," says psychologist Edward Hirt.

18   Another reason why nearly twice as much money is wagered on March Madness than the Super Bowl: More than in other events, NCAA tournament fans simultaneously root for more than one team, triggering a greater likelihood of making multiple bets.

19   With other sports championships you have to wait a week or at least several days between games, but this sports soap opera—with its David versus Goliath battles—continues night and day, providing a stronger hook.

20   So let the games begin. Whatever the final outcome, odds are good that the overall advantage—for mind, body, and spirit—is definitely in your court.

A. UNDERSTANDING THE THESIS AND OTHER MAIN IDEAS

Select the best answer.

_____ 1. Which of the following best states the thesis or central idea of "Are Sports Fans Happier?"

    a. Many professional research studies reveal that rooting passionately for a sports team is good for the mind, body, and soul.

    b. March Madness is a three-week extravaganza that drains productivity at the office and threatens romantic relationships.

    c. Watching sports has many benefits (including the ability to connect with fellow human beings), but it also has some drawbacks.

    d. Employers have begun taking action to prevent workers from watching or betting on sporting events during the workday.

_____ 2. The main idea of paragraph 3 is found in the

    a. first sentence.

    b. second sentence.

    c. third sentence.

    d. last sentence.

_____ 3. Which of the following does the author *not* identify as a benefit of being a sports fan?

    a. Sports fans typically live longer than people who are not sports fans.

    b. Watching sports helps people escape from everyday worries for a while.

    c. Sports give couples something to do together, or time for each person to do his or her "own thing."

    d. Watching sports helps people connect with other human beings.

_____ 4. The topic of paragraph 10 is

    a. short-term productivity losses.

    b. long-term benefits of March Madness in the workplace.

    c. the expressing of emotions.

    d. morale and teamwork.

B. IDENTIFYING DETAILS

Select the best answer.

_____ 1. Which statement is *not* true of the NCAA Basketball Championship?

    a. It is sometimes called "March Madness" or "The Big Dance."

    b. It attracts only hardcore basketball fans.

    c. It lasts approximately three weeks.

    d. More than 60 basketball teams take part in it.

_____ 2. According to the author, two sporting events reach the level of a national holiday. These are March Madness and

    a. the World Series.

    b. the Olympics.

    c. the Stanley Cup.

    d. the Super Bowl.

_____ 3. All of the following researchers are cited in the article *except*

    a. Stuart Fischoff.

    b. Daniel Wann.

    c. Elias Goldenberg.

    d. Edward Hirt.

_____ 4. According to the author, all of the following help explain the popularity of March Madness *except*

    a. fans enjoy rooting for amateur athletes who play passionately and boldly.

    b. college graduates are loyal to the college from which they graduated.

    c. March Madness offers the possibility of unexpected and emotional upsets, which are exciting to watch.

    d. the "brackets" in March Madness betting pools give everyone an equal chance to win the pot.

C. RECOGNIZING METHODS OF ORGANIZATION AND TRANSITIONS

Select the best answer.

_____ 1. The overall pattern of organization used in "Are Sports Fans Happier?" is

    a. definition.

    b. listing.

    c. classification.

    d. process.

_____ 2. The use of the word "However" at the beginning of paragraph 14 indicates that the paragraph will likely use the _____ pattern.

    a. contrast

    b. cause-and-effect

    c. chronological order

    d. order of importance

D. REVIEWING AND ORGANIZING IDEAS: SUMMARIZING

Complete the following summary of paragraphs 3–6 by filling in the missing words or phrases.

Paragraphs 3 and 4: Fans of the NCAA Basketball Championship (also known as _____ or The Big Dance) receive many _____ from following the games. According to Daniel Wann, watching March Madness increases the fans' _____ by helping them bond with other people. Sports fans also have higher levels of self-esteem and lower rates of _____ than people who are not sports fans.

Paragraphs 5 and 6: March Madness attracts people at all levels of _____, from casual fans through hardcore fans. Some of these people watch because they are loyal to their _____, and others watch because they feel inspired by amateur athletes who are not receiving huge _____.

E. READING AND THINKING VISUALLY

Select the best answer.

_____ The author likely included the photo shown on page 269 in order to
  a. imply that March Madness attracts more fans than the Super Bowl.
  b. illustrate one of his key points: that watching sports helps people bond with one another.
  c. show that people enjoy basketball more than they enjoy other sports.
  d. provide examples of business opportunities for entrepreneurs who cater to sports fans.

F. FIGURING OUT IMPLIED MEANINGS

Indicate whether each statement is true (T) or false (F).

_____ 1. Sports fandom has a negative effect on very few marriages.

_____ 2. The author implies that fans of March Madness may find amateur athletes more inspiring than highly paid professional athletes.

_____ 3. Sports fans who need emergency care while watching sporting events may put off going to the hospital so that they can watch the end of the game.

_____ 4. The author implies that employers should prevent workers from watching March Madness games during business hours.

_____ 5. The author is opposed to gambling.

G. THINKING CRITICALLY

Select the best answer.

_____ 1. The writer's primary purpose in "Are Sports Fans Happier?" is to

    a. encourage students to participate in sports.

    b. analyze the reasons that sports fans become so devoted to a particular sport.

    c. discuss the benefits offered by sports fandom.

    d. argue for more national holidays scheduled around sporting events.

_____ 2. The writer supports his ideas primarily by

    a. providing in-depth discussions of different sports.

    b. offering a case study of the life of one specific sports fan.

    c. comparing and contrasting sports in the United States with sports in Europe.

    d. quoting numerous research studies.

_____ 3. The writer's tone can be best described as

    a. cynical.

    b. unbiased.

    c. optimistic.

    d. nostalgic.

_____ 4. In paragraph 4, the author uses the phrase "tribal network" to imply that

    a. the need for social support goes back to the beginnings of humanity.

    b. sports often cause people to act in an uncivilized manner.

    c. more and more people are watching sporting events on the Internet.

    d. many sports teams use Native American tribes as their names (for example, the Florida Seminoles).

_____ 5. What does the author mean by the phrase "Cinderella teams" in paragraph 9?

    a. all-female teams

    b. underdog teams that beat highly favored teams

    c. teams that have a cheerleading squad

    d. teams that have never won a game

H. BUILDING VOCABULARY

Context

Using context and a dictionary, if necessary, determine the meaning of each word as it used in the selection.

_____ 1. hefty (paragraph 2)
   a. humorous
   b. time-consuming
   c. accurate
   d. large

_____ 2. gutsy (paragraph 6)
   a. educated
   b. painful
   c. brave
   d. clumsy

_____ 3. perennial (paragraph 9)
   a. parental
   b. lasting
   c. uncertain
   d. personal

_____ 4. ardent (paragraph 11)
   a. eager
   b. occasional
   c. underpaid
   d. broken

_____ 5. elation (paragraph 13)
   a. suspense
   b. frustration
   c. tenderness
   d. joy

Word Parts

A REVIEW OF ROOTS AND SUFFIXES

PHYSIO means *related to nature and natural phenomena*
LOGY means *the study of*
-AL means *pertaining or referring to*
-ITY refers to *a state, condition, or quality*

Use your knowledge of word parts and the review on the facing page to choose the answer that best defines the boldfaced word in each sentence.

_____ 1. "You have guys hugging each other, cursing at the ref, and bonding by sharing a sense of **commonality**." (paragraph 10)

    a. humor

    b. childhood

    c. sharing

    d. location

_____ 2. "With the thrill of victory, many fans experience bona fide joy—complete with hormonal and other **physiological** changes such as increased pulse and feelings of elation." (paragraph 13)

    a. related to bodily function

    b. psychological

    c. age-related

    d. emotional

Unusual Words/Understanding Idioms

Use the meanings given below to write a sentence using the boldfaced phrase.

1. **Number-crunching** (paragraph 2) entails examining and analyzing a large amount of data to draw accurate conclusions.

    Your sentence: _____

    _____

2. **Idle time** (paragraph 7) means time spent doing nothing.

    Your sentence: _____

    _____

3. **Bragging rights** (paragraph 16) refers to the winning team's "right" to brag about the defeat of a rival.

    Your sentence: _____

    _____

I. SELECTING A LEARNING/STUDY STRATEGY

Assume you will be tested on this reading on an upcoming exam. Evaluate the usefulness of the summaries you completed in Section D. Which other paragraphs from the reading would be useful to summarize?

J. EXPLORING IDEAS THROUGH DISCUSSION AND WRITING

1. Why do you think some sports fans like to root for the "underdog" team?

2. In paragraph 4, the author states that sports fandom provides similar benefits to the social support provided by religious, professional, or other affiliations. In what ways is sports fandom similar to membership in religious or professional associations? In what ways is it different?

3. Do you think sports fans are as devoted to individual sports (such as skating, skiing, or swimming) as they are to team sports (such as football, baseball, or soccer)? Why or why not? Which type of sport do you prefer and why?

K. BEYOND THE CLASSROOM TO THE WEB

Choose your favorite sports team (whether professional or amateur) and visit a Web site maintained by fans of that team. (If you are not a sports fan, choose a local team.) How does the team "give back" to its fans? Why do you think these fans are so devoted to their team?

TRACKING YOUR PROGRESS

Selection 3

Section	Number Correct	Score
A. Thesis and Main Ideas (4 items)	_____ × 4	_____
B. Details (4 items)	_____ × 4	_____
C. Organization and Transitions (2 items)	_____ × 4	_____
E. Reading and Thinking Visually (1 item)	_____ × 4	_____
F. Implied Meanings (5 items)	_____ × 3	_____
G. Thinking Critically (5 items)	_____ × 4	_____
H. Vocabulary		
Context (5 items)	_____ × 3	_____
Word Parts (2 items)	_____ × 3	_____
	Total Score	_____%

10 | Communication/Speech

The field of **communication** is concerned with the exchange of information between individuals and groups through speaking, writing, or nonverbal communication (body language, such as gestures). Communication may be interpersonal, such as that between two persons; may occur within a small group, such as in a group of friends or in a class discussion; and may also be public, in which a speaker addresses an audience. Communication skills are important for success in college, for finding and keeping a rewarding job, and for building and maintaining healthy, strong relationships with family, friends, and co-workers.

By studying communication, you will come to understand those around you and exchange ideas with them more effectively. "Talking to Koko the Gorilla" addresses interspecies communication. "Movie and TV Genres" discusses the most popular types of these communications media. In "Relationships and Technology" you will read about online dating and discover its advantages and disadvantages.

Use the following tips when reading in the communication field.

TIPS FOR READINGS IN COMMUNICATION/SPEECH

- **Pay attention to processes.** In "Talking to Koko the Gorilla," pay attention to the process by which the gorilla has learned to express her thoughts.
- **Pay attention to principles—rules that govern how communication works.** When reading "Relationships and Technology," look for the rules of conduct on which online communication is based.
- **Notice theories (explanations that attempt to describe how or why something happens).** In "Relationships and Technology" the author explains **how** online dating Web sites affect relationships.
- **Be alert for cultural differences.** Not all cultures and ethnic groups follow the same conventions and theories. Do you think the online matchmaking described in "Relationships and Technology" would be considered appropriate in all cultures?
- **Pay attention to language and terminology.** "Movie and TV Genres" contains terminology used to distinguish different media genres and sub-genres.
- **Think critically.** As you read theories, ask challenging questions, such as "Does this information fit with what I already know and have experienced?" For example, when reading "Movie and TV Genres," you might question the accuracy and reliability of documentaries that fall into the "docu-ganda" category.

SELECTION 4

Talking to Koko the Gorilla

Alex Hannaford

Using the steps listed on pages 40–41, preview the reading selection. When you have finished, complete the following items.

1. What animal species is Koko? _____

2. Indicate whether each statement is true (T) or false (F).

    _____   a. Koko lives in the Santa Cruz Mountains of California.

    _____   b. Koko's thought processes are very basic.

MAKING CONNECTIONS

Are you familiar with American sign language (ASL)? Have you seen deaf people using it? Do you know the sign language alphabet? If you know any signs, how do they relate to the words and concepts they express?

READING TIP

As you read, think about your experiences with animals and their ability to communicate. If you have owned a pet, such as a cat or a dog, how has it communicated with you? Did it seem to understand you when you speak? Was it able to understand your emotions?

Talking to Koko the Gorilla

This 40-year-old lowland gorilla understands English and longs for a baby.

1   My location is a closely guarded secret: a ranch somewhere in the Santa Cruz Mountains, several miles outside the small California town of Woodside. Its resident is something of a celebrity. She lives here with a male friend and both value their privacy, so much so that I'm asked to keep absolutely silent as I walk through a grove of towering redwoods up to a little Portakabin. Inside, I'm asked to put on a thin medical mask to cover my nose and mouth, and a pair of latex gloves. Then my guide, Lorraine, tells me to follow another dirt trail to a different outbuilding. It's here that I sit on a plastic chair and look up at an open door, separated from the outside world by a wire fence that stretches the length and width of the frame. And there she is: Koko. A 300-pound lowland gorilla, sitting staring back at me and pointing to an impressive set of teeth.

Koko the gorilla (with one of her keepers) was taught sign language when she was just a year old.

Photo: Bettmann/CORBIS

2 I was told beforehand not to make eye contact initially, as it can be perceived as threatening, and so I glare at the ground. But I can't help stealing brief glances at this beautiful creature. Koko, in case you're not familiar with her story, was taught American sign language when she was about a year old. Now 40, she apparently has a working vocabulary of more than 1,000 signs, and understands around 2,000 words of spoken English. Forty years on, the Gorilla Foundation's Koko project has become the longest continuous interspecies communications program of its kind anywhere.

3 I sign "hello," which looks like a sailor's salute, and she emits a long, throaty growl. "Don't worry, that means she likes you," comes the disembodied voice of Dr. Penny Patterson, the foundation's president and scientific director, from somewhere inside the enclosure. "It's the gorilla equivalent of a purr." Koko grins at me, then turns and signs to Dr. Patterson. "She wants to see your mouth . . . wait, she particularly wants to see your tongue," Dr. Patterson says, and I happily oblige, pulling my mask down, poking my tongue out, and returning the grin. Another soft, deep roar. Dr. Patterson emerges from a side door, closing it behind her, and joins me on the porch. Koko makes a sign. Dr. Patterson translates: "'Visit. Do you . . .' Oh, sweetheart," she says to Koko, then turns to me: "She'd like you to go inside."

sub-Saharan Africa
the area of the African continent south of the Sahara Desert

habitat
natural environment

poaching
illegal hunting

4 Over the years Koko has inadvertently become a poster child for the gorilla conservation movement. There are several subspecies of gorillas, all in **sub-Saharan Africa**, and today, according to the International Union for Conservation of Nature, all are either endangered or critically endangered. They are threatened by disease, the illegal trade in bush meat, and loss of **habitat** due to logging and agricultural expansion. Attempts to educate communities where **poaching** is rife have largely failed; statistics about dwindling numbers of great apes don't resonate with people who can make good money from gorilla meat or body parts, or for whom the logging industry puts dinner on the table.

5 But some conservationists believe stories such as Koko's—of how an "inculturated" gorilla (the word researchers use for primates that have essentially had their own culture suppressed and have adopted a more human-like culture) has actually communicated with us—could be the answer. We should attempt, in other words, to win hearts rather than minds. At 40, Koko could possibly be more relevant than ever. But she's advanced in years, and the Gorilla Foundation is determined to ensure her legacy. That means allowing her to pass on her knowledge of sign language to her offspring, but despite repeated attempts to get her to mate—first with the silverback

Michael and more recently with another, Ndume, her current partner—Koko's keepers' efforts have been in vain.

6   It's rare that anyone gets to meet Koko up close. Most of the staff at the Gorilla Foundation have only ever been outside her enclosure. A handful of celebrities, Leonardo DiCaprio and Robin Williams included, have had the pleasure, but this was to secure publicity for the foundation. I'm told no journalist has spent as long as I will—an hour and a half—in her company. Looming above is a huge three-story enclosure that Koko can access via a hatch. Inside it is Ndume, the male silverback. We can't see each other, but I'm told he is well aware I'm here and I have to keep my voice down, as he's protective of Koko. Inside the kitchen area, I'm still separated from Koko by bars. Watched by Koko's official photographer, Gorilla Foundation co-founder Ron Cohn, I open up the bag of goodies I bought at Toys R Us and flick through a picture book on zoo animals, touching each page and holding it up to her eyes. She then points to the padlock on the door and signs for Dr. Patterson to open it. I sit cross-legged, and Koko shuffles her 300-pound frame toward me.

7   I'm sweating now and still trying desperately not to make eye contact. Suddenly, I feel her leathery hand softly touch mine. She pulls me gently toward her chest, wrapping her arms around me. I can smell her breath—sweet and warm, not unlike a horse's. After she releases me from her embrace, she makes another sign—fists together. "She wants you to follow—to chase her," Dr. Patterson says. Koko lightly takes my hand and places it in the bend in her arm before leading me around the small room, cluttered with soft toys and clothes. I shuffle along the floor so as not to seem threatening, but it's amazing how gentle she is.

8   My wife and I had a baby daughter just three weeks before my visit, and I pull a photo out of my pocket to show her. I've learned the sign—pointing to myself and then making a rocking motion with my arms—to indicate "my baby." Incredibly, Koko takes the photo, looks at it, and kisses it. She then turns, picks up a doll from the mound of toys beside her, and holds it up to me. At one point she tugs lightly on my arm to indicate I'm to lie down beside her. Dr. Patterson says she can sense I'm nervous and does this to make people feel at ease. Another time she turns her back to me and indicates I'm to scratch it for her. She swings herself up onto a large plastic chair and Dr. Patterson turns on a video for her. It's Mary Poppins, and Koko signals that I'm to sit next to her. If my day wasn't surreal enough, it dawns on me that I'm watching Dick Van Dyke while sitting next to a gorilla. After two more hugs,

wielding
using

Koko is coaxed away by Dr. Patterson, **wielding** a nut. And it's over. I stand outside on the porch again and wave good-bye, and she blows me a kiss, then puts her head up to the cage and puckers her lips. I reach out and touch them and then disappear back up the path.

9   The Gorilla Foundation was born in the late 1970s when Dr. Patterson was studying for a Ph.D. in developmental psychology at Stanford University. After discovering a small, undernourished baby gorilla at the San Francisco Zoo, Dr. Patterson persuaded the institution to lend her the animal and started her dissertation on the linguistic capabilities of a lowland gorilla. Two weeks into her

studies, Dr. Patterson noted that Koko was able to make the signs to indicate food and drink. Project Koko, Dr. Patterson's life's work, was born. She makes it clear to me how she feels about gorillas in captivity—40 percent of males die of heart problems before the age of 30, she tells me, something that doesn't happen in the wild—but while it was never her decision for Koko to be born in a zoo, she says, the gorilla's contribution to our understanding of her species has been immeasurable.

10   Dr. Patterson says Koko is extremely sophisticated in her thought processes, using not just sign language but communication cards, books, and multimedia to express herself. Some skeptics have argued that Koko does not understand the meaning behind what she is doing and simply learns to sign because she'll be rewarded. Dr. Patterson admits that in the beginning she, too, thought Koko was simply doing it to "get stuff," but the gorilla began stringing words together to describe objects she didn't know the signs for. A hairbrush, for example, became a "scratch comb"; a mask was an "eye hat"; and a ring was a "finger bracelet." From my own limited time with Koko, I could see reward wasn't her motivation. Yes, she signed to achieve goals, but these goals weren't treats: They were to get me to follow her around the room, to get me to lie down, to get me to play with her—to interact.

11   The idea that Koko might teach sign language to any future offspring is fascinating to researchers. Dr. Patterson says Koko's desire for a baby has evolved over the years. From the age of about 6 she was caring for dolls, and her maternal instincts progressed to living things: a rabbit "wandering around Stanford—obviously a lab escapee"—and then a kitten that Koko named All Ball, eventually the subject of a children's book by Dr. Patterson.

12   "She was very gentle and careful with All Ball," says Dr. Patterson. "She wanted to nurture it." But a few months after All Ball came into Koko's life, the cat escaped from her enclosure and was run over by a car. Dr. Patterson says that when Koko found out, she signed "bad, sad, bad" and "frown, cry, frown." Recently, Dr. Patterson says, Koko has shown no interest in visiting kittens—an indication, she believes, that she is now after the real thing. Through pictures and signs, Koko has indicated that she'd like to raise a child in a group situation. "A mother gorilla and baby in isolation aren't healthy. Zoos have discovered this," Dr. Patterson says. "It takes a village to raise a baby gorilla—just like humans." The ideal scenario is that a zoo or wildlife park loans the Gorilla Foundation a couple of females. Ndume would then impregnate one of them and the three mothers, Koko included, would raise the baby in a group.

13   The book *Koko's Kitten* was published 24 years ago, but now Patterson aims to distribute it in areas in Africa where gorillas are threatened—to teach children there how a great ape can love and care for an animal of another species. We've also learned that great apes, like humans, have the capacity for **empathy**, says Dr. Patterson. "Their politics work like our politics," she says. "If you're not nice, you're out of the group."

empathy
the ability to understand another's feelings

A. UNDERSTANDING THE THESIS AND OTHER MAIN IDEAS

Select the best answer.

_____ 1. Which of the following best states the thesis or central thought of the selection?

   a. Koko the gorilla, who has learned American sign language, is proof that animals born and raised in captivity are capable of human emotions and communication.

   b. The author's experiences with Koko the gorilla make an excellent case for the idea that gorillas can communicate with humans, and the Koko research has raised awareness of efforts dedicated to the conservation of gorillas' natural habitats.

   c. The work of Dr. Penny Patterson of the Gorilla Institute has been instrumental in identifying areas in which human communication and gorilla communication are similar; these efforts are ongoing but need a constant infusion of cash.

   d. Hollywood celebrities have used Koko as a means of generating publicity for themselves; however, Koko's keepers have permitted this because they understand that allowing celebrities access to Koko will aid their fundraising efforts.

_____ 2. The author's purpose in this reading selection is to

   a. convince readers to support the work of Dr. Patterson, the Gorilla Institute, and the San Francisco Zoo.

   b. debunk the myth that animals cannot communicate with humans.

   c. provide a detailed summary of the research conducted with Koko as its subject over the last four decades.

   d. describe his experiences with Koko, discuss gorilla conservation efforts, and explore some of the insights suggested by the Koko research.

_____ 3. The main idea of paragraph 4 is found in the

   a. first sentence.

   b. second sentence.

   c. third sentence.

   d. last sentence.

_____ 4. The topic of paragraph 9 is

   a. Dr. Penny Patterson.

   b. the Gorilla Foundation.

   c. the history of Project Koko.

   d. the San Francisco Zoo.

_____ 5. Which of the following key ideas is *not* supported by the reading?

    a. Gorillas can feel empathy.

    b. As a result of Project Koko, poaching in Africa has greatly decreased.

    c. Although Koko can communicate, she is still a wild animal, and human beings must be cautious around her.

    d. Koko has repeatedly revealed a maternal instinct.

B. IDENTIFYING DETAILS

Select the best answer.

_____ 1. On which continent are all native gorilla species found?

    a. North America

    b. South America

    c. Asia

    d. Africa

_____ 2. The term used by researchers for primates who have developed a human-like culture as a result of their own culture being suppressed is

    a. acculturated.

    b. inculturated.

    c. assimilated.

    d. humanized.

_____ 3. The name of Koko's current mate is

    a. Michael.

    b. Ron.

    c. Ndume.

    d. Leonardo.

_____ 4. All Ball was a

    a. rabbit.

    b. kitten.

    c. gorilla.

    d. chinchilla.

_____ 5. Which signs did Koko make to communicate the idea of "ring"?

    a. pretty picture

    b. hand circle

    c. finger bracelet

    d. round metal

C. RECOGNIZING METHODS OF ORGANIZATION AND TRANSITIONS

Select the best answer.

_____ 1. The primary organizational pattern used in paragraphs 1–9 is
   a. chronological order.
   b. summary.
   c. classification.
   d. comparison and contrast.

_____ 2. Which paragraph makes use of definition?
   a. paragraph 1
   b. paragraph 5
   c. paragraph 9
   d. paragraph 13

_____ 3. The transitional word or phrase used in paragraph 5 to indicate the statement-and-clarification pattern is
   a. suppressed and adopted.
   b. in other words.
   c. should attempt.
   d. despite.

_____ 4. The organizational pattern used in paragraph 10 is
   a. process.
   b. chronological order.
   c. cause-and-effect.
   d. statement and clarification.

D. REVIEWING AND ORGANIZING IDEAS: SUMMARIZING

Complete the following summary of paragraphs 10–12 by filling in the missing words and phrases from the box below.

> advanced   All Ball   books   child   group   maternal   rabbit   support

Dr. Penny Patterson believes that Koko the gorilla uses _____ thought processes, communicating through several methods, including sign language, communication cards, and _____. Although some have argued that Koko uses sign language because she wants something, not because she is truly communicating, Dr. Patterson disagrees. She believes that Koko's combining of different signs to express ideas shows that she is truly communicating. The author's brief experiences with Koko seem to _____ Dr. Patterson's belief.

Dr. Patterson notes that Koko's desire to have a baby has increased over the years. Koko began showing her _____ instinct by adopting first an escaped _____ and then a kitten that she named _____. Koko was very sad when her kitten was run over by a car. Now, however, Koko is not interested in kittens, and Dr. Patterson believes it's because Koko wants a _____ of her own. Dr. Patterson believes a zoo is not the ideal place to raise a baby gorilla; but in a zoo or wildlife park, a _____ of gorillas, including Koko, could work together to raise a baby that was fathered by Ndume.

E. READING AND THINKING VISUALLY

Select the best answer.

_____ 1. The author likely included the photo on page 281 in order to
   a. illustrate Koko's early history.
   b. provide a portrait of Dr. Patterson.
   c. advocate for animal rights.
   d. illustrate the applications of sign language.

_____ 2. Which of the following would be the least relevant illustration to accompany this selection?
   a. the cover of *Koko's Kitten*
   b. an illustration showing how to make the signs for words like *baby, hello,* and *hairbrush*
   c. the gates of the San Diego Zoo
   d. a photo of the adult Koko and Ndume

F. FIGURING OUT IMPLIED MEANINGS

Indicate whether each statement is true (T) or false (F).

_____ 1. Some animals see eye contact as an act of aggression.

_____ 2. The Koko research was sponsored by the Gorilla Foundation.

_____ 3. The author implies that the African logging industry does not care about gorilla conservation.

_____ 4. Koko is mother to two baby gorillas.

_____ 5. In general, it is better for a baby gorilla to be raised by a group of gorillas rather than only by its biological parents.

_____ 6. The politics of gorilla interaction are similar to the politics of human interaction.

_____ 7. The author believes that Koko uses sign languages primarily as a way to "get stuff."

_____ 8. Koko had a positive response to the author, Alex Hannaford.

G. THINKING CRITICALLY

Select the best answer.

_____ 1. The tone of the selection can best be described as

    a. angry.

    b. intolerant.

    c. fascinated.

    d. bemused.

_____ 2. The author's primary purpose for writing the selection is to

    a. argue for severe criminal penalties for those accused or convicted of poaching in protected areas.

    b. provide an in-depth look at Koko's current life in captivity.

    c. explore human-primate communication and how Koko's story is helping conservation efforts.

    d. help the author learn how to communicate better with his own recently born child.

_____ 3. The author supports his central thesis with

    a. personal experience with Koko and interviews with Dr. Penny Patterson.

    b. research citations from a number of highly respected zoological journals.

    c. references to the journalists who have written about Koko over the past forty years.

    d. expert opinion from staff members of zoos across the world.

_____ 4. In paragraph 4, the phrase "bush meat" means

    a. meat that is eaten raw.

    b. meat hunted from wild animals.

    c. meat derived from tree-dwelling primates.

    d. meat from carnivorous animals.

_____ 5. Which of the following statements from the selection is an opinion, not a fact?

    a. "Koko . . . was taught American sign language when she was about a year old." (paragraph 2)

    b. "At 40, Koko could possibly be more relevant than ever." (paragraph 5)

    c. "It's rare that anyone gets to meet Koko up close." (paragraph 6)

    d. "The Gorilla Foundation was born in the late 1970s when Dr. Patterson was studying for a Ph.D. in developmental psychology at Stanford." (paragraph 9)

H. BUILDING VOCABULARY

Context

Using context and a dictionary, if necessary, determine the meaning of each word as it is used in the selection.

_____ 1. glare (paragraph 2)

     a. brightness

     b. lightning

     c. surrender

     d. stare

_____ 2. inadvertently (paragraph 4)

     a. happily

     b. strangely

     c. privately

     d. unintentionally

_____ 3. rife (paragraph 4)

     a. dangerous

     b. unjust

     c. widespread

     d. illegal

_____ 4. coaxed (paragraph 8)

     a. pulled

     b. teased

     c. persuaded

     d. commanded

Word Parts

> ## A REVIEW OF PREFIXES
>
> **INTER-** means *between*.
> **SUB-** means *under or below*.
> **MULTI-** means *many*.

Use your knowledge of word parts to fill in the blanks.

1. *Interspecies* (paragraph 2) communication refers to communication
   _____ two or more species.

2. A *subspecies* (paragraph 4) is a category _____ the larger category of "species."

3. A *multimedia* (paragraph 10) communication method involves the use of
   _____ media, such as video, audio, and written text.

I. SELECTING A LEARNING/STUDY STRATEGY

Write a list of the author's interactions with Koko and what he learned from each.

J. EXPLORING IDEAS THROUGH DISCUSSION AND WRITING

1. Paraphrase paragraphs 4 and 5.

2. How do you feel about wild animals being kept in captivity? Write a paragraph explaining your answer.

3. What does Koko's "growl" mean? In addition to sign language, in what other ways does Koko communicate? Write a paragraph answering these questions.

4. If you have pets (or know someone who does), write an essay describing how these animals communicate their feelings or needs. You may want to consider either the interspecies communication that takes place between two different kinds of pets, or communication between humans and their pets.

5. How effective do you think Koko's story will be in helping to "win hearts and minds"? What makes Koko an appealing "poster child" for the conservation movement? What other methods might the Gorilla Foundation and other conservationists use to educate communities about the plight of gorillas? Write an essay exploring these questions.

K. BEYOND THE CLASSROOM TO THE WEB

Visit the Web site of one of the organizations mentioned in this reading, the Gorilla Foundation. What new or additional information is available about Koko that was not discussed in this reading? Summarize two or three key points and share them with the class.

TRACKING YOUR PROGRESS

Selection 4

Section	Number Correct		Score
A. Thesis and Main Ideas (5 items)	_____	× 3	_____
B. Details (5 items)	_____	× 3	_____
C. Organization and Transitions (4 items)	_____	× 3	_____
E. Reading Thinking Visually (2 items)	_____	× 3	_____
F. Implied Meanings (8 items)	_____	× 2	_____
G. Thinking Critically (5 items)	_____	× 3	_____
H. Vocabulary			
Context (4 items)	_____	× 3	_____
Word Parts (3 items)	_____	× 3	_____
		Total Score	_____%

SELECTION 5

Movie and TV Genres

John Vivian

TEXTBOOK
EXCERPT

PREVIEWING THE READING

Using the steps listed on pages 40–41, preview the reading selection. When you have finished, complete the following items.

1. This reading selection is about _____ and TV _____. The selection also contains a section on _____ genres.

2. List at least five movie genres. _____

_____

3. List at least four television genres. _____

_____

MAKING
CONNECTIONS

What are your favorite TV shows? Your favorite movies or films? How do you decide which movies to see in a movie theater versus which movies you will rent for viewing at home?

READING TIP

As you read, note that the author discusses "motion media" worldwide. Use your own viewing experiences to help you understand definitions, and expand your horizons by paying attention to the examples from other countries, as well as the history of the industry.

genre
category
ergonomics
the study of how
people interact
with their
surroundings; in
this case, the way
people choose to
view motion
media on screens

Movie and TV Genres

1   The products of motion media industries include **genres** that overlap but also include significant distinctions. The lesson: What works on big screens, like in a movie theater, doesn't necessarily work on small screens, like television and hand-held devices. Or at least work differently. One factor is the impossible-to-duplicate impact of larger screens. Another is **ergonomics**. Nobody has the patience to hold a smartphone 14 inches from your face and watch feature-length movies in a single sitting.

Movie Genres

2   Ask someone what a movie is. You'll likely hear a description of what's called feature films that tell stories. Their impact is partly from the overwhelming images on a huge screen. The impact also is from being sealed inside the darkened cocoon of an auditorium. No distractions.

3   **Narrative Films**. Movies that tell stories, much in the tradition of stage plays, are narrative films. These features films are promoted heavily, their titles and actors on marquees. Most are in the 100-minute range. A French magician and inventor, Georges Méliès, pioneered narrative films with fairy tales and science-fiction stories to show in his movie house in 1896. Méliès' *Little Red Riding Hood* and *Cinderella* ran less than 10 minutes—short stories, if you will. Notable innovations in narrative films since the earliest films have been sound, color, and computer-generated imagery.

4   **Talkies**. Earlier audiences were so mesmerized by moving visuals that they didn't mind that the movies were silent. Four upstart moviemakers, the Warner brothers, Albert, Harry, Jack and Sam Warner, changed that in 1927. The Warners' *The Jazz Singer* starring Al Jolson included sound in two segments, 354 words total. Soon theaters everywhere were equipped with loudspeakers. The next year, 1928, the Warners issued *The Singing Fool*, also with Jolson, this time with a full-length soundtrack. The Warners earned 25 times their investment. For 10 years no other movie attracted more people to the box office.

5   **Color**. Overtaking *The Singing Fool* in 1939 was a narrative movie with another technological breakthrough, *Gone with the Wind* with color. Although *Gone with the Wind* is often referred to as the first color movie, the technology had been devised in the 1920s, and *The Black Pirate* with Douglas Fairbanks was far earlier, in 1925. But *GWTW*, as it's called by buffs, was a far more significant film. *GWTW* marked the start of Hollywood's quest for ever-more-spectacular stories and effects to attract audiences—the blockbuster.

6   **Computer-Generated Imagery**. You can imagine why early moviemaker Alfred Clark used a special effect for his 1895 movie *The Execution of Mary Queen of Scots*. "Illusion" was what special effects were called then. Although audiences were amazed, the effects were nothing like today's *CGI*, the shoptalk abbreviation that movie people use for three-dimensional computer-generated imagery. There were CGI scenes in *Star Wars* in 1977, but the technology remained mostly an experimental novelty until 1989 when the pseudopod sea creature created by Industrial Light & Magic for *The Abyss* won an Academy Award.

7   Computer-generated imagery soon became the dominant form of special effect. For stunts, CGI characters began replacing doubles that were nearly indistinguishable from the actors. Crowd scenes were easily created without hiring hundreds of extras. This raised the question of whether movie actors themselves might be replaced by pixels.

8   Movie commentator Neil Petkus worries that some filmmakers may overuse their toy. "CGI effects can be abused and mishandled," Petkus says. "Directors sometimes allow the visual feasts that computers offer to undermine any real content a movie may have had." Petkus faults director George Lucas for going too far in later *Star Wars* movies: "Any interesting character developments that could have occurred in these movies were overwhelmed by constant CGI action sequences."

9   **Animated Films**. The 1920s were pivotal in defining genres of narrative films. In his early 20s, Walt Disney arrived in Los Angeles from Missouri in 1923 with $40 in his pocket. Walt moved in with his brother Roy, and they rounded up $500 and went into the animated film business. In 1928 *Steamboat Willie* debuted in a short film to accompany feature films. The character Willie eventually morphed into Mickey Mouse. Disney took animation to full length with *Snow White and the Seven Dwarfs* in 1937, cementing animation as a subspecies of narrative films.

10   Animated films were labor-intensive, requiring an illustrator to create 1,000-plus sequential drawings for a minute of screen time. Computers changed all that in the 1990s, first with digital effects for movies that otherwise had scenes and actors, notably the *Star Wars* series by George Lucas, then animated features. Disney's *Toy Story* in 1995 was the first movie produced entirely by computers. This new technology led to the **resurgence** of animated films and re-established them as a box office staple.

resurgence
increase to
earlier levels of
popularity

11   **Documentaries**. Nonfiction film explorations of historical or current events and natural and social phenomena go back to 1922 and Robert Flaherty's look into Eskimo life. With their informational thrust, early documentaries had great credibility. Soon, though, propagandists were exploiting the credibility of documentaries with point-of-view nonfiction. Propagandist films found large audiences in World War II, including Frank Capra's seven 50-minute films in the *Why We Fight* series.

12   **Little Movies**. New structures have evolved for moviemaking newcomers to interest the distribution units of major studios in their work. A model for these so-called little movies is the Sundance Film Festival in Park City, Utah. Every January, Hollywood dispatches teams to audition films by independent filmmakers at the event. These are low-budget projects that sometimes bring substantial returns on investment. *The Blair Witch Project*, by a team of University of Central Florida grads, is classic. The movie cost $35,000 to produce. The young colleagues on the project made a killing when scouts from Artisan Entertainment watched a Sundance screening of it in 1998 and paid $1.1 million for distribution rights. For Artisan, the movie generated $141 million at the box office.

Television Genres

13   Television has moved through waves of programming that rise into sudden popularity, then fade. Prime time once was dominated by variety performance shows, then cowboy Westerns, then family dramas, then detective shows. A **perennial** has been situation comedies, called *sitcoms* in industry lingo.

perennial
something that is
enduring

14   **Sitcoms**. Many programs that early television adapted from radio were series with continuing characters in a new, usually dilemmatic situation every week and lots of laugh lines. Soon television was creating original sitcoms, most notably *I Love Lucy*, which ran 197 episodes over nine seasons starting in 1951 followed by special programs through 1960. *Lucy* replays even today. Since 2003 the CBS sitcom *Two and a Half Men* has been a ratings leader with 15 million viewers a week, although there have been questions about whether the numbers can be sustained with Ashton Kutcher replacing Charlie Sheen in the lead for the 2012 season.

15   **Dramatic Series**. The series CSI was a ratings smash for CBS beginning with gruesome leave-nothing-to-the-imagination high-tech investigations into grisly

murders. Other series followed, many like *NCIS* finding large and continuing audiences. Before pathology-themed crime series, there have been other rages in dramatic series. The longest running were Westerns. *Gunsmoke* ran 635 episodes from 1965 to 1975, *Bonanza* 431 episodes from 1959 to 1973. Another genre wave was criminal dramas, led by *Law & Order*, which started a 20-plus season run in 1990.

parlaying
transforming

16   **Reality Shows**. Mark Burnett likes telling the story of **parlaying** his early life experiences as a British Army parachutist, beach T-shirt hawker, Hollywood chauffeur, and nanny into the pioneer prime-time reality show *Survivor*. The key was spotting a 1991 newspaper article about a French adventure contest. With four other members, he created a team, American Pride. Quickly he saw a business opportunity and created a similar race that he called *Eco-Challenge*. That led to *Survivor*, which premiered its 2000 and ushered in a wave of reality programs with contestants in continuing elimination tests and trials. Burnett has created dozens of other shows, including *The Apprentice*.

17   In all, Burnett produced 1,100 hours of television in the decade beginning with the first *Survivor* season. Success begat imitators. Reality-based shows became a major television genre. Dozens of shows followed in the same grain, many with the money-making magic of being relatively low-budget audience-builders that attract big-bucks advertisers. These shows, each with a twist, many on cable networks, included *Storage Wars*, *Top Chef*, *Pawn Stars*, *Deadliest Catch*, and *Ice Road Truckers*. Many combined attractions of the quiz-show genre.

18   **News.** When television emerged as a major medium, people already were watching newsreels at movie houses. These audiovisual features, typically 10 minutes, played with the previews and cartoons before the featured attraction. Network newscasts on television displaced newsreels in the 1950s. Walter Cronkite's evening newscast on CBS was a staple in the lives of Americans from 1962 to 1981.

19   The legacy networks still carry evening newscasts but also have nurtured news-entertainment hybrids like NBC's *Today*, with affiliates piggybacking local programs that mix their own coverage with soft news and fluff.

20   But people no longer need to wait for scheduled newscasts. Since 1980 Cable News Network, CNN for short, has offered around-the-clock news. MSNBC and Fox News Channel came along in 1996. The future of network evening newscasts on the legacy networks may be in question with their aging viewerships and diminishing ratings.

21   **Television Documentaries.** Film documentaries during World War II were propagandist. After the war, however, television journalists sought to bring balance and fairness to documentaries in the 1950s. In part it was that journalists of the just-the-facts mold were doing the documentaries. Also, it was the television networks that underwrote the budgets of these documentaries. Their purpose was to build corporate prestige, not propagandize. A factor in the neutral thrust of most of these documentaries also was the Federal Communications Commission's Fairness Doctrine, a licensing dictate to stations for balance in treating contentions issues.

epitomized
was the perfect
example of

22   The FCC withdrew its Fairness Doctrine in 1987, setting in motion a new rationale for documentaries that, in many cases, seeks not so much to inform as to influence the audience. What emerged was a new-form genre that critics call docu-ganda. Independent filmmaker Michael Moore has **epitomized** the new generation of documentary-makers in movies, first, with *Roger and Me*, a brutal attack on General Motors. Moore's 2004 *Fahrenheit 9/11*, aimed at President Bush's motivations for the

Ken Burns. Documentary producer Ken Burns drew more viewers to PBS with his 1990 Civil War series than any other program in the network's history. He casts his net wide for subjects—baseball, jazz, wars—and consistently delivers definitive treatments. His piece on U.S. national parks debuted in 2009, followed by works on Prohibition, the Dust Bowl, and the Central Park Five convictions.

Iraq war, was the largest-grossing documentary in history—a demonstration of the economic viability of documentaries.

23   Television largely has followed the tradition of the Fairness Doctrine, but the detached, neutral tone has given way to some single point-of-view documentaries. For better or worse? To critics, new-style documentary producer David Zieger says, "Guilty as charged." Zieger raised eyebrows with his *Sir! No Sir!* on the anti-war movement within the military during the Vietnam war and acknowledged his lopsidedness: "If you make a film with both sides, you're going to make a boring film." Film is not journalism, Zieger says.

24   The point-of-view documentaries, whether in movies or television, require viewers to have a high level of media literacy. Competing viewpoints aren't always presented within a single package. Some critics say that the contemporary documentaries that make the biggest splash are, in fact, dangerous because they can dupe viewers into accepting there as the whole truth.

Small-Screen Genres

25   Smartphones and other small-screen devices have been problems for media companies trying to recycle existing products to squeeze out more revenue. Cinemascope doesn't translate well to a laptop, never mind a smartphone. Besides technical issues, there also are very human issues. Rare is the person who will sit through 92 minutes of Jake Kasden's *Bad Teacher*, let alone Paul Johannson's 102-minute screen adaptation of Ayn Rand's 414-page *Atlas Shrugged*. Bad ergonomics doesn't attract audiences.

26   **Video Games**. The most successful genre of small screen content has been the video games designed for-small screen playing. Finnish game maker Rovio sold 12 million copies of Angry Birds in 2010 for Apple iPhones and quickly added versions for Android phones and other touch screen systems.

27   **Quick Drama**. Television networks have tried bridging the attention-span issue of small devices with webisodes—short segments from full-length programs or completely new material, some only three minutes. The webisode concept can be traced to filmmaker Scott Zakarin and his interactive fiction website program *The Spot* in 1995. Zakarin claimed more than 100,000 hits a day, impressive at its time, for his 20s-somethings cast and their beach house dramas. The *Spot* was original drama, in contrast to the later network television attempts to adapt produced-for-television material for small screens.

28   When initiated, the relatively short network webisodes addressed slow Internet downloads. Improved technology has since made television-length programs available for Internet TV, fulfilling the need for on-demand watching.

29   **Live TV**. The universal love affair with small-screen devices made the availability of live television for smartphone and tablet users a no brainer. Subscription-based applications like Netfix, AT&T U-verse Live TV, and Hulu Plus offer instant access to television shows and movies.

30   **Product and Advertising Quality**. Technically and often artistically, the best small-screen motion visuals are produced exclusively for small screens, not adapted from other platforms. This includes videos on products—and also advertising. Just as the advertising industry has long had variations on campaigns for television, radio and print presentation, ad agencies now work to assure a campaign also lends itself to small-screen viewing.

31   **Do-it-yourself Quality**. The weakest small-screen genre technically and artistically comprises post-your-own videos on sites like the original YouTube. By their nature, these are mostly amateur offerings that, when they go viral, are often for the attractions of funny, odd or bizarre content rather than for quality.

32   **APPLYING YOUR MEDIA LITERACY**

- How is it that movies on television fall short of the experience of viewing the same movie in a theater?
- Programming for the expanding cable television market continues. What might be the next genre for television programming and why?
- What kind of moving-image content works well on smartphones and other small-screen devices? Why?

A. UNDERSTANDING THE THESIS AND OTHER MAIN IDEAS

Select the best answer.

_____ 1. Which of the following best states the thesis or central thought of the selection?

    a. While movies and TV programs may appear to be similar, they evolved in very different ways and appeal to completely different audiences.

    b. Movies are the oldest form of motion media, and television is still going strong; but small-screen entertainments are rapidly gaining a large audience.

    c. There are three main types of motion media (movies, television, and motion media on the small screen), and each can be divided into numerous categories.

    d. In the early days of motion media, the two most important advances were the addition of a soundtrack and color production, but today the single most important factor is computer-generated graphics.

_____ 2. The topic of paragraph 8 is

    a. Neil Petkus.

    b. criticisms of over-reliance on CGI.

    c. George Lucas and *Star Wars*.

    d. visual effects.

_____ 3. Which of the following best states the main idea of paragraph 10?

    a. Animation was much loved by a previous generation, but today's moviegoers love a movie with a large number of computer-generated images.

    b. Animation, once a labor-intensive process, is now easily accomplished with computers; in fact, entire films are now made with computers.

    c. The two most important films in U.S. history are *Star Wars* and *Toy Story*.

    d. When the Disney brothers invested their money in an animation studio, they had no idea that computers would someday play such an important role in the film industry.

_____ 4. The topic of paragraph 27 is

    a. Scott Zakarin.

    b. *The Spot*.

    c. TV networks.

    d. webisodes.

B. IDENTIFYING DETAILS

Select the best answer.

_____ 1. Which statement is not true of the early films of George Méliès?
   a. Some were based on fairy tales.
   b. They sometimes had a science-fiction theme.
   c. They debuted in a movie house in 1896.
   d. They usually lasted about 100 minutes.

_____ 2. Mickey Mouse's original name was
   a. Scott.   c. Roy.
   b. Willie.   d. Walt.

_____ 3. The first movie produced entirely by computers was
   a. *Birth of a Nation.*   c. *Snow White and the Seven Dwarfs.*
   b. *Star Wars.*   d. *Toy Story.*

_____ 4. Which statement is true of news?
   a. The earliest news reports lasted about ten minutes.
   b. The audience for TV news programming is growing.
   c. The earliest all-news cable TV channels premiered in 1996.
   d. Most news programming on the major networks today focuses on investigative reporting.

_____ 5. Why does reality TV make money for its producers?
   a. In surveys, most Americans say that reality TV is their favorite television genre.
   b. TV stations can air the same reality TV programs in every country in the world.
   c. Reality TV shows are cheap to produce and attract advertisers.
   d. Merchandise associated with reality TV, such as T-shirts and hats, is very popular with viewers.

_____ 6. The docu-ganda became possible when
   a. Michael Moore received funding from several liberal organizations to create biased movies.
   b. American documentary filmmakers began experiencing greater competition from foreign documentaries produced in Europe and Asia.
   c. propagandists in World War II began using motion media to influence the attitudes and opinions of the American public.
   d. the Federal Communications Commission withdrew its Fairness Doctrine in 1987.

C. RECOGNIZING METHODS OF ORGANIZATION AND TRANSITIONS

Select the best answer.

_____ 1. The overall pattern of organization used in "Movie and TV Genres" is

    a. chronological order.

    b. process.

    c. cause and effect.

    d. classification.

_____ 2. Which transitional words or phrases in paragraph 9 signal use of the chronological order pattern?

    a. In 1923, in 1928, in 1937

    b. arrived in, rounded up

    c. debuted, morphed

    d. went into, took animation to full length

_____ 3. The organizational pattern used in paragraph 12 is

    a. spatial order.

    b. comparison and contrast.

    c. definition.

    d. summary.

D. REVIEWING AND ORGANIZING IDEAS: PARAPHRASING

Complete the following paraphrase of paragraphs 14 and 15 by filling in the missing words or phrases.

Many early TV _____ were based on radio programs. These early shows featured a set of characters in comic situations trying to solve _____. New sitcoms began to be developed specifically for TV; one of the most famous was the wildly successful _____, which ran from 1951 to _____ and remains popular today. *Two and a Half Men* is a successful modern sitcom. In the _____ series category, CBS had a major success with *CSI*, which had many imitators. Earlier successful dramatic series fell into different genres, including _____ (for example, *Gunsmoke* and *Bonanza*) and criminal dramas (including _____, which ran for more than 20 years).

E. READING AND THINKING VISUALLY

Select the best answer.

_____ Which of the following statements is true about the caption to the photo found on page 296 ?

a. The caption focuses on a filmmaker known for his success in creating reality TV series.

b. The caption focuses on a key member of George Lucas's production team.

c. The caption contains information that is not found in the reading.

d. The caption makes it clear that Ken Burns's documentaries are one-sided and have a strongly political agenda.

F. FIGURING OUT IMPLIED MEANINGS

Indicate whether each statement is true (T) or false (F).

_____ 1. The earliest news programming was shown before feature films in movie theaters.

_____ 2. *The Jazz Singer* was the first full-color motion picture.

_____ 3. The author implies that most forms of motion media work equally well on smartphones, television screens, and movie theater screens.

_____ 4. The author suggests that plays evolved into films.

_____ 5. Illusion was the predecessor of computer-generated imagery.

_____ 6. Point-of-view documentaries often tell only one side of the story and therefore require moviegoers to be informed critical thinkers.

_____ 7. Webisodes have been the most successful of the small-screen genres.

_____ 8. In the history of television, the longest running series have been sitcoms.

_____ 9. The author believes that *Gone with the Wind* was the first Hollywood blockbuster.

G. THINKING CRITICALLY

Select the best answer.

_____ 1. The purpose of "Movie and TV Genres" is to

a. provide an overview of the different types of films, television shows, and small-screen entertainments.

b. trace the role of the U.S. government in media-based propaganda in the twentieth century.

c. persuade students to pursue a career in writing, acting, or producing.

d. offer a thorough, detailed history of filmmaking in the United States.

_____ 2. The tone of the reading selection is best described as

    a. humorous.

    b. cynical.

    c. pessimistic.

    d. informative.

_____ 3. Which of the following statements from the reading is a fact, not an opinion?

    a. "Nobody has the patience to hold a smartphone 14 inches from your face and watch feature-length movies in a single sitting." (paragraph 1)

    b. "Earlier audiences were so mesmerized by moving visuals that they didn't mind that the movies were silent." (paragraph 4)

    c. "Nonfiction film explorations of historical or current events and natural and social phenomena go back to 1922 and Robert Flaherty's look into Eskimo life." (paragraph 11)

    d. "Technically and often artistically, the best small-screen motion visuals are produced exclusively for small screens." (paragraph 30)

_____ 4. In paragraph 11, the author states, "Soon, though, propagandists were exploiting the credibility of documentaries with point-of-view nonfiction." He means that

    a. the American public is basically uninformed and therefore easily manipulated.

    b. filmmakers with a specific agenda used documentaries' reputation for fairness in order to present their opinions as the truth.

    c. it is much more difficult to make a documentary (which is a form of nonfiction) than it is to make a feature film that tells a story about fictional characters or events.

    d. documentaries, which were once a highly trusted form of the filmmaker's art, have become much less effective now that producers also create documentaries for TV.

_____ 5. In paragraph 12, the figurative expression "made a killing" means

    a. made a lot of money.

    b. murdered someone.

    c. wrote a screenplay featuring a good deal of violence.

    d. betrayed a friend.

_____ 6. Which of the following phrases from the reading has a negative connotation?

   a. "notable innovations" (paragraph 3)

   b. "industry lingo" (paragraph 13)

   c. "soft news and fluff" (paragraph 19)

   d. "universal love affair" (paragraph 29)

H. BUILDING VOCABULARY

Context

Using context and a dictionary, if necessary, determine the meaning of each word as it is used in the selection.

_____ 1. buffs (paragraph 5)

   a. headbands

   b. historians

   c. fans

   d. scholars

_____ 2. morphed (paragraph 9)

   a. changed

   b. animated

   c. tricked

   d. sued

_____ 3. dispatches (paragraph 12)

   a. discards

   b. dismisses

   c. invests

   d. sends

_____ 4. grisly (paragraph 15)

   a. stained

   b. horrible

   c. visual

   d. fatty

_____ 5. begat (paragraph 17)

   a. created

   b. prevented

   c. followed

   d. balanced

_____ 6. contentious (paragraph 21)

     a. controversial

     b. happy

     c. newsworthy

     d. current

Word Parts

> ### A REVIEW OF PREFIXES, ROOTS, AND SUFFIXES
>
> **AUDIO** means *related to hearing*
> **-LOGY** means *the study of*
> **PATH** means *related to disease*
> **POD** means *foot*
> **PSEUDO-** means *false*

Use your knowledge of word parts and the review above to fill in the blanks and define the boldfaced words in the sentences below.

1. In biology, one-celled animals called amebas move themselves by extending a part of their single cell. This temporary protrusion is called a **pseudopod** (paragraph 6), which literally means _____.

2. **Pathology** (paragraph 15) is the study of _____.

3. An **audiovisual** (paragraph 18) presentation is one that appeals to the audience's sight and _____.

Unusual Words/Understanding Idioms

Use the meanings given below to write a sentence using the boldfaced word or phrase.

1. **Shoptalk** (paragraph 6) means talk about work. For example, a group of mechanics who visit an auto show may "talk shop" about car engines, transmissions, and other car features.

   Your sentence: _____

   _____

2. A **staple** (paragraph 10) is a very common element of something. For example, a staple of the U.S. diet is bread, and a staple of television is the sitcom.

   Your sentence: _____

   _____

3. To call something a **no brainer** (paragraph 29) is to say it is completely obvious.

Your sentence: _____

_____

I. SELECTING A LEARNING/STUDY STRATEGY

Select the best answer.

_____ All of the following are good writing and study strategies for learning the material in this reading *except*

a. creating an outline of the reading.

b. drawing a map of the reading.

c. summarizing the reading.

d. making a list of the movies discussed in the reading.

J. EXPLORING IDEAS THROUGH DISCUSSION AND WRITING

1. Create a time line for the movie industry.

2. Write a paragraph in which you define each of the TV genres introduced in paragraph 13: variety performance shows, cowboy Westerns, family dramas, and detective shows. Provide an example of each.

3. Choose one of the questions asked in paragraph 32 and respond to it in a paragraph.

4. Paragraph 17 discusses the reasons that reality TV shows make money for producers. Why do you think TV watchers enjoy reality TV so much? Write a paragraph or essay answering this question.

5. Choose any one of the genres discussed in this reading, and write an outline for an original production. For example, you might choose "documentary" and decide you would like to make a documentary exploring the role of sports in the social life of a particular high school or college.

K. BEYOND THE CLASSROOM TO THE WEB

Conduct an Internet search for a list of currently available webisodes. Watch two or three of them, then provide a summary of each. What is your opinion of them? Did you enjoy them? Why or why not? What similarities do you see to films and television shows? What differences do you see? Can you imagine webisodes becoming as popular as television programs? Why or why not?

TRACKING
YOUR
PROGRESS

Selection 5

Section	Number Correct	Score
A. Thesis and Main Ideas (4 items)	_____ × 3	_____
B. Details (6 items)	_____ × 3	_____
C. Organization and Transitions (3 items)	_____ × 3	_____
E. Reading and Thinking Visually (1 item)	_____ × 4	_____
F. Implied Meanings (9 items)	_____ × 2	_____
G. Thinking Critically (6 items)	_____ × 3	_____
H. Vocabulary		
Context (6 items)	_____ × 2	_____
Word Parts (3 items)	_____ × 3	_____
	Total Score	_____%

Relationships and Technology

Joseph A. DeVito

TEXTBOOK EXCERPT

Contemporary Issues Reading

Taken from a textbook titled *Interpersonal Messages: Communication and Relationship Skills*, this reading selection discusses the influence of technology on interpersonal relationships.

PREVIEWING THE READING

Using the steps listed on pages 40–41, preview the reading selection. When you have finished, complete the following items.

1. The subject of this selection is _____

2. List two questions you expect to be able to answer after reading this selection:

   a. _____

   b. _____

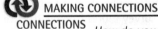

MAKING CONNECTIONS

CONNECTIONS   *How do you typically use the Internet? Estimate what percentage of the total amount of time you spend on the Internet is spent in each of the following categories: social, work, school, entertainment, and news.*

READING TIP

As you read, be sure to highlight the advantages and disadvantages of online relationships.

Relationships and Technology

1   Perhaps even more obvious than culture is the influence of technology on interpersonal relationships. Clearly, online interpersonal relationships are on the increase. The number of Internet users is rapidly increasing, and commercial websites devoted to helping people meet other people are proliferating, making it especially easy to develop online relationships. Such websites as spark.com (www.spark.com), Friend Finder (www.friendfinder.com), Date (www.date.com), Match (www.match.com), Lavalife (www.lavalife.com), and Where Singles Meet (www.wheresinglesmeet.com)

number their members in the millions, making it especially likely that you'll find someone you'd enjoy dating.

2   And not surprisingly, there are websites (for example, www.comparedatingwebsites .com and www.homeandfamilyreview.com/dating.htm) that offer comparisons of the various dating websites, distinguishing between those that are best for serious daters who are looking for lifetime commitment from those that are for people who want to find someone for casual dating. Lavalife, for example, has a pull down menu where you can indicate whether you want a casual date, a relationship, or an intimate encounter. And of course there are dating websites for different **affectional orientations** and different religious preferences.

affectional orientation
an alternative term for sexual or romantic orientation

3   Some dating websites—eharmony.com and perfectmatch.com are perhaps the most notable—have members complete extensive scientific questionnaires about their preferences and personalities which helps further in successfully matching people.

4   Some of these websites, for example, Friend Finder, give free trials so you can test the systems before registering or subscribing. And, to make these websites even more inviting, many of them offer chat rooms, dating and relationship advice, newsletters, and self-tests about love, relationships and dating.

5   Clearly, many people are turning to the Internet to find a friend or romantic partner. And, as you probably know, college students are making the most of sites such as Facebook.com and MySpace.com to meet other students on their own campus. In one study of MOOs (online role-playing games), 93.6 percent of the users formed ongoing friendships and romantic relationships. Some people use the Internet as their only means of interaction; others use it as a way of beginning a relationship and intend to supplement computer talk later with photographs, phone calls, and face-to-face meetings. Interestingly, a *New York Times* survey found that by 2003 online dating was losing its earlier stigma as a last resort for losers.

6   Note that the importance of physical attractiveness enters the face-to-face relationship through nonverbal cues—you see the person's eyes, face, body—and you perceive such attractiveness immediately. In online relationships, just a few years ago, physical attractiveness could have only been signaled through words and descriptions. And in this situation the face-to-face encounter favored those who were physically attractive, whereas the online encounter favored those who were verbally adept at self-presentation. Today, with the numerous social networks such as MySpace, you can post your photo and reveal your attractiveness. Many of the online dating services (such as Friend Finder) now provide you with opportunities to not only post your photograph but also a voice introduction. Of course you still reveal more of yourself in face-to-face encounters, but the differences are clearly diminishing. Table A (p. 309) provides one example of the stages of Internet relationships.

7   Other research on Internet use finds that a large majority of users form new acquaintances, friendships, and romantic partnerships through the Internet. One study, published in 1996, found that almost two-thirds of newsgroup users had formed new relationships with someone they met online. Almost one-third said that they communicated with their partner at least three or four times a week; more than half communicated on a weekly basis. And, a study published in 2006 found that 74 percent of Internet users who identify themselves as single and looking for romantic partners used the Internet for this purpose.

TABLE A ONLINE RELATIONSHIP STAGES

This table represents one attempt to identify the stages that people go through in Internet relationships. As you read down the table, consider how accurately this represents what you know of online relationships. How would you describe the way Internet relationships develop?

STAGE	BEHAVIOR
1. Curiosity	You explore and search for individuals through chat rooms and other online sources.
2. Investigation	You find out information about the individual.
3. Testing	You introduce various topics, looking for common ground.
4. Increasing frequency of contact	You increase the breadth and depth of your relationship.
5. Anticipation	You anticipate face-to-face interaction and wonder what that will bring.
6. Fantasy integration	You create a fantasy of what the person looks like and how the person behaves.
7. Face-to-face meeting	You meet face-to-face, and reality and fantasy meet.
8. Reconfiguration	You adjust the fantasy to the reality and may decide to end the relationship or to pursue it more vigorously.
9. Already separated	If you decide to maintain the relationship, you explore ways you can accomplish this.
10. Long-term relationship	You negotiate the new relationship, whether it will be maintained in its online form or in a new face-to-face form.

Source: This table is adapted from Leonard J. Shedletsky and Joan E. Aitken, *Human Communication on the Internet*, © 2004. Printed and electronically reproduced by permission of Pearson Education, Inc., Upper Saddle River, New Jersey.

8   Women, it seems, are more likely to form relationships on the Internet than men. An early study showed that about 72 percent of women and 55 percent of men had formed personal relationships online. And women are more likely to use the Internet to deepen their interpersonal relationships.

9   As relationships develop on the Internet, network convergence occurs; that is, as a relationship between two people develops, they begin to share their network of other communicators with each other. This, of course, is similar to relationships formed through face-to-face contact. Online work groups also are on the increase and have been found to be more task oriented and more efficient than face-to-face groups. Online groups also provide a sense of belonging that may once have been thought possible only through face-to-face interactions.

Advantages of Online Relationships

10   There are many advantages to establishing relationships online. For example, on-line relationships are safe in terms of avoiding the potential for physical violence or sexually transmitted diseases. Unlike relationships established in face-to-face encounters, in which physical appearance tends to outweigh personality, relationships formed through Internet communication focus on your inner qualities first. Rapport and mutual self-disclosure become more important than physical attractiveness in promoting intimacy. And, contrary to some popular opinions, online relationships rely just as heavily on the ideals of trust, honesty, and commitment as do face-to-face relationships. Friendship and romantic interaction on the Internet are a natural boon to shut-ins and extremely shy people, for whom traditional ways of meeting someone are often difficult. Computer talk is empowering for those with "physical disabilities or disfigurements," for whom face-to-face interactions often are superficial and often end with withdrawal. By eliminating the physical cues, computer talk equalizes the interaction and doesn't put the disfigured person, for example, at an immediate disadvantage in a society in which physical attractiveness is so highly valued. On the Internet you're free to reveal as much or as little about your physical self as you wish, when you wish.

11   Another obvious advantage is that the number of people you can reach is so vast that it's relatively easy to find someone who matches what you're looking for. The situation is like finding a book that covers just what you need from a library of millions of volumes rather than from a collection holding only several thousand.

Disadvantages of Online Relationships

12   Of course, online relationships also have their disadvantages. For one thing, in many situations you can't see the other person. Unless you use a service that enables

"People are more frightened of being lonely than of being hungry, or being deprived of sleep, or having their sexual needs unfulfilled." —Fried Fromm Reichman

you to include photos or exchange photos or meet face-to-face, you won't know what the person looks like. Even if photos are posted or exchanged, how certain can you be that the photos are of the person or that they were taken recently? In addition, in most situations you can't hear the person's voice and this too hinders you as you seek to develop a total picture of the other person. Of course, you can always add an occasional phone call to give you this added information.

13   Online, people can present a false self with little chance of detection. For example, minors may present themselves as adults, and adults may present themselves as children in order to conduct illicit and illegal sexual communications and, perhaps, arrange meetings. Similarly, people can present themselves as poor when they're rich, as mature when they're immature, as serious and committed when they're just enjoying the online experience. Although people can also misrepresent themselves in face-to-face relationships, the fact that it's easier to do online probably accounts for greater frequency of misrepresentation in computer relationships.

14   Another potential disadvantage—though some might argue it is actually an advantage—is that computer interactions may become all-consuming and may substitute for face-to-face interpersonal relationships in a person's life.

15   Perhaps the clearest finding that emerges from all the research on face-to-face and online relationships is that people will seek out and find the relationship that works best for them at a given stage in their lives. For some that relationship will be online, for others face-to-face, for still others a combination. And just as people change, their relationship needs and wants also change, what works now may not work two years from now, and what doesn't work now may be exactly right in a few years.

Source: Joseph A. DeVito, *Interpersonal Messages: Communication and Relationship Skills,* 1st ed., pp. 233–236, © 2008. Printed and electronically reproduced by permission of Pearson Education, Inc., Upper Saddle River, New Jersey.

A. UNDERSTANDING THE THESIS AND OTHER MAIN IDEAS

Select the best answer.

_____ 1. The author's primary purpose in this selection is to
   a. caution people to stay away from online relationships.
   b. promote specific Web sites for online relationships.
   c. describe how technology affects interpersonal relationships.
   d. identify cultural factors that influence interpersonal relationships.

_____ 2. The main idea of paragraph 1 is that
   a. culture has a major impact on interpersonal relationships.
   b. the number of Internet users is rapidly increasing.
   c. some Web sites are especially good at helping people meet.
   d. online interpersonal relationships are on the increase.

_____ 3. The main idea of paragraph 5 is expressed in the

    a. first sentence.

    b. second sentence.

    c. third sentence.

    d. last sentence.

_____ 4. The topic of paragraph 10 is

    a. online relationships.

    b. physical appearance.

    c. face-to-face interactions.

    d. self-disclosure.

_____ 5. The main idea of paragraph 12 is that online it is easy for people to

    a. establish meaningful relationships.

    b. detect misinformation about others.

    c. find someone who matches their needs.

    d. misrepresent themselves.

_____ 6. According to the selection, "network convergence" takes place when two people in an online relationship begin to

    a. look for common ground on a variety of topics.

    b. make plans to meet in person.

    c. share their network of other communicators.

    d. decide whether to continue the relationship.

B. IDENTIFYING DETAILS

Select the best answer.

_____ 1. According to the selection, the term MOOs refers to online

    a. newsgroups.

    b. dating services.

    c. role-playing games.

    d. chat rooms.

_____ 2. All of the following statements about online relationships are true *except*

    a. Men are more likely than women to form online relationships.

    b. Women are more likely than men to use the Internet to deepen their interpersonal relationships.

    c. Online work groups are more task oriented and more efficient than face-to-face groups.

    d. Online groups provide a sense of belonging for their members.

Based on the examples given in the selection, match each Web site in Column A with the description that corresponds to it in Column B.

Column A	Column B
_____ 3. friendfinder.com	a. provides comparisons of the various dating Web sites
_____ 4. lavalife.com	b. has a pull-down menu so users can indicate the type of relationship they seek
_____ 5. eharmony.com	c. allows users to post photographs and voice introductions
_____ 6. homeandfamilyreview .com	d. has members complete scientific questionnaires about their preferences and personalities

C. RECOGNIZING METHODS OF ORGANIZATION AND TRANSITIONS

Complete the following statements by filling in the blanks.

In paragraph 6, the author uses the _____ organizational pattern to discuss the importance of physical appearance in face-to-face encounters versus online relationships. A transitional word that signals this pattern is _____.

D. REVIEWING AND ORGANIZING IDEAS: MAPPING

Complete the following map of paragraphs 10–14 by filling in the blanks.

ONLINE RELATIONSHIPS

ADVANTAGES

1. The potential for _____ _____ or sexually transmitted diseases is avoided.

2. The focus is on _____ rather than physical appearance.

3. Computer talk empowers those for whom traditional ways of meeting are difficult (for example, _____ _____).

4. Because such a huge number of people can be reached, it is relatively easy to find a match.

DISADVANTAGES

1. Many times you will not be able to see what the person looks like.

2. It is hard to form a total picture of someone without seeing or hearing him or her.

3. People may _____ _____ (for example, minors posing as adults or adults posing as children).

4. Computer interactions may become _____ and replace _____.

E. READING AND THINKING VISUALLY

Select the best answer.

_____ 1. Review the photo and caption included with the reading. By including this photo, the author implies that _____ is one of the most common reasons people seek online relationships.

    a. too much free time

    b. loneliness

    c. the desire to get married

    d. boredom

_____ 2. Review Table A, "Online Relationship Stages." In which state do two people adjust their expectations of the other person in the relationship and determine whether or not to continue it?

    a. testing

    b. anticipation

    c. fantasy integration

    d. reconfiguration

F. FIGURING OUT IMPLIED MEANINGS

Indicate whether each statement is true (T) or false (F).

_____ 1. Dating Web sites are designed for people who want a casual relationship only.

_____ 2. Many single Internet users look online for romantic partners.

_____ 3. For many people, online relationships are preferable to face-to-face interactions.

_____ 4. It can be inferred that most people looking for an online relationship are unconcerned about physical appearance.

G. THINKING CRITICALLY

Select the best answer.

_____ 1. The author's tone can best be described as

    a. judgmental.

    b. lighthearted.

    c. concerned.

    d. objective.

_____ 2. The primary purpose of Table A is to

    a. compare the progression of online relationships with relationships based on traditional ways of meeting.

    b. recommend a series of steps for people who are thinking about entering an online relationship.

    c. identify the stages that people often go through in online relationships.

    d. describe acceptable and unacceptable behaviors for online dating.

_____ 3. Which one of the following words has a negative connotation?

    a. self-disclosure

    b. task oriented

    c. interactions

    d. disfigurements

_____ 4. The author supports his thesis by doing all of the following *except*

    a. giving examples and illustrations.

    b. describing his personal experience.

    c. citing research evidence.

    d. providing statistical support.

_____ 5. When the author states that "computer talk equalizes the interaction" (paragraph 10), he means that

    a. even people with limited technological skill can meet others online.

    b. people are more likely to be honest with each other online.

    c. people with physical issues are not at a disadvantage online.

    d. geographic distances do not matter in online relationships.

H. BUILDING VOCABULARY

Context

Using context and a dictionary, if necessary, determine the meaning of each word as it is used in the selection.

_____ 1. proliferating (paragraph 1)

    a. ending

    b. multiplying

    c. altering

    d. continuing

_____ 2. stigma (paragraph 5)

    a. shame

    b. acceptance

    c. positive sign

    d. substitute

_____ 3. adept (paragraph 6)

    a. useless

    b. obvious

    c. skillful

    d. selfish

_____ 4. rapport (paragraph 10)

    a. information

    b. connection

    c. privacy

    d. safety

_____ 5. boon (paragraph 10)

    a. sound

    b. mistake

    c. emotion

    d. benefit

_____ 6. hinders (paragraph 12)

    a. invites in

    b. gets in the way

    c. pushes out

    d. delivers to

Word Parts

A REVIEW OF PREFIXES

NON- means *not*

IL- means *not*

SUPER- means *above*

MIS- means *wrongly*

Match each word in Column A with its meaning in Column B. Write your answers in the spaces provided.

Column A	Column B
_____ 1. nonverbal	a. on the surface
_____ 2. superficial	b. give wrong or misleading information
_____ 3. illicit	c. not spoken
_____ 4. misrepresent	d. not permitted

I. SELECTING A LEARNING/STUDY STRATEGY

Evaluate the effectiveness of the map you completed showing the advantages and disadvantages of online relationships. How else might you organize the material in this selection to study for an exam?

J. EXPLORING IDEAS THROUGH DISCUSSION AND WRITING

1. What do you think of online relationships? If you have met people online, either for friendship or a romantic relationship, has your experience generally been positive or negative? Explain your answer.

2. Make a prediction about the future of online dating. Do you think the current trend will continue? Why or why not?

3. Reread Table A. Discuss whether the table accurately represents what you know about online relationships, and answer the question posed by the author in the table's caption: How would you describe the way Internet relationships develop?

4. Discuss the perception of online dating as "a last resort for losers" (paragraph 5). Do you agree with the 2003 *New York Times* survey that the stigma is disappearing?

K. BEYOND THE CLASSROOM TO THE WEB

Select any dating Web site. Which audience is this dating site seeking to serve? Critically evaluate the Web site's homepage. What does it include (for example, information about the number of "successful matches" made or testimonials from happy couples)? What claims does the Web site make, and are these claims believable?

TRACKING YOUR PROGRESS

Selection 6

Section	Number Correct	Score
A. Thesis and Main Ideas (6 items)	_____ × 4	_____
B. Details (6 items)	_____ × 3	_____
C. Organization and Transitions (2 items)	_____ × 2	_____
E. Reading and Thinking Visually (2 item)	_____ × 1	_____
F. Implied Meanings (4 items)	_____ × 3	_____
G. Thinking Critically (5 items)	_____ × 4	_____
H. Vocabulary		
Context (6 items)	_____ × 2	_____
Word Parts (4 items)	_____ × 2	_____
	Total Score	_____%

11 Arts/Humanities/Literature

The **humanities and arts** are areas of knowledge concerned with human thoughts and ideas and their creative expression in written, visual, or auditory form. They deal with large, global issues such as "What is worthwhile in life?" "What is beautiful?" and "What is the meaning of human existence?" Works of art and literature are creative records of the thoughts, feelings, emotions, or experiences of other people. By studying art and reading literature you can learn about yourself and understand both joyful and painful experiences without going through them yourself. "Censorship of Offensive Art" asks the controversial question, "Should offensive art be censored?" In the short story "Little Brother™" a boy discovers that his Christmas present isn't exactly what he'd hoped it would be. The poem "The Road Not Taken" explores life choices and decision-making.

Use the following tips when reading and studying in the arts, humanities, and literature.

TIPS FOR READING IN THE ARTS/ HUMANITIES/ LITERATURE

- **Focus on values.** Examine social values and think about art's relationship to those values. Should art exist to support those values? In "Censorship of Offensive Art," you will learn about the conflicts that exit between art and social values.
- **Pay attention to the medium.** Words, sound, music, canvas, and clay are all means through which artistic expression occurs. Readings in this chapter are concerned with words and art. Three different vehicles are used in this chapter to express meaning through words: a textbook excerpt, a short story, and a poem.
- **Look for a message or an interpretation.** Works of art and literature express meaning or create a feeling or impression that must be inferred. "The Road Not Taken" addresses issues of decision-making and personal choices. As you read "Little Brother™" try to discover what the author is saying about the role of technology in our lives and relationships.
- **Read literature slowly and carefully.** Rereading may be necessary. Pay attention to the writer's choice of words, descriptions, comparisons, and arrangement of ideas. You should read poems several times.

SELECTION 7

Censorship of Offensive Art
Paul Zelanski and Mary Pat Fisher

TEXTBOOK
EXCERPT

This reading is taken from an art appreciation textbook, *The Art of Seeing*, 8th edition. In the preface to this book, the authors say their goals are "to make art come to life" and to "bring readers to an informed understanding of the arts of the world."

PREVIEWING THE READING

Using the steps listed on pages 40–41, preview the reading selection. When you have finished, complete the following items.

1. The topic of this reading is the _____ of offensive art.

2. Indicate whether each statement is true (T) or false (F).

   _____ a. Nazi Germany was very tolerant of "degenerate art."

   _____ b. The "Sensation" exhibit in Brooklyn, New York, was very controversial.

 MAKING
CONNECTIONS

Censorship is controversial in the United States because many believe it violates the right to free speech, which is part of the Constitution. What attempts at censorship have you witnessed in recent years? (For example, profanity in popular songs is often "wiped out" before these songs receive airplay on the radio.)

READING TIP

As you read, think about censorship from different points of view. For example, suppose you are an artist. How might your attitudes toward censorship differ from those of, say, parents who do not want their children to see disturbing images?

Censorship of Offensive Art

1   DOES THE PURSUIT of art require complete freedom of expression for all artists? Should limits be drawn as to what is acceptable in publicly displayed art or publicly funded art?

prurient
encouraging
excessive interest
in sexual matters

metaphoric
symbolic

aesthetics
concerned with
beauty or the
appreciation of
beauty

2   These questions came to the fore in 1990 in the United States when funding by the National Endowment for the Arts for a traveling exhibition of sexually explicit photographs by Robert Mapplethorpe became the subject of intense debate and even an obscenity court case. It was filed against the director of the Contemporary Art Center in Cincinnati. Jurors were shown only the seven most controversial photographs from the exhibit. They were asked to determine whether they met all three criteria of obscenity, as defined in a 1973 US Supreme Court ruling. The Supreme Court had ruled that a work is obscene if it depicts sexuality "in a patently offensive way," if "the average person, applying contemporary community standards," finds that it appeals to "**prurient** interest," and if it "lacks serious literary, artistic, political, or scientific value."

3   None of the jurors had any background in art appreciation and they did not like the pictures. Nevertheless, they acquitted the director after ten days of expert testimonies designed to prove that Mapplethorpe's work did indeed have serious artistic value and therefore should not be judged legally obscene. The director of the Cleveland Museum of Art argued that the photographs were **metaphoric** "images of rejection, aggression, anxiety." The director of the Walker Art Center in Minneapolis told the jury:

4   "I recognize that they are difficult, I recognize that they are confrontational. I recognize that they tell us things maybe we would rather not hear. But they do shine lights in some rather dark corners of the human psyche. And they symbolize, in disturbing, eloquent fashion, an attitude. And they do reflect an attitude that is not necessarily limited to the artist."

5   One of the jurors later said, "We learned that art doesn't have to be pretty." Nevertheless, the potential for funding for art on the edge to be withdrawn continues to hang over the heads of artists and museums.

6   In 1999, the mayor of New York threatened to withdraw the city's financial support of the Brooklyn Museum of Art, evict it from its premises, and replace its governing board because of its exhibition of the work of ninety-two young British artists, entitled "Sensation." The works included slices of animals in formaldehyde-filled cases, a portrait of a child abuser and murderer made of small children's hand-prints, and statues of children with genitalia where their faces should be. The mayor termed it "sick stuff," and pointed to a work by Chris Ofili, *The Holy Virgin Mary* (Figure 1, p. 322), as being particularly offensive to people of Roman Catholic faith. Ofili's black Madonna is ornamented with cutouts of bullocks and lumps of elephant dung. The resulting controversies involving use of public funds, vested interests, religion, race, moral sensitivities, animal rights, freedom of expression, and mixing of **aesthetics** and politics notwithstanding, the exhibition was held, and record crowds queued up to see it.

7   Art that is intentionally provocative or sensational arouses strong passions around the globe. In 2005, Buenos Aires was rocked by controversy over a retrospective of the anti-religious, explicitly sexual, and politically satirical works of Leon Ferrari. The archbishop of the city declared the exhibition blasphemous, and the cultural center, stallff, and artist received threats of violence. After the exhibit was closed by a judge to avoid hurting people's religious sentiments, the cultural center and city hall won their appeal to reopen it, on the basis of the artist's right to free expression. The

anti-Semitic
anti-Jew

Lenin   8
Vladimir Lenin,
Russian Communist
revolutionary

Stalin
Josef Stalin, Russian
leader from the
1920s until 1953

apocalypse
end of the world

cultural secretary of Buenos Aires observed, "The exhibition may be provocative, but nobody was obliged to see it."

Moscow witnessed violent protests over an exhibition of the work of forty Russian artists exploring religion in Russian life. Held at the Sakharov Museum and Public Center in 2003, the exhibit was entitled "Caution! Religion." The exhibition was vandalized by Orthodox fundamentalists and the organizers were brought to trial in 2005 on charges of provoking religious hatred. Mobs of fundamentalists built altars for prayer vigils in the courthouse corridors and shouted **anti-Semitic** epithets at the defendants. The court demanded that the artists submit statements explaining why they had created their works; one artist had to defend her depiction of Adam and Eve as naked. Psychologists and art historians called by the prosecution said that they detested contemporary art and felt that it should not be shown in public museums. Despite outcries by the international intellectual community, the organizers were found guilty and fined.

9   Controversy erupted again in 2007 in Moscow over an exhibition of political art at the prestigious State Tretyakov Gallery. Among the pieces found most offensive by critics such as the Minister of Culture were photographs of the Blue Noses collective in which members wearing masks of famous people including **Lenin** and **Stalin** were depicted in sexual escapades with each other. Although the show went on in Moscow, many pieces were pulled from the exhibit before it was sent to Paris.

10   Censorship of art has long been an issue. Michelangelo's monumental painting on the end wall of the Sistine Chapel, *The Last Judgment,* was violently attacked in the sixteenth century shortly after it was painted. In the Council of Trent, Roman Catholic Church officials had ruled that sacred images must adhere closely to scriptural descriptions, lest any viewer be misled. Critics felt that Michelangelo had taken too much artistic license. His angels did not have wings, for instance, and the angels blowing trumpets announcing the **apocalypse** were all grouped together, rather than at the four corners of the earth in accordance with scripture. The most controversial aspect of the work was the voluptuous nudity of the figures, which prompted one critic to refer to Michelangelo as "that inventor of filthiness." People tried physically to attack *The Last Judgment.*

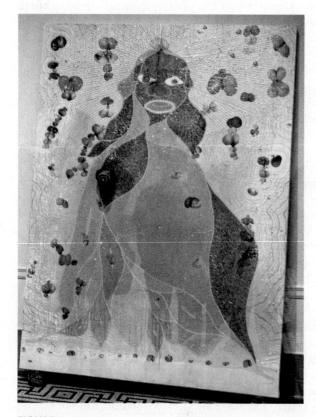

FIGURE 1
Chris Ofili, *The Holy Virgin Mary,* 1996. Paper collage, oil, glitter, polyester resin, map pins, and elephant dung on linen, 96 × 72 ins (244 × 183 cm). Courtesy of the Saatchi Collection.

So as to save the masterpiece, two successive popes ordered that the naked figures should be overpainted with loincloths to cover their genitals and breasts; the bits of clothing now seen did not exist in Michelangelo's original work.

degenerate
corrupt, immoral

11   More recently, in 1937 Nazi Germany confiscated over 16,000 pieces of modern German art of all sorts, burned much of it in a huge fire, and exhibited some of the rest with the label "**Degenerate** Art." At the opening of the exhibit, the president of the Reich Chamber of Visual Arts explained:

12   "We now stand in an exhibition that contains only a fraction of what was bought with the hard-earned savings of the German people and exhibited as art by a large number of museums all over Germany. All around us you see the monstrous off-

ineptitude
lack of skill

spring of insanity, impudence, **ineptitude**, and sheer degeneracy. What this exhibition offers inspires horror and disgust in us all."

Among the works confiscated from German museums were fifty-seven paintings by Wassily Kandinsky.

sacrilege
violation of what is considered sacred or holy

13   Questions arise: What are the ramifications of institutional censorship of artistic creation? Can art be dangerous for social health? Can censorship of art be dangerous for social health? If there should be limits, who should define them? Should the depiction of violence, sexism, racism, or **sacrilege** be censored, or only overt depictions of sexuality?

A. UNDERSTANDING THE THESIS AND OTHER MAIN IDEAS

Select the best answer.

_____ 1. Which of the following best states the thesis or central thought of "Censorship of Offensive Art"?

    a. Russia tends to be more intolerant of edgy or controversial art than the United States is.

    b. The average person is unable to distinguish between art and obscenity.

    c. Censorship of art has been common throughout the ages and continues to raise many questions.

    d. Art is most likely to offend when it mocks or satirizes the key social institutions of religion, politics, and human rights.

_____ 2. The topic of paragraph 6 is

    a. Chris Ofili's *The Holy Virgin Mary*.

    b. the Brooklyn Museum of Art.

    c. politics in New York City.

    d. the controversies created by the "Sensation" exhibit.

_____ 3. The main idea of paragraph 8 is found in the

    a. first sentence.

    b. third sentence.

    c. fourth sentence.

    d. fifth sentence.

_____ 4. The main idea of paragraph 10 is that

    a. Michelangelo is one of the world's greatest, but most controversial, painters.

    b. the Council of Trent established certain guidelines for the artistic portrayal of scripture.

    c. *The Last Judgment* was highly controversial for many reasons.

    d. Catholic popes deemed Michelangelo's paintings obscene and required the artist to change them.

B. IDENTIFYING DETAILS

Select the best answer.

_____ 1. "Censorship of Offensive Art" discusses all of the following artists except

    a. Sandro Botticelli.

    b. Leon Ferrari.

    c. Chris Ofili.

    d. Wassily Kandinsky.

_____ 2. "Caution! Religion" was exhibited in

    a. Brooklyn.

    b. the Vatican.

    c. Moscow.

    d. Nazi Germany.

_____ 3. Which of the following best states the outcome of the obscenity charges brought against the Contemporary Art Center in Cincinnati for exhibiting the photographs of Robert Mapplethorpe?

    a. The director of the Contemporary Art Center was imprisoned.

    b. Robert Mapplethorpe was convicted on obscenity charges but did not serve any jail time.

    c. The work of Robert Mapplethorpe was legally judged as having serious artistic value.

    d. Protestors burned the Contemporary Art Center to the ground before the court case could be decided.

_____ 4. Which piece of art described in the selection was created first?

    a. *The Holy Virgin Mary*

    b. *The Last Judgment*

    c. the Mapplethorpe photographs

    d. the works of Leon Ferrari

C. RECOGNIZING METHODS OF ORGANIZATION AND TRANSITIONS

Select the best answer.

_____ 1. The overall pattern of organization used in "Censorship of Offensive Art" is

    a. classification.

    b. listing.

    c. definition.

    d. comparison and contrast.

_____ 2. The organizational pattern used in paragraph 10 is

    a. summary.

    b. generalization and example.

    c. order of importance.

    d. process.

_____ 3. Which transitional word or phrase in the first sentence of paragraph 6 indicates the use of cause and effect in this sentence?

    a. In 1999

    b. threatened

    c. evict

    d. because

D. REVIEWING AND ORGANIZING IDEAS: MAPPING

Complete the following map of paragraphs 2–8 by filling in the blanks.

ARTIST OR EXHIBIT	DESCRIPTION	PUBLIC RESPONSE AND CONTROVERSIES	OUTCOME
_____ _____	Sexually explicit photographs	Photographs were deemed obscene and a court case was brought	The court decided the photographs had _____ value and were not obscene.
Sensation	Exhibit of the works of 92 British artists, including Chris Ofili's _____ _____	Included many disturbing pieces of art, which the mayor of New York described as " _____ "	The exhibition was held and many people attended.

Continued

ARTIST OR EXHIBIT	DESCRIPTION	PUBLIC RESPONSE AND CONTROVERSIES	OUTCOME
Leon Ferrari	Retrospective of the artist's work that included many anti-religious, explicitly sexual, and politically satirical works	_____ declared the exhibit blasphemous; staff received threats of violence; judge closed the exhibit	The cultural center and city of _____ won an appeal to reopen the exhibit based on the artist's right to free _____ .
_____ _____	Exhibit of the work of 40 Russian artists exploring religion in Russian life	Accused of provoking religious hatred; courts demanded artists submit statements explaining their work; _____ and art historians spoke against contemporary art	Despite outcries by the international intellectual community, the organizers were found _____ and fined.

E. READING AND THINKING VISUALLY

Select the best answer.

_____ 1. The painting shown in Figure 1 on page 322 was displayed in the United States as a part of which exhibit?

   a. "Degenerate Art"

   b. "Caution! Religion"

   c. "Sensation"

   d. "The Leon Ferrari Retrospective"

_____ 2. Which of the following materials was not used to create the painting in Figure 1 on page 322?

   a. map pins

   b. glitter

   c. elephant dung

   d. water color

F. FIGURING OUT IMPLIED MEANINGS

Indicate whether each statement is true (T) or false (F).

_____ 1. The author supports the idea that art should be censored in certain circumstances.

_____ 2. Michelangelo's *The Last Judgment* appears in the Sistine Chapel as the artist originally painted it.

_____ 3. The purpose of the "Degenerate Art" exhibit was to shame both artists and German museums.

_____ 4. In the United States, there is no official legal definition of obscenity.

_____ 5. U.S. court decisions in favor of controversial exhibits have been based on artistic merit and the right to artistic free expression.

_____ 6. Russia seems particularly sensitive to art that touches on political or religious issues.

G. THINKING CRITICALLY

Select the best answer.

_____ 1. The authors' purpose in writing "Censorship of Offensive Art" is to
   a. encourage students to pursue a career in the arts.
   b. raise questions about and discuss key examples of art censorship, examining the controversies and outcomes of these cases.
   c. compare and contrast the U.S. and Russian responses to controversial artists and exhibitions.
   d. provide a complete summary of the history of art censorship from the Renaissance through today.

_____ 2. Which of the following excerpts from the reading is an opinion, not a fact?
   a. "Nevertheless, they acquitted the director after ten days of expert testimony." (paragraph 3)
   b. "In 1999, the mayor of New York threatened to withdraw the city's financial support of the Brooklyn Museum of Art." (paragraph 6)
   c. "Moscow witnessed violent protests over an exhibition of the work of forty Russian artists exploring religion in Russian life." (paragraph 8)
   d. "All around us you see the monstrous offspring of insanity, impudence, ineptitude, and sheer degeneracy." (paragraph 12)

_____ 3. The tone of "Censorship of Offensive Art" is best described as
   a. enraged.
   b. cynical.
   c. solemn.
   d. instructive.

_____ 4. A rhetorical question is a question that an author asks directly, with the goal of stimulating readers to think about the issues under discussion. Which of the following paragraphs is essentially a series of rhetorical questions?

    a. paragraph 6

    b. paragraph 10

    c. paragraph 12

    d. paragraph 13

_____ 5. What do the authors mean by the phrase "art on the edge" in paragraph 5?

    a. art that is exhibited in coastal cities like New York and San Francisco

    b. art that is created by "outsider" artists who are not part of the established art scene

    c. art that is likely to be controversial

    d. art that travels around the country or world as part of a larger exhibit

H. BUILDING VOCABULARY

Context

Using context and a dictionary, if necessary, determine the meaning of each word as it used in the selection.

_____ 1. patently (paragraph 2)

    a. recognizably

    b. protected

    c. patiently

    d. unstable

_____ 2. eloquent (paragraph 4)

    a. persuasive

    b. dark

    c. talkative

    d. controversial

_____ 3. queued up (paragraph 6)

    a. boycotted

    b. lined up

    c. subscribed

    d. supported

_____ 4. blasphemous (paragraph 7)

    a. wholesome

    b. offensive to religion

    c. suitable for adults

    d. understated

_____ 5. epithet (paragraph 8)

    a. gravestone

    b. book

    c. name

    d. rage

_____ 6. monumental (paragraph 10)

    a. famous

    b. overrated

    c. huge

    d. preserved

_____ 7. impudence (paragraph 12)

    a. audacity

    b. immaturity

    c. crime

    d. greed

Word Parts

> ### A REVIEW OF PREFIXES AND ROOTS
>
> **RETRO-** means _backward_
> **SPEC** means _looks_ or _see_
> **TEMP** means _time_

Use your knowledge of word parts and the review above to fill in the blanks in the following sentences.

1. A **contemporary** (paragraph 2) artist is one who lives in modern

   _____.

2. A **retrospective** (paragraph 7) _____ at a specific artist's
career, showing different works from different periods of his or life.

Unusual Words/Understanding Idioms
Use the meanings given below to write a sentence using the boldfaced phrase.

1. To bring something **to the fore** (paragraph 2) means to place it in a leading or conspicuous position.

   Your sentence: _____

   _____

2. **Artistic license** (paragraph 10) refers to an artist's ability to break the strict formal rules of art, writing, or any other creative pursuit in order to suit his or her purposes.

   Your sentence: _____

   _____

I. SELECTING A LEARNING/STUDY STRATEGY

Complete the table in Section D by adding lines that summarize paragraphs 9–12.

J. EXPLORING IDEAS THROUGH DISCUSSION AND WRITING

1. Evaluate the introductory paragraph of this reading. Did it capture your attention? Did it help you better answer the questions in the concluding paragraph?

2. Write a paragraph about *The Holy Virgin Mary*, shown in Figure 1 on page 322. Begin with a description of the piece. Then describe your response to it, explaining whether it was positive or negative and why.

3. In your opinion, what exactly is *art*? What is it not?

4. The censorship of art is one way of banning certain types of expression. We often hear about attempts to ban various forms of expression (such as flag burning, certain articles of clothing, or hate speech). Write a paragraph or essay about a recent controversy regarding censorship. What is your opinion on this particular situation, and why?

K. BEYOND THE CLASSROOM TO THE WEB

Visit the Web site of a major museum, such as the Museum of Modern Art in New York or the Louvre in Paris. Browse through the contemporary art (art from 1980 and beyond) and look for examples of art that might be considered controversial. Print out a copy of the art and discuss it with your classmates. Why would the piece be considered controversial? How do you personally feel about it?

TRACKING YOUR PROGRESS

Selection 7

Section	Number Correct	Score
A. Thesis and Main Ideas (4 items)	_____ × 4	_____
B. Details (4 items)	_____ × 4	_____
C. Organization and Transitions (3 items)	_____ × 4	_____
E. Reading and Thinking Visually (2 items)	_____ × 3	_____
F. Implied Meanings (6 items)	_____ × 3	_____
G. Thinking Critically (5 items)	_____ × 2	_____
H. Vocabulary		
Context (7 items)	_____ × 2	_____
Word Parts (2 items)	_____ × 4	_____
	Total Score	_____%

SELECTION 8

Little Brother™

Bruce Holland Rogers

Bruce Holland Rogers is an American writer of fiction. He has won the Bram Stoker Award for short fiction. (Bram Stoker is the author of the horror classic *Dracula*.) The™ symbol in the story's title means "trademark." A trademark is used to identify the products of a particular company. This story originally appeared in *Strange Horizons*, a weekly online magazine that features science fiction and fantasy stories.

PREVIEWING THE READING

Short stories are not previewed in the same way as textbooks and other reading selections. For this reason, a head note (like the one above) often provides context for reading the story. Based on the head note above, answer the following questions.

1. Into which genre of fiction does the story fit? _____

2. What does the ™ symbol in the story's title mean? _____

 MAKING CONNECTIONS

Do you have any younger brothers or sisters? What do you remember about growing up with them?

READING TIP

As you read, ask yourself: "From whose point of view is this story being told?" How does this point of view help the author save a surprise for the story's last paragraph?

Little Brother™

1   Peter had wanted a Little Brother™ for three Christmases in a row. His favorite TV commercials were the ones that showed just how much fun he would have teaching Little Brother™ to do all the things that he could already do himself. But every year, Mommy had said that Peter wasn't ready for a Little Brother™. Until this year.

2   This year when Peter ran into the living room, there sat Little Brother™ among all the wrapped presents, babbling baby talk, smiling his happy smile, and patting one of the packages with his fat little hand. Peter was so excited that he ran up and gave Little Brother™ a big hug around the neck. That was how he found out about the button. Peter's hand pushed against something cold on Little Brother™'s neck, and suddenly Little Brother™ wasn't babbling any more, or even sitting up. Suddenly, Little Brother™ was **limp** on the floor, as lifeless as any ordinary doll.

limp
floppy, drooping

3   "Peter!" Mommy said.

4   "I didn't mean to!"

5   Mommy picked up Little Brother™, sat him in her lap, and pressed the black button at the back of his neck. Little Brother™'s face came alive, and it wrinkled up as if he were about to cry, but Mommy bounced him on her knee and told him what a good boy he was. He didn't cry after all.

6   "Little Brother™ isn't like your other toys, Peter," Mommy said. "You have to be extra careful with him, as if he were a real baby." She put Little Brother™ down on the floor, and he took tottering baby steps toward Peter. "Why don't you let him help open your other presents?"

7   So that's what Peter did. He showed Little Brother™ how to tear the paper and open the boxes. The other toys were a fire engine, some talking books, a wagon, and lots and lots of wooden blocks. The fire engine was the second-best present. It had lights, a siren, and hoses that blew green gas just like the real thing. There weren't as many presents as last year, Mommy explained, because Little Brother™ was expensive. That was okay. Little Brother™ was the best present ever!

8   Well, that's what Peter thought at first. At first, everything that Little Brother™ did was funny and wonderful. Peter put all the torn wrapping paper in the wagon, and Little Brother™ took it out again and threw it on the floor. Peter started to read a talking book, and Little Brother™ came and turned the pages too fast for the book to keep up.

9   But then, while Mommy went to the kitchen to cook breakfast, Peter tried to show Little Brother™ how to build a very tall tower out of blocks. Little Brother™ wasn't interested in seeing a really tall tower. Every time Peter had a few blocks stacked up, Little Brother™ swatted the tower with his hand and laughed. Peter laughed, too, for the first time, and the second. But then he said, "Now watch this time. I'm going to make it really big."

10   But Little Brother™ didn't watch. The tower was only a few blocks tall when he knocked it down.

11   "No!" Peter said. He grabbed hold of Little Brother™'s arm. "Don't!"

12   Little Brother™'s face wrinkled. He was getting ready to cry.

13   Peter looked toward the kitchen and let go. "Don't cry," he said. "Look, I'm building another one! Watch me build it!"

14   Little Brother™ watched. Then he knocked the tower down.

15   Peter had an idea.

16   When Mommy came into the living room again, Peter had built a tower that was taller than he was, the best tower he had ever made. "Look!" he said.

17   But Mommy didn't even look at the tower. "Peter!" She picked up Little Brother™, put him on her lap, and pressed the button to turn him back on. As soon as he was on, Little Brother™ started to scream. His face turned red.

18　"I didn't mean to!"

19　"Peter, I told you! He's not like your other toys. When you turn him off, he can't move but he can still see and hear. He can still feel. And it scares him."

20　"He was knocking down my blocks."

21　"Babies do things like that," Mommy said. "That's what it's like to have a baby brother."

22　Little Brother™ howled.

23　"He's mine," Peter said too quietly for Mommy to hear. But when Little Brother™ had calmed down, Mommy put him back on the floor and Peter let him **toddle** over and knock down the tower.

toddle
move unsteadily
while learning
to walk

24　Mommy told Peter to clean up the wrapping paper, and she went back into the kitchen. Peter had already picked up the wrapping paper once, and she hadn't said thank you. She hadn't even noticed.

25　Peter wadded the paper into angry balls and threw them one at a time into the wagon until it was almost full. That's when Little Brother™ broke the fire engine. Peter turned just in time to see him lift the engine up over his head and let it drop.

26　"No!" Peter shouted. The windshield cracked and popped out as the fire engine hit the floor. Broken. Peter hadn't even played with it once, and his best Christmas present was broken.

27　Later, when Mommy came into the living room, she didn't thank Peter for picking up all the wrapping paper. Instead, she scooped up Little Brother™ and turned him on again. He trembled and screeched louder than ever.

28　"My God! How long has he been off?" Mommy demanded.

29　"I don't like him!"

30　"Peter, it scares him! Listen to him!"

31　"I hate him! Take him back!"

32　"You are not to turn him off again. Ever!"

33　"He's mine!" Peter shouted. "He's mine and I can do what I want with him! He broke my fire engine!"

34　"He's a baby!"

35　"He's stupid! I hate him! Take him back!"

36　"You are going to learn to be nice with him."

37　"I'll turn him off if you don't take him back. I'll turn him off and hide him someplace where you can't find him!"

38　"Peter!" Mommy said, and she was angry. She was angrier than he'd ever seen her before. She put Little Brother™ down and took a step toward Peter. She would punish him. Peter didn't care. He was angry, too.

39　"I'll do it!" he yelled. "I'll turn him off and hide him someplace dark!"

40　"You'll do no such thing!" Mommy said. She grabbed his arm and spun him around. The spanking would come next.

41　But it didn't. Instead he felt her fingers searching for something at the back of his neck.

A. UNDERSTANDING THE THEME AND MAIN IDEAS

Select the best answer.

_____ 1. One possible theme of the story is that
   a. family is more valuable than material possessions.
   b. it is important to be patient with small children.
   c. technology is replacing human relationships.
   d. brothers should look out for each other.

_____ 2. The climax of the story occurs when
   a. Peter first hugs Little Brother.
   b. Peter's mother leaves the room to cook breakfast.
   c. Peter's mother reaches around to switch him off.
   d. Little Brother breaks the fire engine.

_____ 3. At the end of the story, it is revealed that Peter is
   a. adopted.
   b. an infant.
   c. abused.
   d. a robot.

B. IDENTIFYING DETAILS

Select the best answer.

_____ 1. At the beginning of the story, Peter can best be described as
   a. the oldest of several children.
   b. the youngest of several children.
   c. an only child.
   d. a teenager.

_____ 2. Peter's initial reaction to Little Brother was
   a. excitement.
   b. disappointment.
   c. jealousy.
   d. fear.

_____ 3. When Peter hugged Little Brother, he discovered that Little Brother
   a. was able to talk.
   b. cried when he was held.
   c. was made of plastic.
   d. had a button on his neck.

_____ 4. Peter's mother became angry when

    a. Little Brother broke Peter's new fire engine.

    b. Peter turned off Little Brother.

    c. Peter did not pick up the wrapping paper as she had asked.

    d. Little Brother knocked down Peter's blocks.

C. RECOGNIZING METHODS OF ORGANIZATION AND TRANSITIONS

Select the best answer.

_____ 1. What organizational pattern is used throughout the story?

    a. process

    b. chronological order

    c. classification

    d. cause and effect

_____ 2. The transitional word or phrase in paragraph 27 that implies contrast is

    a. later.

    b. picking up.

    c. instead.

    d. trembled and screeched.

D. REVIEWING AND ORGANIZING IDEAS: SUMMARIZING

Complete the following summary of the story. The first three sentences have been provided for you.

For three years, Peter has been asking for a toy named Little Brother as a Christmas gift. This year, Peter finally got his wish. While hugging his new baby brother, Peter accidentally pushed a button on Little Brother's neck, which caused Little Brother to go slack on the floor.

_____

_____

_____

_____

_____

_____

_____

_____

E. READING AND THINKING VISUALLY

Select the best answer.

_____ 1. A photo is not included with this selection. Which of the following would be the best choice for a photo to accompany the story, one that would stimulate readers' interest but not give away the surprise at the end?

    a. a photo of a mother holding a new baby

    b. a photo of two young boys sitting under a Christmas tree

    c. a photo of the broken fire engine

    d. a photo of a two robots

F. FIGURING OUT IMPLIED MEANINGS

Indicate whether each statement is true (T) or false (F).

_____ 1. The mother in the story believes that Peter is now old enough to have a Little Brother.

_____ 2. Peter receives Little Brother as a Christmas gift because his father has abandoned the family.

_____ 3. Readers see the story mostly through the eyes of Little Brother.

_____ 4. The author exhibits a deep fear of technology.

_____ 5. The author implies that Little Brother acts very much like any real little brother (or sister) would.

_____ 6. One key emotion that Peter exhibits in the story is frustration.

_____ 7. Little Brother does not like being turned off.

G. THINKING CRITICALLY

Select the best answer.

_____ 1. This story is told from the perspective of

    a. Peter's mother.

    b. Little Brother.

    c. a knowledgeable narrator.

    d. Peter.

_____ 2. The setting of the story is

    a. a store at the mall.

    b. Peter's birthday party.

    c. Little Brother's birthday party.

    d. Christmas day at Peter's house.

_____ 3. The tone of this story can best be described as

   a. serious.

   b. comical.

   c. ironic.

   d. tragic.

_____ 4. The phrase "as lifeless as" in paragraph 2 is an example of a

   a. simile.

   b. symbol.

   c. transitional phrase signaling process.

   d. metaphor.

_____ 5. In paragraph 7, the fire engine is described as the "second-best present" that Peter received. By paragraph 26, the fire engine has become Peter's "best present." The author is implying that

   a. modern toys are made cheaply and break quickly.

   b. Peter's mother is already showing favoritism toward the new baby.

   c. Peter's father died on Christmas Eve.

   d. Peter has rapidly discovered that he does not like Baby Brother.

H. BUILDING VOCABULARY

Context

Using context and a dictionary, if necessary, determine the meaning of each word as it is used in the selection.

_____ 1. babbling (paragraph 2)

   a. talking rapidly or foolishly

   b. attempting to speak

   c. pronouncing difficult words

   d. crying loudly

_____ 2. tottering (paragraph 6)

   a. moving unsteadily

   b. walking aggressively

   c. crawling on hands and knees

   d. running rapidly

_____ 3. swatted (paragraph 9)

    a. brushed

    b. hit

    c. looked at

    d. kicked over

_____ 4. trembled (paragraph 27)

    a. froze

    b. yelled

    c. shook

    d. cried

_____ 5. screeched (paragraph 27)

    a. sobbed

    b. kicked

    c. screamed

    d. listened

I. SELECTING A LEARNING/STUDY STRATEGY

In preparation for a class discussion in a literature class, write a brief statement outlining the theme(s) of "Little Brother™."

J. EXPLORING IDEAS THROUGH DISCUSSION AND WRITING

1. Were you surprised by the ending of this story? Discuss what you think will happen next.

2. Why did the author include the trademark symbol (™) in the title and throughout the story?

3. How would the story be different if it were told from the mother's point of view?

4. In addition to Little Brother, what other clues does the author give to reveal that the story is taking place in the future?

5. Evaluate the effectiveness of the story's title. Can you think of other titles that would work for this story?

6. Do you like the science fiction genre? What other fiction genres are you interested in (for example, romance, mystery, adventure, spy thriller)?

K. BEYOND THE CLASSROOM TO THE WEB

Go to the Strange Horizons Web site (the source from which this story was taken). A Web search will help you find it easily. Select another story from the Web site to read, and then write a summary of it.

TRACKING
YOUR
PROGRESS

Selection 8

Section	Number Correct	Score
A. Thesis and Main Ideas (3 items)	_____ × 4	_____
B. Details (4 items)	_____ × 4	_____
C. Organization and Transitions (2 items)	_____ × 4	_____
E. Reading and Thinking Visually (1 item)	_____ × 1	_____
F. Implied Meanings (7 items)	_____ × 4	_____
G. Thinking Critically (5 items)	_____ × 4	_____
H. Vocabulary Context (5 items)	_____ × 3	_____
	Total Score	_____%

The Road Not Taken

Robert Frost

Robert Frost is an American poet known for his poems about rural life. He was awarded the Pulitzer Prize for Poetry four times. He is perhaps best known for his poems about New England, which often examine the relationships between humanity and nature.

PREVIEWING THE READING

Previewing, as described on page 40, does not work well for poetry. Instead of previewing the poem, read it through once to determine its literal content—who is doing what, when, and where? When you have finished, answer the following questions.

1. What decision was the poet/narrator trying to make?

   _____

2. What is the poem's setting?

   _____

 MAKING CONNECTIONS

Think about one of the major decisions you have made in your life. Which options did you face at the time? How did you make your decision? How do you think your decision affected your life? Would you make a different choice if you had to do it all over again?

READING TIP

Read the poem at least twice. The first time, work for literal understanding. What is happening in the poem? The second time, pay more attention to the poem's structure and rhyming pattern.

The Road Not Taken

1   Two roads diverged in a yellow wood,
And sorry I could not travel both
And be one traveler, long I stood
And looked down one as far as I could
5   To where it bent in the undergrowth;

Then took the other, as just as fair,
And having perhaps the better claim
Because it was grassy and **wanted** wear,
Though as for that the passing there
10   Had worn them really about the same,

And both that morning equally lay
In leaves no step had trodden black.
Oh, I kept the first for another day!
Yet knowing how way leads on to way
15   I doubted if I should ever come back.

I shall be telling this with a sigh
Somewhere ages and ages hence:
Two roads diverged in a wood, and I,
I took the one less traveled by,
20   And that has made all the difference.

wanted (line 8)
lacked (line 9)

A. UNDERSTANDING THE THESIS AND OTHER MAIN IDEAS

Select the best answer.

_____ 1. The first stanza implies that the speaker of the poem is

    a. angry with someone in his family.

    b. on a journey.

    c. unable to make a decision.

    d. quite elderly.

_____ 2. Which of the following best states the poem's theme?

    a. One should carefully weigh the pros and cons of every decision.

    b. It is better to take the road less traveled.

    c. The course of one's life is decided by the decisions that one makes.

    d. Making the right choices will prevent regret later in life.

_____ 3. All of the poem's stanzas take place in the past tense except for the _____ stanza.

   a. first

   b. second

   c. third

   d. last

B. IDENTIFYING DETAILS

Select the best answer.

_____ 1. The color of the woods in the first stanza is a clue to

   a. the poet's biases.

   b. the season.

   c. the poet's state of mind.

   d. the precise location of poem's action.

_____ 2. Which lines from the poem imply that the speaker is fairly young?

   a. "And sorry I could not travel both / And be one traveler, long I stood" (stanza 1)

   b. "Because it was grassy and wanted wear, / Though as for that the passing there" (stanza 2)

   c. "Yet knowing how way leads on to way / I doubted if I should ever come back" (stanza 3)

   d. "I shall be telling this with a sigh / Somewhere ages and ages hence:" (stanza 4)

_____ 3. At what time of day does the poem take place?

   a. morning

   b. noon

   c. twilight

   d. midnight

C. RECOGNIZING METHODS OF ORGANIZATION AND TRANSITIONS

Select the best answer.

_____ 1. The overall organizational pattern used in "The Road Not Taken" is

   a. definition.

   b. listing or enumeration.

   c. chronological order.

   d. generalization and example.

_____ 2. What is the dominant pattern of organization in the second stanza?

    a. definition

    b. comparison and contrast

    c. classification

    d. order of importance

_____ 3. Which pattern of organization is implied by the lines "I took the one less traveled by / And that has made all the difference" (lines 19–20)?

    a. cause and effect

    b. comparison and contrast

    c. classification

    d. process

_____ 4. The word in the third stanza that suggests the addition pattern is

    a. and (line 11).

    b. oh (line 13).

    c. yet (line 14).

    d. knowing (line 14).

D. REVIEWING AND ORGANIZING IDEAS: MAPPING

Complete the following map of the poem by filling in the blanks.

1. First stanza

   Speaker stands at a point in the woods where two roads _____ and looks far down one of the roads.

2. Second stanza

   Speaker chooses the second road after _____

3. Third stanza

   Speaker begins to think about the possibility or likelihood that he will _____

4. Fourth stanza

   Speaker looks to the future and realizes that his decision may have a major impact on his life.

E. READING AND THINKING VISUALLY

Select the best answer.

_____ 1. All of the following images would be appropriate to illustrate the poem *except*
  a. a man standing at a crossroads.
  b. a deer standing in the woods.
  c. two versions of the same man: one young, one old.
  d. a man straining his neck to see as far down a path as he can.

F. FIGURING OUT IMPLIED MEANINGS

Indicate whether each statement is true (T) or false (F).

_____ 1. The speaker in the poem makes his choice quickly and spontaneously.

_____ 2. The speaker in the poem implies that both roads are equally attractive.

_____ 3. At the time the speaker makes his choice, nobody had traveled either road that day.

_____ 4. The speaker in the poem believes that he will someday revisit the exact place at which he made his choice.

_____ 5. The poet implies that choice is an unavoidable part of life.

G. THINKING CRITICALLY

Select the best answer.

_____ 1. Which line contains a clue that the poem takes place in autumn?
  a. line 3   c. line 12
  b. line 10   d. line 20

_____ 2. The poem contains several contradictions. Which of these is NOT one of the contradictions found in the poem?
  a. The speaker keeps one road for "another day" but also knows he will never be back.
  b. The speaker says he took the road "less traveled by" but also says that both roads were really worn "about the same."
  c. The speaker seems to think that he made the right decision, but he says that he will tell his story "with a sigh."
  d. The speaker says that he is just "one traveler," but he wishes he could have taken both paths.

H. BUILDING VOCABULARY

Context

Using context and a dictionary if necessary, determine the meaning of each word as it is used in the poem.

_____ 1. diverged (line 1)

    a. disappeared

    b. separated

    c. sloped

    d. ended

_____ 2. undergrowth (line 5)

    a. weeds

    b. lake

    c. vegetation

    d. soil

_____ 3. trodden (line 12)

    a. walked on

    b. destroyed

    c. colored

    d. patterned

_____ 4. hence (line 17)

    a. therefore

    b. ago

    c. however

    d. in the future

I. SELECTING A LEARNING/STUDY STRATEGY

How would you prepare for a class discussion of this poem?

J. EXPLORING IDEAS THROUGH DISCUSSION AND WRITING

1. What kind of mood does the poet create in "The Road Not Taken"? How does he accomplish this?

2. Discuss how you feel about the writing, reading, and study of poetry. How relevant is it to your life?

3. Write a paragraph about a choice you are facing now. How important is this decision? How likely it is to affect your life significantly?

4. Write an essay about a choice you made in the past that has had a significant impact on your life. What other alternatives were available to you? Why did you make the choice you did? Why did you not choose one of the other alternatives?

K. BEYOND THE CLASSROOM TO THE WEB

Do a Google search to locate other poems by Robert Frost. Choose one and compare and contrast it to "The Road Not Taken." How are the two poems similar? How are they different?

TRACKING YOUR PROGRESS

Selection 9

Section	Number Correct	Score
A. Thesis and Main Ideas (3 items)	_____ × 5	_____
B. Details (3 items)	_____ × 5	_____
C. Organization and Transitions (4 items)	_____ × 4	_____
E. Reading and Thinking Visually (1 item)	_____ × 4	_____
F. Implied Meanings (5 items)	_____ × 4	_____
G. Thinking Critically (2 items)	_____ × 5	_____
H. Vocabulary Context (4 items)	_____ × 5	_____
	Total Score	_____%

12 Political Science/Government/History

We live in a political world shaped by history and current events. The economy, the job market, and even television sitcoms are influenced by national and international events. To study political science, government, and history is to understand factors that influence your daily life. Readings in this chapter demonstrate the relevance of these disciplines. In "When Theodore Roosevelt Saved Football," you will read how an American president had an influence on the sport of football. "Camping for Their Lives" addresses the issue of homelessness through a discussion of tent cities. "Reporting the News" provides an in-depth examination of television news and its influence on politics.

Use the following suggestions when reading in the fields of political science, government, and history.

TIPS FOR READING IN POLITICAL SCIENCE/ GOVERNMENT/ HISTORY

- **Focus on the significance of events, both current and historical.** What immediate and long-range effects will or did a particular event, situation, or action have? As you read "When Theodore Roosevelt Saved Football," consider how Roosevelt's actions changed football.

- **Analyze motivations.** What causes people and groups to take action? As you read Reporting the News," consider what factors motivate media coverage of the news.

- **Consider political organizations.** How and why do people organize themselves into political groups and parties? Observe how political power is distributed and who makes important political decisions. As you read "Camping for Their Lives," you will learn about efforts to organize and control those living in tent cities.

- **Be alert for bias and partisanship** (support of a viewpoint or position because it is held by one's political party). As you read "Camping for Their Lives," look for disparate viewpoints on the future of tent cities.

- **Sort facts from opinions.** Opinions and historical interpretation are worthwhile but need to be evaluated. As you read "Reporting the News," observe how the authors provide evidence to support statements of opinion, frequently quoting famous newscasters and journalists.

SELECTION 10

When Theodore Roosevelt Saved Football

Bruce Watson

Bruce Watson is the author of *Freedom Summer: The Savage Season That Made Mississippi Burn and Made America a Democracy*. **His work has appeared in** *The Boston Globe, The Wall Street Journal, The Washington Post,* **and many other publications.**

PREVIEWING THE READING

Using the steps listed on pages 40–41, preview the reading selection. When you have finished, answer the following questions.

1. The Russo-Japanese War ended in _____.

2. Indicate whether each statement is true (T) or false (F).

    _____ a. President Theodore Roosevelt is credited with saving the game of football.

    _____ b. Football today is more dangerous than it was in the early 1900s.

    _____ c. President Theodore Roosevelt was awarded the Nobel Prize for Peace.

MAKING CONNECTIONS

List at least three sports that have a reputation for being violent. Of these, which do you consider the most violent? What rules and regulations, if any, are in place to protect the players' safety? Which sports have a reputation for having the rowdiest fans and spectators?

READING TIP

As you read, notice how the author has cited his sources. Evaluate these sources. Are they reliable and objective? Or are they biased?

When Theodore Roosevelt Saved Football

resounding
echoing

gridirons
football fields

1   In the fall of 1905, shortly after brokering a treaty ending the Russo-Japanese War, President Theodore Roosevelt pursued peace on another battlefield. His campaign, **resounding** from college **gridirons** to the White House, saved the game of football.

revered 2
respected

necessitates
makes necessary

3

4

factions
groups

5

intervened
became involved by
taking action

Roosevelt had not played football while at Harvard, yet he **revered** the game. Its toughness and conquering spirit epitomized what he called "the strenuous life." "Of all games, I personally like football the best," he said. "I have no patience with the people who declaim against it because it **necessitates** rough play and occasional injuries."[1] But by 1905, gridiron injuries were not just "occasional."

Football today stands accused of causing brain damage and spinal injuries, but football in Roosevelt's time was often lethal. With flimsy padding and leather helmets, players bashed heads and piled into human heaps. "Momentum plays"[2] allowed running backs to move before the ball was snapped, hitting linemen at full speed. And with no one allowed to pass the ball, young men smashed into each other again and again. Every game saw several players carried unconscious from the field. During Roosevelt's first term in office, 45 young men died on college or high school gridirons.[3] Each season brought more carnage and calls to ban the game.

The nation's leading football colleges, Harvard, Yale, and Princeton, were divided into pro- and anti-football **factions.** Students loved the game; faculty and college presidents hated it. Harvard had banned football, only to reinstate it due to student demand. Doctors were alarmed by broken bones, concussions, and deaths. Clergymen denounced "foul play" that saw teeth knocked out, noses broken, and fans screaming "Break his neck!" or "Kill him!"[4]

By the fall of 1905, Roosevelt recognized that football was endangered. The muckraking magazine *McClure's* had recently chronicled gridiron corruption, cheating, and the targeting of key players to "put them out of business."[5] Roosevelt's son, Theodore, Jr., a member of Harvard's freshman team, had suffered a black eye, broken arm, and was later knocked unconscious.[6] Each injury to the president's son made headlines. Finally, at the request of prep school headmasters, Roosevelt **intervened.**

A college football player in the early 1900s.

A contemporary college football player.

[1]John S. Watterson III, "Political Football: Theodore Roosevelt, Woodrow Wilson and the Gridiron Reform Movement," *Presidential Studies Quarterly* 25 (Summer 1995): 557.
[2]Ibid, 558.
[3]"Death From Football Playing," *Washington Post,* October 15, 1905, SP2.
[4]Waterson, 556.
[5]Ibid, 559.
[6]"Theodore Hurt in Game," *Washington Post,* November 19, 1905, 3.

denounced
criticized

6   On October 9, Roosevelt called a meeting at the White House. Present were coaches and athletic directors from Harvard, Yale, and Princeton. The men sat around a table in the stately White House dining room. Roosevelt began by praising football and its manly spirit. Then he **denounced** the game's mounting brutality, citing recent dirty plays in Ivy League games. Football had to save itself, the president said, or else the growing outcry would ban the game college by college.[7]

7   The meeting lasted nearly three hours. Yale's Walter Camp, an old friend of Roosevelt's who had defined college football for a generation, agreed with the president. But the Harvard and Princeton men argued that football could not be cleaned up—that roughness was woven into its rules. Roosevelt insisted on reform. He ordered the coaches and athletic directors to sign a pledge "to carry out, in letter and spirit, the rules of the game of football relating to roughness, holding, and foul play."[8] The meeting **adjourned** with no more than the pledge, but it was a beginning.

adjourned
came to an end

8   The violence continued that fall. On a single November afternoon, two high school players and a college halfback were killed.[9] College presidents across the nation called for either reform or banning the game. As the controversy raged, Roosevelt demanded a "gentleman's agreement" among coaches, athletic directors, and "umpires" on the field. Brutality in football, he announced, "should receive the same summary punishment given to a man who cheats at cards or strikes a foul blow in boxing."[10] Rules, he added, should be simplified since "complicated rules allow too many loopholes."[11]

unbefitting
inappropriate

9   In December, Roosevelt attended the annual Army-Navy game. Several years earlier, as Assistant Secretary of the Navy, he had helped restore the popular matchup after it was suspended due to conduct **unbefitting** officers and gentlemen.[12] While watching Army and Navy battle to a 6-6 tie, Roosevelt discussed rule changes with another fan and future president, Princeton's Woodrow Wilson. Off the field, Roosevelt continued to confer with Walter Camp and other officials.

10 As the pressure for reform mounted, two separate committees formed to consider rule changes. The president convinced officials to merge the two committees into one. The new Intercollegiate Athletic Conference (later the NCAA) ultimately made the changes that saved football.

11 In the fall of 1906, when another season began, the president was pleased. The rules committee had modernized the game. First downs were now given for gains of ten yards, reducing the line collisions common when just five yards were needed. Momentum plays were outlawed. "Mass plays" and gang tackling were also banned. And in the most far reaching rule change, a player could take the ball, fade back and *throw* it to another player downfield.

12 The new forward pass did not change football overnight. An incomplete pass led to a 15-yard penalty, and a pass that dropped untouched gave opponents the ball.

---

[7]"Roosevelt Campaign for Football Reform," *New York Times,* October 10, 1905, 1.
[8]"Pledge to the President," *Washington Post,* October 12, 1905, 1.
[9]"Reform Play or Abolish Football," *Boston Globe,* November 26, 1905, 1.
[10]"Is In Favor of Continuing Game," *Boston Globe,* November 21, 1905, 5.
[11]Ibid.
[12]Bruce Watson, "It's More Than Just a Game," *Smithsonian,* (November 1999): 144.

But within a year, the Carlisle Indian School, under Coach Charles "Pop" Warner, used the forward pass to defeat Harvard and other top teams.[13] The growing popularity of passing opened up football and saved countless lives.

13   For his efforts in brokering peace in the Russo-Japanese War, Theodore Roosevelt received the Nobel Peace Prize. He received no such prize for saving football, but decades later, when Russia and Japan were again at war, football had become an American institution.

The NCAA Theodore Roosevelt Award

14   In 1967, to honor his role in forming the National Collegiate Athletic Association, the NCAA established its Theodore Roosevelt Award. The annual award, known as the "Teddy," is given to a former college athlete who has "exemplified most clearly and forcefully the ideals and purposes to which college athletics programs and amateur sports competitions are dedicated."[14] Past winners include former presidents Ronald Reagan, Dwight Eisenhower, George H. W. Bush, comedian Bill Cosby and astronaut Sally Ride.

---

[13]Morrison, op cit.
[14]http://www.ncaa.org/wps/wcm/connect/public/NCAA/Resources/Events/Honors+Calebration/Theodore+Roosevelt+Award

A. UNDERSTANDING THE THESIS AND OTHER MAIN IDEAS

Select the best answer.

_____ 1. Which of the following best states the central thesis of the selection?

a. Of all the team sports played in American history, football is the most deadly.

b. Ivy League universities were once the dominant forces in college football.

c. There have always been two factions in society: those who are pro-football and those who are anti-football.

d. As a result of Theodore Roosevelt's intervention, football is today a much less dangerous sport than it was in the early twentieth century.

_____ 2. The author's primary purpose in "When Theodore Roosevelt Saved Football" is to

a. examine the effects of football on the sport's players and fans.

b. show President Roosevelt's influence on football in the early 1900s.

c. provide information about specific types of football plays, such as momentum plays.

d. analyze the relationships among the U.S. president, university presidents, and sports coaches.

_____ 3. The main idea of paragraph 3 is found in the
    a. first sentence.
    b. third sentence.
    c. fourth sentence.
    d. last sentence.

_____ 4. The topic of paragraph 8 is
    a. injuries sustained by players.
    b. brutality in football.
    c. ongoing violence in football and the controversies surrounding it.
    d. college presidents' response to students' demands regarding campus sports.

_____ 5. The key challenge that President Roosevelt faced was
    a. a deeply divided Congress that did not wish to get involved in regulating college sports.
    b. the idea that college football by its very nature was rough and violent.
    c. opposition from university presidents who feared that students would riot if rules were changed.
    d. his own experiences in playing football for the Yale University team.

B. IDENTIFYING DETAILS

Select the best answer.

_____ 1. Which of the following was _not_ one of the nation's leading football colleges in the early years of the twentieth century?
    a. Princeton
    b. Columbia
    c. Yale
    d. Harvard

_____ 2. Which of the following people has _not_ received the NCAA Theodore Roosevelt Award?
    a. Bill Cosby
    b. Ronald Reagan
    c. Sally Ride
    d. Bill Parcells

_____ 3. President Roosevelt brokered a treaty that ended

    a. the Boer War.

    b. World War II.

    c. the Russo-Japanese War.

    d. the War of 1812.

_____ 4. Theodore Roosevelt once served as

    a. Assistant Secretary of the Navy.

    b. Secretary of the Interior.

    c. Speaker of the House.

    d. Harvard University president.

_____ 5. Which of the following was *not* a change that had come to football by the 1906 season?

    a. Gang tackling was banned.

    b. First downs were given for gains of five yards.

    c. Players could take the ball and throw it to another player downfield.

    d. Line collisions were reduced.

C. RECOGNIZING METHODS OF ORGANIZATION AND TRANSITIONS

Select the best answer.

_____ 1. The overall pattern of organization used in the selection is

    a. definition.

    b. process.

    c. chronological order.

    d. cause and effect.

_____ 2. All of the following transitional phrases signal the selection's main pattern of organization *except* for

    a. in the fall of 1905 (paragraph 1)

    b. on October 9 (paragraph 6)

    c. the president convinced officials (paragraph 10)

    d. decades later (paragraph 13)

_____ 3. The organizational pattern used in paragraph 3 is

    a. summary.

    b. generalization and example.

    c. spatial order.

    d. classification.

_____ 4. Which of the following paragraphs uses the listing or enumeration pattern?

    a. paragraph 1

    b. paragraph 4

    c. paragraph 6

    d. paragraph 13

D. REVIEWING AND ORGANIZING IDEAS: SUMMARIZING

Use the following words to complete the summary of paragraphs 6-7.

ban	coaches	complimenting	gentle
Princeton	unfair	Yale	

On October 9, 1905, the Ivy League colleges sent _____ and athletic directors to a meeting at the White House. President Roosevelt started the meeting by _____ football. Then he criticized the game for its increasing level of violence. He suggested that society would want to _____ the game if action was not taken to prevent players from being badly hurt. Walter Camp, who was affiliated with _____ University, was on the president's side. However, the representatives from _____ and Harvard argued that football was a rough sport and could not be made more _____ . President Roosevelt stood his ground; by the end of the meeting, all of the participants had agreed to enforce existing rules relating to violence and _____ play.

E. READING AND THINKING VISUALLY

Select the best answer.

_____ 1. The author likely chose to include the two photos on page 350 in order to

    a. demonstrate the superiority of football uniforms worn by athletes in the early twentieth century.

    b. make the case that college football players should have access to the same equipment that professional football players have.

    c. illustrate the advances that have been made since the early twentieth century in terms of protecting football players from injury.

    d. persuade readers to support their local college football team.

_____ 2. Which pattern of organization is implied by the two photos on page 350?

    a. definition

    b. comparison and contrast

    c. process

    d. classification

F. FIGURING OUT IMPLIED MEANINGS

Indicate whether each statement is true (T) or false (F).

_____ 1. It is possible that President Roosevelt was motivated to make college football less dangerous because his son was injured playing the game.

_____ 2. The NCAA regards Teddy Roosevelt as a football hero.

_____ 3. President Roosevelt's attempts to reform college football met with immediate success.

_____ 4. The author believes that the forward pass saved lives.

_____ 5. Football uniforms in the early twentieth century did not provide much protection against injury.

_____ 6. Only men have won the NCAA Theodore Roosevelt Award.

_____ 7. The author implies that college administrators and faculty did not like football but allowed the game to be played because it was so popular with students.

_____ 8. The author implies that early football fans enjoyed watching players get hurt.

G. THINKING CRITICALLY

Select the best answer.

_____ 1. The author's tone in the selection can best be described as
a. angry.
b. nostalgic.
c. informative.
d. solemn.

_____ 2. The author cites all of the following sources *except*
a. *Presidential Studies Quarterly.*
b. *The New York Times.*
c. *The Washington Post.*
d. *The Boston Globe.*

_____ 3. The author's audience is
a. historians.
b. the general public, including football fans.
c. politicians and policy makers.
d. student interns.

_____ 4. In paragraph 1, the author writes about "another battlefield." With this piece of figurative language, the author is referring to

a. the killing fields of Cambodia.

b. the war between serious scholars and rowdy sports fans.

c. the lingering effects of the American Civil War.

d. the struggle to make college football safer for players.

_____ 5. A *euphemism* is a word or expression that is substituted for one that may be considered too harsh. A euphemism often seeks to hide an unpleasant truth. In paragraph 5, the euphemism "to put them out of business" means to

a. kill skilled football players.

b. hurt good football players so that they will not be able to play.

c. bankrupt the football team.

d. knock coaches and referees unconscious.

_____ 6. Which statement best summarizes the author's attitude toward Theodore Roosevelt?

a. The author thinks Roosevelt was a mediocre president.

b. The author believes Roosevelt's most important accomplishment was brokering the end of the Russo-Japanese War.

c. The author sees Roosevelt as not only a great political diplomat but also as a sports hero.

d. The author thinks Roosevelt was a better president than George Washington or Abraham Lincoln.

H. BUILDING VOCABULARY

Context

Using context and a dictionary, if necessary, determine the meaning of each word as it is used in the selection.

_____ 1. epitomized (paragraph 2)

a. complained

b. represented

c. criticized

d. turned upside down

_____ 2. declaim (paragraph 2)

a. deny

b. carry a grudge

c. clarify

d. speak

_____ 3. lethal (paragraph 3)
     a. humorous
     b. risky
     c. tiring
     d. deadly

_____ 4. carnage (paragraph 3)
     a. slaughter
     b. meat
     c. rules
     d. popularity

_____ 5. chronicled (paragraph 5)
     a. reported
     b. arranged
     c. understood
     d. denied

_____ 6. stately (paragraph 6)
     a. mathematically
     b. grand
     c. political
     d. hungry

_____ 7. confer (paragraph 9)
     a. belittle
     b. award
     c. consult
     d. argue

Word Parts

> ### A REVIEW OF PREFIXES AND SUFFIXES
>
> **-IZE** means to make.
> **RUSSO-** means related to Russia.

Use your knowledge of word parts to fill in the blanks.

1. To *modernize* (paragraph 11) a set of rules is to make those
   rules _____.

2. The *Russo-Japanese War* (paragraph 1) was fought by Japan and _____.

Unusual Words/Understanding Idioms
Use the meanings given below to write a sentence using the boldfaced word.

Muckraking (paragraph 5) is the act of searching out and making public scandalous information. It sometimes has noble motives (to expose wrongdoing) and sometimes has underhanded motives (for example, to discredit a politician).

_____

_____

A **gentleman's agreement** (paragraph 8) is an understanding that is based on mutual trust. It is generally informal and it is not legally binding. Often, a gentleman's agreement is sealed with a handshake.

_____

_____

A **loophole** (paragraph 8) is a vague area in a set of rules that allows certain types of behavior to slip through. The connotation of the word *loophole* is often negative.

_____

_____

I. SELECTING A LEARNING/STUDY STRATEGY

Suppose you are planning to participate in a class discussion on the topic of "Sports: Then vs. Now." How could you use this reading to prepare for the discussion?

J. EXPLORING IDEAS THROUGH DISCUSSION AND WRITING

1. Sports have a long history of violence. Why do you think sports might bring out violent tendencies in people?

2. Have you ever played football, hockey, or another sport that puts players in physical danger? What types of protective equipment have you used?

3. Write a caption to accompany the two photos on page 350.

4. Write a paragraph in which you agree or disagree with this statement: "Any athlete who intentionally hurts another athlete should be banned from the sport for life."

5. Suppose you are the parent of a child who wants to play on the school football team and perhaps pursue a career in professional football. Write an essay in which you explore the pros and cons of pursuing an athletic career. As a parent, how would you feel about your child playing a potentially dangerous sport?

K. BEYOND THE CLASSROOM TO THE WEB

Search the Web site of a national sports franchise in the sport of choice. Does the team publicize its safety rules and the steps it takes to protect its athletes? Briefly summarize the information and present your summary to the class.

TRACKING
YOUR
PROGRESS

Selection 10

Section	Number Correct	Score
A. Thesis and Main Ideas (5 items)	_____ × 3	_____
B. Details (5 items)	_____ × 3	_____
C. Organization and Transitions (4 items)	_____ × 3	_____
E. Reading and Thinking Visually (2 items)	_____ × 3	_____
F. Implied Meanings (8 items)	_____ × 2	_____
G. Thinking Critically (6 items)	_____ × 3	_____
H. Vocabulary		
Context (7 items)	_____ × 2	_____
Word Parts (2 items)	_____ × 2	_____
	Total Score	_____ %

SELECTION 11

Camping for Their Lives
Scott Bransford

Contemporary
Issues Reading

In this selection, the author describes how tent cities for homeless people have emerged throughout the American West. Read the selection to find out what life is like in a tent city.

PREVIEWING THE READING

Using the steps listed on pages 40–41, preview the reading selection. When you have finished, complete the following items.

1. This selection is about _____.

2. The tent city that is the primary focus of this article is located in

_____.

 MAKING
CONNECTIONS   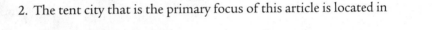 *Where would you live if you could not afford to pay for housing?*

READING TIP

As you read, underline factors that have led to the development of tent cities and highlight words that are used to describe tent cities.

Camping for Their Lives

Call them squatter villages, tent cities, or informal urbanism— more people are calling them home.

1   Marie and Francisco Caro needed a home after they got married, but like many people in California's Central Valley, they didn't have enough money to sign a lease or take out a mortgage. They were tired of sleeping on separate beds in crowded shelters, so they found a slice of land alongside the Union Pacific Railroad tracks in downtown Fresno. The soil was sandy and dry, prone to rising up into clouds when the

autumn winds came. All around, farm equipment factories and warehouses loomed out of the dust, their walls coarse and sun-bleached like desert mountainsides. Even a strong person could wither in a place like this, but if they wanted to build a home, nobody was likely to stop them. So Marie and Francisco gathered scrap wood and took their chances. They raised their tarp roof high like a steeple, then walled off the world with office cubicle dividers. Thieves stayed outside and so did the wind, and the sound of the passing freight trains softened.

2   When I visited the Caros in January, a fire burned in a repurposed oil barrel, warming the cool air, and fresh-cut Christmas tree boughs hung on the walls for decoration. While Francisco chopped wood, Marie confided that she wants to live somewhere else. All she needs is a modest place with a sink and a gas stove, she said, maybe even a television. But until times change, she said, she'll be happy in her self-made abode, cooking on top of the oil barrel, making meals with whatever food God brings. "He gives us bread," said Marie, a Fresno native who quit school in the 10th grade, ashamed of a learning disability that got in the way of her reading. "I'm just waiting for my home."

3   From the well-kept interior of the Caros' place, one can hardly see the jagged rows of tents and shanties on the vacant land around them. About 200 people—primarily

Old Glory
the American flag

poor whites and migrant workers from Mexico—have built informal habitats along the railroad tracks. There are many names for this fledgling city, where **Old Glory** flies from improvised flagpoles and trash heaps rise and fall with the wavering population. To some it's Little Tijuana, but most people call it Taco Flat. Just to the south, under a freeway overpass, there's another camp of roughly equal size called New Jack City where most of the residents are black. Even more makeshift dwellings are scattered throughout the neighborhood nearby. Fresno, which the Brookings Institution ranked in 2005 as the American city with the greatest concentration of poverty, is far from the only place where people are resorting to life in makeshift abodes. Similar encampments are proliferating throughout the West, everywhere from the industrial hub of Ontario, California, to the struggling casino district of Reno, Nevada, and the upscale suburbs of Washington state.

4   In any other country, these threadbare villages would be called slums, but in the United States, the preferred term is *tent city*, a label that implies that they are just a temporary phenomenon. Many journalists, eager to prove that the country is entering the next Great Depression, blame the emergence of these shantytowns on the economic downturn, calling them products of foreclosures and layoffs. While there's some truth to this notion, the fact is that these roving, ramshackle neighborhoods were part of the American cityscape long before the stock market nosedived, and they are unlikely to disappear when prosperity returns. The recent decades of real estate speculation and tough-love social policies have cut thousands of people out of the mainstream markets for work and housing, and the existing network of shelters for the homeless is overburdened and outdated.

vanguard
the forefront or
leading position

5   People such as the Caros are part of a **vanguard** that has been in crisis for years, building squatter settlements as a do-or-die alternative to the places that rejected them. This parallel nation, with a population now numbering at least 2,000 in Fresno alone, was born during the boom times, and it is bound to flourish as the economy falters. "The chickens are coming home to roost," says Larry Haynes, executive director of Mercy House, an organization based in Southern California that serves homeless people. "What this speaks of is an absolute crisis of affordability and accessibility."

6   Against a backdrop of faded industrial buildings and rusty water towers, Taco Flat looks like a relic of a bygone era. These rough-and-ready dwellings, untouched by the luxuries of electricity, sewage lines, and cable connections, seem like an aberration in a country that has grown accustomed to newness. Much of the shock value of tent cities comes from the fact that they force one to do a bit of time travel, revisiting an atmosphere of social disorder that seems more fitting to a Gold Rush-era squatter camp, and a level of destitution that recalls the **Hoovervilles** of the 1930s. Even tent city residents themselves feel trapped in circular trajectories of history, doomed to lives shaped by the threat of lawlessness and the ever-looming peril of relocation.

Hoovervilles
homeless camps
that arose during
the Depression and
were so named
to cast blame on
President Herbert
Hoover

7   Frankie Lynch, one of the self-proclaimed mayors of Taco Flat, has ancestors who fled Oklahoma during the Dust Bowl years, only to discover a new kind of poverty in the farmworker camps of California's Central Valley. Now he's drifting, too, unable to find the construction work that used to pay his bills. "It's just going back to the same thing," says Lynch, 50. "I remember my grandparents and my dad talking about labor camps, and going town to town to work."

incarcerated
put in jail

8   Crime is a concern here—according to county estimates, 41 percent of the homeless population has been **incarcerated** at some point—but the greatest fear for most Taco Flat residents is that they've lost their place in mainstream society, whether as a result of mental or physical illness, of past mistakes, or of the whims of global capitalism. In better times, they might have weathered their troubles, getting by with work in factories, call centers, or construction sites. But those jobs are gone, and many people wonder if they will ever come back.

9   Tent cities have much in common with the squatter camps of the Great Depression, but to simply call them Hoovervilles is to ignore their complexity. To truly understand them, one must look at current trends in the developing world, where informal urbanism—a form of "slum" development that takes place outside the conventions of city planning—is now the predominant mode of city-making. Informal urbanism, characterized by unauthorized occupation of land, makeshift construction, and lack of public utilities, is how many burgeoning nations meet their housing needs. It thrives in places like Fresno, where poverty is **endemic** and there is a wide gap between rich and poor.

endemic
common in a
particular area

10   Rahul Mehrotra, an associate professor in the urban studies and planning department at the Massachusetts Institute of Technology, says there's a kinship between Taco Flat and the squatter settlements of Mumbai, India, where he runs an architectural firm. "It's really a reflection of the government's inability to provide housing affordably across society," Mehrotra says. Informal urbanism also thrives wherever people face exclusion from the mainstream markets for work and shelter, he adds, whether they are excluded for ethnic, economic, or political reasons.

11   This can be seen in Taco Flat's large contingent of undocumented workers, who left their homes in Latin America to find work on the Central Valley's farms and construction sites. As borders tighten and the threat of immigration raids lingers, the act of signing a lease has become more risky, prompting many to forgo formal housing altogether. Undocumented workers are also plagued by low wages, which aren't keeping pace with the rising costs of housing. This hardship has only been exacerbated by jobs disappearing in the Central Valley, where an ongoing drought is turning some of the world's most fertile farmland into a desert. The situation has left Mexican workers like Juan Garcia, 21, suspended between two countries. In neither country is there a guarantee of a livelihood and home is all too often an abstraction. At least in Garcia's native state of Colima, there are always the comforts of family. "It's better in Mexico," Garcia says. "I'm going back."

12   In Fresno and other struggling cities, which perpetually strive to boost tax revenues with development, tent cities are often seen as symbols of criminality and dereliction, glaring setbacks to neighborhood revitalization efforts. That perception is common wherever informal urbanism exists, Mehrotra says, and it often leaves squatter camps on the brink of ruin. "You are always on the edge of demolition," he says. This hit home in Fresno a few years ago, when workers began raiding encampments throughout the city, tearing down makeshift homes and destroying personal property. The city of Fresno and the California Department of Transportation conducted these sweeps in the name of public health, citing citizen complaints about open-air defecation. Yet the raids did nothing to stop tent cities from forming, and they ultimately led to lawsuits. In October 2006, residents who lost their homes in

the raids filed a class-action suit against the city of Fresno and the state of California. A U.S. district judge ordered the defendants to pay $2.3 million in damages.

13   Two hundred miles south of Fresno, there's also been a battle over tent cities in the Inland Empire, an industrial stronghold that stretches out into the deserts east of Los Angeles. Flying into Ontario International Airport, one can see the nucleus of this struggle, in a neighborhood less than a mile from the tarmac. There, on a stretch of vacant land surrounded by aging homes and abandoned orchards, tents are arranged in neat rows. This used to be one of Southern California's largest squatter settlements, an unruly village of tarp and scrap wood that grew until some 400 residents called it home. People moved here from as far away as Florida, recalls Brent Schultz, Ontario's director of housing and neighborhood revitalization.

14   Local officials were disturbed to find out that Ontario was becoming a magnet for the dispossessed, Schultz says. Rather than simply bulldoze the makeshift neighborhood, Ontario officials embarked on a $100,000 campaign to discipline and punish squatters, setting up a formal camp where tarp dwellings became symbols of order. In the spring of last year, police and code enforcement officers issued color-coded bracelets to distinguish Ontario residents from newcomers, then gradually banished the out-of-towners. Then they demolished the shanties and set up an official camp with a chain-link fence and guard shack. Residents were issued IDs and a strict set of rules: no coming and going after 10 P.M., no pets, no children or visitors, no drugs, and no alcohol. About 120 people stuck around, but many left to escape the regimentation. As of July, the population was about 60.

15   "It's like a prison," says Melody Woolsey, 40, who has lived in both versions of the encampment. Schultz, on the other hand, considers the camp one of Ontario's greatest success stories. Some of the camp's residents agree: They say it's a bit like a gated community on a modest scale, a rare haven where one can live affordably without fear of robbery or violence.

16   "Some people come up here and say it looks like a concentration camp, but they don't live here," says Robert, 51, an unemployed factory technician. "They're only looking at it from the outside. I look at it that it's a secure community." Yet the neighborhood is filled with angry people who were excluded from the camp and left to take shelter in cars or in other vacant lots, often under threat of police citations. Many of these outcasts see the camp as a symbol of injustice, a cynical and inauthentic gesture of compassion.

17   For people throughout the American West, the very concept of home is changing, adjusting downward to a reality in which buying cheap land, picking out a subdivision lot, or even renting an apartment has become nothing more than a fancy daydream. That's a painful realization for a region steeped in myths of plenty. But in these hard times, tent cities increasingly are the last province of hope for having a place of one's own. Tent cities like Taco Flat are communities like any other, and if they are neglected, they will be lost to crime, addiction, and illness. Yet whenever officials act to destroy or stifle them with punitive regulations, they not only wipe out the pride of residents struggling to survive, they also jettison a spirit of self-reliance and innovation that could be harnessed to help meet the housing needs of the future.

18   The promise of tent cities begins with their architecture. Makeshift dwellings may not be the dream homes of yesteryear, but they are simple, affordable, and sustainable in their use of salvaged materials. With imaginative designers, they could help solve the present housing crisis, a faster alternative to the process of building shelters and low-income apartment complexes. That possibility is already taking shape in Portland, Oregon, where activists have carved out a space for improvised dwellings in Dignity Village, a community that can house up to 60 people. Founded in 2000 and now approved by the city, it's considered a model by housing advocates worldwide.

19   Beyond the check-in desk in the village's security post, residents find a balance between the human needs for safety and personal freedom. Most are required to do at least 10 hours of community service a week—helping build or remodel homes, for example—but otherwise they set their own schedules. "This isn't a flophouse," says Joe Palinkas, 55. "This is a community place. You support the village by taking care of yourself as if you were on your own." Tent cities also could become a locus for action and dialogue, a place where outreach workers, social service agencies, and everyday citizens can reach out to society's most vulnerable members.

20   Leaders in California's Central Valley might do well to take inspiration from Dignity Village. Instead, planners still see tent cities as obstacles to revitalization. Fresno and Madera counties recently adopted a 10-year plan to end homelessness, and Gregory Barfield, the area's newly appointed homelessness czar, says tent cities aren't part of the picture. "A Dignity Village for us is not the best course of action," says Barfield. "We've got to find out a way to move forward with housing people."

21   But such talk means little to Taco Flat residents like Arthur Barela, 45, who lost his job when the Central Valley's farms began to dry out. For him, the only real home is the one he has made with his blankets, his tent, and his tarp. He still has the strength to keep his place clean, but his frame is nearly skeletal. "Hopefully, things don't get chaotic and things don't get out of hand," says Barela, kneeling before his tent as if in prayer. "Sometimes hunger can make a person do crazy things."

A. UNDERSTANDING THE THESIS AND OTHER MAIN IDEAS

Select the best answer.

_____ 1. The author's primary purpose in this selection is to

a. argue for better social programs on behalf of the homeless population.

b. describe the development of tent cities and the people who live in them.

c. compare modern-day tent cities with the squatter camps of the Depression.

d. criticize people who live in tent cities for not finding jobs and better housing.

_____ 2. The tent city that is the main focus of this article is called

    a. New Jack City.

    b. Hooverville.

    c. the Inland Empire.

    d. Taco Flat.

_____ 3. The topic of paragraph 9 is

    a. squatter camps.

    b. the Great Depression.

    c. informal urbanism.

    d. Hoovervilles.

_____ 4. The main idea of paragraph 17 is that

    a. people in the American West are having to adjust their concept of home.

    b. many people move to the West as their last hope for a place of their own.

    c. tent cities can be destroyed by crime, addiction, illness, or neglect.

    d. officials ruin tent cities whenever they try to impose regulations.

_____ 5. The model community called Dignity Village is located in

    a. Ontario, Canada.

    b. Fresno, California.

    c. Portland, Oregon.

    d. Mumbai, India.

B. IDENTIFYING DETAILS

Indicate whether each statement is true (T) or false (F).

_____ 1. Marie and Francisco Caro live in an abandoned trailer.

_____ 2. The population of Taco Flat is about 200.

_____ 3. In 2005, Fresno was ranked as the American city with the highest concentration of poverty.

_____ 4. The tents and shanties in Taco Flat are equipped with electricity and sewage lines.

_____ 5. According to Fresno county estimates, 41 percent of the homeless population has spent time in jail.

C. RECOGNIZING METHODS OF ORGANIZATION AND TRANSITIONS

Complete the following statements by filling in the blanks.

1. In paragraphs 1 and 2, the author uses the cause-and-effect pattern to describe how Marie and Francisco Caro came to live in a tent city. In their case, the *cause* was their inability to _____ housing and the *effect* was _____ a tent city.

2. In paragraph 9, the author uses the _____ pattern to explain the meaning of the term *informal urbanism.*

3. In paragraphs 15 and 16, two transitions that indicate the contrast organizational pattern are _____ and _____ .

D. REVIEWING AND ORGANIZING IDEAS: MAPPING

Using the descriptions in paragraphs 13 and 14, determine the chronological order of the events below and put them in the correct order on the time line by writing the letters that correspond to the events in the blanks. Some have been done for you.

a. The population of a squatter village in Ontario includes 400 residents.

b. Out-of-towners are gradually banished and shanties are demolished.

c. Many decide to leave because of strict rules.

d. Official camp is established with fence and guard shack.

e. Color-coded bracelets are issued to distinguish Ontario residents from newcomers.

f. Residents are issued IDs and are subject to new rules.

g. Officials begin $100,000 campaign to discipline squatters and create a formal camp.

h. The population declines to about 60 residents.

E. READING AND THINKING VISUALLY

Answer each of the following questions.

1. What details do you notice in the photograph of the tent city on page 362?

_____

2. How does the tent city in the photograph correspond to the descriptions of different tent cities discussed in the selection?

_____

F. FIGURING OUT IMPLIED MEANINGS

For each of the following quotes from the selection, determine whether the bold-faced word has a positive (P) or negative (N) connotation.

_____ 1. "Even a strong person could **wither** in a place like this" (paragraph 1)

_____ 2. "**fresh-cut** Christmas tree boughs hung on the walls for decoration" (paragraph 2)

_____ 3. "these roving, **ramshackle** neighborhoods" (paragraph 4)

_____ 4. "**doomed** to lives shaped by the threat of lawlessness" (paragraph 6)

_____ 5. "symbols of **criminality** and dereliction" (paragraph 12)

_____ 6. "a rare **haven** where one can live affordably" (paragraph 15)

_____ 7. "whenever officials act to destroy or **stifle** them" (paragraph 17)

_____ 8. "The **promise** of tent cities begins with their architecture" (paragraph 18)

_____ 9. "a balance between the human needs for safety and personal **freedom**" (paragraph 19)

_____ 10. "his frame is nearly **skeletal**" (paragraph 21)

G. THINKING CRITICALLY

Select the best answer.

_____ 1. The title "Camping for Their Lives" indicates that most people in tent cities
   a. are having the time of their lives.
   b. have no other options for housing.
   c. are only visiting and are not residents.
   d. prefer the camping lifestyle.

_____ 2. The author supports his thesis with
   a. facts and statistics.
   b. descriptions and examples.
   c. expert opinions.
   d. all of the above.

_____ 3. The author attributes the emergence of tent cities to all of the following *except*

    a. real estate speculation.

    b. tough-love social policies.

    c. the most recent drop in the stock market.

    d. an overloaded and outdated network of homeless shelters.

_____ 4. The author includes the description of Dignity Village in order to

    a. recommend it as a model for affordable communities.

    b. compare and contrast it with the other tent cities in the article.

    c. emphasize the community potential of tent cities.

    d. do all of the above.

_____ 5. The author's overall tone can best be described as

    a. judgmental.

    b. sympathetic.

    c. indifferent.

    d. sarcastic.

H. BUILDING VOCABULARY

Context

Using context and a dictionary, if necessary, determine the meaning of each word as it is used in the selection.

_____ 1. fledgling (paragraph 3)

    a. birdlike

    b. new or beginning

    c. expensive

    d. established

_____ 2. aberration (paragraph 6)

    a. abnormality

    b. observation

    c. recommendation

    d. improvement

_____ 3. destitution (paragraph 6)

    a. structure

    b. comfort

    c. application

    d. poverty

_____ 4. trajectories (paragraph 6)

  a. laws

  b. paths

  c. surfaces

  d. forces

_____ 5. burgeoning (paragraph 9)

  a. allowing

  b. stalling

  c. growing

  d. departing

_____ 6. contingent (paragraph 11)

  a. commitment

  b. group

  c. independent

  d. arrangement

_____ 7. exacerbated (paragraph 11)

  a. made worse

  b. relinquished

  c. suspended

  d. enhanced

_____ 8. regimentation (paragraph 14)

  a. appearance

  b. informality

  c. strict discipline

  d. inconsistency

_____ 9. jettison (paragraph 17)

  a. join

  b. throw away

  c. strain

  d. apply

_____ 10. locus (paragraph 19)

  a. center

  b. dispute

  c. distance

  d. view

Word Parts

A REVIEW OF PREFIXES

RE- means *again*
DIS- means *apart, away, not*
IN- means *not*
UN- means *not*

Use your knowledge of word parts and the review above to fill in the blanks in the following sentences.

1. When an object has been **repurposed** (paragraph 2), it has been adapted so that it can be used _____ for another purpose.

2. To describe workers as **undocumented** (paragraph 11) is to say that they do _____ have the appropriate legal documents, such as immigration or working papers.

3. People who are described as **dispossessed** (paragraph 14) are those who _____ do have homes, property, or possessions.

4. A symbol of **injustice** (paragraph 16) is something that represents an action or treatment that is _____ just or fair.

5. When someone describes a gesture as **inauthentic** (paragraph 16), he or she perceives that it is _____ genuine or sincere.

Unusual Words/Understanding Idioms

Use the meanings given below to write a sentence using the boldfaced word or phrase.

1. Something described as **makeshift** (paragraph 3) is considered a crude and temporary solution made up from whatever is available.

   Your sentence: _____

   _____

2. Someone who says that **the chickens are coming home to roost** (paragraph 5) means that consequences are occurring because of certain actions or mistakes in the past.

   Your sentence: _____

   _____

I. SELECTING A LEARNING/STUDY STRATEGY

Suppose you read this article in preparation for a class discussion on whether or not tent cities are obstacles to revitalization. What techniques would you use to organize the information in the article to support your position?

J. EXPLORING IDEAS THROUGH DISCUSSION AND WRITING

1. Do you detect any bias in this selection? Consider the author's tone, his language, and the evidence he uses to support his position. Does he include opposing viewpoints?

2. According to the selection, leaders in California's Central Valley rejected the idea of a Dignity Village–type tent city (paragraph 20). Why do you think they rejected it?

3. The author quotes a variety of people in the selection, from tent city residents to an urban studies professor to a homelessness czar. Whose opinions did you find most persuasive and why?

4. Compare the introductory paragraphs about the Caros with the last paragraph, about Arthur Barela. Why do you think the author chose to begin and end the article this way?

K. BEYOND THE CLASSROOM TO THE WEB

The reading discusses squatter settlements mostly in North America, but squatters are common in other parts of the world as well. Conduct a Web search for the term favela. What is a favela, and where are favelas found? How are these similar to or different from the squatter settlements discussed in the reading?

TRACKING YOUR PROGRESS

Selection 11		
Section	**Number Correct**	**Score**
A. Thesis and Main Ideas (5 items)	_____ × 4	_____
B. Details (5 items)	_____ × 2	_____
C. Organization and Transitions (5 items)	_____ × 2	_____
F. Implied Meanings (10 items)	_____ × 2	_____
G. Thinking Critically (5 items)	_____ × 4	_____
H. Vocabulary		
Context (10 items)	_____ × 1	_____
Word Parts (5 items)	_____ × 2	_____
	Total Score	_____%

SELECTION 12

Reporting the News

George C. Edwards III, Martin P. Wattenberg, and Robert L. Lineberry

TEXTBOOK EXCERPT

The selection originally appeared in a government textbook, *Government in America*. It was taken from a chapter titled "The Mass Media and the Political Agenda." In the preface to the textbook, the authors say, "We write *Government in America* to provide our readers with a better understanding of our fascinating political system."

PREVIEWING THE READING

Using the steps listed on pages 40–41, preview the reading selection. When you have finished, complete the following items.

1. The topic of this reading is _____.

2. Indicate whether each statement is true (T) or false (F).

_____ a. Most news focuses on everyday occurrences.

_____ b. The media are a key political institution.

MAKING CONNECTIONS

Do you read or watch the news regularly? How much information do the news media really provide about news stories? How many stories are serious, and how many are little more than entertainment?

READING TIP

This selection offers ample opportunity for critical thinking. As you read, think about how the authors' main points help you better understand news reporting.

Reporting the News

1   As journalism students will quickly tell you, news is what is timely and different. It is a man biting a dog, not a dog biting a man. An often-repeated speech on foreign policy or a well-worn statement on the need for immigration reform is less newsworthy than an odd episode. The public rarely hears about the routine ceremonies at state dinners, but when President George Bush threw up all over the Japanese prime

In 2003, during the Iraq War, a number of journalists were embedded with fighting units, meaning that they traveled along with them day after day and literally became part of the unit. Being right in with the action enabled an immediacy of reporting that was never possible before. One much-praised example of embedded reporting was that of NBC's David Bloom, who sent back stunningly clear pictures of what it was like to move through the desert with an infantry division. Sadly, Bloom was one of a number of journalists who died during the conflict with Iraq. He suffered a pulmonary embolism, a condition that may have been brought on by long hours confined to a very small space inside an armored tank.

caucus
a meeting of political party members to select candidates for election

2

minister in 1992, the world's media jumped on the story. Similarly, when Howard Dean screamed to a crowd of supporters after the 2004 Iowa **caucuses**, the major networks and cable news channels played the clip over 600 times in the following four days, virtually obliterating any serious discussion of the issues. In its search for the unusual, the news media can give its audience a peculiar, distorted view of events and policymakers.

Millions of new and different events happen every day; journalists must decide which of them are newsworthy. A classic look into how the news is produced can be found in Edward J. Epstein's *News from Nowhere*, which summarizes his insights from a year of observing NBC's news department from inside the organization. Epstein found that in the pursuit of high ratings, news shows are tailored to a fairly low level of audience sophistication. To a large extent, TV networks define news as what is entertaining to the average viewer. A dull and complicated story would have to be of enormous importance to get on the air; in contrast, relatively trivial stories can make the cut if they are interesting enough. Leonard Downie, Jr., and Robert Kaiser of the *Washington Post* argue that entertainment has increasingly pushed out information in the TV news business. They write that the history of TV news can be summarized in a couple sentences:

As audiences declined, network executives decreed that news had to become more profitable. So news divisions sharply reduced their costs, and tried to raise the entertainment value of their broadcasts.

Regardless of the medium, it cannot be emphasized enough that news reporting is a business in America. The quest for profits shapes how journalists define what is newsworthy, where they get their information, and how they present it. And the pursuit of types of news stories that will attract more viewers or readers also leads to certain biases in what the American public sees and reads.

Finding the News

3   Americans' popular image of correspondents or reporters somehow uncovering the news is accurate in some cases; yet most news stories come from well-established sources. Major news organizations assign their best reporters to particular beats—specific locations from which news often emanates, such as Congress. For example, during the Gulf War in 1991, mere than 50 percent of the lead stories on TV newscasts came from the White House, Pentagon, and State Department beats. Numerous studies of both the electronic and the print media show that journalists rely almost exclusively on such established sources to get their information.

4   Politicians depend on the media to spread certain information and ideas to the general public. Sometimes they feed stories to reporters in the form of trial balloons, information leaked to see what the political reaction will be. For example, a few days prior to President Clinton's admission that he had an "inappropriate relationship" with Monica Lewinsky, top aides to the president leaked the story to Richard Berke of the *New York Times*. The timing of the leak was obvious; the story appeared just before Clinton had to decide how to testify before Kenneth Starr's grand jury. When the public reacted that it was about time he admitted this relationship, it was probably easier for him to do so—at least politically.

symbiotic
a dependent relationship between two parties in which both parties benefit

5   Journalists and politicians have a **symbiotic** relationship, with politicians relying on journalists to get their message out and journalists relying on politicians to keep them in the know. When reporters feel that their access to information is being impeded, complaints of censorship become widespread. During the Gulf War in 1991, reporters' freedom of movement and observation was severely restricted. After the fighting was over, 15 influential news organizations sent a letter to the secretary of defense complaining that the rules for reporting the war were designed more to control the news than to facilitate it. Largely because of such complaints, during the 2003 military campaign to oust Saddam Hussein the Pentagon "embedded" about 500 reporters with **coalition** fighting forces, thus enabling them to report on combat activity as it happened. The result was an increased ability to transmit combat footage. A content analysis by Farnsworth and Lichter found that 35 percent of major TV network stories contained combat scenes compared to just 20 percent in 1991. The public response to this new form of war reporting was largely positive.

coalition
a group of people working together

6   Although journalists are typically dependent on familiar sources, an enterprising reporter occasionally has an opportunity to live up to the image of the crusading truth seeker. Local reporters Carl Bernstein and Bob Woodward of the *Washington*

Post uncovered important evidence about the Watergate break-in and cover-up in the early 1970s. Ever since the Watergate scandal, news organizations have regularly sent reporters on beats to expose the uglier side of government corruption and inefficiency, and journalists have seen such reporting as among their important roles.

7   There are many cases of good investigative reporting making a difference in politics and government. For example, in 1997, the *New York Times* won a Pulitzer Prize for its in-depth reports on how a proposed gold-mining operation threatened the environment of part of Yellowstone National Park. When President Clinton vacationed at nearby Jackson Hole, he decided to go up and see the mine because he had been reading about it in the *New York Times*. Soon afterward, the project was stopped, and the government gave the owners of the property a financial settlement. In 1999, the *Chicago Tribune* documented the experiences of numerous Illinois men sentenced to death who had been convicted on questionable evidence or coerced into confessing. Soon after the series was published, the governor of Illinois suspended all executions in the state. And in 2007, a reporter with the *Birmingham News* won a Pulitzer Prize for his exposure of **cronyism** and corruption in Alabama's two-year college system, resulting in the dismissal of the chancellor and other corrective action.

cronyism
the appointment of unqualified friends and family to positions of authority

Presenting the News

8   Once the news has been "found," it has to be neatly compressed into a 30-second news segment or fit in among other stories and advertisements in a newspaper. If you had to pick a single word to describe news coverage by the news media, it would be *superficial*. "The name of the game," says former White House Press Secretary Jody Powell, "is skimming off the cream, seizing on the most interesting, controversial, and unusual aspects of an issue." Editors do not want to bore or confuse their audience. TV news, in particular, is little more than a headline service. According to former CBS anchor Dan Rather, "You simply cannot be a well-informed citizen by just watching the news on television."

9   Except for the little-watched but highly regarded *NewsHour* on PBS and ABC's late-night *Nightline*, analysis of news events rarely lasts more than a minute. Patterson's study of campaign coverage found that only skimpy attention was given to the issues during a presidential campaign. Clearly, if coverage of political events during the height of an election campaign is thin, coverage of day-to-day policy questions is even thinner. Issues such as reforming the Medicare system, adjusting eligibility levels for food stamps, and regulating the financial services industry are highly complex and difficult to treat in a short news clip. A careful study of media coverage of Bill and Hillary Clinton's comprehensive health care proposal in 1993–94 found that the media focused much more on strategy and who was winning the political game than on the specific policy issues involved. President Obama faced exactly the same problem in his battle to reform America's health care system in 2009–10, frequently admonishing the press, "This isn't about me. This isn't about politics."

10   Strangely enough, as technology has enabled the media to pass along information with greater speed, news coverage has become less thorough. High-tech communication has helped reporters do their job faster but not necessarily better. Newspapers once routinely reprinted the entire text of important political speeches; now the *New*

York Times is virtually the only paper that does so—and even the *Times* has cut back sharply on this practice. In place of speeches, Americans now hear sound bites of 10 seconds or less on TV. The average length of time that a presidential candidate was given to talk uninterrupted on the TV news declined precipitously from 43 seconds in 1968 to just 8 seconds in 2004. Politicians have expressed frustration with sound-bite journalism. For example, President Jimmy Carter told a reporter that

WHY IT MATTERS

The Increasing Speed of News Dissemination

When Samuel Morse sent the first telegraph message from the U.S. Capitol building, he tapped out a question, "What hath God wrought?" The answer back was "What is the news from Washington?" Ever since, the transmission of news via electronic means has become faster and faster. As a result, over time there has been less and less time for deliberative action to deal with long-term problems, and the political agenda has come to focus more on the here and now.

it's a strange thing that you can go through your campaign for president, and you have a basic theme that you express in a 15- or 20-minute standard speech . . . but the traveling press—sometimes exceeding 100 people—will never report that speech to the public. The peripheral aspects become the headlines, but the basic essence of what you stand for and what you hope to accomplish is never reported.

11   Sound-bite journalism has meant both that politicians are unable to present the issues and that they are able to avoid the issues. Why should politicians work to build a carefully crafted case for their point of view when a catchy line will do just as well? And as Walter Cronkite wrote, "Naturally, nothing of any significance is going to be said in seven seconds, but this seems to work to the advantage of many politicians. They are not required to say anything of significance, and issues can be avoided rather than confronted."

12   Over the past decade or so, politicians have found it increasingly difficult to get their message covered on the major networks, as ratings pressures have led to a decrease in political coverage, leaving the field to much-less-watched channels like CNN and MSNBC. The three major networks *together* devoted an average of 12.6 minutes per night to the exceedingly close 2000 presidential election campaign; just half the 24.6 minutes they devoted to the 1992 campaign. Indeed, in the presidential election of 2000, voters had to bypass network television newscasts and watch TV talk shows to hear candidates deliver their messages. George W. Bush was on-screen for a total of 13 minutes during his appearance on *Late Night with David Letterman* on October 19, which exceeded his entire speaking time on all three network news shows during that month. Similarly, Al Gore received more speaking time on his September 14 *Letterman* appearance than he did during the entire month of September on the network evening newscasts.

Cold War
an era of political hostility between the United States and the Soviet Union

13   During the **Cold War**, presidents could routinely obtain coverage for their speeches on the three major networks anytime they requested it. Now, with the networks able to shunt the coverage to CNN and other cable news outlets, it is easy for them to say "no" to even the president. In May 2000, for example, Bill Clinton was rebuffed when he asked for time on ABC, NBC, and CBS to address

U.S.–China relations. "Are you crazy? It's sweeps month!" was one of the responses. In September 2009, Fox opted to show an episode of "So You Think You Can Dance" instead of Obama's address to Congress about health care.

The News and Public Opinion

14   How does the news media's depiction of a threatening, hostile, and corrupt world shape Americans' political opinions and behavior? This question is difficult to answer, as the effects of the news media can be difficult to accurately assess. One reason is that it is hard to separate the media from other influences. When presidents, legislators, and interest groups—as well as news organizations—are all discussing an issue, it is not easy to isolate the opinion changes that come from political leadership from those that come from the news. Moreover, the effect of one news story on public opinion may be trivial but the **cumulative** effect of dozens of news stories may be important.

cumulative
taken together, as a series

15   For many years, students of the subject tended to doubt that the media had more than a marginal effect on public opinion. The "minimal effects hypothesis" stemmed from the fact that early scholars were looking for direct impacts—for example, whether the media affected how people voted. When the focus turned to how the media affect *what Americans think about*, the effects began to appear more significant. In a series of controlled laboratory experiments, Shanto Iyengar and Donald Kinder subtly manipulated the stories participants saw on the TV news. They found that they could significantly affect the importance people attached to a given problem by splicing a few stories about it into the news over the course of a week. Iyengar and Kinder do not maintain that the networks can make something out of nothing or conceal problems that actually exist. But they do conclude that "what television news does, instead, is alter the priorities Americans attach to a circumscribed set of problems, all of which are plausible contenders for public concern." Subsequent research by Miller and Krosnick has revealed that agenda-setting effects are particularly strong among politically knowledgeable citizens who trust the media. Thus, rather than the media manipulating the public, they argue that agenda setting reflects a deliberate and thoughtful process on the part of sophisticated citizens who rely on what they consider a credible institutional source of information.

16   Nonetheless, this agenda-setting effect can have a range of far-reaching consequences. First, by increasing public attention to specific problems, the media influence the criteria by which the public evaluates political leaders. When unemployment goes up but inflation goes down, does public support for the president increase or decrease? The answer could depend in large part on which story the media emphasized. The fact that the media emphasized the country's slow economic growth in 1992 rather than the good news of low inflation and interest rates was clearly instrumental in setting the stage for Bill Clinton's ousting the **incumbent** president, George H. W. Bush, that year. Similarly, the emphasis on the deteriorating economic situation in 2008 rather than the good news about the success of the troop surge in Iraq was clearly an advantage for Obama and a disadvantage for McCain.

incumbent
politician who currently holds an office

17   The media can even have a dramatic effect on how the public evaluates specific events by emphasizing one event over others. When, during a 1976 presidential debate, President Ford incorrectly stated that the Soviet Union did not dominate Eastern Europe, the press gave substantial coverage to Ford's misstatement, and this coverage had an impact on the public. Polls showed that most people did not realize the president had made an error until the press told them so. Afterward, the initial assessment that Ford had won the debate shifted, as voters expressed increased concern about his competence in foreign policymaking. Similarly, the media's focus on misstatements by Al Gore during the first presidential debate of 2000 had an impact on public opinion. In the days immediately following this debate, the percentage who thought that Gore had beaten Bush declined markedly.

18   Much remains unknown about the effects of the media and the news on American political opinion and behavior. Enough is known, however, to conclude that the media are a key political institution. The media control much of the technology that in turn controls much of what Americans believe about politics and government. For this reason, it is important to look at the American policy agenda and the media's role in shaping it.

A. UNDERSTANDING THE THESIS AND OTHER MAIN IDEAS

Select the best answer.

_____ 1. Which of the following best states the thesis or central thought of "Reporting the News"?

a. News is a business that provides much more entertainment than serious political reporting, with a few exceptions; even so, the news influences people's political behaviors.

b. As network television has emphasized reality TV and other types of cheap entertainment, cable news networks have stepped in to undertake serious political reporting.

c. Reporters generally go to well-established contacts for information, but they sometimes uncover injustices that lead to important social and political changes.

d. There is a symbiotic relationship between politicians and reporters, with each relying on the other to bring important information and social agendas to the public's attention.

_____ 2. The main idea of paragraph 1 is found in the

a. first sentence.

b. second sentence.

c. fourth sentence.

d. last sentence.

_____ 3. The topic of paragraph 4 is
   a. President Clinton.
   b. trial balloons.
   c. _The New York Times._
   d. Kenneth Starr's grand jury.

_____ 4. The main idea of paragraph 12 is found in the
   a. first sentence.
   b. second sentence.
   c. third sentence.
   d. last sentence.

_____ 5. The topic of paragraph 15 is
   a. the minimal effects hypothesis.
   b. research into the media's effects on public opinion.
   c. Shanto Iyengar and Donald Kinder.
   d. the roles of knowledgeable citizens in the political process.

B. IDENTIFYING DETAILS

Select the best answer.

_____ 1. Which scandal did Bob Woodward and Carl Bernstein of
   The Washington Post uncover?
   a. Lance Armstrong's use of illegal steroids
   b. Watergate
   c. David Petraeus's affair
   d. Iran-Contra

_____ 2. How long does a typical televised news segment last?
   a. 1 minute or less
   b. 2 minutes
   c. 3 minutes
   d. 5 minutes

_____ 3. The term the authors use to indicate a small piece of information
   that can be conveyed in a very short period of time (ten seconds or
   less) is
   a. beat.
   b. caucus.
   c. sound bite.
   d. trial balloon.

_____ 4. Which presidential candidate benefited from the media's coverage of the country's slow rate of economic growth in 1992?

    a. George H.W. Bush

    b. Bill Clinton

    c. Barack Obama

    d. John McCain

C. RECOGNIZING METHODS OF ORGANIZATION AND TRANSITIONS

Select the best answer.

_____ 1. Which organizational pattern is used in paragraph 7?

    a. generalization and example

    b. process

    c. definition

    d. classification

_____ 2. The organizational pattern used in the "Why It Matters" box titled "The Increasing Speed of News Dissemination" on page 378 is

    a. comparison and contrast.

    b. summary.

    c. listing.

    d. cause and effect.

_____ 3. The transitional word or phrase used to signal the organizational pattern of paragraph 13 is

    a. during the Cold War.

    b. now.

    c. for example.

    d. opted.

D. REVIEWING AND ORGANIZING IDEAS: SUMMARIZING

Complete the following summary of paragraphs 14–18 by filling in the missing words or phrases.

It is difficult to know how exactly the news media affect Americans' political opinions, behaviors, and _____ . It is not easy to separate the media's influence from other influences; and it is hard to trace the effects of any particular news story at any given moment in time. However, while early research showed that the media had only a _____ effect on public opinion, more recent research has shown that the media help set or alter people's _____. Other research has speculated that _____ citizens set the media agenda rather than the other way around. This can have unintended effects. For example, by focusing on something negative that is happening in the economy (such as _____) rather than something positive (such as _____), the media can favor one political figure over another. By reporting on incorrect statements made by politicians, the media can influence how people perceive those politicians. Overall, it is safe to say that the media play a key role in _____.

E. READING AND THINKING VISUALLY

Select the best answer.

_____ The photograph that accompanies the reading was included to demonstrate

a. how desert wars are fought.

b. the dire conditions of war.

c. how soldiers respond to enemy attacks.

d. the dangers embedded journalists face.

F. FIGURING OUT IMPLIED MEANINGS

Indicate whether each statement is true (T) or false (F).

_____ 1. The authors imply that most news organizations are not seeking to earn high profits.

_____ 2. In general, most news programs are produced for a highly educated audience.

_____ 3. Walter Cronkite believed that the current system of news reporting benefits politicians more than it benefits citizens.

_____ 4. Reporters are much more likely to contact established sources for information than to seek out new or unknown sources of information.

_____ 5. The authors imply that the public likes stories in which reporters present the news from the front lines or combat areas of a war zone.

_____ 6. Dan Rather supports the format and style of network news.

_____ 7. The rise of technology has made news agencies more willing to provide in-depth coverage of key issues.

_____ 8. Today, it is easier to find serious discussion of politics on cable channels than on the major TV networks.

_____ 9. The authors imply that the media helped Presidents Clinton and Obama get elected by reporting news that was favorable to their campaigns and unfavorable to their opponents' campaigns.

G. THINKING CRITICALLY

Select the best answer.

_____ 1. The purpose of this reading selection is to

a. criticize network news for its poor coverage of political matters.

b. provide information about the ways news is found and presented in the United States, as well as the effect of news reporting on public opinion and behavior.

c. present the research results generated by several well-known political scientists, then contrast those results with the well-known facts regarding bias in the media.

d. encourage more reporters to undertake serious investigative journalism rather than relying on standard sources for information on topics that are not particularly important to U.S. citizens.

_____ 2. The tone of the selection is best described as

a. humorous.

b. lurid.

c. sarcastic.

d. critical.

_____ 3. Which of the following statements is an opinion, not a fact?

a. "In its search for the unusual, the news media can give its audience a peculiar, distorted view of events and policymakers." (paragraph 1)

b. "Politicians depend on the media to spread certain information and ideas to the general public." (paragraph 4)

c. "George W. Bush was on-screen for a total of 13 minutes during his appearance on *Late Night with David Letterman*." (paragraph 12)

d. "During the Cold War, presidents could routinely obtain coverage for their speeches on the three major networks anytime they requested it." (paragraph 13)

_____ 4. To support their main ideas, the authors quote all of the following credible authorities *except*

    a. Dan Rather.

    b. Walter Cronkite.

    c. Barbara Walters.

    d. Jody Powell.

_____ 5. By using the phrase "at least politically" at the end of paragraph 4, the authors imply that

    a. politicians need to carefully time their admissions of guilt.

    b. President Clinton's admission was easier politically than it was personally.

    c. the news media were biased against Monica Lewinsky.

    d. Kenneth Starr's grand jury was political theater intended to disgrace President Clinton.

H. BUILDING VOCABULARY

Context

Using context and a dictionary, if necessary, determine the meaning of each word as it is used in the selection.

_____ 1. obliterate (paragraph 1)

    a. ignore

    b. interest

    c. distort

    d. destroy

_____ 2. impede (paragraph 5)

    a. run

    b. explode

    c. stand

    d. block

_____ 3. coerce (paragraph 7)

    a. persuade

    b. trick

    c. pull

    d. linger

_____ 4. skimpy (paragraph 9)

    a. buttery

    b. joyful

    c. limited

    d. quick

_____ 5. shunt (paragraph 13)

    a. avoid

    b. lessen

    c. keep

    d. push

_____ 6. marginal (paragraph 15)

    a. spacious

    b. minimal

    c. artificial

    d. level

_____ 7. plausible (paragraph 15)

    a. credible

    b. lost

    c. tender

    d. pleasing

Word Parts

A REVIEW OF PREFIXES

TRANS- means _cross_ or _over_

CIRCUM- means _around_

Use your knowledge of word parts and the review above to fill in the blanks and define the boldfaced word in the following sentences.

1. To **transmit** (paragraph 5) information is to send it out _____ airwaves or radio waves.

2. To **circumscribe** (paragraph 15) a problem is to draw limits _____ it.

Unusual Words/Understanding Idioms

Use the meanings given below to write a sentence using the boldfaced word or phrase.

1. A **well-worn** (paragraph 1) statement is one that has been frequently repeated or used.

   Your sentence: _____

   _____

2. A **leak** (paragraph 4) refers to the intentional or unintentional sharing of secret or sensitive information with the media.

   Your sentence: _____

   _____

I. SELECTING A LEARNING/STUDY STRATEGY

Select the best answer.

_____ 1. This reading contains many facts about the media and their effects on behavior. What would be the best way to learn these facts?

   a. Draw a time line of politics in America.

   b. Read the selection a minimum of eight times.

   c. Skim paragraphs 1–13 but closely read paragraphs 14–18.

   d. Record the facts on a study sheet.

J. EXPLORING IDEAS THROUGH DISCUSSION AND WRITING

1. Write a one-paragraph summary of each of the reading's main sections: "Reporting the News," "Finding the News," "Presenting the News," and "The News and Public Opinion."

2. When you watch the news, read a magazine, or surf the Web, how much attention do you pay to political news? Which political topics are most interesting to you, and why?

3. Examine your campus newspaper. What types of news does it report? Does it cover local, national, or international politics?

4. Much has been written about "media bias." Many people believe that the media are biased along party lines. For example, many believe that *The New York Times* has a liberal bias, while *The Wall Street Journal* has a conservative bias. Watch a newscast or read several articles in a newspaper or magazine. Do you perceive any bias? Write a paragraph or essay exploring your findings.

K. BEYOND THE CLASSROOM TO THE WEB

A popular political Web site is politico.com, which offers a wealth of stories related to politics. Visit the Web site, read an article of your choice, and write a summary of it.

TRACKING
YOUR
PROGRESS

Selection 12

Section	Number Correct	Score
A. Thesis and Main Ideas (5 items)	_____ × 3	_____
B. Details (4 items)	_____ × 4	_____
C. Organization and Transitions (3 items)	_____ × 4	_____
E. Reading and Thinking Visually (1 item)	_____ × 4	_____
F. Implied Meanings (9 items)	_____ × 2	_____
G. Thinking Critically (5 items)	_____ × 3	_____
H. Vocabulary		
Context (7 items)	_____ × 2	_____
Word Parts (2 items)	_____ × 3	_____
	Total Score	_____%

13 Business/Advertising/Economics

Business is a diverse field that includes business management, marketing, finance, statistics, retailing, information systems, and organizational behavior. In general, **business** is concerned with the production and sale of goods and services. All of us are in contact with businesses on a daily basis. When you stop for gas, buy a sandwich, or pick up the telephone, you are involved in a business transaction. In "The Super Bowl: The Mother of All Advertising Events—But Is It Worth It?" you will see how advertising, particularly for the Super Bowl, plays an important role in selling products and services. Studying business can also make you a savvy, better-informed consumer. When you read "Mapping, and Sharing, the Consumer Genome," you will learn how powerful companies collect (and then sell) data about your life, your interests, and your purchases. Business courses can help you make career decisions and discover a wide range of employment opportunities. Business courses also examine the issue of ethnic and cultural diversity because today's workforce consists of individuals from a variety of cultural and ethnic groups. As you read "Product Placement and Advergaming," you will see how product advertisement through placement seeps into popular culture.

Use the following techniques for reading in business.

TIPS FOR READING IN BUSINESS/ ADVERTISING/ ECONOMICS

- **Focus on process.** Many courses in business examine how things work and how things get done. In "Product Placement and Advergaming" you will learn how specific products and brand names are used in movies, television, and other media. In "The Super Bowl: The Mother of All Advertising Events—But Is It Worth It?" you will discover how advertisers build interest in and excitement about their ads.

- **Think about technology and ethics.** Advances in computer technology have revolutionized the way companies do business. Technology can be extremely efficient and effective at figuring out what individuals like to buy (as "Mapping, and Sharing, the Consumer Genome" shows). "Product Placement and Advergaming" talks about advertising through new media, such as YouTube and video games.

- **Consider ethical decision making and social responsibility.** The application of moral standards to business activities and operations is of increasing importance in the field of business. Issues of honesty, fairness, environmental safety, and public health are often discussed in business courses. "Mapping, and Sharing, the Consumer Genome" raises questions about data-collection procedures that may lead to racial profiling. Is such behavior legal? Is it ethical?

389

SELECTION 13

The Super Bowl: The Mother of All Advertising Events—But Is It Worth It?

Philip Kotler and Gary Armstrong

  This reading was taken from the "Advertising and Public Relations" chapter of the textbook *Principles of Marketing*. Read it to learn about the costs and benefits of advertising during the Super Bowl.

PREVIEWING THE READING

Using the steps listed on pages 40–41, preview the reading selection. When you have finished, complete the following items.

1. The subject of this selection is _____

2. The main question you expect to be able to answer after reading this selection is:

_____

 MAKING CONNECTIONS

_____

Do you typically watch the Super Bowl? If so, do you look forward to the commercials as part of your viewing experience or do you ignore them?

READING TIP

As you read, use two different colors of ink to highlight the pros and cons of advertising during the Super Bowl.

The Super Bowl: The Mother of All Advertising Events—But Is It Worth It?

1   The Super Bowl is the mother of all advertising events. Each year, dozens of blue chip advertisers showcase some of their best work to huge audiences around the world. But all this doesn't come cheap. Last year, major advertisers plunked down an average of $2.7 million per 30-second spot and will top $3 million in 2009. Over the past two decades, they've spent over $2 *billion* on just 11.5 hours of Super Bowl

advertising time. But that's just for the air time. Throw in ad production costs—often $1 million or more per showcase commercial—and running even a single Super Bowl ad becomes a super-expensive proposition. Anheuser-Busch ran *seven* spots last year.

2   So every year, as the Super Bowl season nears, up pops the BIG QUESTION: Is Super Bowl advertising worth all that money? Does it deliver a high advertising **ROI**? As it turns out, there's no easy answer to the question.

ROI
return on
investment

3   Advertiser and industry expert opinion varies widely. Super Bowl stalwarts such as Anheuser-Busch, FedEx, General Motors, Career Builder, and the Frito-Lay, Gatorade, and Pepsi-Cola divisions of PepsiCo must think it's a good investment—they come back year after year. But what about savvy marketers such as Unilever, who opted out last year? In a survey of board members of the National Sports Marketing Network, 31 percent said they would recommend Super Bowl ads. But 41 percent said no—Super Bowl ads just aren't worth the money.

4   The naysayers make some pretty good arguments. Super Bowl advertising is outrageously expensive. Advertisers pay 85 percent more per viewer than they'd pay using prime-time network programming. And that $2.7 million would buy a lot of alternative media—for example, 50 different product placements in movies, TV shows, and video games; or two massive billboards in New York's Times Square that would be seen by a million people each day for a year. Beyond the cost, the competition for attention during the Super Bowl is fierce. Every single ad represents the best efforts of a major marketer trying to design a knock-your-socks-off spectacular that will reap high ratings from both critics and consumers. Many advertisers feel

they can get more for their advertising dollar in venues that aren't so crowded with bigger-than-life commercials.

5   Then there's the question of strategic fit. Whereas the Super Bowl might be a perfect advertising event for big-budget companies selling beer, snacks, soft drinks, or sporting goods, it simply doesn't fit the pocketbooks or creative strategies of many other companies and their brands. One media executive likens a Super Bowl ad to a trophy wife: "It makes sense if you are an advertiser with a huge budget," he says. "But if you're an advertiser with a modest budget, that would not be the best use of your money."

6   As for creative fit, consider Unilever's Dove. Three years ago, the company ran a sentimental 45-second commercial from the Dove "Campaign for Real Beauty." The ad was highly rated by consumers and it created considerable buzz—some 400 million impressions of the ad before and after its single appearance on the Super Bowl. But much of that buzz came from publicity surrounding the issue of girls' self-esteem rather than the product. And research showed that the ad produced low levels of involvement with the brand message.

viral
made wildly popular via the Internet

7   Dove got almost equal exposure numbers and more engagement for a lot less money from an outdoor campaign that it ran that same year, and it got a much larger online response from its **viral** "Dove Evolution" and "Onslaught" films, which incurred no media cost at all. "The Super Bowl really isn't the right environment for Dove," says a Unilever executive. The past two years, instead, Dove opted to run consumer-generated ads during the more-female-oriented Academy Awards, an event where beauty brands thrive.

gridiron
football field

8   Still, the Super Bowl has a lot to offer to the right advertisers. It's the most-watched TV event of the year. It plays to a huge and receptive audience—97.5 million viewers who put away their DVR remotes and watch it live, glued to their screens, ads and all. In fact, to many viewers, the Super Bowl ads are more important than what happens on the **gridiron**. Last year, the game itself drew an average 41.6 rating; the ads drew 41.22.

9   "There is no other platform quite like the Super Bowl," says the chief creative officer at Anheuser-Busch. "It's worth it. When you can touch that many households [with that kind of impact] in one sitting, it's actually efficient." In terms of dollars and cents, a study by one research firm found that consumer package-goods firms get a return of $1.25 to $2.74 for every dollar invested in Super Bowl advertising and one Super Bowl ad is as effective as 250 regular TV spots.

10   What's more, for most advertisers, the Super Bowl ad itself is only the centerpiece of something much bigger. Long after the game is over, ad critics, media pundits, and consumers are still reviewing, rehashing, and rating the commercials. It's one of the few sports-related events where "it ain't over when it's over." Thus, measuring the effectiveness of Super Bowl advertising involves a lot more than just measuring eyeballs and reach. "Those 30 seconds of fame are only the tip of the iceberg," says the analyst, "with online views, water-cooler chatter, blog buzz, and USA Today's ratings all below the surface."

11   "The Super Bowl is the only media property where the advertising is as big a story as the content of the show," says Steven Schreibman, vice president of advertising and brand management for Nationwide Financial, "so you want to see how much

you can leverage it." Schreibman is still agog over the response to Nationwide's Super Bowl spot two years ago that featured the hunk Fabio demonstrating that "life comes at you fast." Months afterward, consumers were still visiting Web sites such as ifilm.com to watch the commercial. "We got 1.8 million downloads on [just] that one site," says Schreibman. "Fabio himself keeps me apprised of that."

12   Advertisers don't usually sit back and just hope that consumers will talk about their ads. They build events that help to boost the buzz. For example, year before last, leading up to the Super Bowl at least three advertisers—GM's Chevrolet Division, the NFL, and Doritos—held contests inviting consumers to create their own Super Bowl ads. Doritos' "Crash the Super Bowl Challenge" contest produced more than 1,000 quality entries, considerable media attention, and a bunch of online consumer interest. The winning ad topped the IAG Top 10 Best-Liked Super Bowl Ads list and came in fourth in the *USA Today* Ad Meter rankings.

13   The Super Bowl's largest advertiser, Anheuser-Busch, extends the festivities far beyond game day. It follows up with a postgame e-mail campaign to keep the fires burning. It also hosts a designated Web site where consumers can view all of the company's Super Bowl ads and vote for their favorites via the Web site or text messages.

14   So—back to the original question. Is the Super Bowl advertising really worth the huge investment? It seems that there's no definitive answer—for some advertisers it's "yes": for others, "no." The real trick is in trying to measure the returns. As the title of one recent article asserts, "Measuring Bowl Return? Good Luck!" The writer's conclusion; "For all the time, energy, and angst marketers spend crafting the perfect Super Bowl spot, [that's] a relative breeze compared to trying to prove its return on investment."

A. UNDERSTANDING THE THESIS AND OTHER MAIN IDEAS

Select the best answer.

_____ 1. The central question that the authors address in this selection is:
   a. How much do television ads cost during the Super Bowl?
   b. Do most viewers watch commercials during the Super Bowl?
   c. Is Super Bowl advertising worth the cost?
   d. What is the most popular Super Bowl ad?

_____ 2. The authors' primary purpose is to
   a. persuade companies to advertise during the Super Bowl.
   b. criticize networks for overcharging for Super Bowl ads.
   c. explain why Super Bowl ads cost so much to produce.
   d. discuss the benefits and costs of Super Bowl advertising.

_____ 3. The main point of paragraphs 6 and 7 is that Unilever's Dove ad during the Super Bowl was

    a. overly sentimental.

    b. too expensive.

    c. too female oriented.

    d. not a good fit creatively.

_____ 4. The statement that best expresses the main idea of paragraph 10 is

    a. "for most advertisers, the Super Bowl ad itself is only the centerpiece of something much bigger."

    b. "ad critics, media pundits, and consumers are still reviewing, rehashing, and rating the commercials."

    c. "It's one of the few sports-related events where 'it ain't over when it's over.'"

    d. "Those 30 seconds of fame are only the tip of the iceberg."

_____ 5. The main idea of paragraph 12 is that advertisers

    a. hope that consumers will talk about their ads.

    b. create special events to increase the effect of their ads.

    c. hold contests inviting consumers to make their own Super Bowl ads.

    d. compete with each other for the highest Ad Meter rankings.

B. IDENTIFYING DETAILS

Complete each of the following statements by filling in the blank with the correct numerical amount.

1. Last year, major advertisers paid an average of $ _____ per 30-second spot.

2. Over the past two decades, advertisers have spent more than $_____ on _____ hours of Super Bowl advertising time.

3. Production costs for a single showcase Super Bowl commercial are often $ _____ or more.

4. In a survey of board members of the National Sports Marketing network, _____ percent would recommend Super Bowl ads and _____ percent would not.

5. Advertisers pay _____ percent more per viewer than they would pay using prime-time network programming.

6. Consumer package-goods firms get a return of $ _____ to
   $ _____ for every dollar invested in Super Bowl advertising.

7. One Super Bowl ad is as effective as _____ regular TV spots.

C. RECOGNIZING METHODS OF ORGANIZATION AND TRANSITIONS

Complete the statements by filling in the blanks.

1. In paragraph 3, the phrase that signals that examples will follow is

   _____.

2. In paragraph 5, the authors use the _____ organizational pattern to discuss how Super Bowl advertising may be a good strategic fit
   for some companies and not for others. Two transitions that indicate the
   authors' pattern are _____ and _____.

3. In paragraphs 6 and 7, the authors explain the importance of creative
   fit by contrasting different Dove ad campaigns. The transition that signals Dove's decision to change to a better environment for its product
   is _____.

D. REVIEWING AND ORGANIZING IDEAS: PARAPHRASING

*Complete the following paraphrase of paragraph 8 by filling in the missing words
and phrases.*

The _____ is a good option for the right _____.
More people watch it each year than _____. The Super
Bowl's _____ of _____ million people
watches the _____ and the _____ live. For many, what
happens in the _____ is less important than the _____. Last
year's _____ had an average rating of _____ compared to a rating of _____ for the ads.

E. READING AND THINKING VISUALLY

Answer the following questions.

1. What adjectives would you use to describe the people in the photograph
   that accompanies this reading?

   _____

2. What ideas in the reading does this photograph explain or enhance?

_____

_____

F. FIGURING OUT IMPLIED MEANINGS

Indicate whether each statement is true (T) or false (F).

_____ 1. It can be inferred that Anheuser-Busch spent several million dollars on its Super Bowl ads last year.

_____ 2. Advertisers and industry experts are in complete agreement that Super Bowl advertising is worth the money.

_____ 3. Super Bowl advertising is more appropriate for certain types of products than others.

_____ 4. Super Bowl advertising is a good creative fit for beauty brands like Dove.

_____ 5. Anheuser-Busch believes that Super Bowl ads are worth the investment.

G. THINKING CRITICALLY

Select the best answer.

_____ 1. The authors support their thesis with all of the following *except*
   a. facts.
   b. statistics.
   c. examples.
   d. personal experience.

_____ 2. The title refers to the Super Bowl as "the mother of all advertising events" because it
   a. was the first television event to feature advertising.
   b. is the biggest and most important advertising event.
   c. has generated many other advertising events.
   d. has created a loyal and devoted following.

_____ 3. The authors include the story about Nationwide's Super Bowl ad in paragraph 11 to illustrate
   a. how popular Fabio is with football fans.
   b. how viewers use the Internet to watch commercials.
   c. why advertisers feature well-known celebrities in ads.
   d. how ads continue to generate attention after the Super Bowl.

_____ 4. The conclusion of the selection suggests that

    a. Super Bowl advertising is worth the investment.

    b. Super Bowl advertising is definitely *not* worth the investment.

    c. trying to prove a Super Bowl ad's return on investment is difficult.

    d. marketers spend too much time trying to craft the perfect Super Bowl ad.

_____ 5. The overall tone of this selection can best be described as

    a. disapproving.

    b. serious.

    c. informal.

    d. indignant.

H. BUILDING VOCABULARY

Context

Using context and a dictionary, if necessary, determine the meaning of each word as it is used in the selection.

_____ 1. stalwarts (paragraph 3)

    a. loyal participants

    b. detractors

    c. critics

    d. consumers

_____ 2. savvy (paragraph 3)

    a. difficult

    b. shrewd

    c. picky

    d. similar

_____ 3. massive (paragraph 4)

    a. complex

    b. essential

    c. huge

    d. dark

_____ 4. reap (paragraph 4)

    a. adjust

    b. introduce

    c. allow

    d. collect

_____ 5. incurred (paragraph 7)

    a. forced

    b. brought on

    c. repeated

    d. misplaced

_____ 6. leverage (paragraph 11)

    a. resist

    b. influence

    c. select

    d. disapprove

_____ 7. agog (paragraph 11)

    a. very excited

    b. very confused

    c. against

    d. upset

_____ 8. apprised (paragraph 11)

    a. promised

    b. complained

    c. informed

    d. trained

_____ 9. angst (paragraph 14)

    a. ease

    b. anxiety

    c. power

    d. enjoyment

Word Parts

Complete the following sentence by filling in the blank.

If you know that the prefix *post-* means *after*, then a **postgame** e-mail campaign (paragraph 13) is one that takes place _____ the game.

Unusual Words/Understanding Idioms

Use the meanings given below to write a sentence using the boldfaced phrase.

1. Something that is described as **blue chip** (paragraph 1) is of the highest quality.

Your sentence: _____

_____

2. The phrase **knock-your-socks-off** (paragraph 4) applies when something is astonishingly good.

Your sentence: _____

_____

3. Something that is described as **the tip of the iceberg** (paragraph 10) is just a small, observable part of something much larger.

Your sentence: _____

_____

I. SELECTING A LEARNING/STUDY STRATEGY

Evaluate your highlighting in this reading. How else might you organize information about the pros and cons of advertising during the Super Bowl?

J. EXPLORING IDEAS THROUGH DISCUSSION AND WRITING

1. If you watch the Super Bowl, do you care more about the game or the commercials? After watching a Super Bowl, do you ever re-watch the commercials online or discuss them with friends or co-workers?

2. Consider the different products you use or consume on a regular basis. Which ones do you think would be a good strategic or creative fit for the Super Bowl? Which would be better for the Academy Awards or some other advertising event? Write a paragraph explaining your answers.

3. Describe a commercial that was memorable to you. What features made the commercial appealing? Were you persuaded to buy the product being advertised?

K. BEYOND THE CLASSROOM TO THE WEB

As the world becomes increasingly computer based, advertisers have begun placing electronic ads in many locations. For instance, it is common to get pop-up ads if you are using free e-mail services like Yahoo or Hotmail. More and more YouTube videos now require you to watch at least part of a commercial before you can watch the video. How effective do you think Web advertising is? What can Web advertising accomplish that a Super Bowl ad cannot accomplish? Which types of products are best advertised during the Super Bowl, and which are better advertised on Web sites?

TRACKING YOUR PROGRESS

Selection 13

Section	Number Correct	Score
A. Thesis and Main Ideas (5 items)	_____ × 4	_____
B. Details (10 items)	_____ × 2	_____
C. Organization and Transitions (5 items)	_____ × 2	_____
F. Implied Meanings (5 items)	_____ × 4	_____
G. Thinking Critically (5 items)	_____ × 4	_____
H. Vocabulary		
Context (9 items)	_____ × 1	_____
Word Parts (1 item)	_____ × 1	_____

Total Score _____%

SELECTION 14

Mapping, and Sharing, the Consumer Genome

Natasha Singer

The following article appeared in *The New York Times*, a highly respected newspaper known for its investigative journalism.

PREVIEWING THE READING

Using the steps listed on pages 40–41, preview the reading selection. When you have finished, complete the following items.

1. The company discussed in this reading is _____, based in _____, Arkansas.

2. Indicate whether each statement is true (T) or false (F).

   _____ a. Scott Hughes is fictional.

   _____ b. There is information about almost 190 million households in the Acxiom database.

   _____ c. Acxiom is the largest advertising company in the United States.

   _____ d. Acxiom collects data about race and ethnicity.

 MAKING CONNECTIONS

While surfing the Web, have you ever noticed that the advertisements seem directed toward you, your interests, and your needs? How do you think businesses and Web sites "target" you to receive these ads?

READING TIP

Genome is the scientific term for a complete map of the genetic material found in an organism (for example, the human genome). Here, the term genome is used to describe a complete map of information about consumers, from their age through their address, income level, purchases, and interests.

Mapping, and Sharing, the Consumer Genome

1   It knows who you are. It knows where you live. It knows what you do.

2   It peers deeper into American life than the F.B.I. or the I.R.S., or those prying digital eyes at Facebook and Google. If you are an American adult, the odds are that it knows things like your age, race, sex, weight, height, marital status, education level, politics, buying habits, household health worries, vacation dreams—and on and on.

3   Right now in Conway, Ark, north of Little Rock, more than 23,000 computer servers are collecting, **collating** and analyzing consumer data for a company that, unlike Silicon Valley's marquee names, rarely makes headlines. It's called the Acxiom Corporation, and it's the quiet giant of a multibillion-dollar industry known as database marketing.

collating
combining in proper order

4   Few consumers have ever heard of Acxiom. But analysts say it has amassed the world's largest commercial database on consumers—and that it wants to know much, much more. Its servers process more than 50 trillion data "transactions" a year. Company executives have said its database contains information about 500 million active consumers worldwide, with about 1,500 data points per person. That includes a majority of adults in the United States.

5   Such large-scale data mining and analytics—based on information available in public records, consumer surveys and the like—are perfectly legal. Acxiom's customers have included big banks like Wells Fargo and HSBC, investment services like E-Trade, automakers like Toyota and Ford, department stores like Macy's—just about any major company looking for insight into its customers.

6   For Acxiom, based in Little Rock, the setup is lucrative. It posted profit of $77.26 million in its latest fiscal year, on sales of $1.13 billion.

7   But such profits carry a cost for consumers. Federal authorities say current laws may not be equipped to handle the rapid expansion of an industry whose players often collect and sell sensitive financial and health information yet are nearly invisible to the public. In essence, it's as if the ore of our data-driven lives were being mined, refined and sold to the highest bidder, usually without our knowledge—by companies that most people rarely even know exist.

8   Julie Brill, a member of the Federal Trade Commission, says she would like data brokers in general to tell the public about the data they collect, how they collect it, whom they share it with and how it is used. "If someone is listed as diabetic or pregnant, what is happening with this information? Where is the information going?" she asks. "We need to figure out what the rules should be as a society."

9   Although Acxiom employs a chief privacy officer, Jennifer Barrett Glasgow, she and other executives declined requests to be interviewed for this article, said Ines Rodriguez Gutzmer, director of corporate communications.

10 In March, however, Ms. Barrett Glasgow endorsed increased industry openness. "It's not an unreasonable request to have more transparency among data brokers," she said in an interview with The New York Times. In marketing materials, Acxiom promotes itself as "a global thought leader in addressing consumer privacy issues and earning the public trust."

encrypt
encode, hide

11 But, in interviews, security experts and consumer advocates paint a portrait of a company with practices that privilege corporate clients' interests over those of consumers and contradict the company's stance on transparency. Acxiom's marketing materials, for example, promote a special security system for clients and associates to **encrypt** the data they send. Yet cybersecurity experts who examined Acxiom's Web site for The Times found basic security lapses on an online form for consumers seeking access to their own profiles. (Acxiom says it has fixed the broken link that caused the problem.)

12 In a fast-changing digital economy, Acxiom is developing even more advanced techniques to mine and refine data. It has recruited talent from Microsoft, Google, Amazon.com and Myspace and is using a powerful, multiplatform approach to predicting consumer behavior that could raise its standing among investors and clients.

13 Of course, digital marketers already customize pitches to users, based on their past activities. Just think of "cookies," bits of computer code placed on browsers to keep track of online activity. But Acxiom, analysts say, is pursuing far more comprehensive techniques in an effort to influence consumer decisions. It is integrating what it knows about our offline, online and even mobile selves, creating in-depth behavior portraits in pixilated detail. Its executives have called this approach a "360-degree view" on consumers.

14   "There's a lot of players in the digital space trying the same thing," says Mark Zgutowicz, a Piper Jaffrey analyst. "But Acxiom's advantage is they have a database of offline information that they have been collecting for 40 years and can leverage that expertise in the digital world."

15   Yet some prominent privacy advocates worry that such techniques could lead to a new era of consumer profiling.

16   Jeffrey Chester, executive director of the Center for Digital Democracy, a non-profit group in Washington, says: "It is Big Brother in Arkansas."

17   Scott Hughes, an up-and-coming small-business owner and Facebook denizen, is Acxiom's ideal consumer. Indeed, it created him.

18   Mr. Hughes is a fictional character who appeared in an Acxiom investor presentation in 2010. A frequent shopper, he was designed to show the power of Acxiom's multichannel approach.

19   In the presentation, he logs on to Facebook and sees that his friend Ella has just become a fan of Bryce Computers, an imaginary electronics retailer and Acxiom client. Ella's update prompts Mr. Hughes to check out Bryce's fan page and do some digital window-shopping for a fast inkjet printer.

20   Such browsing seems innocuous—hardly data mining. But it cues an Acxiom system designed to recognize consumers, remember their actions, classify their behaviors and influence them with tailored marketing.

21   When Mr. Hughes follows a link to Bryce's retail site, for example, the system recognizes him from his Facebook activity and shows him a printer to match his interest. He registers on the site, but doesn't buy the printer right away, so the system tracks him online. Lo and behold, the next morning, while he scans baseball news on ESPN.com, an ad for the printer pops up again.

22   That evening, he returns to the Bryce site where, the presentation says, "he is instantly recognized" as having registered. It then offers a sweeter deal; a $10 rebate and free shipping.

23   It's not a random offer. Acxiom has its own classification system, PersonicX, which assigns consumers to one of 70 detailed socioeconomic clusters and markets to them accordingly. In this situation, it pegs Mr. Hughes at a "savvy single"—meaning he's in a cluster of mobile, upper-middle-class people who do their banking online, attend pro sports events, are sensitive to prices—and respond to free-shipping offers.

24   Correctly typecast, Mr. Hughes buys the printer.

25   But the multichannel system of Acxiom and its online partners is just revving up. Later, it sends him coupons for ink and paper, to be redeemed via his cellphone, and a personalized snail-mail postcard suggesting that he donate his old printer to a nearby school.

26   Analysts say companies design these sophisticated ecosystems to prompt consumers to volunteer enough personal data—like their names, e-mail addresses and mobile numbers—so that marketers can offer them customized appeals any time, anywhere.

27   Still, there is a fine line between customization and stalking, while many people welcome the convenience of personalized offers, others may see the surveillance engines behind them as intrusive or even manipulative.

28   "If you look at it in cold terms, it seems like they are really out to trick the customer," says Dave Frankland, the research director for customer intelligence at Forrester Research. "But they are actually in the business of helping marketers make sure that the right people are getting offers they are interested in and therefore establish a relationship with the company."

29   Decades before the Internet as we know it, a businessman named Charles Ward planted the seeds of Acxiom. It was 1969, and Mr. Ward started a data processing company in Conway called Demographics Inc., in part to help the Democratic Party reach voters. In a time when Madison Avenue was deploying one-size-fits-all national ad campaigns, Demographics and its lone computer used public phone books to compile lists for direct mailing of campaign material.

30   Today, Acxiom maintains its own database on about 190 million individuals and 126 million households in the United States. Separately, it manages customer databases for or works with 47 of the Fortune 100 companies. It also worked with the government after the September 2001 terrorist attacks, providing information about 11 of the 19 hijackers.

31   To beef up its digital services, Acxiom recently mounted an aggressive hiring campaign. Last July, it named Scott E. Howe, a former corporate vice president for Microsoft's advertising business group, as C.E.O. Last month, it hired Phil Mui, formerly group product manager for Google Analytics, as its chief product and engineering officer.

millennium
one thousand years

32   In interviews, Mr. Howe has laid out a vision of Acxiom as a new-**millennium** "data refinery" rather than a data miner. That description posits Acxiom as a nimble provider of customer analytics services, able to compete with Facebook and Google, rather than as a stealth engine of consumer espionage.

33   Still, the more that information brokers mine powerful consumer data, the more they become attractive targets for hackers—and draw scrutiny from consumer advocates.

34   This year, Advertising Age ranked Epsilon, another database marketing firm, as the biggest advertising agency in the United States, with Acxiom second. Most people know Epsilon, if they know it at all, because it experienced a major security breach last year, exposing the e-mail addresses of millions of customers of Citibank, JPMorgan Chase, Target, Walgreens and others. In 2003, Acxiom had its own security breaches.

35   But privacy advocates say they are more troubled by data brokers' ranking systems, which classify some people as high-value prospects, to be offered marketing deals and discounts regularly, while dismissing others as low-value—known in industry slang as "waste."

algorithm
computer model

36   Exclusion from a vacation offer may not matter much, says Pam Dixon, the executive director of the World Privacy Forum, a nonprofit group in San Diego, but if marketing **algorithms** judge certain people as not worthy of receiving promotions for higher education or health services, they could have a serious impact.

37   "Over time, that can really turn into a mountain of pathways not offered, not seen and not known about," Ms. Dixon says.

38   Until now, database marketers operated largely out of the public eye. Unlike consumer reporting agencies that sell sensitive financial information about people for

credit or employment purposes, database marketers aren't required by law to show consumers their own reports and allow them to correct errors. That may be about to change. This year, the **F.T.C.** published a report calling for greater transparency among data brokers and asking Congress to give consumers the right to access information these firms hold about them.

F.T.C.
Federal Trade
Commission

39   Acxiom's Consumer Data Products Catalog offers hundreds of details—called "elements"—that corporate clients can buy about individuals or households, to augment their own marketing databases. Companies can buy data to pinpoint households that are concerned, say, about allergies, diabetes or "senior needs." Also for sale is information on sizes of home loans and household incomes.

40   Clients generally buy this data because they went to hold on to their best customers or find new ones—or both.

41   A bank that wants to sell its best customers additional services, for example, might buy details about those customers' social media, Web and mobile habits to identify more efficient ways to market to them. Or, says Mr. Frankland at Forrester, a sporting goods chain whose best customers are 25- to 34-year-old men living near mountains or beaches could buy a list of a million other people with the same characteristics. The retailer could hire Acxiom, he says, to manage a campaign aimed at that new group, testing how factors like consumers' locations or sports preferences affect responses.

42   But the catalog also offers delicate information that has set off alarm bells among some privacy advocates, who worry about the potential for misuse by third parties that could take aim at vulnerable groups. Such information includes consumers' interests—derived, the catalog says, "from actual purchases and self-reported surveys"—like "Christian families," "Dieting/Weight Loss," "Gaming-Casino," "Money Seekers" and "Smoking/Tobacco." Acxiom also sells data about an individual's race, ethnicity and country of origin. "Our Race model," the catalog says, "provides information on the major racial category: Caucasians, Hispanics, African-Americans, or Asians." Competing companies sell similar data.

43   Acxiom's data about race or ethnicity is "used for engaging those communities for marketing purposes," said Ms. Barrett Glasgow, the privacy officer, in an e-mail response to questions.

44   There may be a legitimate commercial need for some businesses, like ethnic restaurant, to know the race or ethnicity of consumers, says Joel R. Reidenberg, a privacy expert and a professor at the Fordham Law School.

45   "At the same time, this is ethnic profiling," he says. "The people on this list, they are being sold based on their ethnic stereotypes. There is a very strong citizen's right to have a veto over the commodification of their profile."

46   He says the sale of such data is troubling because race coding may be incorrect. And even if a date broker has correct information, a person may not want to be marketed to based on race.

47   "Do you know your customers?" Acxiom asks in marketing materials for its shopper recognition system, a program that uses ZIP codes to help retailers confirm consumers' identities—without asking their permission.

48   "Simply asking for name and address information poses many challenges: transcription errors, increased checkout time and, worse yet, losing customers who feel

that you're invading their privacy," Acxiom's fact sheet explains. In its system, a store clerk need only "capture the shopper's name from a check or third-party credit card at the point of sale and then ask for the shopper's ZIP code or telephone number." With that data Acxiom can identify shoppers within a 10 percent margin of error, it says, enabling stores to reward their best customers with special offers. Other companies offer similar services.

circumventing
getting around

49   "This is a direct way of **circumventing** people's concerns about privacy," says Mr. Chester of the Center for Digital Democracy.

50   Ms. Barrett Glasgow of Acxiom says that its program is a "standard practice" among retailers, but that the company encourages its clients to report consumers who wish to opt out.

51   Acxiom has positioned itself as an industry leader in data privacy, but some of its practices seem to undermine that image. It created the position of chief privacy officer in 1991, well ahead of its rivals. It even offers an online request form, promoted as an easy way for consumers to access information Acxiom collects about them.

52   But the process turned out to be not so user-friendly for a reporter for The Times.

53   In early May, the reporter decided to request her record from Acxiom, as any consumer might. Before submitting a Social Security number and other personal information, however, she asked for advice from a cybersecurity expert at The Times. The expert examined Acxiom's Web site and immediately noticed that the online form did not employ a standard encryption protocol—called https—used by sites like Amazon and American Express. When the expert tested the form, using software that captures data sent over the Web, he could clearly see that the sample Social Security number he had submitted had not been encrypted. At that point, the reporter was advised not to request her file, given the risk that the process might expose her personal information.

54   Later in May, Ashkan Soltani, an independent security researcher and former technologist in identity protection at the F.T.C., also examined Acxiom's site and came to the same conclusion. "Parts of the site for corporate clients are encrypted," he says. "But for consumers, who this information is about and who stand the most to lose from data collection, they don't provide security."

55   Ms. Barrett Glasgow says that the form has always been encrypted with https but that on May 11, its security monitoring system detected a "broken redirect link" that allowed unencrypted access. Since then, she says, Acxiom has fixed the link and determined that no unauthorized person had gained access to information sent using the form.

56   On May 25, the reporter submitted online request to Acxiom for her file, along with a personal check, sent by Express Mail, for the $5 processing fee. Three weeks later, no response had arrived.

57   Regulators at the F.T.C. declined to comment on the practices of individual companies. But Jon Leibowitz, the commission chairman, said consumers should have the right to see and correct personal details about them collected and sold by data aggregators.

58   After all, he said, "they are the unseen cyberazzi who collect information on all of us."

A. UNDERSTANDING THE THESIS AND OTHER MAIN IDEAS

Select the best answer.

_____ 1. Which of the following best states the thesis or central idea of the reading selection?

    a. Acxiom, Inc., is the world's largest and most successful data-mining company, with records on the majority of American consumers.

    b. According to the Federal Trade Commission, data mining is legal, but the industry has received strong criticism for invading people's privacy.

    c. Acxiom is a successful company that gathers and sells consumer data, but it has come under fire for some of its practices, including invasion of privacy and ethnic profiling.

    d. Security experts recommend that consumers give up their Facebook accounts and purchase items only from Web sites that begin with the https protocol.

_____ 2. The topic of paragraph 13 is

    a. Acxiom, Inc.

    b. digital marketing.

    c. online activities.

    d. the 360-degree view of consumers.

_____ 3. The implied main idea of paragraph 41 is

    a. Manufacturers of sporting goods are likely to use Acxiom's services.

    b. People who are active on the Web make good clients for banks.

    c. Young men are more likely to respond to customized marketing than young women are.

    d. Businesses can use Acxiom to identify customers based on their habits, activities, and interests.

_____ 4. The main idea of paragraph 42 is found in the

    a. first sentence.

    b. second sentence.

    c. fourth sentence.

    d. last sentence.

B. IDENTIFYING DETAILS

Select the best answer.

_____ 1. A piece of computer code placed on an Internet browser to keep track of activity is a

    a. crawler.

    b. cookie.

    c. commodity.

    d. demographic.

_____ 2. Which of the following companies was founded partly to help the Democratic Party reach voters?

    a. Acxiom

    b. Epsilon

    c. the FTC

    d. Demographics Inc.

_____ 3. Which of the following people is *not* an advocate for better or more transparent practices regarding data collection and sales?

    a. Julie Brill

    b. Ashkan Soltani

    c. Inez Rodriguez Gutzmer

    d. Pam Dixon

_____ 4. What is the purpose of PersonicX?

    a. to help the government identify criminals and terrorists.

    b. to protect consumers' privacy and identity.

    c. to assign consumers to specific socioeconomic clusters.

    d. to allow people to opt out of inclusion in databases.

_____ 5. In the advertising industry, the term "waste" refers to

    a. consumers who are considered "low value" to advertisers.

    b. computers that are outdated and no longer useful.

    c. the amount of trash generated by catalogs and direct-mail pieces.

    d. the part of the advertising budget that has no effect on sales.

C. RECOGNIZING METHODS OF ORGANIZATION AND TRANSITIONS

Select the best answer.

_____ 1. A transitional word or phrase that signals the use of contrast in paragraph 38 is

    a. until now.

    b. unlike.

    c. may be.

    d. access information.

_____ 2. Which organizational pattern is used in paragraphs 40 and 41?

    a. process

    b. classification

    c. generalization and example

    d. definition

_____ 3. Paragraphs 52–56 use the _____ organizational pattern.

    a. summary

    b. chronological order

    c. comparison and contrast

    d. cause-and-effect

D. REVIEWING AND ORGANIZING IDEAS: OUTLINING

Complete the following outline of the reading by filling in the blanks with the correct words or phrases.

ACXIOM

INFORMATION ABOUT THE COMPANY	CONCERNS ABOUT THE COMPANY'S PRACTICES
Based in Little Rock, _____	Security experts say that Acxiom's practices value corporate interests over the privacy interests of consumers
Servers process more than _____ transactions per year	Data mining can lead to a new era of consumer _____
Database contains information about more than _____ million consumers worldwide, including 190 million U.S. consumers and 126 million U.S. households	PersonicX assigns consumers to clusters, which causes certain consumers to be defined as " _____ " (people who do not have much value to advertisers)
_____ include Wells Fargo, Toyota, Macy's	There is a fine line between customization of marketing and _____

(Continued)

ACXIOM

INFORMATION ABOUT THE COMPANY	CONCERNS ABOUT THE COMPANY'S PRACTICES
The company is expanding by hiring people from other successful organizations, such as Microsoft and _____	A company that owns so much valuable information becomes a target for _____
The company's Consumer Data Products catalog offers hundreds of details, called _____, about individuals and households	Database marketers are not required by law to show consumers their own reports and allow them to correct errors
Acxiom has positioned itself as a leader in consumer privacy, creating the position of chief privacy officer in 1991	Some are not comfortable with the idea of segmenting by race or _____, which can lead to racial profiling
	In a recent experiment, researchers found that Acxiom's Web site was not secure, and the company did not respond to a request for the reporter's personal information stored in the Acxiom database

---

E. READING AND THINKING VISUALLY

Select the best answer.

_____ 1. The author likely included the photo on page 402 in order to

    a. illustrate how consumer information is captured and stored in daily life.

    b. hold retail establishments accountable for security breaches.

    c. imply that cashiers' salaries are generally paid by Acxiom.

    d. show how the F.T.C. monitors U.S. businesses.

F. FIGURING OUT IMPLIED MEANINGS

Indicate whether each statement is true (T) or false (F).

_____ 1. The author implies that there may not be much difference between customization and stalking.

_____ 2. The author believes that Acxiom's consumer data is highly secure.

_____ 3. A majority of adults in the United States are a part of Acxiom's database.

_____ 4. The author implies that data-mining activities are illegal.

_____ 5. In the United States, Acxiom has been involved in aiding the War on Terror.

_____ 6. The main customer of database companies like Acxiom and Epsilon is the U.S. government.

_____ 7. Acxiom does not sell data regarding ethnicity and race because this information is too sensitive.

G. THINKING CRITICALLY

Select the best answer.

_____ 1. The purpose of "Mapping, and Sharing, the Consumer Genome" is to

     a. argue for greater government involvement in protecting consumers' privacy.

     b. compare and contrast data-mining practices in the early 1970s with the same practices today.

     c. help students understand the career opportunities in the database marketing industry.

     d. explore the practices and controversies related to the data-mining activities of one successful company.

_____ 2. The tone of the article is best described as

     a. angry.

     b. concerned.

     c. wistful.

     d. longwinded.

_____ 3. To support her main ideas, the author uses of all the following *except*

     a. quotes from government officials.

     b. numbers and statistics.

     c. specific details about the services offered by Acxiom.

     d. quotes from the president of Acxiom.

_____ 4. Which of the following excerpts from the reading is a fact, not an opinion?

     a. "We need to figure out what the rules should be as a society." (paragraph 8)

     b. "It is Big Brother in Arkansas." (paragraph 16)

     c. "It's not a random offer." (paragraph 23)

     d. "There is a very strong citizen's right to have a veto over the commodification of their profile." (paragraph 45)

_____ 5. The word "it" in paragraph 1 refers to

    a. information technology.

    b. Facebook.

    c. your GPS system.

    d. Acxiom.

_____ 6. In paragraph 7, the phrase "it's as if the ore of our data-driven lives were being mined, refined, and sold to the highest bidder" is a

    a. phrase with a positive connotation.

    b. symbol.

    c. metaphor.

    d. personification.

_____ 7. All of the following words or phrases from the reading have negative connotations, _except_

    a. "transparency among data brokers" (paragraph 10).

    b. "correctly typecast" (paragraph 24).

    c. "transcription errors" (paragraph 48).

    d. "unseen cyberazzi" (paragraph 58).

H. BUILDING VOCABULARY

Context

Using context and a dictionary, if necessary, determine the meaning of each word as it is used in the selection.

_____ 1. prying (paragraph 2)

    a. attempting

    b. invasive

    c. impatient

    d. young

_____ 2. lucrative (paragraph 6)

    a. modern

    b. centralized

    c. profitable

    d. expensive

_____ 3. lapse (paragraph 11)

    a. mistake

    b. protocol

    c. form

    d. data

_____ 4. denizen (paragraph 17)

    a. resident

    b. account

    c. profile

    d. setting

_____ 5. deploy (paragraph 29)

    a. create

    b. limit

    c. ruin

    d. use

_____ 6. espionage (paragraph 32)

    a. psychic premonition

    b. spying

    c. cheating

    d. research

_____ 7. augment (paragraph 39)

    a. increase

    b. start

    c. examine

    d. purge

_____ 8. aggregators (paragraph 57)

    a. annoyances

    b. companies

    c. analysts

    d. compilers

Word Parts

> ### A REVIEW OF PREFIXES, ROOTS, AND SUFFIXES
>
> **CONTRA-** means *against* or *opposite*
> **DICT** means *say or tell*
> **MULTI-** means *many*
> **-TION** refers to *a process*

Use your knowledge of word parts to fill in the blanks in the following sentences.

1. To **contradict** (paragraph 11) a statement is to assert the _____ of that statement.

2. A **multiplatform** (paragraph 12) approach makes use of _____ platforms.

3. To engage in **commodification** (paragraph 45) is to make something into a _____.

Unusual Words/Understanding Idioms

Use the meaning given below to write a sentence using the boldfaced phrase.

A **marquee** (paragraph 3) is a rooflike projection over the entrance to a theater. It generally features the names of the stars of a movie or play. Therefore, a **marquee name** is one that is easily recognized.

Your sentence: _____

_____

I. SELECTING A LEARNING/STUDY STRATEGY

Select the best answer.

_____ 1. To prepare for an exam based on this reading, you might effectively use all of the following study strategies *except*

    a. highlighting the reading during your second read-through.

    b. annotating the reading and making marginal notes.

    c. preparing a time line that summarizes the history of Acxiom.

    d. asking and then answering three questions that might be asked on the exam.

J. EXPLORING IDEAS THROUGH DISCUSSION AND WRITING

1. Write a caption to accompany the photograph on page 402.

2. Have you ever purchased a product that you saw advertised on Facebook or another social media site? Or do you tend to ignore these ads? How effectively do you think these sites target your specific interests?

3. How would you feel about companies advertising to you based on your race or ethnic group? For which products or services would this type of advertising be appropriate? For which products or services would it be inappropriate?

4. What steps can you take to ensure your personal information is not captured during transactions or when you are surfing the Web?

K. BEYOND THE CLASSROOM TO THE WEB

Visit Acxiom's Web site and spend some time exploring it. Describe one of Acxiom's services in detail, outlining some of the opportunities it presents as well as some of the ethical challenges.

TRACKING YOUR PROGRESS

Selection 14

Section	Number Correct		Score
A. Thesis and Main Ideas (3 items)	_____	× 4	_____
B. Details (5 items)	_____	× 4	_____
C. Organization and Transitions (3 items)	_____	× 4	_____
E. Reading and Thinking Visually (1 item)	_____	× 3	_____
F. Implied Meanings (7 items)	_____	× 2	_____
G. Thinking Critically (7 items)	_____	× 2	_____
H. Vocabulary			
Context (8 items)	_____	× 2	_____
Word Parts (3 items)	_____	× 3	_____
		Total Score	_____%

SELECTION 15

Product Placement and Advergaming
Michael Solomon

TEXTBOOK
EXCERPT

Taken from a textbook titled *Consumer Behavior*, this reading selection describes how specific products and brand names are used in movies, television, and other media.

REVIEWING THE READING

Using the steps listed on pages 40–41, preview the reading selection. When you have finished, complete the following items.

1. The topic of this selection is _____ .

2. List four questions you might be able to answer after reading this selection.

   a. _____

   b. _____

   c. _____

   d. _____

MAKING
CONNECTIONS *Think about a movie or television show you have seen recently and try to recall whether you noticed the particular products or brands being shown.*

READING TIP

This selection contains many examples of the "what"—in other words, the particular brands and products that appear in different types of media. As you read, be sure to notice the "why"—the reasons given for the use of product placement in each type of media.

Product Placement and Advergaming

1   Back in the day, TV networks demanded that producers "geek" (alter) brand names before they appeared in a show, as when *Melrose Place* changed a Nokia cell phone to a "Nokio." Today, real products pop up everywhere. Many are

aura
atmosphere

well-established brands that lend an **aura** of realism to the action, while others are upstarts that benefit tremendously from the exposure. For example, in the movie version of *Sex and the City* Carrie's assistant admits that she "borrows" her expensive pricey handbags from a rental Web site called Bag Borrow or Steal. The company's head of marketing commented, "It's like the *Good Housekeeping* Seal of Approval. It gives us instant credibility and recognition."

Product Placement

2   Bag Borrow or Steal got a free plug (oops, they got another one here!). In many cases, however, these "plugs" are no accident. Product placement is the insertion of real products in fictional movies, TV shows, books, and plays. Many types of products play starring (or at least supporting) roles in our culture; the most visible brands range from Coca-Cola and Nike apparel to the Chicago Bears football team and the Pussycat Dolls band. The TV shows that feature the most placements include *The Biggest Loser* (it showed about 4,000 brands in just a three-month period), *American Idol* (how subtle is that Coca-Cola glass each judge holds?), *The Apprentice*, *America's Next Top Model*, and *One Tree Hill*. This practice is so commonplace (and profitable) now that it's evolved into a new form of promotion we call branded entertainment, where advertisers showcase their products in longer-form narrative films instead of brief commercials. For example, *SportsCenter* on ESPN showed installments of "The Scout presented by Craftsman at Sears," a 6-minute story about a washed-up baseball scout who discovers a stunningly talented stadium groundskeeper.

3   Product placement is by no means a casual process: Marketers pay about $25 billion per year to plug their brands in TV and movies. Several firms specialize in

Product placement in the Jack Black film *Bernie*

arranging these appearances; if they're lucky they manage to do it on the cheap when they get a client's product noticed by prop masters who work on the shows. For example, in a cafeteria scene during an episode of *Grey's Anatomy* it was no coincidence that the character Izzie Stevens happened to drink a bottle of Izze Sparkling Pomegranate fruit beverage. The placement company that represents PepsiCo paid nothing to insert the prop in that case, but it probably didn't get off so easily when the new brand also showed up in HBO's *Entourage, Big Bang Theory,* and *The New Adventures of Old Christine* on CBS.

4   Today most major releases brim with real products, even though a majority of consumers believe the line between advertising and programming is becoming too fuzzy and distracting (though as we might expect, concerns about this blurring of boundaries are more pronounced among older people than younger). A study reported that consumers respond well to placements when the show's plot makes the product's benefit clear. Similarly, audiences had a favorable impression of when a retailer provided furniture, clothes, appliances, and other staples for struggling families who get help on ABC's *Extreme Makeover: Home Edition.*

5   Although we hear a lot of buzz today about product placement, in reality it's a long-standing cinematic tradition. The difference is that today the placements are more blatant and financially lucrative. In the heyday of the major Hollywood studios, brands such as Bell telephone, Buick, Chesterfield cigarettes, Coca-Cola, De Beers diamonds, and White Owl cigars regularly appeared in films. For example, in a scene in the classic *Double Indemnity* (1944) that takes place in a grocery store, the director Billy Wilder made some products such as Green Giant vegetables face the camera whereas others "mysteriously" were turned around to hide their labels. Indeed, the practice dates at least as far back as 1896, when an early movie shows a cart bearing the brand name Sunlight (a Lever Brothers brand) parked on a street. Perhaps the greatest product placement success story was Reese's Pieces; sales jumped by 65 percent after the candy appeared in the film *E.T.*

6   Some researchers claim that product placement aids consumer decision making because the familiarity of these props creates a sense of cultural belonging while they generate feelings of emotional security. Another study found that placements consistent with a show's plot do enhance brand attitudes, but incongruent placements that aren't consistent with the plot affect brand attitudes *negatively* because they seem out of place.

MARKETING PITFALL

The product placement industry has come under government scrutiny as pressure grows from consumer groups to let viewers know when companies pay to use their products as props. The Federal Communications Commission (FCC) is considering whether it should regulate this practice. Currently shows have to disclose this information but only at the end of the show and in small print. An FCC official says, "You shouldn't need a magnifying glass to know who's pitching you."

Advergaming

7   If you roar down the streets in the *Need for Speed Underground 2* video racing game, you'll pass a Best Buy store as well as billboards that hawk Old Spice and Burger King. *America's Army*, produced by the U.S. government as a recruitment tool, is one of the most successful advergames. Twenty-eight percent of those who visit the *America's Army* Web page click through to the recruitment page.

8   About three-quarters of American consumers now play video games, yet to many marketers the idea of integrating their brands with the stories that games tell is still a well-kept secret. Others including Axe, Mini Cooper, and Burger King have figured this out—they create game narratives that immerse players in the action. Orbitz offers playable banner-games that result in the highest **click-through rate** of any kind of advertising the online travel site does. Even though the game industry brings in more revenue than feature films or music sales, only about 10 percent of marketers execute any promotions in this space.

click-through rate
the percentage of
people who click on
an Internet link

9   Even so, it's likely that the future is bright for advergaming—where online games merge with interactive advertisements that let companies target specific types of consumers. These placements can be short exposures such as a billboard that appears around a racetrack, or they can take the form of branded entertainment and integrate the brand directly into the action. For example, a game that Dairy Queen helped to create called *DQ Tycoon* lets players run their own fast-food franchise. The game requires players to race against the clock to prepare Peanut-Buster Parfaits, take orders, restock the refrigerator, and dip cones.

mushrooming
rapidly increasing

10   The **mushrooming** popularity of user-generated videos on YouTube and other sites creates a growing market to link ads to these sources as well. This strategy is

Mead's branded video game attracted over 10 million players.

Source: From www.miniclip.com. Used by permission of Miniclip (UK) Ltd.

growing so rapidly that there's even a new (trademarked) term for it. Plinking™ is the act of embedding a product or service link in a video.

11   Why is this new medium so hot?

- Compared to a 30-second TV spot, advertisers can get viewers' attention for a much longer time. Players spend an average of 5 to 7 minutes on an advergame site.
- Physiological measures confirm that players are highly focused and stimulated when they play a game.
- Marketers can tailor the nature of the game and the products in it to the profiles of different users. They can direct strategy games to upscale, educated users, while they can gear action games to younger users.
- The format gives advertisers great flexibility because game makers now ship PC video games with blank spaces in them to insert virtual ads. This allows advertisers to change messages on the fly and pay only for the number of game players that actually see them. Sony Corp. now allows clients to directly insert online ads into PlayStation 3 videogames—the in-game ads change over time through a user's Internet connection.
- There's great potential to track usage and conduct marketing research. For example, an inaudible audio signal coded into Activision's *Tony Hawk's Underground 2* skating game on PCs alerts a Nielsen monitoring system each time the test game players view Jeep product placements within the game.

A. UNDERSTANDING THE THESIS AND OTHER MAIN IDEAS

Select the best answer.

_____ 1. The author's primary purpose in this selection is to

    a. discuss the use of real products and brands in movies, television shows, and video games.

    b. compare and contrast product placement in movies and games with controversial advertising methods.

    c. explore the controversies surrounding product placements and advergaming.

    d. describe the latest advances in technology used for film and video game production.

_____ 2. The main idea of paragraph 1 is that

    a. brand names must be altered before they can be used on television.

    b. branded entertainment is taking the place of typical commercials.

      c. *Sex and the City* is the best modern example of product placement techniques.

      d. product placement has become common in our culture.

_____ 3. The topic of paragraph 3 is

      a. Hollywood.

      b. product placement.

      c. popular brands.

      d. popular films.

_____ 4. The main idea of paragraph 9 is found in the

      a. first sentence.

      b. second sentence.

      c. third sentence.

      d. last sentence.

_____ 5. The question answered in the set of bullet points in paragraph 11 is

      a. How can businesses use video games to conduct market research?

      b. Why is advergaming growing in popularity?

      c. How much does product placement cost in comparison to traditional advertising?

      d. How do "virtual advertisements" work?

B. IDENTIFYING DETAILS

Select the best answer.

_____ 1. The act of embedding a product or service link in a video is called

      a. advertorial.

      b. Plinking.

      c. advergaming.

      d. Nielsen monitoring.

_____ 2. Which statement best summarizes consumers' attitude toward product placement?

      a. Because consumers are bombarded with too much advertising, it is almost always unfavorable.

      b. It is favorable when products are placed in movies, but unfavorable when products are placed in video games.

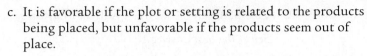

c. It is favorable if the plot or setting is related to the products being placed, but unfavorable if the products seem out of place.

d. It is favorable if the lead actor uses the product, but it is unfavorable if supporting actors or "extras" use the product.

_____ 3. According to the selection, advergaming has been used as a recruitment tool by

a. volunteer organizations.

b. colleges and universities.

c. the U.S. military.

d. children's toy manufacturers.

_____ 4. Which of the following is *not* true of advergaming?

a. Advergaming is most successful when it is directed at teenage boys, who are the main purchasers of video games in the United States.

b. Players are highly focused and stimulated when they are playing a game.

c. Advergaming allows companies to target specific consumer segments, such as children or older adults.

d. In some game systems that work with an Internet connection, ads can be changed over time.

Match each brand with the television show, movie, Web site, or video game in which it appeared, according to the selection.

TV Show, Movie, Web Site, or Video Game	Brand
_____ 5. *Double Indemnity*	**a.** Nokia
_____ 6. *American Idol*	**b.** Sears
_____ 7. *Need for Speed Underground 2*	**c.** Coca-Cola
_____ 8. *Tony Hawk's Underground 2*	**d.** Green Giant vegetables
_____ 9. *Melrose Place*	**e.** Reese's Pieces
_____ 10. *E.T.*	**f.** Burger King
_____ 11. *Grey's Anatomy*	**g.** Jeep
_____ 12. *ESPN Sports Center*	**h.** Izze Sparkling juice

C. RECOGNIZING METHODS OF ORGANIZATION AND TRANSITIONS

Select the best answer.

_____ 1. In paragraph 2, the author explains the meanings of *product placement* and *branded entertainment* using the organizational pattern called

   a. cause and effect.

   b. comparison and contrast.

   c. definition.

   d. process.

_____ 2. In paragraph 2, a word or phrase that signals that the author will illustrate the terms he has defined is

   a. oops.

   b. however.

   c. now.

   d. for example.

_____ 3. In paragraph 5, which organizational pattern does the author use to describe the difference between traditional and modern product placement?

   a. cause and effect

   b. comparison and contrast

   c. classification

   d. enumeration

_____ 4. The transitional word or phrase that signals paragraph 5's organizational pattern is

   a. although.

   b. difference.

   c. for example.

   d. perhaps.

_____ 5. The pattern of organization used in paragraph 11 is

   a. spatial order.

   b. comparison and contrast.

   c. definition.

   d. listing or enumeration.

D. REVIEWING AND ORGANIZING IDEAS: MAPPING

Complete the following maps by filling in the blanks.

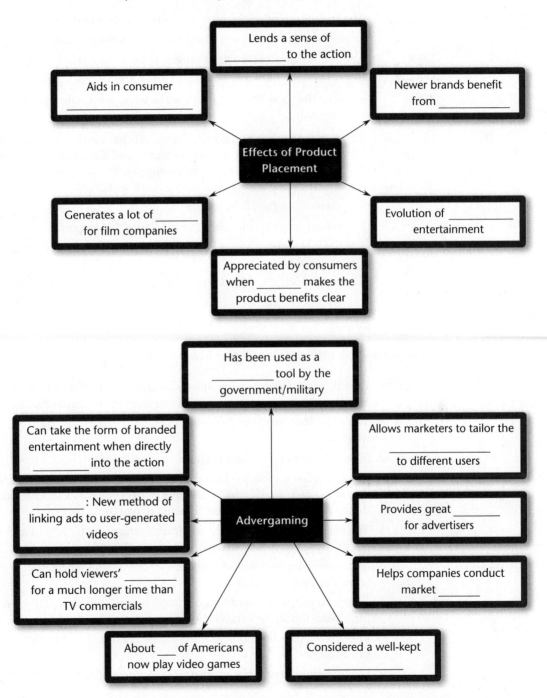

Lends a sense of _____ to the action

Aids in consumer _____

Newer brands benefit from _____

Effects of Product Placement

Generates a lot of _____ for film companies

Evolution of _____ entertainment

Appreciated by consumers when _____ makes the product benefits clear

---

Has been used as a _____ tool by the government/military

Can take the form of branded entertainment when directly _____ into the action

Allows marketers to tailor the _____ to different users

_____ : New method of linking ads to user-generated videos

Advergaming

Provides great _____ for advertisers

Can hold viewers' _____ for a much longer time than TV commercials

Helps companies conduct market _____

About ___ of Americans now play video games

Considered a well-kept _____

E. READING AND THINKING VISUALLY

Select the best answer.

_____ 1. The author included the photo shown on page 418 in order to
   a. emphasize that most product placements sell beverages.
   b. illustrate how product placement is built into a film.
   c. suggest that product placement most often occurs in films.
   d. argue that product placement is the most profitable type of advertising.

_____ 2. Suppose the author wished to include another visual aid with this selection. Knowing that the author's intended audience is first-year college students, which of the following would you recommend the author include?
   a. a scene from *Double Indemnity*
   b. a screen capture from the original "Pong" video game
   c. a screen capture from a popular video game franchise, such as *Prince of Persia*
   d. a scene from an 1890s silent film

F. FIGURING OUT IMPLIED MEANINGS

Indicate whether each statement is true (T) or false (F).

_____ 1. Overall, young people seem more concerned about the blurring line between programming and advertising than older people do.

_____ 2. The most successful product placement of all time took place on *American Idol*.

_____ 3. Most, but not all, product placements are paid for.

_____ 4. In some video games, product placements aren't disguised; they are actually shown as advertisements in a setting (such as a football stadium) that would have advertisements in real life.

_____ 5. The author implies that only large corporations such as Pepsi and Burger King can afford to pay for product placements.

_____ 6. In the early days of television and movies, product placements tended to be more subtle.

_____ 7. American consumers would most likely resent a product placement for suntan lotion on a travel show focusing on island vacations.

_____ 8. Most of the people who play video games are young and fairly uneducated.

_____ 9. Product placement is the most profitable form of advertising.

G. THINKING CRITICALLY

Select the best answer.

_____ 1. The tone of the reading can best be described as

   a. arrogant.

   b. informal.

   c. pessimistic.

   d. sympathetic.

_____ 2. The central thesis is supported by all of the following *except*

   a. examples.

   b. statistical data.

   c. descriptions.

   d. personal experience.

_____ 3. In paragraph 1, the author puts the word "geek" in quotation marks to

   a. show that it is a term used in the advertising business.

   b. imply that unpopular people are more likely to be affected by product placements.

   c. make it clear that he disagrees with the information he is presenting.

   d. create an ironic and sarcastic tone.

_____ 4. When the author says "oops, they got another one here!" in paragraph 2, he means that

   a. he has been paid to advertise the Bag Borrow or Steal Web site.

   b. simply by mentioning the Bag Borrow or Steal Web site, he has advertised it for free.

   c. he is a very strong advocate for product placement, advergaming, and other modern forms of advertising.

   d. he needs to provide a real-world example to have credibility as an author.

_____ 5. In paragraph 5, when the author says that the labels of some products were "mysteriously" hidden from the camera in *Double Indemnity,* he means that

   a. no one is sure why they were turned around.

   b. the hidden product labels were intended to be a mystery to reflect the plot of the movie.

   c. the director intentionally obscured some product labels to draw attention to others, such as Green Giant.

   d. the director was experimenting with special effects during the filming of the movie.

_____ 6. It can be argued that the author is biased in favor of product placement because

    a. he cites many examples of successful product placements.

    b. he is a well-known businessman whose goal is to make as much money as possible.

    c. he understands that today's consumers are much more video oriented than earlier generations were.

    d. he does not offer any serious criticisms of product placement or the negative effects of embedding ads in video games.

H. BUILDING VOCABULARY

Context

Using context and a dictionary, if necessary, determine the meaning of each word as it is used in the selection.

_____ 1. evolved (paragraph 2)

    a. prevented

    b. grew

    c. allowed

    d. performed

_____ 2. brim (paragraph 4)

    a. remove

    b. substitute

    c. are full of

    d. cover up

_____ 3. staples (paragraph 4)

    a. necessities

    b. problems

    c. obstructions

    d. devices

_____ 4. blatant (paragraph 5)

    a. timely

    b. obvious

    c. offensive

    d. private

_____ 5. lucrative (paragraph 5)

    a. profitable

    b. similar

    c. destructive

    d. unnecessary

_____ 6. immerse (paragraph 8)

    a. walk up a steep hill

    b. remove from

    c. serve as a creative force

    d. become deeply involved in

_____ 7. physiological (paragraph 11)

    a. emotional

    b. mental

    c. bodily

    d. unrealistic

Word Parts

> ### A REVIEW OF PREFIXES AND SUFFIXES
>
> **IN-** means *not*
> **-IVE** and **-IC** mean a *state, condition,* or *quality*

Use your knowledge of word parts and the review above to fill in the blanks in the following sentences.

1. If *narrate* means "tell a story," then a **narrative** film (paragraph 2) is one that tells a _____.

2. If the term *cinema* refers to films or movies, then a **cinematic** tradition (paragraph 5) is one having to do with _____.

3. If something is *congruent,* it is fitting or compatible with something else. Therefore, **incongruent** placements in films (paragraph 6) are ones that are _____ with other elements of the film.

4. If something *audible* can be heard, then an **inaudible** audio signal (paragraph 11) _____ be heard.

Unusual Words/Understanding Idioms

Use the meanings given below to write a sentence using the boldfaced word or phrase.

1. To **hawk** something (paragraph 7) is to sell it aggressively. It is an older use of the word and was applied to traveling salespeople who carried their goods around and offered them for sale by shouting on street corners.

   Your sentence: _____

   _____

2. A **banner-game** (paragraph 8) appears in a banner at the top of a Web page. It is usually fairly large and colorful, inviting players to click and play the game.

   Your sentence: _____

   _____

3. An **upscale** consumer (paragraph 11) is well-to-do and has money to spend.

   Your sentence: _____

   _____

4. Something done **on the fly** (paragraph 11) is done quickly and (often) easily.

   Your sentence: _____

   _____

I. SELECTING A LEARNING/STUDY STRATEGY

Predict an essay question about this selection that might be used on an exam.

J. EXPLORING IDEAS THROUGH DISCUSSION AND WRITING

1. Choose one or two television shows to watch for product placement in the next week. Make a list of the products or brands used during the show and indicate whether they were part of the storyline or simply used as props for the characters. If they were props, what do you think they were intended to reveal about the character or story? If they were part of the storyline, what did they add to the plot?

2. Discuss the pros and cons of product placement. For example, do you think using a product that is currently popular will make a movie or TV show seem outdated in a year or two?

3. Why do you think networks no longer require producers to alter brand names?

4. Do you think that product placement has had an effect on your own decisions as a consumer? Why or why not?

5. Do you play video games? If so, have you ever noticed product placements in them? If so, how much attention have you paid to them in comparison to other types of ads (such as TV or radio ads)? What makes you decide whether to pay attention to an ad or not?

K. BEYOND THE CLASSROOM TO THE WEB

One company that has been very successful at product placement is Apple, the creator of the iMac and MacBook personal computers, as well as the iPhone and the iPad. Do a Web search (perhaps using the "Images" option on Google) to find Apple product placements. (You can also use your own experience.) What do you notice about the types of people shown using Apple computers? What does this tell you about the company's marketing strategies and its customers?

TRACKING YOUR PROGRESS

Selection 15

Section	Number Correct		Score
A. Thesis and Main Ideas (5 items)	_____	× 3	_____
B. Details (12 items)	_____	× 2	_____
C. Organization and Transitions (5 items)	_____	× 2	_____
E. Reading and Thinking Visually (2 items)	_____	× 3	_____
F. Implied Meanings (9 items)	_____	× 2	_____
G. Thinking Critically (6 items)	_____	× 2	_____
H. Vocabulary			
Context (7 items)	_____	× 1	_____
Word Parts (4 items)	_____	× 2	_____
		Total Score	_____%

14 Technology in Academic Disciplines

Technology has become an important part of our daily lives. In some cases, technology directly controls our lives. For example, if your car does not start or the bus breaks down, you may miss class. People's lives have been saved by medical technology: for example, when a person's heart has stopped and been restarted by a machine. In other situations, technology influences the quality of our lives. Without technology we would lack many conveniences that we take for granted. For example, we would not have computers, elevators, automated teller machines, or microwave ovens. Technology affects our communication through radio, television, and the Internet; our comfort through furnaces, air conditioners, and plumbing systems; our health through vaccines, drugs, and medical research; and our jobs through computers, copiers, and fax machines. In fact, it is difficult to think of any aspect of our daily lives untouched by technology.

In this chapter you will explore the uses and effects of technology throughout the academic disciplines. As you read "DNA Fingerprinting: Cracking Our Genetic 'Barcode,'" you will learn how DNA fingerprinting works. "Interface Facts" offers insight into the use of video games for academic research across the scientific disciplines. "The Robot Invasion" discusses advances in robotic technology that may change the way companies do business (and individuals do household chores).

Use the following suggestions when reading about technology.

TIPS FOR READING ABOUT TECHNOLOGY

- **Read slowly.** Technical material tends to be factually dense and requires careful, slow reading.
- **Pay attention to technical vocabulary.** All the readings in this chapter include some specialized terminology. Use the definitions in the margin to help you when you get stuck. If you don't understand a word, focus on understanding the main idea and then look up the word later.
- **Focus on process.** Much technical writing focuses on how things work. "DNA Fingerprinting: Cracking Our Genetic 'Barcode,'" explains how DNA fingerprinting works.
- **Use visualization.** Visualization is a process of creating mental pictures or images. As you read, try to picture in your mind the process or procedure that is being described. Visualization makes reading these descriptions easier and will improve your ability to recall details. As you read "The Robot Invasion," try to visualize how "swarming technology" works. To understand how online video games can aid scientific research, visit one of the Web sites discussed in "Interface Facts."

SELECTION 16

DNA Fingerprinting: Cracking Our Genetic "Barcode"

Elaine N. Marieb

TEXTBOOK EXCERPT
Contemporary
Issues Reading

This selection is taken from a textbook titled *Essentials of Human Anatomy and Physiology*, by Elaine N. Marieb, published in 2009. Read the selection to find out about the process known as DNA fingerprinting.

PREVIEWING THE READING

Using the steps listed on pages 40–41, preview the reading selection. When you have finished, complete the following items.

1. The topic of this selection is _____.

2. List at least three questions you expect to be able to answer after reading the selection.

   a. _____

   b. _____

   c. _____

 MAKING CONNECTIONS

What do you already know about DNA fingerprinting? How is it like traditional fingerprinting? With a classmate, make a list of the ways that you think DNA fingerprinting is used in the world today.

READING TIP

As you read, highlight unfamiliar terms and their definitions. If a definition is not given, be sure to look up the term in a dictionary so that you can understand the passage.

DNA Fingerprinting: Cracking Our Genetic "Barcode"

1   The terrorist attacks on New York City's World Trade Center killed more than 3,000 people, their bodies buried in millions of tons of rubble. As weeks passed, it became clear that even if victims could be recovered from the wreckage, their bodies

DNA
deoxyribonucleic acid, the long string of genetic material found in the nucleus of a cell

barcode
a series of vertical bars printed on consumer products to identify the item for pricing and inventory purposes

nucleotides
the basic structural units of nucleic acids such as DNA

2   would probably be mangled, burned, or decomposed to a point where even family members would not recognize them.

In a situation like this, how can we identify individuals with any certainty? The New York Medical Examiner's Office turned to **DNA** fingerprinting, a technique for analyzing tiny samples of DNA taken from semen, skin, blood, or other body tissues. DNA fingerprinting is based on the fact that no two human beings, except for identical twins, possess identical sets of genetic material. In effect, DNA fingerprinting creates a unique genetic "**barcode**" that distinguishes each of us from all other humans. Let's see how it works.

Creating a DNA Profile

3   Recall that DNA contains four **nucleotides**—A, G, C, and T—that form complementary base pairs. In members of the same species, 99.9 percent of DNA is identical. This means that only 0.1 percent of your DNA differs from that of other humans—even close relatives, but this is enough to make you genetically unique. In a DNA string 3 billion units long, that 0.1 percent translates into 3 million variations that differ slightly from everyone else's. Unless you're an identical sibling, your set of DNA is yours alone. DNA fingerprinting involves analyzing an individual's DNA, mapping its unique pattern, and comparing it to other DNA profiles to determine whether there's a match.

4   A standard technique for creating a DNA profile focuses on 13 specific sites on our chromosomes where short segments of nuclear DNA are arranged in a repeating sequence. Although it is theoretically possible that unrelated people could show identical repeats at all 13 sites, the odds are less than 1 in 1 trillion.

5   Sometimes it can be difficult to obtain sufficient nuclear DNA for analysis. DNA samples recovered from crime scenes or disaster sites, for example, are frequently contaminated with dirt, fibers, and debris, or badly decomposed, limiting the amount of testable tissue. DNA retrieval can become a race against time as microbes, enzymes, insects, and environmental factors such as heat and humidity accelerate the process of decomposition.

Sorting and Identifying DNA

6   For DNA to be profiled, it must first be cut into manageable fragments by *restriction enzymes,* enzymes that recognize a specific base sequence and cleave the DNA at this location. This breaks down chromosomes into millions of pieces of different sizes that are then subjected to *gel electrophoresis,* which sorts the pieces by length. The DNA is placed on a gel and positioned in an electric field. The negatively charged fragments of DNA are attracted to the positively charged electrode and migrate toward it. Because the smaller pieces move more quickly than the larger pieces, the fragments end up sorted by size.

7   To locate a specific repeating sequence, researchers make a *DNA probe* with a complementary sequence and tag it with a radioactive compound. Because their sequences are complementary, the probe binds to the site; and when exposed to X-ray film, the image shows dark bands where the probe bound to the DNA.

DNA electrophoresis.
A scientist looking at DNA fragments in an electrophoresis gel.

8   A victim's DNA profile is then compared to known references to find one that matches. In the case of the World Trade Center attack, DNA references were obtained from victims' personal effects (such as toothbrushes and combs), entered into a computer, and sorted to find a match.

DNA Fingerprinting and Forensics

9   DNA fingerprinting has become a vital tool in forensic medicine (the application of medical knowledge to questions of law). For example, DNA fingerprinting is used to identify "John and Jane Does," unknown human remains. The U.S. military takes blood and saliva samples from every recruit so it can identify soldiers killed in the line of duty. DNA fingerprinting can also identify victims of mass disasters such as airplane crashes. The World Trade Center tragedy called for genetic analysis on an unprecedented scale.

10   DNA fingerprinting can prove that a suspect was actually at the scene of a crime. In the United States, some communities now require certain criminal offenders to provide DNA samples, which are classified and stored. DNA profiles can also establish innocence. At least 10 people in the United States have been released from death row after genetic evidence exonerated them.

11   DNA fingerprinting can also verify relationships in cases of disputed property, identify long-lost relatives, and establish paternity, even in paternity cases that are centuries old. For example, historians have fiercely debated whether Thomas Jefferson, our third president, fathered any children by his slave Sally Hemings. Modern DNA researchers entered the fray by profiling Jefferson's Y chromosome. A comparison of 19 genetic markers on the Jefferson Y chromosomes and those of Hemings's descendants found identical matches between the Jefferson line and Hemings's youngest son. Could it be chance? Hardly!

A. UNDERSTANDING THE THESIS AND OTHER MAIN IDEAS

Select the best answer.

_____ 1. The central thesis of this selection is that DNA fingerprinting is
   a. a legal tool primarily for use in the criminal justice system.
   b. a process that makes it possible to identify individuals through their genetic material.
   c. one of several methods used to analyze an individual's DNA.
   d. a new technology that may become useful in the future.

_____ 2. The author's primary purpose is to
   a. compare traditional and DNA fingerprinting.
   b. argue that DNA profiling should be against the law.
   c. describe the process and uses of DNA fingerprinting.
   d. discuss a variety of techniques used in forensic medicine.

_____ 3. The topic of paragraph 2 is
   a. the New York Medical Examiner's Office.
   b. DNA fingerprinting.
   c. identical twins.
   d. genetic barcodes.

_____ 4. According to the selection, DNA fingerprinting involves
   a. analyzing an individual's DNA.
   b. mapping the unique pattern of an individual's DNA.
   c. comparing an individual's DNA profile with others to find a match.
   d. all of the above.

_____ 5. The topic of paragraph 9 is expressed in the
   a. first sentence.
   b. second sentence.
   c. third sentence.
   d. last sentence.

_____ 6. The question that is answered in paragraph 9 is
   a. What is DNA fingerprinting?
   b. How is DNA fingerprinting used in forensic medicine?
   c. How is DNA obtained for matching purposes?
   d. Why is DNA fingerprinting important in criminal cases?

_____ 7. The main idea of paragraph 11 is expressed in the
   a. first sentence.
   b. second sentence.
   c. third sentence.
   d. fourth sentence.

_____ 8. According to the selection, DNA fingerprinting was used to find out whether Thomas Jefferson
   a. had an identical brother.
   b. died of natural causes.
   c. was the son of a slave owner.
   d. fathered a child by Sally Hemings.

B. IDENTIFYING DETAILS

Complete each of the following statements by underlining the correct choice in parentheses.

1. DNA contains (4 / 100) nucleotides that form complementary base pairs.
2. In members of the same species, (0.1 / 99.9) percent of DNA is identical.
3. A DNA string is three (thousand / billion) units long.
4. A standard technique for creating a DNA profile focuses on (4 / 13) specific sites where DNA repeats.
5. The odds of unrelated people showing identical repeats are less than 1 in (3 million / 1 trillion).

C. RECOGNIZING METHODS OF ORGANIZATION AND TRANSITIONS

Select the best answer.

_____ 1. In paragraph 2, the author explains what DNA fingerprinting is by using the organizational pattern called
   a. cause and effect.
   b. definition.
   c. comparison and contrast.
   d. chronological order.

_____ 2. In paragraphs 6–8, the author describes how DNA is sorted and identified using the organizational pattern called
   a. process.
   b. listing.
   c. classification.
   d. comparison and contrast.

_____ 3. In paragraph 9, the transition indicating the author's organizational pattern is

a. has become.

b. for example.

c. also.

d. called for.

D. REVIEWING AND ORGANIZING IDEAS: SUMMARIZING

Use the following words and phrases to complete the summary of paragraphs 6–8.

size	restriction enzymes	probe
gel electrophoresis	X-rays	radioactive compound

The first step in profiling DNA is to break it down using _____
_____. The pieces of chromosomes are then subjected
to _____, which uses an electric field to sort the
pieces by _____. To find a specific repeating sequence, a DNA
_____ with a complementary sequence is made and tagged with
a _____. The probe then binds to the complementary
DNA site and _____ reveal dark bands where the probe and DNA are
bound. Finally, this DNA profile is compared with known references to find a
match.

E. READING AND THINKING VISUALLY

Select the best answer.

_____ 1. The photo on page 435 makes it clear that the electrophoresis process makes use of

a. glass.

b. X-rays.

c. solar energy.

d. fingerprinting technology.

_____ 2. The primary purpose of the photograph on page 435 is to

a. present evidence of the importance of DNA fingerprinting.

b. illustrate how simple the DNA fingerprinting process is.

c. show what DNA electrophoresis looks like.

d. compare DNA fingerprinting to other identification techniques.

F. FIGURING OUT IMPLIED MEANINGS

Indicate whether each statement is true (T) or false (F).

_____ 1. Identifying some victims of the World Trade Center attacks would have been impossible without DNA fingerprinting.

_____ 2. The DNA profiles of siblings and other closely related family members are more similar than those of unrelated people.

_____ 3. The technique is called DNA fingerprinting because it relies primarily on fingerprints for identification.

_____ 4. It is extremely unlikely that unrelated people would have matching DNA profiles.

_____ 5. A person does not need any special training to conduct DNA profiling.

_____ 6. It is impossible to analyze DNA that is more than 100 years old.

_____ 7. In a criminal trial, DNA evidence can establish guilt, but cannot establish innocence.

G. THINKING CRITICALLY

Select the best answer.

_____ 1. The tone of the selection can best be described as
   a. grim.
   b. sympathetic.
   c. informative.
   d. cheerful.

_____ 2. The central thesis of "DNA Fingerprinting: Cracking Our Genetic 'Barcode' " is supported by
   a. facts.
   b. examples.
   c. descriptions.
   d. all of the above.

_____ 3. Of the following phrases, the only one that has a *positive* connotation is
   a. "millions of tons of rubble" (paragraph 1)
   b. "frequently contaminated with dirt" (paragraph 5)
   c. "a vital tool in forensic medicine" (paragraph 9)
   d. "historians have fiercely debated" (paragraph 11)

_____ 4. The author began the selection with a reference to the World Trade Center attacks in order to

    a. compare different types of historical events.

    b. illustrate the importance of DNA fingerprinting.

    c. introduce her own point of view.

    d. establish a setting for the selection.

H. BUILDING VOCABULARY

Context

Using context and a dictionary, if necessary, determine the meaning of each word as it is used in the selection.

_____ 1. accelerate (paragraph 5)

    a. affect

    b. speed up

    c. improve

    d. recover

_____ 2. cleave (paragraph 6)

    a. split

    b. appear

    c. cover

    d. harm

_____ 3. migrate (paragraph 6)

    a. match

    b. show

    c. move

    d. limit

_____ 4. exonerated (paragraph 10)

    a. attacked

    b. cleared

    c. removed

    d. identified

_____ 5. fray (paragraph 11)

    a. tool

    b. location

    c. proof

    d. fight

Word Parts

> ## A REVIEW OF PREFIXES AND SUFFIXES
>
> **DE-** means *away, from*
> **UN-** means *not*
> **PRE-** means *before*
> **-ANT** means *one who*

Use your knowledge of word parts and the review above to fill in the blanks in the following sentences.

1. Something that is **decomposed** (paragraph 1) or in the process of **decomposition** (paragraph 5) is breaking down; it is changing its composition _____ one form to another.

2. If an event happens on an **unprecedented** scale (paragraph 9), it is something that has _____ happened before to such an extent.

3. A person's **descendants** (paragraph 11) may include children, grandchildren, and so on down through a family line. A **descendant** is _____ comes from an ancestor or a race.

Unusual Words/Understanding Idioms
Use the meanings given below to write a sentence using the boldfaced word or phrase.

1. A **barcode** (paragraph 2) is usually an identification given to a product so that it can be priced or identified for inventory. In this selection it refers to our unique set of genetic material.

   Your sentence: _____

   _____

2. When there is a **race against time** (paragraph 5), an urgency exists that makes it important to complete a task before it is too late.

   Your sentence: _____

   _____

I. SELECTING A LEARNING/STUDY STRATEGY

Predict an essay question that might be asked on this selection.

J. EXPLORING IDEAS THROUGH DISCUSSION AND WRITING

1. Evaluate the introduction to the selection. Did it capture your interest? Why or why not?

2. Discuss the title of the selection, "DNA Fingerprinting: Cracking Our Genetic 'Barcode.' " Can you think of another title that would be as effective?

3. Do you think it would be interesting to work in DNA profiling or forensic medicine? Describe why it would or would not appeal to you.

4. Discuss the importance of DNA fingerprinting to the justice system. Do you think that all criminal offenders should be required to provide DNA samples?

K. BEYOND THE CLASSROOM TO THE WEB

As the reading states, DNA testing has become a common technique used in criminal investigations. Conduct a Web search for stories about either (a) a criminal who was captured through DNA evidence, or (b) a falsely accused person who was set free by DNA evidence. Summarize the story in a paragraph or two and share it with the class.

TRACKING YOUR PROGRESS

Selection 16

Section	Number Correct	Score
A. Thesis and Main Ideas (8 items)	_____ × 3	_____
B. Details (5 items)	_____ × 3	_____
C. Organization and Transitions (3 items)	_____ × 2	_____
E. Reading and Thinking Visually (2 items)	_____ × 3	_____
F. Implied Meanings (7 items)	_____ × 3	_____
G. Thinking Critically (4 items)	_____ × 3	_____
H. Vocabulary		
Context (5 items)	_____ × 2	_____
Word Parts (3 items)	_____ × 2	_____
	Total Score	_____ %

SELECTION 17

Interface Facts
Katie L. Burke

This reading selection originally appeared in *The American Scientist*, a magazine of science and technology published by Sigma Xi, The Scientific Research Society.

Using the steps listed on pages 40–41, preview the reading selection. When you have finished, complete the following items.

1. According to the article, _____ games allow people all over the world to take part in scientific research.

2. Indicate whether each statement is true (T) or false (F).
   _____ a. Luis von Ahn is a biologist employed at Carnegie Mellon University.
   _____ b. The field of computerized citizen science is decreasing as a result of new laws that restrict these activities.

MAKING
CONNECTIONS *Have you ever been part of a "flash mob" or "flash event" that you learned about on the Web? Have you taken part in any type of online game, community, or research project?*

READING TIP

Because this reading was taken from a scientific publication, it contains scientific language with which you may not be familiar. Focus on comprehending the reading's key points and not getting bogged down with technical vocabulary.

Interface Facts

Video games allow people all over the world to do scientific research

1   People spend 300 million minutes every day playing Angry Birds, one of the world's most popular video games. What if we could tap into that energy to solve real-world puzzles? In 2003, Carnegie Mellon University computer scientist Luis von

crowdsourcing
the practice of
obtaining services,
ideas, or content
by soliciting
contributions
from a large group
of people (especially
from people online)

extrapolate
formulate a
conclusion from a
set of given facts

DNA
the material in
living cells that
carries genetic
information

Ahn, now known as a **crowdsourcing** pioneer, asked this question and answered it with the ESP Game, in which people score points by giving an image the same label as someone else. By 2006, 10 million images had been labeled, and that year Google bought the game, launching von Ahn's career.

2   In the wake of ESP Game's success, scientists across a variety of fields caught on: When they needed information from large datasets that could not be collected by a computer, people could help. Although public participation in scientific research is not a new idea—for example, the Audubon Society's first Christmas Bird Count took place in 1900—the advent of greater computing power and the Internet have facilitated faster, more widespread information sharing than ever before. Not just hundreds could participate, but hundreds of thousands could interact through a web interface. The field of citizen science took off.

3   The success of early computer-based citizen science projects, such as Stardust@ Home, showed that huge numbers of people around the world were willing to contribute computing power and time to making discoveries. In Galaxy Zoo, launched in 2007, participants classify images of galaxies by shape, and that information is used to **extrapolate** their history. Galaxy Zoo was an unexpected success: Twenty-four hours after the project launched, it was clocking 70,000 classifications per hour. Chris Lintott of Oxford University, one of the creators of Galaxy Zoo, says: "We were completely overwhelmed and pleasantly surprised by the sheer number of people who wanted to help." Galaxy Zoo resulted in discoveries such as the Voorwerp, a strange, giant gas cloud noticed and named by Dutch schoolteacher Hanny Van Arkel. Galaxy Zoo astronomers are using the Hubble Space Telescope to figure out the nature of the Voorwerp and smaller Voorwerp-like gas clouds. "It looks like nothing I've ever seen. They're much more crazy complicated structures than we ever thought," explained Lintott.

4   Collaborating with colleagues from around the world, Lintott went on to create the Zooniverse, an Internet home for popular citizen science projects across disciplines. In the Zooniverse, anyone can participate in research on whale calls, weather as recorded in wartime ship logs or new planets. "These projects create very personal connections to an often quite obscure category of science," Lintott explains. The group has another compelling reason to run these diverse projects: to study what people want to do and what they are good at, Lintott notes. "I was incredibly grateful that all these people wanted to classify galaxies, but I didn't understand what magic thing it was about Galaxy Zoo that made it work. You can think of all the projects in the Zooniverse as an exploration of that space."

5   Online citizen science games are modeled after video games that motivate participants to score points and achieve new tools and levels. For example, FoldIt, a game based on Rosetta@Home and launched in 2008, prompts players to decipher potential 3D protein structures associated with particular pathologies, such as a retroviral protease enzyme key to virus propagation in a form of AIDS found in monkeys. With such high-profile successes, more online citizen science games were launched. In 2010, the Tetris-like game Phylo debuted, prompting players to win points for correctly aligning related **DNA** sequences. Mathieu Blanchette of McGill University, a member of the team that created Phylo, explains, "The main goal of Phylo is to bring together computers and humans, make each do what they are good at, and put the

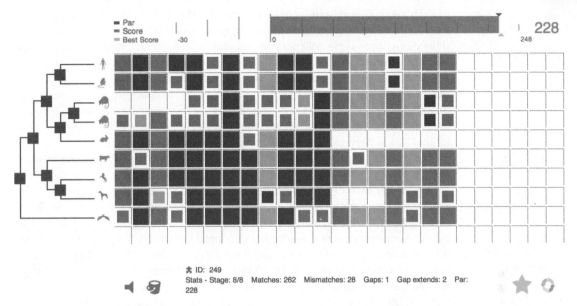

▶ ID: 249
Stats - Stage: 8/8   Matches: 262   Mismatches: 28   Gaps: 1   Gap extends: 2   Par: 228

Phylo is a Tetris-like game, where players win points by correctly aligning related nucleotide sequences. These sequences are chosen because of their relevance to research on human disease and because of computer sequencing software's difficulty in resolving the sequence alignments without people's help. (Photo courtesy of Phylo, McGill University.)

results together to get something better than either could get alone." A March 2012 paper in PloS One announced that 70 percent of the alignments in the game had been improved by the more than 26,000 registered Phylo users, as well as tens of thousands of unregistered users.

6   But what works for one citizen science project will not necessarily work for another. FoldIt players must invest large amounts of time advancing through tutorial levels before they have the skill to contribute to real-life research. Players seem undeterred by this requirement: FoldIt has some 240,000 registered users and counting. Alternatively, Galaxy Zoo and Phylo are interfaces where users need no prior knowledge of the science and can spend a few minutes of their time in order to contribute to research. Said Phylo collaborator Jérôme Waldispühl of McGill University, "The simplest puzzles are as useful as the most complicated ones for improving our alignments." In contrast to FoldIt and Phylo, Galaxy Zoo and other Zooniverse projects are deliberately not structured as games—they lack scores or levels. As Lintott explains, "The instinct to play a game is incredibly powerful, and once you trigger that, it's very easy to switch somebody's motivation from 'I want to help science' to 'I'm playing this game.'" According to Lintott, when that motivation switches, the best and worst players are more likely to stop playing. Therefore, only some online projects benefit from a game interface.

7   Perhaps no one should have been surprised that people participating in these projects do not balk at complex problems, even ones that require programming and simulations. Zooniverse collaborators expanded Galaxy Zoo's idea into Galaxy Zoo Mergers, in which users control simulations of galaxy collisions. "We discovered by accident that if you give access to as much information as you can behind a task, people take it and run an awfully long way. You find people who would never have dreamed of reading textbooks or searching scientific literature wandering through the web because it's their galaxy and they want to know about it. Providing the tools for that sort of deep exploration has become important," says Lintott.

8   The field of computerized citizen science is advancing quickly, altering how research is done as well as how science is perceived and taught. "We're living in a society where human and computer are fully integrated," says Waldispühl. The Zooniverse has recently released a few new projects and will be releasing more in the coming months. Phylo is opening an interface with which researches will be able to submit **genome** sequence alignments they need help improving. Some FoldIt creators went on to launch EteRNA, a game for designing RNA. The Zooniverse team is also using information garnered from their games to improve computers' ability to identify visual patterns, so that the most difficult and unusual tasks are delegated to humans. Lintott predicts, "The next generation of datasets is going to be even bigger, and so we're going to need to split the work between humans and computers, even with hundreds of thousands of people helping."

genome
the complete set of genes or genetic material in an organism

A. UNDERSTANDING THE THESIS AND OTHER MAIN IDEAS

Select the best answer.

_____ 1. Which of the following best states the thesis or central thought of "Interface Facts"?

   a. The founder of crowdsourcing, Luis von Ahn, has become a successful developer of online games.

   b. Internet-based gaming has become an effective method of conducting scientific research, allowing both scientists and non-scientists to take part.

   c. FoldIt, Galaxy Zoo, Stardust, and Phylo have all been successful in helping scientists collect data and information.

   d. The Zooniverse is the next step in social media on the Internet, and it is likely to replace Facebook and text messaging within the next decade.

_____ 2. The main idea of paragraph 3 is found in the

   a. first sentence.

   b. third sentence.

   c. fifth sentence.

   d. last sentence.

_____ 3. The topic of paragraph 5 is
    a. FoldIt.
    b. medical research.
    c. Mathieu Blanchette.
    d. online citizen science games.

_____ 4. The main idea of paragraph 7 is that scientific research games on the Web benefit from providing _____ for the gamers.
    a. chat rooms   c. monetary compensation
    b. deep exploration   d. prizes and rewards

B. IDENTIFYING DETAILS

Match the online citizen-based science projects in Column A with the descriptions in Column B.

Column A	Column B
_____ 1. FoldIt	a. players align related DNA sequences
_____ 2. Galaxy Zoo	b. Web site that is home to popular citizen-science projects across the disciplines
_____ 3. Phylo	c. players classify galaxies by their shape
_____ 4. Zooniverse	d. players receive points when they give an image the same label that other players have given it
_____ 5. ESP Game	e. players work with 3D protein structures

C. RECOGNIZING METHODS OF ORGANIZATION AND TRANSITIONS

Select the best answer.

_____ 1. The overall pattern of organization used in "Interface Facts" is
    a. classification.   c. definition.
    b. summary.   d. listing.

_____ 2. The pattern of organization used in paragraph 1 is
    a. comparison.   c. chronological order.
    b. classification.   d. definition.

_____ 3. The transitional word or phrase used in paragraph 6 to signal the differences between two or more items is
    a. no prior knowledge.   c. in contrast to.
    b. as useful as.   d. therefore.

D. REVIEWING AND ORGANIZING IDEAS: MAPPING

Complete the following map of the reading by filling in the missing words or phrases.

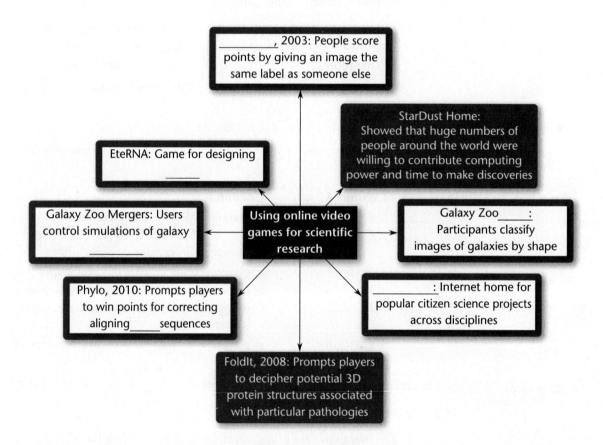

E. READING AND THINKING VISUALLY

Select the best answer.

_____ From the image on page 445 and the description in paragraph 5, you can infer that a "Tetris-like" game is one that

    a. is used primarily by biologists.

    b. asks players to align colored blocks.

    c. permits more than 20,000 players to participate simultaneously.

    d. punishes players who have provided incorrect answers.

F. FIGURING OUT IMPLIED MEANINGS

Indicate whether each statement is true (T) or false (F).

_____ 1. Scientists have been pleasantly surprised by the average person's willingness to help them conduct scientific research.

_____ 2. In general, those who take part in online games geared toward scientific research tend to prefer simpler tasks.

_____ 3. Zooniverse is home to many different citizen-science projects.

_____ 4. Chris Lintott believes that online science research games can help spur interest in science, even among those who are not students or scientists.

_____ 5. The Audubon Society is an organization for people who are interested in birds.

_____ 6. Voorwerp is likely to become the newest planet in our solar system.

_____ 7. A game's best players are usually motivated more by playing the game than by the desire to help science.

G. THINKING CRITICALLY

Select the best answer.

_____ 1. The tone of "Interface Facts" is best described as

    a. optimistic.

    b. cynical.

    c. detached.

    d. solemn.

_____ 2. The author's purpose for writing "Interface Facts" is to

    a. encourage businesses to begin developing Web apps for science games.

    b. describe the growing role of Web-based crowdsourcing in scientific research.

    c. argue against the use of non-scientists in conducting research into diseases and other medical problems.

    d. excite investors about investing their money in citizen-based research.

_____ 3. Which of the following statements from the reading is an opinion, not a fact?

    a. "People spend 300 million minutes every day playing Angry Birds." (paragraph 1)

    b. "The Audubon Society's first Christmas Bird Count took place in 1900." (paragraph 2)

    c. "Galaxy Zoo astronomers are using the Hubble Space Telescope to figure out the nature of the Voorwerp and smaller Voorwerp-like gas clouds." (paragraph 3)

    d. "The instinct to play a game is incredibly powerful." (paragraph 6)

_____ 4. All of the following research scientists are directly quoted in the reading *except* for

    a. Luis von Ahn.

    b. Chris Lintott.

    c. Mathieu Blanchette.

    d. Jérôme Waldispühl.

_____ 5. Which of the following conclusions *cannot* be correctly inferred from "Interface Facts"?

    a. Online video games help scientists draw on the power of other people's brains.

    b. Participants in online gaming often enjoy a "deep" experience in which they are presented with many options and a large amount of information.

    c. Computerized citizen research is appropriate for almost all research studies.

    d. Students who are interested in taking part in citizen research would probably find the Zooniverse Web site a good place to get started.

H. BUILDING VOCABULARY

Context

Using context and a dictionary, if necessary, determine the meaning of each word as it is used in the selection.

_____ 1. pioneer (paragraph 1)

    a. trailblazer

    b. immigrant

    c. manager

    d. computer programmer

_____ 2. advent (paragraph 2)

    a. difficulty

    b. pace

    c. arrival

    d. advantage

_____ 3. obscure (paragraph 4)

    a. acute

    b. sharp

    c. unknown

    d. profitable

_____ 4. balk (paragraph 7)

    a. resist

    b. pay

    c. desire

    d. enjoy

Word Parts

> ### A REVIEW OF PREFIXES AND ROOTS
>
> **PATHO** means _related to disease_
> **UN-** means _not_

Use your knowledge of word parts and the review above to define the boldfaced word in each sentence.

1. In medicine, **pathologies** (paragraph 5) refer to the causes of and symptoms associated with _____.

2. A child who is **undeterred** (paragraph 6) from making mischief is _____ discouraged from engaging in mischievous behaviors that will likely result in unpleasant consequences.

Unusual Words/Understanding Idioms

Use the meanings given below to write a sentence using the boldfaced phrases.

1. **In the wake of** (paragraph 2) is an idiomatic expression that means "following" or "after."

Your sentence: _____

_____

2. A **high-profile** (paragraph 5) person or event is one that attracts a lot of attention or publicity.

Your sentence: _____

_____

I. SELECTING A LEARNING/STUDY STRATEGY

Predict an essay question that might be asked about this reading selection.

J. EXPLORING IDEAS THROUGH DISCUSSION AND WRITING

1. Have you ever used any sort of gaming simulation in one of your college classes? If so, describe your experiences. What was the purpose of the game? What did you learn from it? How did these experiences add to your overall understanding of the field?

2. Suppose you are given a list of the following online research projects: (a) a study about happiness; (b) a project aimed at reinvigorating a troubled area of a city near your home; (c) a study about the ways specific foods affect health and weight. In which project would you be most interested in taking part? Why?

3. In your business class, your instructor gives you the following assignment: Compare and contrast two different advertisements for similar products (for example, two different cars or two different shampoos) and the ways people perceive these advertisements. How might you go about collecting this information?

K. BEYOND THE CLASSROOM TO THE WEB

Visit the Zooniverse Web site at www.zooniverse.org. Select a study that is interesting to you and explore the site. Write a paragraph explaining the study and what it hopes to accomplish.

TRACKING YOUR PROGRESS

Selection 17

Section	Number Correct		Score
A. Thesis and Main Ideas (4 items)	_____	× 3	_____
B. Details (5 items)	_____	× 4	_____
C. Organization and Transitions (3 items)	_____	× 4	_____
E. Reading and Thinking Visually (1 item)	_____	× 4	_____
F. Implied Meanings (7 items)	_____	× 2	_____
G. Thinking Critically (5 items)	_____	× 4	_____
H. Vocabulary			
Context (4 items)	_____	× 3	_____
Word Parts (2 items)	_____	× 3	_____
		Total Score	_____%

The Robot Invasion

Charlie Gillis

The following selection was taken from *Macleans*, a weekly current affairs magazine published in Canada. As you read, consider how the definition of the term *robot* may differ from the way you think about or envision robots.

PREVIEWING THE READING

Using the steps listed on pages 40–41, preview the reading selection. When you have finished, complete the following items.

1. This topic of this reading is _____.

2. Indicate whether each statement is true (T) or false (F).
    _____ a. The author compares robots' activities to those of ants.
    _____ b. Silicon Valley is at the forefront of robotic technology.
    _____ c. Baxter is intended for household use.

MAKING CONNECTIONS

Have you ever seen a robot at work in a factory or on an assembly line? What did it look like? Based on this article, which activities in your daily life can you see robots completing for you?

READING TIP

Although this article is written for the general public, note how it discusses scientific research and breakthroughs. Read with a pen in hand and annotate the selection as you read.

NASA
National
Aeronautics
and Space
Administration

brigade
army squadron

The Robot Invasion

A new breed of small but complex 'learning' robots—working alone or in insect-like swarms—are set to revolutionize manufacturing and labor

1   If you want a glimpse of the future of robotics, and you can't get a tour of **NASA**'s Ames Research Center, try spilling some lunch on your backyard patio. Depending on time of year and location, the inevitable **brigade** of ants will materialize, their

seemingly random movements growing increasingly coordinated as they lug bits of their bonanza away in a martial column—a marvel of low-tech efficiency.

2   Back in the early 1990s, this scenario inspired a far-fetched idea: what if machines could be taught to do the same thing? A large population of relatively simple robots could "swarm" a task we humans would rather forego, like cleaning a banquet hall. Or mining a coal face. Each could be designed to accomplish the most rudimentary functions, robotics experts theorized, such as gathering, carrying and dropping. They'd be equipped with the capacity to share limited information like the quickest routes, or the location of the next payload.

3   Many a scientific career has run aground on the task of mimicking nature, but that imagined future is now within sight. Four months ago, a Canadian computer science professor named Andrew Vardy posted footage on YouTube of toy-sized robots he'd modified to sort plastic pucks randomly placed on a surface the size of a dining table. Over 29 minutes, the devices (they look a bit like tugboats) buzz around their miniature arena, grabbing the pucks and carrying them away. Vardy, who teaches at Memorial University of Newfoundland, is not the first researcher to model mini-bots on insect behavior. Small vehicles equipped with infrared sensors have been taught to hunt, gather and store in laboratories around the world. But Vardy did add a notable wrinkle: his robots could "see" through tiny on-board cameras. By the end of the exercise, they'd sorted the pucks into tidy clusters of red and green.

4   His experiment counts among a series bringing us closer to a day when robots, simple and complex, are part of our daily lives. For decades, engineers and sci-fi writers have forecast a time when autonomous machines would become enough like living creatures to share our homes and work spaces, performing the "three Ds" of human labor—dirty, dangerous and difficult. In doing so, they would unleash a productivity boom, and the visions run from the banal to the inspiring. Human-sized robots might work assembly lines cheek-by-jowl with people. Small submersible 'bots might swarm a contaminated canal, **hoovering** up toxins and heavy metals. "If you really want to stretch the imagination," says Vardy, "you could envision injecting very tiny robots into someone's bloodstream and get them to aggregate undesirable particles, and get [contaminants] out."

hoovering
vacuuming

5   These ambitions were hobbled, though, by a rudimentary problem: the living world's inherent chaos. Without the capacity to respond to random changes in its environment, a robot could be stymied by objects as commonplace as discarded cardboard dropped in their path. Then there was the challenge of getting autonomous machines to work together. Until very recently, robots used in industry required command-and-control by a central computer, their every movement planned and intricately coordinated. The coming generation of robots are expected not only to "learn" their tasks, but to collaborate with each other in pursuit of efficiency and a common goal. "It's not super-exciting learning," says James McLurkin, a computer science professor at Rice University in Houston, and a leading expert on swarm robotics. "They don't walk up to you and say your name. But without it, you couldn't coordinate 1,000 robots."

6   The solutions are coming, though, and as in practically every facet of human enterprise, they're arising from Silicon Valley. The ongoing explosion in microprocessing capacity has allowed researchers like McLurkin to equip robots smaller than a

hamburger with enough chip space to execute a combination of tasks: following a leader, escaping deadlocks and even clearing a floor littered with bread crumbs. Swiss roboticists programmed a squadron of flying "quadrotors" last January to build a six-meter tower in a Paris art gallery, one foam brick at a time. Video of the feat is part of an Internet **meme** featuring the dragonfly-like aircraft, which are equipped with four propellers and capable of omni-directional movement. Quadrotor teams can be seen doing light shows, navigating obstacle courses and—chillingly—ferrying around a submachine gun.

meme
a popular element of culture; "the latest thing"

7   In many ways, they represent the fantastical edge of possibility in robotics. If flying robots can raise a six-meter tower, why not a skyscraper? Or a drilling rig on the Beaufort Sea? The more prosaic applications are already making their way into the marketplace. A Massachusetts company called Kiva Systems has been selling an automated warehousing system since 2005, in which hundreds of orange robots the size of coffee tables whip merchandise from storage to shipping bay. Orders are controlled from a central computer, and the so-called "drive units," which shunt goods around on columns of metal shelving, communicate with each other by wireless signal, ensuring high-demand items are stored closest to the loading area.

8   The system is said to triple distribution productivity, and has been adopted by a host of big-box retailers, including Staples, Best Buy and Crate & Barrel. In March, the online shopping giant Amazon announced it was buying Kiva for $775 million.

9   If scientists can pack so much utility into such a compact package, how long before the larger, **android-style** robots as envisioned by George Lucas debut in our factories and offices? That's the easiest model for most people to picture, thanks to Hollywood. Alas, marrying the digital and human spheres has been no easier for droid makers than for swarm enthusiasts. Humanoid robots built in recent years have simply been too expensive to bring to market, which has restricted the field to military-funded experimental programs, or corporate giants like Honda, which developed a droid-style robot prototype named Asimo as a stunt to promote its car brand.

android-style
resembling humans

10   Enter Baxter, the first commercially available humanoid robot meant for industrial use. Covered in impact-friendly red rubber, and equipped with a computer-screen face, the gangly machine has set the technology world abuzz since its unveiling this summer, because of its unprecedented adaptability (the "it" is intentional; Baxter's

makers are not into anthropomorphizing). A person can program Baxter by simply taking hold of its 11-joint arms and performing a desired task, such as plucking items off a conveyor and placing them in boxes. Baxter can also adjust to unforeseen events, say officials at Rethink Robotics, the Boston-based company that began shipping him last week. If it drops an item, it stops and picks up another. If a human gets in its way, Baxter grinds to a halt instead of serving up a flying elbow.

de facto   11
in practice, in effect

11   Rodney Brooks, the founder of Rethink and Baxter's **de facto** father, credits a series of advancements for bringing his robot to reality, from the advent of cheap microprocessors to the development of new, lightweight materials. The digital photography technology pioneered by the smartphone industry might be the most important of all, he says. Baxter's sensor array includes five such cameras that allow it to "see" objects he'll be handling, and stop when something crosses his line of vision.

12   These breakthroughs made Baxter light and adaptable. More importantly, they drove down its price. At $22,000, Baxter retails for about the cost of a company car—software upgrades included. "We didn't try to design a robot that can do everything, then figure out how much it would cost," Brooks explains. "Instead we designed it with cost in mind. We worked with suppliers to understand what their technologies and capabilities would allow, and what our design constraints were."

13   Brooks, a former Massachusetts Institute of Technology professor, speaks from a position of authority. His first company, iRobotics, brought the world the Roomba, an autonomous vacuum cleaner capable of cleaning while a homeowner isn't even in the house. The firm's genius was to price the device at $200, far below an Electrolux model already on the market in Europe, ensuring millions would sell worldwide. Today, iRobot is credited with putting consumers at ease with the idea of autonomous machines in their midst. YouTube is chock-a-block with videos of laughing babies riding Roombas as the vacuums do their work.

atavistic   14
ancient

C-3PO
friendly robot in the
Stars Wars movies

marauding
wandering in search
of things to steal   15
or people to attack

dystopian
referring to a
dysfunctional world

repatriate
return to a
country of origin   16

prognosticators
predictors

14   Yet friendly as Roomba seems, robots retain their capacity to stoke our most **atavistic** fears. For every friendly android like **C-3PO**, after all, pop culture can offer a platoon of **marauding** killer-bots whose impassive efficiency raises the neck hair (The Terminator). Or some **dystopian** world of people dehumanized by the machines around them (Wall-E). Real-world roboticists spend a lot of time grappling with a hypothesis known as the "uncanny valley," which holds that people are revolted by robots that act almost, but not perfectly, like humans.

15   All of which raises the question of how eager, or ready, we are to welcome them to our midst. While Brooks has been striving to portray Baxter as a tool that will **repatriate** U.S. manufacturing business lost to Asia (even Chinese workers can't toil for free), his invention has unleashed a wave of dread among those who believe it will kill assembly-line positions in America and abroad. "We have reached peak jobs," one glum commenter declared after reading about Baxter on Forbes.com. "From here on out, total employment is only going to go down."

16   The American futurist Thomas Frey recently predicted that two billion jobs worldwide would fall to robots by 2030—about half the employment on Earth. Among the doomed occupations: fishermen, farmers, miners and soldiers. The question, then, is what sort of jobs will replace them, and on this front most **prognosticators** remain upbeat. Frey imagines a world where millions are employed as robot designers, engineers and dispatchers. "It's not intended to be a doom-and-gloom scenario,"

he says. "It's more like a wake-up call. We're going to be transitioning the jobs we have, so we'll need to train people in the skills for the new world that's about to come." Brooks points to history, noting the boost in productivity that has accompanied every technological advancement. "The PC didn't get rid of office workers," he says, "but it changed the jobs that office workers did. I see that as the analogy here."

17   The good news is that there's time to adjust. Richard Vaughan, a computer scientist at Simon Fraser University in Burnaby, B.C., notes that researchers have yet to find a compact energy source capable of powering swarm robots on their imagined missions. Machines like Baxter, meanwhile, will need years of software upgrades before they can replace the dexterity and judgment of assembly-line workers. That's why Vaughan sees a future in a hybrid of the two models: robot teams comprised of machines smart enough to perform a number of tasks well, yet simple enough to mass produce. "The one thing that's getting cheaper is computation," he says. "What you might see is relatively smart robots working together, and that's different from the traditional, minimal [swarm] system, where the robots have a handful of rules they follow mechanically."

18   Whatever shape they take, the dreams of technology's prophets are undeniably in the offing. Last month, a California-based company announced it would spend $3.1 million to develop farm robots capable of weeding lettuce crops. A Japanese engineer named Akira Mita has proposed buildings in which swarm robots follow the occupants from room to room, adjusting temperature, humidity, lighting and music according to the person's mood. That might not be everyone's ideal of how humans should relate to machines: mini-bots that monitor our mood are just a wee bit creepy. But it's proof enough that the future-gazers were right, and a good reason to watch one's potato salad the next time it spills on the deck.

A. UNDERSTANDING THE THESIS AND OTHER MAIN IDEAS

Select the best answer.

_____   1. The thesis or central thought of "The Robot Invasion" is best stated as

a. In the not-too-distant future, robotic technology will completely change society, revolutionizing both factory work and household chores.

b. Robotic technology is best used by the military, by manufacturing companies, and by retail stores that must sort through large amounts of inventory.

c. New advances in robotic technology allow robots to "see" their surroundings, permitting them to do more than ever before; in the coming years, robots are likely to replace humans in certain jobs.

d. In the nations of the developing world, scientists are developing human-like robots called androids to work on assembly lines, conduct research, and care for the elderly; we will see an explosion in android technology over the next few decades.

_____ 2. The topic of paragraph 3 is

    a. YouTube.

    b. robots.

    c. Memorial University.

    d. Andrew Vardy's mini-bots.

_____ 3. The implied main idea of paragraph 10 is

    a. Baxter is designed to look friendly so that it does not frighten human beings.

    b. Rethink Robotics is the company that developed Baxter and brought it to market.

    c. Baxter is now available for sale to businesses and consumers.

    d. Baxter has been introduced with fanfare and has many unique and useful features.

_____ 4. The main idea of paragraph 17 is found in the

    a. first sentence only.

    b. third and fourth sentences.

    c. first and third sentences.

    d. last sentence.

B. IDENTIFYING DETAILS

Select the best answer.

_____ 1. Which of the following is *not* one of the "three D's" of human labor?

    a. difficult

    b. depressing

    c. dirty

    d. dangerous

_____ 2. Which of the following statements is *not* true of Baxter?

    a. It is designed to be affordable by businesses.

    b. It has 11-joint arms.

    c. It is covered in stainless steel.

    d. It was created by the same man who created the Roomba vacuum cleaner.

_____ 3. According to the theory of _____, people are revolted by robots that act almost, but not perfectly, like humans.

    a. the uncanny valley

    b. avionics

    c. swarm tactics

    d. comparative advantage

_____ 4. The occupations that may be "doomed" by the rise of robotic technology include all of the following *except*

    a. miners.

    b. fisherman.

    c. farmers.

    d. secretaries.

_____ 5. Which statement best summarizes the author's approach to robots
that look and act like humans?

    a. Androids are likely to replace human workers within the next 20
years.

    b. Android technology is in its early phases and faces a number of
challenges in human acceptance.

    c. Androids are frequently used in Europe and Asia but are now
becoming more commonplace in the Americas.

    d. Androids are more likely to be programmed with female voices
than male voices, because female voices are more pleasing.

C. RECOGNIZING METHODS OF ORGANIZATION AND TRANSITIONS

Select the best answer.

_____ 1. The overall pattern of organization used in this reading is

    a. comparison and contrast, because the reading is comparing
human labor with robotic labor.

    b. definition, because the reading provides a technical definition of
robotics.

    c. listing, because it provides a series of facts about robots and
robotic technology.

    d. process, because it presents step-by-step information on how
robots are programmed.

_____ 2. Which organizational pattern is used in paragraph 3?

    a. generalization and example

    b. summary

    c. classification

    d. spatial order

_____ 3. Which word or phrase in paragraph 13 signals the use of cause and effect?

    a. position of authority

    b. the firm's genius

    c. is credited with

    d. laughing babies

D. REVIEWING AND ORGANIZING IDEAS: PARAPHRASING

Complete the following paraphrase of paragraphs 3 and 4 by filling in the blanks with the correct words or phrases.

Many experiments that seek to imitate _____ have failed, but progress is being made. Professor Andrew _____ modified several small robots to sort plastic pucks that he'd placed on a table. The robots, which look like tugboats, took _____ minutes to sweep across the table and carry the pucks away. Professor Vardy is not the first scientist to program his robots to behave like _____, but he did do something that has not been done before: He programmed his robots to be able to see and sort colors (red and _____).

Vardy's experiment is the next step in making robots a part of everyday life. Many see robots as machines that will take care of the three D's of human work: dirty, _____, and _____. Using robots for these tasks could greatly increase productivity, with robots even working alongside humans on _____. There is great promise for tiny _____ that can be used in health care (for example, injecting tiny robots into someone's blood).

E. READING AND THINKING VISUALLY

Select the best answer.

_____ 1. The author likely included the two photos on page 455 in order to

    a. warn readers about the dangers of overreliance on technology.

    b. illustrate, compare, and contrast two different types of robotic technologies discussed in the reading.

    c. imply that robots are much more useful (right now) in businesses rather than households.

    d. argue for greater government funding of projects designed to develop robotic technology for military warfare.

F. FIGURING OUT IMPLIED MEANINGS

Indicate whether each statement is true (T) or false (F).

_____ 1. The author worries that robots may be used for violent purposes.

_____ 2. The author implies that many scientists have tried to imitate nature but have failed.

_____ 3. Quadrotor robots are designed to work under water.

_____ 4. Amazon has found that using Kiva robots has increased its productivity by five times.

_____ 5. The author thinks that most human beings will embrace the idea of robots following them from room to room.

_____ 6. A futurist is someone who predicts the future based on current trends and events.

_____ 7. It is likely that human-style robots, or androids, will become common within the next decade.

_____ 8. Unlike earlier generations of robots, Baxter has the ability to "see" its surroundings.

_____ 9. Most of the androids developed to date have been the work of the military or large, successful corporations.

_____ 10. The mini robots designed by Andrew Vardy are based on the behavior of lizards.

_____ 11. Robots made by Kiva Systems are frequently used in warehouses.

_____ 12. The author believes that robots will soon replace human workers on assembly lines.

G. THINKING CRITICALLY

Select the best answer.

_____ 1. The purpose of this reading selection is to

    a. describe Baxter and other robots in detail while providing a cautionary tale about reliance on technology.

    b. summarize the research of key scientists involved in creating robotic technology.

    c. acquaint readers with the history, present state of, and possible future of robotic technology.

    d. look at the predictions made by famous futurists and then evaluate whether these predictions have come true.

_____ 2. The tone of the reading is best described as

    a. frightened.

    b. informative.

    c. skeptical.

    d. distanced.

_____ 3. Which of the following excerpts from the reading is an opinion, not a fact?

    a. "Andrew Vardy posted footage on YouTube of toy-sized robots." (paragraph 3)

    b. "The ongoing explosion in microprocessing capacity has allowed researchers like McLurkin to equip robots smaller than a hamburger with enough chip space to execute a combination of tasks." (paragraph 6)

    c. "Researchers have yet to find a compact energy source capable of powering swarm robots." (paragraph 17)

    d. "Mini-bots that monitor our mood are just a wee bit creepy." (paragraph 18)

_____ 4. The author discusses the scientific work, research, or inventions of all of the following people *except*

    a. Marshall McCluhan.

    b. Andrew Vardy.

    c. Rodney Brooks.

    d. Akira Mita.

_____ 5. The reading uses the phrase "swarm robotics" (paragraph 5) to mean

    a. the use of multiple small robots to attack a problem and solve it piece by piece.

    b. the use of technology to rid houses and businesses of pests, such as bees and termites.

    c. the use of robots to replace human beings as workers on assembly lines.

    d. the development of affordable robotics on a small scale.

_____ 6. In paragraph 10, the author states, "The 'it' is intentional; Baxter's makers are not into anthropomorphizing." He means that

    a. the Baxter robot is currently the most fashionable piece of technology that a business can buy.

    b. Rethink Robotics does not call Baxter "he" or "she" because it does not believe that robots and humans are at all similar.

c. the man who created Baxter, Rodney Brooks, is a humanitarian who sees Baxter as a friend and companion.

d. unlike its predecessors, Baxter can "see" through its vision array, which makes it much more effective at more complicated tasks.

H. BUILDING VOCABULARY

Context

Using context and a dictionary, if necessary, determine the meaning of each word as it is used in the selection.

_____ 1. inevitable (paragraph 1)
- a. large
- b. aggressive
- c. dangerous
- d. unavoidable

_____ 2. rudimentary (paragraph 2)
- a. rude
- b. splendid
- c. troublesome
- d. basic

_____ 3. banal (paragraph 4)
- a. terrifying
- b. poisonous
- c. commonplace
- d. timely

_____ 4. stymied (paragraph 5)
- a. stopped
- b. destroyed
- c. disassembled
- d. used

_____ 5. prosaic (paragraph 7)
- a. small
- b. supportive
- c. matter-of-fact
- d. possible

_____ 6. glum (paragraph 15)

    a. candy

    b. educated

    c. respected

    d. depressed

Word Parts

> **A REVIEW OF PREFIXES**
> _____
>
> **AUTO-** means *one's own*
> **OMNI-** means *all*

Use your knowledge of word parts and the review above to fill in the blanks in the following sentences.

1. **Autonomous** means working on one's own; therefore, in paragraph 4, **autonomous machines** are machines that act independently, or on their _____.

2. **Omni-directional** (paragraph 6) means movement in _____ directions.

Unusual Words/Understanding Idioms

Match the idiomatic boldfaced word or phrase in Column A with its definition in Column B.

Column A	Column B
_____ 1. low-tech (paragraph 1)	a. old-fashioned; not technologically sophisticated
_____ 2. wrinkle (paragraph 3)	b. chattering with excitement and enthusiasm
_____ 3. cheek-by-jowl (paragraph 4)	c. side by side
_____ 4. big-box (paragraph 8)	d. crammed full of things or people
_____ 5. abuzz (paragraph 10)	e. a large retail store known for selling one type of product, such as appliances or sporting goods
_____ 6. chock-a-block (paragraph 13)	f. a useful innovation, information, or piece of advice

I. SELECTING A LEARNING/STUDY STRATEGY

Select the best answer.

_____ 1. Which of the following would not be an effective strategy for reading and studying this selection?

    a. creating a time line of robotic technology, with a brief description of each technological advance

    b. reading the selection twice, highlighting the reading on the second read-through

    c. writing a summary of the reading

    d. creating flash cards of the vocabulary terms defined in the margins

J. EXPLORING IDEAS THROUGH DISCUSSION AND WRITING

1. Keeping the reading's central thought and main ideas in mind, write a caption to accompany the two photos on page 455.

2. Brainstorm a list of daily, tiresome chores. Do any of these chores require absolutely no human thought or decision making? How does your answer to this question relate to some of the main ideas and details in the reading?

3. Evaluate the predictions of Thomas Frey, the futurist quoted in paragraph 16. Do you agree with his predictions? Why or why not? Write a paragraph in which you respond to Frey's predictions.

4. The reading refers to the images of technology and robots that Hollywood has presented to society (paragraph 9). How do movies' presentation of robotic technology match or differ from the facts presented in this reading?

5. Which piece of technology has had the largest impact on your life? How has that technology affected your life?

K. BEYOND THE CLASSROOM TO THE WEB

Conduct an Internet search for Honda's Asimo. Print out a photo of Asimo and share it with your classmates. Summarize its key features.

TRACKING YOUR PROGRESS

Selection 18		
Section	**Number Correct**	**Score**
A. Thesis and Main Ideas (4 items)	_____ × 3	_____
B. Details (5 items)	_____ × 3	_____
C. Organization and Transitions (3 items)	_____ × 2	_____
E. Reading and Thinking Visually (1 item)	_____ × 3	_____
F. Implied Meanings (12 items)	_____ × 2	_____
G. Thinking Critically (6 items)	_____ × 2	_____
H. Vocabulary		
Context (6 items)	_____ × 2	_____
Word Parts (2 items)	_____ × 2	_____
Unusual words (6 items)	_____ × 2	_____
	Total Score	_____%

15 Health-Related Fields

"Nothing can be more important than your health." This is an overused saying, but it remains meaningful. As the medical field and health-care systems become more complex, as medical knowledge expands, and as technology plays an ever-increasing role in diagnosis and treatment, medical personnel, patients, and patients' families face new and difficult challenges, decisions, and dilemmas. In "Medical Technology and Ethical Issues," you will read about how a computer program is used to make decisions about who to treat first in emergency situations. In "When Living Is a Fate Worse Than Death," you will read about the question of whether to end the life of a critically ill child.

While the health field presents many challenges and issues, it also offers new and exciting innovations and opportunities for new treatment options. When reading "A Step Beyond Human," you will learn about changes in the field of prosthetics (artificial limbs) and see what one man has contributed to the field.

Use the following tips when reading in the health-related fields.

TIPS FOR READING IN HEALTH-RELATED FIELDS	

- **Learn necessary terminology.** Each of the articles in this chapter uses some technical and specialized terms. Reading in the field and speaking with health-care professionals will be much easier if you have a mastery of basic terminology.

- **Learn the basics about human body systems.** You have to know how your body works in order to take care of it and to understand readings in the field. For example, in reading "When Living Is a Fate Worse Than Death," you need to know about brain functioning.

- **Read critically.** There are many different viewpoints, different proposed cures, numerous lose-20-pounds-in-a-week diets, and many "miracle" exercise programs. Read critically, ask questions, and look for supporting evidence. As you read "Medical Technology and Ethical Issues," for example, which is about using computers to make decisions about patient treatment and care, ask questions such as "How reliable are these programs?" and "What are the implications if a computer program makes a faulty recommendation?"

Medical Technology and Ethical Issues

SELECTION 19

William E. Thompson and Joseph V. Hickey

**TEXTBOOK
EXCERPT**
Contemporary
Issues Reading

This selection is taken from the health and medicine chapter of the textbook *Society in Focus: An Introduction to Sociology*. Read it to find out about the use of computer technology in determining a patient's treatment in the emergency room.

PREVIEWING THE READING

Using the steps listed on pages 40–41, preview the reading selection. When you have finished, complete the following items.

1. The computer program that is the focus of this selection is referred to as _____ .

2. The title indicates that the authors are interested in the relationship between _____ and _____ .

MAKING CONNECTIONS

What has been your experience with medical technology? Think about the last time you were in a doctor's office, clinic, or hospital and the different forms of technology that were used as part of your medical care.

READING TIP

As you read, highlight the arguments put forth by both critics and supporters of the RIP computer system.

Medical Technology and Ethical Issues

1   With sirens blaring and lights flashing, the ambulance skids to a halt in front of the hospital emergency room entrance. A swarm of medical personnel descend on the ambulance as its drivers and the paramedics who are aboard fling open its door and unload the cargo. The patient is wheeled through the automatic doors of the

triage
the area in a
hospital where a
patient's
condition is
assessed and the
order of treatment
for all patients
is determined
according to
urgency

hospital and rushed down the corridor toward the emergency room **triage**. While nurses and emergency room physicians monitor vital signs and start an intravenous solution, one doctor races over to a desk and hands a clipboard to a staff person who is sitting in front of a computer and who carefully begins to enter data.

2   The computer program is referred to simply as RIP. In emergency rooms across the country and around the world, this computer program is helping doctors make informed decisions about whether to administer life-saving treatments or simply allow patients to die. Using statistical probability, the program analyzes all of the input on a particular patient and makes a prognosis on the likelihood of survival. If the probability is 95 percent or better that the patient is going to die, regardless of treatment, it is recommended that treatment not be administered. However, if the odds are greater than 5 percent that the patient will survive, the computer not only indicates the probability of survival but also prints out recommended treatment procedures. All of this happens in milliseconds.

3   Critics of the new computerized system contend that it is a frightening example of overreliance on computer technology to make decisions that were once reserved for human judgment. Medical ethicist Arthur Caplan of Philadelphia argues that computers should not be used to make decisions about the allocation of medical resources to patients and points out that the computer will be wrong in about 5 percent of all cases. Supporters of the new technology insist that the computer does not make any decisions. Rather, it provides data and information that allow trained medical personnel to make more informed decisions about how to allocate very expensive treatment procedures and how to use most effectively limited medical resources, such as intensive care beds and organs for transplants. Armed with this information, doctors can better determine who should and should not be treated. David Bihari, a critical care specialist in England, points out that because of a lack of intensive care facilities, as many as one in four patients may have to be turned away from British hospitals. A computer program such as RIP provides physicians with vital information about who is most likely to benefit from treatment and who is not.

4   While medical doctors and ethicists debate the merits of using a computer program such as RIP, sociologists are more interested in the social ramifications of such procedures. Decisions about who to treat and how to treat them have always been part of the dynamics of emergency rooms. How important have social variables such as race, gender, age, and social class been in the past? Might a computer be less likely to discriminate on the basis of these and other social characteristics? However, what is lost when the human dimension is subordinated to computer technology in medical decision making? These and other sociological issues are likely to become even more pronounced as more sophisticated medical technology, combined with an increasing demand on medical services, forces physicians and health-care workers around the world to make even more decisions about who should and should not receive their services.

5   Less controversially, emergency rooms across the United States routinely use a doctor-friendly computerized database that, within 60 seconds of inputting symptoms provides a diagnosis and preferred method of treatment in pediatric emergency cases. And what contemporary doctor's office, medical clinic, or hospital would be complete today without computers, X-ray machines, and even sophisticated magnetic resonance imaging and laser technologies?

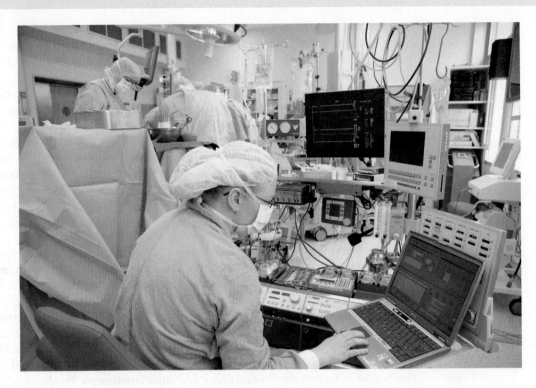

6   The question is not whether technology is going to alter the future course of health and medical care in the United States and around the world but, more important, where we draw the line. Medical ethicists today are debating issues ranging from the use of biogenetic engineering to create life, to the use of fetal organs for transplant and the treatment of Alzheimer's disease, to euthanasia and doctor-assisted suicides. The world was stunned when the parents of a teenage daughter who needed a kidney transplant but couldn't find a perfect match decided to have another child for the express purpose of providing an organ donor. Reports that starving people in developing nations may sell their organs on a black market, from which the organs eventually find their way to the United States and Europe for transplant, provide frightening science fiction–like scenarios for the future. The rapid development of medical knowledge and technology has created what some call an "ethical minefield." From a sociological viewpoint, these and other issues may be ruled on from medical, legal, and religious perspectives but will continue to be debated and ultimately decided in a larger social arena, where attitudes, values, beliefs, and important norms regarding technology, health, and medical care are created, transmitted, and transformed through the process of social interaction.

7   Sociologists have long understood that technology often develops at a much faster rate than the public's ability to grasp its consequences and to rethink the important values, attitudes, norms, and beliefs that surround its uses. Nowhere is this cultural lag more evident than in the case of the revolutionary technological developments in medical and health care. As one sociologist noted, "medical ethics is an arena in which sociologists can revisit issues about the doctor–patient relationship . . . the meaning of death and dying, and the character of the medical profession."

TAKING A CLOSER LOOK

Some people contend that the major purpose of health care and medicine is to sustain and prolong life and that technological developments that allow us to do so should be used without hesitation. Others argue that medical technology has developed at such a rapid pace that the most important issue today is not whether we can sustain and prolong life almost indefinitely, but whether we *should*. On which side of this debate would you most closely align your position? Why? What do you think of computer programs such as RIP? How will they affect emergency room care? What ethical dilemmas are presented by this and other types of medical technology?

A. UNDERSTANDING THE THESIS AND OTHER MAIN IDEAS

Select the best answer.

_____ 1. The authors' primary purpose in this selection is to

    a. debate the use of computerized systems in hospital emergency rooms.

    b. describe the different types of technology used in medical situations.

    c. discuss sociological and ethical issues related to medical technology.

    d. compare critical care procedures in England with those in the United States.

_____ 2. The topic of paragraph 2 is

    a. emergency room care.

    b. the RIP computer program.

    c. health-care workers.

    d. medical technology.

_____ 3. The main idea of paragraph 4 is that sociologists are primarily interested in the

    a. merits of medical technology.

    b. increasing demand on medical services.

    c. human dimension of decision making.

    d. sociological implications of medical technology.

_____ 4. The main argument of supporters of the new computerized system is that it

    a. allows untrained personnel to make high-level decisions.

    b. makes more reliable decisions and fewer mistakes than humans.

    c. provides data to help doctors make more informed decisions.

    d. reduces the possibility of discrimination in treatment decisions.

_____ 5. The statement that best expresses the main idea of paragraph 6 is:

    a. The development of medical technology has created debate about how it should be used.

    b. Medical ethicists are debating the use of biogenetic engineering to create life.

    c. Technology issues must be ruled on from medical, legal, and religious perspectives.

    d. The process of social interaction transforms beliefs about technology and health care.

B. IDENTIFYING DETAILS

Indicate which of the following claims were made by medical ethicist Arthur Caplan (AC) and which were made by critical care specialist David Bihari (DB).

_____ 1. Computers should not be used to make decisions about the allocation of medical resources to patients.

_____ 2. As many as one in four patients may be turned away from British hospitals because of a lack of intensive care facilities.

_____ 3. The computer will be wrong in about 5 percent of all cases.

C. RECOGNIZING METHODS OF ORGANIZATION AND TRANSITIONS

Select the best answer.

_____ 1. In paragraph 1, the organizational pattern the authors use to describe a patient's arrival at the emergency room is

    a. definition.

    b. classification.

    c. cause and effect.

    d. time sequence.

_____ 2. In paragraph 3, the authors use the comparison and contrast pattern to discuss the difference between

    a. supporters and critics of the new computerized system.

    b. expensive treatment procedures and limited resources.

    c. health care in the United States and England.

    d. conventional medical treatment and new medical technology.

_____ 3. The transitional word or phrase in paragraph 3 that indicates examples will follow is

    a. rather.

    b. such as.

    c. as many as.

    d. because.

D. REVIEWING AND ORGANIZING IDEAS: MAPPING

Complete the map (p. 474) of the process described in paragraphs 1 and 2 by filling in the blanks.

E. READING AND THINKING VISUALLY

Answer the following questions.

1. What does the photograph (p. 470) show?

_____

2. What concepts in the selection are illustrated by the photograph?

_____

_____

3. What is the purpose of the box titled "Taking a Closer Look"?

_____

_____

F. FIGURING OUT IMPLIED MEANINGS

Each of the following boldfaced words has a strong positive or negative connotation. Make inferences by indicating whether the word creates a positive (P) or negative (N) image for the reader.

_____ 1. "With sirens **blaring** and lights flashing, the ambulance skids to a halt in front of the hospital emergency room entrance." (paragraph 1)

_____ 2. "Critics of the new computerized system contend that it is a **frightening** example of overreliance on computer technology . . ." (paragraph 3)

_____ 3. "[I]t provides data and information that allow trained medical personnel to make more **informed** decisions . . ." (paragraph 3)

_____ 4. "[E]mergency rooms across the United States routinely use a doctor-**friendly** computerized database . . ." (paragraph 5)

_____ 5. "Reports that **starving** people in developing nations may sell their organs on a black market . . . provide frightening, science fiction–like scenarios." (paragraph 6)

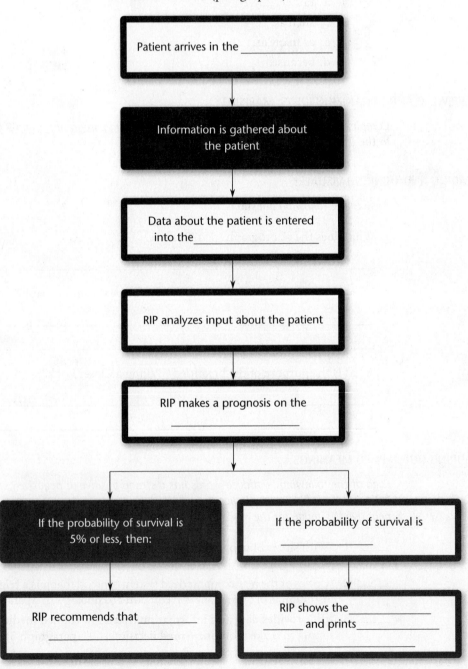

G. THINKING CRITICALLY

Select the best answer.

_____ 1. The authors begin the selection by describing a patient's arrival at the hospital in order to illustrate
   a. the importance of each member of a medical team.
   b. the authors' personal experience in an emergency room.
   c. common mistakes in emergency room procedures.
   d. how computerized technology is used in emergency rooms.

_____ 2. In the first paragraph of the selection, the authors are striving to create a sense of
   a. detachment.
   b. formality.
   c. urgency.
   d. enthusiasm.

_____ 3. The authors pose several questions in paragraph 4 primarily to
   a. persuade the reader that the benefits of medical technology are worth the costs.
   b. get the reader thinking about sociological issues related to medical technology.
   c. demonstrate to the reader that discrimination exists in the health-care system.
   d. remind the reader of the importance of technology in medical decision making.

_____ 4. The phrase "ethical minefield" in paragraph 6 refers to the
   a. explosive growth in the field of medical technology.
   b. hidden and unexpected ethical problems created by medical technology.
   c. use of medical technology in a war setting.
   d. belief that medical technology has caused more harm than good.

_____ 5. The intended audience for this selection is most likely to be
   a. sociology students.
   b. health care professionals.
   c. hospital administrators.
   d. medical ethicists.

H. BUILDING VOCABULARY

Context

Using context and a dictionary, if necessary, determine the meaning of each word as it is used in the selection.

_____ 1. prognosis (paragraph 2)

    a. prediction

    b. allowance

    c. oversight

    d. dismissal

_____ 2. contend (paragraph 3)

    a. nominate

    b. compete

    c. argue

    d. challenge

_____ 3. allocation (paragraph 3)

    a. distribution

    b. connection

    c. opposition

    d. dispute

_____ 4. merits (paragraph 4)

    a. concerns

    b. charges

    c. problems

    d. benefits

_____ 5. ramifications (paragraph 4)

    a. penalties

    b. consequences

    c. conclusions

    d. obstacles

_____ 6. lag (paragraph 7)

    a. region

    b. point

    c. delay

    d. rate

Word Parts

A REVIEW OF PREFIXES, ROOTS, AND SUFFIXES

INTRA   means *within, into, in*
MILLI-   means *thousand*
SUB-   means *under, below*
RE-   means *back, again*
TRANS-   means *cross, over*
SPECT   means *look, see*
LOG   means *study, thought*
-IST   means *one who*

Use your knowledge of word parts and the review above to match each word in Column A with its meaning in Column B.

	Column A	Column B
_____	1. intravenous	a. one who specializes in ethical issues
_____	2. milliseconds	b. placed in a secondary or lower position
_____	3. ethicist	c. consider again
_____	4. sociologist	d. into the vein
_____	5. subordinated	e. sent across
_____	6. perspectives	f. thousandths of a second
_____	7. transmitted	g. viewpoints
_____	8. revisit	h. one who studies society and human behavior

Unusual Words/Understanding Idioms

Use the meanings given below to write a sentence using the boldfaced word or phrase.

1. A **swarm** (paragraph 1) means a large group, especially one that is in motion.

   Your sentence: _____

   _____

2. The term **black market** (paragraph 6) refers to the unlawful buying and selling of goods; in this selection, the "goods" are human organs.

   Your sentence: _____

   _____

I. SELECTING A LEARNING/STUDY STRATEGY

Discuss what method(s) you would use to learn this material in preparation for a multiple-choice test.

J. EXPLORING IDEAS THROUGH DISCUSSION AND WRITING

1. Reread the three questions posed by the authors in paragraph 4 and discuss your response to each one.
2. In the box titled "Taking a Closer Look," the authors ask several questions related to medical technology and ethical issues. Choose one of the questions and write an essay answering it.
3. Evaluate the introduction to this selection. How well did it capture your attention and introduce the topic?

K. BEYOND THE CLASSROOM TO THE WEB

The reading discusses the ethical issues involved with several types of medical technology. Medicine has many other ethical questions related to it, including: Should research on stem cells be permitted? Should people be allowed to end their own lives? Who should get the limited number of donated organs? (Each year, there are many more organs needed than are donated.) Conduct a Web search to find information and differing opinions about one of these topics. Summarize the key controversies and the "pro" and "con" arguments made about the topic.

TRACKING YOUR PROGRESS

Selection 19

Section	Number Correct		Score
A. Thesis and Main Ideas (5 items)	_____	× 4	_____
B. Details (3 items)	_____	× 5	_____
C. Organization and Transitions (3 items)	_____	× 5	_____
F. Implied Meanings (5 items)	_____	× 2	_____
G. Thinking Critically (5 items)	_____	× 4	_____
H. Vocabulary			
Context (6 items)	_____	× 2	_____
Word Parts (8 items)	_____	× 1	_____
		Total Score	_____ %

SELECTION 20

When Living Is a Fate Worse Than Death

Christine Mitchell

Contemporary Issues Reading

This reading first appeared in *Newsweek,* a newsmagazine. The author, a medical ethicist, describes a dilemma faced by hospital staff in treating a young child.

PREVIEWING THE READING

Using the steps listed on pages 40–41, preview the reading selection. When you have finished, complete the following statements.

1. The title indicates that the selection is about a situation in which living is worse than _____.

2. Most of the action in the selection takes place in a _____.

 MAKING CONNECTIONS

Imagine that you are responsible for deciding whether to withhold further treatment from someone who is terminally ill. What factors would you consider in your decision?

READING TIP

As you read, highlight reasons that support the child's right to die.

trachea
the windpipe that carries air from the larynx to the lungs

coded
the action taken by medical professionals to restart a person's heart after it has stopped beating

ICU
the intensive care unit of a hospital

When Living Is a Fate Worse Than Death

1   The baby died last winter. It was pretty terrible. Little Charlotte (not her real name) lay on a high white bed, surrounded by nurses and doctors pushing drugs into her veins, tubes into her **trachea** and needles into her heart, trying as hard as they could to take over for her failing body and brain. She was being **coded**, as they say in the **ICU**. It had happened several times before, but this time it would fail. Her parents, who were working, weren't there.

2   Charlotte was born with too few brain cells to do much more than breathe and pull away from pain. Most of her malformed brain was wrapped in a sac that grew outside her skull and had to be surgically removed to prevent immediate death.

3   Her parents were a young, unmarried couple from Haiti. They loved Charlotte and wanted her to live. The nurses and doctors thought she should be allowed to die peacefully. They recommended that a Do Not Resuscitate order be placed in Charlotte's chart. The new parents disagreed. Surely, they thought, medical care in the United States could save their baby. They bought their daughter a doll.

ER
the emergency room of a hospital

ethicist
a specialist in ethics, the rules or standards guiding the conduct and decisions of members of a profession

4   For 16 months Charlotte bounced back and forth—between hospital, home, the **ER** and pediatric nursing homes. Wherever she was, every time her body tried to die, nurses and doctors staved off death. Each time, Charlotte got weaker.

5   Charlotte's medical team at the hospital asked to talk with the Ethics Advisory Committee and, as the hospital's **ethicist**, I got involved. Is it right to keep doing painful things just to keep Charlotte alive a little longer, her doctors and nurses asked us. To whom are we most obligated: the patient or the family? The committee advised that in this case the parents' rights superseded the caregivers' beliefs about what was right. Painful procedures should be avoided, the panel believed, but the care that Charlotte's parents wanted for her should be provided unless there was a medical consensus that it would not prolong her life. Such a consensus was elusive. There's almost always another procedure that can be tried to eke out a little more time until the patient dies despite everything—as Charlotte did.

6   A week after Charlotte's death, I met with the doctors, nurses and therapists who had done everything they could for her and yet felt terrible about having done too much. We talked for almost two hours about how Charlotte had died.

7   "It was horrible," said a doctor. "We tried to resuscitate her for over an hour. It's the worst thing I've ever done. I actually felt sick." A nurse talked about the holes that were drilled in Charlotte's bones to insert lines they couldn't get in anywhere else.

8   Why didn't Charlotte's parents spare Charlotte—and us—the awfulness of her death? Because they were too young? Too hopeful? Because they were distrustful of white nurses and doctors who they thought might really be saying that their black baby wasn't worth saving? Or because they believed that a "good" death is one in which everything possible has been tried?

9   Why didn't the hospital staff, including the ethics committee, save Charlotte from that kind of death? Maybe we feared that her parents would take us to court, like the mother in Virginia who got a judge to order the hospital to provide lifesaving treatment for her anencephalic baby, who was born without most of her brain. Maybe we were afraid of seeing ourselves in the news—as the staff of a Pennsylvania hospital did when they withdrew life support, against the parents' wishes, from a comatose 3-year-old with fatal brain cancer. Maybe we were thinking about what was best for the parents, not just the child. Maybe we were wrong.

10   The nurse sitting next to me at the meeting had driven two hours from the nursing home where she used to care for Charlotte. She had attended the wake. She said the parents had sobbed; that Dad said he felt terrible because he wasn't there when his little girl died, that Mom still couldn't believe that she was dead.

11   It could have been different. They could have been there holding her. That's the way it happens most of the time in ICUs today. Family and staff make the decision together, machines are removed and death comes gently.

12   As a hospital ethicist, a large part of my job is helping staff and families distinguish between sustaining life and prolonging death. Sometimes I join the staff, as I did that night, in second-guessing decisions and drawing distinctions between the dignified

death of a child held by parents who accept their child's dying, and the death that occurs amid technologically desperate measures and professional strangers.

13   Sooner or later, every person will die. I wish, and the hospital staff I work with wishes, almost beyond telling, that people could know what they are asking when they ask that "everything" be done.

A. UNDERSTANDING THE THESIS AND OTHER MAIN IDEAS

Select the best answer.

_____ 1. The author's primary purpose is to
  a. describe the current technology used in hospitals to prolong life.
  b. explain that hospital personnel grieve along with a patient's family when the patient dies.
  c. contrast the rights of a patient's family with the beliefs of caregivers.
  d. argue that prolonging life is sometimes worse than letting the patient die peacefully.

_____ 2. The main idea of paragraph 3 is that
  a. Charlotte's parents were young and from another country.
  b. Charlotte's parents disagreed with the hospital staff about what was best for her.
  c. a Do Not Resuscitate order should have been placed in Charlotte's chart.
  d. Charlotte's parents believed that U.S. medical care should have been able to save her.

_____ 3. The Ethics Advisory Board ruled that
  a. the Ethics Advisory Committee made the wrong recommendation.
  b. there are many possible procedures that can be done to prolong life.
  c. the hospital staff would have to provide the care that Charlotte's parents wanted for her.
  d. it was difficult to reach a medical consensus about Charlotte's care.

_____ 4. The question that the author is asking in paragraph 9 is
  a. Would Charlotte's parents have taken the hospital staff to court?
  b. Would the hospital staff have been on the news because of their treatment of Charlotte?
  c. Was the staff thinking about what was best for the parents or for Charlotte?
  d. Why didn't the hospital staff do something to change the way that Charlotte died?

_____ 5. The main idea of paragraph 11 is expressed in the

    a. first sentence.

    b. second sentence.

    c. third sentence.

    d. fourth sentence.

B. IDENTIFYING DETAILS

Indicate whether each statement is true (T) or false (F).

_____ 1. Charlotte's parents were from Haiti.

_____ 2. Charlotte was in the hospital because she had developed brain cancer.

_____ 3. Charlotte lived her entire life in the hospital.

_____ 4. The hospital's Ethics Advisory Committee believed the staff should avoid painful procedures for Charlotte.

_____ 5. After Charlotte died, the hospital staff wished that they had tried more techniques to save her.

_____ 6. The nurse who attended the wake said the parents were angry at the hospital.

_____ 7. Charlotte's parents were not at the hospital with Charlotte when she died.

C. RECOGNIZING METHODS OF ORGANIZATION AND TRANSITIONS

Select the best answer.

_____ 1. The organizational pattern that the author uses to describe events in the order in which they occurred during Charlotte's brief life is

    a. time sequence.

    b. definition.

    c. enumeration.

    d. comparison and contrast.

_____ 2. Throughout the reading, the author uses the comparison and contrast organizational pattern to contrast the opinions of

    a. Charlotte's medical team and the Ethics Advisory Committee.

    b. Charlotte's parents and the hospital staff.

    c. Charlotte's parents and the Ethics Advisory Committee.

    d. the hospital ethicist and Charlotte's medical team.

D. REVIEWING AND ORGANIZING IDEAS: PARAPHRASING

Complete the following paraphrases of paragraphs 4 and 11 by filling in the missing words or phrases.

Paragraph 4: Charlotte was moved between the _____, her _____, the hospital's _____, and pediatric _____ for _____ months. Whenever she came close to _____, nurses and _____ were able to hold it off, but she grew _____ each time it happened.

Paragraph 11: Charlotte's _____ could have been different if her _____ had been there holding her. It usually happens like that now in _____. Together, the patient's _____ and the hospital _____ decide to remove the _____ and let _____ come peacefully.

E. READING AND THINKING VISUALLY

Select the best answer.

_____ 1. Unlike many of the reading selections in this book, "When Living Is a Fate Worse Than Death" does not include any visual aids. What is the most likely explanation for why the author did not include a photo of baby Charlotte?

   a. No photos were available of baby Charlotte.

   b. The topic is very sensitive and the author felt that including a photo of baby Charlotte would not be tasteful or respectful of the baby's memory.

   c. The hospital would not permit any photos to be taken of baby Charlotte.

   d. The bereaved parents would not allow any photos of baby Charlotte to be printed.

F. FIGURING OUT IMPLIED MEANINGS

Indicate whether each statement is true (T) or false (F).

_____ 1. Charlotte's parents believed that the medical care in the United States was better than the medical care in Haiti.

_____ 2. Because of her condition at birth, Charlotte always would have been dependent on medical care even if she had survived longer.

_____ 3. It can be inferred that the white hospital staff was prejudiced against the black couple and their baby.

_____ 4. A hospital ethicist helps make decisions about removing life support for terminally ill patients.

_____ 5. The hospital Ethics Advisory Committee thought that Charlotte would eventually get better.

G. THINKING CRITICALLY

Select the best answer.

_____ 1. The author supports her central thesis with
   a. examples.
   b. descriptions.
   c. personal experience.
   d. all of the above.

_____ 2. The tone of the selection can best be described as
   a. angry.
   b. concerned.
   c. objective.
   d. optimistic.

_____ 3. The author wrote the first paragraph in order to
   a. gain sympathy for the baby's parents.
   b. explain why the lifesaving efforts failed.
   c. describe the awfulness of the baby's death.
   d. suggest that every effort had not been made to save the baby's life.

_____ 4. Of the following statements from paragraph 1, the only one that is an *opinion* is
   a. "The baby died last winter."
   b. "It was pretty terrible."
   c. "Charlotte . . . lay on a high white bed, surrounded by nurses and doctors."
   d. "She was being coded."

_____ 5. The author included the statement "They bought their daughter a doll" (paragraph 3) in order to indicate that
   a. the parents were not poor.
   b. Charlotte was able to play.
   c. the parents were hopeful that Charlotte would be all right.
   d. the hospital did not provide toys.

_____ 6. The author speculates that the parents let their child's death happen the way it did because they may have

  a. been too young and hopeful.

  b. distrusted the commitment of white doctors and nurses toward their black baby.

  c. believed that death should come only after every possible procedure had been tried.

  d. all of the above.

_____ 7. In paragraph 12, the author considers the decisions that were made in this case by comparing

  a. her responsibilities as an ethicist with those of the medical caregivers.

  b. her beliefs with those of the parents.

  c. the ICUs of today with the traditional ICUs of the past.

  d. a peaceful, dignified death with the kind that occurs only after desperate medical efforts have failed.

H. BUILDING VOCABULARY

Context
Using context and a dictionary, if necessary, determine the meaning of each word as it is used in the selection.

_____ 1. resuscitate (paragraph 3)

  a. disturb

  b. revive

  c. allow

  d. review

_____ 2. elusive (paragraph 5)

  a. difficult to reach

  b. temporary

  c. permanent

  d. unlucky

_____ 3. eke (paragraph 5)

  a. harm

  b. leave out

  c. draw out

  d. hide

_____ 4. comatose (paragraph 9)

    a. diagnosed

    b. unconscious

    c. terminally ill

    d. recovering

Word Parts

> ### A REVIEW OF PREFIXES AND SUFFIXES
>
> **MAL-**   means *poorly* or *wrongly*
> **SUPER-** means *above*
> **-IST**   means *one who*

Use your knowledge of word parts and the review above to fill in the blanks in the following sentences.

1. The word **malformed** (paragraph 2) means _____

    _____.

2. The word **superseded** (paragraph 5) means to have been put _____ in importance.

3. A person who provides therapy is called a _____ (paragraph 6).

I. SELECTING A LEARNING/STUDY STRATEGY

Select the best answer.

_____ 1. If you were using this article as a source for a paper on the right-to-die issue, which of the following techniques would be most helpful?

    a. highlighting useful information and quotations

    b. drawing a time line

    c. rereading the article

    d. summarizing the parents' opinions

J. EXPLORING IDEAS THROUGH DISCUSSION AND WRITING

1. What do you consider a "good" death?

2. Do you agree more with the author or with those who would do everything possible to prevent, or delay, death?

3. What does the author mean by the phrase "almost beyond telling" (paragraph 13)?

K. BEYOND THE CLASSROOM TO THE WEB

One of the benefits of the Web is its ability to create online "support communities" for those who have suffered a loss or are struggling with personal issues. Sometimes these communities offer bulletin boards where people can ask and answer questions, offer advice, and make suggestions for coping. Think about a common emotional problem people may have (for example, troubled children or the death of a spouse) and conduct a Web search for an online support group. What types of resources does the Web site offer?

TRACKING YOUR PROGRESS

Selection 20

Section	Number Correct	Score
A. Thesis and Main Ideas (5 items)	_____ × 5	_____
B. Details (7 items)	_____ × 3	_____
C. Organization and Transitions (2 items)	_____ × 3	_____
E. Reading and Thinking Visually (1 item)	_____ × 3	_____
F. Implied Meanings (5 items)	_____ × 2	_____
G. Thinking Critically (7 items)	_____ × 3	_____
H. Vocabulary		
Context (4 items)	_____ × 2	_____
Word Parts (3 items)	_____ × 2	_____
	Total Score	_____%

A Step Beyond Human

Andy Greenberg

Andy Greenberg

Contemporary
Issues Reading

This selection first appeared in a December 2009 issue of *Forbes* magazine. Read the article to find out how and why one man is working to transform the field of artificial limbs.

PREVIEWING THE READING

Using the steps listed on pages 40–41, preview the reading selection. When you have finished, complete the following items.

1. The subject of this selection is a man named _____ .

2. List three questions you expect to be able to answer after reading the article.

   a. _____

   b. _____

   c. _____

 MAKING
CONNECTIONS   *Do you know anyone with a disability? Think about how you define "disability."*

READING TIP

As you read, highlight descriptions of the different prosthetic devices developed and/or used by Hugh Herr.

A Step Beyond Human

1   On his way to a lunch meeting a few years ago Hugh Herr was running late. So he parked his Honda Accord in a handicapped parking spot, sprang out of the car and jogged down the sidewalk. Within seconds a policeman called out, asking to see his disability permit. When Herr pointed it out on his dashboard, the cop eyed him suspiciously. "What's your affliction?" he asked dryly.

2   Herr, a slim and unassuming 6-footer with dark, neatly parted hair, took a step toward the officer and responded in an even tone: "I have no [expletive] legs."

Cyborg evangelist: Herr wears a pair of his disability-defying PowerFoot devices.

3

biomechatronics
an applied science combining elements of biology, mechanics, and electronics, as well as robotics and neuroscience

4

prosthetics
artificial limbs

crampons
spikes attached to shoes for ice climbing

5

inertia
in physics, the tendency of a body to maintain its state of rest or uniform motion unless acted upon by an external force

Blurring the boundaries of disability is a trick that Herr, director of the **biomechatronics** group at MIT's Media Lab, has spent the last 27 years perfecting. At age 17 both of Herr's legs were amputated 6 inches below the knee after a rock climbing trip ended in severe frostbite. Today he's one of the world's preeminent **prosthetics** experts. His goal: to build artificial limbs that are superior to natural ones. His favorite test subject: himself. "I like to say that there are no disabled people," says Herr, 45. "Only disabled technology."

Herr swaps his feet out to suit his needs. He generally walks on flat carbon-fiber springs inside his shoes but sometimes replaces them with longer carbon bows for jogging. When he goes rock climbing—often scaling cliffs of expert-level difficulty—he switches to one of multiple pairs of climbing legs he's built himself, including small, rubber feet on aluminum poles that stretch his height beyond 7 feet, spiked aluminum claws that replace **crampons** for ice climbing or tapered polyethylene hatchets that wedge into crevices. "The fact that I'm missing lower limbs is an opportunity," he says. "Between my residual limb and the ground, I can create anything I want. The only limits are physical laws and my imagination."

Over the last several years that imagination has been working overtime. Late next year iWalk, a company Herr founded in 2006, plans to release the PowerFoot One, the world's most advanced robotic ankle and foot. Most prosthetic feet are fixed at a clumsy 90 degrees. The PowerFoot, equipped with three internal microprocessors and 12 sensors that measure force, **inertia** and position, automatically adjusts its angle, stiffness and damping 500 times a second. Employing the same sort of sensory feedback loops that the human nervous system uses, plus a library of known patterns, the PowerFoot adjusts for slopes, dips its toe naturally when walking down stairs, even hangs casually when the user crosses his or her legs.

6   The PowerFoot is the only foot and ankle in the world that doesn't depend on its wearer's energy. With a system of passive springs and a half-pound rechargeable lithium iron phosphate battery, the foot—made of aluminum, titanium, plastic and carbon fiber—provides the same 20-joule push off the ground that human muscles and tendons do. It automatically adjusts the power to the walker's speed, but users can also dial that power up or down with a Bluetooth-enabled phone. (And soon, Herr says, with an iPhone application.) One test subject told Herr that his nonamputated leg often tires before his prosthetic-enhanced one. "This is the first time that the prosthesis is driving the human, instead of the other way around," says Herr.

7   Herr frequently wears a pair of his new creations. The next to try the PowerFoot will be the Department of Defense, which is looking for prostheses for the nearly 1,000 soldiers who have lost limbs in Iraq and Afghanistan. The Veterans Administration and the Army are among the investors who funded his MIT research. Veterans, he argues, also make the perfect early adopters, given their athletic, active lifestyles. "These are remarkable people," says Herr. "If the PowerFoot can work for them, it can work for anyone." iWalk hopes to put the PowerFoot on the general market in 2010, priced in the low five figures. The startup has raised $10.2 million from investors, including General Catalyst Partners and WFD Ventures.

8   Herr's motives extend beyond profit. In 1982 he and a friend climbed Mount Washington in New Hampshire, a place infamous for its unpredictable and nasty weather. They were caught in a snowstorm, losing their way in a near-complete whiteout and subzero temperatures. After three and a half days of crawling along a frozen river, Herr's lower legs were practically destroyed by cold. A member of the rescue team sent after them, 28-year-old Albert Dow, was killed in an avalanche. "I feel a responsibility to use my intellect and resources to do as much as I can to help people. That's Albert Dow's legacy for me," says Herr.

9   Within three months of his amputations Herr was rock climbing with simple prosthetics. Within six months he was in a machine shop, building new feet, using the skills he'd learned at a vocational high school in Lancaster, Pa., where he grew up.

10   While he had previously focused on merely working a trade, Herr became a nearly obsessive student, earning a master's in mechanical engineering at MIT and a Ph.D. in biophysics at Harvard. Once, when his hands suffered from repetitive stress disorder while he was writing his doctoral thesis, he attached a pencil to a pair of sunglass frames and typed with his head. "He's driven to the point of exhaustion, physical degradation," says Rodger Kram, a professor of integrative physiology at the University of Colorado at Boulder, who worked with Herr at Harvard. "Every step he takes, he's forced to think about making prosthetics better."

11   Herr wants to transform how people define disability. Last year he sat on a panel of scientists that confirmed that Oscar Pistorius, a South African sprinter with no legs below the knee, should be allowed to compete in the Olympics. Herr helped discredit arguments that Pistorius got a metabolic advantage from his carbon-fiber legs. (Pistorius missed qualifying by a fraction of a second.)

12   Herr has tasted athletic discrimination, too. Because he uses special climbing prosthetics, many dispute his claim to be the second in the world to free-climb a

Paralympic
related to an
international
competition for
athletes with
disabilities

13

famously challenging pitch near Index Mountain, Wash. "When amputees participate in sports, they call it courageous," he says. "Once you become competitive, they call it cheating." Herr even believes that in the coming decades **Paralympic** athletes will regularly outperform Olympic athletes. We may need special disability laws for humans who decline to have their bodies mechanically enhanced, he says.

"Disabled people today are the test pilots for technology that will someday be pervasive," Herr explains. "Eliminating disability and blurring man and machine will be one of the great stories of this century."

A. UNDERSTANDING THE THESIS AND OTHER MAIN IDEAS

Select the best answer.

_____ 1. The focus of this selection is on Hugh Herr's
   a. ice and rock climbing trips.
   b. athletic achievements.
   c. work with prosthetics.
   d. research at MIT.

_____ 2. The main idea of paragraph 4 is that Herr
   a. uses flat springs in his shoes for walking.
   b. has built his own pair of artificial legs.
   c. has created special prosthetics for ice climbing.
   d. uses different prosthetics for different tasks.

_____ 3. Herr's lower legs were amputated because of
   a. a war injury.
   b. severe frostbite.
   c. a car accident.
   d. bone disease.

_____ 4. The topic of paragraph 5 is
   a. Hugh Herr.
   b. iWalk.
   c. the PowerFoot One.
   d. robotics.

_____ 5. The main idea of paragraph 12 is that Herr
   a. has faced discrimination because of his use of prosthetics.
   b. wants to compete in the Paralympics.
   c. claims to be second in the world to climb Index Mountain.
   d. does not want special disability laws to be enacted.

B. IDENTIFYING DETAILS

Complete the sentences by filling in the blanks.

1. Hugh Herr was _____ years old when his legs were amputated _____ inches below the knee.

2. Herr earned a master's degree in _____ at _____ and a Ph.D. in _____ at _____ .

3. Herr founded a company in _____ called iWalk, which has raised $ _____ million from investors.

4. The Department of _____ is considering the iWalk PowerFoot for _____ who have lost limbs.

C. RECOGNIZING METHODS OF ORGANIZATION AND TRANSITIONS

Complete the following statement by filling in the blanks.

In paragraphs 8 and 9, the author uses the time sequence pattern to describe what happened after Herr and a friend climbed Mount Washington in 1982. Three phrases that signal the passage of time are _____ _____, _____ , and _____ .

D. REVIEWING AND ORGANIZING IDEAS: OUTLINING

Complete the following outline of paragraphs 5 and 6 by filling in the missing words and phrases.

The PowerFoot One

I. Most advanced robotic ankle and foot
    A. Equipped with:

    1. Three internal _____

    2. Twelve sensors measuring _____ , _____ , and position

    B. Automatically adjusts _____ times per second

    1. Angle

    2. _____

    3. _____

C. Makes use of:

    1. Sensory feedback loops

    2. Library of _____

D. Capable of adjusting for slopes and other natural actions

II. Not dependent on _____

  A. Uses a system of passive springs and a rechargeable battery

  B. Made of _____, _____, plastic, and

  _____

  C. Provides the same push as human muscles and tendons

    1. Automatically adjusts power to user's speed

    2. Users can _____ with a phone

E. READING AND THINKING VISUALLY

Complete each of the following items.

1. The purpose of the photograph that accompanies this reading is to

_____

2. The photograph caption refers to Herr as a "cyborg evangelist" because he

_____

F. FIGURING OUT IMPLIED MEANINGS

Indicate whether each statement is true (T) or false (F).

_____ 1. Herr was questioned by a policeman because he had parked illegally.

_____ 2. The policeman could not tell that Herr was disabled.

_____ 3. Herr wants to build prosthetics that are even better than natural limbs.

_____ 4. Herr did not think Oscar Pistorius should be allowed to compete in the Olympics.

_____ 5. According to Herr, Paralympic athletes will one day compete and win against Olympic athletes.

G. THINKING CRITICALLY

Select the best answer.

_____ 1. The tone of this selection can best be described as

    a. humorous.

    b. admiring.

    c. tragic.

    d. solemn.

_____ 2. The "trick" that the author refers to in paragraph 3 is Herr's ability to

    a. change prosthetics depending on his needs.

    b. climb up cliffs of expert-level difficulty.

    c. change people's ideas about what disability means.

    d. create prostheses that feature a variety of functions.

_____ 3. All of the following statements by Herr reveal his attitude toward his disability *except*

    a. "I like to say that there are no disabled people. Only disabled technology."

    b. "The fact that I'm missing lower limbs is an opportunity."

    c. "The only limits are physical laws and my imagination."

    d. "This is the first time that the prosthesis is driving the human."

_____ 4. As described in paragraph 8, the legacy of Albert Dow refers to

    a. an inheritance left to Herr by another disabled climber.

    b. a piece of property left to Herr by one of his distant relatives.

    c. the legal obligation Herr has to an investor in his company.

    d. a sense of responsibility that Herr feels toward a man who died trying to save him.

_____ 5. Of the following words in paragraph 12, the only one with a negative connotation is

    a. special.

    b. courageous.

    c. competitive.

    d. cheating.

H. BUILDING VOCABULARY

Context

Using context and a dictionary, if necessary, determine the meaning of each word as it is used in the selection.

_____ 1. affliction (paragraph 1)

    a. hurry

    b. disability

    c. purpose

    d. approach

_____ 2. preeminent (paragraph 3)

    a. worst

    b. difficult

    c. unknown

    d. top

_____ 3. residual (paragraph 4)

    a. automatic

    b. remaining

    c. unlimited

    d. effective

_____ 4. degradation (paragraph 10)

    a. breakdown

    b. assistance

    c. presentation

    d. reward

_____ 5. pervasive (paragraph 13)

    a. unusual

    b. misunderstood

    c. widespread

    d. expensive

Word Parts

A REVIEW OF PREFIXES AND ROOTS

UN- means *not*

RE- means *back, again*

SUB- means *under, below*

DIS- means *apart, away, not*

LOG means *study, thought*

CRED means *believe*

Use your knowledge of word parts and the review on the preceding page to match each word in Column A with its meaning in Column B.

Column A

_____	1. unassuming
_____	2. rechargeable
_____	3. subzero
_____	4. physiology
_____	5. discredit

Column B

a. below zero

b. the study of the functions of living organisms

c. take away belief in

d. modest, not pretentious

e. able to be energized or charged again

Unusual Words/Understanding Idioms

Use the meanings given below to write a sentence using the boldfaced word.

1. Someone who has **tasted** (paragraph 12) discrimination has experienced it briefly.

   Your sentence: _____

   _____

2. The word **pitch** (paragraph 12) can refer to a throw, a sales talk, an element of sound, a playing field or, as it is used in this selection, a very steep piece of ground.

   Your sentence: _____

   _____

I. SELECTING A LEARNING/STUDY STRATEGY

Assume you will be tested on this article on an upcoming exam. Evaluate your highlighting as well as the outline you completed. How else might you prepare for a test on this material?

J. EXPLORING IDEAS THROUGH DISCUSSION AND WRITING

1. Discuss your initial impression of Herr after reading the opening paragraphs of the selection, and explain how that brief story contributes to your understanding of what kind of person he is. What words would you use to describe Herr?

2. Discuss the meaning of the title, "A Step Beyond Human." Can you think of other titles that might work for this selection?

3. What factors in Herr's life motivate him? Discuss how his life experiences and his attitude make him especially well suited to his work.

K. BEYOND THE CLASSROOM TO THE WEB

Conduct a Web search for information about the U.S. Paralympic team. Choose an athlete you find inspiring and share his or her story with your classmates.

TRACKING YOUR PROGRESS

Selection 21

Section	Number Correct	Score
A. Thesis and Main Ideas (5 items)	_____ × 2	_____
B. Details (10 items)	_____ × 2	_____
C. Organization and Transitions (3 items)	_____ × 5	_____
F. Implied Meanings (5 items)	_____ × 3	_____
G. Thinking Critically (5 items)	_____ × 4	_____
H. Vocabulary		
Context (5 items)	_____ × 2	_____
Word Parts (5 items)	_____ × 2	_____
	Total Score	_____%

16 Life Sciences

The sciences investigate the physical world around us. The **life sciences** are concerned with living organisms—how they grow, develop, and function. The life sciences explore many important questions that affect our daily lives and are essential to our well-being. The study of science is fun and rewarding because you come to understand more about yourself and how you interact with other living things around you. "Can Technology Help Us Put an End to Animal Experimentation?" discusses technological alternatives to animal testing and explores the ethical and practical considerations involved in each option. "Species Extinction: One Found, Many Lost" explores species extinction, examining its leading causes. "And Incredibly Bright" discusses the effects of artificial lighting on the health of human beings and other species.

Use the following suggestions for reading in the life sciences.

TIPS FOR READING IN LIFE SCIENCES

- **Adopt a scientific mind-set.** To read successfully in the sciences, get in the habit of asking questions and seeking answers, analyzing problems, and looking for solutions or explanations. For example, when reading "Species Extinction: One Found, Many Lost," focus on the problem and evidence presented.

- **Learn new terminology.** To read in the sciences, you have to learn the language of science. Science is exact and precise, and scientists use specific terminology to make communication as error free as possible. In "And Incredibly Bright," for example, you will encounter scientific terms that refer to the measurement of light.

- **Focus on cause and effect and process.** Because science is concerned with how and why things happen, cause and effect and process are almost always important. In "Species Extinction: One Found, Many Lost," for example, you will learn about the causes of species extinction.

SELECTION 22

Can Technology Help Us Put an End to Animal Experimentation?

George Dvorsky

This selection was originally published on i09, a Web site that describes itself as a "daily publication that covers science, science fiction, and the future." The author, George Dvorsky, is a Canadian bioethicist and a contributing editor at io9.

PREVIEWING THE READING

Using the steps listed on pages 40–41, preview the reading selection. When you have finished, complete the following items.

1. The three R's of animal testing are _____, _____, and _____.

2. Most technological alternatives to animal testing are coming from the fields of _____, _____, and _____.

MAKING
CONNECTIONS

What are your opinions on the ethics of animal testing? Do you think it is acceptable to test medical treatments on animals? Why or why not?

READING TIP

The author of the selection is a bioethicist. Use word parts to define the term bioethics. How do the author's background and qualifications affect your perception of the reliability of this reading?

Can Technology Help Us Put an End to Animal Experimentation?

1   Nobody likes the idea of experimenting on animals. It seems like the definition of inhumanity, especially when you consider the growing evidence that animals have awareness just like us. But there's no doubt that the human race has gained incalculable benefits from the scientific testing of animals. Most scientists don't want to rule out animal testing, because we just don't have any decent alternatives.

2   Until now. Technology is finally coming up with solutions that could eliminate the practice altogether.

3   Putting an end to animal experimentation is more than just a matter of ethics. A growing number of scientists and clinicians are challenging the use of animal models on medical and scientific grounds. A 2006 study in JAMA concluded that, "patients and physicians should remain cautious about **extrapolating** the findings of prominent animal research to the care of human disease," and that "even high-quality animal studies will replicate poorly in human clinical research."

extrapolating
extending

4   Two years ago, independent studies published in PLOS showed that only animal trials with positive results tend to get published, and that only two stroke treatments out of 500 verified that animal models actually worked on humans.

5   Making matters worse is the fact that mice are used in nearly 60% of all experiments. As Slate's Daniel Engber argues, mice are among the most unreliable test subjects, when it comes to approximating human biological processes. But most scientists are reluctant to move away from this tried-and-true model, mostly because mice are cheap, docile, and good subjects for genetic engineering experiments. They're also denied many of the rights afforded to other animals. Still, Engber points out, "It's not at all clear that the rise of the mouse—and the million research papers that resulted from it—has produced a revolution in public health."

6   Given these problems, and combined with the overarching ethics question, it's clear that something better has to come along. Thankfully, the process of replacing animal models is largely underway—an effort that began over 50 years ago.

The three R's of animal testing

7   Back in 1959, English scientists William Russell and Rex Burch conducted a study to see how animals were being treated at the hands of research scientists. To make their assessments, they looked at the degree of "humaneness" or "inhumaneness"

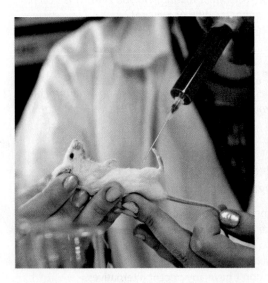

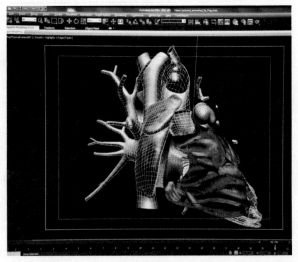

afforded
granted

that was **afforded** to the animals during testing. By analyzing the work being done by scientists in this way, Russell and Burch sought to create a set of guidelines that could be used to reduce the amount of suffering inflicted on laboratory animals.

8   To that end, they proposed the three R's of animal testing: Reduction, Refinement, and Replacement.

9   By practicing reduction, scientists were asked to acquire high quality data using the smallest possible number of animals. Experiments needed to be designed so that they could continue to **yield** valuable results, while minimizing (if not eliminating) the need for endless repetition of the same tests. Consequently, scientists were told to work closer with statisticians (to better understand the required level of statistical significance) and to refer to previous studies that had essentially performed the same tests.

yield
produce

10   Refinement was simply the idea that more humanitarian approaches were required. It was a call to reduce the severity of distress, pain, and fear experienced by many lab animals.

11   More significant, however, was the suggestion that scientists replace their lab animals with non-sentient animals—things like microorganisms, metazoan parasites, and certain plants. The less **cognitively** sophisticated the animal, it was thought, the less capacity it had to experience emotional, physical, and psychological distress.

cognitively
related to the
process of
acquiring
knowledge

12   Since the publication of Russell and Burch's guidelines, a number of scientists and bioethicists have put these policies into practice. But now, as more sophisticated tools emerge, scientists have been given entirely new options for testing—options that will enable them to honor the "R" of replacement.

Technological alternatives

13   Most of these new alternatives that are emerging are coming from the fields of biotechnology, hi-res scanning, and computer science.

14   Take research laboratory CeeTox, for example. They're using human cell-based *in vitro* (lab grown) models to predict the toxicity of drugs, chemicals, cosmetics, and consumer products—tests that are replacing the need to pump potentially hazardous chemicals into animals' stomachs, lungs, and eyes. Likewise, biotech firm Hurel has developed a lab-grown human liver that can be used to break down chemicals.

15   There's also MatTek's *in vitro* 3D human skin tissue that's being used by the National Cancer Institute, the U.S. military, private companies, and a number of universities. Their virtual skin is proving to be an excellent substitute for the real thing, allowing scientists to conduct burn research, and to test cosmetics, radiation exposure, and so on.

16   The development of non-invasive brain scanning techniques is also enabling scientists to work on human test subjects. Technologies such as MRI, fMRI, EEG, PET, and CT are replacing the need to perform vivisections on the brains of rats, cats, and monkeys.

17   Likewise, the practice of microdosing, where volunteers are given extremely small one-time drug doses, is allowing researchers to work ethically with humans.

18   There's also the tremendous potential for computer models—and this is very likely where the future of drug testing and other scientific research lies. And this is a revolution that's already well underway.

19   The first heart models were developed 13 years ago, kickstarting efforts into the development of simulated lungs, the musculoskeletal system, the digestive system, skin, kidneys, the lymphatic system—and even the brain.

20   Today, computer simulations are being used to test the efficacy of new medications on asthma, though laws still require that all new drugs get verified in animal and humans tests before licensing. Models are also being used to simulate human metabolism in an effort to predict plaque build-up and cardiovascular risk. These same systems are also being used to evaluate drug toxicity—tests that would have normally involved the use of lab animals. And as we reported a few months ago, new computer simulations can even help scientists predict the negative side effects of drugs. All this is just the tip of the iceberg.

21   This said, not everyone agrees that computer simulations are the way to go. Some people feel that simulations can never truly paint an accurate picture of what they're trying to model—that it's a classic case of "garbage in, garbage out." The basic reasoning is that scientists can't possibly simulate something they don't truly understand. Consequently, if their models are off by even just a little bit, the entire simulation will diverge dramatically from reality.

intractable
hard to control

22   But even though these problems are real, they're not necessarily **intractable**— nor are they deal breakers. It may very well turn out that the margin of error achieved in computer simulations will be comparable (or better) than the current margin of error when testing animal models. And given the rate of technological advance, both in biotechnology and information technology, it's even conceivable that we can simulate the intricate complexity that makes up organisms with extreme accuracy. And at that point, animal experimentation won't even seem like a sensible option.

A. UNDERSTANDING THE THESIS AND OTHER MAIN IDEAS

Select the best answer.

_____ 1. Which of the following best states the thesis or central thought of the selection?

a. The medical research industry has a long history of conducting experiments on animals, and medical researchers are required to follow the three R's when conducting their experiments.

b. There are two sides to the animal-experimentation controversy; one side believes such research is necessary for the benefit of humanity, while the other side believes that the results of animal research do not necessarily apply to human beings.

c. Since the 1950s, medical researchers have been encouraged to follow the three R's of animal testing, but current and future developments in computer modeling and simulations may make animal research obsolete.

d. There is a hierarchy of experimental animals; mammals such as pigs and monkeys are generally treated with the most respect, while lower-order animals, such as protozoans and parasites, receive the cruelest treatment.

_____ 2. The author's primary purpose is to

    a. convince readers that animal testing is unethical.

    b. illustrate the unethical research practices of pharmaceutical companies.

    c. imply that the best subjects for drug efficacy tests are human beings.

    d. examine the history of the ethics of animal experimentation and look to the future.

_____ 3. The topic of paragraph 5 is

    a. the medical research of Daniel Engber.

    b. the overall status of public health in the United States and Canada.

    c. issues and controversies surrounding the use of mice in experiments.

    d. the use of computer models to simulate the biological processes of mice and other rodents.

_____ 4. The main idea of paragraph 21 is found in the

    a. first sentence.

    b. second sentence.

    c. third sentence.

    d. last sentence.

_____ 5. Which of the following conclusions is _not_ supported by the reading?

    a. It is unlikely that all the research conducted on mice has increased overall public health.

    b. It is unlikely that microorganisms can feel pain.

    c. While computer models offer much promise, they likely have limitations; and for that reason, some experiments on animals are likely to continue.

    d. Although _in vitro_ technology may be successful at growing human organs, those organs should be used for transplants, not for experimentation.

B. IDENTIFYING DETAILS

Select the best answer.

_____ 1. Which of the following is not one of the "three R's" of animal testing put forth by Rex Burch and William Russell?

    a. replacement   c. reproduction

    b. reduction   d. refinement

_____ 2. Which human organ has the biotech firm Hurel grown in a lab?

    a. heart   c. liver

    b. lung   d. kidney

_____ 3. Which of the following sources is *not* cited in the article?

    a. Lancet   c. Slate

    b. JAMA   d. PLOS

_____ 4. The animal most commonly used in experiments is the

    a. rat.   c. monkey.

    b. pig.   d. mouse.

_____ 5. The author sees _____ as the future of drug testing.

    a. refinement

    b. overseas research

    c. computer simulations

    d. bioengineering

C. RECOGNIZING METHODS OF ORGANIZATION AND TRANSITIONS

Select the best answer.

_____ 1. The organizational pattern used in paragraph 3 is

    a. classification.

    b. statement and clarification.

    c. comparison and contrast.

    d. process.

_____ 2. The main organizational patterns used in the sub-heading "The three R's of animal testing" (paragraphs 7–12) are

    a. chronological order and spatial order.

    b. enumeration and definition.

    c. spatial order and comparison/contrast.

    d. cause/effect and process.

_____ 3. All of the following patterns of organization are used in the sub-heading "Technological alternatives" (paragraphs 13–22) *except*

    a. listing.

    b. generalization and example.

    c. definition.

    d. classification.

_____ 4. The transitional word or phrase in paragraph 14 that signals supporting evidence for the main idea presented in paragraph 13 is

    a. for example.

    b. *in vitro* models.

    c. replacing.

    d. likewise.

D. REVIEWING AND ORGANIZING IDEAS: MAPPING

Complete the following map of the selection by filling in the missing words and phrases.

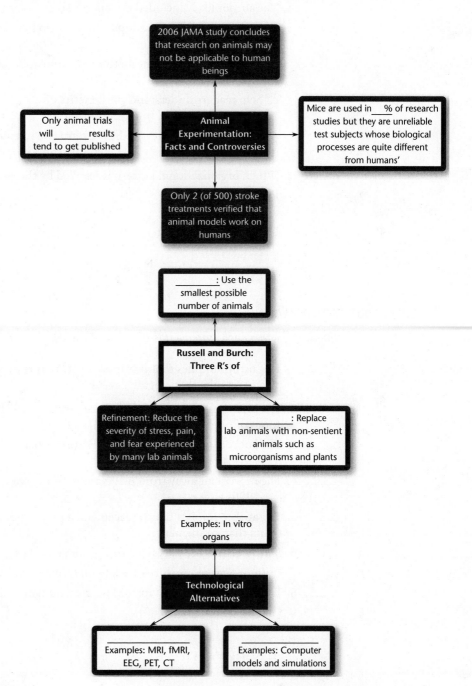

E. READING AND THINKING VISUALLY

Select the best answer.

_____ 1. The author likely included the photos shown on page 500 in order to
   a. encourage readers to adopt animals who have been the subject of medical experiments.
   b. illustrate two different methods of (and approaches to) conducting medical research.
   c. help readers understand the benefits of using computers to simulate the biological functions of mice.
   d. imply that mice offer the best alternative to computer modeling, which is in its infancy and therefore cannot be deemed reliable.

_____ 2. Which organizational pattern is implied by the two photos on page 500?
   a. definition
   b. comparison/contrast
   c. classification
   d. process

F. FIGURING OUT IMPLIED MEANINGS

Indicate whether each statement is true (T) or false (F).

_____ 1. The author implies that it is more likely that researchers will report positive results than negative results.

_____ 2. The biological processes of mice are similar to the biological processes of humans.

_____ 3. The author implies that researchers treat other animals with more respect than they treat mice.

_____ 4. The movement away from using animals in research began in the late 1990s.

_____ 5. The author implies that replacement is more important for animal rights than refinement.

_____ 6. *In vitro* organs are harvested from human bodies.

_____ 7. Current laws require drug testing on humans and animals.

_____ 8. The author implies that microdosing on humans is an ethical practice.

G. THINKING CRITICALLY

Select the best answer.

_____ 1. The tone of the reading can best be described as

    a. informative and optimistic.

    b. angry and vindictive.

    c. gentle and humorous.

    d. puzzled and curious.

_____ 2. Which of the following best states the author's attitude toward animal testing?

    a. He is vehemently opposed to medical research being conducted on any animal.

    b. He understands both sides of the argument but hopes that new technologies will greatly reduce animal testing.

    c. He completely supports research on non-mammals, but he is more conflicted about research on mammals.

    d. He is impatient with animal-rights activists who do not understand that human progress depends to a certain extent on animal experimentation.

_____ 3. All of the following excerpts from the reading are facts *except*

    a. "Nobody likes the idea of experimenting on animals." (paragraph 1)

    b. "Only two stroke treatments out of 500 verified that animals models actually worked on humans." (paragraph 4)

    c. "Their virtual skin is proving to be an excellent substitute for the real thing." (paragraph 15)

    d. "The first heart models were developed 13 years ago." (paragraph 19)

_____ 4. Paragraph 21 uses the figurative phrase "garbage in, garbage out." This phrase means

    a. "What you see is what you get."

    b. "The ends justify the means."

    c. "Results are only as good as the information used to create them."

    d. "There are two sides to every story, and both sides need to be told."

H. BUILDING VOCABULARY

Context

Using context and a dictionary, if necessary, determine the meaning of each word as it is used in the selection.

_____ 1. replicate (paragraph 3)

    a. copy

    b. fail

    c. research

    d. predict

_____ 2. docile (paragraph 5)

    a. dumb

    b. inexpensive

    c. small

    d. mild

_____ 3. toxicity (paragraph 14)

    a. potency

    b. unpredictability

    c. naturalness

    d. strength of poison

_____ 4. efficacy (paragraph 20)

    a. price

    b. strength

    c. effectiveness

    d. legality

_____ 5. diverge (paragraph 21)

    a. examine

    b. drive

    c. limit

    d. separate

_____ 6. conceivable (paragraph 22)

    a. pregnant

    b. possible

    c. likely

    d. angry

Word Parts

> ## A REVIEW OF PREFIXES AND ROOTS
>
> **IN-** means not.
> **MICRO-** means small.
> **VIV** means living.

Use your knowledge of word parts to fill in the blanks in the following sentences.

1. *Incalculable* (paragraph 1) benefits are benefits that cannot be

   _____.

2. Experiments on *microorganisms* (paragraph 11) involve research on organisms that are very _____.

3. *Vivisections* (paragraph 16) are performed while an animal is _____.

Unusual Words/Understanding Idioms

Use the meanings given below to write a sentence using the boldfaced word.

1. **Kickstarting** (paragraph 19) a process means getting it started through decisive, focused action.

   _____

   _____

2. The idiomatic phrase **tip of the iceberg** (paragraph 20) refers to the comparatively small part of something that can be seen, while the rest (the much larger part) remains hidden.

   _____

   _____

I. SELECTING A LEARNING/STUDY STRATEGY

To prepare for a class discussion or exam about the reading, prepare a detailed outline.

J. EXPLORING IDEAS THROUGH DISCUSSION AND WRITING

1. Write a caption to accompany the two photos that appear on page 500.
2. In paragraph 1, the author refers to "the growing evidence that animals have awareness just like us." Do you own (or have you owned) a pet? How would you describe its "awareness"? Did it seem to feel emotion and pain?

3. Assume for the sake of this question that animal testing will continue to be necessary in some research studies. Write a paragraph in which you provide guidelines for how test animals should be treated.

4. Write an essay in which you explain your stance on animal testing.

K. BEYOND THE CLASSROOM TO THE WEB

Search the Web for articles (including blogs) that discuss animal rights. How reliable do you find the information in each source? Is each source biased or unbiased? Look carefully at tone and use of language, as well as the images provided. How successful is each Web site at conveying its opinions or point of view?

TRACKING YOUR PROGRESS

Selection 22

Section	Number Correct	Score
A. Thesis and Main Ideas (5 items)	_____ × 3	_____
B. Details (5 items)	_____ × 3	_____
C. Organization and Transitions (4 items)	_____ × 3	_____
E. Reading and Thinking Visually (2 items)	_____ × 3	_____
F. Implied Meanings (8 items)	_____ × 2	_____
G. Thinking Critically (4 items)	_____ × 3	_____
H. Vocabulary		
Context (6 items)	_____ × 3	_____
Word Parts (3 items)	_____ × 2	_____
	Total Score _____%	

SELECTION 23

Species Extinction: One Found, Many Lost

Teresa Audesirk, Gerald Audesirk, and Bruce E. Byers

TEXTBOOK EXCERPT

This selection is taken from an introductory biology textbook used by many nursing, allied health, and biology majors. Read it to discover how and why animals and other life forms become extinct.

PREVIEWING THE READING

Using the steps listed on pages 40–41, preview the reading selection. When you have finished, complete the following items.

1. The topic of this selection is _____.
2. List one question you expect to be able to answer after reading the selection. _____

 MAKING CONNECTIONS

While extinction is a scientific term, it is a concept that most people already understand. Perhaps the best-known mass extinction is that of the dinosaurs, but can you think of any other, more modern examples?

READING TIP

Some students find it difficult to read science textbooks because they contain so much unfamiliar vocabulary. While reading the selection, first try to determine the meaning of unknown words through context. If you get stuck on a particular word, check the meaning in a dictionary before you continue. Scientific knowledge builds on key concepts; if you don't understand the basics, you are unlikely to grasp the selection's main ideas. Make sure you understand the concept of adaptation.

Species Extinction: One Found, Many Lost

1   The steep, rain-drenched slopes of Vietnam's Annamite Mountains are remote and forbidding, cloaked in tropical mists that lend an air of mystery and conceal-ment to the forested peaks. As it turns out, this remote refuge conceals a most aston-ishing biological surprise: the saola, a hoofed, horned mammal that was unknown to

science until the early 1990s. The discovery of a new species of large mammal at this late date was a complete shock. After centuries of human exploration and exploitation of every corner of the world's forests, deserts, and savannas, scientists were certain that no large mammal species could have escaped detection. As long ago as 1812, French naturalist Georges Cuvier wrote that "there is little hope of discovering new species of large quadrupeds." And yet, the saola—3 feet high at the shoulder, weighing up to 200 pounds and sporting 20-inch black horns—remained hidden in Annamite Mountain forests, outside the realm of scientific knowledge.

2   Ironically, we have discovered the lost world of Vietnamese animals at a moment when that world is in danger of disappearing. Economic development in Vietnam has brought logging and mining to ever more remote regions of the country; and Annamite Mountain forests are being cleared at an unprecedented rate. The increasing local human population means that animals are hunted heavily; most of our knowledge of the saola comes from carcasses found In local markets. All of the newly discovered mammals of Vietnam are quite rare, seen only infrequently even by local hunters. Fortunately, the Vietnamese government has established a number of national parks and nature preserves in key areas. Only time will tell if these measures are sufficient to ensure the survival of the mysterious mammals of the Annamites.

What Causes Extinction?

3   Every living organism must eventually die, and the same is true of species. Just like individuals, species are "born" (through the process of speciation), persist for some period of time, and then perish. The ultimate fate of any species is extinction, the death of the last of its members. In fact, at least 99.9% of all the species that have ever existed are now extinct. The natural course of evolution, as revealed by **fossils**, is continual turnover of species as new ones arise and old ones become extinct.

fossil
the remains of a prehistoric organism preserved in rock

4   The immediate cause of extinction is probably always environmental change, in either the nonliving or the living parts of the environment. Environmental changes that can lead to extinction include habitat destruction and increased competition among species. In the face of such changes, species with small geographic ranges or highly specialized adaptations are especially susceptible to extinction.

Localized Distribution Makes Species Vulnerable

5   Species vary widely in their range of distribution and, hence, in their vulnerability to extinction. Some species, such as herring gulls, white-tailed deer, and humans, inhabit entire continents or even the whole Earth; others, such as the Devil's Hole pupfish (Figure A), have extremely limited ranges. Obviously, if a species

Sao La

The saola, unknown to science until 1992, is one of a number of previously undiscovered species recently found in the mountains of Vietnam.

Figure A: Very localized distribution can endanger a species. The Devil's Hole pupfish is found in only one spring-fed water hole in the Nevada desert. This and other isolated small populations are at high risk of extinction.

inhabits only a very small area, any disturbance of that area could easily result in extinction. If Devil's Hole dries up due to a drought or well drilling nearby, its pupfish will immediately vanish. Conversely, wide-ranging species will not succumb to local environmental catastrophes.

Overspecialization Increases the Risk of Extinction

6   Another factor that may make a species vulnerable to extinction is overspecialization. Each species evolves adaptations that help it survive and reproduce in its environment. In some cases, these adaptations include specializations that favor survival in a particular and limited set of environmental conditions. The Karner blue butterfly, for example, feeds only on the blue lupine plant (Figure B, p. 514). The butterfly is therefore found only where the plant thrives. But the blue lupine has become quite rare because its habitat of sandy, open woods and clearings in northeast North America has been largely replaced by farms and development. If the lupine disappears, the Karner blue butterfly will surely become extinct along with it.

Interactions with Other Species May Drive a Species to Extinction

7   Interactions such as competition and predation serve as agents of natural selection. In some cases, these same interactions can lead to extinction rather than to adaptation.

isthmus   8
a narrow strip of
land with sea on both
sides

Organisms compete for limited resources in all environments. If a species' competitors evolve superior adaptations and the species doesn't evolve fast enough to keep up, it may become extinct. A particularly striking example of extinction through competition occurred in South America, beginning about 2.5 million years ago. At that time, the **isthmus** of Panama rose above sea level and formed a land bridge between North America and South America. After the previously separated continents were connected, the mammal species that had evolved in isolation on each continent were able to mix. Many species did indeed expand their ranges, as North American mammals moved southward and South American mammals moved northward. As they moved, each species encountered resident species that occupied the same kinds of habitats and exploited the same kinds of resources. The ultimate result of the ensuing competition was that the North American species diversified and underwent an adaptive radiation that displaced the vast majority of the South American species, many of which went extinct. Clearly, evolution had bestowed on the North American species some (as yet unknown) set of adaptations that enabled their descendants to exploit resources more efficiently and effectively than their South American counterparts could.

Figure B: Extreme specialization places species at risk. The Karner blue butterfly feeds exclusively on the blue lupine, found in dry forests and clearings in the northeastern United States. Such behavior specialization renders the butterfly extremely vulnerable to any environmental change that may exterminate its single host plant species.

Habitat Change and Destruction Are the Leading Causes of Extinction

9   Habitat change, both contemporary and prehistoric, is the single greatest cause of extinctions. Present-day habitat destruction due to human activities is proceeding at a rapid pace. Many biologists believe that we are presently in the midst of the fastest-paced and most widespread episode of species extinction in the history of life. Loss of tropical forests is especially devastating to species diversity. As many as half the species presently on Earth may be lost during the next 50 years as the tropical forests that contain them are cut for timber or to clear land for cattle and crops.

HAVE YOU EVER WONDERED

HOW MANY SPECIES INHABIT THE PLANET?

One way to determine the number of species on Earth might be to simply count them. You could comb the scientific literature to find all the species that scientists have discovered and named, and then tally up the total number. If you did that, you'd end up with a count of roughly 1.5 million species. But you still wouldn't know how many species are on Earth.

Why doesn't counting work? Because most of the planet's species remain undiscovered. Relatively few scientists are engaged in the search for new species, and many undiscovered species are small and inconspicuous, or live in poorly explored habitats such as the floor of the ocean or the topmost branches of tropical rain forests. So, no one knows the actual number of species on Earth. But biologists agree that the number must be much higher than the number of named species. Estimates range from 2 million to 100 million or more.

A. UNDERSTANDING THE THESIS AND OTHER MAIN IDEAS

Select the best answer.

_____ 1. The central thesis of the selection is that

　　a. finding a new species is rare, but species extinction is very common for a number of reasons.

　　b. extinction is the result of environmental destruction.

　　c. mammals are more resilient species than birds and fish, especially the mammals that live in mountainous regions.

　　d. competition for resources leads to evolution.

_____ 2. The authors' main purpose in "Species Extinction: One Found, Many Lost" is to

　　a. explain how species adapt to their surroundings.

　　b. relate their travel experiences in the mountains of Vietnam.

　　c. get students involved in volunteer activities for environmental awareness.

　　d. describe the finding of a new species as well as the causes of species extinction.

_____ 3. One of the "mysterious mammals of the Annamites" is the

　　a. koala.

　　b. blue lupine.

　　c. saola.

　　d. white-tailed deer.

_____ 4. The best estimate of the number of species that exist on Earth is
     a. 500,000.
     b. 2–100 million.
     c. 8–10 million.
     d. 1.5 million.

_____ 5. The ultimate fate of all species is
     a. extinction.
     b. evolution.
     c. habitat destruction.
     d. adaptation.

_____ 6. The leading causes of extinction are
     a. volcanic eruptions.
     b. asteroids striking the Earth.
     c. habitat change and destruction.
     d. global warming and flooding.

_____ 7. The main idea of paragraph 8 is found in the
     a. first sentence.
     b. second sentence.
     c. third sentence.
     d. last sentence.

B. IDENTIFYING DETAILS

Select the best answer.

_____ 1. Which species does not inhabit an entire continent or the whole Earth?
     a. humans
     b. pupfish
     c. herring gulls
     d. white-tailed deer

_____ 2. Which species relies on the blue lupine for its food?
     a. Karner blue butterfly
     b. pupfish
     c. saola
     d. cuvier

_____ 3. The immediate cause of species extinction is
    a. competition for food.
    b. human hunting practices.
    c. growth in human population.
    d. environmental change.

_____ 4. The authors provide the example of the Panamanian land bridge to explain
    a. how overspecialization leads to extinction.
    b. localized distribution.
    c. the death of species in the Amazon rain forest.
    d. extinction through competition.

_____ 5. All of the following can lead to extinction _except_
    a. overspecialization.
    b. localized distribution.
    c. high birth rates within a species.
    d. interaction with other species.

_____ 6. The natural habitat of the Karner blue butterfly is
    a. northeastern North America.
    b. South America.
    c. Vietnam.
    d. desert-like climates.

C. RECOGNIZING METHODS OF ORGANIZATION AND TRANSITIONS

Complete the sentences by filling in the blanks.

1. The overall organizational pattern used in paragraphs 3–9 is _____ _____.

Now, considering how you completed sentence 1, complete sentences 2 and 3.

2. The four _____ are localized distribution, overspecialization, interactions with other species, and habitat change and destruction.

3. The _____ is extinction.

4. Which boldfaced heading within the reading clearly signals the organizational pattern used? _____

D. REVIEWING AND ORGANIZING IDEAS: PARAPHRASING

Complete the following paraphrases by filling in the missing words or dates.

Paragraphs 1 and 2: As long ago as _____, scientists thought they had discovered all the _____ on Earth. But in the early _____ a horned mammal called a _____ was discovered in the _____ Mountains in _____. But the _____ of this species is not guaranteed because the _____ in which it lives are being cleared, and the animal is heavily _____.

Paragraphs 3–9: All species will become _____ at some point. Most species die out as a result of changes in the _____; the greatest cause of extinction is _____. _____ distribution makes some species vulnerable; if the species lives in one particular area, then the disturbance of that area can lead to _____. Species that are _____ to a particular environment are also vulnerable. Interactions such as _____ for resources and death at the hands of _____ can also lead to extinction.

E. READING AND THINKING VISUALLY

Select the best answer.

_____ 1. The author chose to include Figure A, the photo of the pupfish, in order to

    a. provide an illustration of a species vulnerable to extinction due to localized distribution.

    b. make the point that fish and other marine life are more in danger of extinction than land-based mammals.

    c. illustrate a species that is already extinct as a result of habitat destruction or change.

    d. show one of the few remaining members of a species that is already 99.9 percent extinct.

_____ 2. According to Figure A, which of the following is *not* the pupfish's native habitat?

    a. Nevada

    b. the rain forest

    c. the desert

    d. Devil's Hole

_____ 3. The author included Figure B, the photo of the Karner blue butter-fly, as an example of

    a. the destruction of species as a result of habitat change.

    b. a species with localized distribution.

    c. competition for resources between the butterfly and the lupine.

    d. a species that has engaged in extreme specialization.

_____ 4. In Figure B, the caption refers to a "host" plant species. In this con-text, *host* means

    a. the dry forests in which the butterfly lives.

    b. an extremely specialized species limited to one geographic area.

    c. a species on which another species relies for its existence.

    d. the northeastern United States.

F. FIGURING OUT IMPLIED MEANINGS

Indicate whether each statement is true (T) or false (F).

_____ 1. Less than 1 percent of the species that have ever existed still exist today.

_____ 2. The author implies that the Karner blue butterfly gets its color from the plant it feeds on.

_____ 3. In all environments, all resources are limited.

_____ 4. The authors imply that natural occurrences, such as volcanoes and earthquakes, are the major causes of habitat destruction.

_____ 5. About half of Earth's species live in tropical rain forests.

_____ 6. The saola's existence was not discovered until 1812.

_____ 7. Evolutionary processes provided South American species with a set of adaptations that gave them an advantage over North American species.

_____ 8. The authors imply that changes in the nonliving environment are more destructive to species than changes in the living environment.

_____ 9. Wide-ranging species tend to be heavily affected by local environ-mental disasters.

G. THINKING CRITICALLY

Select the best answer.

_____ 1. The tone of this selection is best described as

    a. angry.

    b. scientific.

    c. pessimistic.

    d. sympathetic.

_____ 2. Which word in paragraph 1 might hint at the authors' belief that humans pursue their own interests at the expense of all other species?

a. concealment

b. mystery

c. exploitation

d. shock

_____ 3. The authors use the quote from Georges Cuvier in paragraph 1 in order to

a. describe how surprised scientists were by the discovery of the saola.

b. hint that the scientific method is less than reliable.

c. suggest that the saola must have evolved as a modern species after 1812.

d. provide support for the idea that mountain wildlife must be preserved.

_____ 4. Based on paragraph 3, which of the following statements would the authors most likely agree with?

a. Only the strongest species survive extinction.

b. Insect and amphibian species (such as cockroaches and frogs) are likely to survive much longer than mammals.

c. Humans will die out at some point.

d. Life on Earth will eventually come to an end as a result of mass extinctions.

_____ 5. What is the best definition of *range* as the term is used in paragraph 5?

a. a mountainous area

b. a continent

c. the area in which a species lives

d. a landmass and the bodies of water it touches

_____ 6. When the authors say that "Interactions such as competition and predation serve as agents of natural selection" (paragraph 7), they mean that

a. endangered species are best protected within natural wildlife preserves.

b. modern zoos provide the re-creations of the natural environment that animals need in order to reproduce.

c. the single most important influence on extinction is human–animal interaction.

d. species can become extinct if they are weaker than other species that prey on them or other species eat all the available food.

_____ 7. Why have the authors included the box titled "How Many Species Inhabit the Planet?" with this selection?

    a. to fill up some additional space that otherwise would have been left empty on the page

    b. to explain why the answer to this question is much trickier than the average person would think

    c. to criticize scientists for severely undercounting the number of species left on Earth

    d. to encourage students to volunteer for causes that seek to protect endangered species

_____ 8. Which of the following is the best example of informed opinion?

    a. The discovery of a new species of large mammal at this late date was a complete shock. (paragraph 1)

    b. Each species evolves adaptations that help it survive and reproduce in its environment. (paragraph 6)

    c. Present-day habitat destruction due to human activities is proceeding at a rapid pace. (paragraph 9)

    d. Many biologists believe that we are presently in the midst of the fastest-paced and most widespread episode of species extinction in the history of life. (paragraph 9)

H. BUILDING VOCABULARY

Context

Using context and a dictionary, if necessary, determine the meaning of each word as it is used in the selection.

_____ 1. savannas (paragraph 1)

    a. oceans

    b. icebergs

    c. islands

    d. grasslands

_____ 2. unprecedented (paragraph 2)

    a. rapid

    b. surprising

    c. never happened before

    d. occurring quite soon

_____ 3. habitat (paragraph 4)

    a. jungle trees

    b. natural home

    c. urban location

    d. recurring event

_____ 4. drought (paragraph 5)

    a. prolonged dry spell

    b. hurricane

    c. earthquake

    d. high level of humidity

_____ 5. tally (see first paragraph in the box on p. 515)

    a. kill

    b. divide

    c. estimate

    d. add

_____ 6. inconspicuous (see second paragraph in the box on p. 515)

    a. in large numbers

    b. air-breathing

    c. not attracting attention

    d. gray-colored

Word Parts

> **A REVIEW OF PREFIXES**
>
> **QUAD-** means *four*
> **PRE-** means *before*

Use your knowledge of word parts and the review above to fill in the blanks in the following sentences.

1. If the root *ped* means "foot," then a **quadruped** (paragraph 1) has _____ feet.

2. Something that occurred in **prehistoric** times (paragraph 9) took place _____ written history.

I. SELECTING A LEARNING/STUDY STRATEGY

Select the best answer.

_____ 1. The best way to study and learn this reading would be to

    a. create flash cards with key vocabulary.

    b. outline the selection.

    c. watch a video about the extinction of a particular species.

    d. draw a diagram of the extinction process.

J. EXPLORING IDEAS THROUGH DISCUSSION AND WRITING

1. According to the selection, it is not uncommon for species to go extinct. But technologies can go extinct as well. For example, how many people still use telephones with cords? How many people own black and white TVs? Can you think of any other technologies that have become or are becoming extinct?

2. What do you think motivates people to want to protect endangered species? For example, most people would argue that the bald eagle, a longtime symbol of America, should be protected. But suppose we were to learn that cockroaches or bedbugs were about to go extinct. Would anyone care? Why or why not?

3. To what other areas of life or society might the concept of "extinction" be applied? For example, do words go extinct as new words are created? (Think, for example, about words that older people use. Will they still be in use 50 years from now?) Do certain social customs go extinct as society changes? (For example, do men still feel compelled to stand up when a woman leaves the table, the way they used to in the 1940s and 1950s?)

K. BEYOND THE CLASSROOM TO THE WEB

Recent scientific advances may allow scientists to bring extinct species back to life. Conduct a Web search on this topic. What process would scientists have to follow in order to bring back an extinct species? What are the arguments for and against bringing back extinct species?

TRACKING YOUR PROGRESS

Selection 23

Section	Number Correct	Score
A. Thesis and Main Ideas (7 items)	_____ × 4	_____
B. Details (6 items)	_____ × 3	_____
C. Organization and Transitions (4 items)	_____ × 2	_____
E. Reading and Thinking Visually (4 items)	_____ × 1	_____
F. Implied Meanings (9 items)	_____ × 2	_____
G. Thinking Critically (8 items)	_____ × 2	_____
H. Vocabulary		
Context (6 items)	_____ × 1	_____
Word Parts (2 items)	_____ × 1	_____
	Total Score	_____ %

SELECTION 24

And Incredibly Bright

Holly Haworth

This selection was taken from *Earth Island Journal*, a quarterly magazine. The magazine says its mission statement is to "combine investigative journalism and thought-provoking essays that make the subtle but profound connections between the environment and other contemporary issues."

PREVIEWING THE READING

Using the steps listed on pages 40–41, preview the reading selection. When you have finished, complete the following items.

1. According to this selection, artificial lighting has blotted out the

   _____.

2. Indicate whether each statement is true (T) or false (F).

   _____ a. Alienation from the night sky is limited to the Los Angeles area.

   _____ b. As a result of artificial lighting, stars are easier to observe.

   _____ c. Artificial light affects many species, not just humans.

MAKING CONNECTIONS

Tonight, when it is dark outside, go outdoors and look at the sky. Can you see the stars? Notice how much artificial light surrounds you. Would you expect more artificial light in an urban (city) environment or a rural (country) environment? Why?

READING TIP

Science relies on research to formulate conclusions. As you read, keep track of the research studies cited by the author, and use a pen to underline the key conclusions of each study.

And Incredibly Bright

We have blotted out the night sky

1   In 1994, when an earthquake knocked out power in Los Angeles, many residents called 911 to express concern about a "giant, silvery cloud" in the sky. In fact, what they were looking at—perhaps for the first time—was the Milky Way (Figure 1). On

Figure 1: The Milky Way.

cosmos
universe

other nights, the vast city's millions of electric lights faded out the glowing band of stars that has connected people to the **cosmos** for millennia.

2   This alienation from the night sky is not restricted to L.A. residents. Nearly two-thirds of Americans now live in places where the Milky Way is no longer visible. Our cities and suburbs are so brightly lit that on any given night only 1 percent of Americans have a view of the sky unpolluted by artificial light. The range and reach of our lights is increasing every year—at a rate that experts say will cancel out every dark sky in the contiguous United States in just over a decade. Soon, all of America will have lost sight of the Milky Way. There is little global-scale data on artificial night sky brightness, but researchers at the US National Optical Astronomy Observatory in Arizona say more than one-fifth of the world's population has already lost "naked-eye visibility" of the Milky Way.

3   What does this loss of natural darkness mean? In the past few decades, astrono-

repercussions
results

mers, medical researchers, and ecologists have been discovering the myriad, disturbing **repercussions** an artificially illuminated world has on us and on all life on Earth.

4   For astronomers, the increase of artificial night lighting—which causes light to reflect off the moisture and dust in the air and creates a glow in the sky—means the stars and planets are harder to observe. Among other things, light glare increases the difficulty of detecting potentially dangerous asteroids.

5   The most worrisome research on human health links nighttime light exposure to increased risk of breast cancer. The first scientist to break ground in that area was Dr. Richard Stevens, who published a report in 1987 that drew a connection between breast cancer and night-shift work. Twenty years later, in 2007, the World Health Organization, too, concluded that prolonged night-shift work could lead to cancer.

circadian
recurring naturally
on a 24-hour cycle

6   Now, new research shows that that not only working at night, but simply being in what Harvard scientist Itai Kloog calls the "modern urbanized sleeping habitat," is a risk. Recent studies led by Kloog show a significant association between nighttime brightness and incidence of breast cancer. Most scientists believe this has something to do with the body's ability to produce melatonin—a hormone secreted at night by the pineal gland that helps balance the reproductive, thyroid, and adrenal hormones and regulates the body's **circadian** rhythm of sleeping and waking. Melatonin reduces the body's nocturnal production of estrogen—a hormone that can stimulate growth of cancer cells. It has also been shown to slow or stop the growth of several types of cancer cells. Exposure to nighttime light, even at low levels, can seriously impede melatonin production. A 2011 Ohio State University study found that chronic exposure to dim light at night could also affect our immune system's ability to respond to illness.

diurnal
active in daytime

7   Humans aren't the only ones impacted by light pollution. In fact, we may be far more adaptable to it than other species. "We have a bias as **diurnal** creatures that we don't realize how much wildlife is active at night," says Chad Moore, the US National Park Service's Night Sky program manager.

8   While we still don't know enough about the full ecological consequences of light pollution, scientists are finding increasing evidence that artificial light disrupts the natural activities of many species, affecting how they forage, communicate, and even reproduce.

fry
young fish

9   Researchers have found, for example, that sockeye salmon **fry** stop swimming downstream when exposed to any light above 0.1 lux (the standard measurement for lighting) and often end up in slow-moving waters near the shore, which makes them vulnerable to predators. Some slow-flying bat species are finding it difficult to feed themselves since there are fewer hours of unalloyed darkness available to them and also because the insects that they like to eat swarm around lights at night.

10   In coastal areas, thousands of hatchling sea turtles that crawl out of their shells at night get disoriented by lights from beachfront homes and resorts and never make it to the safety of the sea. And every year, millions of bedazzled birds fly into our cities' lighted high-rises and communication towers and die. A 2012 study by Travis Longcore and Catherine Rich of the Urban Wildlands Group and colleagues found that about 6.8 million birds die in North America every year by flying too close to the static red lights on communication towers and colliding with cables that hold up the tall structures. Earlier this year they published another study that breaks down those deaths by species, something that hasn't been done before. "There aren't just birds out there, there are many hundreds of different species of birds," says Longcore, who along with Rich co-edited the book, *Ecological Consequences of Artificial Night Lighting.*

11   While it would be difficult to do away with night lighting, which makes much of our modern lifestyle possible, research shows as much as half of the light we project is wasted—it points up at the sky instead of illuminating the street below. Simple ways to minimize such waste and reduce light pollution include turning lights off when not in use and lighting our streets and outdoors with cutoff lights that point only downward.

12   Although research on the full impact of light pollution is ongoing, Moore thinks we should act now to reclaim the night. "It would be a mistake to think we need to have information on every particular species before we can act," he says. "We know enough now that we can say anytime we spill light into the sky, we're putting animals and wildlife at risk, and we're probably putting ourselves at risk."

A. UNDERSTANDING THE THESIS AND OTHER MAIN IDEAS

Select the best answer.

_____ 1. Which of the following sentences best states the thesis or central thought of "And Incredibly Bright"?

    a. Artificial nighttime lighting has been linked to an increased risk of breast cancer as well as problems with the human immune system.

    b. Nighttime lighting not only blots out the night sky, it also has negative effects on humans and other species.

    c. The effects of nighttime lighting are many, but none is more important than the problems it creates by making asteroids difficult to identify.

    d. Humans, who are diurnal, are affected by artificial nighttime lighting, but nocturnal creatures (such as bats and sea turtles) are affected more by artificial daytime lighting.

_____ 2. Which of the following sentences best states the implied main idea of paragraph 2?

    a. All over the world, the Milky Way is invisible to people.

    b. In general, people who live in a city environment see less of the night sky than people who live in a rural or country environment.

    c. As a result of nighttime artificial lighting, which increases every year, people across the United States and the globe are unable to see the night sky.

    d. At the current rate, nobody in America will be able to see the night sky twenty years from now.

_____ 3. The main idea of paragraph 6 is found in the

    a. first sentence.

    b. second sentence.

    c. fourth sentence.

    d. last sentence.

_____ 4. Which of the following sentences best states the implied main idea of paragraph 10?

    a. Nighttime lighting leads to the deaths of animals from many species, from sea turtles to birds.

    b. The U.S. government should fund more habitats for particular species, such as sea turtles.

    c. Travis Longcore and Catherine Rich have limited their scientific studies to bird species.

    d. According to *Ecological Consequences of Artificial Night Lighting*, the airline industry is responsible for the death of almost 7 million birds per year.

_____ 5. The topic of paragraph 11 is

    a. the modern lifestyle.

    b. night lighting.

    c. light waste and pollution.

    d. light.

B. IDENTIFYING DETAILS

Match the scientific term in Column A with its definition in Column B.

Column A	Column B
_____ 1. diurnal	a. measurement of light
_____ 2. melatonin	b. hormone that can stimulate the growth of cancer cells
_____ 3. estrogen	c. active during the day
_____ 4. lux	d. natural hormone that regulates sleep and waking
_____ 5. nocturnal	e. active at night

C. RECOGNIZING METHODS OF ORGANIZATION AND TRANSITIONS

Select the best answer.

_____ 1. The overall pattern of organization used in "And Incredibly Bright" is

    a. process.

    b. cause and effect.

    c. classification.

    d. comparison and contrast.

_____ 2. The organizational pattern used in paragraphs 8 and 9 is

    a. summary.

    b. definition.

    c. generalization and example.

    d. order of importance.

_____ 3. Two transitional words or phrases that signal the addition pattern in paragraph 10 are

    a. thousands, millions.

    b. found, published.

    c. and, another.

    d. get disoriented, flying too close.

D. REVIEWING AND ORGANIZING IDEAS: OUTLINING

Complete the following outline of the reading.

I. Artificial Nighttime Lighting: Basic Facts

    A. After 1994 Los Angeles _____, people reported seeing a silvery cloud that was actually the Milky Way

    B. Two-thirds of Americans cannot see the _____

    C. Range and rates of lights are increasing every year

    D. More than _____ of world's population cannot see the Milky Way

II. Scientific Research and Observations

    A. Richard Stevens, _____: connection between night-shift work and breast cancer

    B. _____, 2007: confirmed link between prolonged night-shift work and cancer

    C. Itai Kloog, Harvard

        1. Modern urbanized _____ habitat is a risk

        2. Significant association between nighttime brightness and _____

        _____

          i. Decrease in production of _____

    D. Ohio State University, 2011: Chronic exposure to dim light at night can affect body's _____ system

    E. Unspecified researchers

        1. Salmon fry stop swimming downstream when exposed to light above 0.1 lux

        2. _____ have difficulty feeding themselves

3. _____ hatchlings get disoriented and do not make it to the water

F. Travis Longcore and _____, 2012: 6.8 million birds die in North America every year by flying too close to lights

III. Possible Solutions

A. Minimize light waste and _____

B. Chad Moore, U.S. National Park Service: The time to act is now

E. READING AND THINKING VISUALLY

Select the best answer.

_____ 1. According to the reading, what percentage of the world's population has lost "naked-eye visibility" of the image shown in Figure 1 on page 525?
   a. one-fifth
   b. one-quarter
   c. one-half
   d. two-thirds

_____ 2. Approximately what percentage of Americans live in places where they can look at the night sky and see the image in Figure 1 on page 525?
   a. 20 percent (one-fifth)
   b. 33 percent (one-third)
   c. 67 percent (two-thirds)
   d. 1 percent

F. FIGURING OUT IMPLIED MEANINGS

Indicate whether each statement is true (T) or false (F).

_____ 1. The author of this selection, Holly Haworth, supports the idea of energy conservation.

_____ 2. Human beings are generally nocturnal.

_____ 3. The "giant, silvery cloud" that many Los Angeles residents saw in 1994 was actually the majesty of the night sky, unpolluted by artificial light.

_____ 4. Artificial light reduces the number of insects available for bats to eat.

_____ 5. Night-shift work can cause cancer because artificial light reduces the body's production of melatonin.

_____ 6. Artificial light interferes with humans' ability to view the night sky because artificial light leads to poor nighttime vision.

_____ 7. Young sockeye salmon often end up in fast-moving waters as a result of artificial light.

G. THINKING CRITICALLY

For items 1–4, indicate whether each statement is a fact (F) or an opinion (O).

_____ 1. "Our cities and suburbs are so brightly lit that on any given night only 1 percent of Americans have a view of the sky unpolluted by artificial light." (paragraph 2)

_____ 2. "The most worrisome research on human health links nighttime light exposure to increased risk of breast cancer." (paragraph 5)

_____ 3. "In fact, we may be far more adaptable to it [light pollution] than other species." (paragraph 7)

_____ 4. "It would be a mistake to think we need to have information on every particular species before we can act." (paragraph 12)

For items 5–8, select the best answer.

_____ 5. The purpose of "And Incredibly Bright" is to

    a. encourage readers to move to rural (country) areas where they can view the glories of the night sky.

    b. discuss the effects of artificial light on various species, including humans, birds, and other living creatures.

    c. help students understand key concepts in astronomy, such as lux, asteroids, and the Milky Way.

    d. encourage scientists to undertake more research regarding the role of artificial lighting in human cancers.

_____ 6. The tone of the article is best described as

    a. informal.

    b. informative.

    c. skeptical.

    d. angry.

_____ 7. The author uses all of the following to support her main ideas *except*

    a. scientific research.

    b. statistics and data.

    c. personal experience.

    d. quotes from scientific professionals.

_____ 8. According to the article, which of the following effects has *not* been linked to artificial lighting?

    a. less production of melatonin

    b. a diminished immune system

    c. poor performance on the job

    d. incidence of breast cancer

H. BUILDING VOCABULARY

Context

Using context and a dictionary, if necessary, determine the meaning of each word as it is used in the selection.

_____ 1. vast (paragraph 1)

    a. ancient

    b. populated

    c. huge

    d. electrified

_____ 2. contiguous (paragraph 2)

    a. bordering

    b. ongoing

    c. intimidating

    d. rural

_____ 3. myriad (paragraph 3)

    a. old

    b. unpleasant

    c. many

    d. far-reaching

_____ 4. nocturnal (paragraph 6)

    a. natural

    b. nighttime

    c. increased

    d. female

_____ 5. chronic (paragraph 6)

    a. repeated

    b. small amount

    c. untimely

    d. synchronized

_____ 6. unalloyed (paragraph 9)

    a. intense

    b. frightening

    c. productive

    d. pure

_____ 7. static (paragraph 10)

    a. unmoving

    b. electrical

    c. large

    d. suspended

Word Parts

> ### A REVIEW OF ROOTS AND SUFFIXES
>
> **ASTRO** or **ASTER** means *star*
> **ANN** or **ENN** means *year*
> **ECO** means *earth*
> **MIL** means *thousand*
> **-ER** means *one who*
> **-LOGY** means *the study of*

Use your knowledge of word parts and the review above to choose the answer that best defines the boldfaced word in the sentences below.

_____ 1. **Millennia** (paragraph 1) are periods of _____.

    a. 30 seconds

    b. 10 minutes

    c. 1,000 years

    d. 5 centuries

_____ 2. An **astronomer** (paragraph 3) is one who studies _____.

    a. stars

    b. astrology

    c. animals

    d. light

_____ 3. An **ecologist** (paragraph 3) studies _____.

    a. the human body

    b. the earth

    c. the universe

    d. water

Unusual Words/Understanding Idioms

Use the meanings given below to write a sentence using the boldfaced phrase.

1. **Global-scale data** (paragraph 2) refers to information that is collected across the world.

   Your sentence: _____

   _____

2. To **break ground** (paragraph 5) means to do something new and innovative that is likely to have a positive benefit. The adjective form of this phrase is **groundbreaking**.

   Your sentence: _____

   _____

I. SELECTING A LEARNING/STUDY STRATEGY

Predict two exam questions that might be asked about the reading.

J. EXPLORING IDEAS THROUGH DISCUSSION AND WRITING

1. What exactly does the author mean by the phrase "modern urbanized sleeping habitat" (paragraph 6)? Write a paragraph explaining this phrase.
2. Paragraph 11 outlines some suggestions for eliminating light pollution and waste. Write a paragraph in which you offer some additional suggestions for reducing unnecessary light in your home, on your campus, or at your job.
3. Summarize the negative effects of artificial lighting.
4. Evaluate the author's use of her sources. Which of her statements are not supported by specific scientific research or a quotation from a respected scientist at a credible institution?
5. How would your life (and society) change if electric light were not widely available? Write an essay in which you explore the possibilities.

K. BEYOND THE CLASSROOM TO THE WEB

The selection makes reference to several scientific or governmental organizations, including The U.S. National Optical Astronomy Observatory, the World Health Organization, and the Urban Wildlands Group. Visit the Web site of one of these organizations and look for the group's mission statement (usually found by clicking on the link that says "About" or "About Us"). What are the organization's goals? In your opinion, are the materials on the organization's Web site biased or unbiased? Explain your answer.

**TRACKING
YOUR
PROGRESS**

Selection 24

Section	Number Correct	Score
A. Thesis and Main Ideas (5 items)	_____ × 4	_____
B. Details (5 items)	_____ × 3	_____
C. Organization and Transitions (3 items)	_____ × 3	_____
E. Reading and Thinking Visually (2 items)	_____ × 3	_____
F. Implied Meanings (7 items)	_____ × 2	_____
G. Thinking Critically (8 items)	_____ × 2	_____
H. Vocabulary		
Context (7 items)	_____ × 2	_____
Word Parts (3 items)	_____ × 2	_____
	Total Score	_____%

17 Physical Sciences/Mathematics

The **physical sciences** are concerned with the properties, functions, structure, and composition of matter, substances, and energy. They include physics, chemistry, astronomy, physical geography, and geology. **Mathematics** is the study of relationships among numbers, quantities, and shapes using signs, symbols, and proofs (logical solutions of problems). Often mathematics and physical science work together to address interesting questions important to our life and well-being. "A Statistician's View: What Are Your Chances of Winning the Powerball Lottery?" uses mathematics to examine a popular American pastime for some, an addiction for others—playing a lottery. "'Hope It's in Your Backyard!'" discusses a controversial method of extracting natural gas from the ground. "Additional Renewable-Energy Options" examines new ways to harvest and channel energy.

Use the following suggestions for reading in the physical sciences and mathematics.

TIPS FOR READING IN PHYSICAL SCIENCES/ MATHEMATICS

- **Read slowly and reread if necessary.** Both mathematics and the physical sciences are technical and detailed. Do not expect to understand everything on your first reading. When reading "A Statistician's View: What Are Your Chances of Winning the Powerball Lottery?" you might read it once to grasp the author's overall position on lotteries and then reread, concentrating on the role mathematics plays in examining the issue.

- **Focus on new terminology.** To read mathematics and the physical sciences, you have to learn the language of science. Mathematics and physical sciences are exact and precise, using terminology to make communication as error free as possible. In "Hope It's in Your Backyard!" you will encounter technical terms such as hydraulic fracturing, greenhouse gas, carbon dioxide, and climate change. Understanding the precise meanings of these terms mean will help you better evaluate media coverage of global warming.

- **Use writing to learn.** Reading alone is often not sufficient for learning mathematics and physical sciences. While highlighting and annotating a text work well for many subjects, they do not for math and science textbooks, where everything seems important. Try writing; express ideas in your own words. This method will test your understanding, too. If you cannot explain an idea in your own words, you probably do not understand it. After reading "Additional Renewable-Energy Options," try to summarize in your own words each alternative energy option.

One of the most challenging things to read in mathematics textbooks is word problems. This task requires both reading skills and knowledge of mathematics, as well as reasoning skills. To read and solve word problems more effectively, use the following steps.

TIPS FOR READING WORD PROBLEMS

- **Identify what is being asked for.** You may need to read the problem several times in order to do so. Often the information asked for occurs at the end of the problem.

- **Locate the useful information contained in the problem.** Underline useful information. Many problems also contain irrelevant information that will not help you solve the problem; cross out this information. Also note what information you do not have.

- **Visualize the problem.** Draw a picture or diagram that will make the problem real and practical. Label its parts, and include measurements and any other relevant information.

- **Estimate your answer.** Decide what would and would not be a reasonable answer.

- **Decide how to solve the problem.** Recall formulas you have learned that are related to the problem. You may have to translate ordinary words into mathematical language. For example, the phrase *percent of* usually suggests multiplication; the words *decreased by* mean subtraction.

- **Solve the problem.** Set up an equation and choose variables to represent unknown quantities.

- **Verify your answer.** Compare your answer with your estimate. If there is a large discrepancy, it is a signal that you have made an error. Be sure to check your arithmetic.

SELECTION 25

A Statistician's View: What Are Your Chances of Winning the Powerball Lottery?

Ronald L. Wasserstein

Ronald L. Wasserstein is executive director of the American Statistical Association, the main association for statisticians and related professionals in the United States. An expert on state lotteries, he is a former statistics professor at Washburn University.

PREVIEWING THE READING

Using the steps listed on pages 40–41, preview the reading selection. When you have finished, answer the following questions.

1. In November 2012, the largest Powerball jackpot on record was worth _____.

2. Indicate whether each statement is true (T) or false (F).

_____ a. To play Powerball, a player selects five numbers between 1 and 89.

_____ b. Your chance of winning the lottery with a single ticket is 1 in 75 million.

_____ c. The author's purpose for writing is to discourage people from buying lottery tickets.

 MAKING CONNECTIONS

Have you ever played the lottery, or do you play it regularly? What type(s) of lottery tickets do you buy (for example, lotto-like games or scratch-off tickets)? Do you think the odds of winning at a scratch-off game are better than winning a state lottery? Where can you find information about your odds of winning each type of game?

READING TIP

This selection is fairly short, but it requires a fairly slow reading pace. Take the time to think about the author's way of describing the size of the numbers he is writing about. Do these descriptions better help you understand your odds of winning the Powerball jackpot?

A Statistician's View: What Are Your Chances of Winning the Powerball Lottery?

1   In November 2012, a Missouri couple and an Arizona man shared the largest Powerball jackpot ever—$587 million. An article about the Missouri couple—Mark and Cindy Hill—appeared in *The Huffington Post* on February 25 telling a wonderful story about how the couple is using their winnings to benefit their community. Such stories lead us to daydream about what we might do if we won all that money.

2   What are your chances of winning? A quick look at the Powerball Web site tells you the probability of winning the jackpot is 1 in 175,223,510. To see where that number comes from, imagine purchasing every number combination. In Powerball, a player first picks five different whole numbers between 1 and 59. One could make a list of all the possibilities, starting with (1, 2, 3, 4, 5), (1, 2, 3, 4, 6), and so on all the way through (55, 56, 57, 58, 59). But it would take a long time to make that list, because it has more than five million entries! Indeed, mathematics tells us the number of ways to choose five distinct numbers from 1 to 59 is 5,006,386.

3   After choosing the five numbers between 1 and 59, the player then picks another number between 1 and 35 that is called the Powerball. So, we multiply the 5,006,386 by 35 and see that there are 175,223,510 possible Powerball combinations. For simplicity, let's be generous and round off to an even 175,000,000.

4   Your chance of winning the lottery on a single ticket is one in 175 million. That seems tiny, and it is. In fact, it is so small that it is difficult for us to grasp. Understanding how small this number is provides the key to understanding how likely—or unlikely—it is you will become the next big winner of the Powerball jackpot.

5   For some reason, we tend to associate unlikely events with a specific physical phenomenon. "I have a better chance of being struck by lightning," we often say. But that does not provide much of a basis for comparison. We realize being struck by lightning is unlikely, but we have no sense of how unlikely, and of course the chance of being struck by lightning is much different for a farmer than a coal miner.

6   The problem with grasping the smallness of "1 in 175 million" is that we never see 175 million distinct objects. It is easy to grasp 1 in 50, for example, because we can imagine ourselves with 49 other people in a room. We can get our minds around 1 in 75,000 (roughly) by visualizing the crowd of people at the Super Bowl and imagining ourselves being the one person selected from that crowd to win a prize. But one in 175 million cannot be readily visualized.

7   Here is an example I have used in classrooms all over the country, and it is way more fun than thinking about being struck by lightning! Imagine 175 million freshly minted one-dollar bills are being delivered to my house near Washington, D.C. One of those dollar bills is specially marked as the "lucky dollar bill." You get to pick a dollar bill, and if you happen to pick the lucky dollar bill, you win all the dollar bills.

8   A straightforward mathematical calculation using the dimensions of a dollar bill reveals it will take two semi-trailers to deliver the 175,000,000 dollar bills to my house. Once these arrive, they will have to be unloaded, of course, so you will have

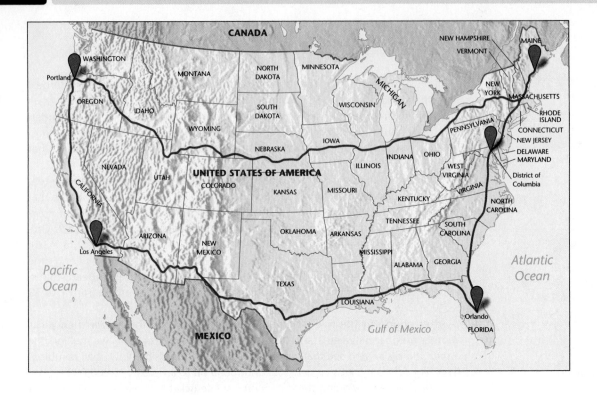

a fair chance to pick the lucky dollar bill. So, we will lay them out end to end. How long will that line of dollar bills go?

9   If we start from my house, we'll have enough dollar bills to go all the way south to Disney World in Orlando [Florida]. Then we'll still have enough to go clear across the country to Disneyland [in California]! But, even then, we are not out of dollar bills, so we can go north and make it all the way to Portland, Oregon. Still, we have dollar bills, enough to make it all the way east to Portland, Maine. And, fortunately, we'll have enough to make it back to my house near DC, completing the loop.

10   Do we have any dollars bills left? Yes! We would still have enough dollar bills to go all the way around the loop a second time!

11   Now imagine that you walk, bike or drive for as long as you want around the double loop, and when you decide to stop, you stoop over and pick up one dollar bill. Your chance of selecting the lucky dollar bill is one in 175 million, the same as your chance of winning the Powerball jackpot!

12   Your chance of ever winning this big jackpot is impossibly small. It isn't going to happen.

13   It is not my purpose or place to discourage people from buying lottery tickets. I just want everyone to understand their chances as fully and accurately as possible.

—Wasserstein, *Huffington Post*

A. UNDERSTANDING THE THESIS AND OTHER MAIN IDEAS

Select the best answer.

_____ 1. Which of the following best states the central thesis of the selection?

a. You are more likely to get struck by lightning (or experience some other natural disaster) than to win the Powerball jackpot.

b. The best use of lottery winnings is donating the money to benefit the community.

c. People who play the lottery are simply wasting their money.

d. Mathematics and some visualization can help you understand why your odds of winning the Powerball jackpot are so tiny.

_____ 2. The author's primary purpose is to

a. convince students to major in mathematics or statistics.

b. put pressure on states to offer more lottery-type contests.

c. help readers understand why their odds of winning a lottery jackpot are impossibly small.

d. argue that the money collected from the sale of lottery tickets should be used to help rehabilitate addicted gamblers.

_____ 3. According to the selection, the odds of winning the Powerball jackpot are

a. 1 in 49 million.

b. 1 in 59 million.

c. 1 in 129 million.

d. 1 in 175 million.

_____ 4. The main idea of paragraph 6 can be found in the

a. first sentence.

b. second sentence.

c. third sentence.

d. first and last sentences.

_____ 5. The topic of paragraphs 9–10 is

a. the length of a trail composed of 175 million dollar bills.

b. the geography of lottery use (that is, the states where the lottery is most popular).

c. the methods used to transport currency around the United States.

d. key points of interest on the east and west coasts of the United States.

B. IDENTIFYING DETAILS

Select the best answer.

_____ 1. Answer this question without doing any math. 5,006,386 times 35 equals:

a. about 30 million.

b. about 50 million.

c. about 100 million.

d. about 175 million.

_____ 2. In which two states did the winners of the November 2012 Power-ball jackpot live?

a. Oregon and Maine

b. Washington, DC and Florida

c. California and Florida

d. Arizona and Missouri

_____ 3. When buying a Powerball ticket, you must select the "Powerball." Which of the following is *not* one of your options for the Powerball?

a. 8

b. 23

c. 34

d. 59

_____ 4. Which of the following variables does the author use to calculate how many trucks would be needed to bring 175 million dollar bills to his house?

a. the weight of the dollar bills

b. the date the dollar bills were minted

c. the dimensions of the dollar bills

d. the degree to which the dollar bills are crushed or folded

_____ 5. All of the following are key points of the "dollar bill loop" described by the author *except*

a. Seattle, Washington.

b. Washington, DC.

c. Portland, Maine.

d. Orlando, Florida.

C. RECOGNIZING METHODS OF ORGANIZATION AND TRANSITIONS

Select the best answer.

_____ 1. The organizational pattern by which the author explains the probability of winning the jackpot in paragraphs 2–3 is
    a. process.
    b. spatial order.
    c. definition.
    d. enumeration.

_____ 2. The primary organizational pattern of paragraphs 4–11 is
    a. comparison and contrast.
    b. statement and clarification.
    c. classification.
    d. cause and effect.

_____ 3. The transitional phrase that hints at the organizational pattern beginning in paragraph 4 is
    a. your chance
    b. that seems
    c. in fact
    d. provides the key

D. REVIEWING AND ORGANIZING IDEAS: PARAPHRASING

Complete the following paraphrase of paragraphs 4–5 from the selection by filling in the blanks.

The odds of one lottery ticket winning the Powerball jackpot are 1 in _____ million, which means extremely tiny odds. These odds are so _____ that they are hard for us to understand, but comprehending this number is essential to understanding why you probably will not win the next big jackpot. Many people think they can better grasp the likelihood of rare events by comparing them to the odds of something that happens in the physical world, such as _____. However, this is not a valid comparison because getting struck by lightning depends on many different _____.

E. READING AND THINKING VISUALLY

Select the best answer.

_____ 1. The author likely included the map shown with the reading (p. 540) in order to

    a. explain how popular the lottery is across the United States.

    b. show the loop of dollar bills that he describes in the second half of the reading.

    c. imply that the lottery is much more popular in the United States than it is in Canada.

    d. illustrate a loop of approximately 175,000 miles.

_____ 2. The loop shown in the map travels through all of the following U.S. states *except*

    a. Texas.

    b. South Carolina.

    c. Kansas.

    d. New York.

F. FIGURING OUT IMPLIED MEANINGS

Indicate whether each statement is true (T) or false (F).

_____ 1. It is easy to understand your odds of winning the Powerball jackpot by comparing them to your odds of experiencing an earthquake.

_____ 2. The author of this article is or was a teacher.

_____ 3. An extremely large number of possible number combinations in Powerball leads to very tiny odds of winning.

_____ 4. Approximately 175 million people attend the Super Bowl each year.

_____ 5. The author lives in the nation's capital.

_____ 6. You must fully complete the circuit shown on the map on page 540 twice to pass every dollar bill on the path described by the author.

_____ 7. To help readers understand the article, the author simplifies some of the numbers involved.

G. THINKING CRITICALLY

Select the best answer.

_____ 1. The tone of the selection can best be described as

    a. angry.

    b. condescending.

    c. cynical.

    d. informative.

_____ 2. All of the following excerpts from the reading are facts *except*

    a. "Your chance of winning the lottery on a single ticket is in one in 175 million" (paragraph 4).

    b. "But that does not provide much of a basis of comparison." (paragraph 5)

    c. "It will take two semi-trailers to deliver the 175,00,000 dollar bills to my house." (paragraph 8)

    d. "We would still have enough dollar bills left to go all the way around the loop a second time." (paragraph 10)

_____ 3. The author uses all of the following to support his thesis *except*

    a. mathematical examples and reasoning.

    b. details of how the Powerball lottery is played.

    c. citations from mathematical journals.

    d. a map that helps readers visualize how far 175 million one-dollar bills would stretch.

_____ 4. According to the author, "the chance of being struck by lightning is much different for a farmer than a coal miner" (paragraph 5). Who is more likely to be struck by lightning and why?

    a. The farmer is more likely to be struck because he works out-doors, exposed to the weather.

    b. The farmer is more likely to be struck because farming is a more dangerous occupation than mining.

    c. The miner is more likely to be struck because metals under-ground attract lightning.

    d. The miner is more likely to be struck because the ground con-ducts electricity.

_____ 5. In which paragraph does the author explicitly state his purpose for writing the piece?

    a. paragraph 1   c. paragraph 7

    b. paragraph 2   d. paragraph 13

H. BUILDING VOCABULARY

Context

Using context and a dictionary, if necessary, determine the meaning of each word as it used in the selection.

_____ 1. probability (paragraph 2)

    a. mathematics

    b. likelihood

    c. ratio

    d. statistics

_____ 2. phenomenon (paragraph 5)

    a. drawback

    b. occurrence

    c. promise

    d. timeframe

_____ 3. grasp (paragraph 6)

    a. hold

    b. understand

    c. simplify

    d. decide

_____ 4. minted (paragraph 7)

    a. mined

    b. made

    c. crusted

    d. spicy

Word Parts

A REVIEW OF SUFFIXES

-IAN means "one who."

Use your knowledge of word parts to fill in the blank.

1. A **statistician** (title) is one who studies _____.

Unusual Words/Understanding Idioms

Use the meanings given below to write a sentence using the boldfaced phrase.

1. **Rounding off** (paragraph 3) is a mathematical term for taking a complicated number and making it slightly lower or slightly higher to make it easier to read and understand. For example, 15,231 might be rounded off (or rounded down) to 15,000.

_____

_____

2. To **get one's mind around** something (paragraph 6) is to understand it. The connotation is one of a difficult concept that is difficult to understand at first.

_____

_____

I. SELECTING A LEARNING/STUDY STRATEGY

How might you prepare for a class discussion based on this reading?

J. EXPLORING IDEAS THROUGH DISCUSSION AND WRITING

1. Do you find the author's way of explaining large numbers helpful? Why or why not?
2. After reading this article, are you less likely to buy lottery tickets in the future? Why or why not? Write a paragraph answering these questions.
3. Write a summary of the article.
4. Write an essay in which you answer this question: Why do so many people play the lottery?

K. BEYOND THE CLASSROOM TO THE WEB

Does your state have a lottery? If so, visit the lottery commission's Web site for information about the games offered. Which of these do you have the best chance of winning? The lowest chance of winning? Do you see a relationship between the size of the prizes and the likelihood of winning them? If so, describe that relationship.

TRACKING YOUR PROGRESS

Selection 25

Section	Number Correct		Score
A. Thesis and Main Ideas (5 items)	_____	× 3	_____
B. Details (5 items)	_____	× 3	_____
C. Organization and Transitions (3 items)	_____	× 4	_____
E. Reading and Thinking Visually (2 items)	_____	× 4	_____
F. Implied Meanings (5 items)	_____	× 2	_____
G. Thinking Critically (5 items)	_____	× 4	_____
H. Vocabulary			
Context (4 items)	_____	× 3	_____
Word Parts (1 item)	_____	× 4	_____
		Total Score	_____ %

SELECTION 26

"Hope It's in Your Backyard!"

Neil deMause

This selection is taken from *Extra!*, a monthly magazine published by FAIR (Fairness & Accuracy in Reporting). FAIR monitors the reporting of the national media. According to FAIR's mission statement, the organization "maintains a regular dialogue with reporters at news outlets across the country, providing constructive critiques when called for and applauding exceptional, hard-hitting journalism."

PREVIEWING THE READING

Using the steps listed on pages 40–41, preview the reading selection. When you have finished, complete the following items.

1. The topic of this selection is press coverage of the natural-gas extraction technique known as _____.

2. Indicate whether each statement is true (T) or false (F).

   _____ a. Overall, it appears that the media do not consistently report on the troublesome aspects of fracking.

   _____ b. Sue Tierney is outspoken about her support for fracking.

3. Which of the following sources are *not* cited in the reading? Check all that apply.

   _____ a. *Newsweek*

   _____ b. *The Washington Post*

   _____ c. *Scientific American*

   _____ d. *The New York Times*

 MAKING CONNECTIONS   *If you drive a car, what recent trends have you seen in gasoline prices? How does the price of gasoline relate to the topic of this reading?*

READING TIP

This article is written much like a college research paper. It summarizes the reporting of several resources and then draws a conclusion from it. Note how the author of this article, Neil deMause, use quotes from the original sources to offer support for his main ideas.

"Hope It's in Your Backyard!"

Gushing over fracking ignores climate crisis

1   One of the difficulties of reporting on climate change is its incremental nature: It's hard to expect every media mention of someone driving a car or running an air conditioner to include a note about its effects on the environment. Yet even when the climate impacts of an action are unambiguous and central to a story, reporters all too often avoid the subject.

2   Take the natural-gas extraction technique of hydraulic fracturing (**Extra**!, 2/12). Better known as "fracking," the process involves cracking open underground rock layers containing oil and gas deposits by blasting them with a high-pressure chemical **slurry**. Of the many troubling side effects of fracking—which run from groundwater contamination to increased earthquake activity—one of the most worrisome is its impact on climate change.

slurry
a mixture of fine particles suspended in water

3   Any drilling for fossil fuels means more carbon will eventually be released into the atmosphere, but fracking's effect on climate is compounded by the fact that the drilling process can create huge **methane** leaks: A study by Cornell scientists Robert Howarth and Anthony Ingraffea estimated that fracked wells leak 40 to 60 percent more methane than conventional wells (**Scientific American,** 1/20/12). Because methane is 20 times as potent a **greenhouse gas** as carbon dioxide, the National Center for Atmospheric Research has estimated that at these levels of leakage, switching from oil to natural gas consumption would significantly worsen global warming over the next several decades (**Climate Progress**, 9/9/11).

methane
a polluting gas

greenhouse gas
a type of airborne gas that has been linked to climate change

4   Outside of scientific and environmental media, however, you'd be hard-pressed to find any discussion of the climate change risk in tracking coverage, much of which has instead followed the fossil fuel industry's line that the technique is the first step to a future of cheap energy.

5   In an article on the spread of fracking to Europe and China, for example, **Time** magazine (5/21/12) cited the International Energy Agency as predicting that "the world could be entering a golden age of gas, in which inexpensive natural gas replaces coal as the electricity source of choice." Aside from a brief mention of concerns over groundwater contamination by the chemicals used in fracking—listed as one of the "obstacles" to more widespread adoption of the technology—no downsides were noted, while increased mining of natural gas was discussed as a way for smaller countries to become energy-independent of oil-rich nations. "Fracking," concluded **Time**'s Bryan Walsh, "is here to stay."

6   **USA Today** (5/15/12) was even more optimistic about a fracked future, running a front-page story headlined "U.S. Energy Independence Is No Longer Just a Pipe Dream," that raved about the glorious future that will result from fracked natural gas. The advent of fracking in Williamsport, Pennsylvania, the paper reported, has transformed a "once-sleepy chunk of north-central Pennsylvania" into the star of "an emerging national energy rush," with companies rushing to move to town and new hotels in the works. The paper went on to list what it called "an improbable-sounding **litany** of good things" that could result from fracked wells—from falling gas prices to independence from foreign oil to an economic boom that would (according to one report) create 3.6 million new jobs—but failed to mention a single environmental concern.

litany
list

7   Meanwhile, an enthusiastic **ABC World News** report (5/10/12) on "new drilling techniques [that] find oil in your backyard" avoided even saying the name hydraulic fracturing (though a longer Web report did). Instead, correspondent Sharyn Alfonsi interviewed Kansas farmers whose oil royalties "could be" as much as $500,000 a month. At the end of the segment, Alfonsi displayed a map of frackable sites, gushing that there could be "2 trillion barrels of oil in our backyards." To which Diane Sawyer replied: "Hope it's in your backyard!"—and then urged viewers to consult a map on the **ABC News** website to see if fracking riches could be theirs, too.

8   Reports like these faithfully echo the talking points of the fossil fuel industry: The American Petroleum Institute's fracking page states confidently, "Shale energy is the answer. It creates jobs, stimulates the economy and provides a secure energy future for America."

9   Other media outlets have been more cautious about proclaiming a glorious fracking future: The **Associated Press** (5/20/12) noted that while some New York farmers look longingly at the lucrative drilling leases that have gone to their neighbors in fracking-friendly Pennsylvania, others worry about well-water contamination and the destruction of farmland for mining roads and pipelines. But even lengthy series on the fracking controversy, such as the **New York Times'** ongoing "Drilling Down" (starting 2/26/11) and **NPR**'s "The Fracking Boom: Missing Answers" (5/14–17/12), have focused solely on the problems of ground water and air pollution without touching on climate questions.

NPR
National Public
Radio

10   One rare exception was an **NPR Morning Edition** story (5/17/12) by Elizabeth Shogren that followed a National Oceanic and Atmospheric Administration scientist who discovered a huge plume of methane north of Denver, ultimately tracing it to new fracking wells in northeastern Colorado. "We need to know a lot about methane itself, which is natural gas, if we're worried about climate change," energy consultant Sue Tierney told Shogren. "Fifty years from now, are we really going to be wondering it we really screwed up because we went on this big gas boom?" It's a question that the media should be asking now, not half a century on.

—deMause, *Extra!*

BY THE NUMBERS

90 Years	Estimated supply of domestic natural gas at current consumption levels
24 Trillion	Cubic feet of natural gas used annually in the United States
26 percent	Amount of the nation's electricity generated by natural gas in 2011
11,400	New wells fractured each year to produce natural gas
14,000	Wells re-fractured each year to produce natural gas
5	States that have enacted hydraulic fracturing related legislation this session
24	States that have introduced legislation addressing hydraulic fracturing
137	Bills introduced that address hydraulic fracturing

—Pless, *State Legislatures Magazine*

A. UNDERSTANDING THE THESIS AND OTHER MAIN IDEAS

Select the best answer.

_____ 1. Which of the following best states the thesis or central thought of "Hope It's in Your Backyard!"?

   a. While fracking offers many advantages for extracting natural gas from the earth, it also contributes to climate change.

   b. NPR *Morning Edition* and *The New York Times* are pro-environmental media organizations that present the most unbiased reporting on fracking, while all other media are supported by the energy industry.

   c. Although it seems clear that fracking contributes to climate change, many media outlets focus on the positive aspects of this technology; even the sources that report on the problems with fracking tend to ignore the climate-change effects.

   d. Fracking has the potential to become a leading source of energy production in the United States, but other countries, such as China and India, are proceeding with much more caution with regard to fracking.

_____ 2. Which of the following sources did not run a news report that focused primarily on the advantages of fracking?

   a. *USA Today*

   b. Associated Press

   c. *Time*

   d. NPR *Morning Edition*

_____ 3. The topic of paragraph 3 is

   a. Robert Howarth and Anthony Ingraffea.

   b. drilling for fossil fuels.

   c. the National Center for Atmospheric Research.

   d. the effects of fracking on global warming.

_____ 4. The main idea of paragraph 10 is found in the

   a. first sentence.

   b. second sentence.

   c. third sentence.

   d. last sentence.

B. IDENTIFYING DETAILS

Select the best answer.

_____ 1. The town in Pennsylvania that has recently experienced an economic boom as a result of fracking is
  a. Williamsport.
  b. Philadelphia.
  c. Pittsburgh.
  d. Harrisburg.

_____ 2. According to the American Petroleum Institute, what is the solution to America's energy problems?
  a. wind energy
  b. solar energy
  c. shale energy
  d. geothermal energy

_____ 3. The article discusses all of the following possible negative effects of fracking *except* for
  a. destruction of farmland.
  b. increased likelihood of earthquakes.
  c. nuclear waste.
  d. water contamination.

_____ 4. The article discusses all of the following possible positive effects of fracking *except* for
  a. energy independence.
  b. the creation of new jobs.
  c. falling gas prices.
  d. a decrease in the U.S. deficit.

C. RECOGNIZING METHODS OF ORGANIZATION AND TRANSITIONS

Select the best answer.

_____ 1. The overall pattern of organization used in "Hope It's in Your Backyard!" is
  a. listing.
  b. process.
  c. classification.
  d. spatial order.

_____ 2. The pattern of organization used in paragraph 2 is

    a. chronological order.

    b. definition.

    c. cause and effect.

    d. summary.

_____ 3. The two transitional words or phrases that signal the cause-and-effect pattern used in paragraph 3 are

    a. process, estimated.

    b. the fact that, 40 to 60 percent more.

    c. means, because.

    d. compounded, significantly worsen.

D. REVIEWING AND ORGANIZING IDEAS: MAPPING

Complete the following map of the conclusion of each source cited in the reading.

PARAGRAPH	SOURCE	CONCLUSION
3	Scientific American	A _____ University study estimates that fracked wells leak _____ percent more methane than conventional wells.
3	Climate Progress	According to the _____, switching from oil to natural gas consumption might significantly increase global warming as a result of the _____ released into the atmosphere.
5	_____	According to the International Energy Agency, inexpensive natural gas could replace _____ and coal and help smaller countries become independent from oil-rich countries.
_____	USA Today	Fracking has helped Williamsport, Pennsylvania, experience economic growth; other possible results are falling _____ prices, independence from _____ oil, and the creation of jobs.
7	_____ _____	Referred to the results of fracking as "oil in your _____" and urged viewers to consult a map showing whether they can become wealthy from fracking on their property.
_____	Associated Press	Some New York farmers envy the fracking contracts that are making people in Pennsylvania wealthy, but they also worry about the contamination of well _____ and the destruction of _____.
_____	_____ _____	Reporter Elizabeth Shogren followed Sue Tierney, a scientist at the National Oceanic and Atmospheric Administration, who expressed concern that fracking offers short-term benefits but may have _____ consequences in the long run.

E. READING AND THINKING VISUALLY

Using the "By the Numbers" box on page 550, select the best answer.

_____ 1. Fracking creates _____ new wells each year.
   a. 14,000
   b. 11,400
   c. 137
   d. 24

_____ 2. At current consumption levels, the U.S. supply of natural gas will
   last approximately _____ years.
   a. 5
   b. 26
   c. 90
   d. 137

F. FIGURING OUT IMPLIED MEANINGS

Indicate whether each statement is true (T) or false (F).

_____ 1. Methane is a natural gas.

_____ 2. The American Petroleum Institute is dedicated to exploring the
   advantages and disadvantages of fracking.

_____ 3. Fracked wells release much less methane than conventional wells.

_____ 4. Natural gas is a cheaper source of energy than electricity or coal.

_____ 5. The *USA Today* article was biased in favor of fracking.

_____ 6. *New York Times* coverage of the fracking issue has emphasized water
   and pollution issues rather than climate change.

_____ 7. Methane is a greenhouse gas, but carbon dioxide is not.

_____ 8. Pennsylvania is more open to fracking activities than New York State.

G. THINKING CRITICALLY

Select the best answer.

_____ 1. The author's purpose in this reading selection is to
   a. examine, summarize, and critique the reporting of the news
      media on the issue of fracking.
   b. support local initiatives for alternative forms of energy, such as
      wind energy and solar energy.
   c. argue for increased government regulation of hydraulic fractur-
      ing activities.
   d. present scientific research on fracking's effects on the natural
      environment.

_____ 2. The tone of "Hope It's in Your Backyard!" could best be described as

    a. hopeful.

    b. indirect.

    c. awestruck.

    d. critical.

_____ 3. Which of the following reports offered the most positive view of fracking?

    a. "Drilling Down" in _The New York Times_

    b. "The Fracking Boom: Missing Answers," on NPR

    c. "U.S. Energy Independence Is No Longer Just a Pipe Dream," _USA Today_

    d. NPR _Morning Edition_, May 17, 2012

_____ 4. Which of the following passages from the reading selection is an opinion, not a fact?

    a. "Any drilling for fossil fuels means more carbon will eventually be released into the atmosphere." (paragraph 3)

    b. "Methane is 20 times as potent a greenhouse gas as carbon dioxide." (paragraph 3)

    c. "Shale energy is the answer." (paragraph 8)

    d. "Some New York farmers look longingly at the lucrative drilling leases that have gone to their neighbors in fracking-friendly Pennsylvania." (paragraph 9)

_____ 5. The author uses all of the following words or phrases ironically _except_ for

    a. "scientific and environmental media" (paragraph 4)

    b. " 'could be' as much as $500,000 a month" (paragraph 7)

    c. "Hope it's in your backyard!" (paragraph 7)

    d. "glorious fracking future" (paragraph 9)

H. BUILDING VOCABULARY

Context

Using context and a dictionary, if necessary, determine the meaning of each word as it used in the selection.

_____ 1. unambiguous (paragraph 1)

    a. dangerous

    b. unreported

    c. clear

    d. secondary

_____ 2. compounded (paragraph 3)

    a. interested

    b. increased

    c. understood

    d. learned

_____ 3. potent (paragraph 3)

    a. strong

    b. deadly

    c. important

    d. well-known

_____ 4. downside (paragraph 5)

    a. loss

    b. lining

    c. data

    d. drawback

_____ 5. advent (paragraph 6)

    a. banning

    b. discovery

    c. advantage

    d. arrival

_____ 6. lucrative (paragraph 9)

    a. profitable

    b. energy-intensive

    c. luxurious

    d. frightening

Word Parts

A REVIEW OF ROOTS

HYDRO means water

Use your knowledge of word parts and the review above to choose the answer that best defines the boldfaced word in the following sentence.

_____ 1. A **hydraulic** (paragraph 2) process is one that makes use of

    a. electricity.

    b. gas.

    c. water.

    d. drills.

Unusual Words/Understanding Idioms

Use the meanings given below to write a sentence using the boldfaced phrases.

1. To be **hard-pressed** (paragraph 4) is to experience difficulty.

    Your sentence: _____

    _____

2. The phrase **golden age** (paragraph 5) often refers to a period of peace, prosperity, or happiness.

    Your sentence: _____

    _____

I. SELECTING A LEARNING/STUDY STRATEGY

Predict two exam questions that might be asked about the reading.

J. EXPLORING IDEAS THROUGH DISCUSSION AND WRITING

1. Do you think that media that report only on the positive effects of fracking are necessarily biased? Why or why not?

2. What exactly is the greenhouse effect? Write a paragraph explaining what it is and how it works. (You will likely need to do some research to answer this question.)

3. Does a fracking industry exist in your state? Write a paragraph or two answering this question. If your state does permit fracking, what seem to be the effects so far? If your state does not permit fracking, are you in favor of or against it? Why?

4. Locate any of the original articles or news reports listed in this reading. Read or watch the entire report and write a summary of it. Has the author of "Hope It's in Your Backyard!" left out any details? If so, which ones?

K. BEYOND THE CLASSROOM TO THE WEB

Conduct a Web search for information about a form of alternate energy that you find interesting (for example, solar energy or wind energy). Then prepare a brief paper or a class presentation about its pros and cons.

TRACKING YOUR PROGRESS

Selection 26

Section	Number Correct	Score
A. Thesis and Main Ideas (4 items)	_____ × 4	_____
B. Details (4 items)	_____ × 3	_____
C. Organization and Transitions (3 items)	_____ × 4	_____
E. Reading and Thinking Visually (2 items)	_____ × 4	_____
F. Implied Meanings (8 items)	_____ × 2	_____
G. Thinking Critically (5 items)	_____ × 3	_____
H. Vocabulary		
Context (6 items)	_____ × 3	_____
Word Parts (1 item)	_____ × 3	_____
	Total Score	_____%

SELECTION 27

Additional Renewable-Energy Options

Richard T. Wright and Dorothy F. Boorse

TEXTBOOK
EXCERPT
—————
Contemporary
Issues Reading

This selection originally appeared in a textbook titled *Environmental Science: Toward a Sustainable Future.* Read it to learn about several options for renewable energy.

PREVIEWING THE READING

Using the steps listed on pages 40–41, preview the reading selection. When you have finished, complete the following items.

1. This selection is about _____

2. The three main types of renewable-energy options that are discussed in the selection are:

   a. _____

   b. _____

   c. _____

 MAKING
CONNECTIONS *Describe what the term "renewable energy" means to you. What renewable-energy options do you think are most worth pursuing? Why?*

READING TIP

As you read, highlight descriptions of how different types of renewable-energy options are designed to work, as well as any limitations of each option.

Additional Renewable-Energy Options

1   Aside from water, wind, biomass, and hydrogen energy, there are other renewable-energy options that are worth pursuing.

Geothermal Energy

2   In various locations in the world, such as the northwestern corner of Wyoming (now Yellowstone National Park), there are springs that yield hot, almost boiling,

water. Natural steam vents and other thermal features are also found in such areas. They occur where the hot, molten rock of Earth's interior is close enough to the surface to heat groundwater, particularly in volcanic regions. Using such naturally heated water or steam to heat buildings or drive turbogenerators is the basis of geothermal energy. In 2008, geothermal energy provided over 10,000 MW of electrical power (equivalent to the output of 10 large nuclear or coal-fired power stations) in countries as diverse as Nicaragua, the Philippines, Kenya, Iceland, and New Zealand. Today the largest single facility is in the United States at a location known as The Geysers, 70 miles (110 km) north of San Francisco (Figure A). With over 2,900 MW from geothermal energy, the United States is the world leader in the use of this energy source; new projects in the development stage will increase this to over 6,000 MW. As impressive as this application of geothermal energy is, nearly double the amount is being used to directly heat homes and buildings, largely in Japan and China.

3   A recent study by MIT suggested that the United States employ an emerging technology called enhanced geothermal systems (EGS). EGS involves drilling holes several miles deep into granite that holds temperatures of 400 degrees or more and injecting water under pressure into one hole where it absorbs heat from the rock and, as steam, flows up another shaft to a power plant where it generates electricity. Such plants already exist in Australia, Europe, and Japan. This underground heat is widespread in the United States, unlike the present limited geothermal sources. The MIT team proposed

FIGURE A GEOTHERMAL ENERGY.
One of the 15 geothermal power plants operated by Calpine Corporation at The Geysers in Sonoma and Lake Counties, California. Calpine's geothermal plants at The Geysers are capable of producing 725 megawatts of power, or about 21 percent of California's non-hydroelectric green energy.

a $1 billion investment to exploit the EGS potential, predicting that by 2050 some 100 gigawatts (GW) of electrical power could be developed in this way.

Heat Pumps

4   A less spectacular, but far more abundant, energy source than the large geothermal power plants exists anywhere pipes can be drilled into the Earth. Because the ground temperature below six feet or so remains constant, the Earth can be used as part of a heat exchange system that extracts heat in the winter and uses the ground as a heat sink in the summer. Thus, the system can be used for heating and cooling and does away with the need for separate furnace and air-conditioning systems. As Figure B shows, a geothermal heat pump (GHP) system involves loops of buried pipes filled with an antifreeze solution, circulated by a pump connected to the air handler (a box containing a blower and a filter). The blower moves house air through the heat pump and distributes it throughout the house via ductwork.

5   Four elementary schools in Lincoln, Nebraska, installed GHP systems for their heating and cooling. Their energy cost savings were 57% compared with the cost of conventional heating and cooling systems installed in two similar schools. Taxpayers will save an estimated $3.8 million over the next 20 years with the GHP systems. According to the EPA, these systems are by far the most cost-effective energy-saving systems available. Although they are significantly more expensive to install than conventional heating and air-conditioning systems, they are trouble free and save money over the long run. New heat pump installations in the United Sates are growing at an annual rate of 20% per year, with almost 1 million installed by 2008.

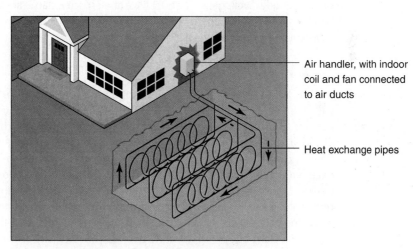

Air handler, with indoor coil and fan connected to air ducts

Heat exchange pipes

FIGURE B GEOTHERMAL HEAT PUMP SYSTEM.
The pipes buried underground facilitate heat exchange between the house and the Earth. This system can either cool or heat a house and can be installed almost anywhere, although at a higher initial cost than a conventional heating, ventilation, and air-conditioning system.

Tidal and Wave Power

6   A phenomenal amount of energy is inherent in the twice-daily rise and fall of the ocean tides, brought about by the gravitational pull of the Moon and the Sun. Many imaginative schemes have been proposed for capturing this limitless, pollution-free source of energy. The most straightforward idea is the tidal barrage, in which a dam is built across the mouth of a bay and **turbines** are mounted in the structure. The incoming tide flowing through the turbines would generate power. As the tide shifted, the blades would be reversed so that the outflowing water would continue to generate power.

turbines
machines that use rotating blades to convert a fast-moving flow of air, water, or other fluid into power

7   In about 30 locations in the world, the shoreline topography generates tides high enough—20 feet (6 m) or more—for this kind of use. Large tidal power plants already exist in two of those places: France and Canada. The only suitable location in North America is the Bay of Fundy, where the Annapolis Tidal Generating Station has operated since 1984, at 20-MW capacity. Thus, this application of tidal power has potential only in certain localities, and even there, it would not be without adverse environmental impacts. The barrage would trap sediments, impede the migration of fish and other organisms, prevent navigation, alter the circulation and mixing of saltwater and freshwater in estuaries, and perhaps have other, unforeseen ecological effects.

8   Other techniques are being explored that harness the currents that flow with the tides. For example, in 2006, Verdant Power installed six 15-foot-tall underwater turbines to harness the tidal energy of the East River in New York City; unfortunately, the currents were too strong for the blades and sheared off the tips. After another attempt also failed, Verdant has installed another turbine that has held up and is generating power for a nearby supermarket. The city plans to add many more turbines if all goes well, generating 10 MW of electricity. San Francisco is eyeing a similar scheme to tap the energy of the 400 billion gallons of water that flow under the Golden Gate Bridge with every tide.

Ocean Waves

9   Standing on the shore of any ocean, an observer would have to be impressed with the energy arriving with each wave, generated by offshore winds. It might be possible to harness some of this energy, but the technological challenge is daunting. The ideal location is one that receives the wave's force before it hits the shoaling sea floor, is close enough to shore to facilitate hookup with transmission cables, and is deep enough so that the equipment will not crash on the sea floor during storm turbulence. In the United States, the Pacific Northwest provides these conditions, and the Pacific Gas and Electric Company has contracted with Finavera Renewables to install the nation's first, admittedly small, wave power plant off the coast of northern California. Eight buoys will generate two MW of electricity as they bob up and down with the waves, expanding and contracting a hose that pumps pressurized water through a turbine. There are other proposed mechanisms for capturing wave energy, and it is fair to say that this technology is in the early research-and-development stage. The U.S. DOE is supporting research on ocean energy on a 50% cost-share basis.

Ocean Thermal-Energy Conversion

10   Over much of the world's oceans, a **thermal gradient** of about 20°C (36°F) exists between surface water heated by the Sun and the colder deep water. Ocean thermal-energy conversion (OTEC) is the name of an experimental technology that uses this temperature difference to produce power. The technology involves using the warm surface water to heat and vaporize a low-boiling-point liquid such as ammonia. The increased pressure of the vaporized ammonia would drive turbogenerators. The ammonia vapor leaving the turbines would then be recondensed by cold water pumped up from as much as 300 feet (100 m) deep and returned to the start of the cycle.

thermal gradient
the rate of temperature change over a specified distance

11   Various studies indicate that OTEC power plants show little economic promise—unless, perhaps, they can be coupled with other, cost-effective operations. For example, in Hawaii, a shore based OTEC plant uses the cold, nutrient-rich water pumped from the ocean bottom to cool buildings and supply nutrients for vegetables in an aquaculture operation, in addition to cooling the condensers in the power cycle. Even so, interest in duplicating such operations is minimal at present.

Final Thoughts

12   Our look at current energy policy indicates that the United States is making a serious effort to address the need to develop renewable-energy sources and to improve the efficiency of current energy use. This policy also continues the effort to move toward a hydrogen economy. What about the global targets of achieving stable atmospheric levels of greenhouse gases and a long-term sustainable-energy policy? Unfortunately, current policy also promotes further use and development of fossil fuel energy. It's "business as usual" for the fossil fuel industries. How can that be changed?

13   One development that has caught everyone's attention in recent years is the rising price of gasoline. Until recently, the United States was the only industrialized country that has seen fit to keep gasoline prices remarkably low. Fuel in all other highly developed countries is so heavily taxed that it costs consumers upward of $6 per gallon—unlike U.S. prices, which were below $1.50 for 12 of the last 18 years. When gasoline rose to $3 a gallon in 2005, consumers began to turn away from gas-guzzling sport-utility vehicles and muscle cars and have been opting for the rising number of gasoline-electric hybrid cars appearing on the lots of many car manufacturers. This supports the suggestion of a number of economists and environmental groups that we should be paying more—much more—for gasoline (and other fossil fuels). To accomplish this, we would need a policy change: a carbon tax—that is, a tax levied on all fuels according to the amount of carbon dioxide that they produce when consumed. Such a tax, proponents believe, would provide both incentives to use renewable sources, which would not be taxed, and disincentives to consume fossil fuels. It is hard to imagine any step that would be more effective (or more controversial) in reducing greenhouse gas emissions in the United States. A number of European countries have already adopted such a tax.

14   Are the preceding developments, even the suggested carbon tax, enough to enable us to achieve a sustainable-energy system and to mitigate global climate change? Very likely, no. Yet many of them are moving us in the stewardly direction that is vital to the future of the global environment.

—Wright and Boorse, *Environmental Science*, pp. 415-418

A. UNDERSTANDING THE THESIS AND OTHER MAIN IDEAS

Select the best answer.

_____ 1. The authors' primary purpose is to
   a. explain the importance of reducing the use of fossil fuels.
   b. identify factors that contribute to global climate change.
   c. suggest ways to improve energy conservation and efficiency.
   d. describe a variety of renewable-energy options.

_____ 2. The topic of paragraph 3 is
   a. renewable-energy options.
   b. enhanced geothermal systems (EGS).
   c. underground heat.
   d. emerging technologies.

_____ 3. The term **tidal barrage** describes a system in which
   a. turbines are mounted in a dam built across the mouth of a bay.
   b. holes are drilled several miles deep into granite.
   c. the warm surface water of the ocean is used to vaporize a low-boiling-point liquid.
   d. cold, nutrient-rich water is pumped from the ocean bottom.

_____ 4. The authors' purpose in paragraph 13 is to
   a. complain about the rising cost of gasoline.
   b. suggest ways to reduce greenhouse gas emissions.
   c. explain what a carbon tax is and why it is needed.
   d. compare the United States with other industrialized countries.

_____ 5. According to the selection, current energy policy in the United States is doing all of the following *except*
   a. addressing the need to develop renewable-energy sources.
   b. attempting to improve the efficiency of current energy use.
   c. discouraging further use and development of fossil fuel energy.
   d. continuing the effort to move toward a hydrogen economy.

B. IDENTIFYING DETAILS

Indicate whether each statement is true (T) or false (F).

_____ 1. The largest single geothermal energy facility is located in the Philippines.

_____ 2. Power plants using enhanced geothermal systems (EGS) already exist in Australia, Europe, and Japan.

_____ 3. Geothermal heat pump (GHS) systems are being used to heat and cool four elementary schools in Lincoln, Nebraska.

_____ 4. GHS systems are much less expensive to install than conventional heating and cooling systems.

_____ 5. New heat pump installations are growing at a rate of 20% per year in the United States.

_____ 6. Large tidal power plants are being used in 30 locations around the world.

_____ 7. The only tidal power plant in North America is in the Bay of Fundy.

_____ 8. The first wave power plant in the United States will be installed off the coast of Alaska.

_____ 9. The U.S. Department of Energy shares the costs of ocean energy research.

_____ 10. The EPA considers ocean thermal-energy conversion (OTEC) the most cost-effective energy-saving system available.

C. RECOGNIZING METHODS OF ORGANIZATION AND TRANSITIONS

Select the best answer.

_____ 1. The overall pattern of organization in this selection is

    a. listing.

    b. cause and effect.

    c. comparison and contrast.

    d. order of importance.

_____ 2. In paragraph 4, the pattern the authors use to describe how a geothermal heat pump (GHP) system works is

    a. definition.

    b. process.

    c. classification.

    d. listing.

_____ 3. In paragraph 8, the pattern the authors use to describe other techniques for using tidal power is

    a. comparison and contrast.

    b. generalization and example.

    c. classification.

    d. chronological order.

_____ 4. In paragraph 11, the transition that indicates that the authors will illustrate an idea is

    a. unless.

    b. perhaps.

    c. for example.

    d. in addition.

D. REVIEWING AND ORGANIZING IDEAS: OUTLINING

Complete the following outline of paragraphs 2–11 of the selection by filling in the missing words or phrases.

I. Geothermal Energy

    A. Naturally heated water or steam

        1. Occurs where Earth's _____ is near the surface

    B. _____

        1. Holes drilled into hot granite

        2. Existing plants in _____

    C. Geothermal heat pumps

        1. Earth used as part of a _____

        2. Eliminate need for _____

II. Tidal and Wave Power

    A. _____

        1. Uses dam with turbines to harness power

        2. Limited to locations with tides over _____

        3. Adverse _____

    B. Ocean waves

        1. Early research-and-development stage

III. _____

    A. Uses temperature difference between _____

    B. Little economic promise

E. READING AND THINKING VISUALLY

Complete each of the following sentences.

1. The photograph in Figure A most closely corresponds to the material under the heading _____.

2. According to the caption for Figure A, the Calpine Corporation operates _____ geothermal units in Sonoma and Lake Counties, California.

3. The purpose of Figure B is to illustrate a _____

4. Figure B shows that heat exchange pipes are located _____

_____.

F. FIGURING OUT IMPLIED MEANINGS

Indicate whether each statement is true (T) or false (F).

_____ 1. The study by MIT supports the idea that enhanced geothermal systems are a good potential source of electricity.

_____ 2. Geothermal heat pump (GHP) systems are not likely to gain acceptance in the United States.

_____ 3. The tidal barrage system may have several negative environmental effects.

_____ 4. Attempts to use the tidal energy of the East River to generate power have all failed.

_____ 5. The U.S. Department of Energy is supportive of research on ocean energy.

_____ 6. Ocean thermal-energy conversion power plants are too expensive unless they are part of other cost-effective operations.

G. THINKING CRITICALLY

Select the best answer.

_____ 1. The tone of the selection can best be described as

    a. informative.

    b. pessimistic.

    c. amused.

    d. sensational.

_____ 2. The title of this selection implies that

    a. the renewable-energy options in this selection are unlikely to succeed.

    b. solar and wind energy are the only realistic options for renewable energy.

    c. there are other renewable-energy options in addition to the ones described in this selection.

    d. the public prefers to continue using gasoline and other fossil fuels rather than renewable-energy options.

_____ 3. The central thesis of this selection is supported primarily by

    a. interviews with researchers.

    b. facts and statistics.

    c. expert opinions.

    d. the authors' personal experience.

_____ 4. The audience for this selection is most likely to be

    a. geothermal scientists.

    b. politicians.

    c. renewable-energy experts.

    d. students in environmental science.

H. BUILDING VOCABULARY

Context

Using context and a dictionary, if necessary, determine the meaning of each word as it is used in the selection.

_____ 1. molten (paragraph 2)

    a. surface

    b. deep

    c. melted

    d. variable

_____ 2. exploit (paragraph 3)

    a. complicate

    b. utilize

    c. expose

    d. waste

_____ 3. inherent (paragraph 6)

    a. part of

    b. prevented by

    c. separate from

    d. restricted

_____ 4. adverse (paragraph 7)

    a. pleasing

    b. accurate

    c. familiar

    d. harmful

_____ 5. impede (paragraph 7)

    a. attack

    b. improve

    c. obstruct

    d. promote

_____ 6. daunting (paragraph 9)

    a. careful

    b. intimidating

    c. limiting

    d. threatening

_____ 7. opting (paragraph 13)

    a. changing

    b. advancing

    c. choosing

    d. avoiding

_____ 8. mitigate (paragraph 14)

    a. make less severe

    b. remove

    c. build up

    d. prolong

Word Parts

A REVIEW OF ROOTS AND PREFIXES

GEO means *earth*
DICT means *tell, say*
GRAPH means *write*
VERS means *turn*
ANTI- means *against*
PRE- means *before*
DU- means *two*
PRO- means *for, in favor of*
DIS- means *apart, away, not*
CONTRO- means *against, opposite*

Match each word in Column A with its meaning in Column B.

Column A   **Column B**

_____ 1. geothermal   a. the physical features of a place or region

_____ 2. predicting   b. causing public dispute or debate

_____ 3. antifreeze   c. saying what will happen in the future

_____ 4. topography   d. having to do with the Earth's temperature

_____ 5. duplicating   e. factors intended to discourage or deter certain actions

_____ 6. proponents   f. a substance that lowers the freezing point of a liquid

_____ 7. disincentives   g. making two of; copying

_____ 8. controversial   h. those in favor of an idea

I. SELECTING A LEARNING/STUDY STRATEGY

Discuss methods of studying the outline shown on page 566 in preparation for an exam that covers this reading.

J. EXPLORING IDEAS THROUGH DISCUSSION AND WRITING

1. What did you already know about different types of renewable energy? Which of the ones described in the selection seemed most likely to become a reality? Explain your answer.

2. What are the pros and cons of tidal power? Write a summary based on the information in the selection.

3. Why do the authors call the current energy policy "business as usual" for the fossil fuel industries? What do they mean by their use of the word *stewardly*? Reread the last three paragraphs of the selection and discuss what the authors reveal about their feelings toward U.S. energy policy, climate change, and the future of the global environment.

K. BEYOND THE CLASSROOM TO THE WEB

Conduct a Web search for the U.S. Department of Energy's Office of Energy Efficiency and Renewable Energy (EERE) Web site. After you have spent some time exploring different aspects of the site, write a paragraph explaining which of the clean energy technologies described on the site seems most likely to succeed, and why.

TRACKING YOUR PROGRESS

Selection 27

Section	Number Correct	Score
A. Thesis and Main Ideas (5 items)	_____ × 4	_____
B. Details (10 items)	_____ × 2	_____
C. Organization and Transitions (4 items)	_____ × 2	_____
F. Implied Meanings (6 items)	_____ × 2	_____
G. Thinking Critically (4 items)	_____ × 2	_____
H. Vocabulary		
Context (8 items)	_____ × 2	_____
Word Parts (8 items)	_____ × 2	_____
	Total Score	_____%

18 Career Fields

Opportunities in a variety of career fields are rapidly expanding; new fields are being created and many existing fields are showing increased demand for workers. As the workplace changes, workers are often asked to shift to new fields, requiring them to adapt, retrain, and acquire new or updated skills.

In addition to the health-related fields (see Chapter 15), growing fields include education, criminal justice, and travel and tourism. The readings in this chapter are representative of these three career fields. As you read "Lift the Cell Phone Ban," you will see how teachers are encouraged to adapt new technology, specifically cell phones, to enhance classroom learning. "Trial Lawyers Cater to Jurors' Demands for Visual Evidence" addresses a trend within the criminal justice field—the presentation of trial evidence in a visual format. While reading "Eco-tourism," you will learn about this new trend in tourism as well as locations across the globe that are attracting eco-tourists.

Use the following suggestions when reading about career fields.

TIPS FOR READING IN CAREER FIELDS

- **Pay attention to processes and procedures.** Many career fields involve completing a task, such as teaching a lesson, filing a crime report, or planning trips or excursions. Usually there are written rules and/or unwritten expectations about how things are done. Notice details, sequence, and format.

- **Learn the terminology that is introduced in your readings.** You will need to be able to speak and write the language of your field in order to communicate with co-workers. When reading "Trial Lawyers Cater to Jurors' Demands for Visual Evidence " you will see terms such as *plantiff*, *forensic pathology*, and *animated recreation* for example.

- **Read slowly and reread as needed.** Textbooks in many career fields are highly factual and packed with information. Do not expect to understand or remember everything with only one reading.

- **Use visualization to create mental images or pictures.** As you read descriptions, such as those of the popular eco-tourist destinations in "Eco-tourism," visualize examples.

SELECTION 28

Lift the Cell Phone Ban

David Rapp

Contemporary Issues Reading

This article originally appeared in *Administr@tor,* a magazine for teachers and administrators. Read it to discover how some schools are experimenting with the use of cell phones in the classroom.

PREVIEWING THE READING

Using the steps listed on pages 40–41, preview the reading selection. When you have finished, complete the following items.

1. This selection is primarily about _____

   _____

2. Based on the four boldfaced headings, list four topics that will be discussed in the reading. The first one is provided for you.

   a. Cell phones as a solution to classroom problems or issues

   b. _____

   c. _____

   d. _____

   _____

 MAKING CONNECTIONS

Do any of your instructors have specific policies regarding cell phone use in your classes? Do you find these policies fair, or do you think they are too restrictive? Can you think of any instances where a cell phone might be useful in a particular class?

READING TIP

As you read, keep track of the pros and cons of cell phone usage in the classroom.

Lift the Cell Phone Ban

Stop thinking classroom disruption. Start thinking powerful (and free) teaching tool.

Cell phones could become the next big learning tool in the classroom. So why have schools been so slow to embrace them?

curriculum
program of study

1   Without a doubt, cell phones can cause serious disruption in the classroom. From urgent text messages flying across the room to lessons interrupted by rap-song ringtones, these gadgets are responsible for nationwide frustration among educators. And, in extreme cases, students have used their cell phones to cheat on tests and harass other students, even during class time. While such disturbances are certainly a nuisance in school, not all teachers see cell phones as the enemy. In fact, for some, they've become a teaching solution.

Cell Phone Solution

2   Between the alarms, calls, and text-messaging, it's easy to see why some classrooms have implemented a no-cell phone policy. But educators know that with students, cell phone use is inevitable, so why not use the devices for good? Many schools in Asia and the United Kingdom—where they've been using high-speed 3G, or third-generation, cellular networks years longer than the United States—have already turned cell phones into teaching tools. Recently, several school districts in North America have done the same. At the Craik School in Saskatchewan, Canada, such an experiment turned into an integral part of the **curriculum**.

3   Craik's program started with a discussion in the staff room between the school's principal, Gord Taylor, and teacher Carla Dolman. Many of the children had received cell phones for Christmas, and the phones had become a distraction. "So we tossed out the idea of rather than looking at them as an evil thing," says Taylor, "that we look at them as a tool for learning." They realized that the text message and alarm functions would be useful for reminding students of homework assignments and tests, for example. They decided to run a pilot project with eighth and ninth graders.

Testing the Waters

4   Initially, only about 40 percent of the class had cell phones, but kids who had them were willing to share. The text message function was mainly used at first, but as Dolman became more familiar with the myriad functions, it became clear that these gadgets had a lot more classroom potential. Video and sound recording came into play, and the phones' Bluetooth networking capabilities allowed for easy information sharing. Dolman found they worked perfectly for her classes' "lit circles," in which the students divide into smaller groups to discuss different aspects of a particular book. Previously, she found it difficult to monitor each of the different groups simultaneously. But kids who had video functions on their phones could record their discussions then Bluetooth them to Dolman's phone, and she could watch each individual discussion, without missing a moment.

minimal
small in number

5   Dolman says such problems like class disruption were **minimal**. "It's a stereotype of teenagers—that you can't trust them with a cell phone. Our experience was that if you give them the opportunity to use them, and you give them guidelines to go with that use, you won't have problems."

6   Principal Taylor agrees. "The one thing we really stressed with the kids was the whole idea of appropriate use," he says. "They make darn sure that the volume is turned off. A lot of adults need to learn that."

7   As for the kids, they loved using the phones for class work, but parents in the district have had mixed reactions, says Taylor. "Some thought we were crazy, and were very strongly opposed to it, and some embraced the idea initially. As time went on, about 90 percent came to say it was a good idea. They didn't see it as a gadget, or as a replacement for learning, they saw it as a tool for learning."

8   Taylor's colleagues have been more enthusiastic. "In our school division there are about 90 principals and about 600 teachers, and I would say that out of the principals, there were about 15 to 20 that really were gung-ho and wanted to know what we were doing." The rest, Taylor says, thought the program was innovative and at least worth a try. "There were no negative thoughts on it whatsoever."

Learning Curves

9   Taylor sees the cell phone as a necessary tool to teach to kids. "We would be burying our heads in the sand if we said that cell phones were not a part of everyday life," he says. "I don't know a businessman out there who doesn't carry a cell phone. I don't know a lawyer or accountant out there who doesn't carry a cell phone. Why wouldn't we have them in schools?"

10   Given the example of the Craik School, why haven't more American teachers embraced cell phone use in the classroom? In fact, few U.S. schools are even considering their use. Liz Kolb, author of the recently released book *Toys to Tools: Connecting Student Cell Phones to Education*, says that Americans have traditionally seen cell phones as nothing more than a social toy. "We hear stories about students using cell phones in negative ways, like posting videos of teachers to YouTube, or cheating via text messaging," she says.

inhibiting
preventing

11   Many teachers simply don't know the teaching potential cell phones have, Kolb says. "There are some teachers who have never sent a text message, so the fear of their students knowing more than them about a tool in the classroom is often very **inhibiting**." Professional development, Kolb says, is a necessity for normalizing the idea of classroom cell phones.

Corporate Help

12   Matt Cook, a math and science teacher in the Keller Independent School District, near Fort Worth, Texas, knows his cell phone inside and out. He's used it to document results in his classroom. In fact, his familiarity with cell phone tech sparked his imagination, and led him to get in touch with Verizon and AT&T, as well as software company GoKnow, based in Ann Arbor, Michigan. All three companies have agreed to donate technology to the district for a pilot program to use cell phones in fifth-grade classrooms. (Other cell phone companies are certainly interested in classroom possibilities. Qualcomm has a similar program in the works called K-Nect.)

13   "I firmly believe that to prepare kids for their future, we need to start speaking the language of kids," says Cook. "They're using this stuff anyway—let's teach them how to use it productively."

14   The GoKnow software turns the students' smartphones into computers, allowing students to use word processors, spreadsheets, and art programs, among others, on their cell phones. For example, every child learns the concept of the water cycle: how water moves on, above, and below Earth's surface through the processes of evaporation, condensation, precipitation, and so on. With GoKnow's cell-based applications, a student could draw a concept map showing the relationship between the processes, create an animation illustrating how it all looks, and write up a text report on what they've learned—all centralized on a desktop-like interface on the smartphone's screen.

15   At the end of the day, the students can upload all their work online. "The kids sync their phone up to the server. The parents can look at the work they've done, and the teachers can make annotations and grade the work, all online," says Cook.

16   Elliot Soloway, founder of GoKnow, sees the key to popularizing cell phone use in classrooms is to make it easy to integrate into a school's existing curriculum. GoKnow's software has been engineered to make the process as easy as possible, he says. "We can do this in eight minutes with a teacher. Sit down with your paper-and-pencil lesson, and we're going to show you how to transform that lesson into a cell phone–based lesson you can integrate with your existing curriculum."

17   Soloway says that if the Keller program is successful, smartphones could become a part of the curriculum in neighboring districts. "We've talked to other districts in Texas that are watching," he says. If cell phones in classrooms do catch on, the schools would, in effect, be getting low-cost computers into their students' hands.

18   Dolman thinks that the possibilities for cell phones will only increase as kids become more familiar with the technology. "The more we discover what we can do with them, the more valuable they are. If you can **harness** what students are interested in, you have massive amounts of potential. And if you can get that into the classroom, you're set."

harness
capture and use

A. UNDERSTANDING THE THESIS AND OTHER MAIN IDEAS

Select the best answer.

_____ 1. The central thesis of the selection is that

    a. cell phones in the classroom are annoying and disruptive.

    b. today's students enjoy using modern technologies.

    c. teachers who use cell phones in the classroom help their school districts save money.

    d. cell phones can be an effective teaching and learning tool when used properly.

_____ 2. The author's primary purpose is to

    a. discourage instructors from allowing cell phone use in the classroom.

    b. open up the minds of teachers, parents, and school administrators to the idea of using cell phones in the classroom.

    c. emphasize the way cell phones can be used in science education.

    d. describe the differing attitudes between the U.S. and Canadian educational systems with regard to cell phones.

_____ 3. The main idea of paragraph 8 is

    a. Overall, principals in Saskatchewan, Canada, are open to or enthusiastic about the idea of using cell phones in the classroom.

    b. In general, teachers are more interested in the classroom use of cell phones than administrators are.

    c. The majority of principals are highly interested in finding ways to use cell phones in education.

    d. A great deal of negativity surrounds the idea of using cell phones in the classroom.

_____ 4. The topic of paragraph 10 is

    a. Liz Kolb's book, _Toys to Tools_.

    b. social media sites such as YouTube and Facebook.

    c. U.S. schools' attitudes toward cell phones in the classroom.

    d. cheating that occurs through text messaging.

_____ 5. The main idea of paragraph 14 is

    a. the water cycle is best illustrated through animations viewed on a cell phone.

    b. cell phones are best used for creating concept maps.

    c. GoKnow software turns students' smartphones into computers.

    d. the screens of cell phones are the ideal size for educational applications.

B. IDENTIFYING DETAILS

Select the correct answer.

_____ 1. Which Canadian province is discussed in the reading?

    a. Alberta

    b. Quebec

    c. Saskatchewan

    d. British Columbia

_____ 2. The staff of the Craik School discovered that cell phones' alarm functions can be used to

    a. remind students about tests and homework assignments.

    b. ensure that students arrive to class on time.

    c. time experiments during scientific lab classes.

    d. count down the amount of time left during tests.

_____ 3. Which statement best summarizes the attitude of the parents whose children attend the Craik School?

    a. The parents were extremely supportive of the idea of using cell phones when the idea was first suggested.

    b. While early attitudes varied from skeptical to enthusiastic, as time went on the vast majority of parents came to embrace the idea of cell phones as learning tools.

    c. Parents were open to the idea of using cell phones in the classroom as long as companies such as GoKnow paid the associated costs.

    d. The parents originally supported the idea of using cell phones for education, but have come to see the technology primarily as a "toy" used for socializing.

_____ 4. Which of the following companies did not donate technology to the Keller Independent School District in Fort Worth, Texas?

    a. AT&T

    b. Verizon

    c. GoKnow

    d. Qualcomm

_____ 5. Which of the following people does not work for a school district?

    a. Carla Dolman

    b. Gord Taylor

    c. Elliot Soloway

    d. Matt Cook

_____ 6. According to Liz Kolb, which factor is critical in helping U.S. teachers adjust to the idea of using cell phones in the classroom?

    a. professional development

    b. financial incentives

    c. free software donated by local companies

    d. parental support

C. RECOGNIZING METHODS OF ORGANIZATION AND TRANSITIONS

Select the best answer.

_____ 1. The reading examines educational practices in two countries, Canada and the United States, and finds that U.S. teachers tend to be less open to the idea of using cell phones as educational tools. For this reason, we might say one pattern of organization used in the reading is

   a. definition.

   b. comparison and contrast.

   c. spatial order.

   d. order of importance.

_____ 2. The transitional word or phrase used to signal the statement-and-clarification pattern in paragraph 1 is

   a. without a doubt.

   b. in extreme cases.

   c. for some.

   d. in fact.

D. REVIEWING AND ORGANIZING IDEAS: OUTLINING

Complete the following outline of paragraphs 1–8 by filling in the missing words and phrases.

Lift the Cell Phone Ban

A. Cell Phone Solution

   1. Reasons for no-cell-phone policy: alarms, calls, _____

   2. Some North American educators have begun using cell phones as teaching tools.

      Example: _____ in Saskatchewan, Canada

B. Testing the Waters

   1. At first only _____ % of students had cell phones, but students were willing to share

   2. At first, _____ were the key function used

   3. Later, _____ came into play

   4. Teacher Dolman's experience: Few disruptions if students are given _____ for cell phone use

   5. Parental reactions: At first _____ , later more enthusiastic

   6. Educator reactions: Very _____

E. READING AND THINKING VISUALLY

Select the best answer.

_____ 1. The author most likely chose to include the illustration shown on page 574 in order to

   a. stress that cell phones are an extremely common technology.

   b. illustrate the many education-based applications of cell phones.

   c. suggest that cell phones are a better choice than computers for the classroom.

   d. show the basic configuration of most cell phones.

_____ 2. Look closely at the illustration on page 574. Which of the following academic subjects or disciplines is not represented by the icons that appear alongside the cell phone?

   a. geography

   b. art

   c. psychology

   d. filmmaking

F. FIGURING OUT IMPLIED MEANINGS

Indicate whether each statement is true (T) or false (F).

_____ 1. In general, cellular networks are more developed in Europe and Asia than they are in the United States.

_____ 2. Instructors have found that students are usually unwilling to share their cell phones with students who don't own cell phones of their own.

_____ 3. Principal Taylor implies that adults are just as guilty of rude cell phone use as students are.

_____ 4. The "lit circles" discussed in paragraph 4 were most likely part of a science class.

_____ 5. The title of the reading makes it clear that the author favors the use of cell phones in the classroom.

_____ 6. In general, the author believes that students cannot be trusted to use cell phones in an ethical and responsible manner.

_____ 7. Teachers can be trained to use GoKnow software in just a few minutes.

G. THINKING CRITICALLY

Select the best answer.

_____ 1. The tone of the reading can best be described as

    a. angry.

    b. optimistic.

    c. humorous.

    d. sarcastic.

_____ 2. A *rhetorical question* is a question a writer or speaker asks directly, often as a starting point for a discussion. Which of the following rhetorical questions is not found in the reading?

    a. So why have schools been slow to embrace them?

    b. But educators know that with students, cell phone use is inevitable, so why not use the devices for good?

    c. Why have parents in the United States been so unwilling to support the use of cell phones in the classroom?

    d. Given the example of the Craik School, why haven't more American teachers embraced cell phone use in the classroom?

_____ 3. What is a "lit circle" (paragraph 4)?

    a. a study group that meets at night

    b. a mathematical concept

    c. a literary discussion group

    d. an iPhone application

_____ 4. According to the reading, what is the primary purpose of Bluetooth technology?

    a. tutoring in grammar and writing

    b. networking and information sharing

    c. simulating scientific phenomena

    d. socializing and interpersonal communication

_____ 5. What does the author mean by the phrase *social toy* in paragraph 10?

    a. communication device

    b. overpriced electronic assistant

    c. access point for entry into MySpace or Facebook

    d. device used primarily for socializing rather than study or work

_____ 6. Liz Kolb implies that U.S. teachers do not want to use cell phones in the classroom as a result of

    a. their own insecurities.

    b. research suggesting that cell phones are not effective learning tools.

    c. a sense of competition with Canadian teachers.

    d. a fear of modern technology.

_____ 7. The author ends the reading with a(n)

    a. fact.

    b. statistic.

    c. informed opinion.

    d. example based on the author's experience.

H. BUILDING VOCABULARY

Context

Using context and a dictionary, if necessary, determine the meaning of each word as it is used in the selection.

_____ 1. nuisance (paragraph 1)

    a. annoyance

    b. forbidden item

    c. highlight

    d. noise

_____ 2. integral (paragraph 2)

    a. mathematical

    b. expensive

    c. essential

    d. technological

_____ 3. myriad (paragraph 4)

    a. complicated

    b. advanced

    c. multimedia

    d. many

_____ 4. colleagues (paragraph 8)

    a. students

    b. bosses

    c. co-workers

    d. principals

Word Parts

> ### A REVIEW OF PREFIXES AND SUFFIXES
>
> **TRANS-** means *to change substantially*
> **-IZE** means *to make*

Use your knowledge of word parts and the review above to fill in the blanks in the following sentences.

1. To **popularize** (paragraph 16) cell phone use in classrooms is to _____ cell phone use popular.

2. To **transform** (paragraph 16) a paper-and-pencil lesson into a cell phone–based lesson is to _____ its format drastically from one based on paper to one based on technology.

Unusual Words/Understanding Idioms

Use the meanings given below to write a sentence using the boldfaced phrase.

1. To be **gung-ho** (paragraph 8) about something is to be very enthusiastic about it.

   Your sentence: _____

   _____

2. To **bury your head in the sand** (paragraph 9) is to deny reality.

   Your sentence: _____

   _____

3. A **pilot program** (paragraph 12) is a program that is being run on an experimental basis.

   Your sentence: _____

   _____

I. SELECTING A LEARNING/STUDY STRATEGY

Select the best answer.

_____ 1. In preparing for an class discussion based on this article, it would be most helpful to

    a. reread it several times.

    b. write a detailed outline

    c. draw a map

    d. write a list of questions and reactions

_____ 2. Which of the following would be the most likely essay exam question based on this article?

    a. Compare and contrast cell phones and laptops as effective teaching tools.

    b. Explain how and why cell phones are effective teaching tools.

    c. Justify distributing cell phones to all students who cannot afford them.

    d. Explain why the use of cell phones is often discouraged.

J. EXPLORING IDEAS THROUGH DISCUSSION AND WRITING

1. Describe an experience in which one of your instructors reacted to a student using a cell phone in class. How did your instructor handle the situation? What would you have done differently, if anything?

2. The reading specifies scientific simulations of the water cycle (paragraph 14) as one application that can be viewed on a cell phone. Alone or with a group, come up with a list of at least three additional suggestions for using cell phones in your college classes. For each suggestion, specify the course in which you would use it.

K. BEYOND THE CLASSROOM TO THE WEB

Cell phones have evolved into "smartphones" that allow users not only to make phone calls, but also to surf the Web, make movies, and find their way around a city with sophisticated mapping technologies. These capabilities are made possible by computer applications, sometimes called "apps." Look at your cell phone provider's Web site and list three or four apps you find interesting and applicable to your college courses. Briefly describe how each works and what its benefits would be. If you don't own a cell phone or smart phone, do a Web search for Apple's iPhone and describe some of its available apps.

**TRACKING
YOUR
PROGRESS**

Selection 28

Section	Number Correct	Score
A. Thesis and Main Ideas (5 items)	_____ × 4	_____
B. Details (6 items)	_____ × 4	_____
C. Organization and Transitions (2 items)	_____ × 2	_____
E. Reading and Thinking Visually (2 items)	_____ × 3	_____
F. Implied Meanings (7 items)	_____ × 2	_____
G. Thinking Critically (7 items)	_____ × 2	_____
H. Vocabulary		
Context (4 items)	_____ × 3	_____
Word Parts (2 items)	_____ × 3	_____
	Total Score	_____%

SELECTION 29

Trial Lawyers Cater to Jurors' Demands for Visual Evidence

Sylvia Hsieh

This reading originally appeared in *Lawyers USA*. The author was a staff writer for the magazine.

PREVIEWING THE READING

Using the steps listed on pages 40–41, preview the reading selection. When you have finished, complete the following items.

1. According to the article, trial lawyers cater to jurors' demands for _____ evidence.

2. Indicate whether each statement is true (T) or false (F).

    _____ a. Today's jurors like to see visual evidence in the courtroom.

    _____ b. It can be difficult to get a courtroom judge to allow visual evidence at trial.

MAKING CONNECTIONS

Have you ever served on a jury? If so, how recently? What types of evidence were presented? How convincing were they?

READING TIP

This reading offers quotations by experts in the legal field. Be sure to evaluate these critically, noticing how each is used to support the author's main points.

Trial Lawyers Cater to Jurors' Demands for Visual Evidence

1   As jurors demand slicker, speedier, sound bite-like presentation of trial evidence, lawyers are hiring visual artists, computer graphic designers, and illustrators to transform piles of documents into light, sound, and images. While words, paper, and argument are the tools that lawyers are most comfortable employing, jurors expect a courtroom display bordering on entertainment. Video games, smart phones, and legal TV shows have all fed these expectations. "Jurors have the expectation of all the

plaintiff
in a court case, the person who files suit

2

mediation and arbitration
methods of resolving a legal dispute without going to court

whiz-bang gadgetry of *CSI: Miami* and want to know why you can't get a whole case done with less time for commercials," said Rubin Guttman, a **plaintiffs'** personal injury attorney in Cleveland.

The lower cost of technology has fueled greater competition among providers of visual evidence and made such evidence almost a must for any size case. "You literally can't go to trial without some type of presentation in 30-second sound bites and attention-grabbers to make a point: animations, graphics, videos. It's more and more like the Discovery Channel," said Dan Copfer, president of Visual Evidence/ E-Discovery in Cleveland.

3   Not only is visual evidence not just for the Goliaths anymore; it's also not just for jury trials. Lawyers are also going increasingly visual in **mediation and arbitration**. In one recent example, Copfer's company was hired to create visual evidence for a small California company with 10-12 employees in a mandatory mediation against a large corporation over a contract dispute. "This little company can afford to pay a few dollars. The cost of technology has gone way down. It's an even playing field," said Copfer, whose team consists of graphic artists and illustrators from the Cleveland Institute of Art.

This graphic was created to demonstrate different scenarios based on witness reports of a vehicle accident.

"Every case can be visual"

4   According to Brian Carney, every legal case can be turned into a visual story. Carney, a former prosecutor, noticed over a decade ago that juries weren't grasping evidence in criminal cases and his office wasn't presenting evidence in a way that made it easy for juries to understand. Carney was also a videographer, and he started a multimedia department to help prosecutors present their cases in more visually appealing ways. He now owns WIN Interactive in Quincy, Mass., a provider of visual presentations for lawyers in criminal and civil cases. Criminal cases naturally lend themselves to visual storytelling, he said. "A crime happened at a scene, the defendant ran away, was arrested, and hid evidence somewhere else. A crime is inherently a visual case," Carney said.

5   Michael Moore, a prosecutor with the Beadle County State's Attorney in Huron, S.D., said he

uses video graphics to bring to life abstract concepts like timing and distance. "I can have a computer graphic artist design a model to show the shooter was 10 feet away from the victim and show the pattern of the shot. It looks like a modern video game like *Grand Theft Auto* that looks 3D," said Moore. Moore said he also uses electronically converted crime scene sketches to help illustrate officers' testimony from their perspective. "When an officer testifies he saw this piece of evidence, like a blood splat, he can point to the screen and say, 'This is where I was standing,' so the jury can see exactly what [the officer] was looking at from his **vantage point**," Moore said.

vantage point
place or position 6
offering a good view
of something

Even cases that lawyers think of as strictly document-based—like a business case—can be communicated through visual media. Michael Diamant, a business attorney, recently hired graphic artists to create video animation of organic molecules in a patent case over cement molecules. "The animation showed [the] complex . . . combination of molecules [covered by the patent]. The other side said there was only one configuration," said Diamant, a partner at Taft Stettinius & Hollister in Cleveland. "What I'm trying to do with the jury is to focus the issue so they can understand [it] in a clear graphic way, and take away all the noise around it," he said. "Visual artists come up with pretty creative ideas how to do it. . . . Sometimes I tell them exactly what I want. Sometimes I tell them the problem and they give me a bunch of different thoughts." One of the downsides to going visual at trial is cost. Expenses can range anywhere from $5,000 to $50,000, which some cases cannot justify, Diamant said. "You've got to have value, because the client is going to pay for it. Even if you win the case, they will have fewer dollars net in their pocket," he noted.

Evidentiary challenges

7   Hiring visual and computer artists may be great for juries, but it can be a challenge to get by judges as gatekeepers of evidence. "Artists have great ideas, but a lot of them are inadmissible," said Carney. His team is made up of 3D animation modeling artists and two lawyers with graphics backgrounds in video, computer programming, and illustration.

8   In closing arguments in the notorious Michael Skakel murder trial, Carney created a controversial audio-visual montage that used edited portions of Skakel's own recorded voice describing his feeling of "panic" dubbed over gruesome photos of the victim, Martha Moxley. On appeal, the defense argued that the **montage** confused the jury into thinking Skakel's "panic" referred to the murder, when he was really only worried he had been seen masturbating in a tree where the victim was found. The Connecticut Supreme Court upheld the audio-visual montage as "not deceptive," finding that all of the audio and photos had already been admitted into evidence. (State v. Skakel, 888 A.2d 985 (Conn. 2006).)

montage
collection of
separate items,
edited together to
create a continuous
whole

9   Copfer says that 90 percent of the visual evidence his company creates for trial lawyers is for demonstrative purposes to illustrate a point, and never makes it back to the jury room. For visual evidence that you do want to get admitted, you need to have the artists designing the visuals work closely with your experts.

10   In a homicide case that Moore prosecuted alleging that a homeowner murdered an intruder by repeatedly shooting him in the back as he ran away, both his expert and his graphic designer contributed to an animated recreation of the events. "I had the forensic pathologist review photos of the crime scene, ballistic tests of the shotgun and the police report, and he rendered an opinion about the muzzled target distance and angle of the victim when he was shot," said Moore. "When I got the report, I immediately thought that I needed to have a computer graphics designer to [render] visually . . . what this expert was saying." However, in order to get the animated interpretation into evidence, he had the designer create computer graphics for the time of each gunshot but not for the time between shots. "My expert could only tell the distance between the shooter and the victim at the time each shot happened. He didn't know what happened between shots one and two," said Moore, noting that the jury convicted the **defendant**.

defendant
in a court case, the person who is accused

11   Moore said that he has lost *Daubert* challenges when he has tried to admit computer graphics created when an expert enters numbers into a software program. "If you have accident reconstruction software, it's based on a formula where you plug in the speeds and times, then the computer generates a simulation of the accident or crime. It's not truly their opinion; they are putting in numbers and can't articulate how it happened. I've had that successfully challenged," he said.

pitfall
unexpected danger or difficulty

12   Another **pitfall** is to go crazy and try to turn every bit of evidence into a visual. "Lawyers can get overenthusiastic about creating visuals. They forget they have to be directly connected to the evidence," warned Carney. And if everything is turned into a video, jurors will soon tire of it. "On the one hand, they want to be entertained. But you can't run an hour's worth of video testimony because they're used to switching channels," said Diamant.

A. UNDERSTANDING THE THESIS AND OTHER MAIN IDEAS

Select the best answer.

_____ 1. Which of the following best states the central thesis of the selection?

a. Visual evidence can be used very effectively to reach jurors in courtroom cases, but such evidence must adhere to the rules of evidence and should not be overdone.

b. Regardless of the court case or the financial limitations of plaintiffs and defendants, both sides should use visual evidence to strengthen their case.

c. Dan Copfer, Brian Carney, and Michael Diamant are all former lawyers who have become entrepreneurs in the growing field of visual evidence.

d. Jurors must be very careful when weighing visual evidence, because this evidence is often created by computer simulations that may not represent the situation accurately.

_____ 2. The author's primary purpose is to

    a. discuss a trend in the way lawyers are choosing to present evidence in court cases.

    b. persuade students to major in forensics or another law-centered career.

    c. list some of the ways that video-based evidence is being used in the courtroom.

    d. help readers better understand the complicated rules of evidence that judges must enforce.

_____ 3. The main idea of paragraph 8 is that

    a. multimedia evidence should not be used in murder trials.

    b. Michael Skakel murdered Martha Moxley.

    c. audiovisual presentations can mislead a jury.

    d. modern videographers do not adhere to a code of ethics.

_____ 4. Which of the following statements is true of the heading, "Every case can be visual," which appears before paragraph 4?

    a. This heading would better serve as the title of the article.

    b. This heading serves as the implied main idea of paragraphs within it.

    c. This heading is flawed because it focuses only on the visual without any reference to the audio.

    d. This heading emphasizes that all lawyers must work within their clients' financial constraints.

_____ 5. Which of the following statements is *not* supported by the reading?

    a. The lower costs associated with technology have made visual evidence more affordable to many lawyers and their clients.

    b. Video evidence is used mostly on the behalf of plaintiffs.

    c. Before presenting visual evidence in a courtroom trial, lawyers must make sure it meets the rules of evidence.

    d. Video evidence can be used not only in criminal cases but also in cases related to intellectual property questions (for example, patent cases).

B. IDENTIFYING DETAILS

Select the best answer.

_____ 1. According to the article, all of the following have led jurors to expect a courtroom display bordering on entertainment *except*
a. legal television shows.
b. video games.
c. smart phones.
d. glossy magazines.

_____ 2. Before becoming the owner of WIN Interactive, Brian Carney was a
a. visual artist.
b. partner in a large law firm.
c. prosecutor.
d. television executive.

_____ 3. According to the selection, which of the following is *not* true of today's juries?
a. They are more likely to acquit defendants than to convict defendants.
b. They have been influenced by crime TV shows like *CSI: Miami*.
c. They get bored if they are presented with too much visual evidence.
d. They want to be entertained when they are sitting on a jury.

_____ 4. A *Daubert* challenge, referred to in paragraph 11, likely refers to a legal challenge regarding
a. lawyers' compensation.
b. the reliability of software programs.
c. the admissibility of evidence.
d. the right to privacy.

_____ 5. Which of the following currently works as an attorney at a law firm?
a. Taft Stettinius
b. Dan Copfer
c. Michael Moore
d. Michael Diamant

C. RECOGNIZING METHODS OF ORGANIZATION AND TRANSITIONS

Select the best answer.

_____ 1. The overall organizational pattern used in the reading is
   a. cause and effect.
   b. listing.
   c. process.
   d. classification.

_____ 2. The organizational pattern used in paragraph 1 is primarily
   a. chronological order.
   b. spatial order.
   c. cause and effect.
   d. definition.

_____ 3. The pattern of organization used in paragraph 3 is
   a. summary.
   b. generalization and example.
   c. comparison and contrast.
   d. process.

_____ 4. The transitional word or phrase that signals the organizational
   pattern of paragraph 3 is
   a. not only
   b. in one recent example
   c. mandatory remediation
   d. an even playing field

_____ 5. A pattern of organization used in paragraph 4 is
   a. definition.
   b. addition.
   c. classification.
   d. chronological order.

D. REVIEWING AND ORGANIZING IDEAS: OUTLINING

Complete the following outline of the selection by filling in the missing words and phrases.

I. Introduction
   A. Jurors demand slicker, _____ sound bites during trials
      1. Lawyers are hiring visual artists, graphic designers, _____

2. Jurors want to be entertained

3. Jurors' expectations are created by _____, smart phones, TV

4. Lower cost of technology has fueled competition among providers of visual evidence

5. Visual evidence is used in jury trials, _____, and arbitration

6. Even smaller companies can afford to pay for visual evidence

II. Every Case Can Be Visual

    1. Brian Carney: Former prosecutor who used visual evidence in trials

      a. Criminal cases lend themselves to _____ storytelling

    2. _____: Prosecutor who uses videos to explain abstract concepts

      a. Can use graphics to illustrate officers' testimony

    3. _____: Business attorney, partner at law firm

      a. Used visual evidence in a patent case

      b. Sees the cost of "going visual at trial" as possibly high

III. _____

    1. Visual evidence can be _____

    2. Visual evidence can be deceptive

      a. Important case: _____ murder trial

        i. Supreme Court upheld audiovisual montage as not deceptive

    3. Artists should work closely with lawyers to make sure rules of _____ are followed

IV. Closing Ideas

    1. Lawyers can overdo the visual presentations

    2. Jurors will get bored if everything is presented in a video

E. READING AND THINKING VISUALLY

Select the best answer.

_____ 1. The author likely chose to use the photo shown on page 587 in order to

    a. suggest that video testimony is more effective in a courtroom than audio testimony is.

    b. imply that only guilty parties need to use visual evidence.

    c. illustrate evidence from cases prosecuted by Michael Moore of the Beadle County State Attorney's office.

    d. provide a specific example of an audiovisual presentation used in a real court case.

_____ 2. The situation illustrated in the graphic on page 587 involved a(n)

    a. kidnapping.

    b. drug dealing.

    c. vehicle accident.

    d. terrorism.

F. FIGURING OUT IMPLIED MEANINGS

Indicate whether each statement is true (T) or false (F).

_____ 1. The graphic artists at Visual Evidence/E-Discovery are talented amateurs.

_____ 2. Most crimes can be thought of and presented visually.

_____ 3. The author implies that artists are often creative but do not necessarily know the legal rules of evidence.

_____ 4. Michael Skakal was accused of killing someone.

_____ 5. The author implies that accident reconstruction software is infallible.

_____ 6. Martha Moxley was murdered.

_____ 7. The author implies that jurors have a short attention span.

_____ 8. Most of the visual evidence shown in the courtroom is viewed again in the jury room.

G. THINKING CRITICALLY

Select the best answer.

_____ 1. The tone of the reading can best be described as

    a. respectful.

    b. skeptical.

    c. humorous.

    d. informative.

_____ 2. The author's attitude toward using visual evidence in the courtroom is

    a. neutral.

    b. positive.

    c. negative.

    d. biased.

_____ 3. All of the following statements from the reading are opinions *except*

    a. "Jurors have the expectation of all the whiz-bang gadgetry of *CSI: Miami* and want to know why you can't get a whole case done with less time for commercials." (paragraph 1)

    b. "A crime is inherently a visual case." (paragraph 4)

    c. "The other side said there was only one configuration." (paragraph 6)

    d. "Lawyers can get overenthusiastic about creating visuals." (paragraph 12)

_____ 4. Paragraph 8 uses the following citation: State v. Skakel, 888 A.2d 985 (Conn. 2006). This is a reference to a(n)

    a. Internet site.

    b. legal journal.

    c. article that originally appeared in a Connecticut newspaper.

    d. specific court case.

_____ 5. In paragraph 3, the phrase "even playing field" means

    a. litigation related to sports injuries.

    b. a situation where all parties have equal opportunity to win or succeed.

    c. technology that allows the poor and oppressed to vote.

    d. educational opportunities that allow artists to pursue careers in the legal profession.

_____ 6. In paragraph 6, Michal Diamant states, "Even if you win the case, [clients] will have fewer dollars net in their pocket." He means that

    a. it can be costly to produce visual evidence, and those costs will be deducted from any settlements that clients receive as a result of their court case.

    b. in all jury cases, the lawyers make the lion's share of the money while the plaintiffs and defendants pay all the costs.

    c. some legal victories come at great expense, not only to the people involved but also to society at large.

    d. while winning a court case can be a very emotional moment, in the long run everybody loses because of the high cost of the U.S. legal system.

H. BUILDING VOCABULARY

Context

Using context and a dictionary, if necessary, determine the meaning of each word as it used in the selection.

_____ 1. mandatory (paragraph 3)
   a. binding
   b. personal
   c. legal
   d. required

_____ 2. abstract (paragraph 5)
   a. artistic
   b. short version
   c. mathematical science
   d. theoretical

_____ 3. noise (paragraph 6)
   a. loudness
   b. color
   c. clutter
   d. emotion

_____ 4. gruesome (paragraph 8)
   a. close-up
   b. hidden
   c. horrifying
   d. large

_____ 5. alleging (paragraph 10)
   a. proving
   b. underplaying
   c. accusing
   d. hinting

Word Parts

A REVIEW OF PREFIXES, ROOTS, AND SUFFIXES

IN- means not.
MULTI- means many.
SPEC means look or see.
-IBLE refers to a state, condition, or quality.

Use your knowledge of word parts to fill in the blanks.

1. A *multimedia* (paragraph 4) presentation makes use of _____ media.

2. A *perspective* (paragraph 5) is a way of _____ something.

3. *Inadmissible* (paragraph 7) evidence cannot be _____ into evidence.

Unusual Words/Understanding Idioms

Use the meanings given below to write a sentence using the boldfaced word.

1. The phrase **sound bite** (paragraph 1) is often used in the media. It means a brief extract from a recorded interview. It has taken on the connotation of a statement that is compact and glib (shallow and insincere).

   _____

   _____

2. **Goliaths** (paragraph 3) refer to very powerful people or organizations. This is a reference to the giant Goliath from the Bible.

   _____

   _____

I. SELECTING A LEARNING/STUDY STRATEGY

Discuss methods of studying the outline shown on pages 592–593 in preparation for an exam that covers this reading.

J. EXPLORING IDEAS THROUGH DISCUSSION AND WRITING

1. Do you watch any crime dramas on television? If so, what do you like about them and why do you watch them? Write a paragraph explaining your opinion.
2. If you watch crime dramas on TV, write a paragraph giving a criminal three tips on what *not* to do at a crime scene.
3. Much of this reading uses legal language and vocabulary. Paraphrase paragraph 10 using your own words.
4. In paragraph 1, the author states that video games, smart phones, and legal TV shows have fed jurors' expectations for a courtroom environment that is entertaining. Write an essay in which you explain how each of these types of media may have affected jurors' expectations.

5. Have you ever served on a jury? If so, describe the experience. Was it interesting, boring, provocative? What kinds of evidence did the prosecutor present, and was the evidence convincing? If you haven't served on a jury, suppose you are serving at a murder trial. What kinds of evidence would you need to see in order to find the defendant guilty?

K. BEYOND THE CLASSROOM TO THE WEB

This reading makes many references to "admissible evidence." Conduct a Web search for this phrase and make a list of types of evidence. In one column, place the types of evidence that are admissible. In another column, place the types of evidence that are not admissible. What does the phrase "fruit of the poisonous tree" mean?

TRACKING YOUR PROGRESS

Selection 29		
Section	**Number Correct**	**Score**
A. Thesis and Main Ideas (5 items)	_____ × 3	_____
B. Details (5 items)	_____ × 3	_____
C. Organization and Transitions (5 items)	_____ × 2	_____
E. Reading and Thinking Visually (2 items)	_____ × 5	_____
F. Implied Meanings (8 items)	_____ × 2	_____
G. Thinking Critically (6 items)	_____ × 3	_____
H. Vocabulary		
Context (5 items)	_____ × 2	_____
Word Parts (3 items)	_____ × 2	_____
	Total Score	_____%

SELECTION 30

Eco-tourism

John R. Walker and Josielyn T. Walker

TEXTBOOK
EXCERPT

This reading originally appeared in *Tourism: Concepts and Practices*, a textbook for students who are preparing for careers in the tourism and hospitality industries. In their preface, the authors write, "This textbook is written to empower you and help you on your way to becoming a future leader of this great industry. *Tourism: Concepts and Practices* will give you an overview of the world's largest and fastest growing industry groupings."

PREVIEWING THE READING

Using the steps listed on pages 40–41, preview the reading selection. When you have finished, complete the following items.

1. This reading defines and discusses _____.

2. Indicate whether each statement is true (T) or false (F).

   _____ a. This reading explains who eco-tourists are.

   _____ b. This reading concentrates on why native peoples object to eco-tourism.

 MAKING CONNECTIONS

How do you think tourists affect local economies, both positively and negatively? Have you ever thought about the ways tourism may be linked to social realities like poverty, pollution, jobs, standards of living, education, and the environment?

READING TIP

To understand tourism, it is essential to understand geography. Locate each place discussed in the reading on a map.

Eco-tourism

What Is Eco-tourism?

1   The Ecotourism Society in Bennington, Vermont, suggests a simplified (and widely used) definition of eco-tourism: "Responsible travel to natural areas that conserves the environment and sustains the well-being of the host people." Dr. David Weaver,

a respected eco-tourism author and scholar, defines eco-tourism as: "A form of tourism that fosters learning experiences and appreciation of the natural environment, or some component thereof, within its associated cultural context. It is managed in accordance with industry best practice to attain environmentally and socio-culturally sustainable outcomes as well as financial viability."

Who Are Eco-tourists?

2   The International Ecotourism Society developed a profile of the average eco-tourist from a survey among travelers in North America. The survey found that most eco-tourists were between the ages of 35 and 54 years, with variations resulting from factors such as activity and cost. There was no difference between male and female eco-tourists, although men and women preferred to participate in different activities. Whereas males tended to be more interested in specialist activities and outdoor adventure, females preferred general interest experiences. It has been assumed that eco-tourists are more highly educated than the average traveler is. The survey found this assumption to be generally true, with 82 percent being college graduates.

3   No major differences were found between the average tourist and the eco-tourist when it came to household composition. Most of the people in the surveys live as couples. However, the survey found that more general tourists live as couples with children compared to eco-tourists, who have the tendency to live alone. When it is time to travel, fewer eco-tourists travel alone and instead travel in groups. However whether they travel alone or in a group also depends on the type of experience and the destination. Many prefer to travel as couples, with participants from the same household or from different households. Most eco-tourists (60 percent) preferred to travel as a couple, with only 15 percent preferring to travel with their families, and 13 percent alone.

4   The average length of each eco-tourism trip was found to be 8 to 14 days, during which a majority of travelers were willing to spend more than other tourists usually are. More precisely, most were willing to spend between $2,000 and $3,000 per trip. The length of the trip varied depending on the type of experience, the planned activities, and the destination. The survey showed that eco-tourists tend to stay longer at a location compared to general tourists, with stays ranging from two weeks to a month or longer. Just as the general tourist, most eco-tourists seem to prefer to travel during the summer months. However, a higher percentage of eco-tourists compared to general tourists were willing to travel during the winter months. Eco-tourists generally are more frequent travelers than the general traveler is. The survey revealed that most eco-tourists look for (1) a wilderness setting, (2) the opportunity to view wildlife, and (3) an area in which they can

Eco-tourists hiking on a trail in the rainforest.

participate in hiking and/or trekking. Motivating factors are mainly the opportunity to enjoy scenery and nature, as well as new places and experiences. Other things of priority include local food produced with local ingredients, friendly hospitality, as well as organized opportunities to spend time with local people.

Eco-tourism Activities

5   What often comes to mind when people think about eco-tourism is the vision of a middle-aged couple in flannel shirts and hiking boots strolling around the wilderness with a pair of binoculars, hoping to spot a rare bird. Although a number of tourists engage in that stereotypical activity, there are many other opportunities for fun and action.

6   These opportunities might include a guided tour through the rain forest, witnessing the magical world under the sea, rafting roaring rapids, or participating in a cultural event. As with all tourism, the types of available activities depend on the destination. If traveling in Norway, visitors have the opportunity to go on a whale or elk safari, whereas in Kenya they will encounter giraffes, or elephants, or zebras. In Brazil, they can explore the rainforest, and in the Middle East, a lush oasis.

7   Wildlife watching is popular in just about every location in the world. Encountering exotic animals is exciting, especially when they are in their natural environment. In less dense areas, bike tours are popular. These are more interactive, especially if the tourists take little luggage with them and opt for staying at small, locally run hotels. This also allows for participating in local cultural events, which could include watching a ceremonial dance, going to a traditional wedding, or learning how to cook the local food specialties. Actually participating in an event is even more rewarding for both the tourist and the host community.

8   In coastal areas, snorkeling and scuba diving are extremely popular, and available depending on the fragility of the local marine life and its ecosystem. Boat tours and canoe rides are also commonly found on the coast and in areas adjacent to rivers, marshes, and lakes. Travelers can take an airboat ride in the Florida Everglades or a quiet canoe trip among alligators. Even better, they can experience a specialist cruise, with lectures and snorkeling, to Ecuador's Galapagos Islands, the famous site where Charles Darwin developed his theory of evolution.

9   Eco-tourism trips keep travelers busy and active. No matter where the destination is, there is always something to see and do. Even when there are few or no activities planned for a day, eco-tourists can find plenty to do, such as visiting local markets, taking photographs of the scenery and the people, or even lying in a hammock and enjoying what the environment has to offer.

flora
plant life

fauna
animal life

10   Some important reasons why people go on eco-tourism vacations are to participate in conservation and preservation efforts, to learn about the **flora** and **fauna** of an area, and to become familiar with the culture of the host community. Bird watching is popular in many locations in the world. Being able to see exotic species of animals is exciting, especially if the chances of getting a second glimpse of the animal are almost impossible. Probably the most popular activity of an eco-tourism vacation is walking or hiking through parks and other designated areas, which provides excellent possibilities for travelers to experience the natural beauty that

surrounds the host people, as well as to have a firsthand look at the host community and their lifestyle.

11   Photography is usually a welcomed hobby as well. Travelers encounter plenty of photo opportunities while on an eco-tourism trip. Pictures can be taken in just about every location and of just about anything that comes into view. However, if eco-tourists plan to photograph animals, they need to be very patient because wild animals tend to hide or move along rather quickly. They may also be afraid of bright lights, which is the reason why some parks and attractions prohibit flash photography. In addition, eco-tourists must be aware of the host community's norms for photographs; some cultures are against photos, and others might charge tourists for the opportunity to photograph community members.

12   Some eco-tourists take an eco-tourism vacation to study a specific issue or topic. For instance, eco-tourism is an excellent way to learn about a certain culture or reinforce learning of a new language. Other people take eco-tourism trips to find out more about a specific type of plant or animal life at the destination. Archaeologists and other scientists sometimes go on eco-tourism "vacations" to study the history and present culture of the area, as well as its development throughout its years of existence. Excavation projects are abundant in areas such as Tikal, Quintana Roo, Peru, Greece, Egypt, and other regions of the world that have a hidden mystery behind their culture. No matter what the destination or the activity, eco-tourism has a lot to offer the traveler and the host community.

Important Eco-tourism Destinations

13   There is no definite or correct answer to the question of which eco-tourism destinations are best. Although good eco-tourism sites are too numerous and varied to list here, we try to highlight some of the most popular and interesting ones. Although North America may not be considered a top eco-tourism destination, it has abundant national parks and unique and beautiful places such as the Everglades that are prime locations for a wide variety of eco-tourism and nature tourism activities.

14   Some of Central America's most popular eco-areas include the many tropical rainforests and sites of Mayan ruins. Belize and Costa Rica are often referred to as pioneers of eco-tourism because they began promoting large-scale tourism in the 1980s when eco-tourism first became popular. Belize and Costa Rica have many parks, beaches, and lush tropical forests that are protected by the government and prominent organizations such as the World Tourism Organization (WTO) and the United Nations Environment Programme (UNEP), allowing for greater conservation and preservation efforts to be practiced. Mundo Maya is one of the region's most successful eco-tourism projects. It is unique in that it is a joint endeavor of the countries in which Maya civilization was, and still is, found. These countries include Belize, El Salvador, Guatemala, Honduras, and parts of Mexico. Tourists can climb the massive stone pyramids, sit in one of the housing rooms, hike through the jungles, and watch for exotic birds and howler monkeys, among other animals. In some places, tourists can even see the coral reefs of the Caribbean coastline. The great thing about

Mundo Maya is that the traveler can visit one area or country at a time, or enjoy a package featuring some or all countries and major attractions at once.

15   Costa Rica has, over the years, been a model of eco-tourism, with abundant natural wonders. The country contains 5 percent of the world's biodiversity within just 0.035 percent of the earth's surface. Also, large areas of the country are set aside as national parks, and there are plans to plant 5 million trees each year and become a carbon-neutral country by 2023. Costa Rica has, in comparison with other countries, more of a range of eco-tourism offerings, from rustic to luxurious, from counterculture to **indigenous** culture, from spiritual to scientific, from purely Costa Rican to undeniably North American, from European to **eclectic** cross-cultural blends.

indigenous
native

eclectic
wide-ranging,
diverse

16   The vast continent of South America also has a myriad of eco-tourism areas of growing popularity and importance. More tourists are finding their way into the lush jungles and down the Amazon River in Brazil, where they get to go on exciting and informative adventures with the local population of the Amazon. Ecuador is also becoming popular for eco-tourism.

17   One of the most popular eco-tourism destinations of all time, and indeed the one often cited as the place where eco-tourism originated, is the Galapagos Islands, located some 600 hundred miles off the coast of Ecuador. Interestingly, it was Charles Darwin who brought attention to the islands when he wrote about them in *On the Origin of Species by Means of Natural Selection,* published in 1859. Darwin noted that the wildlife with no natural **predators** were usually "tame," and that many of the islands had developed their own unique species of animals, birds, and plants. UNESCO declared the Galapagos a World Heritage site in 1978, which says a lot about its uniqueness and importance.

predators
animals that prey on
other animals

18   Europe has been criticized for a lack of sustainability, but when we look away from the congested areas of, for example, London, Rome, and Paris, plenty of destinations focus on eco-tourism. In particular, tours to explore the ancient ruins, architecture, and cultures of Turkey and Greece are a popular choice. In addition, the largely untouched natural areas and distinctive culture of the Scandinavian countries are growing in recognition and importance.

19   Travelers who want to explore Asia can join an eco-tour to the snow-capped Himalayas in Nepal or the sultry jungles of Thailand. More places, such as Malaysia, Thailand, and the Philippines, are developing their tourism programs based on environmental conservation and protection. Looking for Shangri-la? The former hidden kingdom of the Hunza Valley in Pakistan has been opened for eco-tourism, allowing a select number of tourists to see the 700-year-old Hunza Fort and village. The project has been internationally acclaimed as an outstanding example of sustainable tourism.

20   More adventures await travelers in Africa, where the tourism industry, especially eco-tourism, has been growing tremendously over the past years. The most popular activity is the safari, which lets visitors get up close and personal with exotic wildlife including elephants, gazelles, lions, tigers, cheetahs, and countless others. Kenya is an important destination for safaris, as are Tanzania, South Africa, Botswana, and Malawi. Chumbe, a tiny island nature reserve off the coast of Tanzania, is another African hotspot. This eco-resort offers many activities. For example, travelers can snorkel the rare coral reef and explore the rain forest. At night, they can sleep in

Eco-tourists in Tanzania, Africa, can appreciate lions in their natural setting as well as several other animal species.

an ecologically self-sustaining hut, complete with solar panels, rainwater tanks, and a composting toilet.

21   Australia is home to an impressive variety of eco-friendly places, including the Great Barrier Reef, which is perhaps the most famous. The "Leave No Trace" program ensures that visitors act in a responsible manner. Visitors to the Great Barrier Reef can enjoy activities such as snorkeling, fishing, diving, hiking, camping, and much more with many certified eco-friendly companies.

22   The massive glaciers of Antarctica are subject to increasing interest and attention. These days, many regions of the world are designating their attractions as eco-tourism sites. Vacationers are becoming more adventurous and are visiting remote, exotic places. They are participating in activities that hopefully affect nature, host communities, and themselves in a positive manner.

23   From Yellowstone National Park in the United States to the Mayan Ruins of Tikal in Guatemala; from the Amazon River in Brazil to the vast safari lands of Kenya; from the snow-capped Himalayas in Nepal to the sultry jungles of Thailand; from the Great Barrier Reef in Australia to the massive ice glaciers in Antarctica—it seems that eco-tourism is taking place in all corners of the world. Some sort of eco-tourism activity is happening in almost every country of the world. A majority of these destinations are found in developing countries, and it seems only natural, considering that they are the home to exotic ecosystems.

—Walker and Walker, Tourism, pp. 376, 386–389, 392–394

A. UNDERSTANDING THE THESIS AND OTHER MAIN IDEAS

Select the best answer.

_____ 1. Which of the following best states the thesis or central thought of the reading selection?

   a. Although most eco-tourism takes place in exotic locations, eco-tourism can also be found in places with cooler climates, like Europe and North America.

   b. Eco-tourists fit a very distinct profile that distinguishes them from typical or general tourists.

   c. Eco-tourism is socially and environmentally friendly tourism; many different activities and locations are available to the distinct set of people who choose eco-tourism.

       d. The key activities preferred by eco-tourists are boating, walking, going on safari, taking part in local ceremonies, eating local foods, and visiting culturally important ruins.

_____ 2. The main idea of paragraph 14 is found in the

       a. first sentence.

       b. fourth sentence.

       c. sixth sentence.

       d. last sentence.

_____ 3. The topic of paragraph 19 is

       a. the jungles of Thailand.

       b. Asia.

       c. sustainable tourism.

       d. eco-tourist destinations in Asia.

_____ 4. According to the various definitions in paragraph 1, which of the following is not a part of eco-tourism?

       a. appreciation of the natural environment

       b. visits to depressed urban areas in underdeveloped countries

       c. well-being of the host people

       d. management according to the best practices of the tourism industry

_____ 5. While many activities are available to eco-tourists, overall the single most popular activity is

       a. snorkeling.

       b. taking part in local cultural events.

       c. hiking.

       d. eating at local restaurants.

B. IDENTIFYING DETAILS

For questions 1–4, select the best answer.

_____ 1. Which of the following statements is *not* generally true of eco-tourists?

       a. They are more likely to live alone.

       b. They tend to travel in couples.

       c. They tend to be recent college graduates.

       d. Their trips usually last 8–14 days.

_____ 2. Charles Darwin developed his theory of evolution in
_____, which is often considered the birthplace of
eco-tourism.

    a. the Galapagos Islands

    b. Belize

    c. Australia

    d. Malawi

_____ 3. In which U.S. state are the Everglades located?

    a. New York

    b. California

    c. Colorado

    d. Florida

_____ 4. Which of the following countries was _not_ home to a part of Mayan
civilization?

    a. Mexico

    b. Argentina

    c. Belize

    d. Guatemala

For questions 5–8, match each eco-tourist destination in Column A with its location in Column B.

Column A	**Column B**
_____ 5. Great Barrier Reef	a. Pakistan
_____ 6. Hunza Valley (Shangri-la)	b. Nepal
_____ 7. Chumbe	c. Tanzania
_____ 8. Himalayas (mountains)	d. Australia

C. RECOGNIZING METHODS OF ORGANIZATION AND TRANSITIONS

Select the best answer.

_____ 1. In paragraph 1, the word _____ clearly points to the
_____ pattern.

    a. defines, definition

    b. suggests, listing

    c. conserves, process

    d. attain, cause and effect

_____ 2. The overall organizational pattern used in paragraphs 2–4 is
_____, but the paragraphs also make use of
_____.

   a. process, definition
   b. statement and clarification, comparison and contrast
   c. classification, chronological order
   d. cause and effect, summary

_____ 3. The overall pattern used to organize paragraphs 5–12 is

   a. order of importance.
   b. listing.
   c. definition.
   d. comparison and contrast.

D. REVIEWING AND ORGANIZING IDEAS: MAPPING

Complete the following partial map of the reading by filling in the blanks with the correct words or phrases.

What Is Eco-tourism?

_____ definition: responsible travel to
natural areas that conserves the environment and sustains that
well-being of the hosts

Dr. David Weaver's definition: tourism that fosters learning
and _____ of the environment, managed in
accordance with _____

_____

Between _____ years old

Men interested in specialist activities and _____
adventure

Women interested in general experiences

More highly _____ than general travelers

Many live alone but travel in _____

Average trip is _____ to 14 days

More willing to spend money than average tourists

Stay at a location _____ than average tourists

Prefer summer travel

Motivations are to enjoy scenery and _____, to _____
_____, and have new experiences

E. READING AND THINKING VISUALLY

Select the best answer.

_____ 1. The photograph on page 600 is included in the reading to
   a. demonstrate a popular ecotourism activity and environment.
   b. define who eco-tourists are.
   c. describe the risks of eco-tourism.
   d. show eco-tourists working together.

_____ 2. The purpose of the photograph on page 604 is to
   a. encourage readers to appreciate for African wildlife.
   b. explain the impact of eco-tourism.
   c. demonstrate how wildlife responds to eco-tourists.
   d. illustrate what eco-tourists might see on an African safari.

F. FIGURING OUT IMPLIED MEANINGS

Indicate whether each statement is true (T) or false (F).

_____ 1. Eco-tourism is most popular in the autumn.

_____ 2. Eco-tourists should understand the cultural norms surrounding the taking of photographs before they arrive at their destination.

_____ 3. Eco-tourism only takes place in remote unpopulated areas of Third World countries.

_____ 4. The authors imply that eco-tourism can be responsible for increasing the appreciation of local ethnic cultures.

_____ 5. In general, eco-tourists are less educated than general travelers.

_____ 6. By "sustainability," the authors mean a set of practices that do not harm people or the land.

G. THINKING CRITICALLY

Select the best answer.

_____ 1. The purpose of this reading selection is to
   a. encourage students to pursue a career in travel and tourism.
   b. expand the reader's knowledge regarding world geography, including the economic and political systems of various countries.
   c. provide an overview of eco-tourism: its definition, participants, activities, and locations.
   d. criticize the governments of North America and Europe for their unwillingness to fund national parks and eco-tourist activities.

_____ 2. The tone of this reading selection is best described as

    a. solemn.

    b. apathetic.

    c. old-fashioned.

    d. informative.

_____ 3. All of the following excerpts from the reading are facts, except for one, which is an opinion. Which is the opinion?

    a. "Eco-tourists generally are more frequent travelers than the general traveler is." (paragraph 4)

    b. "Encountering exotic animals is exciting, especially when they are in their natural environment." (paragraph 7)

    c. "Excavation projects are abundant in areas such as Tikal, Quintana Roo, Peru, Greece, Egypt, and other regions of the world that have a hidden mystery behind their culture." (paragraph 12)

    d. "The country [Costa Rica] contains 5 percent of the world's biodiversity within just 0.035 percent of the earth's surface." (paragraph 15)

_____ 4. The profile of eco-tourists in paragraphs 2–4 is based on

    a. a survey of travelers.

    b. the authors' research.

    c. U.S. government data.

    d. the number of passports issued.

_____ 5. The phrase "host community" as used throughout the reading (for example, in paragraph 10) means

    a. a country with strict wildlife conservation laws.

    b. the mayor of a local village.

    c. a destination that is welcoming tourists.

    d. the person sponsoring a local cultural event.

H. BUILDING VOCABULARY

Context

Using context and a dictionary, if necessary, determine the meaning of each word as it used in the selection.

_____ 1. fosters (paragraph 1)

    a. explains

    b. defines

    c. encourages

    d. diminishes

_____ 2. composition (paragraph 3)

   a. participation

   b. costs

   c. makeup

   d. activities

_____ 3. abundant (paragraph 12)

   a. plentiful

   b. controversial

   c. underfunded

   d. ancient

_____ 4. lush (paragraph 14)

   a. alcoholic

   b. thick

   c. hot

   d. colorful

_____ 5. rustic (paragraph 15)

   a. rusty

   b. poorly kept

   c. country

   d. fragrant

_____ 6. myriad (paragraph 16)

   a. many

   b. diverse

   c. pleasant

   d. pyramid-shaped

Word Parts

A REVIEW OF PREFIXES AND SUFFIXES

ECO means *earth*

-IST means *one who*

-LOGY means *the study of*

Use your knowledge of word parts and the preceding review to fill in the blanks and define the boldfaced words in the sentences below.

1. **Ecosystems** (paragraph 8) are the various _____ systems that keep the planet and its people alive.

2. An **archaeologist** (paragraph 12) is one who _____ human history and prehistory through the excavation of sites and the analysis of artifacts and other physical remains of our human ancestors.

Unusual Words/Understanding Idioms

Use the meanings given below to write a sentence using the boldfaced word or phrase.

1. A **joint venture** or **joint endeavor** (paragraph 14) involves two or more parties working together, usually for mutual benefit.

   Your sentence: _____

   _____

2. **Pioneers** (paragraph 14) is a term that refers to those who were first to take part in something, such as the beginnings of eco-tourism.

   Your sentence: _____

   _____

I. SELECTING A LEARNING/STUDY STRATEGY

1. Now that you have read the selection, go back and reread it as if you were preparing for an exam. Highlight the reading in a way that would help you review the material.
2. Alone or with a small group of classmates, brainstorm two questions that might be asked on an essay exam about the reading.

J. EXPLORING IDEAS THROUGH DISCUSSION AND WRITING

1. An eco-friendly vacation might end up being more expensive than staying at a nice hotel in a major tourist city (for example, London or Paris). Why do you think this is the case?
2. Suppose you have decided to sign up for an eco-friendly tour. Prepare a list of ten things you should do before you leave for the trip.

3. Research a natural conservation area in your city, county, or state. Will it appeal to eco-tourists? Write a paragraph describing the area, what it has to offer, and why it would (or would not) appeal to eco-tourists.

4. Write a paraphrase of paragraph 1 or 17.

K. BEYOND THE CLASSROOM TO THE WEB

Conduct a Web search for a company that offers eco-tourist trips. Choose a location that is interesting to you. What sorts of activities are available to people who visit that location? How much does the trip cost? What information does the Web site provide to help you prepare for the trip and decide whether it is the right choice for you?

TRACKING YOUR PROGRESS

Selection 30		
Section	**Number Correct**	**Score**
A. Thesis and Main Ideas (5 items)	_____ × 3	_____
B. Details (8 items)	_____ × 3	_____
C. Organization and Transitions (3 items)	_____ × 2	_____
E. Reading and Thinking Visually (2 items)	_____ × 3	_____
F. Implied Meanings (6 items)	_____ × 3	_____
G. Thinking Critically (5 items)	_____ × 3	_____
H. Vocabulary		
Context (6 items)	_____ × 2	_____
Word Parts (2 items)	_____ × 2	_____
	Total Score	_____%

Classroom Simulation: Textbook Reading and Writing

Discipline: Communication
Course: Interpersonal Communication

Textbooks are one of the most important parts of most college courses. This classroom simulation is designed to show you how to use your textbook most effectively within the framework of a sample college course. It walks you through a series of typical classroom activities, all of which are based on a textbook excerpt, which is treated as a reading assignment for one class session.

The textbook used in this simulation is from an interpersonal communications textbook. Most communications courses share a common goal: to provide information about the various aspects of human communication. Many students take communications courses as electives because the field is applied. That is, the course offers many opportunities for students to apply what they've learned to their own lives and relationships.

This part of *Reading Across the Disciplines* provides you with a series of activities that you are likely to encounter in a typical communications course. These activities include:

- Reading a textbook chapter
- Preparing for the lecture
- Participating in class
- Writing about the reading
- Taking quizzes and exams on the topic

The textbook chapter featured in the pages that follow is an excerpt from *The Interpersonal Communication Book*, 13th edition, by Joseph A. DeVito. The selection comes from Chapter 9, "Interpersonal Relationship Stages, Theories, and Communication."

Note: As you complete the activities in this part, you will be using the SQ3R method described in Chapter 2. The writing activities add a fourth R, React, to the SQ3R method.

PREPARING FOR THE LECTURE

Your instructor tells your class that she will devote all of next week to the topic of interpersonal relationships and how they develop. She assigns the chapter excerpt reprinted here on pages 618–635 and asks students to come to class prepared to discuss it. You check the course syllabus and see that she plans to spend Monday lecturing on the topic. On Wednesday, the class will break into small groups and take part in collaborative learning exercises.

ACTIVITY 1   Previewing the Text (Survey)

Using the steps listed on pages 40–41, preview the reading selection. When you have finished, complete the following items.

1. The title of the chapter is "Interpersonal Relationship Stages, Theories, and Communication." What exactly does *interpersonal* mean? How can you use word parts to decipher the meaning? _____

_____

2. What is the most important contributor to human happiness?

_____

3. What are the six stages of a relationship?

_____

4. Name at least four strategies for communicating in a developing relationship.

_____

_____

5. List at least four strategies for repairing a troubled relationship.

_____

_____

_____

ACTIVITY 2   Previewing the Visual Aids (Survey)

Preview the visual aids included with the textbook selection, and then answer the following questions.

1. What is a parasocial relationship?

_____

_____

2. What is the topic of Table 9.1 (page 623)? _____

3. Which factors make it more likely that couples who meet on the Internet will remain together? _____

_____

_____

4. True or false? College students today have less empathy than college students from the 1980s and 1990s. _____

ACTIVITY 3   Working with Textbook Features to Help Increase Your Comprehension (Survey)

Examine the features included in the textbook and think about how you can use them to help you study and learn. Answer the following questions.

1. What is the purpose of the feature "Why read this chapter?" at the top of page 619 ?

_____

_____

2. The chapter includes several photos labeled "Viewpoints." Each concludes with several questions. What is the purpose of these

questions? How can answering them help you better learn the topics in the chapter?

_____

_____

_____

3. What is the overall goal of the boxed insert on page 625?

_____

_____

4. What is the black box in the lower-left corner of page 622?

_____

_____

_____

_____

5. List at least two features of the textbook that ask readers to examine their own lives and behaviors.

_____

_____

_____

6. The author uses several bulleted lists (for example, pages 628 and 631). In general, what purpose do these lists serve?

_____

_____

ACTIVITY 4   Activating Background Knowledge (Survey and Question)

As you complete your preview of the chapter, activate your background knowledge by thinking about the following questions.

1. Which parts of your life are most important to your happiness? For example: family, friends, money, success, hobbies?

2. Think about a current or former friendship or relationship. Examine it in terms of the relationship stages discussed on pages 621–627 and in Figure 9.1. How did you meet? How did your relationship grow and develop? Is it still going strong, or has it deteriorated? Did the

relationship ever experience a problem that is now in the past? If so, how did you resolve the situation, or did the relationship end?

3. When you meet another person whom you like, how do you determine whether you wish to pursue that relationship as a friendship or a romance?

4. Sometimes relationships "break." What are some possible causes of these breaks?

5. Suppose you have just met a new person. How is your behavior different with that person from how it is with people you have known for a long time?

READING THE ASSIGNMENT

Now that you have previewed the selection and activated your background knowledge, read the selection.

ACTIVITY 5 Asking Questions about the Reading (Question, Read, and Recite)

As you read each heading, turn it into a question that you think the section will answer. Write these questions in the margin. For example, for the heading titled "Relationship Stages" on page 621, you might ask the question, "What are the stages of a typical relationship?" After you read each section, look away from the page and try to answer the questions you wrote down.

ACTIVITY 6 Highlighting as You Read

Read and highlight the selection; assume you are preparing for a multiple choice quiz on the chapter.

CHAPTER

9

■ ■ ■ ■

Interpersonal Relationship Stages, Theories, and Communication

Relationship Stages

Relationship Theories

Relationship Communication

Sally is getting ready to meet someone face-to-face who she met on Match.com; so far, they've only communicated over the Internet. She likes what she has learned about this person and would like to see the relationship make it to the next stage. To make this happen, she's going to have to admit that she lied about her age and a few other things. She has to decide how to communicate these admissions in some way. See how her choices play out in the video "Coming Clean" (www.mycommunicationlab.com).

Why read this chapter?

Because you'll learn about:

- the stages that relationships go through.
- the reasons you develop relationships.
- the communication patterns in relationship development, deterioration, and repair.

Because you'll learn to:

- navigate through relationships stages more comfortably and effectively.
- evaluate and assess your own relationships.
- communicate more effectively in developing, deteriorating, and repairing relationships.

Contact with other human beings is so important that when you're deprived of it for long periods, depression sets in, self-doubt surfaces, and you may find it difficult to manage even the basics of daily life. Research shows clearly that the most important contributor to happiness—outranking money, job, and sex—is a close relationship with one other person (Freedman, 1978; Laroche & deGrace, 1997; Lu & Shih, 1997). The desire for relationships is universal; interpersonal relationships are important to men and to women, to homosexuals and to heterosexuals, to young and to old (Huston & Schwartz, 1995).

A good way to begin the study of interpersonal relationships is to examine your own relationships (past, present, or those you look forward to) by asking yourself what your relationships do for you. What are the advantages and the disadvantages? Focus on your own relationships in general (friendship, romantic, family, and work); focus on one particular relationship (say, your life partner or your child or your best friend); or focus on one type of relationship (say, friendship), and respond to the following statements by indicating the extent to which your relationship(s) serve each of these functions. Visualize a 10-point scale on which 1 indicates that your relationship(s) never serves this function, 10 indicates that your relationship(s) always serves this function, and the numbers in between indicate levels between these extremes. You may wish to do this twice—once for your face-to-face relationships and once for your online relationships.

_____ 1. My relationships help to lessen my loneliness.
_____ 2. My relationships help me gain in self-knowledge and in self-esteem.
_____ 3. My relationships help enhance my physical and emotional health.
_____ 4. My relationships maximize my pleasures and minimize my pains.
_____ 5. My relationships help me to secure stimulation (intellectual, physical, and emotional).

Let's elaborate just a bit on each of these commonly accepted advantages of interpersonal communication.

1. One of the major benefits of relationships is that they help to lessen loneliness (Rokach, 1998; Rokach & Brock, 1995). They make you feel that someone cares, that someone likes you, that someone will protect you, that someone ultimately will love you.

2. Through contact with others you learn about yourself and see yourself from different perspectives and in different roles—as a child or parent, as a coworker, as a manager, as a best friend, for example. Healthy interpersonal relationships help enhance self-esteem

and self-worth. Simply having a friend or romantic partner (at least most of the time) makes you feel desirable and worthy.

3. Research consistently shows that interpersonal relationships contribute significantly to physical and emotional health (Goleman, 1995a; Pennebacker, 1991; Rosen, 1998; Rosengren, 1993) and to personal happiness (Berscheid & Reis, 1998). Without close interpersonal relationships you're more likely to become depressed—and this depression, in turn, contributes significantly to physical illness. Isolation, in fact, contributes as much to mortality as high blood pressure, high cholesterol, obesity, smoking, or lack of physical exercise (Goleman 1995a).

4. The most general function served by interpersonal relationships, and the function that encompasses all the others, is that of maximizing pleasure and minimizing pain. Your good friends, for example, will make you feel even better about your good fortune and less hurt when you're confronted with hardships.

5. As plants are heliotropic and orient themselves to light, humans are stimulotropic and orient themselves to sources of stimulation (Davis, 1973). Human contact is one of the best ways to secure this stimulation—intellectual, physical, and emotional. Even an imagined relationship seems better than none.

Now, respond to these sentences as you did to the above.

_____ 6. My relationships put uncomfortable pressure on me to expose my vulnerabilities.
_____ 7. My relationships increase my obligations.
_____ 8. My relationships prevent me from developing other relationships.
_____ 9. My relationships scare me because they may be difficult to dissolve.
_____ 10. My relationships hurt me.

These statements express what most people would consider disadvantages of interpersonal relationships.

6. Close relationships put pressure on you to reveal yourself and to expose your vulnerabilities. While this is generally worthwhile in the context of a supporting and caring relationship, it may backfire if the relationship deteriorates and these weaknesses are used against you.

7. Close relationships increase your obligations to other people, sometimes to a great extent. Your time is no longer entirely your own. And although you enter relationships to spend more time with these special people, you also incur time (and perhaps financial) obligations with which you may not be happy.

8. Close relationships can lead you to abandon other relationships. Sometimes the other relationship involves someone you like, but your partner can't stand. More often, however, it's simply a matter of time and energy; relationships take a lot of both, and you have less to give to these other and less intimate relationships.

9. The closer your relationships, the more emotionally difficult they are to dissolve—a feeling which may be uncomfortable for some people. If a relationship is deteriorating, you may feel distress or depression. In some cultures, for example, religious pressures may prevent married couples from separating. And if lots of money is involved, dissolving a relationship can often mean giving up the fortune you've spent your life accumulating.

10. And, of course, your partner may break your heart. Your partner may leave you—against all your pleading and promises. Your hurt will be in proportion to how much you care and need your partner. If you care a great deal, you're likely to experience great hurt. If you care less, the hurt will be less—it's one of life's little ironies.

To complement this discussion of the disadvantages of interpersonal relationships, we'll look also at what has come to be called the "dark side of interpersonal relationships" in the following chapter.

Relationship Stages

It's useful to look at interpersonal relationships as created and constructed by the individuals. That is, in any interpersonal relationship—say, between Pat and Chris—there are actually several relationships: (1) the relationship that Pat sees, (2) the relationship as Chris sees it, (3) the relationship that Pat wants and is striving for, (4) the relationship that Chris wants. And of course there are the many relationships that friends and relatives see and that they reflect back in their communications; for example, the relationship that Pat's mother, who dislikes Chris, sees and reflects in her communication with Pat and Chris is very likely to influence Pat and Chris in some ways. And then there's the relationship that a dispassionate researcher/observer would see. Looked at in this way, there are many interpersonal relationships in any interpersonal relationship.

This is not to say that there is no *real* relationship; it's just to say that there are many real relationships. And because there are these differently constructed relationships, people often disagree about a wide variety of issues and evaluate the relationship very differently. Regularly, on *Jerry Springer* and *Maury,* you see couples who view their relationship very differently. The first guest thinks all is going well until the second guest comes on and explodes—often identifying long-held dissatisfactions and behaviors that shock the partner.

One of the most obvious characteristics of relationships is that they occur in stages, moving from initial contact to greater intimacy and sometimes to dissolution. You and another person don't become intimate friends immediately upon meeting. Rather, you build an intimate relationship gradually, through a series of steps or stages. The same is true of most relationships (Mongeau & Henningsen, 2008).

The six-stage model presented in Figure 9.1 (p. 232) describes the main stages in most relationships. As shown in the figure, the six stages of relationships are contact, involvement, intimacy, deterioration, repair, and dissolution with each having an early and a late phase. The arrows represent the movements that take place as relationships change. Let's first examine the six stages and then we'll look at the types of relationship movements.

Contact

At the initial phase of the **contact** stage, there is some kind of *perceptual contact*—you see, hear, read a message from, view a photo or video, or perhaps smell the person. From this you form a mental and physical picture—gender, approximate age, beliefs and values, height, and so on. After this perception, there is usually *interactional contact.* Here the contact is superficial and relatively impersonal. This is the stage at which you exchange basic information that is preliminary to any more intense involvement ("Hello, my name is Joe"), or you might send someone a request to be a friend. Here you initiate interaction ("May I join you?") and engage in invitational communication ("May I buy you a latte?"). The contact stage is the time of "first impressions." According to some researchers, it's at this stage—within the first four minutes of initial interaction—that you decide whether you want to pursue the relationship (Zunin & Zunin, 1972).

Involvement

At the **involvement** stage of a relationship, a sense of mutuality, of being connected, develops. Here you experiment and try to learn

VIEWPOINTS Parasocial relationships are relationships that audience members perceive themselves to have with media personalities (Giles, 2001; Giles & Maltby, 2004; Rubin & McHugh, 1987). At times viewers develop these relationships with real media personalities—Wendy Williams, Anderson Cooper, or Lady Gaga, for example; and at other times the relationship is with a fictional character— an investigator on *CSI,* a scientist on *Bones,* or a doctor on a soap opera. What's your view of parasocial relationships? Are there advantages to these relationships? Disadvantages? What's your experience with parasocial relationships?

FIGURE 9.1
A Six-Stage Model of Relationships

Because relationships differ so widely, it's best to think of any relationship model as a tool for talking about relationships rather than as a specific map that indicates how you move from one relationship position to another. As you review this figure, consider, for example, if you feel that other steps or stages would further explain what goes on in relationship development.

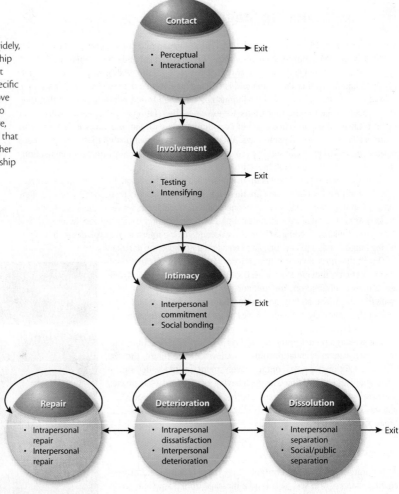

Contact
- Perceptual
- Interactional
→ Exit

Involvement
- Testing
- Intensifying
→ Exit

Intimacy
- Interpersonal commitment
- Social bonding
→ Exit

Repair
- Intrapersonal repair
- Interpersonal repair

Deterioration
- Intrapersonal dissatisfaction
- Interpersonal deterioration

Dissolution
- Interpersonal separation
- Social/public separation
→ Exit

more about the other person. At the initial phase of involvement, a kind of *testing* goes on. You want to see whether your initial judgment proves reasonable. So you may ask questions: "Where do you work?" "What are you majoring in?" If you want to get to know the person even better, you might continue your involvement by intensifying your interaction and by beginning to reveal yourself, though in a preliminary way. In a dating relationship, you might use a variety of strategies to help you move to the next stage and perhaps to intimacy. For example, you might increase contact with your partner; give your partner tokens of affection such as gifts, cards, or flowers; increase your own personal attractiveness; do things that suggest intensifying the relationship, such as flirting or making your partner jealous; and become more sexually intimate (Tolhuizen, 1989). Table 9.1 provides a look at some of the popular ways we flirt.

For cyberflirting, see "Cyberflirting, etc." at tcbdevito.blogspot.com. How do you see cyberflirting? What cyberflirting techniques do you find most interesting?

Intimacy

At the **intimacy** stage, you commit yourself still further to the other person and establish a relationship in which this individual becomes your best or closest friend, lover, or companion.

TABLE 9.1	How to Flirt and Not to Flirt

Here are a few nonverbal and verbal ways people flirt and some cautions to observe. The most general caution, which applies to all the suggestions, is to recognize that different cultures view flirting very differently and to observe the prevailing cultural norms.

Flirtatious Messages	Cautions
Maintain an open posture; face the person; lean forward; tilt your head to one side (to get a clearer view of the person you're interested in).	Don't move so close that you make it uncomfortable for the other person.
Make eye contact and maintain it for a somewhat longer than normal time; raise your eyebrows to signal interest; blink and move your eyes more than usual; wink.	Be careful that your direct eye contact doesn't come off as leering or too invasive, and avoid too much blinking—people will think you have something wrong with your eyes.
Smile and otherwise displace positive emotions with your facial expressions.	Avoid overdoing this; laughing too loud at lame jokes is probably going to appear phony.
Touch the person's hand.	Be careful that the touching is appropriate and not perceived as intrusive.
Mirror the other's behaviors.	Don't overdo it. It will appear as if you're mimicking.
Introduce yourself.	Avoid overly long or overly cute introductions.
Ask a question (most commonly, "Is this seat taken?").	Avoid sarcasm or joking; these are likely to be misunderstood.
Compliment ("great jacket").	Avoid any compliment that might appear too intimate.
Be polite; respect the individuals positive and negative face needs.	But, don't be overly polite; it will appear phony.

Both the quantity and the quality of your interpersonal exchanges increase (Emmers-Sommer, 2004), and, of course, you also talk more and in greater detail about the relationship (Knobloch, Haunani, & Theiss, 2006). You also come to share each other's social networks—a practice followed by members of widely different cultures (Gao & Gudykunst, 1995). And, not surprisingly, your relationship satisfaction also increases with the move to this stage (Siavelis & Lamke, 1992).

The intimacy stage usually divides itself into two phases. In the *interpersonal commitment* phase the two people commit themselves to each other in a private way. In the *social bonding* phase the commitment is made public—perhaps to family and friends, perhaps to the public at large. Here you and your partner become a unit, an identifiable pair. The Understanding Interpersonal Theory & Research box on page 235 looks at this process of commitment in more detail.

INTERPERSONAL CHOICE POINT

Meeting the Parents

You're dating someone from a very different culture and have been invited to meet the parents and have a traditional ethnic dinner. What are some of the things you might do to make this potentially difficult situation go smoothly?

 Deterioration

The **relationship deterioration** stage is characterized by a weakening of the bonds between the friends or lovers. The first phase of deterioration is usually *intrapersonal dissatisfaction*: You

VIEWPOINTS Some cultures consider sexual relationships to be undesirable outside of marriage; others see sex as a normal part of intimacy and chastity as undesirable. Intercultural researchers (Hatfield & Rapson, 1996, p. 36) recall a meeting at which colleagues from Sweden and the United States were discussing ways of preventing AIDS. When members from the United States suggested teaching abstinence, Swedish members asked, "How will teenagers ever learn to become loving, considerate sexual partners if they don't practice?" "The silence that greeted the question," note the researchers, "was the sound of two cultures clashing." How have your cultural beliefs and values influenced what you consider appropriate relationship and sexual behavior?

begin to experience personal dissatisfaction with everyday interactions and begin to view the future with your partner more negatively. If this dissatisfaction grows, you pass to the second phase, *interpersonal deterioration.* You withdraw and grow farther and farther apart. You share less of your free time. When you're together, there are more awkward silences, fewer disclosures, less physical contact, and a lack of psychological closeness. Conflicts become more common and their resolution more difficult. On social network sites, the deterioration stage is perhaps seen most clearly in the decline in frequency of comments, pokes, and thumbs-up liking.

Repair

Some relationship partners, sensing deterioration, may pursue the **relationship repair** stage. Others, however, may progress—without stopping, without thinking—to dissolution.

At the first repair phase, *intrapersonal repair,* you may analyze what went wrong and consider ways of solving your relational difficulties. You might, at this stage, consider changing your behaviors or perhaps changing your expectations of your partner. You might also evaluate the rewards of your relationship as it is now and the rewards to be gained if your relationship ended.

Should you decide that you want to repair your relationship, you might discuss this with your partner at the *interpersonal repair* phase—you might talk about the problems in the relationship, the changes you wanted to see, and perhaps what you'd be willing to do and what you'd want your partner to do. This is the stage of negotiating new agreements and new behaviors. You and your partner might try to repair your relationship by yourselves, or you might seek the advice of friends or family or perhaps go for professional counseling.

Dissolution

At the **relationship dissolution** stage, the bonds between the individuals are broken. In the beginning, dissolution usually takes the form of *interpersonal separation,* in which you may move into separate apartments and begin to lead lives apart from each other. If this separation proves acceptable and if the original relationship isn't repaired, you enter the phase of *social or public separation.* If the relationship is a marriage, this phase corresponds to divorce. Avoidance of each other and a return to being "single" are among the primary characteristics of dissolution. On Facebook this would be the stage where you defriend the person and/or block that person from accessing your profile.

Dissolution also is the stage during which the ex-partners begin to look upon themselves as individuals rather than halves of a pair. They try to establish a new and different life, either alone or with another person. Some people, it's true, continue to live psychologically with a relationship that has already been dissolved; they frequent old meeting places, reread old love letters, daydream about all the good times, and fail to extricate themselves from a relationship that has died in every way except in their memory.

INTERPERSONAL CHOICE POINT
Ending the Relationship

You want to break up your eight-month romantic relationship and still remain friends. What are the possible contexts in which you might do this? What types of things can you say that might help you accomplish your dual goal?

Understanding *Interpersonal Theory & Research*

RELATIONSHIP COMMITMENT

An important factor influencing the course of relationship deterioration (as well as relationship maintenance) is the degree of commitment that you and your relationship partner have toward each other and toward the relationship. Not surprisingly, commitment is especially strong when individuals are satisfied with their relationship and grows weaker as individuals become less satisfied (Hirofumi, 2003). Three types of commitment are often distinguished and can be identified from your answers to the following questions (Johnson, 1973, 1982, 1991; Knapp & Taylor, 1994; Knapp & Vangelisti, 2009; Kurdek, 1995):

- Do I have a **desire** to stay in this relationship? Do I have a desire to keep this relationship going?
- Do I have a moral **obligation** to stay in this relationship?
- Do I have to stay in this relationship? Is it a **necessity** for me to stay in this relationship?

All relationships are held together, in part, by commitment based on desire, obligation, or necessity, or on some combination of these factors. And the strength of the relationship, including its resistance to possible deterioration, is related to your degree of commitment. When a relationship shows signs of deterioration and yet there's a strong commitment to preserving it, you may well surmount the obstacles and reverse the process. For example, couples with high relationship commitment will avoid arguing about minor grievances and also will demonstrate greater supportiveness toward each other than will those with lower commitment (Roloff & Solomon, 2002). Similarly, those who have great commitment are likely to experience greater jealousy in a variety of situations (Rydell, McConnell, & Bringle, 2004). When commitment is weak and the individuals doubt that there are good reasons for staying together, the relationship deteriorates faster and more intensely.

Working with Theories and Research

Has commitment or the lack of it (on the part of either or both of you) ever influenced the progression of one of your relationships? What happened?

In cultures that emphasize continuity from one generation to the next—as in, say, China—interpersonal relationships are likely to be long-lasting and permanent. Those who maintain long-term relationships tend to be rewarded, and those who break relationships tend to be punished. But in cultures in which change is seen as positive—as in, say, the United States—interpersonal relationships are likely to be more temporary (Moghaddam, Taylor, & Wright, 1993). Here the rewards for long-term relationships and the punishments for broken relationships will be significantly less.

Movement among the Stages

Relationships are not static; we move from one stage to another largely as a result of our interpersonal interactions. Three general kinds of movement may be identified.

VIEWPOINTS ⤧ Popular myth would have us believe that most heterosexual love affairs break up as a result of the man's outside affair. But the research does not support this (Blumstein & Schwartz, 1983; cf., Janus & Janus, 1993). When surveyed as to the reason for breaking up, only 15 percent of the men indicated that it was their interest in another partner, whereas 32 percent of the women noted this as a cause of the breakup. These findings are consistent with their partners' perceptions as well: 30 percent of the men (but only 15 percent of the women) noted that their partner's interest in another person was the reason for the breakup. These findings are surely dated. What do you think we'd find if the same survey were done today? More important, why do you think differences exist at all?

For an interesting article on moving from involvement to intimacy, see "From Dating to Mating" at tcbdevito.blogspot.com. Any further suggestions?

Stage Movement The six-stage model illustrates the kinds of movement that take place in interpersonal relationships. In the model, you'll note three types of arrows:

- The **exit arrows** show that each stage offers the opportunity to exit the relationship. After saying "Hello" you can say "Goodbye" and exit. And, of course, you can end even the most intimate of relationships.
- The **vertical arrows** between the stages represent the fact that you can move to another stage: either to a stage that is more intense (say, from involvement to intimacy) or to a stage that is less intense (say, from intimacy to deterioration).
- The **self-reflexive arrows**—the arrows that return to the beginning of the same level or stage—signify that any relationship may become stabilized at any point. You may, for example, continue to maintain a relationship at the intimate level without its deteriorating or going back to the less intense stage of involvement. Or you may remain at the "Hello, how are you?" stage—the contact stage—without getting any further involved.

As you can imagine, movement from one stage to another depends largely on your communication skills—for example, your abilities to initiate a relationship, to present yourself as likable, to express affection, to self-disclose appropriately, and, when necessary, to dissolve the relationship with the least possible amount of acrimony (Dindia & Timmerman, 2003). These issues are covered in the last section of this chapter, "Relationship Communication" (pp. 247–254).

Turning Points Movement through the various stages takes place both gradually and in leaps. Often, you progress from one stage to another gradually. You don't jump from contact to involvement to intimacy; rather, you progress gradually, a few degrees at a time. In addition to this gradual movement, there are relationship turning points (Baxter & Bullis, 1986). These are significant relationship events that have important consequences for the individuals and the relationship and may turn its direction or trajectory. For example, a relationship that is progressing slowly might experience a rapid rise after the first date, the first kiss, the first sexual encounter, or the first meeting with the partner's child.

Turning points are often positive, as the examples above would indicate. But, they can also be negative. For example, the first realization that a partner has been unfaithful, lied about past history, or revealed a debilitating addiction would likely be significant turning points for many romantic relationships.

Not surprisingly, turning points vary with culture. In some cultures the first sexual experience is a major turning point; in others it's a minor progression in the normal dating process.

What constitutes a turning point will also vary with your relationship stage. For example, an expensive and intimate gift may be a turning point at the involvement or the repair stage, an ordinary event if you're at the intimate stage and such gifts are exchanged regularly, and an inappropriate gift if given too early in the relationship.

The Relationship License Movement of a somewhat different type can be appreciated by looking at what is called the **relationship license**—the license or permission to break some relationship rule as a result of your relationship stage. As the relationship develops, so does the relationship license; as you become closer and approach the intimacy stage, you have greater permission to say and do things that you didn't have at the contact or involvement stage. The license becomes broader as the relationship develops and becomes more restrictive as the relationship deteriorates. For example, long-term friends or romantic couples (say at the intimacy stage) may taste each other's food in a restaurant or may fix each other's clothing or pat each other on the rear. These are violations of rules that normally hold for non-intimates, for casual acquaintances or people in the initial stages of a relationship. In relationships that are deteriorating, the licenses become more limited or may be entirely withdrawn.

In some relationships the license is reciprocal; each person's license is the same. In other relationships it's nonreciprocal; one person has greater license than the other. For example, perhaps one person has license to come home at any time but the other is expected to stay on schedule. Or one person has license to spend the couple's money without explanation but the other has no such right. Or one perhaps has the right to be unfaithful but the other doesn't. For example, in some cultures men are expected to have intimate relationships with many women, whereas women are expected to have relationships only with a legally approved partner. In this case a nonreciprocal license is built into the culture's rules.

Part of the art of relationship communication—as you move through the various stages—is to negotiate the licenses that you want without giving up the privacy you want to retain. This negotiation is almost never made explicit; most often it is accomplished nonverbally and in small increments. The license to touch intimately, for example, is likely to be arrived at through a series of touches that increase gradually, beginning with touching that is highly impersonal.

INTERPERSONAL CHOICE POINT
Reducing Uncertainty

You've been dating this person on and off for the last six months but you'd now like to move this relationship to a more exclusive arrangement. You're just not sure how your partner would feel about this. What are some of the things you might do to reduce the uncertainty and ambiguity? Specifically, what might you say to get some indication of whether your partner would or would not like to move this relationship toward greater intimacy?

Ethics in Interpersonal Communication

YOUR OBLIGATION TO REVEAL YOURSELF

If you're in a close relationship, your influence on your partner is considerable, so you may have an obligation to reveal certain things about yourself. Conversely, you may feel that the other person—because he or she is so close to you—has an ethical obligation to reveal certain information to you. At what point in a relationship—if any—do you feel you would have an ethical obligation to reveal each of the 10 items of information listed here? Visualize a relationship as existing on a continuum, from initial contact at 1 to extreme intimacy at 10; and use the numbers from 1 to 10 to indicate at what point you would feel your romantic partner or friend would have a right to know each type of information about you. If you feel you would never have the obligation to reveal this information, use 0.

At what point do you have an ethical obligation to reveal the following information to a romantic partner (say of a year or two) and a close friend?

Romantic Partner	Friend	
_____	_____	Age
_____	_____	History of family genetic disorders
_____	_____	HIV status
_____	_____	Past sexual experiences
_____	_____	Marital history
_____	_____	Annual salary and net financial worth
_____	_____	Affectional orientation
_____	_____	Attitudes toward other races and nationalities
_____	_____	Religious beliefs
_____	_____	Past criminal activity or incarceration

ETHICAL CHOICE POINT

You're in a romantic relationship and your partner presses you to reveal your past sexual experiences. You really don't want to (you're not very proud of your past) and furthermore, you don't think it's relevant to your current relationship. Today, your partner asks you directly to reveal this part of your past. What are your ethical obligations here? Are there certain aspects that you ethically need to reveal and others aspects that you are not ethically bound to reveal?

Relationship Communication

Communication is the life-blood of relationships—without communication relationships could not exist. And without effective communication, effective relationships could not exist. With effective communication, however, you stand a much better chance of experiencing relationships that are productive, satisfying, supportive, open, honest, and possess all the characteristics you want in a relationships. Here we look at some of the communication patterns and guides to effectiveness in developing, deteriorating, and repairing relationships.

Communicating in Developing Relationships

Much research has focused on the communication that takes place as you make contact, become involved, and reach intimacy (Ayres, 1983; Canary & Stafford, 1994; Canary, Stafford, Hause, & Wallace, 1993; Dainton & Stafford, 1993; Dindia & Baxter, 1987; Guerrero, Eloy, & Wabnik, 1993). Here are some examples of how people communicate as they develop and seek to maintain their relationships, presented in the form of suggestions for more effective interpersonal relationships. As a preface, it should be noted that these messages may be sent over any of the available communication channels. Because many relationships develop online (Match.com commercials claim that one out of five relationships begin online), and because online contact is so easy to maintain even when partners are widely separated geographically, a great deal of relationship communication occurs through e-mail, Facebook postings, instant messaging, texting, and tweeting.

VIEWPOINTS One study found that of people who met on the Internet, those who meet in places of common interest, who communicate over a period of time before they meet in person, who manage barriers to greater closeness, and who manage conflict well are more likely to stay together than couples who do not follow this general pattern (Baker, 2002). Based on your own experiences, how would you predict which couples would stay together and which would break apart?

- **Be nice.** Researchers call this *prosocial behavior.* You're polite, cheerful, and friendly; you avoid criticism; and you compromise even when it involves self-sacrifice. Prosocial behavior also includes talking about a shared future; for example, talking about a future vacation or buying a house together. It also includes acting affectionately and romantically.
- **Communicate.** You call just to say, "How are you?" or send cards or letters. Sometimes communication is merely "small talk" that is insignificant in itself but is engaged in because it preserves contact. Also included would be talking about the honesty and openness in the relationship and talking about shared feelings. Responding constructively in a conflict (even when your partner may act in ways harmful to the relationship) is another type of communicative maintenance strategy (Rusbult & Buunk, 1993).
- **Be open.** You engage in direct discussion and listen to the other—for example, you self-disclose, talk about what you want from the relationship, give advice, and express empathy.
- **Give assurances.** You assure the other person of the significance of the relationship—for example, you comfort the other, put your partner first, and express love.
- **Share joint activities.** You spend time with the other—for example, playing ball, visiting mutual friends, doing specific things as a couple (even cleaning the house), and sometimes just being together and talking with no concern for what is done. Controlling (eliminating or reducing) extrarelational activities would be another type of togetherness behavior (Rusbult & Buunk, 1993). Also included here would be ceremonial behaviors; for example, celebrating birthdays and anniversaries, discussing past pleasurable times, and eating at a favorite restaurant.

- **Be positive.** You try to make interactions pleasant and upbeat—for example, holding hands, giving in to make your partner happy, and doing favors. At the same time, you would avoid certain issues that might cause arguments.
- **Focus on improving yourself.** For example, you work on making yourself look especially good and attractive to the other person.
- **Be empathic.** This skill is covered in the accompanying Understanding Interpersonal Skills box.

Understanding *Interpersonal Skills*

EMPATHY

Empathy is feeling what another person feels from that person's point of view without losing your own identity. Empathy enables you to understand emotionally what another person is experiencing. (To sympathize, in contrast, is to feel *for* the person—to feel sorry or happy for the person, for example.) Women, research shows, are perceived as more empathic and engage in more empathic communication than do men (Nicolai & Demmel, 2007). So following these suggestions may come more easily to women.

Communicating Empathy. Empathy is best expressed in two distinct parts: thinking empathy and feeling empathy (Bellafiore, 2005). In thinking empathy you express an understanding of what the other person means. For example, when you paraphrase someone's comment, showing that you understand the meaning the person is trying to communicate, you're communicating thinking empathy. The second part is feeling empathy; here you express your feeling of what the other person is feeling. You demonstrate a similarity between what you're feeling and what the other person is feeling. Often you'll respond with both thinking and feeling empathy in the same brief response; for example, when a friend tells you of problems at home, you may respond by saying, for example, "Your problems at home do seem to be getting worse. I can imagine how you feel so angry at times."

Here are a few more specific suggestions to help you communicate both your feeling and your thinking empathy more effectively (Authier & Gustafson, 1982).

- **Be clear.** Make it clear that you're trying to understand, not to evaluate, judge, or criticize.
- **Focus.** Maintain eye contact, an attentive posture, and physical closeness to focus your concentration. Express involvement through facial expressions and gestures.
- **Reflect.** In order to check the accuracy of your perceptions and to show your commitment to understanding the speaker, reflect back to the speaker the feelings that you think are being expressed. Offer tentative statements about what you think the person is feeling; for example, "You seem really angry with your father" or "I hear some doubt in your voice."
- **Disclose.** When appropriate, use your own self-disclosures to communicate your understanding; but be careful that you don't refocus the discussion on yourself.
- **Address mixed messages.** At times you may want to identify and address any mixed messages that the person is sending as a way to foster more open and honest communication. For example, if your friend verbally expresses contentment but shows nonverbal signs of depression, it may be prudent to question the possible discrepancy.
- **Acknowledge importance.** Make it clear that you understand the depth of a person's feelings.

Working with Interpersonal Skills

In what situations would you appreciate others showing empathy? What specifically might they do to demonstrate this empathy?

Communicating in Deteriorating Relationships

Like communication in developing relationships, communication in deteriorating relationships involves special patterns and special strategies of disengagement.

Communication Patterns These patterns are in part a response to the deterioration; you communicate the way you do because you feel that your relationship is in trouble. However, these patterns are also causative: The communication patterns you use largely determine the fate of your relationship. Here are a few communication patterns that are seen during relationship deterioration.

■ **Withdrawal.** Nonverbally, withdrawal is seen in the greater space you need and in the speed with which tempers and other signs of disturbance arise when that space is invaded. Other nonverbal signs of withdrawal include a decrease in eye contact and touching; less similarity in clothing; and fewer displays of items associated with the other person, such as bracelets, photographs, and rings (Knapp & Vangelisti, 2009; Miller & Parks, 1982). Verbally, withdrawal is marked by a decreased desire to talk and especially to listen. At times, you may use small talk not as a preliminary to serious conversation but as an alternative, perhaps to avoid confronting the serious issues.

VIEWPOINTS Research reported in *Science Daily* (www.sciencedaily.com) finds that college students today have less empathy than did college students from the 1980's and 1990's. In fact, researchers claim that today's students are 40 percent less empathic than students from the 80's and 90's. How would you describe your peers in terms of empathy?

■ **Decline in self-disclosure.** Self-disclosing communications decline significantly. If the relationship is dying, you may think self-disclosure not worth the effort. Or you may limit your self-disclosures because you feel that the other person may not accept them or can no longer be trusted to be supportive and empathic.

■ **Deception.** Deception increases as relationships break down. Sometimes this takes the form of clear-cut lies which you or your partner may use to avoid arguments over such things as staying out all night, not calling, or being seen in the wrong place with the wrong person. At other times lies may be used because of a feeling of shame; you may not want the other person to think less of you. One of the problems with deception is that it has a way of escalating, eventually creating a climate of distrust and disbelief.

■ **Positive and negative messages.** During deterioration there's an increase in negative and a decrease in positive messages. Once you praised the other's behaviors, but now you criticize them. Often the behaviors have not changed significantly; what has changed is your way of looking at them. What once was a cute habit now becomes annoying; what once was "different" now becomes inconsiderate. When a relationship is deteriorating, requests for pleasurable behaviors decrease ("Will you fix me my favorite dessert?") and requests to stop unpleasant or negative behaviors increase ("Will you stop whistling?") (Lederer, 1984). Even the social niceties that accompany requests get lost as they deteriorate from "Would you please make me a cup of coffee, honey?" to "Get me some coffee, will you?" to "Where's my coffee?"

Strategies of Disengagement Another dimension of communicating in relationship deterioration focuses on the strategies people use in breaking up a relationship. When you wish to exit a relationship, you need some way of explaining this—to yourself as well as to your partner. You need a strategy for getting out of a relationship that you no longer find satisfying or profitable. A few such strategies are presented in the list that follows (Cody, 1982). As you read down the list, note that your choice of a strategy will depend on your goal. For example, you're more likely to remain friends if you use de-escalation than if you use justification or avoidance (Banks, Altendorf, Greene, & Cody, 1987).

Dear John,

VIEWPOINTS As more relationships are established and maintained online, more of them are also dissolved online. How would you describe the "rules" for breaking up online versus face-to-face? What are the major differences?

- The use of a **positive tone** to preserve the relationship and to express positive feelings for the other person. For example, "I really care for you a great deal, but I'm not ready for such an intense relationship."
- **Negative identity management** to blame the other person for the breakup and to absolve yourself of the blame for the breakup. For example, "I can't stand your jealousy, your constant suspicions, your checking up on me. I need my freedom."
- **Justification** to give reasons for the breakup. For example, "I'm going away to college for four years; there's no point in not dating others."
- **De-escalation** to reduce the intensity of the relationship. For example, you might avoid the other person, cut down on phone calls, or reduce the amount of time you spend together. Or you might de-escalate to reduce the exclusivity and hence the intensity of the relationship and say, for example, "I'm just not ready for an exclusive relationship. I think we should see other people."

Dealing with a Breakup   Regardless of the specific reason for the end of the relationship, relationship breakups are difficult to deal with; invariably they cause stress and emotional problems, and they may actually create as much pain in a person's brain as physical injuries (Eisenberger, Lieberman, & Williams, 2003). Women, it seems, experience greater depression and social dysfunction than men after relationship dissolution (Chung, Farmer, Grant, Newton, Payne, Perry, Saunders, Smith, & Stone, 2002). Consequently, it's important to give attention to self-repair. Here are a few suggestions to ease the difficulty that is sure to be experienced, whether the breakup is between friends or lovers or occurs because of death, separation, or the loss of affection and connection.

- **Break the loneliness–depression cycle.** Instead of wallowing in loneliness and depression, be active, do things. Engage in social activities with friends and others in your support system. Many people feel they should bear their burdens alone. Men, in particular, have been taught that this is the only "manly" way to handle things. But seeking the support of others is one of the best antidotes to the unhappiness caused when a relationship ends. Tell your friends and family of your situation—in only general terms, if you prefer—and make it clear that you want support. Seek out people who are positive and nurturing. Avoid negative individuals who will paint the world in even darker tones. Make the distinction between seeking support and seeking advice. If you feel you need advice, seek out a professional.
- **Take time out.** Resist the temptation to jump into a new relationship while the old one is still warm or before a new one can be assessed with some objectivity. At the same time, resist swearing off all relationships. Neither extreme works well. Also, take time out for yourself. Renew your relationship with yourself. If you were in a long-term relationship, you probably saw yourself as part of a team, as part of a couple. Now get to know yourself as a unique individual—standing alone at present but fully capable of entering a meaningful relationship in the near future.
- **Bolster your self-esteem.** When relationships fail, self-esteem often declines. This seems especially true for those who did not initiate the breakup (Collins & Clark, 1989). You may feel guilty for having caused the breakup or inadequate for not holding on to the relationship. You may feel unwanted and unloved. Your task is to regain a positive self-image. Recognize, too, that having been in a relationship that failed—even if you view yourself as the main cause of the breakup—does not mean that you are a failure. Neither does it mean

that you cannot succeed in a new and different relationship. It does mean that something went wrong with this one relationship. Ideally, it was a failure from which you have learned something important about yourself and about your relationship behavior.

- **Remove or avoid uncomfortable relationship symbols.** After any breakup, there are a variety of reminders—photographs, gifts, and letters, for example. Resist the temptation to throw these out. Instead, remove them. Give them to a friend to hold or put them in a closet where you won't see them. If possible, avoid places you frequented together. These symbols will bring back uncomfortable memories. After you have achieved some emotional distance, you can go back and enjoy these as reminders of a once pleasant relationship. Support for this suggestion comes from research showing that the more vivid your memory of a broken love affair—a memory greatly aided by these relationship symbols— the greater your depression is likely to be (Harvey, Flanary, & Morgan, 1986).
- **Become mindful of your own relationship patterns.** Avoid repeating negative patterns. Many people repeat their mistakes. They enter second and third relationships with the same blinders, faulty preconceptions, or unrealistic expectations with which they entered earlier involvements. Instead, use the knowledge gained from your failed relationship to prevent repeating the same patterns. At the same time, don't become a prophet of doom. Don't see in every relationship vestiges of the old. Don't jump at the first conflict and say, "Here it goes all over again." Treat the new relationship as the unique relationship it is. Don't evaluate it through past experiences. Use past relationships and experiences as guides, not filters.

Communication in Relationship Repair

If you wish to save a relationship, you may try to do so by changing your communication patterns and, in effect, putting into practice the insights and skills learned in this course. First, we'll look at some general ways to repair a relationship, and second, we'll examine ways to deal with repair when you are the only one who wants to change the relationship.

Interpersonal Repair   We can look at the strategies for repairing a relationship in terms of the following six suggestions, whose first letters conveniently spell out the word *REPAIR*, a useful reminder that repair is not a one-step but a multistep process (see Figure 9.3).

FIGURE 9.3
The Relationship Repair Wheel

The wheel seems an apt metaphor for the repair process; the specific repair strategies—the spokes—all work together in constant process. The wheel is difficult to get moving, but once in motion it becomes easier to turn. Also, it's easier to start when two people are pushing, but it is not impossible for one to move it in the right direction. What metaphor do you find helpful in thinking about relationship repair?

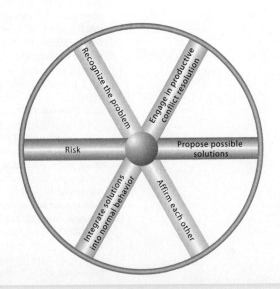

Recognize the Problem   Your first step is to identify the problem and to recognize it both intellectually and emotionally. Specify what is wrong with your present relationship (in concrete terms) and what changes would be needed to make it better (again, in specific terms). Create a picture of your relationship as you would want it to be, and compare that picture to the way the relationship looks now. Specify the changes that would have to take place if the ideal picture were to replace the present picture.

Also try to see the problem from your partner's point of view and to have your partner see the problem from yours. Exchange these perspectives, empathically and with open minds. Try, too, to be descriptive when discussing grievances, taking special care to avoid such troublesome terms as "always" and "never." Own your feelings and thoughts; use *I*-messages and take responsibility for your feelings instead of blaming your partner.

Engage in Productive Communication and Conflict Resolution   Interpersonal communication skills such as those discussed throughout the text (for example, other-orientation, openness, confidence, immediacy, expressiveness, and empathy, considered in Understanding Interpersonal Skills boxes) are especially important during repair and are an essential part of any repair strategy. Here are several suggestions to refresh your memory.

- Look closely for relational messages that will help clarify motivations and needs. Respond to these messages as well as to the content messages.
- Exchange perspectives and see the situation as your partner does.
- Practice empathic and positive responses, even in conflict situations.
- Own your feelings and thoughts. Use *I*-messages and take responsibility for these feelings.
- Use active listening techniques to help your partner explore and express relevant thoughts and feelings.
- Remember the principle of irreversibility; think carefully before saying things you may later regret.
- Keep the channels of communication open. Be available to discuss problems, negotiate solutions, and practice new and more productive communication patterns.

Similarly, the skills of effective interpersonal conflict resolution are crucial in any attempt at relationship repair. If partners address relationship problems by deploying productive conflict resolution strategies, the difficulties may be resolved and the relationship may actually emerge stronger and healthier. If, however, unproductive and destructive strategies are used, then the relationship may well deteriorate further. The nature and skills of conflict resolution are considered in depth in Chapter 11.

Pose Possible Solutions   After the problem is identified, discuss solutions—possible ways to lessen or eliminate the difficulty. Look for solutions that will enable both of you to win. Try to avoid "solutions" in which one person wins and the other loses. With such win–lose solutions, resentment and hostility are likely to fester.

Affirm Each Other   Any strategy of relationship repair should incorporate supportiveness and positive evaluations. For example, happy couples engage in greater positive behavior exchange: They communicate more agreement, approval, and positive affect than do unhappy couples (Dindia & Fitzpatrick, 1985). Clearly, these behaviors result from the positive feelings the partners have for each other. However, it can also be argued that these expressions help to increase the positive regard each person has for the other.

One way to affirm another is to talk positively. Reverse negative communication patterns. For example, instead of withdrawing, talk about the causes of and the possible cures for your disagreements and problems. Reverse the tendency to hide your inner self. Disclose your feelings. Compliments, positive stroking, and all the nonverbals that say "I care" are especially important when you wish to reverse negative communication patterns.

Cherishing behaviors are an especially insightful way to affirm another person and to increase favor exchange (Lederer, 1984). **Cherishing behaviors** are those small gestures you enjoy receiving from your partner (a smile, a wink, a squeeze, a kiss). Cherishing behaviors should be (1) specific and positive, (2) focused on the present and future rather than related to issues about which the partners have argued in the past, (3) capable of being performed daily, and (4) easily executed. People can make a list of the cherishing behaviors they each wish to receive and then exchange lists. Each person then performs the cherishing behaviors desired by the partner. At first, these behaviors may seem self-conscious and awkward. In time, however, they will become a normal part of interaction.

Integrate Solutions into Normal Behavior Often solutions that are reached after an argument are followed for only a very short time; then the couple goes back to their previous, unproductive behavior patterns. Instead, integrate the solutions into your normal behavior; make them an integral part of your everyday relationship behavior. For example, make the exchange of favors, compliments, and cherishing behaviors a part of your normal relationship behavior.

Risk Take risks in trying to improve your relationship. Risk giving favors without any certainty of reciprocity. Risk rejection by making the first move to make up or by saying you're sorry. Be willing to change, adapt, and take on new tasks and responsibilities. Risk the possibility that a significant part of the problem is you—that you're being unreasonable or controlling or stingy and that this is causing problems and needs to be changed.

Intrapersonal Repair One of the most important avenues to relationship repair originates with the principle of punctuation (see Chapter 1) and the idea that communication is circular rather than linear (see Chapter 1; Duncan & Rock, 1991). Let's consider an example involving Pat and Chris: Pat is highly critical of Chris; Chris is defensive and attacks Pat for being insensitive, overly negative, and unsupportive. If you view the communication process as beginning with Pat's being critical (that is, the stimulus) and with Chris's attacks being the response, you have a pattern such as occurs in Figure 9.4 (A).

   With this view, the only way to stop the unproductive communication pattern is for Pat to stop criticizing. But what if you are Chris and can't get Pat to stop being critical? What if Pat doesn't want to stop being critical?

   You get a different view of the problem when you see communication as circular and apply the principle of punctuation. The result is a pattern such as appears in Figure 9.4 (B).

FIGURE 9.4

(A) A Stimulus–Response View of Relationship Problems

This view of the relationship process implies that one behavior is the stimulus and one behavior is the response. It implies that a pattern of behavior can be modified only if you change the stimulus, which will produce a different (more desirable) response.

(B) A Circular View of Relationship Problems

Note that in this view of relationships, as distinguished from that depicted in Figure 9.4 (A), relationship behaviors are seen in a circular pattern; no specific behavior is singled out as a stimulus and none as a response. The pattern can thus be broken by interference anywhere along the circle.

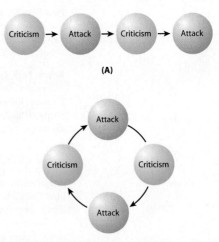

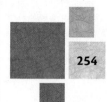

254   PART 3   Interpersonal Relationships

Note that no assumptions are made about causes. Instead, the only assumption is that each response triggers another response; each response depends in part on the previous response. Therefore, the pattern can be broken at any point: Chris can stop Pat's criticism, for example, by not responding with attacks. Similarly, Pat can stop Chris's attacks by not responding with criticism.

In this view, either person can break an unproductive cycle. Clearly, relationship communication can be most effectively improved when both parties change their unproductive patterns. Nevertheless, communication can be improved even if only one person changes and begins to use a more productive pattern. This is true to the extent that Pat's criticism depends on Chris's attacks and to the extent that Chris's attacks depend on Pat's criticism.

REVIEWING THE READING ASSIGNMENT

Now that you have read the selection, you should reread it in order to strengthen your comprehension and knowledge.

ACTIVITY 7 Reviewing Your Highlighting and Annotating the Reading (Review)

After you have read the complete selection once, review your highlighting. Add any annotations that will help you review the selection when you prepare for a quiz or exam on the material.

ATTENDING THE LECTURE AND PARTICIPATING IN CLASS

No two professors will emphasize the exact same material in their lectures. This is true for several reasons. First, professors have a wide range of interests. Second, instructors often complain that the term is much too short for them to cover everything they'd like to talk about. For that reason, they have to pick and choose the topics they will cover in class. (Often, they rely on the textbook to fill in the gaps.)

We asked several communications professors to share their strategies for teaching the material in the "Interpersonal Relationship Stages, Theories, and Communication" chapter that you just read. Some of their responses are shown on the following page.

INSTRUCTORS' COMMENTS ON TEACHING THE CHAPTER

"I'd begin my lecture with the photo of Lady Gaga and her fans. We live in a society that is dominated by the media and celebrities, and I'd like students to think critically about their 'relationships' with celebrities. Social media like Twitter can lend the impression that people are friends with celebrities or with people they have never met. I'd like my students to consider not only how modern social media is changing relationships, but also how celebrities are using Facebook and Twitter to build a fan base and increase their own fame."

"I love Table 9.1 on how to flirt and how not to flirt. Many of my students are very interested in romance, and this would be fun to discuss in class. I would go a few steps beyond the table, though, and ask students to talk about why certain types of flirtation work while other types make people uncomfortable. I find that getting students' interest this way really increases class participation."

"I like to focus on theory in my class, so I would organize the lecture around Figure 9.1. It's an excellent summary of the stages in a relationship, and I'd want my students to come away from the lecture with a strong knowledge of each stage. While I think the material on relationship communication is important, I just don't have time to cover it. I would expect students to have read this material, however, and I would certainly ask about it on the exam."

"My area of research is empathy. I don't think this topic is discussed enough in the textbook, but it is an area that needs much more attention. I believe that many of today's social problems are created by a lack of empathy, so I want to go into more detail on the topic. For that reason, the box on page 249 [630] is very important to me, and I will spend much of the lecture talking about current examples and other research on empathy. I expect students to read the complete chapter, though, and I will save 15 minutes at the end of my lecture to answer questions that students might have about the textbook selection."

ACTIVITY 8   Participating in Class

Prepare a list of five questions that you would ask in class about the selection. Compare these with your classmates' questions. Did many of you ask the same or similar questions? What purposes might these questions serve, other than stimulating classroom discussion?

ACTIVITY 9   Classroom Activity—Self-Revelation

Complete the Ethics in Interpersonal Communication survey on page 627 ("Your Obligation to Reveal Yourself"). Then discuss your results with a group of classmates. Do any specific trends emerge? In other words, do you find areas of general agreement? If so, on which topics? Take an average of the scores and write those into the questionnaire. (To figure the average, add everyone's score for each line and divide by the number of people in your group.) Choose a group leader to present your findings to the class. What type of graphic or visual aid might you create to present your findings?

ACTIVITY 10 Classroom Activity—Avoiding Negative Behaviors

Review the heading titled "Dealing with a Breakup" on pages 631–632. This section focuses on positive methods of dealing with a breakup. With a group of classmates, brainstorm a list of behaviors you should avoid after breaking up with a romantic partner. Present this list to the class. Did the groups come up with similar suggestions?

WRITING ABOUT THE READING

Students often have two purposes for writing in response to a reading. The first purpose is to help them learn the material better. Many studies have shown that writing greatly aids comprehension. The second purpose is to react to the reading. Reactions can be informal (journal entries, freewriting, and so on) or formal (paragraphs, essays, or longer papers on a specific topic). Sometimes the instructor assigns a specific topic or a specific question to which students must respond. Other times, students must come up with their own topic.

ACTIVITY 11 Paraphrasing

Choose one of the following activities to complete.

1. Paraphrase the section titled "The Relationship License" on pages 626–627.

2. Paraphrase the section titled "Strategies of Disengagement" on pages 630–631.

3. Paraphrase the section titled "Engage in Productive Communication and Conflict Resolution" on page 633.

ACTIVITY 12 Summarizing

Choose one of the following activities to complete.

1. Write a summary of the section titled "Relationship Stages" on pages 621–627.

2. Write a summary of the section titled "Relationship Communication" on pages 628–635.

ACTIVITY 13   Outlining

Prepare an outline of the reading selection, using the format shown on page 168.

ACTIVITY 14   Freewriting / Journal Entry (React)

When you freewrite, you sit down and just begin writing. Freewriting is an informal way of responding to a reading. It allows you to begin exploring your ideas and reactions without worrying about grammar, punctuation, or spelling. Many writers find that freewriting is an excellent way to begin getting their thoughts on paper. A journal is a notebook in which you record ideas, reactions, and freewrites. React to the reading selection by freewriting on one of these topics:

1. breaking up a relationship

2. making new friends

3. men's and women's styles of communication

4. helping friends get through a difficult time

5. problems in friendships: what can be forgiven, what cannot be forgiven, and why

ACTIVITY 15   Writing Paragraphs and Essays (React)

Write a paragraph or essay in which you answer one of the following "Interpersonal Choice Point" questions found in the reading.

1. Meeting the Parents: You're dating someone from a very different culture and have been invited to meet the parents and have a traditional ethnic dinner. What are some of the things you might do to make this potentially difficult situation go smoothly?

2. Ending the Relationship: You want to break up your eight-month romantic relationship and still remain friends. What are the possible contexts in which you might do this? What types of things can you say that might help you accomplish your dual goal?

3. Reducing Uncertainty: You've been dating this person on and off for the last six months but you'd now like to move this relationship to a more exclusive arrangement. You're just not sure how your partner would feel about this. What are some of the things you might do to reduce the uncertainty and ambiguity? Specifically, what might you say to get some indication of whether your partner would or would not like to move this relationship toward greater intimacy?

ACTIVITY 16 Brainstorming Research Topics

In many courses, you will be asked to write a long paper (perhaps as long as ten pages). For these papers, you are often expected to choose your own topic. Based on the reading, brainstorm a list of five possible topics you might like to research and write about. Then revisit your list and choose the topic you like best. Why did you eliminate the other topics? Why did you choose the specific topic that you selected?

TAKING QUIZZES

To make sure students have read the assignment, instructors often give quizzes based on the reading selection. These quizzes usually focus on the reading's key points or main ideas. The goal of these quizzes is not to trick you but rather to make sure you have read the selection. For this reason, the quiz questions usually focus on key (vocabulary) terms and concepts. If you have read the selection, it should be easy to do well on the quiz.

ACTIVITY 17 Quiz: Relationship Stages, pages 621–627

Select the best answer.

_____ 1. At which stage of a relationship do you commit yourself to the other person, establishing a close friendship or romantic relationship?

    a. contact

    b. involvement

    c. intimacy

    d. deterioration

_____ 2. The opposite of relationship repair is

    a. social bonding.

    b. interactional contact.

    c. relationship license.

    d. relationship dissolution.

_____ 3. The parties in a relationship often have "permission" to break certain relationship rules as a result of the particular relationship stage in which they find themselves. This "permission" is sometimes called

    a. self-reflexivity.

    b. the relationship license.

    c. public choice.

    d. reciprocity.

_____ 4. The six stages of a relationship are _____, involvement, intimacy, deterioration, _____, and dissolution.

    a. testing, avoidance

    b. reciprocity, turning points

    c. contact, repair

    d. flirting, neutrality

_____ 5. All of the following are good examples of turning points in a relationship, *except*

    a. the first kiss.

    b. having a friend in common.

    c. a revelation that a partner has been unfaithful.

    d. the realization that a partner has an addiction problem.

ACTIVITY 18   Quiz: Relationship Communication, pages 628–635

Indicate whether each statement is true (T) or false (F).

_____ 1. Communication is essential to a healthy relationship, whether that relationship is friendship, familial, or romantic.

_____ 2. Prosocial behavior simply means "being nice."

_____ 3. The ability to feel what another person feels, from that person's point of view, without losing your own identity is called sympathy.

_____ 4. Increased eye contact is often a sign of withdrawal from a relationship.

_____ 5. As a relationship deteriorates, deception sometimes increases.

_____ 6. Telling your romantic partner that you would like to start seeing other people is a method of de-escalation.

_____ 7. To get over a failed relationship, it is best to spend a good deal of time by yourself.

_____ 8. The best way to get over a romantic break-up is to start dating again.

_____ 9. To begin repairing a relationship, you must first recognize and define the problem.

_____ 10. In a healthy relationship, a wink can be considered a cherishing behavior.

TAKING THE EXAM

Exams are often an important part of determining your grade. While some exams feature mostly objective (true/false, multiple-choice, short-answer, fill-in-the-blank) questions, many require writing and critical thinking.

ACTIVITY 19   Brainstorming Essay Exam Questions

Use the headings within the reading to prepare a list of three possible exam questions. (Note: If you used the SQ3R method, you have already brainstormed these questions and practiced answering them.)

ACTIVITY 20   Taking an Essay Exam: Comprehension and Analysis

Select one of the following questions and answer it. Because most exams have a time limit, make sure you can answer this question fully in 15 minutes or less.

1. When happens when a relationship begins to deteriorate? Which two options are available to the participants in that relationship? Describe the deterioration process and outline the available options. To support your key points, you may use personal experience.

2. John and Mary have been married a long time and have a happy, supportive relationship. When John and Mary banter with each other, they often say things that shock their friends. John jokingly says, "I am filing for a divorce if you don't buy me an expensive present" while Mary says, with a smile, "Well, if you won't mow the lawn, I'll ask my lover to do it." What relationship option are John and Mary exercising? How do their behaviors violate the typical "rules" of a relationship? Is John and Mary's behavior reciprocal? If so, why? If not, why not? Offer three additional examples of this type of behavior.

3. List and explain four strategies for coping with a breakup.

4. Some communication specialists use the acronym REPAIR to help them remember the six facets of repairing a relationship. What does each letter in REPAIR stand for? Briefly explain each letter and apply it to this situation: Two long-time friends have grown apart; one has gotten married and is raising a family, while the other friend remains single. The single friend feels that her now-married friend does not make time for her any more.

ACTIVITY 21 Taking an Essay Exam: Critical Thinking

Some essay exams ask for critical thinking and synthesis. Answer the following question in 15 minutes or less.

Your textbook includes several "Viewpoints" features that ask for your opinion on a number of topics. Choose one of the following "Viewpoints" questions and answer it, demonstrating how the textbook concepts apply to your answer. You may use personal experience to support your answer.

1. What's your view of parasocial relationships? Are there advantages to these relationships? Disadvantages? What's your experience with parasocial relationships? (See photo, page 621.)

2. How have your cultural beliefs and values influenced what you consider appropriate relationship and sexual behavior? (See photo, page 624.)

3. One study found that of people who met on the Internet, those who meet in places of common interest, who communicate over a period of time before they meet in person, who manage barriers to greater closeness, and who manage conflict well are more likely to stay together than couples who do not follow this general pattern. Based on your own experiences, how would you predict which couples would stay together and which would break apart? (See photo, page 628.)

4. Research reported in *Science Daily* finds that college students today have less empathy than did college students from the 1980s and 1990s. In fact, researchers claim that today's students are 40 percent less empathic than students from the 80s and 90s. How would you describe your peers in terms of empathy? (See photo, page 630.)

Credits

Text Credits

5: Joan Salge Blake, *Nutrition and You: MyPlate Edition*, 2nd ed. San Francisco: Pearson Benjamin Cummings, 2012, pp. 226, 273; **6:** Mark Krause and Daniel Corts, *Psychological Science: Modeling Scientific Literacy*, 1st ed., p. 385, © 2012. Printed and electronically reproduced by permission of Pearson Education, Inc., Upper Saddle River, New Jersey; **6:** Mark Krause and Daniel Corts, *Psychological Science: Modeling Scientific Literacy*, 1st ed., p. 384, © 2012. Printed and electronically reproduced by permission of Pearson Education, Inc., Upper Saddle River, New Jersey; **7:** Courtland L. Bovée and John V. Thill, *Business in Action*, 6th ed. Upper Saddle River, NJ: Pearson, p. 222; **25:** Tim Curry, Robert Jiobu, and Kent Schwirian, *Sociology for the Twenty-First Century*, 3rd ed. Upper Saddle River, NJ: Pearson Prentice Hall, 2002, p. 207; **26:** Screen shot reprinted by permission of University of New Haven; **32:** Google and the Google logo are registered trademarks of Google Inc., used with permission; **41:** Joseph A. DeVito, *The Interpersonal Communication Book*, 13th ed., pp. 143–144, © 2013. Printed and electronically reproduced by permission of Pearson Education, Inc., Upper Saddle River, New Jersey; **44:** Joan O'C. Hamilton, "Treating Wounded Soldiers: Polytrauma," *Stanford* magazine, November/December 2009. Excerpted from the original article titled "Mission Critical" in *Utne Reader*. Reprinted with permission from Stanford magazine, published by Stanford Alumni Association, Stanford University; **48:** Mary Ann Schwartz and BarBara Marliene Scott, *Marriages and Families: Diversity and Change*, 7th ed. Upper Saddle River, NJ: Pearson, 2012, p. 212; **56:** F. Philip Rice and Kim Gale Dolgin, *The Adolescent: Development, Relationships, and Culture*, 10th ed. Boston: Allyn and Bacon, 2002, pp. 250–251; **58:** Gerald Audesirk, Teresa Audesirk, and Bruce E. Byers, *Life on Earth*, 3rd ed. Upper Saddle River, NJ: Pearson Prentice Hall, 2003, pp. 622–624, 632; **60:** Mark C. Carnes and John A. Garraty, *The American Nation: A History of the United States*, 11th ed. New York: Pearson Longman, 2003, p. 267; **62:** Suzanne G. Marshall, Hazel O. Jackson, and M. Sue Stanley, *Individuality in Clothing Selection and Personal Appearance*, 7th ed. Upper Saddle River, NJ: Pearson Prentice Hall, 2012, p. 111; **68:** William J. Germann and Cindy L. Stanfield, *Principles of Human Physiology*. San Francisco: Benjamin

Cummings, 2002, p. 174; **75:** Gerald Audesirk, Teresa Audesirk, and Bruce E. Byers, *Life on Earth*, 3rd ed. Upper Saddle River, NJ: Pearson Prentice Hall, 2003, p. 237; **82:** Walter E. Volkomer, *American Government*, 14th ed. Boston: Pearson, 2013, p. 114; **82:** Jeffrey Bennett, Megan Donahue, Nicholas Schneider, and Mark Voit, *The Essential Cosmic Perspective*, 6th ed. San Francisco: Pearson Addison-Wesley, 2012, p. 150; **82:** Stephen P. Robbins and Mary Coulter, *Management*, 11th ed. Upper Saddle River, NJ: Pearson Prentice Hall, 2012, p. 362; **83:** H. W. Brands, T. H. Breen, R. Hal Williams, and Ariela J. Gross, *American Stories: A History of the United States*, 2nd ed. Boston: Pearson, 2012, p. 481; **83:** Daniel Limmer and Michael F. O'Keefe, *Emergency Care*, 12th ed. Upper Saddle River, NJ: Pearson Brady, 2012, p. 828; **84:** Walter E. Volkomer, *American Government*, 14th ed. Boston: Pearson, 2013, p. 242; **85:** Diane Sukiennik, Lisa Raufman, and William Bendat, *The Career Fitness Program: Exercising Your Options*, 10th ed. Upper Saddle River, NJ: Pearson Prentice Hall, 2013, pp. 50–51; **85:** Jeffrey Bennett, Megan Donahue, Nicholas Schneider, and Mark Voit, *The Essential Cosmic Perspective*, 6th ed. San Francisco: Pearson Addison-Wesley, 2012, p. 48; **86:** Edward J. Tarbuck and Frederick K. Lutgens, *Earth: An Introduction to Physical Geology*, 10th ed. Upper Saddle River, NJ: Pearson Prentice Hall, 2011, p. 74; **86:** David Krogh, *Biology: A Guide to the Natural World*, 5th ed. San Francisco: Pearson Benjamin Cummings, 2011, p. 319; **87:** Joseph A. DeVito, *The Interpersonal Communication Book*, 13th ed., p. 161, © 2013. Printed and electronically reproduced by permission of Pearson Education, Inc., Upper Saddle River, New Jersey; **87:** John D. Carl, *Think Sociology*, 1st ed., p. 122, © 2010. Adapted and electronically reproduced by permission of Pearson Education, Inc., Upper Saddle River, New Jersey; **87:** George C. Edwards III, Martin P. Wattenberg, and Robert L. Lineberry, *Government in America: People, Politics, and Policy*, 15th ed., p. 608, © 2011. Printed and electronically reproduced by permission of Pearson Education, Inc., Upper Saddle River, New Jersey; **88:** Frederic H. Martini and Edwin F. Bartholomew, *Essentials of Anatomy and Physiology*, 6th ed. San Francisco: Pearson Benjamin Cummings, 2013, p. 3; **88:** Patrick Frank, *Prebles' Artforms: An Introduction to the Visual Arts*,

9th ed. Upper Saddle River, NJ: Pearson Prentice Hall, 2009, p. 104; **88:** Ronald J. Ebert and Ricky W. Griffin, *Business Essentials*, 7th ed. Upper Saddle River, NJ: Pearson Prentice Hall, 2009, p. 161; **88:** George C. Edwards III, Martin P. Wattenberg, and Robert L. Lineberry, *Government in America: People, Politics, and Policy*, 14th ed., p. 306, © 2009. Adapted and electronically reproduced by permission of Pearson Education, Inc., Upper Saddle River, New Jersey; **88:** Joseph A. DeVito, *Human Communication: The Basic Course*, 9th ed. Boston: Pearson Allyn and Bacon, 2003, p. 217; **89:** Ronald J. Ebert and Ricky W. Griffin, *Business Essentials*, 4th ed. Upper Saddle River, NJ: Pearson Prentice Hall, 2003, p. 64; **89:** Barbara Miller, *Cultural Anthropology*, 2nd ed. Boston: Pearson Allyn & Bacon, 2004, pp. 144–145; **89:** Paul G. Hewitt, *Conceptual Physics*, 9th ed. San Francisco: Addison Wesley, 2002, p. 39; **90:** Michael R. Solomon, *Consumer Behavior: Buying, Having, and Being*, 10th ed. Upper Saddle River, NJ: Pearson, 2013, p. 73; **90:** Rebecca J. Donatelle, *Health: The Basics*, 5th ed. San Francisco: Pearson Benjamin Cummings, 2003, p. 105; **95:** George C. Edwards III, Martin P. Wattenberg, and Robert L. Lineberry, *Government in America: People, Politics, and Policy*, 15th ed., p. 639, © 2011. Printed and electronically reproduced by permission of Pearson Education, Inc., Upper Saddle River, New Jersey; **95:** Frederic H. Martini and Edwin F. Bartholomew, *Essentials of Anatomy and Physiology*, 6th ed. San Francisco: Pearson Benjamin Cummings, 2013, p. 283; **96:** Michael R. Solomon, *Consumer Behavior: Buying, Having, and Being*, 10th ed. Upper Saddle River, NJ: Pearson, 2013, p. 565; **96:** John W. Hill, Terry W. McCreary, and Doris K. Kolb, *Chemistry for Changing Times*, 13th ed. Upper Saddle River, NJ: Pearson Prentice Hall, 2013, p. 16; **96:** Gary Armstrong and Philip Kotler, *Marketing: An Introduction*, 11th ed., p. 103, © 2013. Printed and electronically reproduced by permission of Pearson Education, Inc., Upper Saddle River, New Jersey; **101:** Jeffrey Jensen Arnett, *Human Development: A Cultural Approach*. Boston: Pearson, 2012, p. 459; **102:** Michael R. Solomon, *Consumer Behavior: Buying, Having, and Being*, 5th ed. Upper Saddle River, NJ: Prentice Hall, 2002, p. 184; **103:** Jeffrey Bennett et al., *The Cosmic Perspective*, Brief Edition. San Francisco: Addison Wesley Longman, 2000, p. 28; **103:** Rebecca J. Donatelle, *Health: The Basics*, Green Edition, 9th ed. San Francisco: Pearson Benjamin Cummings, 2011, p. 280; **104:** Courtland L. Bovée and John V. Thill, *Business in Action*, 6th ed. Upper Saddle River, NJ: Pearson Prentice Hall, 2013, p. 20; **104:** James M. Rubenstein, *Contemporary Human Geography*, 2nd ed. Upper Saddle River, NJ: Pearson Prentice Hall, 2013, p. 214; **105:** John Vivian, *The Media of Mass Communication*, 11th ed., p. 378, © 2013. Printed and electronically reproduced by permission of Pearson Education, Inc., Upper Saddle River, New Jersey; **105:** James M. Henslin, *Sociology: A Down-to-Earth Approach*, 11th ed. Boston: Pearson, 2012, p. 81; **105:** George C. Edwards III, Martin P. Wattenberg, and Robert L. Lineberry, *Government in America: People, Politics, and Policy*, 10th ed. New York: Pearson Longman, 2002, p. 422; **106:** Ronald J. Ebert and Ricky W. Griffin, *Business Essentials*,

7th ed. Upper Saddle River, NJ: Pearson Prentice Hall, 2009, p. 188; **107:** Elaine N. Marieb, *Human Anatomy and Physiology*, 5th ed. San Francisco: Pearson Benjamin Cummings, 2001, p. 9; **107:** Joseph A. DeVito, *Messages: Building Interpersonal Communication Skills*, 5th ed. Boston: Allyn and Bacon, 2002, p. 161; **109:** Diane Sukiennik, Lisa Raufman, and William Bendat, *The Career Fitness Program: Exercising Your Options*, 10th ed. Upper Saddle River, NJ: Pearson Prentice Hall, 2013, p. 185; **115:** X. J. Kennedy and Dana Gioia, *Literature: An Introduction to Fiction, Poetry, Drama, and Writing*, 11th ed. New York: Pearson Longman, 2010, p. 762; **116:** Barbara Miller, *Cultural Anthropology*, 2nd ed. Boston: Pearson Allyn & Bacon, 2004, pp. 308–309; **117:** Michael Bade and Robin Parkin, *Essential Foundations of Economics*, 6th ed. Boston: Pearson Addison Wesley, 2013, p. 205; **118:** Frederick K. Lutgens and Edward J. Tarbuck, *The Atmosphere: An Introduction to Meteorology*, 12th ed. Upper Saddle River, NJ: Pearson Prentice Hall, 2013, pp. 131–132; **119:** Lawrence Snyder, *Fluency with Information Technology: Skills, Concepts, and Capabilities*, 5th ed. Boston: Pearson Addison Wesley, 2013, p. 51; **119:** Jeffrey Bennett, Megan Donahue, Nicholas Schneider, and Mark Voit, *The Essential Cosmic Perspective*, 6th ed. San Francisco: Pearson Addison-Wesley, 2012, pp. 412–413; **120:** Robert A. Divine et al., *America Past and Present*, Combined Volume, 9th ed. New York: Pearson Longman, 2011, p. 596; **121:** Gary Nash et al., *The American People: Creating a Nation and a Society*. New York: Pearson Longman, 2006, pp. 611–613; **122:** H. W. Brands, T. H. Breen, R. Hal Williams, and Ariela J. Gross, *American Stories: A History of the United States*, 2nd ed. Boston: Pearson, 2012, p. 807; **123:** Michael R. Solomon, *Consumer Behavior: Buying, Having, and Being*, 10th ed. Upper Saddle River, NJ: Pearson, 2013, p. 95; **123:** George C. Edwards III, Martin P. Wattenberg, and Robert L. Lineberry, *Government in America: People, Politics, and Policy*, 15th ed. New York: Pearson Longman, 2011, p. 627; **124:** Rebecca J. Donatelle, *Access to Health*, 7th ed. San Francisco: Pearson Benjamin Cummings, 2002, p. 264; **124:** James M. Rubenstein, *Contemporary Human Geography*, 2nd ed. Upper Saddle River, NJ: Pearson Prentice Hall, 2013, pp. 278–279; **125:** Joan Salge Blake, *Nutrition and You: MyPlate Edition*, 2nd ed. San Francisco: Pearson Benjamin Cummings, 2012, pp. 52–56; **126:** David Krogh, *Biology: A Guide to the Natural World*, 5th ed. San Francisco: Pearson Benjamin Cummings, 2011, p. 526; **126:** Frederic H. Martini and Edwin F. Bartholomew, *Essentials of Anatomy and Physiology*, 6th ed. San Francisco: Pearson Benjamin Cummings, 2013, p. 312; **128:** Frederick K. Lutgens and Edward J. Tarbuck, *The Atmosphere: An Introduction to Meteorology*, 12th ed. Upper Saddle River, NJ: Pearson Prentice Hall, 2013, p. 454; **129:** Daniel Limmer and Michael F. O'Keefe, *Emergency Care*, 12th ed. Upper Saddle River, NJ: Pearson Brady, 2012, p. 533; **129:** Rebecca J. Donatelle, *Access to Health*, 7th ed. San Francisco: Pearson Benjamin Cummings, 2002, p. 516; **131:** James M. Henslin, *Sociology: A Down-to-Earth Approach*, 11th ed. Boston: Pearson, 2012, p. 78; **132:** James N. Danziger, *Understanding the Political World: A*

Comparative Introduction to Political Science, 11th ed. New York: Pearson, 2013, p. 87; **132:** Jeffrey Bennett, Megan Donahue, Nicholas Schneider, and Mark Voit, *The Essential Cosmic Perspective*, 6th ed. San Francisco: Pearson Addison-Wesley, 2012, pp. 325-326; **133:** Michael Levens, *Marketing: Defined, Explained, Applied*, 2nd ed. Upper Saddle River, NJ: Pearson Prentice Hall, 2012, p. 228; **134:** Courtland L. Bovée and John V. Thill, *Business in Action*, 6th ed. Upper Saddle River, NJ: Pearson Prentice Hall, 2013, p. 80; **135:** Jeffrey Jensen Arnett, *Human Development: A Cultural Approach*. Boston: Pearson, 2012, pp. 200-201; **137:** James M. Rubenstein, *Contemporary Human Geography*, 2nd ed. Upper Saddle River, NJ: Pearson Prentice Hall, 2013, p. 131; **138:** Frederic H. Martini and Edwin F. Bartholomew, *Essentials of Anatomy and Physiology*, 6th ed. San Francisco: Pearson Benjamin Cummings, 2013, p. 271; **138:** William J. Germann and Cindy L. Stanfield, *Principles of Human Physiology*. San Francisco: Benjamin Cummings, 2002, pp. 606-607; **138:** Jay S. Albanese, *Criminal Justice*, 5th ed. Upper Saddle River, NJ: Pearson Prentice Hall, 2013, p. 421; **139:** Rebecca J. Donatelle, *Health: The Basics*, 5th ed. San Francisco: Pearson Benjamin Cummings, 2003, p. 324; **140:** Edward F. Bergman and William H. Renwick, *Introduction to Geography: People, Places, and Environment*, 2nd ed. Upper Saddle River, NJ: Pearson Prentice Hall, 2002, p. 185; **140:** Walter E. Volkomer, *American Government*, 14th ed. Boston: Pearson, 2013, p. 344; **141:** Stephen F. Davis and Joseph J. Palladino, *Psychology*, 3rd ed. Upper Saddle River, NJ: Pearson Prentice Hall, 2000, p. 210; **141:** Edward F. Bergman and William H. Renwick, *Introduction to Geography: People, Places, and Environment*, 2nd ed. Upper Saddle River, NJ: Pearson Prentice Hall, 2002, p. 182; **143:** James M. Rubenstein, *Contemporary Human Geography*, 2nd ed. Upper Saddle River, NJ: Pearson Prentice Hall, 2013, p. 89; **143:** James M. Henslin, *Social Problems*, 5th ed. Upper Saddle River, NJ: Pearson Prentice Hall, 2000, p. 93; **143:** Edward F. Bergman and William H. Renwick, *Introduction to Geography: People, Places, and Environment*, 2nd ed. Upper Saddle River, NJ: Pearson Prentice Hall, 2002, p. 197; **144:** Jay S. Albanese, *Criminal Justice*, 5th ed. Upper Saddle River, NJ: Pearson Prentice Hall, 2013, p. 370; **144:** Rebecca J. Donatelle, *My Health: An Outcomes Approach*, 1st ed., p. 23, © 2013. Printed and electronically reproduced by permission of Pearson Education, Inc., Upper Saddle River, New Jersey; **155:** Carl Dahlman, William H. Renwick, and Edward Bergman, *Introduction to Geography: People, Places, and Environment*, 5th ed. Upper Saddle River, NJ: Pearson Prentice Hall, 2011, p. 95; **155:** Stephen P. Robbins and Mary Coulter, *Management*, 11th ed. Upper Saddle River, NJ: Pearson Prentice Hall, 2012, p. 79; **156:** James A. Fagin, *Criminal Justice*, 2nd ed. Boston: Pearson Allyn and Bacon, 2007, p. 78; **156:** Ronald J. Ebert and Ricky W. Griffin, *Business Essentials*, 4th ed. Upper Saddle River, NJ: Pearson Prentice Hall, 2003, p. 71; **157:** John D. Carl, *Think Sociology*, 1st ed., pp. 228-231, © 2010. Printed and electronically reproduced by permission of Pearson Education, Inc., Upper Saddle River, New Jersey; **166:** Barbara Miller, *Cultural Anthropology*,

2nd ed. Boston: Pearson Allyn & Bacon, 2004, p. 302; **166:** William E. Thompson and Joseph V. Hickey, *Society in Focus: An Introduction to Sociology*, 4th ed. Boston: Allyn and Bacon, 2002, p. 355; **169:** William E. Thompson and Joseph V. Hickey, *Society in Focus: An Introduction to Sociology*, 4th ed. Boston: Allyn and Bacon, 2002, p. 285; **171:** Alex Thio, *Sociology: A Brief Introduction*, 5th ed. Boston: Pearson Allyn and Bacon, 2003, pp. 35-36; **172:** James A. Fagin, *Criminal Justice*, 2nd ed. Boston: Pearson Allyn and Bacon, 2007, p. 152; **174:** Daniel Limmer and Michael F. O'Keefe, *Emergency Care*, 12th ed. Upper Saddle River, NJ: Pearson Brady, 2012, p. 36; **175:** H. W. Brands, T. H. Breen, R. Hal Williams, and Ariela J. Gross, *American Stories: A History of the United States*, 2nd ed. Boston: Pearson, 2012, pp. 735-736; **176:** James M. Rubenstein, *Contemporary Human Geography*, 2nd ed. Upper Saddle River, NJ: Pearson Prentice Hall, 2013, p. 296; **183:** David Batstone, excerpt from "Katja's Story: Human Trafficking Thrives in the New Global Economy," *Sojourners Magazine*, June 2006. © 2006 David Batstone. Reprinted by permission of the author; **186:** John J. Macionis, *Society: The Basics*, 12th ed., p. 216, © 2013. Printed and electronically reproduced by permission of Pearson Education, Inc., Upper Saddle River, New Jersey; **187:** William J. Germann and Cindy L. Stanfield, *Principles of Human Physiology*. San Francisco: Benjamin Cummings, 2002, p. 185; **187:** Joseph A. DeVito, *Human Communication: The Basic Course*, 12th ed. Boston: Pearson Allyn & Bacon, 2012, p. 52; **188:** John W. Hill, Terry W. McCreary, and Doris K. Kolb, *Chemistry for Changing Times*, 13th ed. Upper Saddle River, NJ: Pearson Prentice Hall, 2013, p. 446; **188:** Patrick Frank, *Prebles' Artforms: An Introduction to the Visual Arts*, 9th ed. Upper Saddle River, NJ: Pearson Prentice Hall, 2009, p. 37; **189:** James A. Fagin, *Criminal Justice*, 2nd ed. Boston: Pearson Allyn and Bacon, 2007, pp. 245-246; **192:** Norm Christensen, *The Environment and You*. Upper Saddle River, NJ: Pearson Prentice Hall, 2013, p. 118; **193:** Robert L. Lineberry and George C. Edwards, *Government in America: People, Politics, and Policy*, 4th ed. Glenview, IL: Scott Foresman, 1989, p. 540; **194:** Rebecca J. Donatelle, *My Health: An Outcomes Approach*, 1st ed., p. 131, © 2013. Adapted and electronically reproduced by permission of Pearson Education, Inc., Upper Saddle River, New Jersey; **194:** Rebecca J. Donatelle, *My Health: An Outcomes Approach*, 1st ed., p. 161, © 2013. Adapted and electronically reproduced by permission of Pearson Education, Inc., Upper Saddle River, New Jersey; **194:** William E. Thompson and Joseph V. Hickey, *Society in Focus: An Introduction to Sociology*, 7th ed., p. 383, © 2011. Adapted and electronically reproduced by permission of Pearson Education, Inc., Upper Saddle River, New Jersey; **195:** Jay S. Albanese, *Criminal Justice*, 5th ed. Upper Saddle River, NJ: Pearson Prentice Hall, 2013, pp. 435-436; **198:** Ambrose Bierce, *The Devil's Dictionary* (1911); **199:** Marge Thielman Hastreiter, "Not Every Mother Is Glad Kids Are Back in School," *Buffalo Evening News*, 1991. Reprinted by permission of the author; **202:** Bess Armstrong, in Angela Bonavoglia, ed., *The Choices We Made: 25 Women and Men Speak*

Out About Abortion. New York: Random House, 1991, p. 165; **202:** Roger LeRoy Miller, Daniel K. Benjamin, and Douglass C. North, *The Economics of Public Issues*, 16th ed. New York: Pearson Addison-Wesley, 2010, p. 10; **204:** Richard Paul Janaro and Thelma C. Altschuler, *The Art of Being Human: The Humanities as a Technique for Living*, 10th ed. New York: Pearson Longman, 2012, p. 183; **207:** William Blake, "London" from *Songs of Experience* (1794); **207:** Jane Kenyon, excerpt from "The Suitor" from *Collected Poems*. Copyright © 2005 by The Estate of Jane Kenyon. Reprinted with the permission of The Permissions Company, Inc. on behalf of Graywolf Press, www.graywolfpress.org; **208:** Percy Bysshe Shelley, *Adonais: An Elegy on the Death of John Keats* (1821); **208:** William Shakespeare, *As You Like It* 2.7.138142; **208:** Gustave Flaubert, "The Legend of Saint Julian the Hospitaller" (1838); **220:** John J. Macionis, *Society: The Basics*, 12th ed., Figure 12.4, p. 313, © 2013. Printed and electronically reproduced by permission of Pearson Education, Inc., Upper Saddle River, New Jersey; **222:** Center for Nutrition Policy and Promotion, April 2005, www.mypyramid.gov. An organization of the U.S. Department of Agriculture. In Donatelle, *Health: The Basics*, Green Edition, 9th ed. Pearson, 2011, p. 257; **223:** Gary Armstrong and Philip Kotler, *Marketing: An Introduction*, 11th ed., Table 11.1, p. 326, © 2013. Printed and electronically reproduced by permission of Pearson Education, Inc., Upper Saddle River, New Jersey; **225:** Ronald J. Ebert and Ricky W. Griffin, *Business Essentials*, 8th ed., p. 38, © 2011. Printed and electronically reproduced by permission of Pearson Education, Inc., Upper Saddle River, New Jersey; **226:** Jenifer Kunz, *THINK Marriages and Families*, 1st ed., p. 173, © 2011. Printed and electronically reproduced by permission of Pearson Education, Inc., Upper Saddle River, New Jersey; **227:** William E. Thompson and Joseph V. Hickey, *Society in Focus: An Introduction to Sociology*, 7th ed., p. 282, © 2011. Printed and electronically reproduced by permission of Pearson Education, Inc., Upper Saddle River, New Jersey; **227:** George C. Edwards III, Martin P. Wattenberg, and Robert L. Lineberry, *Government in America: People, Politics, and Policy*, 14th ed., p. 201, © 2009. Printed and electronically reproduced by permission of Pearson Education, Inc., Upper Saddle River, New Jersey; **229:** John D. Carl, *Think Sociology*, 1st ed., p. 271, © 2010. Reprinted and electronically reproduced by permission of Pearson Education, Inc., Upper Saddle River, New Jersey; **230:** Michael R. Solomon, Mary Anne Poatsy, and Kendall Martin, *Better Business*, 1st ed., Figure 7-5, p. 205, © 2010. Printed and electronically reproduced by permission of Pearson Education, Inc., Upper Saddle River, New Jersey; **230:** J. David Bergeron, Gloria Bizjak, Chris Le Baudour, and Keith Wesley, *First Responder*, 8th ed., Figure 9.5, p. 257, © 2009. Printed and electronically reproduced by permission of Pearson Education, Inc., Upper Saddle River, New Jersey; **232:** Elaine N. Marieb, *Essentials of Human Anatomy and Physiology*, 7th ed., p. 106, © 2003. Printed and electronically reproduced by permission of Pearson Education, Inc., Upper Saddle River, New Jersey; **232:** Elaine N. Marieb, *Essentials of*

Human Anatomy and Physiology, 7th ed., Figure 4.9, p. 106, © 2003. Printed and electronically reproduced by permission of Pearson Education, Inc., Upper Saddle River, New Jersey; **234:** The Geography of American Poverty. U.S. Census Bureau, 2008. In Carl, *Think Sociology*. Pearson, 2010, pp. 122; **235:** John D. Carl, *Think Sociology*, 1st ed., pp. 200–201, © 2010. Adapted and electronically reproduced by permission of Pearson Education, Inc., Upper Saddle River, New Jersey; **237:** Rebecca J. Donatelle, *My Health: An Outcomes Approach*, 1st ed., p. 73, © 2013. Printed and electronically reproduced by permission of Pearson Education, Inc., Upper Saddle River, New Jersey; **237:** Rebecca J. Donatelle, *My Health: An Outcomes Approach*, 1st ed., p. 73, © 2013. Printed and electronically reproduced by permission of Pearson Education, Inc., Upper Saddle River, New Jersey; **246:** William E. Thompson and Joseph V. Hickey, *Society in Focus: An Introduction to Sociology*, 7th ed., pp. 573–574, 580–581, © 2011. Printed and electronically reproduced by permission of Pearson Education, Inc., Upper Saddle River, New Jersey; **257:** Kelly J. Welch, *Family Life Now*, 2nd ed. 2010 Census Update, pp. 326–328, © 2012. Printed and electronically reproduced by permission of Pearson Education, Inc., Upper Saddle River, New Jersey; **268:** Sid Kirchheimer, "Are Sports Fans Happier?" article © SEPS licensed by Curtis Licensing, Indianapolis, IN. All rights reserved; **280:** Alex Hannaford, "Talking to Koko the Gorilla," as appeared in *The Week*, October 14, 2011. A longer version appeared originally in the *London Telegraph*, September 17, 2011. © Telegraph Media Group Ltd. 2011; **292:** John Vivian, *Media of Mass Communication*, 11th ed., pp. 157–163, © 2013. Printed and electronically reproduced by permission of Pearson Education, Inc., Upper Saddle River, New Jersey; **307:** Joseph A. DeVito, *Interpersonal Messages: Communication and Relationship Skills*, 1st ed., pp. 233–236, © 2008. Printed and electronically reproduced by permission of Pearson Education, Inc., Upper Saddle River, New Jersey; **309:** Leonard Shedletsky and Joan E. Aitken, *Human Communication on the Internet*, 1st ed., Figure 8.1, p. 159, © 2004. Adapted and electronically reproduced by permission of Pearson Education, Inc., Upper Saddle River, NJ; **320:** Paul J. Zelanski and Mary Pat Fisher, *The Art of Seeing*, 8th ed., pp. 30–31, © 2011. Adapted and electronically reproduced by permission of Pearson Education, Inc., Upper Saddle River, New Jersey; **332:** Bruce Holland Rogers, "Little Brother™" copyright © Bruce Holland Rogers. From *Strange Horizons*, October 30, 2000. Used by permission of the author; **342:** Robert Frost, "The Road Not Taken" from *Mountain Interval*. New York: Henry Holt, 1921; **349:** Bruce Watson, "When Theodore Roosevelt Saved Football." First appeared in *History Channel Magazine*. © 2011 Bruce Watson. Reprinted by permission of the author; **361:** Scott Bransford, "Camping for Their Lives" as appeared in *Utne Reader*, excerpted from the original article "Tarp Nation," *High Country News*, March 16, 2009. © 2009 by Scott Bransford. Reproduced by permission of the author; **374:** George C. Edwards III, Martin P. Wattenberg, and Robert L. Lineberry, *Government* *in America: People, Politics, and Policy*, 15th ed., pp. 211–217, © 2011. Adapted and electronically reproduced by permission of Pearson Education, Inc., Upper Saddle River, New Jersey; **390:** Philip Kotler and Gary Armstrong, *Principles of Marketing*, 13th ed., pp. 445–446, © 2010. Printed and electronically reproduced by permission of Pearson Education, Inc., Upper Saddle River, New Jersey; **402:** Natasha Singer, "Mapping, and Sharing, the Consumer Genome." From *The New York Times*, June 16, 2012. © 2012 The New York Times. All rights reserved. Used by permission and protected by the Copyright Laws of the United States. The printing, copying, redistribution, or retransmission of this Content without express written permission is prohibited. www.nytimes.com; **417:** Michael R. Solomon, *Consumer Behavior*, 9th ed., pp. 584–587, © 2011. Printed and electronically reproduced by permission of Pearson Education, Inc., Upper Saddle River, New Jersey; **420:** From www.miniclip.com. Used by permission of Miniclip (UK) Ltd.; **433:** Elaine N. Marieb, *Essentials of Human Anatomy and Physiology*, 9th ed., pp. 57–58, © 2009. Printed and electronically reproduced by permission of Pearson Education, Inc., Upper Saddle River, New Jersey; **443:** Katie L. Burke, "Interface Facts," *American Scientist*, November–December 2012, pp. 463–465. © 2012 Sigma Xi, The Scientific Research Society. Reprinted with permission; **445:** Screen shot of Phylo. © McGill University 2013. Reprinted with permission; **453:** Charlie Gillis, "The Robot Working-Class Invasion," *Maclean's*, October 17, 2012. © 2012 Rogers Media. Reprinted with permission; **468:** William E. Thompson and Joseph V. Hickey, *Society in Focus: An Introduction to Sociology*, 7th ed., pp. 625–628, © 2011. Adapted and electronically reproduced by permission of Pearson Education, Inc., Upper Saddle River, New Jersey; **479:** Christine Mitchell, "When Living Is a Fate Worse Than Death." From *Newsweek*, August 28, 2000. © 2000 The Newsweek/Daily Beast Company LLC. All rights reserved. Used by permission and protected by the Copyright Laws of the United States. The printing, copying, redistribution, or retransmission of this Content without express written permission is prohibited. www.newsweek.com; **488:** Andy Greenberg, "A Step Beyond Human." From *Forbes*, December 14, 2009. © 2009 Forbes. All rights reserved. Used by permission and protected by the Copyright Laws of the United States. The printing, copying, redistribution, or retransmission of this Content without express written permission is prohibited. www.forbes.com; **499:** George Dvorsky, "Can Technology Help Us Put an End to Animal Experimentation?" io9.com, September 5, 2012. © Gawker Media 2012. Reprinted with permission; **511:** Teresa Audesirk, Gerald Audesirk, and Bruce E. Byers, *Biology: Life on Earth*, 9th ed., pp. 303, 312–315, © 2011. Printed and electronically reproduced by permission of Pearson Education, Inc., Upper Saddle River, New Jersey; **524:** Holly Haworth, "And Incredibly Bright: We have blotted out the night sky." Originally published in *Earth Island Journal*, Spring 2013. www.earthislandjournal.org. Reprinted by permission of the publisher; **539:** Ronald L. Wasserstein, "A Statistician's

View: What Are Your Chances of Winning the Powerball Lottery?" *Huffington Post*, May 16, 2013. Reprinted by permission of the author; **549:** Neil DeMause, "Hope It's in Your Backyard!" First published in *Extra!*, the magazine of FAIR (Fairness & Accuracy in Reporting, Inc.), July 2012. Reprinted by permission of the publisher; **550:** By the Numbers, from Jacquelyn Pless, "A New Method of Extracting Natural Gas Has Yielded a Bounty of Supply, along with Health and Environmental Concerns," *State Legislatures Magazine*, May 2012. © National Conference of State Legislatures. Reprinted by permission; **559:** Richard T. Wright and Dorothy F. Boorse, *Environmental Science: Toward a Sustainable Future*, 11th ed., pp. 415–418, © 2011. Printed and electronically reproduced by permission of Pearson Education, Inc., Upper Saddle River, New Jersey; **573:** David Rapp, "Lift the Cell Phone Ban." Text and illustration from *Scholastic Administrator*, January 2009 issue. Copyright © 2009 by Scholastic Inc. Reprinted by permission of Scholastic Inc; **586:** Sylvia Hsieh, "Trial Lawyers Cater to Jurors' Demands for Visual Evidence," *Lawyers USA*, May 2012. Reprinted with permission from The Dolan Co., 10 Milk Street, 10th Floor, Boston, MA 02108. © 2012; **599:** John R. Walker and Josielyn T. Walker, *Tourism: Concepts and Practices*, 1st ed., pp. 376, 386–389, 392–394, © 2011. Printed and electronically reproduced by permission of Pearson Education, Inc., Upper Saddle River, New Jersey; **618:** Joseph A. DeVito, *The Interpersonal Communication Book*, 13th ed., pp. 228–237, 247–254, © 2013. Printed and electronically reproduced by permission of Pearson Education, Inc., Upper Saddle River, New Jersey.

Photo Credits

1(BL): Blend Images/Getty Images; **1 (CL):** Jim Beckel, The Oklahoman/AP Images; **1 (CL):** Jim Beckel, The Oklahoman/AP Images; **1(CR):** D. Hurst/Alamy; **2(BL):** Jim MacMillan/AP Images; **2(C):** Masterpics/Alamy; **2(TL):** Ramón Espelt Photography/Flickr/Getty Images; **3(TR):** Bruce Coleman INC./Alamy; **3(CR):** Blueringmedia/Fotolia; **3(TL):** David R. Frazier Photolibrary, Inc./Alamy; **3(CL):** Peter Arnold Inc./Alamy; **4:** West Coast Surfer/Getty Images; **9:** Ra2 Studio/Fotolia; **13:** Bill Bachmann/Science Source; **15:** SPL/Science Source; **18:** David R. Frazier Photolibrary, Inc./Alamy; **22:** Andrew Holt/Alamy; **29:** Peathegee Inc/Blend Images/Corbis; **34:** BKMCphotography/Shutterstock; **37(BR):** Diego Cervo/Shutterstock; **37(CR):** Diego Cervo/Shutterstock; **45:** Eric Risberg/AP Images; **97:** Chris Madden/Cartoon Stock; **99:** Samuel Acosta/Shutterstock; **158:** Silvio Tamberi/Fotolia; **159:** Vladimir Mucibabic/Fotolia; **180:** Bob Daemmrich/The Image Works; **181:** Christina Dicken, News-Leader/AP Images; **185:** David Borchart/The New Yorker Collection/www.cartoonbank.com; **218:** Yann Guichaoua/SuperStock; **219:** Exactostock/SuperStock; **247:** Imagebroker.net/SuperStock; **257:** Dennis MacDonald/PhotoEdit, Inc.; **269:** Comstock/Thinkstock; **281:** Gorilla Foundation/

Index